Teach
Yourself
Visual C++™ 4

in 21 Days

Teach Yourself
Visual C++™ 4
in 21 Days

Ori Gurewich
Nathan Gurewich

SAMS
PUBLISHING

201 West 103rd Street
Indianapolis, Indiana 46290

Copyright © 1996 by Sams Publishing

FIRST EDITION

International Standard Book Number: 0-672-30795-2

Library of Congress Catalog Card Number: 95-74776

99   98   97   96   4   3   2   1

Interpretation of the printing code: the rightmost double-digit number is the year of the book's printing; the rightmost single-digit, the number of the book's printing. For example, a printing code of 96-1 shows that the first printing of the book occurred in 1996.

Composed in AGaramond and MCPdigital by Macmillan Computer Publishing

Printed in the United States of America

Trademarks

Publisher and President	*Richard K. Swadley*
Acquisitions Manager	*Greg Wiegand*
Development Manager	*Dean Miller*
Managing Editor	*Cindy Morrow*
Marketing Manager	*Gregg Bushyeager*

Acquisitions Editor
Christopher Denny

Development Editor
Kelly Murdock

Software Development Specialist
Steve Flatt

Production Editor
Lisa M. Lord

Technical Reviewer
Vincent W. Mayfield

Editorial Coordinator
Bill Whitmer

Technical Edit Coordinator
Lynette Quinn

Formatter
Frank Sinclair

Editorial Assistants
Sharon Cox
Andi Richter
Rhonda Tinch-Mize

Cover Designer
Tim Amrhein

Book Designer
Gary Adair

Production Team Supervisor
Brad Chinn

Production
Carol Bowers, Michael Brumitt, Jeanne Clark, Judy Everly, Jason Hand, Sonya Hart, Mike Henry, Ayanna Lacey, Paula Lowell, Donna Martin, Bobbi Satterfield, Laura Smith, SA Springer, Josette Starks, Andrew Stone, Tim Taylor, Susan Van Ness, Mark Walchle, Colleen Williams

Indexer
Chris Cleveland

Overview

Contents

Week 2 at a Glance

8 Displaying Bitmaps

9 Displaying Text in Different Fonts

Acknowledgments

We would like to thank Chris Denny, acquisitions editor at Sams Publishing, for asking us to write this book, and especially for the various suggestions and recommendations he made during the development and production of the book. We would also like to thank Lisa Lord, the production editor of this book; Kelly Murdock, the development editor; the production and art departments of Sams; and all the other people at Sams Publishing who helped in the development and production of this book.

Thanks also to Microsoft Corporation, which supplied us with technical information and various betas and upgrades of the software product. In particular, thanks to Mr. Summeet Shrivastava from Microsoft Corporation.

About the Authors

Ori Gurewich and Nathan Gurewich are well-known authors of several best-selling books about Visual C++, Visual Basic for Windows, C/C++ programming, multimedia programming, database design and programming, and other topics.

Ori Gurewich holds a bachelor's degree in electrical engineering from Stony Brook University, Stony Brook, New York. His background includes working as a senior software engineer and a software consultant engineer for companies developing professional multimedia and Windows applications. He is an expert in the field of PC programming and network communications and has developed various multimedia algorithms for the PC. Ori Gurewich can be contacted at:

CompuServe: CompuServe ID 72072,312
Microsoft Network: MSN ID Ori_Gurewich
Internet: Ori_Gurewich@msn.com

Nathan Gurewich holds a master's degree in electrical engineering from Columbia University, New York, and a bachelor's degree in electrical engineering from Hofstra University, Long Island, New York. Since the introduction of the PC, he has been involved in the design and implementation of commercial software packages for the PC. He is an expert in the field of PC programming and in providing consulting services on programming, local and wide area networks, database management and design, and software marketing. Nathan Gurewich can be contacted at:

CompuServe: CompuServe ID 75277,2254
Microsoft Network: MSN ID Nathan_Gurewich
Internet: Nathan_Gurewich@msn.com

Introduction

Using Visual C++ to Develop Professional Windows Applications

Welcome to the fascinating world of programming powerful, professional Windows applications with the Microsoft Visual C++ 4 package.

Windows is currently the most popular operating system for the PC; consequently, almost all vendors ship their PCs with a mouse and the Windows operating system already installed. In this book, *Teach Yourself Visual C++ 4 in 21 Days*, you'll learn how to develop state-of-the-art Windows applications by using the Visual C++ package. This means you'll have to write code using the C/C++ programming language, but don't worry! Even if you've never used C/C++ before, you'll be able to use this book. Why? Because this book comes with a tutorial that teaches you C/C++ quickly in Appendixes A, B, and C. As you'll soon see, you'll write your first Windows program with Visual C++ in Chapter 1 of this book!

Why Use Windows? Why Use Visual C++?

There are several reasons why Windows has become so popular in a relatively short time:

- Windows lets you write *device-independent programs.* This means that while you're writing the application, you don't have to concern yourself with what type of printer, mouse, monitor, keyboard, sound card, CD-ROM drive, or other devices your users own. Your application will work fine, no matter what hardware your users have. So does this mean, for example, that your user can have *any* sound card? Not at all! It is your user's responsibility to install the sound card into his or her PC. During the installation, Windows asks the user to install the appropriate drivers, then either accepts or rejects the sound card. Windows will accept the sound card if the hardware and the software (drivers) your user received from the sound card vendor were used according to Windows requirements. Once Windows accepts the sound card, the Windows applications you write should work with that sound card. The same applies for other devices such as the printer, the monitor, and the CD-ROM drive.

- A lot of code is already installed in your user's PC. Once Windows is installed, the PC contains much Windows-related software. This code exists on your PC (the developer's PC) and on your users' PCs. This means that before you even start writing the first line of code yourself, your user already has more than half your program in his or her PC! Not only do you not have to write this code, you don't even have to distribute that code to your users.

- Standard user interface. The user-interface mechanism is the same for all Windows applications. Without reading your application's documentation, your users know

how to execute your application, they can use the icon on the corner of the application's window to minimize the window, they know the meaning of the OK and Cancel buttons, they know what the About dialog box is, and they understand many other features of your program before you even start writing it!

These reasons for using Windows are applicable no matter what programming language you use for developing the application. Why should you use Visual C++ for writing Windows applications and not "regular" C with the SDK (Software Developer Kit) for Windows? The answer to this question is provided in the following sections.

What Is Visual C++?

The *C++* in this book's title means you have to use C/C++ for writing the code. However, this book assumes no previous C/C++ experience. That's why the book includes a tutorial (see Appendixes A, B, and C). During the course of this book, you will learn all the C++ techniques you need to write professional, powerful Windows applications.

Now that you know the meaning of the *C++* in *Visual C++*, what does *Visual* mean? It means you'll accomplish many of your programming tasks by using the keyboard and the mouse to visually design and write your applications. You'll select controls such as pushbuttons, radio buttons, and scrollbars with the mouse, drag them to your application's window, and size them—and you'll be able to see your application as you build it (this is called *design time*). In other words, you'll be able to see what your application will look like before you execute it. This is a great advantage because it saves you considerable time (you can see your application without compiling/linking it), and you can change your mind about the placement and size of edit boxes, pushbuttons, and other objects by simply using the mouse.

ClassWizard: What Is That?

The most powerful feature of Visual C++ is a "wizard" called *ClassWizard*. ClassWizard writes code for you! In the industry, this type of program is often referred to as a CASE (computer-aided software engineering) program. Of course, ClassWizard is not a magic program—you have to tell it what you want it to write for you. For example, suppose you visually placed a pushbutton in your application's window with the mouse. Once you have placed the button, you want to write code that's executed whenever the user clicks that button. This is the time to use ClassWizard. By choosing various options in ClassWizard's window, you tell ClassWizard to prepare all the overhead code. ClassWizard responds by preparing all the overhead code and then showing you where to insert your own code. Therefore, your job is to write your code in the area ClassWizard prepared. In addition to ClassWizard, Visual C++ is equipped with other wizards, such as the AppWizard. You'll learn about all these wizards during the course of this book.

What Are OLE Controls?

One of the main advantages of using Visual C++ 4 is the ability to use OLE (object linking and embedding) controls. OLE controls are pieces of software that you can easily "plug" into your Visual C++ programs. In modern modular programming (such as Visual C++), the trend is to "pick up" OLE controls and plug them into your programs. OLE controls let you perform sophisticated and powerful operations quickly. In Chapters 18 and 19, "Creating Your Own OLE Control (Parts I and II)," you'll learn how to design and use your own OLE controls.

In this book, you'll also learn how to make a two-dimensional (2-D) drawing with a regular text editor, such as WordPad in Windows 95. You'll then "plug" an OLE control into your program that converts the 2-D drawing to a three-dimensional (3-D) picture. You'll finally write your own code that lets your user "travel" inside the 3-D picture! In addition, you can place sprite objects in the 3-D picture and animate them; as your user "travels" inside the 3-D picture, he or she will encounter these animated sprite objects. In other words, you'll be able to design your own DOOM-like program. All these tasks can be accomplished quickly, thanks to OLE technology.

The programs you'll be creating in Chapter 20, "Using the Multimedia OLE Control," and Chapter 21, "Games and 3-D Virtual Reality," require special OLE controls. These controls, as well as other files to enhance your programs, can be downloaded from CompuServe or the Internet. (See "Free Online Code Offer" on the last page of this book for specific information on downloading these files.)

Conventions Used in This Book

The following typographic conventions are used in this book:

- Statements, functions, variables, events, and any text you type or see on the screen appear in a `computer` typeface.
- *Italics* highlight technical terms when they first appear in the text and are sometimes used to emphasize important points.
- Code that you type in yourself appears in a **bold computer** typeface. This book also sets off code that you enter with these "flags":

```
/////////////////////////
// MY CODE STARTS HERE
/////////////////////////


............................
... Your code appears here ...
............................


/////////////////////////
// MY CODE ENDS HERE
/////////////////////////
```

Visual C++ Is Fun

Visual C++ is an interesting, fun package to use because it lets you develop sophisticated Windows applications in a short time, so relax and prepare yourself for a pleasant journey!

In Week 1, you'll realize that Visual C++ is very easy to use. Yes, on the first day of this week you'll jump into the Visual C++ water! You'll actually write your first Visual C++ program.

On the second day, you'll learn how to write a Visual C++ program that uses the edit box control and the check box control. You'll learn how to visually create a dialog box that uses these controls and how to attach code to their events.

On the third day, you'll learn how to use OLE controls. You'll learn what OLE controls are and how to incorporate them into your Visual C++ programs.

On the fourth day, you'll learn how to detect and use mouse and keyboard operations from within your Visual C++ programs. In particular, you'll learn how to create a program that lets the user draw with the mouse.

On the fifth day, you'll learn how to design menus and incorporate them into your Visual C++ programs.

On the sixth day, you'll learn how to create and use predefined and custom-made dialog boxes.

On the seventh day, you'll learn how to create programs that draw graphics. You'll also learn how to install and use a timer.

Writing Your First Visual C++ Application

Today you'll write your first Visual C++ program! This involves two steps:

- The visual design step
- The code-writing step

In the *visual design step*, you design the appearance of your program. You use the Visual C++ tools to place various objects (such as pushbuttons, scrollbars, radio buttons, and so on) in your programs' windows. During the visual design step, you don't write any code.

In the *code-writing step*, you write code using the Visual C++ text editor and the C++ programming language.

The Hello.EXE Program

In this chapter, you'll write a Visual C++ program called Hello.EXE. Before you start writing it, however, first specify what the Hello.EXE program should look like and what it should do.

- When you start the Hello.EXE program, its window should look like the one shown in Figure 1.1.

Figure 1.1.
The window of the Hello.EXE program.

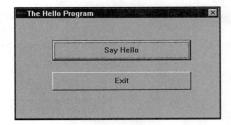

- The Hello.EXE program includes two pushbuttons: Say Hello and Exit. When you click the Say Hello button, a HELLO message box appears. (See Figure 1.2.)

Figure 1.2.
The HELLO message box.

- To close the HELLO message box, click its OK button. Then click the Exit pushbutton to terminate the Hello.EXE program.

Now that you know what the Hello.EXE program should look like and how it should behave, you can start designing it. In the following sections, you'll design the Hello.EXE program by following step-by-step instructions.

Creating a Directory for the Hello.EXE Program Files

Before you start creating the project file and program files of the Hello.EXE program, first create a directory on your hard drive where the Hello.EXE files will reside.

☐ Use the Windows Explorer of Windows 95 to create the directory C:\TYVCProg\Programs\CH01.

Creating the Project of the Hello.EXE Program

The first thing you have to do when you start a new Visual C++ program is create the project of the program. To create the project of the Hello.EXE program, follow these steps:

☐ Start the Microsoft Developer Studio. The icon of the Microsoft Developer Studio resides in the Microsoft Visual C++ 4.0 program group. (See Figure 1.3.)

Figure 1.3.

Executing the Microsoft Developer Studio.

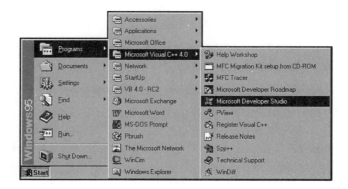

What is the Microsoft Developer Studio? It is the essence of the Visual C++ package. Using the Microsoft Developer Studio, you'll create, execute, and maintain your Visual C++ programs. It includes all the tools you'll need to develop these programs.

After you execute the Microsoft Developer Studio, its main window appears, as shown in Figure 1.4. (Depending on the desktop setting of your Visual C++, the window of your Microsoft Developer Studio may look a little different from the one shown in Figure 1.4.)

5

Figure 1.4.

The main window (desktop) of the Microsoft Developer Studio.

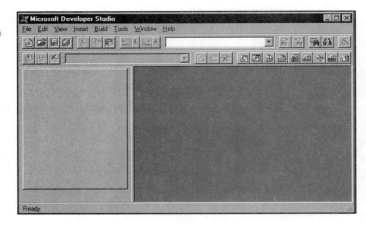

> **Note:** You write and maintain your Visual C++ programs by using the Microsoft Developer Studio. The names "Developer Studio" and "Visual C++" are inter-changeable; however, all the steps in the following sections and throughout this book will use "Visual C++" instead of "Developer Studio".

Now create the project of the Hello.EXE program:

☐ Select New from the File menu of Visual C++.

Visual C++ responds by displaying the New dialog box. (See Figure 1.5.)

Figure 1.5.

The New dialog box.

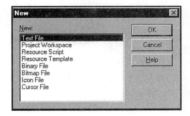

☐ Select Project Workspace in the New dialog box, then click the OK button.

Visual C++ responds by displaying the New Project Workspace dialog box. (See Figure 1.6.)

You'll use the New Project Workspace dialog box to tell Visual C++ the type of project and the name of the project you want to create.

Figure 1.6.
The New Project Workspace dialog box.

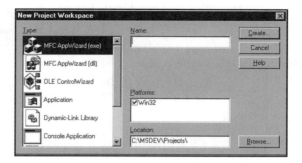

☐ Make sure the MFC AppWizard (exe) item is selected in the Type list box.

By selecting MFC AppWizard (exe), you are telling Visual C++ that you want to create an EXE program. Now tell Visual C++ in which directory the project and program files will be saved:

☐ Click the Browse button at the lower-right corner of the New Project Workspace dialog box.

Visual C++ responds by displaying the Choose Directory dialog box. (See Figure 1.7.)

Figure 1.7.
The Choose Directory dialog box.

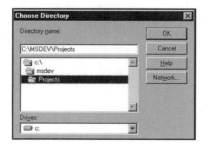

☐ Use the Choose Directory dialog box to select the C:\TYVCProg\Programs\CH01 directory, then click the OK button. (You will not save the project and program files into the default directory that Visual C++ suggests. Rather, you'll save the files into the C:\TYVCProg\Programs\CH01 directory.)

Next, tell Visual C++ the name of the project you want to create:

☐ Type Hello in the Name box of the New Project Workspace dialog box.

You have finished specifying the project type, project location, and project name for the Hello.EXE program. Your New Project Workspace dialog box should now look like the one shown in Figure 1.8.

Figure 1.8.
Specifying the project type, project location, and project name.

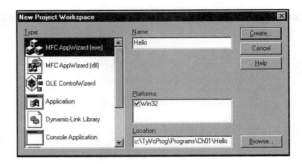

☐ Click the Create button of the New Project Workspace dialog box.

Visual C++ responds by displaying the MFC AppWizard - Step 1 dialog box. (See Figure 1.9.)

Figure 1.9.
The MFC AppWizard - Step 1 dialog box.

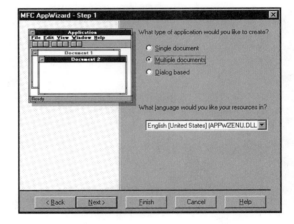

What is MFC AppWizard? *MFC AppWizard* is a powerful "wizard" that writes the skeleton code of your program for you. Instead of writing overhead code every time you start writing a new program, you can use MFC AppWizard to write it for you.

In the following steps, you'll use the dialog boxes of MFC AppWizard to specify various characteristics of the program you want to create. Once you are done, MFC AppWizard will create the skeleton code of your program for you.

MFC AppWizard currently displays the MFC AppWizard - Step 1 dialog box shown in Figure 1.9. In this dialog box, you specify the type of application you want to create and the language you would like to use for the program's resources.

☐ Click the "Dialog based" radio button of the MFC AppWizard - Step 1 dialog box.

By selecting the Dialog based radio button, you are telling MFC AppWizard that you want to create a *dialog-based program*, which means that the main window of the Hello program is a dialog box. As you saw earlier in Figure 1.1, the Hello.EXE program's main window is a dialog box with two pushbuttons: Say Hello and Exit.

☐ Leave the Language combo box at the default setting: English [United States](APPWZENU.DLL).

Your MFC AppWizard - Step 1 dialog box should now look like the one shown in Figure 1.10.

Figure 1.10.
The MFC AppWizard - Step 1 dialog box.

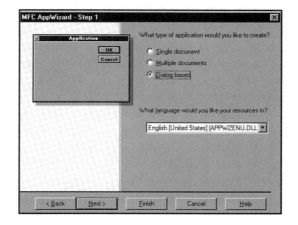

☐ Click the Next button to advance to the next MFC AppWizard dialog box.

The MFC AppWizard - Step 2 of 4 dialog box appears. (See Figure 1.11.)

Figure 1.11.
The MFC AppWizard - Step 2 of 4 dialog box.

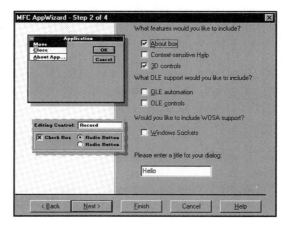

As you can see, the MFC AppWizard - Step 2 of 4 dialog box lets you specify whether various features should be included in the program. This dialog box also lets you specify the title of the program's dialog box (the main window).

☐ Set the MFC AppWizard - Step 2 of 4 dialog box as shown in Figure 1.12. Leave all the check boxes at the default settings and set the title of the dialog box to The Hello Program.

Figure 1.12.

The MFC AppWizard - Step 2 of 4 dialog box.

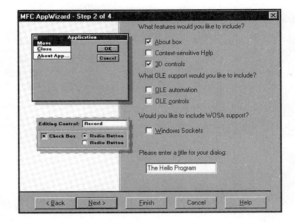

☐ Click the Next button to advance to the next MFC AppWizard dialog box.

The MFC AppWizard - Step 3 of 4 dialog box appears. (See Figure 1.13.)

Figure 1.13.

The MFC AppWizard - Step 3 of 4 dialog box.

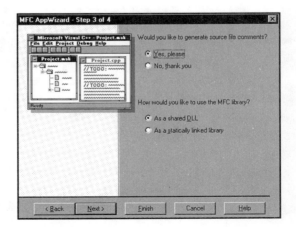

As you can see, the MFC AppWizard - Step 3 of 4 dialog box asks you two questions:

1. Would you like to generate source file comments?
2. How would you like to use the MFC library?

☐ Answer the two questions as shown in Figure 1.13.

By using the settings shown in Figure 1.13, you are specifying the following:

1. When MFC AppWizard creates the skeleton code of the program for you, it will include comments. Including comments in the skeleton files will help you understand the code that MFC AppWizard writes for you (in case you want to review it).

2. The program that MFC AppWizard creates for you will use a dynamic link library (DLL), not a statically linked library. Using a DLL gives you the advantage of having a smaller EXE file.

☐ Click the Next button to advance to the next MFC AppWizard dialog box.

The MFC AppWizard - Step 4 of 4 dialog box appears. (See Figure 1.14.)

Figure 1.14.
The MFC AppWizard - Step 4 of 4 dialog box.

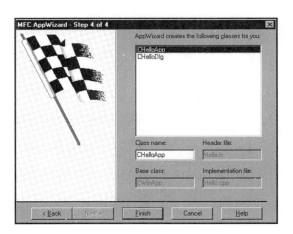

As you can see, the MFC AppWizard - Step 4 of 4 dialog box tells you what classes and files MFC AppWizard will create for you. You don't have to change any of the settings in this dialog box.

☐ Click the Finish button to tell MFC AppWizard to create the project and skeleton files of the Hello program.

The New Project Information dialog box appears. (See Figure 1.15.)

Figure 1.15.
*The New Project Informa-
tion dialog box.*

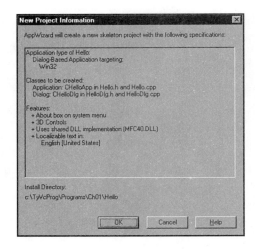

The New Project Information dialog box summarizes all the specifications you made in the
previous steps.

☐ Click the OK button of the New Project Information dialog box.

> *Visual C++ responds by creating all the skeleton files of the Hello program in the directory
> C:\TYVCProg\Programs\CH01\Hello. Finally, the Visual C++ window appears, as
> shown in Figure 1.16.*

Figure 1.16.
*The Visual C++ window
after creating the project of
the Hello program.*

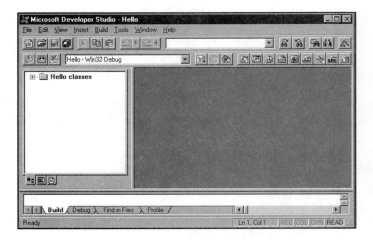

1

Note: Depending on Visual C++'s desktop settings, your Visual C++ desktop may look different from the window shown in Figure 1.16.

The dialog box at the left side of the window, which contains the text `Hello classes`, is called the Project Workspace dialog box. If you don't see the Project Workspace dialog box in your Visual C++ desktop, then select Project Workspace from the View menu of Visual C++.

You'll learn about the Project Workspace dialog box (what it is and how to use it) later in this chapter.

As shown in Figure 1.16, the title of your Visual C++ window is now `Microsoft Developer Studio - Hello`. The "Hello" in the title indicates that you are currently working on the Hello project.

Compiling and Linking the Hello Program

Believe it or not, although you haven't written a single line of code yet, you already have a working Windows program. The skeleton code that MFC AppWizard wrote for you actually does something. To see this code in action, you need to compile and link the Hello program and then execute it.

Follow these steps to compile and link the Hello program:

☐ Select Set Default Configuration from the Build menu of Visual C++.

Visual C++ responds by displaying the Default Project Configuration dialog box. (See Figure 1.17.)

Figure 1.17.
The Default Project Configuration dialog box.

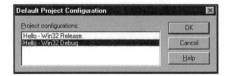

You use the Default Project Configuration dialog box to specify how Visual C++ will generate the EXE file of the project. If you set the Default Project Configuration dialog box to `Win32 Debug` (as in Figure 1.17), then Visual C++ will generate an EXE file with the code lines needed for debugging. However, if you set the Default Project Configuration dialog box to `Win32 Release`, then no debugging code will be embedded in the EXE file.

☐ Select Hello - Win32 Release in the Default Project Configuration dialog box, then click the OK button.

Although you haven't written a single line of code yet, try compiling and linking the program at this early stage of the development.

To create the Hello.EXE file, do the following:

☐ Select Build Hello.EXE from the Build menu.

Visual C++ responds by compiling and linking the files of the Hello program and creating the Hello.EXE file.

Note: In the preceding step you were instructed to compile and link the Hello program by selecting Build Hello.EXE from the Visual C++ Build menu. You can also compile and link the program by selecting Rebuild All from the Build menu.

When you select Build Hello.EXE from the Build menu, only the files changed since the last time you compiled the program are compiled. When you select Rebuild All from the Build menu, all the program files are compiled (whether or not the files were changed since the last compilation).

Sometimes, your project may go out of sequence and Visual C++ will "think" that files that need to be compiled should not be compiled. In such cases, you can force Visual C++ to compile all the files by selecting Rebuild All from the Build menu.

☐ Select Execute Hello.EXE from the Build menu to execute the Hello.EXE program.

Visual C++ responds by executing the Hello.EXE program. The main window of the Hello.EXE program appears, as shown in Figure 1.18.

Figure 1.18.
The main window of the Hello.EXE program.

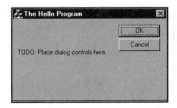

As you can see, the skeleton code that MFC AppWizard wrote for you created a simple EXE program whose main window contains two pushbuttons (OK and Cancel) and displays the text `TODO: Place dialog controls here.`

Notice that the title of the program's window is The Hello Program, which you specified in the MFC AppWizard - Step 2 of 4 dialog box. (Refer back to Figure 1.12.)

The Hello.EXE program also includes an About dialog box because you used Step 2 of the MFC AppWizard to include an About dialog box in the program. (Refer back to Figure 1.12.) To see the About dialog box of the Hello.EXE program, follow these steps:

☐ Open the system menu of the Hello.EXE program by clicking the small icon at the upper-left corner of the application window.

The Hello.EXE program responds by displaying its system menu. (See Figure 1.19.)

Figure 1.19.
The system menu of the Hello.EXE program.

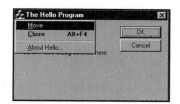

☐ Select About Hello from the system menu.

The Hello.EXE program responds by displaying the About Hello dialog box. (See Figure 1.20.)

Figure 1.20.
The About Hello dialog box.

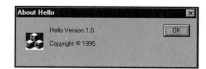

☐ Close the About dialog box by clicking its OK button.

☐ Terminate the Hello.EXE program by clicking the × icon at the upper-right corner of the program's window.

As you have just seen, the skeleton code that MFC AppWizard wrote for you produced a working Windows program. Of course, at this point the Hello.EXE program does not look and behave like you want it to. In the following sections, you'll use the Visual C++ tools to customize the Hello.EXE program until it looks and behaves like you want it to.

Note: In the preceding steps you executed the Hello.EXE program by selecting Execute Hello.EXE from the Visual C++ Build menu.

> The Hello.EXE program is a regular Windows EXE file, so you can also execute it directly from Windows just as you execute any other Windows EXE file (for example, by using Windows Explorer).
>
> Visual C++ placed the Hello.EXE file in your C:\TYVCProg\Programs\CH01\ Hello\Release directory because you set the default project configuration to Win32 - Release before compiling and linking the files of the Hello project. If you had set the default project configuration to Win32 - Debug, Visual C++ would have placed the Hello.EXE file in the Debug subdirectory—C:\TYVCProg\Programs\CH01\ Hello\Debug.

The Visual Implementation of the Hello.EXE Program

As discussed at the beginning of this chapter, writing a Visual C++ program involves two steps: the visual design step and the code-writing step. You'll now perform the visual design step. You'll use the visual design tools of Visual C++ to customize the main window of the Hello.EXE program until it looks like the one shown back in Figure 1.1.

Take a look at the desktop of Visual C++. Your Visual C++ desktop should currently look like the one shown in Figure 1.21.

Figure 1.21.
The Visual C++ desktop with the Project Workspace dialog box of the Hello project.

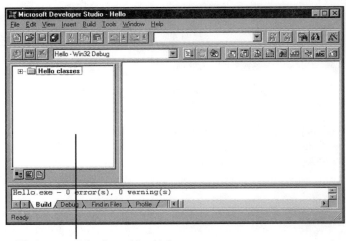

The Project Workspace dialog box of the Hello program

As shown in Figure 1.21, the dialog box at the left side of the Visual C++ window is called the Project Workspace dialog box. Remember to select Project Workspace from the View menu if you don't see the Project Workspace dialog box.

As its name implies, the Project Workspace dialog box, shown in Figure 1.22, is the place for managing all aspects of your project. For example, you can use the Project Workspace dialog box to view a list of all your project files or to open any of your project files.

Figure 1.22.
The Project Workspace dialog box.

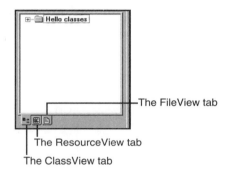

The FileView tab

The ResourceView tab

The ClassView tab

As shown in Figures 1.21 and 1.22, the bottom of the Project Workspace dialog box has three tabs: ClassView, ResourceView, and FileView. The ClassView tab lets you view and edit the project's classes. The ResourceView tab lets you view and edit the project's resources (for example, dialog boxes, menus, icons, BMP pictures). You use the ResourceView tab for the visual design of your program. The FileView tab lets you view and edit any of the project files.

Right now you want to use the visual aspect of the Hello.EXE program, so you need to use the ResourceView tab:

☐ Click the ResourceView tab of the Project Workspace dialog box.

Your Project Workspace dialog box should now look like the one shown in Figure 1.23.

As shown in Figure 1.23, the Project Workspace dialog box displays the text Hello resources.

☐ Double-click the Hello resources item to list all the resources of the Hello project (or click the + icon to the left of the Hello resources item).

   Visual C++ responds by expanding the Hello resources item to list several subitems. (See Figure 1.24.)

As shown in Figure 1.24, the subitems under the Hello resources item are various resources types: Dialog, Icon, String Table, and Version. Right now, your objective is to visually design the dialog box that serves as the main window of the Hello program. Therefore, you have to expand the Dialog item:

☐ Double-click the Dialog item (or click the + icon to the left of the Dialog item). Visual C++ responds by expanding the Dialog item—two subitems are listed beneath it. (See Figure 1.25.)

Figure 1.23.
Selecting the ResourceView tab.

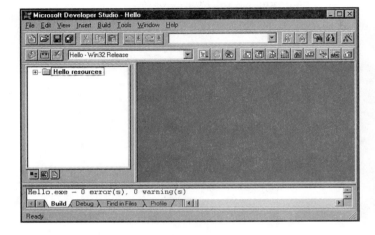

Figure 1.24.
Expanding the Hello resources item.

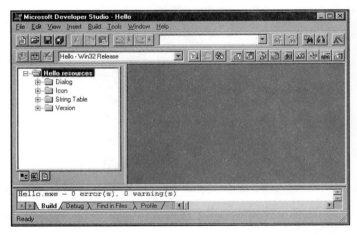

As you can see, there are two subitems under the Dialog item: IDD_ABOUTBOX and IDD_HELLO_DIALOG. As you might have guessed, IDD_ABOUTBOX is the ID of the Hello program's About dialog box, and IDD_HELLO_DIALOG is the ID of the dialog box that serves as the main window of the Hello program.

☐ Double-click the IDD_HELLO_DIALOG item to customize the dialog box serving as the Hello program's main window.

Figure 1.25.
Expanding the Dialog item.

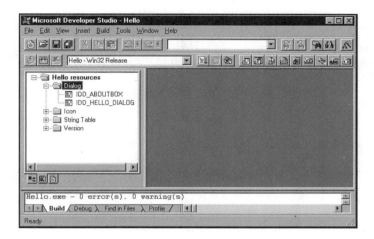

Visual C++ responds by displaying the IDD_HELLO_DIALOG dialog box in design mode, ready for you to customize. (See Figure 1.26.)

Figure 1.26.
IDD_HELLO_DIALOG in design mode (before customization).

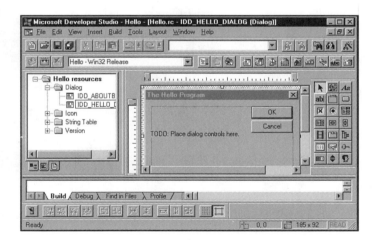

As you can see, the IDD_HELLO_DIALOG dialog box contains three controls: an OK pushbutton, a Cancel pushbutton, and the text TODO: Place dialog controls here. Your objective is to customize the IDD_HELLO_DIALOG dialog box so that it will look like the one shown back in Figure 1.1.

Begin the customization by deleting the OK pushbutton, deleting the Cancel pushbutton, and deleting the TODO: Place dialog controls here. text:

☐ Click the OK pushbutton in the IDD_HELLO_DIALOG dialog box, then press the Delete key.

Visual C++ responds by removing the OK button from the IDD_HELLO_DIALOG dialog box.

☐ Click the Cancel pushbutton in the IDD_HELLO_DIALOG dialog box, then press the Delete key.

Visual C++ responds by removing the Cancel button from the IDD_HELLO_DIALOG dialog box.

☐ Click the text TODO: Place dialog controls here. in the IDD_HELLO_DIALOG dialog box, then press the Delete key.

Visual C++ responds by removing the text TODO: Place dialog controls here. from the IDD_HELLO_DIALOG dialog box.

Your IDD_HELLO_DIALOG dialog box is now empty. (See Figure 1.27.)

Figure 1.27.
IDD_HELLO_DIALOG after removing the controls.

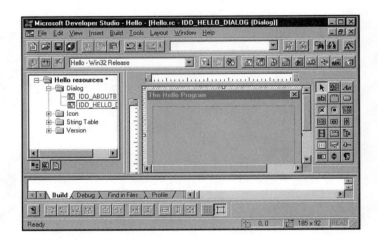

In the following steps, you'll place two pushbutton controls in the IDD_HELLO_DIALOG dialog box; to do this, you'll use the Controls toolbar of Visual C++. (See Figure 1.28.)

Figure 1.28.
The Controls toolbar of Visual C++.

> **Note:** If you do not see the Controls toolbar on your Visual C++ desktop, then do the following:
>
> ☐ Select Toolbars from the View menu of Visual C++.
>
> *Visual C++ will respond by displaying the Toolbars dialog box. (See Figure 1.29.)*
>
> ☐ Make sure the Controls check box has a check mark in it. If it doesn't, click to place a check mark in it.
>
> ☐ Close the Toolbars dialog box by clicking its OK button.
>
> *Visual C++ will respond by displaying the Controls toolbar.*

Figure 1.29.
The Toolbars dialog box.

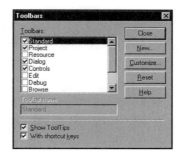

Follow these steps to place a pushbutton in the IDD_HELLO_DIALOG dialog box:

☐ Click the pushbutton tool, shown enlarged in Figure 1.30, in the Controls toolbar of Visual C++.

Figure 1.30.
The pushbutton tool in the
Controls toolbar.

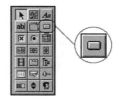

☐ Now click in the IDD_HELLO_DIALOG dialog box where you want the pushbutton control to appear.

Visual C++ responds by placing a pushbutton control at the point where you clicked the mouse. (See Figure 1.31.)

Figure 1.31.

Placing a pushbutton control in the IDD_HELLO_DIALOG dialog box.

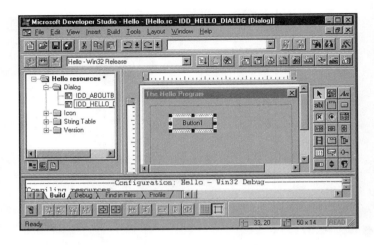

The pushbutton caption is currently `Button1`. As shown in Figure 1.1, it should be `Say Hello`. Here is how you change the pushbutton caption:

☐ Right-click on the Button1 pushbutton control. (That is, place the mouse cursor over the pushbutton and click the mouse's right button.)

> *Visual C++ responds by displaying a pop-up menu next to the Button1 control. (See Figure 1.32.)*

Figure 1.32.

The pop-up menu displayed after you right-click the Button1 control.

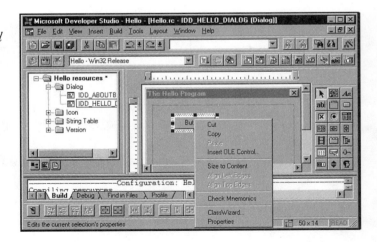

☐ Select Properties from the pop-up menu.

> *Visual C++ responds by displaying the Push Button Properties dialog box. (See Figure 1.33.)*

Figure 1.33.
The Push Button Properties dialog box.

As shown in Figure 1.33, the Caption box contains the text Button1. Here is how you change the caption:

☐ Click in the Caption box and replace the text Button1 with the text Say Hello.

Your Push Button Properties dialog box should now look like the one shown in Figure 1.34.

Figure 1.34.
Changing the caption to Say Hello.

☐ Close the Push Button Properties dialog box by clicking the × icon at the upper-right corner of the window.

Your IDD_HELLO_DIALOG dialog box should now look like the one shown in Figure 1.35—the pushbutton's caption is Say Hello.

Figure 1.35.
The pushbutton's new caption.

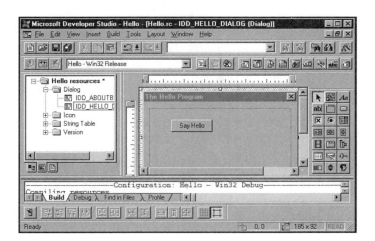

As shown back in Figure 1.1, the Say Hello button should be wider than it is in Figure 1.35. Here is how you change the width of the Say Hello button:

☐ Make sure the Say Hello button is selected (by clicking it), then drag any of the handles on the button's right edge to the right until the button is the desired width. (The handles are the solid black squares on the rectangle enclosing the button.)

Similarly, to increase the height of the Say Hello button, do the following:

☐ Make sure the Say Hello button is selected, then drag any of the handles on the bottom edge of the button downward until the button is the desired height.

The enlarged Say Hello button is shown in Figure 1.36.

Figure 1.36.
Enlarging the Say Hello button.

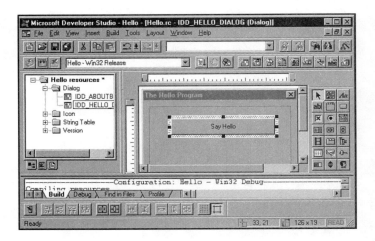

You can also move the Say Hello button to any location in the dialog box by clicking the button and dragging it with the mouse.

When you placed the button in the dialog box, Visual C++ automatically assigned IDC_BUTTON1 as a default ID for the button. However, you should change the button's ID to make it easier to identify it as the ID for the Say Hello button (for example, IDC_SAYHELLO_BUTTON). Here is how you do that:

☐ Right-click the Say Hello button, then select Properties from the pop-up menu.

   Visual C++ responds by displaying the Push Button Properties dialog box. (Refer back to Figure 1.34.)

☐ Click in the ID box and replace the text IDC_BUTTON1 with the text IDC_SAYHELLO_BUTTON.

From now on, Visual C++ will refer to the Say Hello button as IDC_SAYHELLO_BUTTON.

You are almost done with the visual design of the IDD_HELLO_DIALOG dialog box. As shown back in Figure 1.1, the dialog box should also contain an Exit pushbutton. Follow these steps to add the Exit pushbutton:

☐ Place a new button in the dialog box by clicking the pushbutton tool in the Controls toolbar, then clicking anywhere in the IDD_HELLO_DIALOG dialog box.

☐ Move the new button below the Say Hello button by clicking and dragging it.

☐ Make the new button the same size as the Say Hello button by dragging its handles.

Note: For your convenience, while you are designing the IDD_HELLO_DIALOG dialog box, you can display it in full-screen mode by doing the following:

☐ Select Full Screen from the Visual C++ View menu.

Visual C++ will respond by displaying the IDD_HELLO_DIALOG dialog box in full-screen mode—the whole screen will be used for designing the dialog box.

☐ To cancel the full-screen mode, simply press the Esc key.

Now change the properties of the new button as follows:

☐ Right-click the new button and select Properties from the pop-up menu.

☐ Set the Caption property to Exit.

☐ Set the ID property to IDC_EXIT_BUTTON.

Your IDD_HELLO_DIALOG dialog box should now look like the one shown in Figure 1.37.

Figure 1.37.
IDD_HELLO_DIALOG with the Say Hello and Exit pushbuttons.

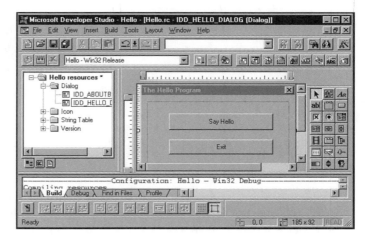

Congratulations! You have finished the visual design of the Hello program.

☐ Save your work by selecting Save All from the File menu.

Seeing Your Visual Design in Action

Although you haven't written any code yet, you have finished the visual design of the Hello.EXE program. To see your visual design in action, follow these steps:

☐ Select Build Hello.EXE from the Build menu.

Visual C++ responds by compiling and linking the Hello program.

Once Visual C++ finishes compiling and linking the program, you can execute the program:

☐ Select Execute Hello.EXE from the Build menu.

Visual C++ responds by executing the Hello.EXE program. The main window of Hello.EXE appears, as shown in Figure 1.38.

Figure 1.38.
The main window of the Hello.EXE program.

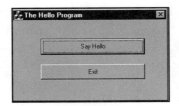

As you can see, the main window of the Hello.EXE program (the IDD_HELLO_DIALOG dialog box) appears just as you designed it—with a Say Hello pushbutton and an Exit pushbutton.

☐ Click the Say Hello and Exit buttons.

As you can see, nothing happens when you click the Say Hello and Exit buttons because you haven't attached any code to them. You'll attach code to these buttons in the following sections.

☐ Terminate the Hello.EXE program by clicking the × icon at the upper-right corner of the program's window.

Attaching Code to the Say Hello Pushbutton

As you have seen, at this point nothing happens when you click the Say Hello and Exit pushbuttons. In this section, you'll attach code to the Say Hello pushbutton so the program will do what it's supposed to do when you click the button. In the next section, you'll attach code to the Exit pushbutton.

When you click the Say Hello pushbutton, the Hello.EXE program should display a HELLO message box. (Refer back to Figure 1.2.) Follow these steps to attach code to the Say Hello button:

☐ Select ClassWizard from the View menu.

Visual C++ responds by displaying the MFC ClassWizard dialog box. (See Figure 1.39.)

Figure 1.39.
The MFC ClassWizard dialog box.

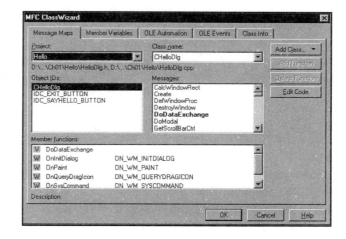

What is ClassWizard? ClassWizard is another powerful "wizard" that lets you attach code to the controls of your program very easily. In the following steps, you'll use ClassWizard to attach code to the Say Hello pushbutton.

As shown in Figure 1.39, the top of ClassWizard's dialog box has five tabs: Message Maps, Member Variables, OLE Automation, OLE Events, and Class Info.

☐ Make sure the Message Maps tab is selected.

☐ Make sure the Class name drop-down list box at the top of the ClassWizard dialog box is set to CHelloDlg.

The CHelloDlg class is the class associated with the IDD_HELLO_DIALOG dialog box (the main window of the Hello program). This class was created for you by MFC AppWizard when you created the Hello project. Therefore, the code you attach to the Say Hello pushbutton will be written in the CHelloDlg class.

You will now use ClassWizard to write the code that's automatically executed whenever you click the Say Hello pushbutton. Here is how you do that:

☐ Select IDC_SAYHELLO_BUTTON in the Object IDs list box of the ClassWizard dialog box.

Your MFC ClassWizard dialog box should now look like the one shown in Figure 1.40.

Figure 1.40.

Selecting the IDC_SAYHELLO_BUTTON item in the Object IDs list box.

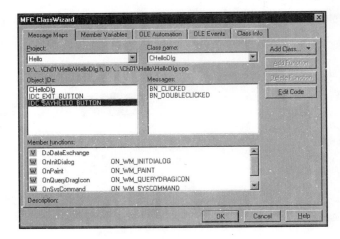

In the preceding step, you selected the IDC_SAYHELLO_BUTTON object because you want to attach code to the Say Hello pushbutton (recall that IDC_SAYHELLO_BUTTON is the ID you assigned to the Say Hello button).

The Messages list box (to the right of the Object IDs list) lists messages representing events associated with the currently selected object. As shown in Figure 1.40, there are two possible events (messages) associated with the IDC_SAYHELLO_BUTTON pushbutton: BN_CLICKED and BN_DOUBLECLICKED. BN_CLICKED represents the event "the user clicked the pushbutton"; BN_DOUBLECLICKED represents the event "the user double-clicked the pushbutton."

You want to attach code to the event "the user clicked the Say Hello pushbutton." You have already selected IDC_SAYHELLO_BUTTON in the Object IDs list box, so now you need to perform this step:

☐ Select the BN_CLICKED item in the Messages list box.

Your MFC ClassWizard dialog box should now look like the one shown in Figure 1.41— IDC_SAYHELLO_BUTTON is selected in the Object IDs list box, and BN_CLICKED is selected in the Messages list box.

Next, you have to tell ClassWizard to add the function corresponding to the event you just selected. This function is executed automatically whenever you click the Say Hello button. Here is how you do that:

☐ Click the Add Function button of ClassWizard.

> *ClassWizard responds by displaying the Add Member Function dialog box. (See Figure 1.42.)*

Figure 1.41.
Selecting BN_CLICKED *in the Messages list box.*

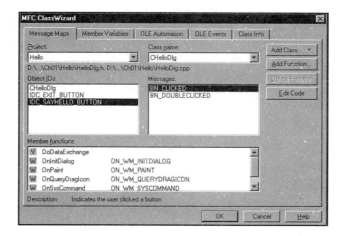

Figure 1.42.
The Add Member Function dialog box.

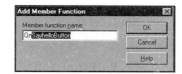

As shown in Figure 1.42, ClassWizard suggests naming the new function OnSayhelloButton.

☐ Click the OK button to accept the default name that ClassWizard suggests.

> *ClassWizard responds by adding the function* OnSayhelloButton() *to the Hello program. This function will be automatically executed whenever you click the Say Hello pushbutton.*

ClassWizard wrote only the code that declares the OnSayhelloButton() function and the skeleton of the function. It is your job to write the code in the OnSayhelloButton() function. To do that, follow these steps:

☐ Click the Edit Code button of ClassWizard.

> *ClassWizard responds by opening the file HelloDlg.cpp with the function* OnSayhelloButton() *ready for you to edit. (See Figure 1.43.)*

☐ Write code in the OnSayhelloButton() function so that it will look like this:

```
void CHelloDlg::OnSayhelloButton()
{

// TODO: Add your control notification handler code here

////////////////////////////
// MY CODE STARTS HERE
////////////////////////////
```

```
MessageBox("Hello! This is my first Visual C++ program.");

/////////////////////////
// MY CODE ENDS HERE
/////////////////////////

}
```

☐ Save your work by selecting Save All from the File menu.

Figure 1.43.

The OnSayhelloButton() *function, ready for editing.*

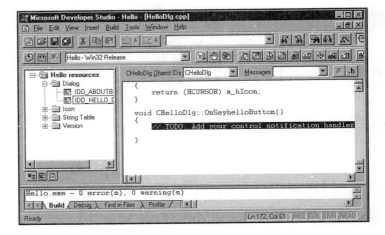

Note: As you have just seen, when you use MFC ClassWizard to attach code to a control, you type your code in a skeleton of the function that ClassWizard writes for you.

To make it easy for you to distinguish between code that Visual C++ wrote for you and code that you type yourself, the following convention is used in this book:

Code that you type yourself is presented in the following manner:

```
/////////////////////////
// MY CODE STARTS HERE
/////////////////////////


.............................
... Your code appears here ...
.............................


/////////////////////////
// MY CODE ENDS HERE
/////////////////////////
```

The **MY CODE STARTS HERE** and **MY CODE ENDS HERE** comments will help you distinguish between code that Visual C++ wrote for you and code that you type.

The code you typed in the `OnSayhelloButton()` function is very simple (one line):

```
MessageBox("Hello! This is my first Visual C++ program.");
```

It uses the `MessageBox()` function to display a message box with the text `Hello! This is my first Visual C++ program`.

To see the code you attached to the Say Hello pushbutton in action, follow these steps:

☐ Select Build Hello.EXE from the Build menu.

   Visual C++ responds by compiling and linking the Hello program.

Once Visual C++ finishes compiling and linking the program, you can execute it:

☐ Select Execute Hello.EXE from the Build menu.

   Visual C++ responds by executing the Hello.EXE program. The main window of Hello.EXE appears, as shown back in Figure 1.38.

☐ Click the Say Hello pushbutton.

   As expected, the Hello.EXE program responds by displaying a HELLO message box. (See Figure 1.44.) The code you attached to the Say Hello pushbutton is working!

Figure 1.44.
Displaying the HELLO message box.

☐ Close the HELLO message box by clicking its OK button.

☐ Try to click the Exit pushbutton.

Of course, nothing happens when you click the Exit pushbutton because you haven't attached code to it yet. You'll attach code to the Exit pushbutton in the following section.

☐ Terminate the Hello.EXE program by clicking the × icon at the upper-right corner of the program's window.

Attaching Code to the Exit Pushbutton

At this point, nothing happens when you click the Exit pushbutton. In this section, you'll attach code to the Exit pushbutton so that the Hello.EXE program will terminate when you click the button. Follow these steps to attach code to the Exit pushbutton:

☐ Select ClassWizard from the View menu of Visual C++.

   Visual C++ responds by displaying the MFC ClassWizard dialog box. (Refer back to Figure 1.39.)

☐ Make sure the Message Maps tab is selected.

☐ Make sure the Class name drop-down list box at the top of the ClassWizard dialog box is set to CHelloDlg.

In the preceding step, you were instructed to select the CHelloDlg class in the ClassWizard dialog box because you're going to attach code to the Exit pushbutton, which is in the IDD_HELLO_DIALOG dialog box. The IDD_HELLO_DIALOG dialog box is associated with the CHelloDlg class. Therefore, the code you attach to the Exit pushbutton will be written in the CHelloDlg class.

☐ Select IDC_EXIT_BUTTON in the Object IDs list of the ClassWizard dialog box (because you are attaching code to the Exit pushbutton).

☐ Select BN_CLICKED in the Messages list box to attach code to the BN_CLICKED event of the Exit pushbutton.

Your MFC ClassWizard dialog box should now look like the one shown in Figure 1.45—IDC_EXIT_BUTTON is selected in the Object IDs list box, and BN_CLICKED is selected in the Messages list box.

Figure 1.45.

Selecting IDC_EXIT_BUTTON in the Object IDs list box and BN_CLICKED in the Messages list box.

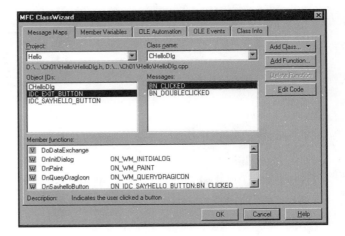

By selecting IDC_EXIT_BUTTON in the Object IDs list box and BN_CLICKED in the Messages list box, you are specifying that you want to attach code to the event "the user clicked the Exit pushbutton." That is, you want to attach code to the Click event of the Exit pushbutton.

Next, tell ClassWizard to add the function corresponding to the event you just selected—the function executed automatically whenever you click the Exit button. Here is how you do that:

☐ Click the Add Function button of ClassWizard.

  ClassWizard responds by displaying the Add Member Function dialog box. ClassWizard suggests naming the new function OnExitButton.

☐ Click the OK button of the Add Member Function dialog box to accept the default name that ClassWizard suggests.

  ClassWizard responds by adding the function OnExitButton() *to the Hello program. This function will be executed automatically whenever you click the Exit pushbutton.*

To write code in the OnExitButton() function, do the following:

☐ Click the Edit Code button of ClassWizard.

  ClassWizard responds by opening the file Hello.cpp with the function OnExitButton() *ready for you to edit.*

☐ Write code in the OnExitButton() function so that it will look like this:

```
void CHelloDlg::OnExitButton()
{
// TODO: Add your control notification handler code here

/////////////////////////
// MY CODE STARTS HERE
/////////////////////////

OnOK();

/////////////////////////
// MY CODE ENDS HERE
/////////////////////////

}
```

☐ Save your work by selecting Save All from the File menu.

The code you typed in the OnExitButton() function is very simple (one line):

```
OnOK();
```

This statement closes the IDD_HELLO_DIALOG dialog box of the Hello program by calling the OnOK() member function of the CHelloDlg class. The OnOK() member function works like an OK button—it closes the dialog box. Because the IDD_HELLO_DIALOG dialog box serves as the main window of the Hello program, closing it by calling the OnOK() function terminates the program.

> **Note:** The reason you can call the OnOK() member function of the CHelloDlg class from the OnExitButton() function is that OnExitButton() is also a member function of the CHelloDlg class. Recall that when you added the OnExitButton() function by using ClassWizard, you specified that the class name is CHelloDlg, as shown in Figure 1.45.
>
> The OnOK() function is actually a member function of the MFC class CDialog. When Visual C++ created the CHelloDlg class for you, Visual C++ derived the CHelloDlg class from the MFC class CDialog. Therefore, the CHelloDlg class inherited the OnOK() member function from its parent, CDialog.

To see the code you attached to the Exit pushbutton in action, follow these steps:

☐ Select Build Hello.EXE from the Build menu.

> *Visual C++ responds by compiling and linking the Hello program.*

Once Visual C++ finishes compiling and linking the program, you can execute it:

☐ Select Execute Hello.EXE from the Build menu.

> *Visual C++ responds by executing the Hello.EXE program. The main window of Hello.EXE appears, as shown back in Figure 1.38.*

☐ Click the Exit pushbutton.

> *As expected, the Hello.EXE program responds by terminating. The code you attached to the Exit pushbutton is working!*

Customizing the Icon of the Hello.EXE Program

The icon of the Hello.EXE program is the small picture at the upper-left corner of the program's window. The Hello program's icon is currently the default icon that Visual C++ created when you generated the skeleton of the program. (See Figure 1.46.)

You can change the default icon that Visual C++ created for the program as follows:

☐ Select the ResourceView tab of the Project Workspace dialog box.

Figure 1.46.
*The default icon created for
the Hello.EXE program.*

 Note: If for some reason the Project Workspace dialog box is not open on the Visual C++ desktop, then you can display it by selecting Project Workspace from the View menu.

☐ In the Project Workspace dialog box, expand the Icon item by double-clicking it, then double-click the IDR_MAINFRAME item listed under the Icon item. (See Figure 1.47.)

Figure 1.47.
*Selecting the
IDR_MAINFRAME item.*

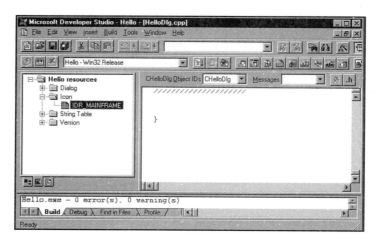

Visual C++ responds by displaying the icon of the Hello.EXE program in design mode. (See Figure 1.48.)

You can now use the Graphics toolbar and Colors toolbar of Visual C++ to replace the default picture of Hello.EXE's icon with your own drawing. The Graphics and Colors toolbars of Visual C++ are shown in Figure 1.49.

Figure 1.48.
The icon of the Hello.EXE program in design mode.

Figure 1.49.
The Graphics and Colors toolbars of Visual C++.

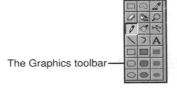

The Graphics toolbar

The Colors toolbar

If you do not see the Graphics toolbar or Colors toolbar on your Visual C++ desktop, then do the following to display them:

☐ Select Toolbars from the View menu of Visual C++.

  Visual C++ will respond by displaying the Toolbars dialog box. (Refer back to Figure 1.29.)

☐ Make sure the Graphics check box and the Colors check box have check marks in them. If they don't, click them to place a check mark.

☐ Close the Toolbars dialog box by clicking its OK button.

  Visual C++ will respond by displaying the Graphics toolbar and Colors toolbar.

Note: You use the Graphics toolbar and the Colors toolbar of Visual C++ just as you use similar toolbars in other drawing programs. For example, you can use the eraser tool of the Graphics toolbar to erase the drawing.

Remember, you can display the icon in full-screen mode by selecting Full Screen from the View menu. To cancel the full-screen mode, press the Esc key.

Note: Figure 1.50 shows the icon of the Hello.EXE program in design mode after the default drawing has been replaced with a simple drawing of the word "Hello."

Once you finish customizing the icon of the Hello program, you can see your visual design in action by compiling and linking the Hello project and then executing the Hello.EXE program.

Figure 1.50.
The icon of the Hello.EXE program in design mode (after customization).

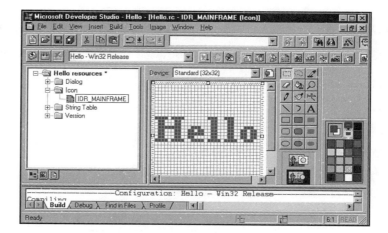

Opening an Old Project

Suppose you work on the Hello project for a while, then you quit Visual C++, and later you want to resume working on the Hello project. In this case, you would have to start Visual C++ and load the Hello project. The following step-by-step tutorial illustrates how to open an old Visual C++ project:

☐ Quit Visual C++ by selecting Exit from the File menu.

In the preceding step you are instructed to quit Visual C++ so that you'll get a real "feel" for starting Visual C++ and opening an old project.

☐ Start Visual C++ as you did in the beginning of this chapter by starting the Microsoft Developer Studio. (The icon is in the Microsoft Visual C++ program group.)

The Visual C++ desktop appears.

To open the Hello project, do the following:

☐ Select Open Workspace from the File menu.

> *Visual C++ responds by displaying the Open Project Workspace dialog box.*

☐ Use the Open Project Workspace dialog box to select the
C:\TYVCProg\Programs\CH01\Hello\Hello.MDP project workspace file.

> *Visual C++ responds by opening the Project Workspace of the Hello program.*

You can now use the ResourceView tab of the Project Workspace dialog box to customize the
resources of the Hello program, just as you did at the beginning of this chapter.

Following a Properties Table

In this chapter you have been instructed to perform the visual design of the Hello.EXE program
by following detailed step-by-step instructions. However, in subsequent chapters, instead of
using step-by-step instructions, you'll be instructed to perform the visual design of the programs
by following a *properties table*.

Table 1.1 is a typical example of a properties table. This table is the properties table of the
IDD_HELLO_DIALOG dialog box of the Hello.EXE program.

**Table 1.1. The properties table of the IDD_HELLO_DIALOG
dialog box.**

Object	Property	Setting
Dialog Box	**ID**	**IDD_HELLO_DIALOG**
Push Button	**ID**	**IDC_SAYHELLO_BUTTON**
	Caption	Say Hello
Push Button	**ID**	**IDC_EXIT_BUTTON**
	Caption	Exit

Following a properties table to design a dialog box is easy. All you have to do is place the listed
controls in the dialog box and set their properties as specified in the table.

Summary

In this chapter, you have written your first Visual C++ program. You have learned that writing
a Visual C++ program involves two steps: the visual design step and the code-writing step.

As you have seen, performing the visual design of your program with Visual C++ is easy. You use the ResourceView tab of the Project Workspace dialog box to open the resource you want to customize (for example, a dialog box) and then use the Visual C++ tools to perform your visual design.

Once you finish the visual design, attach code to the controls you created during the visual design by using ClassWizard.

Q&A

Q **The About dialog box, shown in Figure 1.20, that Visual C++ created for the Hello.EXE program is nice. However, I'd like to customize this dialog box. For example, I'd like to include my own copyright notice in this dialog box. How do I do that?**

A You can customize the About dialog box that Visual C++ created for the Hello.EXE program just as you customized the IDD_HELLO_DIALOG dialog box. Here is how you do that:

☐ Open the project workspace of the Hello program (if it's not open already). You open the project workspace by selecting Open Workspace from the File menu, then selecting the C:\TYVCProg\Programs\CH01\Hello\Hello.MDP workspace file.

☐ If you do not see the Project Workspace dialog box in your desktop, then select Project Workspace from the View menu.

☐ Select the ResourceView tab of the Project Workspace dialog box, expand the Hello resources item, expand the Dialog item, and finally double-click the IDD_ABOUTBOX item under the Dialog item.

   Visual C++ responds by displaying the About dialog box of the Hello program in design mode.

You can now use the Controls toolbar to customize the About dialog box. For example, you can use the static text tool of the Controls toolbar to add your own text to the About dialog box. The static text tool is shown magnified in Figure 1.51.

You place the static text control in the dialog box the same way you placed the pushbutton control—click the static text tool in the Controls toolbar, then click in the dialog box.

To set the text of the static text control, right-click the static text control in the dialog box, select Properties from the pop-up menu, then set the Caption property of the control to the desired text.

Figure 1.51.
The static text tool in the Controls toolbar.

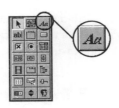

Q The main window of the Hello.EXE program has an × icon at its upper-right corner, but it does not include the Minimize and Maximize boxes that many Windows programs have. How can I change the main window of the Hello.EXE program so that it includes the Minimize and Maximize boxes?

A To add Minimize and Maximize boxes to the main window of the Hello.EXE program (the IDD_HELLO_DIALOG dialog box), set the Maximize box and Minimize box properties of the IDD_HELLO_DIALOG dialog box to TRUE. Here is how you do that:

☐ Open the project workspace of the Hello program (if it's not open already) by selecting Open Workspace from the File menu, then selecting the C:\TYVCProg\Programs\CH01\Hello\Hello.MDP workspace file.

☐ If you don't see the Project Workspace dialog box in your desktop, then select Project Workspace from the View menu.

☐ Select the ResourceView tab of the Project Workspace dialog box, expand the Hello resources item, expand the Dialog item, and finally double-click the IDD_HELLO_DIALOG item under the Dialog item.

> *Visual C++ responds by displaying the IDD_HELLO_DIALOG dialog box in design mode.*

You need to change the Maximize box and Minimize box properties of the IDD_HELLO_DIALOG dialog box. Here is how you do that:

☐ Right-click the mouse in any free area—not occupied by a control—in the IDD_HELLO_DIALOG dialog box.

☐ Select Properties from the pop-up menu.

> *Visual C++ responds by displaying the Dialog Properties dialog box.*

☐ Select the Styles tab of the Dialog Properties dialog box. (See Figure 1.52.)

☐ Place a check mark in the Minimize box and Maximize box check boxes.

> That's it! Your IDD_HELLO_DIALOG dialog box now includes the Maximize and Minimize boxes. (See Figure 1.53.)

Figure 1.52.
The Styles tab of the Dialog Properties dialog box.

Figure 1.53.
IDD_HELLO_DIALOG with the Maximize and Minimize boxes.

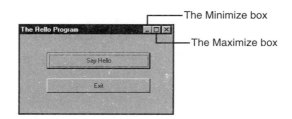

— The Minimize box

— The Maximize box

Quiz

1. What are the two steps in the design process of a Visual C++ program?
2. What is a dialog-based program?
3. Describe the steps you take to open the IDD_HELLO_DIALOG dialog box of the Hello program so you can visually customize it.
4. What is ClassWizard?

Exercise

The main window of the Hello.EXE program currently has two pushbuttons in it: Say Hello and Exit. Add a third pushbutton called Beep to the main window of the program. Attach code to the BN_CLICKED event of the Beep pushbutton so that the PC will beep when the user clicks this button.

Hint: This is the statement that causes the PC to beep:

```
MessageBeep((WORD)-1);
```

Quiz Answers

1. The two steps in the design process of a Visual C++ program are the visual design step and the code-writing step.
2. A dialog-based program has a dialog box for the program's main window.
3. To open the IDD_HELLO_DIALOG dialog box in design mode, do the following:

☐ Select the ResourceView tab of the Project Workspace dialog box, expand the Hello resources item, expand the Dialog item, and finally double-click the IDD_HELLO_DIALOG item under the Dialog item.

> *Visual C++ will respond by displaying the IDD_HELLO_DIALOG dialog box in design mode.*

4. ClassWizard is a powerful "wizard" that enables you to attach code to controls very easily. For example, in the Hello program you used ClassWizard to attach code to the Click events of the Say Hello and Exit pushbuttons.

Exercise Answer

To add the Beep pushbutton, follow these steps:

☐ Open the project workspace of the Hello program by selecting Open Workspace from the File menu, then selecting the C:\TYVCProg\Programs\CH01\Hello\Hello.MDP workspace file.

☐ If you do not see the Project Workspace dialog box in your desktop, then select Project Workspace from the View menu.

☐ Select the ResourceView tab of the Project Workspace dialog box, expand the Hello resources item, expand the Dialog item, and finally double-click the IDD_HELLO_DIALOG item under the Dialog item.

> *Visual C++ responds by displaying the IDD_HELLO_DIALOG dialog box in design mode.*

☐ Place a new pushbutton control in the IDD_HELLO_DIALOG dialog box.

☐ Right-click the new pushbutton control, select Properties from the pop-up menu, then set the properties of the new pushbutton as follows:

```
ID: IDD_BEEP_BUTTON
Caption: Beep
```

Remember, choose Full Screen from the View menu to display the IDD_HELLO_DIALOG dialog box in full-screen mode and enlarge the dialog box by dragging its handles.

Now attach code to the Click event of the Beep pushbutton as follows:

☐ Select ClassWizard from the View menu.

> *Visual C++ responds by displaying the MFC ClassWizard dialog box.*

☐ Make sure the Message Maps tab is selected.

☐ Make sure the Class name drop-down list box at the top of the ClassWizard dialog box is set to CHelloDlg.

In the preceding step, you were instructed to select the CHelloDlg class in the ClassWizard dialog box to attach code to the Beep pushbutton; the Beep pushbutton is in the IDD_HELLO_DIALOG dialog box, which is associated with the CHelloDlg class. Therefore, the code you attach to the Beep pushbutton will be written in the CHelloDlg class.

☐ Select IDC_BEEP_BUTTON in the Object IDs list of the ClassWizard dialog box to attach code to the Beep pushbutton.

☐ Select BN_CLICKED in the Messages list box to attach code to the BN_CLICKED event of the Exit pushbutton.

By selecting IDC_BEEP_BUTTON in the Object IDs list box and BN_CLICKED in the Messages list box, you are specifying that you want to attach code to the event "the user clicked the Beep pushbutton."

☐ Click the Add Function button of ClassWizard.

> *ClassWizard responds by displaying the Add Member Function dialog box. ClassWizard suggests naming the new function* OnBeepButton.

☐ Click the OK button of the Add Member Function dialog box to accept the default name that ClassWizard suggests.

> *ClassWizard responds by adding the function* OnBeepButton() *to the Hello program. This function will be executed automatically whenever the user clicks the Beep pushbutton.*

To write the code in the OnBeepButton() function, do the following:

☐ Click the Edit Code button of ClassWizard.

> *ClassWizard responds by opening the file HelloDlg.cpp, with the function* OnBeepButton() *ready for you to edit.*

☐ Write code in the OnBeepButton() function so that it will look like this:

```
void CHelloDlg::OnBeepButton()
{
// TODO: Add your control notification handler code here

//////////////////////////
// MY CODE STARTS HERE
//////////////////////////

MessageBeep((WORD)-1);

//////////////////////////
// MY CODE ENDS HERE
//////////////////////////

}
```

☐ Save your work by selecting Save All from the File menu.

The code you typed in the `OnBeepButton()` function is very simple (one line):

```
MessageBeep((WORD)-1);
```

This statement causes the PC to beep through the PC speaker. To see (and hear) the Beep pushbutton in action, follow these steps:

☐ Select Build Hello.EXE from the Build menu.

Visual C++ responds by compiling and linking the Hello program.

Once Visual C++ finishes compiling and linking the program, you can execute it:

☐ Select Execute Hello.EXE from the Build menu.

Visual C++ responds by executing the Hello.EXE program. The main window of Hello.EXE appears.

☐ Click the Beep pushbutton.

As expected, the Hello.EXE program responds by beeping. The code you attached to the `Click` *event of the Beep pushbutton is working!*

☐ Terminate the Hello.EXE program by clicking its Exit pushbutton.

Controls, Properties, and Events

In the previous chapter, you wrote a Visual C++ program that uses the pushbutton control. You learned how to place a pushbutton control in a dialog box and how to attach code to the `BN_CLICKED` event of the pushbutton control.

In this chapter, you'll get experience with other controls. You'll learn how to write a Visual C++ program that uses the edit box control and the check box control. You'll learn how to visually design a dialog box that uses these controls and how to attach code to the events of these controls.

The Test.EXE Program

In this chapter, you'll write a Visual C++ program called Test.EXE, which illustrates how to write Visual C++ programs that use two popular Windows controls: the edit box and the check box. But before you start writing the Test.EXE program, first review what it should look like and what it should do:

- When you start the Test.EXE program, its window should look like the one shown in Figure 2.1.

Figure 2.1.

The window of the Test.EXE program.

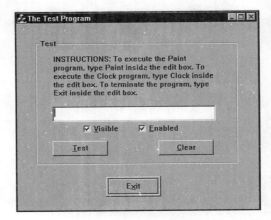

- The window of the Test.EXE program includes several controls: a static text control with instructions text, an edit box, two check boxes (Visible and Enabled), and three pushbuttons (Test, Clear, and Exit). (A static text control is used for displaying text.)
- As specified by the instructions text, if you type the word Paint in the edit box, the Test program executes the Windows Paint program. If you type the word Clock in the edit box, the Test program executes the Windows Clock program. And if you type the word Exit in the edit box, the Test program terminates. You don't have to press Enter after typing the word. As soon as you type the last letter of the word, Test.EXE responds by executing the appropriate program.

- When you click the Test button, the Test.EXE program displays the text This is a test! in the edit box. (See Figure 2.2.) When you click the Clear button, the Test.EXE program clears the edit box.

Figure 2.2.
Displaying text in Test.EXE's edit box.

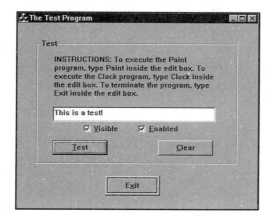

- As shown in Figure 2.1, the Visible and Enabled check boxes have check marks in them when you start the program. When you remove the check mark from the Visible check box, the edit box becomes invisible. (See Figure 2.3.) To make the edit box visible again, place a check mark in the Visible check box.

Figure 2.3.
Removing the check mark from the Visible check box.

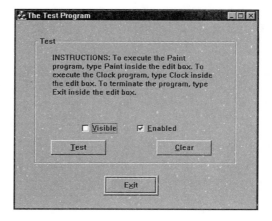

- When you remove the check mark from the Enabled check box, the edit box becomes disabled. The text is dimmed, and you can't change its value. (See Figure 2.4.) To enable the edit box again, place a check mark in the Enabled check box.

Figure 2.4.
*Removing the check mark
from the Enabled check box.*

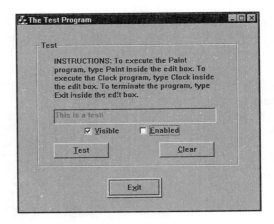

- When you click the Exit pushbutton, the Test.EXE program terminates.

Now that you know what the Test.EXE program should look like and what it should do, you can start designing this program.

Creating the Project of the Test.EXE Program

Follow these steps to create the project and skeleton files of the Test.EXE program:

☐ Use the Windows Explorer of Windows 95 to create the directory C:\TYVCProg\Programs\CH02.

☐ Start Visual C++. (Recall that to start Visual C++, you execute the Microsoft Developer Studio.)

☐ Select New from the File menu.

    Visual C++ responds by displaying the New dialog box.

☐ Select Project Workspace from the New dialog box and then click the OK button.

    Visual C++ responds by displaying the New Project Workspace dialog box.

☐ Select MFC AppWizard (exe) from the Type list.

☐ Type Test in the Name box.

☐ Click the Browse button and select the C:\TYVCProg\Programs\CH02 directory.

☐ Click the Create button.

    Visual C++ responds by displaying the MFC AppWizard - Step 1 window.

☐ Set the MFC AppWizard - Step 1 window as shown in Figure 2.5 to create a dialog-based application.

Figure 2.5.
The MFC AppWizard - Step 1 window.

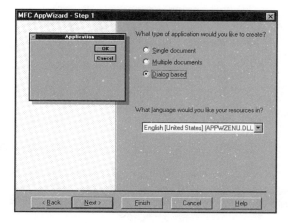

☐ Click the Next button of the Step 1 window.

Visual C++ responds by displaying the MFC AppWizard - Step 2 of 4 window.

☐ Set the MFC AppWizard - Step 2 of 4 window, as shown in Figure 2.6, to set the dialog box's title to The Test Program.

Figure 2.6.
The MFC AppWizard - Step 2 of 4 window.

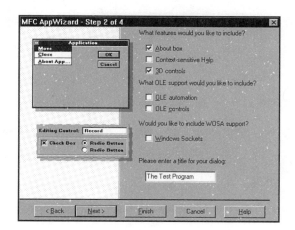

☐ Click the Next button.

Visual C++ responds by displaying the Step 3 of 4 window.

☐ Set the Step 3 of 4 options as shown in Figure 2.7.

Figure 2.7.
*The MFC AppWizard -
Step 3 of 4 window.*

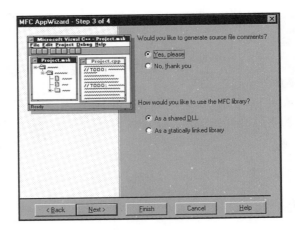

☐ Click the Next button.

> *Visual C++ responds by displaying the Step 4 of 4 window. (See Figure 2.8.)*

Figure 2.8.
*The MFC AppWizard -
Step 4 of 4 window.*

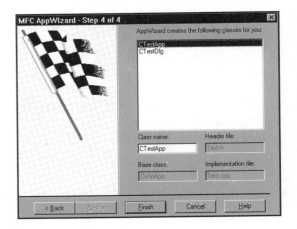

☐ Click the Finish button.

> *Visual C++ responds by displaying the New Project Information window.*

☐ Click the OK button of the New Project Information window.

☐ Select Set Default Configuration from the Build menu of Visual C++.

> *Visual C++ responds by displaying the Default Project Configuration dialog box.*

☐ Select Test - Win32 Release in the Default Project Configuration dialog box, then click the OK button.

That's it! You've finished creating the project file and skeleton files of the Test program.

The Visual Design of the Test Program

You'll now visually design the dialog box that serves as the main window of the Test program (the IDD_TEST_DIALOG dialog box).

☐ Select Project Workspace from the View menu.

☐ Select the ResourceView tab of the Project Workspace window.

☐ Expand the Test resources item.

☐ Expand the Dialog item.

☐ Double-click the IDD_TEST_DIALOG item.

> *Visual C++ responds by displaying the IDD_TEST_DIALOG dialog box in design mode.*

☐ Delete the OK button, Cancel button, and text in the IDD_TEST_DIALOG dialog box.

☐ Design the IDD_TEST_DIALOG dialog box according to Table 2.1. When you finish designing the dialog box, it should look like Figure 2.9.

Note: Table 2.1 instructs you to place several controls in the IDD_TEST_DIALOG dialog box and to set certain properties of these controls. If you forgot how to place controls in a dialog box or how to set the properties of controls, refer back to Chapter 1, "Writing Your First Visual C++ Application."

If you don't see the Controls toolbar on your Visual C++ desktop, then select Toolbars from the View menu and place a check mark in the Controls check box.

If you aren't sure whether a certain tool in the Controls toolbar is the right tool, then do the following:

☐ Place the mouse cursor over the tool in the Controls toolbar.

> *Visual C++ will respond by displaying a small yellow rectangle that shows the tool's name. For example, if you move the mouse cursor over the tool of the edit box control, Visual C++ will display a yellow rectangle with the text* Edit Box.

Remember, you can display the IDD_TEST_DIALOG dialog box in full-screen mode by selecting Full Screen from the View menu. Cancel the full-screen mode by pressing the Esc key.

Table 2.1. The properties table of the IDD_TEST_DIALOG dialog box.

Object	Property	Setting
Dialog Box	ID	**IDD_TEST_DIALOG**
	Caption	The Test Program
	Font	System, Size 10 (General tab)
	Minimize box	Checked (Styles tab)
	Maximize box	Checked (Styles tab)
Group Box	ID	**IDC_STATIC**
	Caption	Test
Static Text	ID	**IDC_STATIC**
	Caption	INSTRUCTIONS: To execute the Paint program, type Paint inside the edit box. To execute the Clock program, type Clock inside the edit box. To terminate the program, type Exit inside the edit box.
Edit Box	ID	**IDC_TEST_EDIT**
Check Box	ID	**IDC_VISIBLE_CHECK**
	Caption	&Visible
Check Box	ID	**IDC_ENABLED_CHECK**
	Caption	&Enabled
Push Button	ID	**IDC_TEST_BUTTON**
	Caption	&Test
Push Button	ID	**IDC_CLEAR_BUTTON**
	Caption	&Clear
Push Button	ID	**IDC_EXIT_BUTTON**
	Caption	E&xit
	Client edge	Checked (Extended Styles tab)
	Static edge	Checked (Extended Styles tab)
	Modal frame	Checked (Extended Styles tab)

Figure 2.9.
Customizing the
IDD_TEST_DIALOG
dialog box.

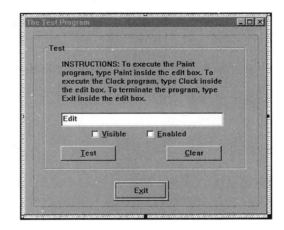

The following list explains, in more detail, how to use the properties table for the IDD_TEST_DIALOG dialog box:

1. The first object listed in Table 2.1 is the IDD_TEST_DIALOG dialog box itself. You set its Minimize box and Maximize box properties to Checked as follows:

☐ Right-click any free area in the dialog box and select Properties from the pop-up menu.

☐ Select the Styles tab of the Dialog Properties dialog box and place a check mark in the Minimize box and Maximize box check boxes.

After you place a check mark in the Minimize box and Maximize box check boxes, the IDD_TEST_DIALOG dialog box will have a Minimize box and a Maximize box in the upper-right corner. During runtime, you can use these boxes to minimize or maximize the dialog box.

2. Table 2.1 instructs you to set the Font property of the IDD_TEST_DIALOG dialog box to System, Size 10. You do that as follows:

☐ Right-click any free area in the dialog box and select Properties from the pop-up menu.

☐ Select the General tab of the Properties dialog box, click the Font button, and set the font to System, Size 10.

The Font property of the dialog box specifies the font type and size used for the text of all the controls you'll place in the dialog box.

3. The second object listed in Table 2.1 is a group box control. The group box control is used for cosmetic reasons only. In Figure 2.9, the group box control is the frame enclosing the Instructions static text control, the edit box control, the Visible and Enabled check box controls, and the Test and Clear pushbutton controls. Set the Caption property of the group box control to Test by following these steps:

☐ Right-click the frame of the static text control and select Properties from the pop-up menu.

☐ After you place the group box control in the dialog box, you can move it to any location by dragging its frame. You can also set its size by dragging its handles.

4. The Caption properties of the check box controls and pushbutton controls include the & character. For example, Table 2.1 specifies that the Caption property of the Exit pushbutton should be E&xit. The & character before the *x* underlines the letter *x* in E&xit. This means that during the execution of the program, pressing Alt+X produces the same results as clicking the Exit button.

5. Use the Extended Styles tab of the Properties dialog box to set the Client edge, Static edge, and Modal frame properties of the Exit pushbutton control to Checked. These properties affect only the visual appearance of the control. Once you set them, you'll see their effects on the pushbutton.

You've finished the visual design of the IDD_TEST_DIALOG dialog box. To see your visual design in action, follow these steps:

☐ Select Build Test.EXE from the Build menu.

☐ Select Execute Test.EXE from the Build menu.

Visual C++ responds by executing the Test.EXE program. The main window of Test.EXE appears, as shown in Figure 2.10.

Figure 2.10.
The main window of the Test.EXE program.

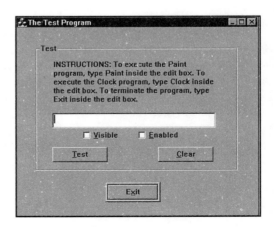

As you can see, the main window of the Test.EXE program (the IDD_TEST_DIALOG dialog box) appears just as you designed it.

☐ Experiment with the controls in the program's window.

As you can see, you can type in the edit box, you can check and uncheck the check boxes, and you can click the pushbuttons. Of course, none of the controls are doing what they're supposed to do because you haven't attached any code yet. You'll attach code to the controls later in this chapter.

☐ Terminate the Test.EXE program by clicking the × icon at the upper-right corner.

Attaching Variables to the Edit Box and Check Box Controls

In this section, you need to attach variables to the edit box control and to the two check box controls, so you can use the variables to access these controls when you write the program's code. These variables are used for reading and writing data to and from the controls.

Follow these steps to attach a variable to the IDC_TEST_EDIT edit box control:

☐ Select ClassWizard from the View menu.

Visual C++ responds by displaying the MFC ClassWizard dialog box.

☐ Select the Member Variables tab of the MFC ClassWizard dialog box. (See Figure 2.11.)

Figure 2.11.
Selecting ClassWizard's Member Variables tab.

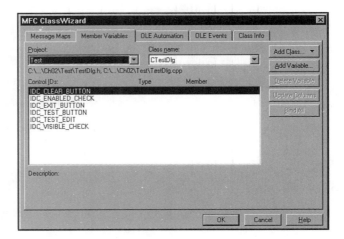

☐ Make sure that the Class name drop-down list box is set to CTestDlg.

The CTestDlg class is the class associated with the IDD_TEST_DIALOG dialog box, which serves as the main window of the Test program. Since you are attaching a variable to a control in the IDD_TEST_DIALOG dialog box, the variable will be a data member of the CTestDlg class.

☐ Select IDC_TEST_EDIT in the Object IDs list to attach a variable to the IDC_TEST_EDIT edit box.

☐ Click the Add Variable button.

Visual C++ responds by displaying the Add Member Variable dialog box. (See Figure 2.12.)

Figure 2.12.
The Add Member Variable dialog box.

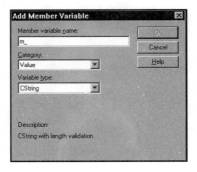

☐ Set the Add Member Variable dialog box as follows:

Member variable name:	m_TestEdit
Category:	Value
Variable type:	CString

☐ Click the OK button of the Add Member Variable dialog box.

You've now attached a variable to the IDC_TEST_EDIT edit box control.

Note: In the preceding steps, you attached a variable of type CString to the IDC_TEST_EDIT edit box. CString is an MFC class specifically designed for storing and manipulating strings of characters. You can store a string in a variable of type CString and then use the member functions of the CString class to manipulate the string.

Next, attach a variable to the IDC_VISIBLE_CHECK check box control:

☐ Select IDC_VISIBLE_CHECK in the Object IDs list box, click the Add Variable button, then set the Add Member Variable dialog box as follows:

Member variable name:	m_VisibleCheck
Category:	Value
Variable type:	BOOL

☐ Click the OK button of the Add Member Variable dialog box.

Finally, attach a variable to the Enabled check box control:

☐ Select IDC_ENABLED_CHECK in the Object IDs list box, click the Add Variable button, then set the Add Member Variable dialog box as follows:

Member variable name:	m_EnabledCheck
Category:	Value
Variable type:	BOOL

☐ Click the OK button of the Add Member Variable dialog box.

☐ Click the OK button of the MFC ClassWizard dialog box.

So, putting it all together, you attached a variable of type CString to the IDC_TEST_EDIT edit box and named it m_TestEdit. When you write the program code, you'll use this variable to read and write strings into the IDC_TEST_EDIT edit box.

You attached a variable of type BOOL to the IDC_VISIBLE_CHECK check box and named it m_VisibleCheck. When you write the program code, you'll use this variable to access the IDC_VISIBLE_CHECK check box.

You also attached a variable of type BOOL to the IDC_ENABLED_CHECK check box and named it m_EnabledCheck. When you write the program code, you'll use this variable to access the IDC_ENABLED_CHECK check box.

All these variables are data members of the CTestDlg class (the class associated with the IDD_TEST_DIALOG dialog box). In the following sections, you'll write code that makes use of these variables.

Writing Code That Initializes the Dialog Box Controls

When you start a dialog-based program, you want some of the controls in the program's main window to have certain initial settings. For example, in the Test.EXE program, you want the

Visible and Enabled check boxes to have check marks in them. (Refer back to Figure 2.1.) Follow these steps to write the code that initializes the Visible and Enabled check boxes:

☐ Select ClassWizard from the View menu.

Visual C++ responds by displaying the MFC ClassWizard dialog box.

☐ Select the Message Maps tab of ClassWizard.

☐ Use the ClassWizard dialog box to make the following selection:

Class name:	CTestDlg
Object ID:	CTestDlg
Message:	WM_INITDIALOG

Your MFC ClassWizard dialog box should now look like Figure 2.13.

Figure 2.13.
Selecting the WM_INITDIALOG *event with ClassWizard.*

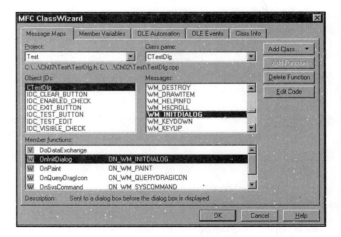

As its name implies, WM_INITDIALOG is the event "initialize the dialog box." Therefore, the code you attach to the WM_INITDIALOG event is responsible for initializing the dialog box.

☐ Click the Edit Code button of ClassWizard.

Visual C++ responds by opening the file TestDlg.cpp with the function OnInitDialog() *ready for you to edit.*

The OnInitDialog() function already has some code written by Visual C++. You'll type your own code below this comment line:

```
// TODO: Add extra initialization here
```

☐ Write the following code in the OnInitDialog() function:

```
BOOL CTestDlg::OnInitDialog()
{
CDialog::OnInitDialog();
...
...
...

// TODO: Add extra initialization here

/////////////////////////
// MY CODE STARTS HERE
/////////////////////////

// Set the variable of the IDC_VISIBLE_CHECK
// check box to TRUE.
m_VisibleCheck = TRUE;

// Set the variable of the IDC_ENABLED_CHECK
// check box to TRUE.
m_EnabledCheck = TRUE;

// Update the screen.
UpdateData(FALSE);

/////////////////////////
// MY CODE ENDS HERE
/////////////////////////

return TRUE;  // return TRUE  unless you set the focus
              // to a control
}
```

☐ Save your work by selecting Save All from the File menu.

The first statement you typed in the OnInitDialog() function sets the variable m_VisibleCheck to a value of TRUE:

```
m_VisibleCheck = TRUE;
```

The m_VisibleCheck variable is of type BOOL (boolean), which means it can have a value of either TRUE or FALSE. By setting m_VisibleCheck to TRUE, you are specifying that you want the IDC_VISIBLE_CHECK check box to have a check mark in it. If you want to remove a check mark from a check box, set the variable to FALSE.

The next statement sets the variable m_EnabledCheck to a value of TRUE:

```
m_EnabledCheck = TRUE;
```

By setting m_EnabledCheck to TRUE, you are specifying that you want the IDC_ENABLED_CHECK check box to have a check mark in it.

At this point, the variables of the two check box controls are updated with the values you want the controls to display. However, the controls themselves aren't yet updated with the values of the variables. To actually transfer the values of the variables into the controls (to display onscreen), you need to use the UpdateData() function with FALSE as its parameter. Therefore, the last statement you typed in the OnInitDialog() function updates the screen with the new values of the variables:

```
// Update the screen.
UpdateData(FALSE);
```

After the preceding statement is executed, the current contents of the variable m_VisibleCheck will be transferred into the IDC_VISIBLE_CHECK check box, and the current contents of the variable m_EnabledCheck will be transferred into the IDC_ENABLED_CHECK check box.

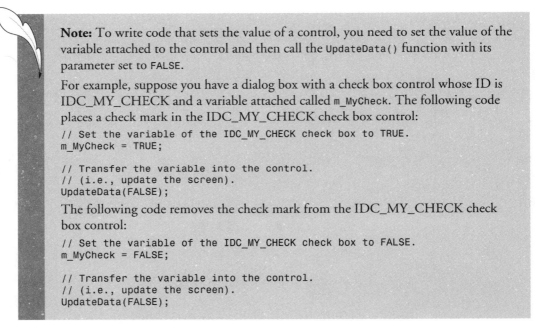

Note: To write code that sets the value of a control, you need to set the value of the variable attached to the control and then call the UpdateData() function with its parameter set to FALSE.

For example, suppose you have a dialog box with a check box control whose ID is IDC_MY_CHECK and a variable attached called m_MyCheck. The following code places a check mark in the IDC_MY_CHECK check box control:

```
// Set the variable of the IDC_MY_CHECK check box to TRUE.
m_MyCheck = TRUE;

// Transfer the variable into the control.
// (i.e., update the screen).
UpdateData(FALSE);
```

The following code removes the check mark from the IDC_MY_CHECK check box control:

```
// Set the variable of the IDC_MY_CHECK check box to FALSE.
m_MyCheck = FALSE;

// Transfer the variable into the control.
// (i.e., update the screen).
UpdateData(FALSE);
```

To see the initialization code you typed in the OnInitDialog() function in action, follow these steps:

☐ Select Build Test.EXE from the Build menu.

☐ Select Execute Test.EXE from the Build menu.

Visual C++ responds by executing the Test.EXE program. The main window of Test.EXE appears, as shown in Figure 2.14.

As you can see, the initialization code you wrote in the OnInitDialog() function works! Both the Visible check box and the Enabled check box have check marks in them.

☐ Terminate the Test.EXE program by clicking the × icon at the upper-right corner.

Figure 2.14.
*The main window of the
Test.EXE program.*

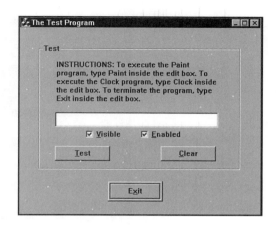

Attaching Code to the *BN_CLICKED* Event of the Exit Pushbutton

At this point, when you click the Exit pushbutton, nothing happens. In this section, you'll attach code to the BN_CLICKED event of the Exit pushbutton so the program will do what it's supposed to do—terminate the Test.EXE program. Remember, the BN_CLICKED event occurs when you click the control.

Follow these steps to attach code to the BN_CLICKED event of the Exit pushbutton:

☐ Select ClassWizard from the View menu.

   Visual C++ responds by displaying the MFC ClassWizard dialog box.

☐ Select the Message Maps tab of ClassWizard.

☐ Use the ClassWizard dialog box to select the following event:

Class name:	CTestDlg
Object ID:	IDC_EXIT_BUTTON
Message:	BN_CLICKED

Your MFC ClassWizard dialog box should now look like Figure 2.15.

☐ Click the Add Function button of ClassWizard and name the new function OnExitButton.

☐ Click the Edit Code button of ClassWizard.

   *Visual C++ responds by opening the file TestDlg.cpp with the function OnExitButton()
   ready for you to edit.*

Figure 2.15.
Selecting the BN_CLICKED
event of the
IDC_EXIT_BUTTON
pushbutton.

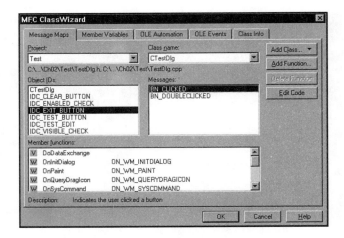

☐ Write the following code in the OnExitButton() function:

```
void CTestDlg::OnExitButton()
{
// TODO: Add your control notification handler code here

//////////////////////////
// MY CODE STARTS HERE
//////////////////////////

// Terminate the program.
OnOK();

//////////////////////////
// MY CODE ENDS HERE
//////////////////////////

}
```

☐ Save your work by selecting Save All from the File menu.

The code you typed in the OnExitButton() function is made up of a single statement:

```
OnOK()
```

This statement terminates the program by calling the OnOK() function, which terminates the program by closing the dialog box.

To see the code you attached to the BN_CLICKED event of the Exit pushbutton in action, follow these steps:

☐ Select Build Test.EXE from the Build menu.

☐ Select Execute Test.EXE from the Build menu.

Visual C++ responds by executing the Test.EXE program.

☐ Click the Exit pushbutton.

As expected, the Test.EXE program responds by terminating. The code you attached to the Exit pushbutton is working!

Attaching Code to the *BN_CLICKED* Event of the Test Pushbutton

When you click the Test pushbutton, the Test.EXE program should display the text This is a test! in the IDC_TEST_EDIT edit box. (Refer back to Figure 2.2.) Follow these steps to attach code to the BN_CLICKED event of the Test pushbutton that performs this task:

☐ Select ClassWizard from the View menu.

Visual C++ responds by displaying the MFC ClassWizard dialog box.

☐ Select the Message Maps tab of ClassWizard.

☐ Use the ClassWizard dialog box to select the following event:

Class name:	CTestDlg
Object ID:	IDC_TEST_BUTTON
Message:	BN_CLICKED

☐ Click the Add Function button of ClassWizard and name the new function OnTestButton.

☐ Click the Edit Code button of ClassWizard.

Visual C++ responds by opening the file TestDlg.cpp with the function OnTestButton() ready for you to edit.

☐ Write the following code in the OnTestButton() function:

```
void CTestDlg::OnTestButton()
{
// TODO: Add your control notification handler code here

/////////////////////////
// MY CODE STARTS HERE
/////////////////////////

// Fill the variable of the IDC_TEST_EDIT edit box
// with the text: "This is a test!".
m_TestEdit = "This is a test!";

// Update the screen.
UpdateData(FALSE);
```

```
/////////////////////
// MY CODE ENDS HERE
/////////////////////

}
```

☐ Save your work by selecting Save All from the File menu.

The code you typed in the `OnTestButton()` function is made up of two statements. The first statement fills the `m_TestEdit` variable attached to the IDC_TEST_EDIT edit box with the string `"This is a test!"`:

```
m_TestEdit = "This is a test!";
```

The second statement updates the screen:

```
UpdateData(FALSE);
```

As discussed earlier, calling the `UpdateData()` function with its parameter set to `FALSE` updates the dialog box controls with the values of the variables attached to the controls. So after the preceding statement is executed, the text `This is a test!` will be displayed in the IDC_TEST_EDIT edit box.

To see the code you attached to the `BN_CLICKED` event of the Test pushbutton in action, follow these steps:

☐ Select Build Test.EXE from the Build menu.

☐ Select Execute Test.EXE from the Build menu.

  Visual C++ responds by executing the Test.EXE program.

☐ Click the Test pushbutton.

  As expected, the Test.EXE program responds by displaying the text `This is a test!` in the IDC_TEST_EDIT edit box.

☐ Terminate the Test.EXE program by clicking the Exit button.

Attaching Code to the *BN_CLICKED* Event of the Clear Pushbutton

When you click the Clear pushbutton, the Test.EXE program should clear the IDC_TEST_EDIT edit box. Follow these steps to attach code to the `BN_CLICKED` event of the Clear pushbutton that performs this task:

☐ Select ClassWizard from the View menu.

  Visual C++ responds by displaying the MFC ClassWizard dialog box.

☐ Select the Message Maps tab of ClassWizard.

☐ Use the ClassWizard dialog box to select the following event:

Class name:	CTestDlg
Object ID:	IDC_CLEAR_BUTTON
Message:	BN_CLICKED

☐ Click the Add Function button of ClassWizard and name the new function `OnClearButton`.

☐ Click the Edit Code button of ClassWizard.

Visual C++ responds by opening the file TestDlg.cpp with the function `OnClearButton()` *ready for you to edit.*

☐ Write the following code in the `OnClearButton()` function:

```
void CTestDlg::OnClearButton()
{
// TODO: Add your control notification handler code here

/////////////////////////
// MY CODE STARTS HERE
/////////////////////////

// Fill the variable of the IDC_TEST_EDIT edit box
// with NULL.
m_TestEdit = "";

// Update the screen.
UpdateData(FALSE);

/////////////////////////
// MY CODE ENDS HERE
/////////////////////////

}
```

☐ Save your work by selecting Save All from the File menu.

The code you typed in the `OnClearButton()` function is made up of two statements. The first statement fills the `m_TestEdit` variable attached to the IDC_TEST_EDIT edit box with a NULL string:

```
m_TestEdit = "";
```

The second statement updates the screen, so that the new value of the `m_TestEdit` variable will be transferred to the IDC_TEST_EDIT edit box:

```
UpdateData(FALSE);
```

To see the code you attached to the BN_CLICKED event of the Clear pushbutton in action, follow these steps:

☐ Select Build Test.EXE from the Build menu.

☐ Select Execute Test.EXE from the Build menu.

Visual C++ responds by executing the Test.EXE program.

☐ Type something in the edit box.

☐ Click the Clear button.

As expected, the Test.EXE program responds by clearing the text you typed in the edit box—the edit box is filled with a NULL string.

☐ Terminate the Test.EXE program by clicking the Exit button.

Attaching Code to the *BN_CLICKED* Event of the Visible Check Box

When you remove the check mark from the Visible check box, the Test.EXE program should hide the IDC_TEST_EDIT edit box from view; when you check the Visible check box, the Test.EXE program should make the IDC_TEST_EDIT edit box visible. You'll now attach code to the BN_CLICKED event of the Visible check box that performs these tasks.

Note: The BN_CLICKED event of a check box control occurs when you place or remove a check mark in the check box.

Follow these steps to attach code to the BN_CLICKED event of the Visible check box:

☐ Select ClassWizard from the View menu.

Visual C++ responds by displaying the MFC ClassWizard dialog box.

☐ Select the Message Maps tab of ClassWizard.

☐ Use the ClassWizard dialog box to select the following event:

Class name:	CTestDlg
Object ID:	IDC_VISIBLE_CHECK
Message:	BN_CLICKED

☐ Click the Add Function button of ClassWizard and name the new function OnVisibleCheck.

☐ Click the Edit Code button of ClassWizard.

Visual C++ responds by opening the file TestDlg.cpp with the function `OnVisibleCheck()` *ready for you to edit.*

☐ Write the following code in the `OnVisibleCheck()` function:

```
void CTestDlg::OnVisibleCheck()
{
// TODO: Add your control notification handler code here

//////////////////////////
// MY CODE STARTS HERE
//////////////////////////

// Update the variables of the controls
// (the screen contents are transferred
// to the variables of the controls).
UpdateData(TRUE);

// If the IDC_VISIBLE_CHECK check box is checked, make
// the IDC_TEST_EDIT edit box visible. Otherwise, hide the
// IDC_TEST_EDIT edit box.
if (m_VisibleCheck==TRUE)
   GetDlgItem(IDC_TEST_EDIT)->ShowWindow(SW_SHOW);
else
   GetDlgItem(IDC_TEST_EDIT)->ShowWindow(SW_HIDE);

//////////////////////////
// MY CODE ENDS HERE
//////////////////////////

}
```

☐ Save your work by selecting Save All from the File menu.

The first statement you typed in the `OnVisibleCheck()` function updates the variables of the controls with the current contents of the screen:

`UpdateData(TRUE);`

When you call the `UpdateData()` function with its parameter set to `TRUE`, the current values of the controls on the screen are transferred to the variables attached to the controls.

> **Note:** When you call the `UpdateData()` function with its parameter set to `TRUE`, you update the variables:
>
> `UpdateData(TRUE);`
>
> That is, you transfer the current contents of the onscreen controls into the variables attached to the controls.

> When you call the `UpdateData()` function with its parameter set to `FALSE`, you update the screen:
>
> `UpdateData(FALSE);`
>
> That is, you transfer the current values of the variables attached to the controls to the onscreen controls.

The first statement you typed in the `OnVisibleCheck()` function transfers the current contents of the controls onscreen into the variables attached to the controls:

`UpdateData(TRUE);`

After the preceding statement is executed, the variable `m_VisibleCheck` is filled with the current value of the IDC_VISIBLE_CHECK check box. If you place a check mark in the IDC_VISIBLE_CHECK check box, then `m_VisibleCheck` will be filled with the value `TRUE`; if you remove the check mark, then `m_VisibleCheck` will be filled with the value `FALSE`.

The remaining code you typed in the `OnVisibleCheck()` function uses an `if…else` statement to evaluate the `m_VisibleCheck` variable:

```
if (m_VisibleCheck==TRUE)
    GetDlgItem(IDC_TEST_EDIT)->ShowWindow(SW_SHOW);
else
    GetDlgItem(IDC_TEST_EDIT)->ShowWindow(SW_HIDE);
```

If the IDC_VISIBLE_CHECK check box is currently selected, then the preceding `if` condition is satisfied and the statement under the `if` is executed:

`GetDlgItem(IDC_TEST_EDIT)->ShowWindow(SW_SHOW);`

This statement uses the `ShowWindow()` function to make the IDC_TEST_EDIT edit box visible. When its parameter is set to `SW_SHOW`, the control is made visible.

If, however, the IDC_VISIBLE_CHECK check box is not selected, then the statement under the `else` is executed:

`GetDlgItem(IDC_TEST_EDIT)->ShowWindow(SW_HIDE);`

This statement uses the `ShowWindow()` function to make the IDC_TEST_EDIT edit box invisible. When its parameter is set to `SW_HIDE`, the control is hidden.

Notice that in the preceding statements, the `ShowWindow()` function is being executed on this statement:

`GetDlgItem(IDC_TEST_EDIT)`

The `GetDlgItem()` function returns a pointer to the control whose ID is supplied as the function's parameter. For example, `GetDlgItem(IDC_TEST_EDIT)` returns a pointer to the

IDC_TEST_EDIT edit box control. Therefore, the following statement will hide the IDC_TEST_EDIT edit box control from view:

```
GetDlgItem(IDC_TEST_EDIT)->ShowWindow(SW_HIDE);
```

To summarize, here is how the code in the `OnVisibleCheck()` function works: When you check or uncheck the Visible check box, its `BN_CLICKED` event occurs, and the `OnVisibleCheck()` function is automatically executed. If you check the Visible check box, then the code in the `OnVisibleCheck()` function makes the IDC_TEST_EDIT edit box visible; if you uncheck it, however, then the code in the `OnVisibleCheck()` function hides the IDC_TEST_EDIT edit box from view.

To see the code you attached to the `BN_CLICKED` event of the Visible check box in action, follow these steps:

☐ Select Build Test.EXE from the Build menu.

☐ Select Execute Test.EXE from the Build menu.

   Visual C++ responds by executing the Test.EXE program.

☐ Experiment with the Visible check box.

   As expected, the Test.EXE program shows or hides the IDC_TEST_EDIT edit box when you check and uncheck the Visible check box.

☐ Terminate the Test.EXE program by clicking the Exit button.

Attaching Code to the *BN_CLICKED* Event of the Enabled Check Box

When you uncheck the Enabled check box, the Test.EXE program disables the IDC_TEST_EDIT edit box; conversely, when you check the Enabled check box, the IDC_TEST_EDIT edit box is enabled. The `BN_CLICKED` event of the Enabled check box performs these tasks, so you'll follow the same steps you did for the Visible check box to attach code to it.

☐ Just as you did for the Visible check box, choose ClassWizard from the View menu, select ClassWizard's Message Maps tab, and select the following event in the ClassWizard dialog box:

Class name:	CTestDlg
Object ID:	IDC_ENABLED_CHECK
Message:	BN_CLICKED

☐ Click the Add Function button, name the new function `OnEnabledCheck`, and click the Edit Code button.

Visual C++ responds by opening the file TestDlg.cpp with the function `OnEnabledCheck()` *ready for you to edit.*

☐ Write the following code in the `OnEnabledCheck()` function:

```
void CTestDlg::OnEnabledCheck()
{
// TODO: Add your control notification handler code here

//////////////////////////
// MY CODE STARTS HERE
//////////////////////////

// Update the variables of the controls.
// (the screen contents are transferred
// to the variables of the controls).
UpdateData(TRUE);

// If the IDC_ENABLED_CHECK check box is checked, enable
// the IDC_TEST_EDIT edit box. Otherwise, disable the
// IDC_TEST_EDIT edit box.
if (m_EnabledCheck==TRUE)
   GetDlgItem(IDC_TEST_EDIT)->EnableWindow(TRUE);
else
   GetDlgItem(IDC_TEST_EDIT)->EnableWindow(FALSE);

//////////////////////////
// MY CODE ENDS HERE
//////////////////////////

}
```

☐ Select Save All from the File menu to save your work.

The code in the `OnEnabledCheck()` function works the same way as the code in the `OnVisibleCheck()` function. When you check or uncheck the Enabled check box, its `BN_CLICKED` event occurs, and the `OnEnabledCheck()` function is automatically executed. The first statement in the `OnEnabledCheck()` function updates the variables of the controls with the current onscreen contents:

```
UpdateData(TRUE);
```

After this statement is executed, the `m_EnabledCheck` variable is filled with the current value of the IDC_ENABLED_CHECK check box. Therefore, placing a check mark in the Enabled check box fills `m_EnabledCheck` with the value TRUE. The remaining code uses an `if…else` statement to evaluate the `m_EnabledCheck` variable:

```
if (m_EnabledCheck==TRUE)
   GetDlgItem(IDC_TEST_EDIT)->EnableWindow(TRUE);
else
   GetDlgItem(IDC_TEST_EDIT)->EnableWindow(FALSE);
```

If the Enabled check box is checked, then the preceding `if` condition is satisfied and the statement under the `if` is executed:

```
GetDlgItem(IDC_TEST_EDIT)->EnableWindow(TRUE);
```

This statement uses the `EnableWindow()` function to enable or disable the IDC_TEST_EDIT edit box. Therefore, when the parameter of the `EnableWindow()` function is set to `TRUE`, the control is enabled.

If the Enabled check box isn't checked, then the statement under the `else` is executed. When the parameter is set to `FALSE`, the control is disabled:

```
GetDlgItem(IDC_TEST_EDIT)->EnableWindow(FALSE);
```

The `EnableWindow()` function is being executed on the following statement:

```
GetDlgItem(IDC_TEST_EDIT)
```

As it did in the Visible check box, `GetDlgItem(IDC_TEST_EDIT)` returns a pointer to the IDC_TEST_EDIT edit box control and uses the following statement to disable the edit box control:

```
GetDlgItem(IDC_TEST_EDIT)->EnableWindow(FALSE);
```

To see the code you attached to the `BN_CLICKED` event of the Enabled check box in action, follow these steps:

☐ Select Build Test.EXE from the Build menu.

   Visual C++ responds by compiling and linking the Test.EXE program.

☐ Select Execute Test.EXE from the Build menu.

   Visual C++ responds by executing the Test.EXE program.

☐ Experiment with the Enabled check box, then click the Exit button to terminate the Test.EXE program.

   As expected, when you check and uncheck the Enabled check box, the Test.EXE program enables and disables the IDC_TEST_EDIT edit box.

Attaching Code to the *EN_CHANGE* Event of the Edit Box Control

The `EN_CHANGE` event of an edit box control occurs when you change the contents of the edit box by entering or deleting characters. In this section, you'll attach code to the `EN_CHANGE` event of the IDC_TEST_EDIT edit box. This code will perform the following three tasks:

- Execute the Windows Paint program when you type Paint in the edit box.
- Execute the Windows Clock program when you type Clock in the edit box.
- Terminate the program when you type Exit in the edit box.

Follow these steps to attach code to the EN_CHANGE event of the IDC_TEST_EDIT edit box:

☐ Select ClassWizard from the View menu, select ClassWizard's Message Maps tab, and select the following event in the ClassWizard dialog box:

Class name:	CTestDlg
Object ID:	IDC_TEST_EDIT
Message:	EN_CHANGE

☐ Click the Add Function button, name the new function OnChangeTestEdit, and click the Edit Code button.

Visual C++ responds by opening the file TestDlg.cpp with the function OnChangeTestEdit() ready for you to edit.

☐ Write the following code in the OnChangeTestEdit() function:

```
void CTestDlg::OnChangeTestEdit()
{
// TODO: Add your control notification handler code here

/////////////////////////
// MY CODE STARTS HERE
/////////////////////////

// Update the variables of the controls.
UpdateData(TRUE);

// Fill the variable UpperValue with the uppercase string
// of the IDC_TEST_EDIT edit box.
CString UpperValue;
UpperValue = m_TestEdit;
UpperValue.MakeUpper();

// If the user typed Paint in the edit box, execute the
// Paint program (pbrush.exe) and clear the IDC_TEST_EDIT
// edit box.
if (UpperValue=="PAINT")
    {
    system("pbrush.exe");
    m_TestEdit="";
    UpdateData(FALSE);
    }

// If the user typed Clock in the edit box, execute the
// Clock program (clock.exe) and clear the IDC_TEST_EDIT
// edit box.
```

```
if (UpperValue=="CLOCK")
    {
    system("clock.exe");
    m_TestEdit="";
    UpdateData(FALSE);
    }

// If the user typed Exit in the edit box, terminate
// the program and clear the IDC_TEST_EDIT
// edit box.
if (UpperValue=="EXIT")
    {
    OnOK();
    }

//////////////////////
// MY CODE ENDS HERE
//////////////////////

}
```

☐ Save your work by selecting Save All from the File menu.

The first statement in the OnChangeTestEdit() function updates the variables of the controls with the current onscreen contents:

```
UpdateData(TRUE);
```

After this statement is executed, the m_TestEdit variable of the IDC_TEST_EDIT edit box is filled with the current value of the IDC_TEST_EDIT edit box. For example, if you type the word Hello in the IDC_TEST_EDIT edit box, then m_TestEdit will be filled with the string "Hello".

These are the next three statements:

```
// Fill the variable UpperValue with the uppercase string
// of the IDC_TEST_EDIT edit box.
CString UpperValue;
UpperValue = m_TestEdit;
UpperValue.MakeUpper();
```

This statement creates a variable called UpperValue of type CString:

```
CString UpperValue;
```

This statement fills the variable UpperValue with the value of the m_TestEdit variable:

```
UpperValue = m_TestEdit;
```

Recall that when you attached the m_TestEdit variable to the IDC_TEST_EDIT edit box, you specified that m_TestEdit is of type CString. Therefore, the variable UpperValue holds the contents of the IDC_TEST_EDIT edit box.

The next statement executes the MakeUpper() member function of the CString class on the UpperValue variable:

```
UpperValue.MakeUpper();
```

As its name implies, the MakeUpper() function converts the string's lowercase characters to uppercase characters. For example, if the variable initially contained the string "Hello", then the MakeUpper() function would convert the variable to hold the string "HELLO". Therefore, if you type Paint in the edit box at this point, then UpperValue is filled with the string "PAINT".

The remaining code you typed in the OnChangeTestEdit() function uses three if statements to evaluate the UpperValue variable:

```
// If the user typed Paint in the edit box, execute the
// Paint program (pbrush.exe) and clear the IDC_TEST_EDIT
// edit box.
if (UpperValue=="PAINT")
    {
    system("pbrush.exe");
    m_TestEdit="";
    UpdateData(FALSE);
    }

// If the user typed Clock in the edit box, execute the
// Clock program (clock.exe) and clear the IDC_TEST_EDIT
// edit box.
if (UpperValue=="CLOCK")
    {
    system("clock.exe");
    m_TestEdit="";
    UpdateData(FALSE);
    }

// If the user typed Exit in the edit box, terminate
// the program and clear the IDC_TEST_EDIT
// edit box.
if (UpperValue=="EXIT")
    OnOK();
```

If the uppercase conversion of what you typed in the IDC_TEST_EDIT edit box is "PAINT", then the condition of the first if statement is satisfied and the following three statements are executed:

```
system("pbrush.exe");
m_TestEdit="";
UpdateData(FALSE);
```

This statement uses the system() function to execute the EXE file of the Paint program (PBRUSH.EXE):

```
system("pbrush.exe");
```

Note that in the preceding statement the full pathname of the program is not specified.

Therefore, the system() function will execute the PBRUSH.EXE file in your \Windows directory.

The next two statements fill the IDC_TEST_EDIT edit box with a NULL string:

```
m_TestEdit="";
UpdateData(FALSE);
```

This is done so that after Test.EXE executes the Paint program, the IDC_TEST_EDIT edit box will be cleared.

If the uppercase conversion of what you typed in the IDC_TEST_EDIT edit box is "CLOCK", then the condition of the second if statement is satisfied and the following three statements are executed:

```
system("clock.exe");
m_TestEdit="";
UpdateData(FALSE);
```

This statement executes the EXE file of the Clock program (CLOCK.EXE):

```
system("clock.exe");
```

These two statements clear the IDC_TEST_EDIT edit box:

```
m_TestEdit="";
UpdateData(FALSE);
```

If the uppercase conversion of what you typed in the IDC_TEST_EDIT edit box is "EXIT", then the condition of the third if statement is satisfied and the following statement is executed to terminate the program:

```
OnOK();
```

To see the code you attached to the EN_CHANGE event of the IDC_TEST_EDIT edit box in action, follow these steps:

☐ Select Build Test.EXE from the Build menu.

☐ Select Execute Test.EXE from the Build menu.

Visual C++ responds by executing the Test.EXE program.

☐ Type Paint in the IDC_TEST_EDIT edit box.

The Test.EXE program responds by executing the Windows Paint program.

☐ Terminate the Paint program by clicking the × icon at the upper-right corner.

☐ Type Clock in the IDC_TEST_EDIT edit box.

The Test.EXE program responds by executing the Windows Clock program.

☐ Terminate the Clock program by clicking the × icon at the upper-right corner.

☐ Type Exit in the IDC_TEST_EDIT edit box.

The Test.EXE program responds by terminating.

Summary

In this chapter, you have gained some experience with controls, and you have written a program that uses the edit box control, the check box control, and the pushbutton control.

As you have seen, writing a program that uses a control amounts to placing the control in the dialog box, setting the control's properties, and attaching code to the events of the control.

Q&A

Q During the design of the Test program, I attached a variable to the edit box control and to the check box controls. But I didn't have to attach variables to the pushbutton controls. Why not?

A You attached variables to the edit box and check box controls so you could write code that reads and writes values to and from these controls. In the case of the pushbutton control, you don't have to read and write values to or from this control (because a pushbutton does not have text in it to be read or written into).

Q The Test.EXE program illustrates how to disable or enable and hide or show an edit box control. What about other controls? What code do I have to write to disable or enable and hide or show controls like pushbuttons, check boxes, and so on?

A With other types of controls, you use the same code you used with the edit box control. For example, suppose your program includes a pushbutton control whose ID is IDC_MY_BUTTON. The following statements illustrate how to disable or enable and hide or show the IDC_MY_BUTTON pushbutton:

```
// Hide the IDC_MY_BUTTON pushbutton.
GetDlgItem(IDC_MY_BUTTON)->ShowWindow(SW_HIDE);

// Make the IDC_MY_BUTTON pushbutton visible.
GetDlgItem(IDC_MY_BUTTON)->ShowWindow(SW_SHOW);

// Disable the IDC_MY_BUTTON pushbutton.
GetDlgItem(IDC_MY_BUTTON)->EnableWindow(FALSE);

// Enable the IDC_MY_BUTTON pushbutton.
GetDlgItem(IDC_MY_CONTROL)->EnableWindow(TRUE);
```

Quiz

1. Explain what the following statement does:

   ```
   UpdateData(FALSE);
   ```

2. Explain what the following statement does:

   ```
   UpdateData(TRUE);
   ```

3. Suppose your program includes an edit box control whose ID is IDC_MY_EDIT, and you attached a variable of type CString called m_MyEdit to the IDC_MY_EDIT edit box. Describe what the following code does:

   ```
   m_MyEdit = "Hello";
   UpdateData(FALSE);
   ```

4. Suppose your program includes a check box control whose ID is IDC_MY_CHECK, and you attached a variable of type BOOL called m_MyCheck to the IDC_MY_CHECK check box. Describe what the following code does:

   ```
   m_MyCheck = TRUE;
   UpdateData(FALSE);
   ```

5. Suppose your program includes an edit box control whose ID is IDC_MY_EDIT, and you attached a variable of type CString called m_MyEdit to the IDC_MY_EDIT edit box. Describe what the following code does:

   ```
   UpdateData(TRUE);
   MessageBox(m_MyEdit);
   ```

6. When does the BN_CLICKED event of a check box control occur?

7. When does the EN_CHANGE event of a check box control occur?

8. Explain how to make a control visible and invisible during runtime.

9. Explain how to make a control enabled and disabled during runtime.

Exercise

Currently, when you type Paint in the edit box of the Test.EXE program, it executes the Windows Paint program. When you type Clock in the edit box, the Test.EXE program executes the Windows Clock program, and when you type Exit in the edit box, the Test.EXE program terminates.

Add code to the Test.EXE program so that when you type Beep in the edit box, your PC will beep.

Hint: This is the statement that causes the PC to beep:

```
MessageBeep((WORD)-1);
```

Quiz Answers

1. The following statement updates the controls onscreen (in the dialog box) with the current values of the variables attached to the controls:

   ```
   UpdataData(FALSE);
   ```

   After the preceding statement is executed, the values of the variables attached to the controls are transferred to the corresponding controls onscreen.

2. The following statement updates the variables attached to the controls with the current values of the controls themselves:

   ```
   UpdataData(TRUE);
   ```

   After the preceding statement is executed, the current settings of the controls onscreen are transferred to the corresponding variables attached to the controls.

3. The following statement fills the m_MyEdit variable of the IDC_MY_EDIT edit box with the string "Hello":

   ```
   m_MyEdit = "Hello";
   ```

   This statement transfers the contents of the m_MyEdit variable to the IDC_MY_EDIT edit box:

   ```
   UpdateData(FALSE);
   ```

   The preceding two statements display the text Hello in the IDC_MY_EDIT edit box.

4. The following statement fills the m_MyCheck variable of the IDC_MY_CHECK check box with the value TRUE:

   ```
   m_MyCheck = TRUE;
   ```

   And this statement transfers the contents of the m_MyCheck variable to the IDC_MY_CHECK check box:

   ```
   UpdateData(FALSE);
   ```

   When a value of TRUE is transferred to a check box control, a check mark is placed in the check box, so the preceding two statements place a check mark in the IDC_MY_CHECK check box.

5. The following statement transfers the current contents of the IDC_MY_EDIT edit box control into the m_MyEdit variable attached to the control:

   ```
   UpdateData(TRUE);
   ```

   And this statement displays a message box with the contents of the m_MyEdit variable:

   ```
   MessageBox(m_MyEdit);
   ```

   The preceding two statements display a message box showing the current contents of the IDC_MY_EDIT edit box.

6. The BN_CLICKED event of a check box control occurs when you place or remove a check mark in the check box control.

7. The EN_CHANGE event of an edit box control occurs when you change the contents of the edit box.

8. To hide or show a control, you can use the ShowWindow() function. For example, suppose you have a control whose ID is IDC_MY_CONTROL. To hide the IDC_MY_CONTROL control, execute the ShowWindow() function as follows:

```
GetDlgItem(IDC_MY_CONTROL)->ShowWindow(SW_HIDE);
```

To make the IDC_MY_CONTROL control visible, execute the ShowWindow() function as follows:

```
GetDlgItem(IDC_MY_CONTROL)->ShowWindow(SW_SHOW);
```

9. To enable and disable a control, you can use the EnableWindow() function. For example, suppose you have a control whose ID is IDC_MY_CONTROL. To disable the IDC_MY_CONTROL control, execute the EnableWindow() function as follows:

```
GetDlgItem(IDC_MY_CONTROL)->EnableWindow(FALSE);
```

To enable the IDC_MY_CONTROL control, execute the EnableWindow() function as follows:

```
GetDlgItem(IDC_MY_CONTROL)->EnableWindow(TRUE);
```

Exercise Answer

To enhance the Test.EXE program so you can make your PC beep when you type Beep in the edit box control, add the following code to the end of the OnChangeTestEdit() function in the TestDlg.cpp file:

```
// If the user typed Beep in the edit box, beep and
// clear the IDC_TEST_EDIT edit box.
if (UpperValue=="BEEP")
    {
    MessageBeep((WORD)-1);
    m_TestEdit="";
    UpdateData(FALSE);
    }
```

After you add this code to the end of the OnChangeTestEdit() function, it will look like this:

```
void CTestDlg::OnChangeTestEdit()
{
// TODO: Add your control notification handler code here

//////////////////////////
// MY CODE STARTS HERE
//////////////////////////
```

```
// Update the variables of the controls.
UpdateData(TRUE);

// Fill the variable UpperValue with the uppercase string
// of the IDC_TEST_EDIT edit box.
CString UpperValue;
UpperValue = m_TestEdit;
UpperValue.MakeUpper();

// If the user typed Paint in the edit box, execute the
// Paint program (pbrush.exe) and clear the IDC_TEST_EDIT
// edit box.
if (UpperValue=="PAINT")
   {
   system("pbrush.exe");
   m_TestEdit="";
   UpdateData(FALSE);
   }

// If the user typed Clock in the edit box, execute the
// Clock program (clock.exe) and clear the IDC_TEST_EDIT
// edit box.
if (UpperValue=="CLOCK")
   {
   system("clock.exe");
   m_TestEdit="";
   UpdateData(FALSE);
   }

// If the user typed Exit in the edit box, terminate
// the program and clear the IDC_TEST_EDIT
// edit box.
if (UpperValue=="EXIT")
   {
   OnOK();
   }

// If the user typed Beep in the edit box, beep and
// clear the IDC_TEST_EDIT edit box.
if (UpperValue=="BEEP")
   {
   MessageBeep((WORD)-1);
   m_TestEdit="";
   UpdateData(FALSE);
   }

/////////////////////
// MY CODE ENDS HERE
/////////////////////

}
```

To see (and hear) the code you added to the OnChangeTestEdit() function in action, follow these steps:

☐ Select Build Test.EXE from the Build menu.

☐ Select Execute Test.EXE from the Build menu.

Visual C++ responds by executing the Test.EXE program.

☐ Type Beep in the edit box.

As expected, the Test.EXE program responds by beeping and clearing the edit box. Type Beep once again in the edit box, and your PC will beep again.

☐ Terminate the Test.EXE program by clicking its Exit pushbutton or by typing Exit in the edit box.

2

Using OLE Controls and the Component Gallery

In the previous two chapters, you wrote Visual C++ programs that use standard Visual C++ controls. In this chapter, you'll learn what OLE controls are and how to use them in your Visual C++ programs. This chapter also shows you how to incorporate an OLE control into your project by using the Component Gallery feature of Visual C++.

What Is an OLE Control?

The standard Visual C++ controls you've used in the previous two chapters are in the Controls toolbar (for example, the pushbutton control, the check box control, the edit box control, and so on). A control has both properties and events. For example, the pushbutton control has the Caption property and the BN_CLICKED event. The code you attach to a control's event is executed automatically when the event occurs. When you attach code to the BN_CLICKED event of a pushbutton, for example, this code is automatically executed whenever you click the pushbutton.

Wouldn't it be nice if you could use other controls (made by third-party vendors) in addition to Visual C++ standard controls? Well, that's what OLE (*object linking and embedding*) controls are all about. An *OLE control* is a file with the extension OCX (for example, MyButton.OCX). Visual C++ and other visual programming languages enable you to incorporate the OLE control into your program and use it just as you use standard Visual C++ controls. You can place OLE controls in your program's dialog boxes, set the properties of OLE controls, and attach code to the events of OLE controls.

When you use an OLE control in your program, the OLE file typically resides in the \Windows\System directory, but it can also exist in the directory the program is run from. An OLE control is like a dynamic linked library (DLL)—it's linked to your program dynamically.

OLE controls extend Visual C++'s out-of-the-box features. They enable you to easily write sophisticated, state-of-the-art programs. In Chapter 20, "Using the Multimedia OLE Control," and Chapter 21, "Games and 3-D Virtual Reality," you'll learn how to use OLE controls for creating multimedia and 3-D virtual reality programs.

In this chapter, you'll learn how to add an OLE control, already included with Visual C++, to your Visual C++ program and how to use this control in the program.

The Table.EXE Program

In this chapter, you'll write a Visual C++ program called Table.EXE that illustrates how to write a Visual C++ program that uses an OLE control. The Table.EXE program uses the Grid OLE control, which helps you write programs that display data in tabular format. The Grid OLE control is included with Visual C++; its filename is Grid32.OCX. The "32" in the filename indicates that this is a 32-bit OLE control.

Before you start writing the Table.EXE program, first review what the Table.EXE program should look like and what it should do.

- When you start the Table.EXE program, its window should look like the one shown in Figure 3.1.

Figure 3.1.
The window of the Table.EXE program.

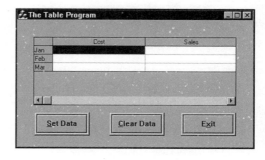

- The window of the Table.EXE program contains an empty table and three pushbuttons: Set Data, Clear Data, and Exit. As you may have guessed, the table shown in Figure 3.1 is the Grid control. To fill the table with data, you click the Set Data button. (See Figure 3.2.)

Figure 3.2.
The Table.EXE program fills the table with data.

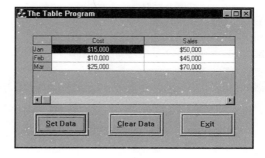

- When you click the Clear Data button, the Table.EXE program clears the data in the table, as shown in Figure 3.1; when you click the Exit pushbutton, the Table.EXE program terminates.

Now that you know what the Table.EXE program should look like and what it should do, you can start creating it.

Creating the Project of the Table.EXE Program

Follow these steps to create the project and skeleton files of the Table.EXE program:

☐ Create the directory C:\TYVCProg\Programs\CH03 and start Visual C++.

☐ Select New from the File menu.

Visual C++ responds by displaying the New dialog box.

☐ Select Project Workspace, then click the OK button.

Visual C++ responds by displaying the New Project Workspace dialog box.

☐ Select MFC AppWizard (exe) from the Type list, enter Table in the Name box, and click the Browse button.

☐ Select the C:\TYVCProg\Programs\CH03 directory and click the Create button.

Visual C++ responds by displaying the MFC AppWizard - Step 1 window.

☐ In the Step 1 window, choose the option to create a dialog-based application, then click the Next button.

Visual C++ responds by displaying the MFC AppWizard - Step 2 of 4 window.

☐ In the Step 2 window, set the title of the dialog box to The Table Program and place a check mark in the OLE Controls check box. (See Figure 3.3.) When you're done, click the Next button.

Figure 3.3.
The MFC AppWizard - Step 2 of 4 window.

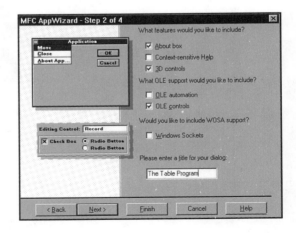

Note: Make sure you place a check mark in the OLE Controls check box, as shown in Figure 3.3, because the program you're creating will use an OLE control. In the previous two chapters, you didn't choose this option because the programs you created didn't use OLE controls.

Visual C++ responds by displaying the Step 3 of 4 window.

☐ In the Step 3 window, choose "Yes, please" to generate source file comments and "As a shared DLL" to use a dynamic link library. Click the Next button when you're done.

Visual C++ responds by displaying the Step 4 of 4 window.

☐ In the Step 4 window, notice that AppWizard created the CTableApp and CTableDlg classes for you. Click the Finish button.

Visual C++ responds by displaying the New Project Information window.

☐ Click the OK button, then select Set Default Configuration from the Build menu.

Visual C++ responds by displaying the Default Project Configuration dialog box.

☐ Select Table - Win32 Release in the Default Project Configuration dialog box, then click the OK button.

That's it! You've finished creating the project and skeleton files of the Table program.

Copying the Grid OLE Control to Your Windows System Directory

As discussed earlier, the Table.EXE program will use the Grid OLE control, but first you need to copy the Grid32.OCX file into your \Windows\System directory.

☐ Use the Windows Explorer to copy the Grid32.OCX file from the \Msved\Redist\OCX directory of the Visual C++ CD-ROM into your \Windows\System directory.

Registering the Grid OLE Control

Before you can use the Grid OLE control, you have to register it with Windows. The Test Container program is used to register and test OLE controls. Follow these steps to register the Grid OLE control:

☐ Select OLE Control Test Container from the Tools menu.

Visual C++ responds by running the Test Container program, as shown in Figure 3.4.

Figure 3.4.

The Test Container
program.

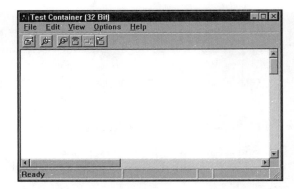

Note: If you have problems starting the Test Container program from Visual C++, then you can start it directly from Windows:

☐ Use the Windows Explorer or select Run from the Start menu to execute the C:\MSDEV\BIN\TSTCON32.EXE file, which is the EXE file of the Test Container program.

☐ Select Register Controls from the File menu of Test Container.

Test Container responds by displaying the Controls Registry dialog box. (See Figure 3.5.)

Figure 3.5.

The Controls Registry
dialog box.

The Controls Registry dialog box lists all the OLE controls currently registered in your Windows system. To register the Grid OLE control, do the following:

☐ Click the Register button of the Controls Registry dialog box.

Test Container responds by displaying the Register Controls dialog box. (See Figure 3.6.)

Figure 3.6.
*The Register Controls
dialog box.*

☐ In this dialog box, select the file C:\Windows\System\Grid32.OCX, then click the Open
button.

> *Test Container responds by registering the Grid OLE control and then displaying the
> Controls Registry again.*

☐ You can check whether the Grid OLE control is registered by looking for the filename
C:\Windows\System\Grid32.OCX in the Control File column:

Control Name	Control File
MSGrid.Grid	C:\WINDOWS\SYSTEM\GRID32.OCX

This item is shown highlighted in Figure 3.7.

Figure 3.7.
*The GRID32.OCX file
listed in the Controls
Registry.*

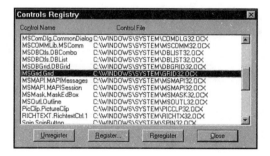

☐ Click the Close button, then select Exit from Test Container's File menu to end the
program.

Now that the Grid OLE control is registered, you can incorporate it into the Table.EXE
program in the following sections.

The Visual Design of the Table Program

You'll now visually design the dialog box that serves as the main window of the Table program (the IDD_TABLE_DIALOG dialog box):

☐ Select Project Workspace from the View menu, then select the ResourceView tab.

☐ Expand the Table resources item, expand the Dialog item, and double-click the IDD_TABLE_DIALOG item.

> *Visual C++ responds by displaying the IDD_TABLE_DIALOG dialog box in design mode.*

☐ Delete the OK button, Cancel button, and text in the IDD_TABLE_DIALOG dialog box.

You'll now place a Grid OLE control in the IDD_TABLE_DIALOG dialog box:

☐ Right-click any free area in the IDD_TABLE_DIALOG dialog box, then select Insert OLE Control from the pop-up menu.

> *Visual C++ responds by displaying the Insert OLE Control dialog box. (See Figure 3.8.)*

Figure 3.8.
The Insert OLE Control dialog box.

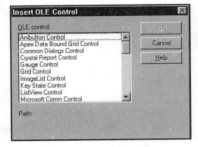

The Insert OLE Control dialog box lists all the OLE controls currently registered in your system.

☐ Select the Grid Control item in the Insert OLE Control dialog box. (See Figure 3.9.)

Figure 3.9.
Selecting the Grid OLE control.

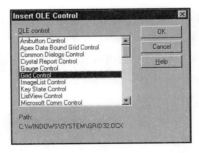

☐ Click the OK button of the Insert OLE Control dialog box.

Visual C++ responds by placing the Grid OLE control in the IDD_TABLE_DIALOG dialog box. (See Figure 3.10.)

Figure 3.10.
Placing the Grid OLE control.

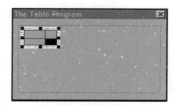

You can now treat the Grid control just as you treat a standard Visual C++ control. You can drag it with the mouse to move it, you can size it by dragging its handles, and you can set its properties by right-clicking the control and selecting Properties from the pop-up menu.

☐ Design the IDD_TABLE_DIALOG dialog box by using the specifications in Table 3.1. When you're done, the dialog box should look like the one shown in Figure 3.11.

To make the IDD_TABLE_DIALOG dialog box look like the one shown in Figure 3.11, you will have to increase its width and height. Remember, you do this by dragging the dialog box's handles with the mouse. You can also display the dialog box in full-screen mode to make designing easier—remember to choose Full Screen from the View menu and press Esc when you're done.

Table 3.1. The properties table of the IDD_TABLE_DIALOG dialog box.

Object	Property	Setting
Dialog Box	**ID**	**IDD_TABLE_DIALOG**
	Caption	The Table Program
	Font	System, Size 10
	Minimize box	Checked (Styles tab)
	Maximize box	Checked (Styles tab)
Grid Control	**ID**	**IDC_SALES_GRID**
	Row	4 (Control tab)
	Col	3 (Control tab)
Push Button	**ID**	**IDC_SETDATA_BUTTON**
	Caption	&Set Data

Table 3.1. continued

Object	Property	Setting
	Client edge	Checked (Extended Styles tab)
	Static edge	Checked (Extended Styles tab)
	Modal frame	Checked (Extended Styles tab)
Push Button	**ID**	**IDC_CLEARDATA_BUTTON**
	Caption	&Clear Data
	Client edge	Checked (Extended Styles tab)
	Static edge	Checked (Extended Styles tab)
	Modal frame	Checked (Extended Styles tab)
Push Button	**ID**	**IDC_EXIT_BUTTON**
	Caption	E&xit
	Client edge	Checked (Extended Styles tab)
	Static edge	Checked (Extended Styles tab)
	Modal frame	Checked (Extended Styles tab)

Figure 3.11.
*IDD_TABLE_DIALOG
in design mode.*

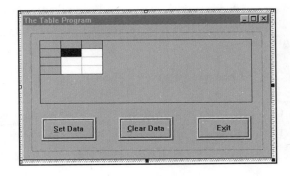

Keep the following points in mind as you're using Table 3.1:

- The first object listed in Table 3.1 is the IDD_TABLE_DIALOG dialog box itself. You set its Minimize box and Maximize box properties to Checked as follows:

  ☐ Right-click any free area in the dialog box and select Properties from the pop-up menu.

  ☐ Select the Styles tab of the Properties dialog box and place a check mark in the Minimize box and Maximize box check boxes.

After you place a check mark in the Minimize box and Maximize box check boxes, the IDD_TABLE_DIALOG dialog box will have a Minimize box and a Maximize box in its upper-right corner. During runtime, you can use them to minimize or maximize the dialog box.

- The Font property specifies the font type and size used for the text of all the controls you'll place in the dialog box. Table 3.1 instructs you to set the Font property of the IDD_TABLE_DIALOG dialog box to System, Size 10. You do that as follows:

  ☐ Right-click any free area in the dialog box and select Properties from the pop-up menu.

  ☐ Select the General tab of the Properties dialog box, click the Font button, and set the font to System, Size 10.

- The second object listed in Table 3.1 is the Grid control. Table 3.1 instructs you to set the ID of the Grid control to IDC_SALES_GRID. Of course, you can use any name for an ID, but the Grid control will be used for displaying sales figures, so IDC_SALES_GRID is an appropriate name.

- Table 3.1 instructs you to set the Rows property of the Grid control to 4 and the Cols property to 3. These properties, found in the Control tab of the Properties dialog box, specify the number of rows and columns that the Grid control should have.

- Table 3.1 specifies setting the Client edge, Static edge, and Modal frame properties of the three pushbutton controls to Checked. These properties, found in the Extended Styles tab of the Properties dialog box, are cosmetic properties—they affect only the visual appearance of the control.

- As shown in Figure 3.11, you have to increase the default width and height of the Grid control. When you do this, the width and height of the cells in the Grid control do not increase. Don't worry, though—you'll set the width and height of the cells when you write the program's code.

You've finished the visual design of the IDD_TABLE_DIALOG dialog box. To see it in action, follow these steps:

☐ Select Build Table.EXE from the Build menu.

Note: When you select Build Table.EXE from the Build menu, only the files that have been changed since the last time you compiled the program are compiled. However, sometimes your project may go out of sequence and Visual C++ will "think" that files needing to be compiled shouldn't be compiled. As a result, the linker may fail. In such cases, you can force Visual C++ to compile all the files by selecting Rebuild All from the Build menu.

☐ Select Execute Table.EXE from the Build menu.

Visual C++ responds by executing the Table.EXE program. The main window of Table.EXE appears, as shown in Figure 3.12.

Figure 3.12.
The main window of the Table.EXE program.

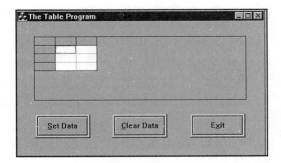

As you can see, the main window of the Table.EXE program (the IDD_TABLE_DIALOG dialog box) looks just as you designed it. Remember, you'll be widening the cells in the Grid control later when you write the program's code.

☐ Terminate the Table.EXE program by clicking the × icon at the upper-right corner.

Attaching a Variable to the Grid Control

You'll now attach a variable to the Grid control, so you can use the variable later to access the properties of the Grid control. Follow these steps to attach a variable to the IDC_SALES_GRID Grid control:

☐ Select ClassWizard from the View menu.

Visual C++ responds by displaying the MFC ClassWizard dialog box.

☐ Select the Member Variables tab of the MFC ClassWizard dialog box. (See Figure 3.13.)

☐ Make sure that the Class name list box is set to CTableDlg.

The CTableDlg class is associated with the IDD_TABLE_DIALOG dialog box (the main window of the Table program). Because you're going to attach a variable to a control in the IDD_TABLE_DIALOG dialog box, the Class name list box should be set to CTableDlg. As a result, the variable will be a data member of the CTableDlg class.

☐ Select IDC_SALES_GRID in the Object IDs list to attach a variable to the IDC_SALES_GRID Grid control, then click the Add Variable button.

Visual C++ responds by displaying the message box shown in Figure 3.14.

Figure 3.13.
Selecting the Member Variables tab of ClassWizard.

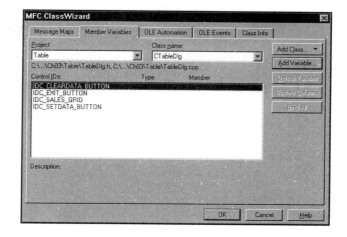

3

Figure 3.14.
The message box displayed after you try to attach a variable to the Grid control.

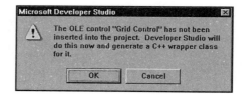

The message box in Figure 3.14 tells you that before you can attach a variable to the Grid control, Visual C++ first needs to create a class for the Grid control.

☐ Click the OK button.

Visual C++ responds by displaying the Confirm Classes dialog box. (See Figure 3.15.)

Figure 3.15.
The Confirm Classes dialog box.

The Confirm Classes dialog box tells you that the name of the class Visual C++ is going to create is `CGridCtrl`, the .cpp file of the `CGridCtrl` class will be GridCtrl.cpp, and the .h file of the `CGridCtrl` class will be GridCtrl.h.

The variable you attach to the Grid control will be of type `CGridCtrl`. The `CGridCtrl` class will have member functions you can use to access the properties of the Grid control.

☐ Click the OK button of the Confirm Classes dialog box.

Visual C++ responds by creating the `CGridCtrl` class, then the Add Member Variable dialog box opens. (See Figure 3.16.)

Figure 3.16.
The Add Member Variable dialog box.

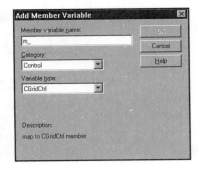

☐ Set the Add Member Variable dialog box as follows:

Member variable name:	`m_SalesGrid`
Category:	`Control`
Variable type:	`CGridCtrl`

☐ Click the OK button of the Add Member Variable dialog box, then click the OK button of the ClassWizard dialog box.

You've finished attaching a variable to the IDC_SALES_GRID Grid control!

Note: In the preceding steps, Visual C++ created a class for the Grid control and added this class to the project of the Table.EXE program. Visual C++ also placed the tool of the Grid OLE control in the Controls toolbar. (See Figure 3.17.) If you want to place another Grid control in the IDD_SALES_DIALOG dialog box, you can, just as you place a standard Visual C++ control—click the tool in the Controls toolbar, then click anywhere in the dialog box.

Figure 3.17.
The Controls toolbar with the tool of the Grid OLE control.

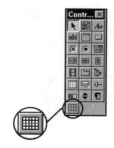

Putting it all together, you have attached a variable of type `CGridCtrl` to the IDC_SALES_GRID Grid control and named it `m_SalesGrid`. In the following sections, you'll write the code of the Table.EXE program and use the `m_SalesGrid` variable to access the properties of the Grid control.

Writing the Code That Initializes the Grid Control

You'll now write the code that initializes the IDC_SALES_GRID Grid control and attach it to the `WM_INITDIALOG` event, which is the event "initialize the dialog box." Follow these steps to write the code that initializes the dialog box:

☐ Select ClassWizard from the View menu, select the Message Maps tab, and use the ClassWizard dialog box to select the following event:

Class name:	CTableDlg
Object ID:	CTableDlg
Message:	WM_INITDIALOG

Your MFC ClassWizard dialog box should now look like the one shown in Figure 3.18.

☐ Click the Edit Code button of ClassWizard.

> *Visual C++ responds by opening the file TableDlg.cpp with the function `OnInitDialog()` ready for you to edit. Remember, you can view and edit code in full-screen mode (select Full Screen from the View menu and press Esc to cancel the full-screen mode).*

The `OnInitDialog()` function already has some code written by Visual C++. You'll type your own code below this comment line:

```
// TODO: Add extra initialization here
```

Figure 3.18.

Selecting the WM_INITDIALOG *event.*

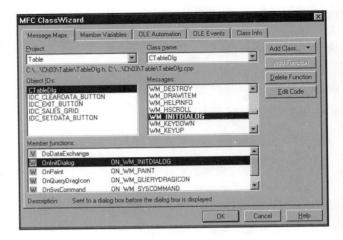

☐ Write the following code in the OnInitDialog() function:

```
BOOL CTableDlg::OnInitDialog()
{
CDialog::OnInitDialog();
...
...
...

// TODO: Add extra initialization here

///////////////////////////
// MY CODE STARTS HERE
///////////////////////////

// Set the width of column 0 to 500.
m_SalesGrid.SetColWidth(0,500);

// Set the width of column 1 to 2500.
m_SalesGrid.SetColWidth(1,2500);

// Set the width of column 2 to 2500.
m_SalesGrid.SetColWidth(2,2500);

// Set the alignment of Col 1 to centered.
m_SalesGrid.SetFixedAlignment(1, 2);
m_SalesGrid.SetColAlignment(1, 2);

// Set the alignment of Col 2 to centered.
m_SalesGrid.SetFixedAlignment(2, 2);
m_SalesGrid.SetColAlignment(2, 2);

// Fill cell x=0,y=1 with the text "Jan".
m_SalesGrid.SetCol(0);
m_SalesGrid.SetRow(1);
m_SalesGrid.SetText("Jan");
```

```
// Fill cell x=0,y=2 with the text "Feb".
m_SalesGrid.SetCol(0);
m_SalesGrid.SetRow(2);
m_SalesGrid.SetText("Feb");

// Fill cell x=0,y=3 with the text "Mar".
m_SalesGrid.SetCol(0);
m_SalesGrid.SetRow(3);
m_SalesGrid.SetText("Mar");

// Fill cell x=1,y=0 with the text "Cost".
m_SalesGrid.SetCol(1);
m_SalesGrid.SetRow(0);
m_SalesGrid.SetText("Cost");

// Fill cell x=2,y=0 with the text "Sales".
m_SalesGrid.SetCol(2);
m_SalesGrid.SetRow(0);
m_SalesGrid.SetText("Sales");

/////////////////////
// MY CODE ENDS HERE
/////////////////////

return TRUE;  // return TRUE  unless you set the focus
              // to a control
}
```

☐ Save your work by selecting Save All from the File menu.

The code you typed in the `OnInitDialog()` function initializes the IDD_SALES_GRID Grid control by setting its various properties. The first statement in the `OnInitDialog()` function uses the `SetColWidth()` function to set the width of Column 0, the leftmost column, of the Grid control:

```
m_SalesGrid.SetColWidth(0,500);
```

The preceding statement executes the `SetColWidth()` function on the `m_SalesGrid` variable you attached to the IDC_SALES_GRID Grid control. The `SetColWidth()` function (a member function of the `CGridCtrl` class) sets the width of the column specified by the function's first parameter to the width specified by the function's second parameter. Therefore, the preceding statement sets the width of Column 0 of the Grid control to `500`.

When you write programs that use the Grid control, you can determine the widths of the Grid control columns by trial and error. Try setting the width of the columns to various values (in your code), then execute the program and see whether the columns are the correct width.

The next statement sets the width of Column 1 to `2500`:

```
m_SalesGrid.SetColWidth(1,2500);
```

Then, the next statement sets the width of Column 2 to `2500`:

```
m_SalesGrid.SetColWidth(2,2500);
```

The next two statements use the SetFixedAlignment() and SetColAlignment() functions to set the text alignment of Column 1 of the Grid control to centered:

```
m_SalesGrid.SetFixedAlignment(1, 2);
m_SalesGrid.SetColAlignment(1, 2);
```

From now on, when you write text in any of the cells of Column 1, the text will be automatically centered.

This statement sets the alignment of the topmost cell of Column 1 to a value of 2, which corresponds to "centered alignment":

```
SetFixedAlignment(1, 2);
```

The topmost cell of Column 1 is the cell containing the text Cost. (Refer back to Figure 3.1.) It's also called the *fixed cell* because it remains in the same place even when you're scrolling the rows.

This statement sets the alignment of the rest of the cells of Column 1 to a value of 2:

```
m_SalesGrid.SetColAlignment(1, 2);
```

To summarize, these two statements set the alignment of Column 1 of the Grid control to a value of 2, which corresponds to centered alignment:

```
m_SalesGrid.SetFixedAlignment(1, 2);
m_SalesGrid.SetColAlignment(1, 2);
```

Therefore, text entered into any of the cells of Column 1 will be centered.

Similarly, the next two statements you typed in the OnInitDialog() function set the alignment of Column 2 of the Grid control to centered alignment:

```
m_SalesGrid.SetFixedAlignment(2, 2);
m_SalesGrid.SetColAlignment(2, 2);
```

The next three statements fill the cell whose x-y coordinate is x=0, y=1 with the text Jan:

```
m_SalesGrid.SetCol(0);
m_SalesGrid.SetRow(1);
m_SalesGrid.SetText("Jan");
```

The SetCol() function specifies the x-coordinate of the cell, the SetRow() function specifies the y-coordinate, and the SetText() function actually puts the text in the cell.

The next three statements fill the cell whose x-y coordinate is x=0, y=2 with the text Feb:

```
m_SalesGrid.SetCol(0);
m_SalesGrid.SetRow(2);
m_SalesGrid.SetText("Feb");
```

The next three statements fill the cell whose x-y coordinate is x=0, y=3 with the text Mar:

```
m_SalesGrid.SetCol(0);
m_SalesGrid.SetRow(3);
m_SalesGrid.SetText("Mar");
```

The next three statements fill the cell whose x-y coordinate is x=1, y=0 with the text Cost:

```
m_SalesGrid.SetCol(1);
m_SalesGrid.SetRow(0);
m_SalesGrid.SetText("Cost");
```

Finally, the last three statements fill the cell whose x-y coordinate is x=2, y=0 with the text Sales:

```
m_SalesGrid.SetCol(2);
m_SalesGrid.SetRow(0);
m_SalesGrid.SetText("Sales");
```

To see the initialization code you typed in the OnInitDialog() function in action, follow these steps:

☐ Select Build Table.EXE from the Build menu.

☐ Select Execute Table.EXE from the Build menu.

> *Visual C++ responds by executing the Table.EXE program. The main window of Table.EXE appears, as shown in Figure 3.19.*

Figure 3.19.
The main window of the Table.EXE program.

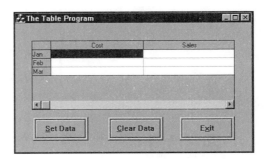

As you can see, the initialization code you wrote in the OnInitDialog() function works! The cells of Columns 1 and 2 of the Grid control have been widened, and the cells of Column 0 and Row 1 of the Grid control are filled with text. Also, the text in the cells of Columns 1 and 2 is centered. (The leftmost column is considered Column 0 and the topmost row is considered Row 0.)

☐ Terminate the Table.EXE program by clicking the × icon.

Attaching Code to the *BN_CLICKED* Event of the Set Data Pushbutton

In the `OnInitDialog()` function, you wrote the code that fills the cells of Column 0 and Row 0 of the Grid control. You'll now write the code that fills the remaining cells of the Grid control. Follow these steps to attach this code to the `BN_CLICKED` event of the Set Data pushbutton:

☐ Select ClassWizard from the View menu, select the Message Maps tab, and use the ClassWizard dialog box to select the following event:

> | | |
> |---:|:---|
> | Class name: | `CTableDlg` |
> | Object ID: | `IDC_SETDATA_BUTTON` |
> | Message: | `BN_CLICKED` |

☐ Click the Add Function button, name the new function `OnSetdataButton`, then click the Edit Code button.

> *Visual C++ responds by opening the file TableDlg.cpp with the function* `OnSetdataButton()` *ready for you to edit.*

☐ Write the following code in the `OnSetdataButton()` function:

```
void CTableDlg::OnSetdataButton()
{
// TODO: Add your control notification handler code here

/////////////////////////
// MY CODE STARTS HERE
/////////////////////////

// Fill cell x=1,y=1 with the text "$15,000".
m_SalesGrid.SetCol(1);
m_SalesGrid.SetRow(1);
m_SalesGrid.SetText("$15,000");

// Fill cell x=1,y=2 with the text "$10,000".
m_SalesGrid.SetCol(1);
m_SalesGrid.SetRow(2);
m_SalesGrid.SetText("$10,000");

// Fill cell x=1,y=3 with the text "$25,000".
m_SalesGrid.SetCol(1);
m_SalesGrid.SetRow(3);
m_SalesGrid.SetText("$25,000");

// Fill cell x=2,y=1 with the text "$50,000".
m_SalesGrid.SetCol(2);
m_SalesGrid.SetRow(1);
m_SalesGrid.SetText("$50,000");

// Fill cell x=2,y=2 with the text "$45,000".
m_SalesGrid.SetCol(2);
m_SalesGrid.SetRow(2);
m_SalesGrid.SetText("$45,000");
```

```
// Fill cell x=2,y=3 with the text "$70,000".
m_SalesGrid.SetCol(2);
m_SalesGrid.SetRow(3);
m_SalesGrid.SetText("$70,000");

/////////////////////
// MY CODE ENDS HERE
/////////////////////

}
```

☐ Save your work by selecting Save All from the File menu.

The code you typed in the OnSetdataButton() function is very simple. It uses the SetCol(), SetRow(), and SetText() functions to fill the cells of the Grid control with text.

To see the code you attached to the BN_CLICKED event of the Set Data pushbutton, follow these steps:

☐ Select Build Table.EXE from the Build menu.

☐ Select Execute Table.EXE from the Build menu.

Visual C++ responds by executing the Table.EXE program.

☐ Click the Set Data pushbutton.

As expected, the Table.EXE program responds by filling the cells of the Grid control with data. (See Figure 3.20.)

Figure 3.20.
Filling all the cells of the Grid control with data.

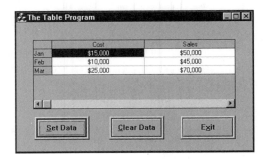

Notice that you can't change the data in the cells of the Grid control by typing in them. If you want to enable the user to enter his or her own text in the Grid control's cells, then you have to write additional code. (See the second question in the "Q&A" section at the end of this chapter.)

☐ Terminate the Table.EXE program by clicking the × icon.

Attaching Code to the *BN_CLICKED* Event of the Clear Data Pushbutton

You'll now attach code to the BN_CLICKED event of the Clear Data pushbutton. This code will clear the text from all the cells of the Grid control, except the cells in Row 0 and Column 0. Follow these steps:

☐ Select ClassWizard from the View menu, select the Message Maps tab, and use the ClassWizard dialog box to select the following event:

Class name:	CTableDlg
Object ID:	IDC_CLEARDATA_BUTTON
Message:	BN_CLICKED

☐ Click the Add Function button, name the new function OnCleardataButton, and click the Edit Code button.

Visual C++ responds by opening the file TableDlg.cpp with the function OnCleardataButton() *ready for you to edit.*

☐ Write the following code in the OnCleardataButton() function:

```
void CTableDlg::OnCleardataButton()
{
// TODO: Add your control notification handler code here

/////////////////////////
// MY CODE STARTS HERE
/////////////////////////

// Fill the cells of column 1 with NULL strings.
short i;
m_SalesGrid.SetCol(1);
for (i=1; i<4; i++)
    {
    m_SalesGrid.SetRow(i);
    m_SalesGrid.SetText("");
    }

// Fill the cells of column 2 with NULL strings.
m_SalesGrid.SetCol(2);
for (i=1; i<4; i++)
    {
    m_SalesGrid.SetRow(i);
    m_SalesGrid.SetText("");
    }

/////////////////////////
// MY CODE ENDS HERE
/////////////////////////

}
```

☐ Save your work by selecting Save All from the File menu.

The first block of code you typed uses a `for` loop to fill all the cells of Column 1 (except the cell in Row 0) with NULL strings:

```
short i;
m_SalesGrid.SetCol(1);
for (i=1; i<4; i++)
    {
    m_SalesGrid.SetRow(i);
    m_SalesGrid.SetText("");
    }
```

The statement before the `for` loop sets the Grid control's Col property to 1:

```
m_SalesGrid.SetCol(1);
```

Consequently, all the subsequent calls to the `SetText()` function in the `for` loop will be performed on cells in Column 1.

In the `for` loop itself, each iteration of the loop fills a different cell in Column 1 with a NULL string:

```
for (i=1; i<4; i++)
    {
    m_SalesGrid.SetRow(i);
    m_SalesGrid.SetText("");
    }
```

In the first iteration, the cell whose y-coordinate is y=1 is filled with a NULL string. In the second iteration, the cell whose y-coordinate is y=2 is filled with a NULL string, and so on.

The second block of code in the `OnSetdataButton()` function uses a `for` loop to fill all the cells of Column 2 (except the cell in Row 0) with NULL strings:

```
m_SalesGrid.SetCol(2);
for (i=1; i<4; i++)
    {
    m_SalesGrid.SetRow(i);
    m_SalesGrid.SetText("");
    }
```

To see the code you attached to the BN_CLICKED event of the Clear Data pushbutton in action, follow these steps:

☐ Select Build Table.EXE from the Build menu.

☐ Select Execute Table.EXE from the Build menu.

Visual C++ responds by executing the Table.EXE program.

☐ Click the Set Data pushbutton.

The Table.EXE program responds by filling the cells of the Grid control with data, as shown previously in Figure 3.20.

☐ Click the Clear Data pushbutton.

As expected, all the Grid control's cells (except in Column 0 and Row 0) are filled with NULL strings.

☐ Terminate the Table.EXE program by clicking the × icon.

Attaching Code to the *BN_CLICKED* Event of the Exit Pushbutton

When you click the Exit pushbutton, the Table.EXE program should terminate. Follow these steps to attach code to the BN_CLICKED event of the Exit pushbutton:

☐ Select ClassWizard from the View menu, select the Message Maps tab, and use the ClassWizard dialog box to select the following event:

Class name:	CTableDlg
Object ID:	IDC_EXIT_BUTTON
Message:	BN_CLICKED

☐ Click the Add Function button, name the new function OnExitButton, and click the Edit Code button.

> *Visual C++ responds by opening the file TableDlg.cpp with the function* OnExitButton() *ready for you to edit.*

☐ Write the following code in the OnExitButton() function:

```
void CTableDlg::OnExitButton()
{
// TODO: Add your control notification handler code here

/////////////////////////
// MY CODE STARTS HERE
/////////////////////////

// Terminate the program.
OnOK();

/////////////////////////
// MY CODE ENDS HERE
/////////////////////////

}
```

☐ Save your work by selecting Save All from the File menu.

The code in the OnExitButton() function is made up of a single statement that terminates the program:

OnOK()

Recall from Chapter 2, "Controls, Properties, and Events," that the OnOK() function terminates the program by closing the dialog box.

The Table.EXE program is now finished! To see the code you attached to the BN_CLICKED event of the Exit pushbutton in action, follow these steps:

☐ Select Build Table.EXE from the Build menu.

☐ Select Execute Table.EXE from the Build menu.

> *Visual C++ responds by executing the Table.EXE program.*

☐ Click the Exit pushbutton.

> *As expected, the Table.EXE program responds by terminating.*

Using the Component Gallery to Add an OLE Control

During the visual design of the IDD_TABLE_DIALOG dialog box, you inserted the Grid OLE control in the dialog box by right-clicking a free area and selecting Insert OLE Control from the pop-up menu. Visual C++ responded by placing the Grid OLE control in the dialog box. Later, when you attached a variable to the Grid control, Visual C++ created a class for the Grid control, added the files of this class to the project of the Table.EXE program, and placed the tool of the Grid OLE control in the Controls toolbar. (Refer back to Figure 3.17.)

Another way to insert an OLE control into a dialog box is to use the Component Gallery feature. To do this, follow these steps:

☐ Display the dialog box in design mode.

☐ Select Component from the Insert menu.

> *Visual C++ responds by displaying the Component Gallery dialog box.*

☐ Select the OLE Controls tab of the Components Gallery dialog box.

☐ In the OLE Controls tab, select the OLE control you want to insert in the dialog box, then click the Insert button.

> *Visual C++ responds by displaying the Confirm Classes dialog box, telling you the name of the class that will be added for the OLE control and the names of the .cpp file and .h file of the class.*

☐ Click the OK button of the Confirm Classes dialog box.

> *Visual C++ responds by adding the selected OLE control to your project and placing the tool of this OLE control in the Controls toolbar.*

☐ Click the Close button of the Components Gallery dialog box.

You can now place the OLE control in the dialog box just as you place standard Visual C++ controls:

☐ Click the tool of the OLE control you added to the project in the Controls toolbar, then click in any free area in the dialog box.

Visual C++ responds by placing the OLE control in the dialog box at the point where you clicked the mouse.

Summary

In this chapter, you have learned how to incorporate an OLE control into your Visual C++ programs. Using an OLE control is similar to using a standard Visual C++ control: You place the control in a dialog box, set its properties, and attach code to its events.

You have also learned how to use the Component Gallery to insert an OLE control into a dialog box.

Q&A

Q In the Table.EXE program, I didn't attach any code to the events of the Grid OLE control. Does the Grid OLE control have events? If so, how do I attach code to its events?

A Yes, the Grid OLE control has events. You can attach code to its events just as you attach code to events of standard Visual C++ controls—use the Message Maps tab of ClassWizard.

To see a list of the events of the Grid OLE control, follow these steps:

☐ Open the project workspace of the Table.EXE program if it's not open already. (Select Open Workspace from the File menu, then select the C:\TYVCProg\Programs\CH03\Table\Table.MDP file.)

☐ Select ClassWizard from the View menu, select the Message Maps tab, and use the ClassWizard dialog box to make the following selection:

        Class name: CTableDlg
        Object ID: IDC_SALES_GRID

Your ClassWizard dialog box should now look like the one shown in Figure 3.21—all the events of the Grid control are listed in the Messages list box.

As shown in Figure 3.21, the Grid control has events associated with it. Some of the names of these events are self-explanatory. For example, the `Click` event occurs when you click the Grid control, and the `DblClick` event occurs when you double-click the Grid control.

Figure 3.21.

Listing the events of the Grid OLE control.

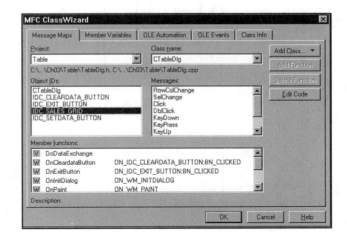

3

Q In the Table.EXE program, I can't place my own text in the cells of the Grid control. Can I write a spreadsheet-like program with the Grid OLE control so I can enter my own data in the cells?

A Yes. To enter your own data, you can attach code to the DblClick event of the Grid control. When you double-click a certain cell in the Grid control, the code you attach will display a small dialog box, asking you to type the data to be entered in the cell. The code will take your input and place it in the cell by using the SetData() function. The SetData() function will place the data in the currently selected cell.

But what code do you write to display this dialog box? In Chapter 6, "Dialog Boxes," you'll learn how to design and display your own custom dialog boxes.

Q What code do I write to make an OLE control invisible?

A To make an OLE control invisible, you can execute the ShowWindow() function on the variable you attached to the control. For example, in the Table.EXE program, the following statement would make the Grid control invisible:

```
m_SalesGrid.ShowWindow(SW_HIDE);
```

Similarly, the following statement would make the Grid control visible:

```
m_SalesGrid.ShowWindow(SW_SHOW);
```

Q Why would I ever want to make an OLE control invisible?

A In some cases, you may want your programs to use the functions of a certain OLE control but not want the user to see the OLE control. When you make the OLE control invisible, the user won't see it, but your program can use the properties and events of the control.

Quiz

1. An OLE control enables object linking and embedding and has the extension OCX (for example, MyControl.OCX).

    a. True
    b. False

2. The filename of the OLE control used in the Table.EXE program is Grid32.OCX.

    a. True
    b. False

3. Suppose the variable attached to the Grid OLE control is called m_MyGrid. Describe what the following statements do:

```
m_MyGrid.SetCol(2);
m_MyGrid.SetRow(3);
m_MyGrid.SetText("Hello");
```

Exercise

Currently, when you double-click the Grid control in the Table.EXE program, nothing happens. Enhance the Table.EXE program so that when you double-click the Grid control, the program displays a message box showing the text in the cell that was double-clicked.

Hint: To get the text of the cell, you can execute the GetText() member function of the CGridCtrl class on the m_SalesGrid variable of the Grid control.

Quiz Answers

1. True.

2. True.

3. The statements fill the cell in the Grid control whose x-y coordinate is x=2, y=3 with the text Hello.

Exercise Answer

To enhance the Table.EXE program so that when you double-click the Grid control, the program displays a message box showing the text in the cell that was double-clicked, do the following:

☐ Attach code to the DblClick event of the IDC_SALES_GRID Grid control. The code will consist of a single statement:

```
MessageBox( m_SalesGrid.GetText() );
```

The Mouse and the
Keyboard

In this chapter, you'll learn how to write Visual C++ programs that use the mouse and the keyboard. In particular, you'll create the Draw and MyKey programs.

The Draw Program

The Draw program illustrates how you can write a program that uses the mouse for drawing, but before writing the Draw program yourself, first review its specifications.

• When you start the program, the window shown in Figure 4.1 appears.

Figure 4.1.
The window of the Draw program.

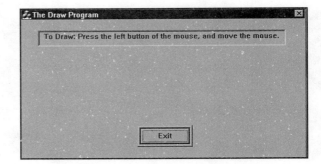

• When you move the mouse while holding down the left mouse button, the Draw program draws according to your mouse movements. Figure 4.2 shows how you can use the Draw program to write something.

Figure 4.2.
Writing with the Draw program.

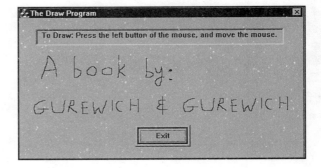

• When you click the Draw program's Exit button, the Draw program terminates.

Creating the Project of the Draw Program

Follow these steps to create the project of the Draw program:

☐ Create the C:\TYVCProg\Programs\CH04 directory, start Visual C++, and select New from the File menu.

> *Visual C++ responds by displaying the New dialog box.*

☐ Select Project Workspace from the New dialog box, then click the OK button.

> *Visual C++ responds by displaying the New Project Workspace.*

☐ Select MFC AppWizard (exe) from the Type list and enter Draw in the Name box. Then click the Browse button, select the C:\TYVCProg\Programs\CH04 directory, and click the Create button.

> *Visual C++ responds by displaying the MFC AppWizard - Step 1 window.*

☐ In Step 1 of the MFC AppWizard, click the "Dialog based" radio button (because you want to create a dialog-based application), then click the Next button to advance to the Step 2 window.

☐ In Step 2 of the MFC AppWizard, place a check mark in the About box and 3-D controls check boxes and enter the title Draw for the dialog box. When you're done, click the Next button to advance to the Step 3 window.

☐ In Step 3 of the MFC AppWizard, select the "Yes, please" radio button (because you want Visual C++ to generate source file comments) and the "As a shared DLL" radio button. Click the Next button to advance to the Step 4 window.

☐ Click the Finish button of the Step 4 window, then click the OK button of the New Project Information dialog box.

☐ Select Set Default Configuration from the Build menu.

> *Visual C++ responds by displaying the Default Project Configuration dialog box.*

☐ Set the project to Draw Win32 - Release.

That's it! You've finished creating the Draw project.

The Visual Design of the Draw Program

You'll now visually design the window of the Draw program with the following steps:

☐ Select Project Workspace from the View menu to display the Project Workspace window, then select the ResourceView tab. Next, expand the Draw resources item, expand the Dialog item, and double-click the IDD_DRAW_DIALOG item.

Visual C++ responds by displaying the IDD_DRAW_DIALOG dialog box in design mode.

☐ Delete the OK and Cancel buttons and the TODO static text of the IDD_DRAW_DIALOG dialog box.

☐ Design the IDD_DRAW_DIALOG dialog box according to Table 4.1. When you finish designing the dialog box, it should look like Figure 4.1.

Table 4.1. The properties table of the IDD_DRAW_DIALOG dialog box.

Object	Property	Setting
Dialog Box	**ID**	**IDD_DRAW_DIALOG**
	Caption	The Draw Program
	Font	System, Size 10
Push Button	**ID**	**IDC_EXIT_BUTTON**
	Caption	Exit
	Client edge	Checked (Extended Styles tab)
	Static edge	Checked (Extended Styles tab)
	Modal frame	Checked (Extended Styles tab)
Static Text	**ID**	**IDC_INSTRUCTION_STATIC**
	Align Text	Center (Styles tab)
	Static edge	Checked (Extended styles tab)
	Client edge	Checked (Extended styles tab)
	Caption	To Draw: Press the left button of the mouse, and move the mouse.

Attaching Code to the *BN_CLICKED* Event of the Exit Button

You'll now attach code to the BN_CLICKED event of the Exit button.

☐ Select ClassWizard from the View menu.

Visual C++ responds by displaying the MFC ClassWizard dialog box.

☐ Select the Message Maps tab and use the ClassWizard dialog box to select the following event:

> Class name: CDrawDlg
> Object ID: IDC_EXIT_BUTTON
> Message: BN_CLICKED

☐ Click the Add Function button, name the new function OnExitButton, and click the Edit Code button.

> *Visual C++ responds by opening the file DrawDlg.cpp with the function OnExitButton()*
> *ready for you to edit.*

☐ Write the following code in the OnExitButton() function:

```
void CDrawDlg::OnExitButton()
{
// TODO: Add your control notification handler code here

////////////////////////
// MY CODE STARTS HERE
////////////////////////

// Terminate the program
OnOK();

////////////////////////
// MY CODE ENDS HERE
////////////////////////

}
```

Attaching Code to the *WM_MOUSEMOVE* Event of the Dialog Box

You'll now attach code to the WM_MOUSEMOVE event of the dialog box, which is automatically executed whenever you move the mouse.

☐ Select ClassWizard from the View menu, select the Message Maps tab, and use the ClassWizard dialog box to select the following event:

> Class name: CDrawDlg
> Object ID: CDrawDlg
> Message: WM_MOUSEMOVE

☐ Click the Add Function button to create the new function OnMouseMove, then click the Edit Code button.

> *Visual C++ responds by opening the file DrawDlg.cpp with the function OnMouseMove()*
> *ready for you to edit.*

☐ Write the following code in the `OnMouseMove()` function:

```
void CDrawDlg::OnMouseMove(UINT nFlags, CPoint point)
{
// TODO: Add your message handler code here and/or call
// default

//////////////////////////
// MY CODE STARTS HERE
//////////////////////////

if ( (nFlags & MK_LBUTTON) == MK_LBUTTON )
{

// Create a dc object
CClientDC  dc(this);

// Draw a pixel
dc.SetPixel(point.x,
            point.y,
            RGB(0,0,0) );


} //end of if

//////////////////////////
// MY CODE ENDS HERE
//////////////////////////

CDialog::OnMouseMove(nFlags, point);
}
```

☐ Select Save All from the File menu to save your work.

The code you typed in the `OnMouseMove()` function is an `if` statement:

```
if ( (nFlags & MK_LBUTTON) == MK_LBUTTON )
{

/// This code is executed, provided that
/// the mouse was moved while the left
/// button of the mouse is pressed down.

}
```

The `OnMouseMove()` function is executed whenever you move the mouse. The first parameter of the `OnMouseMove()` function is `nFlags`, which indicates whether certain keyboard keys (such as Ctrl and Shift) and mouse buttons were pressed while the mouse was moved.

The `&` operation (bitwise AND operation) examines whether the left mouse button is pressed down while the mouse is moved; if it is, then the code under the `if` statement is executed.

Note: If you are unfamiliar with the bitwise AND operation, note the following:

Suppose that MyFlag is equal to 00111111—it consists of 8 bits. You want to determine whether the rightmost bit is equal to 0 or 1. You can make this determination as follows (assuming that RIGHT_MOST is a constant equal to 00000001):

```
if ( (MyFlag & RIGHT_MOST) == RIGHT_MOST )
{
// This code is executed, provided that the rightmost
// bit of MyFlag is equal to 1.
}
```

Therefore, when you use AND on 00111111 with 00000001, the result is 00000001:

```
00111111 & 00000001 = 00000001
```

In a similar manner, you can perform the AND operation to determine the value of any bit location in MyFlag. For example, if 3RD_FROM_RIGHT is a constant equal to 00000100, then you can determine whether the third bit from the right of MyFlag is equal to 1 as follows:

```
if ( (MyFlag & 3RD_FROM_RIGHT ) == 3RD_FROM_RIGHT )
{
// This code is executed, provided that the 3rd bit from
// the right of MyFlag is equal to 1.
}
```

Therefore, the code under the `if` statement is executed whenever you move the mouse while the left button is held down.

The code you typed under the `if` statement creates a device context object:

```
CClientDC  dc(this);
```

You can think of the *device context* (dc) as an imaginary screen that resides in memory. Once you create the dc, you can draw into it as if it were a regular screen. You can draw pixels, lines, geometrical shapes, and so on. Whatever you draw in the dc is transferred to the real screen.

The next statement you typed draws a pixel in the dc:

```
dc.SetPixel(point.x,
            point.y,
            RGB(0,0,0) );
```

The dc is an imaginary screen in memory, but if you could look at it now, you'd see a pixel drawn in it. The SetPixel() function draws the pixel at the location specified by the first and second parameters of the SetPixel() function. point.x is the horizontal coordinate of the mouse cursor, and point.y is the vertical coordinate. For example, if point.x is equal to 100 and point.y is equal to 200, the pixel will be drawn 100 pixels to the right of the window's left edge and 200 pixels below the window's top edge.

But what are the values of point.x and point.y? The second parameter of the OnMouseMove() function is point, which holds the coordinates of the mouse cursor at the time the OnMouseMove() function is executed. Therefore, the SetPixel() function draws the pixel at the location of the mouse cursor.

The third parameter of the SetPixel() function is the returned value of the RGB() function, which indicates the color of the pixel that SetPixel() draws.

The *R* in RGB stands for red, the *G* stands for green, and the *B* stands for blue. The RGB() function has three parameters: the first indicates the amount of red in the resulting color, the second indicates the amount of green, and the third indicates the amount of blue. You can generate any color by "mixing" the red, green, and blue colors. For example, to indicate the color red, use RGB(255,0,0).

Each color can have a maximum value of 255 and a minimum value of 0. RGB(255,0,0) is red because the value for red is at its maximum, and the green and blue amounts are 0. Similarly, RGB(0,255,0) is green and RGB(0,0,255) is blue.

You should recognize two additional colors by inspecting the RGB() function. White is represented by RGB(255,255,255), the maximum amounts of red, green, and blue. Black is generated as RGB(0,0,0), the result of no red, green, or blue. Therefore, the third parameter of SetPixel() indicates that the pixel should be drawn in black.

Drawing a Picture Point by Point

To see your code in action, follow these steps:

☐ Compile and link the Draw program.

☐ Execute the Draw program.

☐ While holding the left mouse button down, drag the mouse.

Draw responds by drawing pixels according to the mouse movement.

☐ Practice with the Draw program, then click the Exit button to terminate it.

Checking the Mouse Status

The OnMouseMove() function is executed whenever you move the mouse, but your PC can't respond to each and every mouse movement. Why? Because if your CPU was busy executing the OnMouseMove() function in response to each and every mouse movement, it couldn't perform any other tasks. Instead of executing the OnMouseMove() function every time the mouse is moved, Windows checks the mouse cursor location periodically. If the mouse cursor is at a different location than it was during the previous check, then a *flag* is set indicating the mouse was moved.

The new coordinates of the mouse cursor, as well as key presses and button clicks, are noted and saved.

When the OnMouseMove() function is executed, the point parameter indicates the coordinates of the mouse cursor during the last position check, and nFlags indicates the status of certain keys and mouse buttons. Remember that the CPU can perform other tasks between executions of the OnMouseMove() function. However, if you move the mouse quickly, the OnMouseMove() function won't be executed for each new location of the mouse during the movement. You can prove it to yourself as follows:

☐ Execute the Draw program and move the mouse as shown in Figure 4.3—begin by moving the mouse slowly, then increase the speed of your mouse movement.

Figure 4.3.

Varying your mouse movement speed.

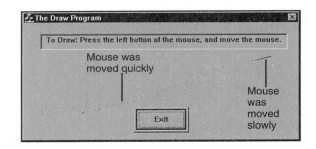

There are many points on the right side of the window shown in Figure 4.3. Why? Since you moved the mouse very slowly, the OnMouseMove() function was executed many times. Each execution of OnMouseMove() causes a pixel to be drawn at the new mouse location.

When the mouse was moved very quickly, only a few points were drawn along its path. Why? Because the OnMouseMove() function was executed only a few times during the mouse movement.

Enhancing the Draw Program

If you've ever drawn with Paint (Window 95) or Paintbrush (Windows NT and Windows 3.1x), you might have noticed that, unlike the Draw program, the lines drawn when you move the mouse are solid. In the Draw program, you have to move the mouse very slowly to draw a solid line. In this section, you'll try enhancing your Draw program so it performs more like Paint or Paintbrush.

You're going to attach code that makes it seem as if the lines are drawn according to the mouse movement—the same trick used by Paint and Paintbrush. The code will connect the points with straight lines. It will look as though the program draws lines at each point along the mouse path, but in reality, the program simply "connects the dots" drawn by the Draw program. If you move the mouse very quickly along the path shown in Figure 4.4, you would expect the program to draw the line along that path. Since the mouse was moved very quickly, however, the resulting line looks very different than it should. (The same situation occurs when using programs such as Paint and Paintbrush.)

Figure 4.4.
Drawing by connecting the dots.

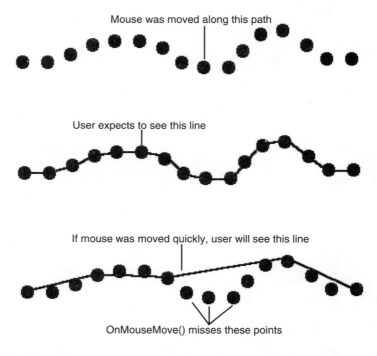

Mouse was moved along this path

User expects to see this line

If mouse was moved quickly, user will see this line

OnMouseMove() misses these points

To connect the pixels with lines, the `OnMouseMove()` function needs to know the previous coordinates of the mouse. You'll now declare two member variables, `m_PrevX` and `m_PrevY`, which will be used to hold the coordinates of the mouse cursor.

☐ Display the DrawDlg.h file by opening the Project Workspace, clicking the FileView tab, expanding the Dependencies item, and double-clicking the DrawDlg.h item.

☐ Add the declaration of the `m_PrevX` and `m_PrevY` member variables to the constructor function (in the DrawDlg.h file) as follows:

```
// DrawDlg.h : header file
//
/////////////////////////////////////////////////////
// CDrawDlg dialog

class CDrawDlg : public CDialog
{
// Construction
public:
CDrawDlg(CWnd* pParent = NULL);  // standard constructor
```

```
//////////////////////
// MY CODE STARTS HERE
//////////////////////

int m_PrevX;
int m_PrevY;

//////////////////////
// MY CODE ENDS HERE
//////////////////////

....
....
....
};
```

☐ Modify the OnMouseMove() function in the DrawDlg.cpp file:

```
void CDrawDlg::OnMouseMove(UINT nFlags, CPoint point)
{
// TODO: Add your message handler code here
// and/or call default

//////////////////////
// MY CODE STARTS HERE
//////////////////////

if ( (nFlags & MK_LBUTTON) == MK_LBUTTON )
{

// Create a dc object
CClientDC   dc(this);

// Draw a pixel
// dc.SetPixel(point.x,
//             point.y,
//             RGB(0,0,0) );


dc.MoveTo(m_PrevX, m_PrevY);
dc.LineTo(point.x, point.y);

m_PrevX = point.x;
m_PrevY = point.y;

}

//////////////////////
// MY CODE ENDS HERE
//////////////////////

CDialog::OnMouseMove(nFlags, point);
}
```

The code you typed first comments out the SetPixel() function:

```
// Draw a pixel
// dc.SetPixel(point.x,
```

```
//              point.y,
//              RGB(0,0,0) );
```

Then the `MoveTo()` and `LineTo()` functions are executed:

```
dc.MoveTo(m_PrevX, m_PrevY);
dc.LineTo(point.x, point.y);
```

To draw a line, you use the `MoveTo()` function to indicate the starting point. The coordinates of the line's starting point are the previous coordinates of the mouse cursor. Then you execute the `LineTo()` function; its parameters indicate the line's endpoint, which is the current coordinates of the mouse cursor.

You also updated the `m_PrevX` and `m_PrevY` member variables with the current mouse cursor coordinates; the next time the `OnMouseMove()` function is executed, the `m_PrevX` and `m_PrevY` variables are updated:

```
m_PrevX = point.x;
m_PrevY = point.y;
```

> **Note:** The previous coordinates of the mouse (`m_PrevX` and `m_PrevY`) were declared as *data member variables* to maintain the values of `m_PrevX` and `m_PrevY` during the life of the program. `OnMouseMove()` updates the values of `m_PrevX` and `m_PrevY`. After the execution of `OnMouseMove()`, the values of `m_PrevX` and `m_PrevY` are not lost—they are updated on the next execution of `OnMouseMove`.

☐ Compile, link, and execute the Draw program.

☐ Draw something with the Draw program.

As you can see in Figure 4.5, now the dots are connected with straight lines.

Figure 4.5.
Connecting the dots with straight lines.

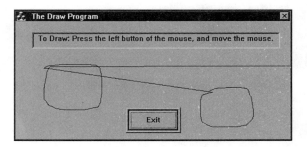

☐ Experiment with the Draw program, then click its Exit button to terminate the program.

Revising the Draw Program

Did you notice that there's something wrong with the current version of Draw? The program always draws a straight line as the first line that is drawn. Why is this happening? In OnMouseMove() you added code that connects the previous mouse location with the current mouse location. The previous mouse coordinates are m_PrevX and m_PrevY, but when you start the program, m_PrevX and m_PrevY aren't updated yet. You might also notice that you can't draw two separate circles like the ones shown in Figure 4.6, because when you start drawing the second circle, a straight line will connect the last point of the first circle to the first point of the second circle.

Figure 4.6.

Drawing two circles with the Draw program.

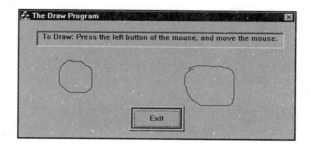

To solve the problems of the Draw program, you need to attach code to the WM_LBUTTONDOWN event, which occurs whenever you press the left mouse button.

☐ Choose ClassWizard from the View menu, select the Message Maps tab, and use the ClassWizard dialog box to select the following event:

Class name:	CDrawDlg
Object ID:	CDrawDlg
Message:	WM_LBUTTONDOWN

☐ Click the Add Function button to create the new function OnLButtonDown, then click the Edit Code button.

Visual C++ responds by opening the file DrawDlg.cpp with the function OnLButtonDown() ready for you to edit.

☐ Write the following code in the OnLButtonDown() function:

```
void CDrawDlg::OnLButtonDown(UINT nFlags, CPoint point)
{
// TODO: Add your message handler code here
// and/or call default

/////////////////////////
// MY CODE STARTS HERE
/////////////////////////
```

```
m_PrevX = point.x;
m_PrevY = point.y;
/////////////////////////
// MY CODE ENDS HERE
/////////////////////////

CDialog::OnLButtonDown(nFlags, point);
}
```

The code you typed updates the m_PrevX and m_PrevY member variables. Note that the OnLButtonDown() function has the same parameters as the OnMouseMove() function. The point parameter indicates the current mouse position when the left mouse button is pressed. Now when you start drawing, the m_PrevX and m_PrevY variables are updated with the current mouse position.

☐ Compile, link, and execute the Draw program.

☐ Draw the two circles shown previously in Figure 4.6.

As you can see, now it's possible to draw two separate circles. When you start drawing the second circle, you press the left mouse button down at the first point of the second circle. This causes the execution of the OnLButtonDown() function, which updates m_PrevX and m_PrevY with the coordinates of the first point of the second circle.

☐ Experiment with the Draw program, then click the Exit button to terminate the program.

The MyKey Program

The Draw program demonstrates how you can attach code to the MouseMove and LButtonDown events. You can also attach code to keyboard events. The MyKey program demonstrates how to do this, but before you start designing the program, review its specifications:

- When you start the MyKey program, the window shown in Figure 4.7 appears.

Figure 4.7.
The MyKey program.

- When you press a key on the keyboard, a message box displays the values of various flags representing the key that was pressed.

Creating the MyKey Project

You'll now create the MyKey project with the following steps:

☐ Create the C:\TYVCProg\Programs\CH04 directory.

☐ Start Visual C++, then select New from the File menu.

Visual C++ responds by displaying the New dialog box.

☐ Open a new project workspace, select the MFC AppWizard item, and enter MyKey in the Name box.

☐ Click the Browse button, select the C:\TYVCProg\Programs\CH04 directory, and click the Create button.

Visual C++ responds by displaying the MFC AppWizard Step 1 dialog box.

☐ Click the "Dialog based" radio button of the Step 1 window to create a dialog-based application, then click the Next button to advance to the Step 2 window.

☐ In Step 2 of the MFC AppWizard, select the options for an About box and 3-D controls and enter the title MyKey for the dialog box. When you're done, click the Next button to advance to the Step 3 window.

☐ In Step 3 of the MFC AppWizard, select the "Yes, please" radio button (because you want Visual C++ to place comments) and the "As a shared DLL" radio button. Then click the Next button to advance to the Step 4 window.

☐ Click the Finish button of the Step 4 window, then click the OK button of the New Project Information dialog box.

Visual C++ responds by creating the MyKey project and all its associated files.

☐ Select Set Default Configuration from the Build menu.

Visual C++ responds by displaying the Default Project Configuration dialog box.

☐ Set the project to MyKey Win32 - Release.

That's it! You've finished creating the MyKey project.

The Visual Design of the MyKey Program

You'll now visually design the window of the MyKey program:

☐ Select Project Workspace from the View menu, click the ResourceView tab, expand the MyKey resources item, expand the Dialog item, and finally double-click the IDD_MYKEY_DIALOG item.

Visual C++ responds by displaying the IDD_MYKEY_DIALOG dialog box in design mode.

☐ Delete the OK button, Cancel button, and TODO text in the IDD_MYKEY_DIALOG dialog box.

☐ Design the IDD_MYKEY_DIALOG dialog box according to Table 4.2. When you finish designing the dialog box, it should look like Figure 4.7.

Table 4.2. The properties table of the IDD_MYKEY_DIALOG dialog box.

Object	Property	Setting
Dialog Box	**ID**	**IDD_MYKEY_DIALOG**
	Caption	The MyKey Program
	Font	System, Size 10
	Client edge	Checked (Extended Styles tab)
	Static edge	Checked (Extended Styles tab)
Static Text	**ID**	**IDC_INSTRUCTION_STATIC**
	Caption	Press keys on the keyboard
	Align text	Center (Styles tab)
	Client edge	Checked (Extended Styles tab)
	Static edge	Checked (Extended Styles tab)
	Disabled	Checked (General)

Attaching Code to the Keyboard Events

You'll now attach code that's executed whenever you press keys on the keyboard:

☐ Select ClassWizard from the View menu, select the Message Maps tab, and use the ClassWizard dialog box to select the following event:

Class name:	CMyKeyDlg
Object ID:	CMyKeyDlg
Message:	WM_KEYDOWN

☐ Click the Add Function button to create the new function OnKeyDown(), then click the Edit Code button.

Visual C++ responds by opening the file MyKeyDlg.cpp with the function OnKeyDown() ready for you to edit.

☐ Write the following code in the OnKeyDown() function:

```
void CMyKeyDlg::OnKeyDown(UINT nChar, UINT nRepCnt, UINT nFlags)
{
// TODO: Add your message handler code here
// and/or call default

/////////////////////////
// MY CODE STARTS HERE
/////////////////////////

char   strnChar[10];
char   strnRepCnt[10];
char   strnFlags[10];

CString  strKeyPressed;

itoa(nChar,   strnChar,   10);
itoa(nRepCnt, strnRepCnt, 10);
itoa(nFlags,  strnFlags,  10);

strKeyPressed = (CString)"You pressed the key: " +
                "\n" +
                "nChar=" +
                strnChar +
                "\n" +
                "nRepCnt=" +
                strnRepCnt +
                "\n" +
                "nFlags="+
                strnFlags;

MessageBox(strKeyPressed);


/////////////////////////
// MY CODE ENDS HERE
/////////////////////////

CDialog::OnKeyDown(nChar, nRepCnt, nFlags);
}
```

Take a look at the parameters of the OnKeyDown() function:

```
void CMyKeyDlg::OnKeyDown(UINT nChar, UINT nRepCnt, UINT nFlags)
{
…
…
…
}
```

The first parameter of OnKeyDown() is nChar, which specifies the code of the pressed key. The second parameter, nRepCnt, represents the number of times the key was pressed down repeatedly. For example, if you hold the *A* key down and keep pressing it, the nRepCnt parameter of the OnKeyDown() function would hold the number of times the PC considered the *A* key pressed.

The third parameter of the OnKeyDown() function is nFlags, which specifies a number representing special keys (such as the Alt key, the function keys, and so on).

The code you typed declares three strings:

```
char    strnChar[10];
char    strnRepCnt[10];
char    strnFlags[10];
```

They will hold the strings corresponding to the nChar, nRepCnt, and nFlags parameters.

Then you declared the strKeyPressed variable as a variable of type CString:

```
CString    strKeyPressed;
```

Next, you update the strKeyPressed variable with a string that will be displayed whenever you press a key on the keyboard. The nChar parameter is converted to a string:

```
itoa(nChar, strnChar, 10);
```

Note: Use the itoa() function to convert a number to a string. For example, to convert the number MyNumber to a string named sNumber, first declare the sNumber as a string:

```
char    sNumber[5];
```

In the preceding statement, five characters were allocated to the sNumber string. Then you can use the itoa() function to updated the sNumber string as follows:

```
itoa(sNumber, Number, 10);
```

The third parameter of the itoa() function is 10 because you are specifying that the number supplied as the second parameter of itoa() is a decimal number.

You then convert the nRepCnt and nFlags numbers to strings as follows:

```
itoa(nRepCnt, strnRepCnt, 10);
itoa(nFlags,  strnFlags,  10);
```

Now that the three parameters of the OnKeyDown() function are stored as strings, you can update the strKeyPressed string as follows:

```
strKeyPressed = (CString)"You pressed the key: " +
                "\n" +
                "nChar=" +
                strnChar +
                "\n" +
                "nRepCnt=" +
                strnRepCnt +
                "\n" +
                "nFlags="+
                strnFlags;
```

\n is the line-feed character.

Finally, you display the strKeyPressed string with the MessageBox() function as follows:

```
MessageBox(strKeyPressed);
```

(The \n character you inserted in the strKeyPressed string causes the string to be displayed on multiple lines.)

☐ Compile, link, and execute the MyKey program.

☐ Press a key on your keyboard, and notice that the message box displays the contents of the OnKeyDown() function's parameters corresponding to the pressed key.

☐ Experiment with the MyKey program, then click the × icon on the upper-right corner to terminate the MyKey program.

> **Note:** It's important to note that you were instructed to disable the static text control in the MyKey window during design time. Why? Because you want the messages that correspond to pressing the keys to reach the IDD_MYKEY_DIALOG dialog box and be processed by the OnKeyDown() function. If the dialog box contains an enabled control, the messages corresponding to the key press will reach the control that has keyboard focus (instead of reaching the OnKeyDown() function of the IDD_MYKEY_DIALOG dialog box).

Summary

In this chapter, you have designed and executed the Draw program, a program that uses the mouse for drawing. As you have seen, the Draw program uses the OnMouseMove() function to execute code whenever you move the mouse. The Draw program also uses the OnLButtonDown() function, a function executed whenever you press the left mouse button.

You have also designed and executed the MyKey program, a program that detects which keys you pressed on the keyboard.

Q&A

Q Are there other mouse messages I can use?

A Yes. In this chapter, you have learned about the WM_MOUSEMOVE message (generated whenever you move the mouse) and the WM_LBUTTONDOWN message (generated whenever you press the left mouse button). Other messages you may find useful are the WM_LBUTTONDBLCLK message (generated whenever you double-click the mouse) and the

LBUTTONUP message (generated whenever you release the left mouse button). Use ClassWizard to examine the messages associated with the IDD_DRAW_DIALOG dialog box, and notice other mouse-related messages, such as WM_RBUTTONUP and WM_RBUTTONDOWN.

Q Are there other keyboard messages I can use?

A In this chapter, you use the WM_KEYDOWN message (generated whenever you press a key on the keyboard). Use ClassWizard to examine other keyboard-related messages of the IDD_MYKEY_DIALOG dialog box. For example, the WM_KEYUP message is generated when a key is released.

Quiz

1. The OnKeyDown() function is executed whenever you press:

   a. The left mouse button.

   b. A key on the keyboard.

   c. None of the above.

2. nChar is the parameter of the OnKeyDown() function, and the ASCII code of the *A* character is 65. When you press the A key, nChar is equal to what?

3. RGB(0,0,255) represents the color _____.

4. RGB(123,211,98) represents the color _____.

Exercises

1. What code will you write that is executed whenever the second bit from the right of a variable called HerFlag is equal to 1? Assume that a constant is declared as 2ND_FROM_RIGHT and that this constant is equal to 00000010.

2. Modify the Draw program so that it will draw thick red lines when you draw with the mouse. Note: New information is introduced in the answer of this exercise. Follow the steps presented there.

Quiz Answers

1. b.

2. 65

3. Blue

4. I don't know if this color has a name, but it's a mixture of red, green, and blue (the color is actually green with some yellow in it).

Exercise Answers

1. Here is the code that accomplishes this:

```
if ( (HerFlag & 2ND_FROM_RIGHT) == 2ND_FROm_RIGHT)
{
// This code is executed whenever the second
// bit from the right of HerFlag is equal
// to 1.
}
```

2. The Draw program draws lines (in the OnMouseMove() function) by using the LineTo() function as follows:

```
dc.LineTo(point.x, point.y);
```

But what color will be used for drawing the line? And what is the thickness of the line that will be drawn with the LineTo() function? Since you didn't specify any particular pen, the default pen will be used, which is a solid black pen that is 1 pixel wide.

☐ Modify the OnMouseMove() function:

```
void CDrawDlg::OnMouseMove(UINT nFlags, CPoint point)
{
// TODO: Add your message handler code here
// and/or call default

//////////////////////////
// MY CODE STARTS HERE
//////////////////////////

if ( (nFlags & MK_LBUTTON) == MK_LBUTTON )
{

// Create a dc object
CClientDC dc(this);

// Create a new pen (solid, 10 pixels, red).
CPen NewPen(PS_SOLID,
            10,
            RGB(255,0,0) );

// Select the pen.
dc.SelectObject(&NewPen);

// Draw a pixel
// dc.SetPixel(point.x,
//             point.y,
//             RGB(0,0,0) );

dc.MoveTo(m_PrevX, m_PrevY);
dc.LineTo(point.x, point.y);

m_PrevX = point.x;
m_PrevY = point.y;

}
```

4

```
////////////////////////
// MY CODE ENDS HERE
////////////////////////
```

```
CDialog::OnMouseMove(nFlags, point);
}
```

The code you added creates a new pen called `NewPen` of type `CPen`:

```
// Create a new pen (solid, 10 pixels, red).
CPen NewPen(PS_SOLID,
            10,
            RGB(255,0,0) );
```

The new pen is declared as a solid red pen, 10 pixels wide.

Then the `SelectObject()` function is executed to apply the new pen:

```
// Select the pen.
dc.SelectObject(&NewPen);
```

It's not enough to declare the new pen. You must also put the new pen in use by executing the `SelectObject()` function.

The rest of the code in the `OnMouseMove()` function remains the same:

```
dc.MoveTo(m_PrevX, m_PrevY);
dc.LineTo(point.x, point.y);
```

The line will be drawn as a solid red line that is 10 pixels wide.

☐ Compile, link, and execute the program.

☐ Use the mouse to draw and notice that the lines are solid red and 10 pixels wide. (See Figure 4.8.)

Figure 4.8.

Using the enhanced version of the Draw program.

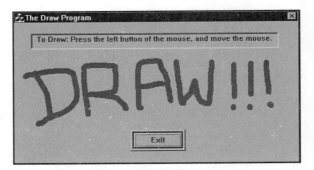

5

Menus

So far you've written programs without menus, but now you'll learn how to add a menu to your Visual C++ program.

The Speed.EXE Program

In this chapter, you'll write a program called Speed.EXE that illustrates how to write a Visual C++ program that includes a menu. Before you start writing the Speed.EXE program, first review what the Speed.EXE program should look like and what it should do.

- When you start the Speed.EXE program, its window should look like the one in Figure 5.1.

Figure 5.1.
The window of the Speed.EXE program.

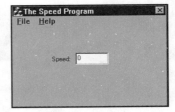

- As shown in Figure 5.1, the window of the Speed.EXE program contains an edit box where you can type a numeric value. The Speed.EXE program also includes two pop-up menus: File and Help. (See Figures 5.2 and 5.3.)

Figure 5.2.
The File menu of the Speed.EXE program.

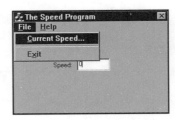

Figure 5.3.
The Help menu of the Speed.EXE program.

- When you select Current Speed from the File menu, the program displays a message box showing the numeric value specified in the edit box. When you select About from the Help menu, the program displays an About dialog box. (See Figure 5.4.)

Figure 5.4.
The About dialog box of the Speed.EXE program.

- When you select Exit from the File menu, the program terminates.

Now that you know what the Speed.EXE program should look like and what it should do, start creating this program.

Creating the Project of the Speed.EXE Program

Follow these steps to create the project and skeleton files of the Speed.EXE program:

☐ Create the directory C:\TYVCProg\Programs\CH05, start Visual C++, choose New from the File menu, and select Project Workspace from the New dialog box and click the OK button.

Visual C++ responds by displaying the New Project Workspace dialog box.

☐ Select MFC AppWizard (exe) from the Type list and enter Speed in the Name box.

☐ Click the Browse button, select the C:\TYVCProg\Programs\CH05 directory, and click the Create button.

Visual C++ responds by displaying the MFC AppWizard - Step 1 window.

☐ In the Step 1 window, choose the option to create a dialog-based application, then click the Next button.

☐ In Step 2, enter The Speed Program as the title of the dialog box. Make sure the buttons for "About box" and "3D controls" are selected, then click the Next button.

☐ In Step 3, choose the "Yes, please" radio button to generate comments and the "As a shared DLL" radio button, then click the Next button.

☐ In Step 4, notice that AppWizard has created the CSpeedApp and CSpeedDlg classes for you. When you're done, click the Finish button.

Visual C++ responds by displaying the New Project Information window.

☐ Click the OK button, choose Set Default Configuration from the Build menu, select Speed - Win32 Release in the Default Project Configuration dialog box, then click the OK button.

That's it! You've finished creating the project and skeleton files of the Speed program.

Creating the Menu of the Speed Program

Follow these steps to create the menu of the Speed program:

☐ Select Project Workspace from the View menu, select the ResourceView tab, and expand the Speed resources item.

Your Project Workspace window should now look like Figure 5.5.

Figure 5.5.
The Project Workspace window with the ResourceView tab selected.

As shown in Figure 5.5, the project of the Speed program currently includes four types of resources: Dialog, Icon, String Table, and Version. However, you want to design a menu, so you need to insert a menu resource to the project. Here is how you do that:

☐ Right-click the Speed resources item in the Project Workspace window and select Insert from the pop-up menu.

Visual C++ responds by displaying the Insert Resource dialog box. (See Figure 5.6.)

Figure 5.6.
The Insert Resource dialog box.

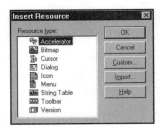

☐ Select Menu, then click the OK button of the dialog box.

Visual C++ responds by inserting a new blank menu in the project and displaying it in design mode, ready for you to edit. (See Figure 5.7.)

Figure 5.7.
Inserting a new blank menu in design mode.

The title of the leftmost pop-up menu is currently blank.

The menu bar

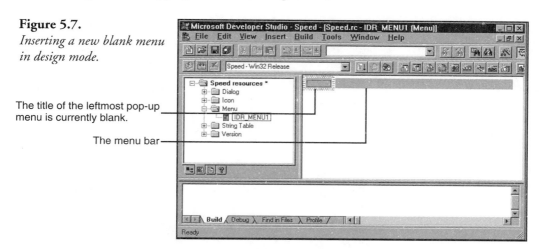

As you can see in Figure 5.7, the title of the Visual C++ window includes the text IDR_MENU1 (Menu). This means that the menu Visual C++ created for you has the ID IDR_MENU1. The menu bar is currently blank; you'll be customizing it until it looks like the one shown in Figures 5.2 and 5.3. The leftmost side of the menu bar has a small blank rectangle surrounded by black dots. This rectangle represents the title of the leftmost pop-up menu of the menu bar. Follow these steps to set its title to File:

☐ Double-click the leftmost rectangle of the menu bar.

Visual C++ responds by displaying the Menu Item Properties dialog box. (See Figure 5.8.)

Figure 5.8.
Displaying the Menu Item Properties dialog box.

After you double-click the leftmost rectangle of the menu bar, the Menu Item Properties dialog box appears.

☐ Set the Caption field to &File.

Notice as you type in the Caption field that the title of the leftmost pop-up menu changes accordingly. Your menu bar should now look like the one shown in Figure 5.9.

Figure 5.9.
Setting the title of the leftmost pop-up menu to File.

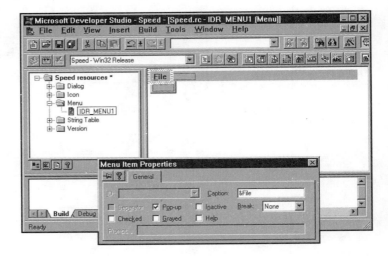

The *F* in "File" is underlined because you prefixed File with the & character. Consequently, the File pop-up menu will open when you press Alt+F on the keyboard during runtime.

As shown in Figure 5.9, there's now a small empty rectangle under the File menu title. This rectangle represents the caption of the first menu item of the File menu. (If you don't see this rectangle on your screen, click the File title). To set the caption of the first item in the File pop-up menu, do the following:

☐ Double-click the blank rectangle under the File title.

Visual C++ responds by opening the Menu Item Properties dialog box again so you can set the caption of the first menu item of the File pop-up menu.

☐ Set the Caption field to &Current Speed....

Your IDR_MENU1 menu should look like the one in Figure 5.10. The caption of the first menu item is now set to Current Speed.

The *C* in "Current Speed" is prefixed with the & character. During runtime, you can press C on the keyboard to select the Current Speed menu item when the File pop-up menu is open.

As shown in Figure 5.10, the Menu Item Properties dialog box also has an ID field. However, you don't have to set the ID of the menu item. Visual C++ will automatically assign an ID for each menu item you add to the pop-up menu. To make sure Visual C++ automatically assigned an ID to the Current Speed menu item, do the following:

Figure 5.10.

Setting the caption of the first File menu item to Current Speed.

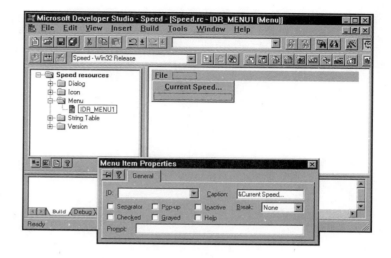

☐ Double-click the Current Speed item of the File pop-up menu.

> *Visual C++ responds by opening the Menu Item Properties dialog box again. (See Figure 5.11.)*

As you can see, Visual C++ assigned ID_FILE_CURRENTSPEED as an ID for the Current Speed menu item. (You can't see the last *D* in ID_FILE_CURRENTSPEED because the ID field isn't wide enough.)

Figure 5.11.

Checking the ID of the Current Speed menu item.

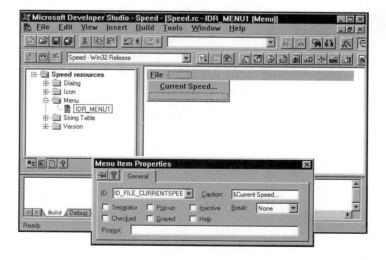

The next menu item to add to the File pop-up menu is a separator bar. As shown back in Figure 5.2, there's a separator bar between the Current Speed menu item and the Exit menu item. To add the separator bar, do the following:

☐ Double-click the blank rectangle under the Current Speed menu item.

> *Visual C++ responds by again displaying the Menu Item Properties dialog box so you can add a separator bar.*

☐ Place a check mark in the Separator check box. (See Figure 5.12.)

> *Visual C++ responds by inserting a separator bar below the Current Speed menu item.*

Figure 5.12.

Adding a separator bar.

The last menu item to add is the Exit menu item. Follow these steps to add the Exit menu item to the File pop-up menu:

☐ Double-click the blank rectangle under the separator bar of the File pop-up menu.

> *Visual C++ responds by again displaying the Menu Item Properties dialog box so you can set the caption of File's third menu item.*

☐ Set the Caption field to E&xit.

The File pop-up menu is finished! Your IDR_MENU1 menu should now look like the one shown in Figure 5.13.

As shown in Figure 5.3, the menu of the Speed.EXE program should also include a Help pop-up menu; follow these steps to add one:

☐ Double-click the small rectangle on the menu bar to the right of the File pop-up menu title.

☐ Set the Caption field in the Menu Item Properties dialog box to &Help.

Your IDR_MENU1 menu should now look like the one shown in Figure 5.14.

As shown in Figure 5.3, the Help pop-up menu should include only one menu item: About. Follow these steps to add the About menu item to the Help pop-up menu:

☐ Double-click the blank rectangle under the Help title.

Figure 5.13.
The IDR_MENU1 menu after finishing the File pop-up menu.

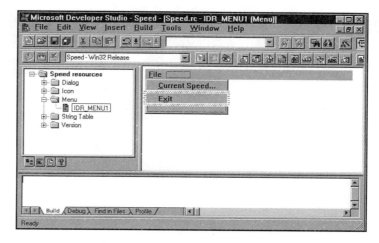

Figure 5.14.
Setting the title of the second pop-up menu to Help.

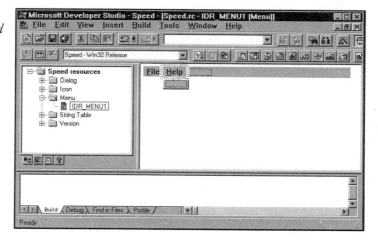

> *Visual C++ responds by again displaying the Menu Item Properties dialog box so you can set the caption of Help's first menu item.*

☐ Set the Caption field to &About....

That's it! You've finished the Help pop-up menu of the IDR_MENU1 menu. (See Figure 5.15.)

The last thing to do before you've finished the design of the IDR_MENU1 menu is to associate the IDR_MENU1 menu with a class. Here is how you do that:

☐ Select ClassWizard from the View menu.

> *Visual C++ responds by displaying the Adding a Class dialog box. (See Figure 5.16.)*

Figure 5.15.
Adding the About menu item.

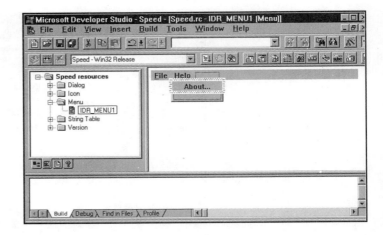

Visual C++ displays the Adding a Class dialog box because you're working on the IDR_MENU1 menu, which isn't currently associated with any class.

Figure 5.16.
The Adding a Class dialog box.

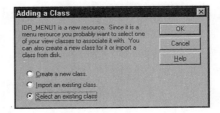

☐ Select the "Select an existing class" radio button in the Adding a Class dialog box, then click the OK button.

Visual C++ responds by displaying the Select Class dialog box. (See Figure 5.17.)

Figure 5.17.
The Select Class dialog box.

☐ Select the CSpeedDlg class in the Class List box, then click the Select button. (Note: Do not use the default setting of CAboutDlg shown in Figure 5.17. Rather, select the CSpeedDlg item, then click the Select button.)

Visual C++ responds by displaying the MFC ClassWizard dialog box. (See Figure 5.18.)

Figure 5.18.
The MFC ClassWizard dialog box.

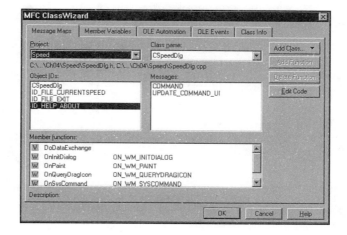

☐ Click the OK button of the MFC ClassWizard dialog box.

That's it! You've finished associating the IDR_MENU1 menu with a class.

Why did you associate the IDR_MENU1 menu with the CSpeedDlg class and not with another class? Because the CSpeedDlg class is associated with the IDD_SPEED_DIALOG dialog box that serves as the program's main window. Therefore, the code you attach later to the menu items of the IDR_MENU1 menu can access member functions and data members associated with the IDD_SPEED_DIALOG dialog box.

The Visual Design of the IDD_SPEED_DIALOG Dialog Box

In the previous section, you designed the IDR_MENU1 menu and associated it with the CSpeedDlg class. In this section, you'll visually design the IDD_SPEED_DIALOG dialog box— the main window of the program. You'll place controls in the dialog box and attach the IDR_MENU1 menu by following these steps:

☐ Select the ResourceView tab of the Project Workspace window.

☐ Expand the Speed resources item, expand the Dialog item, and double-click the IDD_SPEED_DIALOG item.

Visual C++ responds by displaying the IDD_SPEED_DIALOG dialog box in design mode.

☐ Delete the OK button, Cancel button, and text in the IDD_SPEED_DIALOG dialog box.

☐ Place a static text control in the IDD_SPEED_DIALOG dialog box and set its Caption property to Speed:.

☐ Place an edit box control in the IDD_SPEED_DIALOG dialog box and set its ID to IDC_SPEED_EDIT.

Your IDD_SPEED_DIALOG dialog box should now look like the one in Figure 5.19.

Figure 5.19.
IDD_SPEED_DIALOG after customization.

To finish the visual design of IDD_SPEED_DIALOG, attach the IDR_MENU1 menu you designed earlier to the IDD_SPEED_DIALOG dialog box. Here is how you do that:

☐ Right-click any free area in the IDD_SPEED_DIALOG dialog box and select Properties from the pop-up menu.

Visual C++ responds by displaying the Dialog Properties dialog box. (See Figure 5.20.)

Figure 5.20.
The Dialog Properties dialog box.

Use the Menu drop-down list under the Caption field to select the menu you want to attach to the dialog box:

☐ Click the down-arrow next to the Menu drop-down list and select the IDR_MENU1 menu.

Your Dialog Properties dialog box should now look like the one in Figure 5.21.

Figure 5.21.
Setting the Menu drop-down list to IDR_MENU1.

☐ Save your work by selecting Save All from the File menu.

You've finished the visual design of the IDD_SPEED_DIALOG dialog box and attached the IDR_MENU1 menu. To see your visual design in action, follow these steps:

☐ Select Build Speed.EXE from the Build menu.

☐ Select Execute Speed.EXE from the Build menu.

> *Visual C++ responds by executing the Speed.EXE program. The main window is shown in Figure 5.22.*

Figure 5.22.
The main window of the Speed.EXE program.

As you can see, the main window of the Speed.EXE program is just as you designed it—it includes the text Speed: and an edit box control, and the menu you designed is attached.

☐ Experiment with the File menu and the About menu. (Refer back to Figures 5.2 and 5.3.)

Of course, when you select a menu item, nothing happens because you haven't attached code to the menu items yet. You'll attach code to the menu items later in this chapter.

☐ Terminate the Speed.EXE program by clicking the × icon.

Attaching a Variable to the Edit Box Control

You need to attach a variable to the IDC_SPEED_EDIT edit box control so that when you write the program's code, you can use this variable to read the contents of the edit box control. To do this, follow these steps:

☐ In the Member Variables tab of ClassWizard, make the following selections:

Class name:	CSpeedDlg
Control ID:	IDC_SPEED_EDIT

☐ Click the Add Variable button and set the variable as follows:

Variable name:	m_SpeedEdit
Category:	Value
Variable type:	int

☐ Click the OK button of the Add Member Variable dialog box.

Your MFC ClassWizard dialog box should now look like the one shown in Figure 5.23.

Figure 5.23.
Attaching the m_SpeedEdit variable to the edit box.

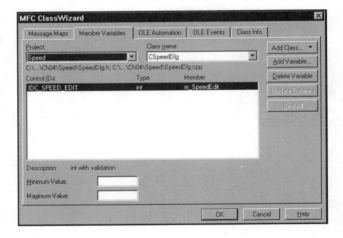

Since you specified the m_SpeedEdit variable as type int (numeric), Visual C++ lets you specify the minimum value and maximum value for the variable.

☐ Set the Minimum Value and Maximum Value fields at the bottom of the ClassWizard dialog box as follows:

Minimum Value:	0
Maximum Value:	100

These settings mean that during runtime, you can type values only in the range from 0 to 100 in the IDC_SPEED_EDIT edit box.

☐ Click ClassWizard's OK button.

Attaching Code to the *EN_CHANGE* Event of the Edit Box Control

You'll now attach code to the EN_CHANGE event of the IDC_SPEED_EDIT edit box, which occurs when you change the contents of the edit box by entering or deleting characters.

☐ Select ClassWizard from the View menu. In the Message Maps tab, select the following event:

Class name:	CSpeedDlg
Object ID:	IDC_SPEED_EDIT
Message:	EN_CHANGE

☐ Click the Add Function button, name the new function OnChangeSpeedEdit, and click the Edit Code button.

Visual C++ responds by opening the file SpeedDlg.cpp with the function OnChangeSpeedEdit() *ready for you to edit.*

☐ Write the following code in the OnChangeSpeedEdit() function:

```
void CSpeedDlg::OnChangeSpeedEdit()
{
// TODO: Add your control notification handler code here

/////////////////////////
// MY CODE STARTS HERE
/////////////////////////

// Update the variable of the IDC_SPEED_EDIT.
UpdateData(TRUE);

/////////////////////////
// MY CODE ENDS HERE
/////////////////////////

}
```

☐ Save your work by selecting Save All from the File menu.

The single statement you typed in the OnChangeSpeedEdit() function updates the variables of the controls with the controls' current contents:

```
UpdateData(TRUE);
```

Therefore, after the preceding statement is executed, the m_SpeedEdit variable will be updated with the value you enter in the IDC_SPEED_EDIT edit box.

5

Attaching Code to the Current Speed Menu Item of the File Menu

You'll now attach code to the Current Speed menu item of the File menu that will display a message box with the current value entered in the IDC_SPEED_EDIT edit box:

☐ Display the IDR_MENU1 menu in design mode by double-clicking the IDR_MENU1 item in the Project Workspace window or by selecting Speed.rc-IDR_MENU1[Menu] from the Window menu.

☐ Select ClassWizard from the View menu. In the Message Maps tab, select the following event:

Class name:	CSpeedDlg
Object ID:	ID_FILE_CURRENTSPEED
Message:	COMMAND

Your ClassWizard dialog box should now look like the one shown in Figure 5.24.

Figure 5.24.
Selecting the COMMAND *event of the Current Speed menu item.*

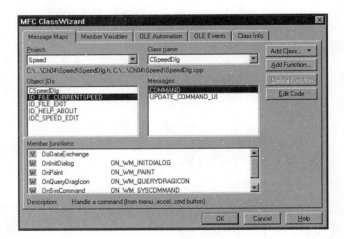

The COMMAND event of a menu item occurs whenever you select that menu item. Therefore, the code you'll attach to the COMMAND event of the Current Speed menu item will be automatically executed whenever you select the Current Speed menu item.

☐ Click ClassWizard's Add Function button, name the new function OnFileCurrentspeed, then click the Edit Code button.

Visual C++ responds by opening the file SpeedDlg.cpp with the function
OnFileCurrentspeed() ready for you to edit.

☐ Write the following code in the `OnFileCurrentspeed()` function:

```
void CSpeedDlg::OnFileCurrentspeed()
{

// TODO: Add your command handler code here

/////////////////////////
// MY CODE STARTS HERE
/////////////////////////

// Convert the numeric value of m_SpeedEdit into a string.
char strSpeed[15];
itoa(m_SpeedEdit, strSpeed, 10);

// Display the speed.
MessageBox(strSpeed);

/////////////////////////
// MY CODE ENDS HERE
/////////////////////////

}
```

☐ Save your work by selecting Save All from the File menu.

The first two statements you entered in the `OnFileCurrentspeed()` function convert the integer value stored in the `m_SpeedEdit` variable into a string:

```
char strSpeed[15];
itoa(m_SpeedEdit, strSpeed, 10);
```

The next statement uses the `MessageBox()` function to display the string value:

```
MessageBox(strSpeed);
```

To see the code you attached to the Current Speed menu item in action, follow these steps:

☐ Select Build Speed.EXE from the Build menu.

☐ Select Execute Speed.EXE from the Build menu.

Visual C++ responds by executing the Speed.EXE program.

☐ Type any integer value from 0 to 100 in the edit box.

☐ Select Current Speed from the File menu of the Speed.EXE program.

As expected, the Speed.EXE program responds by displaying a message box with the value you typed in the edit box.

☐ Close the message box by clicking its OK button.

☐ Terminate the Speed.EXE program by clicking the × icon.

Attaching Code to the Exit Menu Item of the File Menu

You'll now attach code to the Exit menu item of the File menu to terminate the program. Follow these steps:

☐ Display the IDR_MENU1 menu in design mode.

☐ Select ClassWizard from the View menu. In the Message Maps tab, select the following event:

Class name:	CSpeedDlg
Object ID:	ID_FILE_EXIT
Message:	COMMAND

☐ Click the Add Function button, name the new function OnFileExit, and click the Edit Code button.

Visual C++ responds by opening the file SpeedDlg.cpp with the function OnFileExit() *ready for you to edit.*

☐ Write the following code in the OnFileExit() function:

```
void CSpeedDlg::OnFileExit()
{
// TODO: Add your command handler code here

/////////////////////////
// MY CODE STARTS HERE
/////////////////////////

// Terminate the program.
OnOK();

/////////////////////////
// MY CODE ENDS HERE
/////////////////////////

}
```

☐ Save your work by selecting Save All from the File menu.

The single statement in the OnFileExit() function terminates the program by calling the OnOK() function. Recall from previous chapters that the OnOK() function terminates the program by closing the dialog box.

To see the code you attached to the Exit menu item in action, follow these steps:

☐ Select Build Speed.EXE from the Build menu.

☐ Select Execute Speed.EXE from the Build menu.

Visual C++ responds by executing the Speed.EXE program.

☐ Select Exit from the File menu of the Speed.EXE program.

As expected, the Speed.EXE program responds by terminating.

Attaching Code to the About Menu Item of the Help Menu

You'll now attach code to the About menu item of the Help menu that will display the About dialog box of the Speed.EXE program. Follow these steps:

☐ Display the IDR_MENU1 menu in design mode.

☐ Select ClassWizard from the View menu. In the Message Maps tab, select the following event:

> Class name: CSpeedDlg
> Object ID: ID_HELP_ABOUT
> Message: COMMAND

☐ Click the Add Function button, name the new function OnHelpAbout, and click the Edit Code button.

> *Visual C++ responds by opening the file SpeedDlg.cpp with the function OnHelpAbout() ready for you to edit.*

☐ Write the following code in the OnHelpAbout() function:

```
void CSpeedDlg::OnHelpAbout()
{

// TODO: Add your command handler code here

/////////////////////////
// MY CODE STARTS HERE
/////////////////////////

// Create an object of class CAboutDlg
CAboutDlg dlg;

// Display the About dialog box.
dlg.DoModal();

/////////////////////////
// MY CODE ENDS HERE
/////////////////////////

}
```

☐ Save your work by selecting Save All from the File menu.

The first statement you entered in the `OnFileExit()` function creates an object called `dlg` of class `CAboutDlg`:

```
CAboutDlg dlg;
```

The `CAboutDlg` class was created by Visual C++ when you created the project and skeleton files of the program. This class is associated with the About dialog box that Visual C++ created for you.

The second statement displays the About dialog box by executing the `DoModal()` member function on the `dlg` object:

```
dlg.DoModal();
```

As its name implies, the `DoModal()` function displays the dialog box as a modal dialog box. This means that while the dialog box is displayed, you cannot make other windows of the program active.

The Speed.EXE program is finished! To see the code you attached to the About menu item in action, follow these steps:

☐ Select Build Speed.EXE from the Build menu.

☐ Select Execute Speed.EXE from the Build menu.

> *Visual C++ responds by executing the Speed.EXE program.*

☐ Select About from the Help menu of the Speed.EXE program.

> *As expected, the Speed.EXE program responds by displaying the About dialog box.*

☐ Close the About dialog box by clicking its OK button.

☐ Terminate the Speed.EXE program by selecting Exit from its File menu.

Summary

In this chapter, you have learned how to incorporate a menu into a dialog-based program. You have learned how to design a menu, how to associate the menu with the class of the dialog box serving as the program's main window, how to attach the menu to the dialog box, and how to attach code to the menu items.

Q&A

Q In the Speed.EXE program, I associated the IDR_MENU1 menu with the CSpeedDlg class. Why the CSpeedDlg class and not another class?

A The `CSpeedDlg` class is the class associated with the IDD_SPEED_DIALOG dialog box, the main window of the Speed.EXE program. Because you associate the IDR_MENU1 with the `CSpeedDlg` class, when you attach code to the menu items, the code can access data members and member functions of the `CSpeedDlg` class. This means that the code you attach to the menu items can access the data members attached to the controls of the IDD_SPEED_DIALOG dialog box.

Quiz

1. A separator bar is a horizontal line that separates menu items.

    a. True

    b. False

2. When does the COMMAND event of a menu item occur?

3. Suppose you add a new menu item to the IDR_MENU1 menu of the Speed.EXE program, and its ID is ID_MY_MENUITEM. Describe the steps needed to attach code to the ID_MY_MENUITEM menu item.

Exercise

Enhance the Speed.EXE program by adding a new menu item to the Help menu of the Speed program and setting its caption to Say Hello. Attach code to the Say Hello menu item so that the program will display a Hello message box when you select this menu item.

Quiz Answers

1. True.

2. The COMMAND event of a menu item occurs when you select it.

3. To attach code to the ID_MY_MENUITEM menu item of the Speed.EXE program, do the following:

☐ Display the IDR_MENU1 menu in design mode.

☐ Select ClassWizard from the View menu. In the Message Maps tab, select the following event:

Class name:	CSpeedDlg
Object ID:	ID_MY_MENUITEM
Message:	COMMAND

☐ Click the Add Function button, name the new function `OnMyMenuitem`, and click the Edit Code button.

☐ Write code in the OnMyMenuitem() function. This code will be automatically executed whenever you select the ID_MY_MENUITEM menu item.

Exercise Answer

To add the Say Hello menu item to the Help menu of the Speed.EXE program, do the following:

☐ Display the IDR_MENU1 menu in design mode.

☐ Click the Help menu title in the IDR_MENU1 menu bar.

☐ Click the small blank rectangle under the About menu item of the Help pop-up menu.

Visual C++ responds by displaying the Menu Item Properties dialog box, so you can set the caption of the new menu item.

☐ Set the Caption field to &Say Hello.

Next, attach code to the Say Hello menu item:

☐ Make sure the IDR_MENU1 menu is currently displayed by double-clicking the IDR_MENU1 item in the Project Workspace window.

☐ Select ClassWizard from the View menu. In the Message Maps tab, select the following event:

Class name:	CSpeedDlg
Object ID:	ID_HELP_SAYHELLO
Message:	COMMAND

☐ Click the Add Function button, name the new function OnHelpSayhello, and click the Edit Code button.

☐ Write the following code in the OnHelpSayhello() function:

```
void CSpeedDlg::OnHelpSayhello()
{
// TODO: Add your control notification handler code here

/////////////////////////
// MY CODE STARTS HERE
/////////////////////////

// Display a Hello message box.
MessageBox("Hello");

/////////////////////////
// MY CODE ENDS HERE
/////////////////////////

}
```

Dialog Boxes

In this chapter, you'll learn how to create and display dialog boxes from within your Visual C++ programs and how to use predefined and custom-made dialog boxes.

Types of Dialog Boxes

You can display two types of dialog boxes:

- Predefined dialog boxes
- Custom-made dialog boxes

Predefined dialog boxes are also called *message boxes*. Their appearance has already been defined, so you can make only minor changes to them. Custom-made dialog boxes, on the other hand, are dialog boxes you define and design, so you have full control over their appearance and behavior.

The MyMsg Program

You'll now design and create the MyMsg program, a program that uses predefined dialog boxes. Before creating the MyMsg program, review its specifications:

- When you execute the program, the window shown in Figure 6.1 appears.

Figure 6.1.
The window of the MyMsg program.

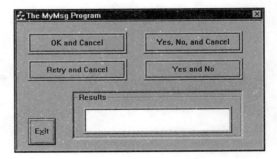

- You can click any of the four buttons in the upper portion of the window to display various message boxes. For example, after clicking the Yes and No button, the message box shown in Figure 6.2 appears. The edit box shown in Figure 6.1 will display the name of the button you clicked. You can click the other buttons to experiment with other message boxes that have different icons and buttons.

Figure 6.2.
*The message box displayed
after clicking the Yes and No
button.*

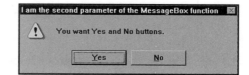

Creating the Project of the MyMsg Program

You'll now create the project of the MyMsg program:

☐ Create the C:\TYVCProg\Programs\CH06 directory.

☐ Start Visual C++ and select New from the File menu.

    Visual C++ responds by displaying the New dialog box.

☐ Select the Project Workspace item, then click the OK button.

    Visual C++ responds by displaying the New Project Workspace dialog box.

☐ Select the MFC AppWizard (exe) item and type MyMsg in the Name box.

☐ Click the Browse button, select the C:\TYVCProg\Programs\CH06 directory, and click the Create button.

    Visual C++ responds by displaying the MFC AppWizard - Step 1 window.

☐ In Step 1, use the default setting to create a dialog-based application, then click the Next button.

☐ In Step 2, use the default settings and enter MyMsg as the title for the dialog box. When you're done, click the Next button.

☐ In Step 3, use the default settings and click the Next button.

☐ In Step 4, notice that AppWizard has created the CMyMsgApp and CMyMsgDlg classes for you. When you're done, click the Finish button, then click the OK button of the Project Information window.

☐ Select Set Default Configuration from the Build menu, then select the MyMsg - Win32 Release item.

That's it! Visual C++ has created the MyMsg project and all its associated files.

6

The Visual Design of the MyMsg Program

You'll now visually design the main window of the MyMsg program by following these steps:

☐ In the Project Workspace, click the ResourceView tab and expand the MyMsg resources item, then the Dialog item. Finally, double-click the IDD_MYMSG_DIALOG dialog box.

Visual C++ responds by displaying the IDD_MYMSG_DIALOG dialog box in design mode.

☐ Delete the OK button, Cancel button, and TODO text from the IDD_MYMSG_DIALOG dialog box.

☐ Design the IDD_MYMSG_DIALOG dialog box according to Table 6.1. When you finish, it should look like Figure 6.1 in design mode.

Table 6.1. The properties table of the IDD_MYMSG_DIALOG dialog box.

Object	Property	Setting
Dialog Box	**ID**	**ID_MYMSG_DIALOG**
	Caption	The MyMsg Program
	Font	System, Size 10 (General tab)
	Client edge	Checked (Extended Styles tab)
	Static edge	Checked (Extended Styles tab)
Push Button	**ID**	**IDC_EXIT_BUTTON**
	Caption	E&xit
Push Button	**ID**	**IDC_OKCANCEL_BUTTON**
	Caption	OK and Cancel
	Client edge	Checked (Extended Styles tab)
	Static edge	Checked (Extended Styles tab)
	Modal frame	Checked (Extended Styles tab)
Push Button	**ID**	**IDC_YESNO_BUTTON**
	Caption	Yes and No
	Client edge	Checked (Extended Styles tab)
	Static edge	Checked (Extended Styles tab)
	Modal frame	Checked (Extended Styles tab)

Object	Property	Setting
Push Button	**ID**	**IDC_YESNOCANCEL_BUTTON**
	Caption	Yes, No, and Cancel
	Client edge	Checked (Extended Styles tab)
	Static edge	Checked (Extended Styles tab)
	Modal frame	Checked (Extended Styles tab)
Push Button	**ID**	**IDC_RETRYCANCEL_BUTTON**
	Caption	Retry and Cancel
	Client edge	Checked (Extended Styles tab)
	Static edge	Checked (Extended Styles tab)
	Modal frame	Checked (Extended Styles tab)
Group Box	**ID**	**IDC_RESULTS_STATIC**
	Caption	Results
	Client edge	Checked (Extended Styles tab)
	Static edge	Checked (Extended Styles tab)
Edit Box	**ID**	**IDC_RESULTS_EDIT**
	Multiline	Checked (Styles tab)
	Client edge	Checked (Extended Styles tab)
	Static edge	Checked (Extended Styles tab)
	Modal frame	Checked (Extended Styles tab)
	Align text	Center (Styles tab

Attaching a Variable to the Edit Box

You'll now attach a variable to the IDC_RESULTS_EDIT edit box.

☐ In the Member Variables tab of ClassWizard, make the following selection:

Class name:	CMyMsgDlg
Control ID:	IDC_RESULTS_EDIT

☐ Click the Add Variable button and set the variable as follows:

Variable name:	m_ResultsEdit
Category:	Value
Variable type:	string

☐ Click the OK button of the Add Member Variable dialog box, then click the OK button of ClassWizard.

Attaching Code to the Exit Button

You'll now attach code to the BN_CLICKED event of the Exit button:

☐ In the Message Maps tab of ClassWizard, select the following event:

Class name:	CMyMsgDlg
Object ID:	IDC_EXIT_BUTTON
Message:	BN_CLICKED

☐ Click the Add Function button, name the new function OnExitButton, and click the Edit Code button.

Visual C++ responds by opening the file MyMsgDlg.cpp with the function OnExitButton() *ready for you to edit.*

☐ Write the following code in the OnExitButton() function:

```
void CMyMsgDlg::OnExitButton()
{
// TODO: Add your control notification handler code here


/////////////////////////
// MY CODE STARTS HERE
/////////////////////////

// Terminate the program
OnOK();

/////////////////////////
// MY CODE ENDS HERE
/////////////////////////

}
```

Attaching Code to the *BN_CLICKED* Event of the OK and Cancel Button

You'll now attach code to the BN_CLICKED event of the IDC_OKCANCEL_BUTTON button:

☐ In the Message Maps tab of ClassWizard, select the following event:

Class name:	CMyMsgDlg
Object ID:	IDC_OKCANCEL_BUTTON
Message:	BN_CLICKED

☐ Click the Add Function button, name the new function OnOkcancelButton, and click the Edit Code button.

> *Visual C++ responds by opening the file MyMsgDlg.cpp with the function* OnOkcancelButton() *ready for you to edit.*

☐ Write the following code in the OnOkcancelButton() function:

```
void CMyMsgDlg::OnOkcancelButton()
{
// TODO: Add your control notification handler code here

/////////////////////////
// MY CODE STARTS HERE
/////////////////////////

int iResults;

iResults =
MessageBox
    (
    "You want Ok and Cancel buttons.",
    "I am the second parameter of the MessageBox function",
     MB_OKCANCEL + MB_ICONSTOP
     );

if (iResults==IDOK)
{
m_ResultsEdit = "You clicked the OK button!";
UpdateData(FALSE);
}


if (iResults==IDCANCEL)
{
m_ResultsEdit = "You clicked the Cancel button!";
UpdateData(FALSE);
}

/////////////////////////
// MY CODE ENDS HERE
/////////////////////////

}
```

The code you typed declares an integer variable:

```
int iResults;
```

The iResults variable will hold an integer corresponding to the button you clicked in the message box displayed by the MyMsg program.

6

The MessageBox() function is then executed as follows:

```
iResults =
  MessageBox
    (
    "You want Ok and Cancel buttons.",
    "I am the second parameter of the MessageBox function",
     MB_OKCANCEL + MB_ICONSTOP
     );
```

The returned value from MessageBox() is assigned to the iResults variable. Later in this function, you'll use if statements to examine the value of iResults.

The MessageBox() function has three parameters. The first is a string that appears in the message box, the second is a string that appears as the caption of the message box, and the third parameter of MessageBox() is the following:

```
MB_OKCANCEL + MB_ICONSTOP
```

MB_OKCANCEL is a constant that tells the MessageBox() function to display two buttons in the message box: the OK button and the Cancel button. MB_ICONSTOP is a constant that tells the MessageBox() function to display the Stop icon in the message box.

The MessageBox() function returns an integer, which is assigned to the iResults variable. A series of two if statements are then executed to examine the value of iResults. The code under the first if statement is executed if you click the OK button of the message box:

```
if (iResults==IDOK)
{
m_ResultsEdit = "You clicked the OK button!";
UpdateData(FALSE);
}
```

The code under the preceding if statement updates the m_ResultsEdit variable (the variable of the edit text box); then the edit box is updated with the UpdateData() function.

Therefore, the edit box displays text telling you that you clicked the OK button. The code under the second if statement is executed if you click the Cancel button of the message box:

```
if (iResults==IDCANCEL)
{
m_ResultsEdit = "You clicked the Cancel button!";
UpdateData(FALSE);
}
```

The code under the second if statement is similar to the code under the first if statement, except that it displays this text:

```
"You clicked the Cancel button!";
```

☐ Select Save All from the File menu to save your work.

☐ Compile, link, and execute the MyMsg program.

☐ Click the OK and Cancel button.

MyMsg responds by displaying the message box shown in Figure 6.3.

Note that the × icon is displayed in the message box because the third parameter of the MessageBox() function contains the MB_ICONSTOP constant. Also, the message box contains the OK and Cancel buttons because the third parameter of the MessageBox() function indicates OK and Cancel buttons.

Figure 6.3.
The message box displayed after you click the OK and Cancel button.

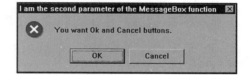

☐ Click the OK button of the message box.

MyMsg responds by updating the edit box, as shown in Figure 6.4.

Figure 6.4.
The text displayed after you click the OK button of the message box.

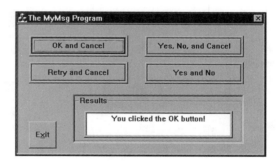

☐ Click the OK and Cancel button.

MyMsg responds by displaying the message box shown in Figure 6.3.

☐ Click the Cancel button of the message box.

MyMsg responds by updating the edit box with a string telling you that you clicked the Cancel button of the message box. (See Figure 6.5.)

☐ Experiment with the MyMsg program, then click the Exit button to terminate the program.

Figure 6.5.

The text displayed after you click the Cancel button of the message box.

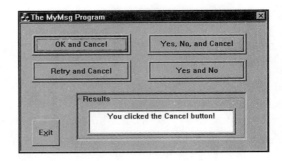

Attaching Code to the *BN_CLICKED* Event of the Yes, No, and Cancel Button

You'll now attach code to the BN_CLICKED event of the IDC_YESNOCANCEL_BUTTON button:

☐ In the Message Maps tab of ClassWizard, select the following event:

Class name:	CMyMsgDlg
Object ID:	IDC_YESNOCANCEL_BUTTON
Message:	BN_CLICKED

☐ Click the Add Function button, name the new function OnYesnocancelButton, and click the Edit Code button.

Visual C++ responds by opening the file MyMsgDlg.cpp with the function OnYesnocancelButton() ready for you to edit.

☐ Write the following code in the OnYesnocancelButton() function:

```
void CMyMsgDlg::OnYesnocancelButton()
{
// TODO: Add your control notification handler code here

/////////////////////////
// MY CODE STARTS HERE
/////////////////////////

int iResults;

iResults =
    MessageBox (

  "You want Yes, No, and Cancel buttons.",
  "I am the second parameter of the MessageBox function",
   MB_YESNOCANCEL + MB_ICONINFORMATION

            );
```

```
if (iResults==IDYES)
{
m_ResultsEdit = "You clicked the Yes button!";
UpdateData(FALSE);
}


if (iResults==IDNO)
{
m_ResultsEdit = "You clicked the No button!";
UpdateData(FALSE);
}


if (iResults==IDCANCEL)
{
m_ResultsEdit = "You clicked the Cancel button!";
UpdateData(FALSE);
}


/////////////////////////
// MY CODE ENDS HERE
/////////////////////////

}
```

The code you typed is similar to the code in the OnOkcancelButton() function, except that this is the third parameter of the MessageBox() function:

```
MB_YESNOCANCEL + MB_ICONINFORMATION
```

The preceding constants mean that the message box includes the Yes, No, and Cancel buttons (MB_YESNOCANCEL) and that the icon displayed in the message box is the Information icon (MB_ICONINFORMATION). Also, the first parameter of the MessageBox() function displays text indicating that you clicked the IDC_YESNOCANCEL_BUTTON button:

```
iResults =
    MessageBox (

    "You want Yes, No, and Cancel buttons.",
    "I am the second parameter of the MessageBox function",
    MB_YESNOCANCEL + MB_ICONINFORMATION

                );
```

A series of three if statements are executed. The code under the first if statement is executed if you clicked the Yes button:

```
if (iResults==IDYES)
{
m_ResultsEdit = "You clicked the Yes button!";
UpdateData(FALSE);
}
```

The code under the second `if` statement is executed if you clicked the No button:

```
if (iResults==IDNO)
{
m_ResultsEdit = "You clicked the No button!";
UpdateData(FALSE);
}
```

The code under the third `if` statement is executed if you clicked the Cancel button:

```
if (iResults==IDCANCEL)
{
m_ResultsEdit = "You clicked the Cancel button!";
UpdateData(FALSE);
}
```

☐ Select Save All from the File menu to save your work.

☐ Compile, link, and execute the MyMsg program.

☐ Click the Yes, No, and Cancel button and make sure the MyMsg program is working properly. For example, when the message box is displayed, click the Yes button of the message box. The edit box of the MyMsg main window should contain text confirming that you clicked the Yes button.

☐ Experiment with the MyMsg program, then click its Exit button to terminate the program.

Attaching Code to the *BN_CLICKED* Event of the Retry and Cancel Button

You'll now attach code to the `BN_CLICKED` event of the IDC_RETRYCANCEL_BUTTON button:

☐ In the Message Maps tab of ClassWizard, select the following event:

Class name:	CMyMsgDlg
Object ID:	IDC_RETRYCANCEL_BUTTON
Message:	BN_CLICKED

☐ Click the Add Function button, name the new function `OnRetrycancelButton`, and click the Edit Code button.

Visual C++ responds by opening the file MyMsgDlg.cpp with the function `OnRetrycancelButton()` *ready for you to edit.*

☐ Write the following code in the `OnRetrycancelButton()` function:

```
void CMyMsgDlg::OnRetrycancelButton()
{
// TODO: Add your control notification handler code here

//////////////////////
// MY CODE STARTS HERE
//////////////////////

int iResults;

iResults =
     MessageBox (

     "You want Retry and Cancel buttons.",
     "I am the second parameter of the MessageBox function",
      MB_RETRYCANCEL + MB_ICONQUESTION

                    );

if (iResults==IDRETRY)
{
m_ResultsEdit = "You clicked the Retry button!";
UpdateData(FALSE);
}


if (iResults==IDCANCEL)
{
m_ResultsEdit = "You clicked the Cancel button!";
UpdateData(FALSE);
}

//////////////////////
// MY CODE ENDS HERE
//////////////////////

}
```

The code you typed is similar to the code in the previous section. Note that now the parameters of the `MessageBox()` function are as follows:

```
iResults =
     MessageBox (

     "You want Retry and Cancel buttons.",
     "I am the second parameter of the MessageBox function",
      MB_RETRYCANCEL + MB_ICONQUESTION

                    );
```

6

The constant MB_ICONQUESTION, part of the third parameter of MessageBox(), causes the Question icon to appear in the message box. The MB_RETRYCANCEL constant, also part of the third parameter of MessageBox(), causes the MessageBox() function to display the Retry and Cancel buttons.

A series of two if statements are then executed. The code under the first if statement is executed if you clicked the Retry button:

```
if (iResults==IDRETRY)
{
m_ResultsEdit = "You clicked the Retry button!";
UpdateData(FALSE);
}
```

The code under the second if statement is executed if you clicked the Cancel button:

```
if (iResults==IDCANCEL)
{
m_ResultsEdit = "You clicked the Cancel button!";
UpdateData(FALSE);
}
```

☐ Select Save All from the File menu to save your work.

☐ Compile, link, and execute the MyMsg program.

☐ Click the Retry and Cancel button and make sure the MyMsg program works properly. For example, when the message box is displayed, click its Retry button. The edit box of the MyMsg main window should contain text confirming you clicked the Retry button.

☐ Experiment with the MyMsg program, then click its Exit button to terminate the program.

Attaching Code to the *BN_CLICKED* Event of the Yes and No Button

You'll now attach code to the BN_CLICKED event of the IDC_YESNO_BUTTON button:

☐ In the Message Maps tab of ClassWizard, select the following event:

Class name:	CMyMsgDlg
Object ID:	IDC_YESNO_BUTTON
Message:	BN_CLICKED

☐ Click the Add Function button, name the new function OnYesnoButton, and click the Edit Code button.

Visual C++ responds by opening the file MyMsgDlg.cpp with the function OnYesnoButton() *ready for you to edit.*

☐ Write the following code in the `OnYesnoButton()` function:

```
void CMyMsgDlg::OnYesnoButton()
{
// TODO: Add your control notification handler code here

/////////////////////////
// MY CODE STARTS HERE
/////////////////////////

int iResults;

iResults =
    MessageBox (

  "You want Yes and No buttons.",
  "I am the second parameter of the MessageBox function",
  MB_YESNO + MB_ICONEXCLAMATION

              );

if (iResults==IDYES)
{
m_ResultsEdit = "You clicked the Yes button!";
UpdateData(FALSE);
}


if (iResults==IDNO)
{
m_ResultsEdit = "You clicked the No button!";
UpdateData(FALSE);
}


/////////////////////////
// MY CODE ENDS HERE
/////////////////////////

}
```

The code you typed is similar to the code in previous sections. The message box is displayed as follows:

```
iResults =
    MessageBox (

  "You want Yes and No buttons.",
  "I am the second parameter of the MessageBox function",
  MB_YESNO + MB_ICONEXCLAMATION

              );
```

The third parameter of `MessageBox()` indicates that the Exclamation icon (`MB_ICONEXCLAMATION`) will be displayed and the Yes and No button will be included in the message box (`MB_YESNO`).

6

A series of two `if` statements is executed. The code under the first `if` statement is executed if you clicked the Yes button of the message box:

```
if (iResults==IDYES)
{
m_ResultsEdit = "You clicked the Yes button!";
UpdateData(FALSE);
}
```

The code under the second `if` statement is executed if you clicked the No button of the message box:

```
if (iResults==IDNO)
{
m_ResultsEdit = "You clicked the No button!";
UpdateData(FALSE);
}
```

☐ Select Save All from the File menu to save your work.

☐ Compile, link, and execute the MyMsg program.

☐ Click the Yes and No button and check that the MyMsg program works properly. For example, when the message box is displayed, click its Yes button. The edit box of the MyMsg main window should display text confirming you clicked the Yes button.

☐ Experiment with the MyMsg program, then click its Exit button to terminate the program.

> **Note:** You can also add *modality constants* to the third parameter of the `MessageBox()`. If you do not specify a modality constant, then the default is used, which is `MB_APPLMODAL`. This makes the message box a modal dialog box, meaning you can't switch to other windows in the same application unless you first close the message box.
>
> Another option is `MB_SYSTEMMODAL`, a constant that makes the message box a system modal, which means you can't switch to another window of any application unless the message box is closed.

The MyCus Program

The MyMsg program illustrated how to display predefined message boxes. An alternative method for displaying dialog boxes is to use custom-made dialog boxes, illustrated in the MyCus program. Before starting to design the MyCus program, review its specifications:

• When you start the MyCus program, the window shown in Figure 6.6 appears.

Figure 6.6.
The main window of the MyCus program.

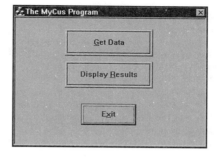

- When you click the Get Data button, the MyCus program displays the custom-made dialog box shown in Figure 6.7. You can then enter data into the edit box.

Figure 6.7.
The custom-made dialog box.

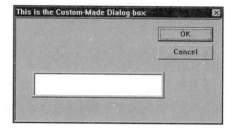

- When you close the custom-made dialog box, the main window of the MyCus program appears again. You can then click the Display Results button to display the text entered in the edit box. For example, if you typed the text This is a test in the edit box, the message box displayed after clicking the Display Results button is shown in Figure 6.8.

Figure 6.8.
The message box displayed after clicking the Display Results button.

Creating the Project of the MyCus Program

Open a new project workspace to create the project of the MyCus program:

☐ Select the MFC AppWizard (exe) item and type MyCus in the Name box.

☐ Click the Browse button, select the C:\TYVCProg\Programs\CH06 directory, and click the Create button.

> *Visual C++ responds by displaying the MFC AppWizard - Step 1 window.*

☐ In Step 1, use the default setting to create a dialog-based application, then click the Next button.

☐ In Step 2, use the default settings and enter MyCus as the dialog box title. When you're done, click Next.

☐ In Step 3, use the default settings, then click Next.

☐ In the Step 4 window, notice that AppWizard created the CMyCusApp and CMyCusDlg classes for you. When you're done, click the Finish button.

☐ Select Set Default Configuration from the Build menu and select the MyCus - Win32 Release item.

That's it! Visual C++ has created the MyCus project and all its associated files.

The Visual Design of the MyCus Program

You'll now visually design the main window of the MyCus program:

☐ In the Project Workspace, click the ResourceView tab and expand the MyCus resources item, then the Dialog item. Finally, double-click the IDD_MYCUS_DIALOG dialog box.

> *Visual C++ responds by displaying the IDD_MYCUS_DIALOG dialog box in design mode.*

☐ Delete the OK button, Cancel button, and TODO text.

☐ Design the IDD_MYCUS_DIALOG dialog box according to Table 6.2. When you finish designing the dialog box, it should look like Figure 6.6.

Table 6.2. The properties table of the IDD_MYCUS_DIALOG dialog box.

Object	Property	Setting
Dialog Box	**ID**	**IDD_MYCUS_DIALOG**
	Caption	The MyCus Program
	Font	System, Size 10
	Client edge	Checked (Extended Styles tab)
	Static edge	Checked (Extended Styles tab)

SAMS
Sams
Learning
Center
SAMS
PUBLISHING

Object	Property	Setting
Push Button	**ID**	**IDC_EXIT_BUTTON**
	Caption	E&xit
Push Button	**ID**	**IDC_GETDATA_BUTTON**
	Caption	&Get Data
	Client edge	Checked (Extended Styles tab)
	Static edge	Checked (Extended Styles tab)
	Modal frame	Checked (Extended Styles tab)
Push Button	**ID**	**IDC_DISPLAYRESULTS_BUTTON**
	Caption	Display &Results
	Client edge	Checked (Extended Styles tab)
	Static edge	Checked (Extended Styles tab)
	Modal frame	Checked (Extended Styles tab)

Attaching Code to the *BN_CLICKED* Event of the Exit Button

You'll now attach code to the BN_CLICKED event of the Exit button:

☐ In the Message Maps tab of ClassWizard, select the following event:

Class name:	CMyCusDlg
Object ID:	IDC_EXIT_BUTTON
Message:	BN_CLICKED

☐ Click the Add Function button, name the new function OnExitButton, then click the Edit Code button.

Visual C++ responds by opening the file MyCusDlg.cpp with the function OnExitButton() ready for you to edit.

☐ Write the following code in the OnExitButton() function:

```
void CMyCusDlg::OnExitButton()
{
// TODO: Add your control notification handler code here

////////////////////////
// MY CODE STARTS HERE
////////////////////////

OnOK();
```

6

```
///////////////////////
// MY CODE ENDS HERE
///////////////////////

}
```

The code you typed terminates the program.

The Visual Design of the Custom-Made Dialog Box

Currently, the MyCus program has two dialog boxes: the IDD_MYCUS_DIALOG dialog box, the main window of the MyCus program, and the IDD_ABOUTBOX dialog box, the About box of the MyCus program. To display the About box, click the small icon at the upper-left corner of the window, then select About from the system menu that pops up.

You'll now add a third dialog box to the MyCus program that will be displayed when you click the Get Data button:

☐ In the Project Workspace, click the ResourceView tab and expand the MyCus resources item, then the Dialog item. Make sure there are two dialog boxes items under the Dialog item.

☐ Right-click the Dialog item.

   Visual C++ responds by displaying a menu.

☐ Select Insert Dialog from the menu.

   Visual C++ responds by inserting another dialog box to the MyCus project. The ID of the new dialog box is IDD_DIALOG1.

Follow these steps to customize the IDD_DIALOG1 dialog box:

☐ Right-click the IDD_DIALOG1 dialog box, select Properties from the menu that pops up, and change the ID property from IDD_DIALOG1 to IDD_CUSTOM_DIALOG.

☐ Set the Caption property of the IDD_CUSTOM_DIALOG to This is the Custom-Made Dialog box.

> **Note:** When you create programs in this book, you are typically instructed to create dialog-based programs, in which a dialog box serves as the main window of the program. For example, IDD_MYCUS_DIALOG is a dialog box that serves as the main window of the MyCus program. Furthermore, you're instructed to delete the TODO text, OK button, and Cancel button of the dialog box.

However, the IDD_CUSTOM_DIALOG dialog box is displayed after clicking a button in the IDD_MYCUS_DIALOG dialog box. The IDD_CUSTOM_DIALOG dialog box serves as a dialog box for getting users' input. Typically, such a dialog box needs the OK button and the Cancel button, so don't delete its OK and Cancel buttons.

Placing an Edit Box in the Custom-Made Dialog Box

You'll now place an edit box in the IDD_CUSTOM_DIALOG dialog box:

☐ Place an edit box control in the IDD_CUSTOM_DIALOG dialog box.

☐ Set the ID property of the edit box to IDC_MYDATA_EDIT.

☐ Set the following properties of the edit box (for cosmetic reasons):

Property	Setting
Client edge	Checked (Extended Styles tab)
Static edge	Checked (Extended Styles tab)
Modal frame	Checked (Extended Styles tab)

Associating the Custom-Made Dialog Box with a Class

Dialog boxes have to be associated with classes. For example, the IDD_MYCUS_DIALOG is associated with the CMyCusDlg class, which Visual C++ added when the program and skeleton files of the project were created. CMyCusDlg was created as a derived class from the CDialog class, which has many useful member functions. Therefore, CMyCusDlg will inherit these member functions.

Follow these steps to verify that CMyCusDlg is indeed a derived class of CDialog:

☐ Make sure the IDD_MYCUS_DIALOG item is highlighted in the Project Workspace window.

☐ Double-click the IDD_MYCUS_DIALOG item to display the dialog box in design mode.

☐ Right-click in a free area in the dialog box and select ClassWizard from the menu that pops up.

6

Visual C++ responds by displaying the MFC ClassWizard window.

☐ Click the Class Info tab.

Visual C++ responds by displaying the Class Info tab shown in Figure 6.9.

Figure 6.9.
The Class Info tab.

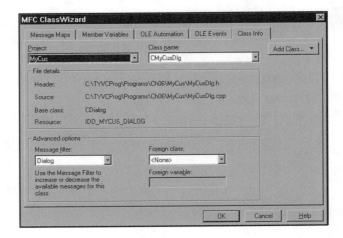

As you can see from Figure 6.9, the base class of `CMyCusDlg` is indeed `CDialog`.

You'll now create a class for the IDD_CUSTOM_DIALOG dialog box using `CDialog` as the base class:

☐ Close the MFC ClassWizard window.

☐ Double-click the IDD_CUSTOM_DIALOG item under the Dialog item in the Project Workspace window.

Visual C++ responds by displaying the IDD_CUSTOM_DIALOG dialog box in design mode.

☐ Select ClassWizard from the View menu.

Instead of displaying the MFC ClassWizard window, Visual C++ responds by displaying the Adding a Class window shown in Figure 6.10 because the IDD_CUSTOM_DIALOG dialog box doesn't have a class associated with it yet.

Figure 6.10.
The Adding a Class window.

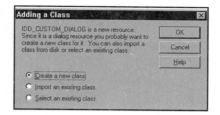

☐ Make sure the "Create a new class" button is selected, then click the OK button.

Visual C++ responds by displaying the Create New Class window shown in Figure 6.11.

Figure 6.11.
The Create New Class window.

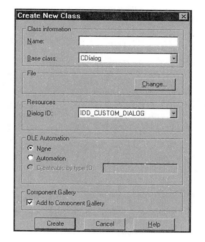

☐ Set the Name box under "Class information" to CCustDlg and make sure the Base class list box is set to CDialog. (See Figure 6.12.)

Whenever Visual C++ creates a class, it also creates two files associated with the class. For example, when Visual C++ created the CMyCusDlg class for the IDD_MYCUS_DIALOG dialog box, it created the MyCusDlg.cpp and MyCusDlg.h files. So if you named the class of IDD_CUSTOM_DIALOG CCustDlg, what are the names of the .cpp and .h files that Visual C++ will create? This is how you find out:

☐ Click the Change button of the Create New Class window.

Visual C++ responds by displaying the Change Files dialog box shown in Figure 6.13.

Figure 6.12.
Setting the class name of
IDD_CUSTOM_DIALOG
to CCustDlg.

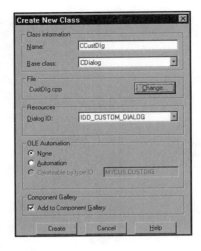

Figure 6.13.
The Change Files
dialog box.

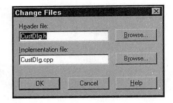

As shown in Figure 6.13, the two files associated with the CCustDlg class are CustDlg.h and CustDlg.cpp.

☐ Click the OK button of the Change Files dialog box.

☐ Click the Create button of the Create New Class window.

   Visual C++ responds by opening the MFC ClassWizard window.

☐ Click the OK button to close the MFC ClassWizard window.

Attaching a Variable to the Edit Box of IDD_CUSTOM_DIALOG

During the visual design of the IDD_CUSTOM_DIALOG dialog box, you added the IDC_MYDATA_EDIT edit box. You'll now attach a member variable to this edit box:

☐ In the Member Variables tab of ClassWizard, set the Class name to CCustDlg and select the IDC_MYDATA_EDIT item.

   The MFC ClassWizard window should now look like the one shown in Figure 6.14.

Figure 6.14.

Attaching a member variable to the IDC_MYDATA_EDIT edit box.

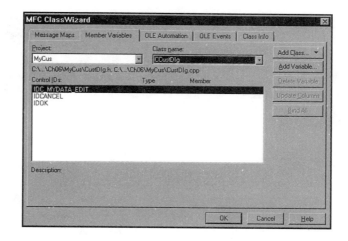

☐ Click the Add Variable button and select the following options in the Add Member Variable dialog box:

Variable name:	`m_MyDataEdit`
Category:	`Value`
Variable type:	`CString`

Your Add Member Variable dialog box should now look like Figure 6.15.

Figure 6.15.

Adding the `m_MyDataEdit` *member variable.*

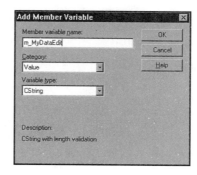

☐ Click the OK button of the Add Member Variable dialog box.

☐ Click the OK button of the MFC ClassWizard window.

Creating an Object of Class *CCustDlg*

You have visually designed the IDD_CUSTOM_DIALOG dialog box and associated it with the CCustDlg class. In this section and the next, you'll write code in the CMyCusDlg class (the MyCusDlg.cpp and MyCusDlg.h files)—the class associated with the main window of the program, the IDD_MYCUS_DIALOG dialog box. This code will be responsible for displaying the IDD_CUSTOM_DIALOG dialog box.

First create the m_dlg object, an object of class CCustDlg:

```
CCustDlg m_dlg;
```

What does it mean to create an object m_dlg of class CCustDlg? It means you'll create a dialog box whose visual appearance is the same as the IDD_CUSTOM_DIALOG dialog box. Follow these steps to create the m_dlg object:

☐ In the Project Workspace, click the FileView tab, expand the Dependencies item, and double-click the MyCusDlg.h item.

Visual C++ responds by opening the MyCusDlg.h file.

☐ Insert the following code in the CMyCusDlg class declaration (in the MyCusDlg.h file):

```
class CMyCusDlg : public CDialog
{
// Construction
public:
// standard constructor
CMyCusDlg(CWnd* pParent = NULL);

/////////////////////////////
// MY CODE STARTS HERE
/////////////////////////////

CCustDlg m_dlg;

/////////////////////////////
// MY CODE ENDS HERE
/////////////////////////////

...
...
...


};
```

The preceding code declares m_dlg as a data member of the CMyCusDlg class because you want m_dlg to be visible from any member function of the CMyCusDlg class. For example, when you attach code to the BN_CLICKED event of the buttons in IDD_MYCUS_DIALOG, you'll be able to use m_dlg from within your code.

You declared m_dlg as an object of class CCustDlg. Although you know that CCustDlg is the class associated with the IDD_CUSTOM_DIALOG dialog box, the compiler doesn't. Therefore, when the compiler compiles the MyCusDlg.cpp file and encounters CCustDlg, you'll get a compiling error!

Remember that when you created the CCustDlg class, the CustDlg.h file was created. (Refer back to Figure 6.13.) In fact, Visual C++ declared the CCustDlg class in the CustDlg.h file. To avoid compiling errors, all you have to do is use the #include statement as follows:

☐ Add the #include statement at the beginning of the MyCusDlg.h file:

```
// MyCusDlg.h : header file
//

/////////////////////////
// MY CODE STARTS HERE
/////////////////////////

#include "CustDlg.h"

/////////////////////////
// MY CODE ENDS HERE
/////////////////////////

....
..…..
..…..
```

Attaching Code to the *BN_CLICKED* Event of the Get Data Button

You'll now attach code to the BN_CLICKED event of the IDC_GETDATA_BUTTON button. When you click this button, the IDD_CUSTOM_DIALOG dialog box should appear.

☐ In the Message Maps tab of ClassWizard, select the following event:

Class name:	CMyCusDlg
Object ID:	IDC_GETDATA_BUTTON
Message:	BN_CLICKED

☐ Click the Add Function button, name the new function OnGetdataButton, and click the Edit Code button.

Visual C++ responds by opening the file MyCusDlg.cpp with the function OnGetdataButton() *ready for you to edit.*

6

☐ Write the following code in the `OnGetdataButton()` function:

```
void CMyCusDlg::OnGetdataButton()
{
// TODO: Add your control notification handler code here

////////////////////////////
// MY CODE STARTS HERE
////////////////////////////


// Display the IDD_CUSTOM_DIALOG dialog box
m_dlg.DoModal();

////////////////////////////
// MY CODE ENDS HERE
////////////////////////////

}
```

The code you typed displays the `m_dlg` dialog box as a modal dialog box:

```
m_dlg.DoModal();
```

> **Note:** A *modal dialog box* must be closed before you can switch to another window in the same application. For example, you can click the Get Data button to display the custom-made dialog box. Once the custom-made dialog box is displayed, you cannot return to the main window of the application, unless you close the custom-made dialog box.

Attaching Code to the *BN_CLICKED* Event of the Display Results Button

You'll now attach code to the IDC_DISPLAYRESULTS_BUTTON of the IDD_MYCUS_DIALOG dialog box:

☐ In the Message Maps tab of ClassWizard, select the following event:

Class name:	CMyCusDlg
Object ID:	IDC_DISPLAYRESULTS_BUTTON
Message:	BN_CLICKED

☐ Click the Add Function button, name the new function `OnDisplayresultsButton`, and click the Edit Code button.

Visual C++ responds by opening the file MyCusDlg.cpp with the function `OnDisplayresultsButton()` *ready for you to edit.*

☐ Write the following code in the `OnDisplayresultsButton()` function:

```
void CMyCusDlg::OnDisplayresultsButton()
{
// TODO: Add your control notification handler code here

///////////////////////////
// MY CODE STARTS HERE
///////////////////////////


// Display the data that the user entered
MessageBox(m_dlg.m_MyDataEdit);

///////////////////////////
// MY CODE ENDS HERE
///////////////////////////

}
```

The code you typed displays a message box:

```
MessageBox( m_dlg.m_MyDataEdit );
```

Note how the text of the edit box is provided as the parameter of the `MessageBox()` function—`m_MyDataEdit` is the member variable you attached to the IDC_MYDATA_EDIT edit box in IDD_CUSTOM_DIALOG. Therefore, the text of the edit box is denoted as follows:

```
m_dlg.m_MyDataEdit
```

☐ Compile, link, and execute the MyCus program.

☐ Click the Get Data button.

MyCus responds by displaying the custom-made dialog box.

☐ Type something in the edit box, then click the OK button of the custom-made dialog box.

☐ Click the Display Results button.

MyCus responds by displaying a message box showing the text you typed in the edit box.

☐ Experiment with the MyCus program, then click the Exit button to terminate it.

6

Summary

In this chapter, you have designed and created two programs:

- MyMsg, a program that uses predefined dialog boxes.
- MyCus, a program that uses custom-made dialog boxes.

As you've seen, using predefined dialog boxes is easier, but you have limited control over their appearance and behavior. On the other hand, you can go to the trouble of designing your own custom-made dialog boxes, which means more work, but also more control over how the dialog boxes look and what they do.

Q&A

Q Should I use predefined dialog boxes or custom-made dialog boxes?

A It depends on the particular application you are developing. For example, suppose you are prompting the user with a message such as `insert diskette into disk drive a:`, `then click the OK button`. This is a simple instruction to the user, so a predefined dialog box is appropriate.

However, if your program needs to accept some data from the user (such as checking or unchecking a check box, setting a radio button, and so on), you'll have to use a custom-made dialog box that lets the user enter the data.

Q The MyCus program uses the following `MessageBox()` function to display a message box:

```
MessageBox( m_dlg.m_MyDataEdit );
```

I thought that the `MessageBox()` function had three parameters. What happened to the other two parameters?

A The `MessageBox()` function does have three parameters. If you supply only the first parameter, the message box will appear with no icon and its caption will be the same as the program name. (Refer back to Figure 6.8.) When you're developing applications, you should supply the second and third parameters of the `MessageBox()` function. However, during the study of Visual C++, you'll find that the `MessageBox()` function can frequently be used to display values for the purpose of debugging and understanding the material. In these cases, when the `MessageBox()` function is used for the sole purpose of displaying values, there's no need to supply the second and third parameters.

Quiz

1. You can close the custom-made dialog box by clicking its OK button or its Cancel button. What is the difference between these two methods of closing the custom-made dialog box in the MyCus program?

2. Why were you instructed not to delete the OK and Cancel buttons of the custom-made dialog box of the MyCus program?

Exercise

Enhance the MyCus program so that when the user clicks the Exit button, the program does not immediately terminate. Rather, the program displays a message box asking the user if he or she really wants to terminate the program.

Quiz Answers

1. You can answer this question by performing the following experiment:

☐ Start the MyCus program.

☐ Click the Get Data button.

☐ Type Testing!!! in the edit box.

☐ Click the OK button of the custom-made dialog box.

☐ Now click the Get Data button again.

As you can see, the edit box contains the text Testing!!!!. In other words, because you previously closed the custom-made dialog box by clicking its OK button, the value you typed in the edit box is maintained.

☐ In the edit box of the custom-made dialog box, type NOT TESTING!!!.

☐ Click the Cancel button of the custom-made dialog box.

☐ Click the Get Data button.

As you can see, the edit box contains the text Testing!!! because you previously closed the custom-made dialog box by clicking its Cancel button. Therefore, the text you typed in the edit box is not maintained; the old value that existed in the edit box is maintained.

2. Data attached to controls in the IDD_CUSTOM_DIALOG dialog box will maintain their values if you click the OK button of the custom-made dialog box. If you click the Cancel button, the values of the controls in the IDD_CUSTOM_DIALOG dialog box remain as they were the last time the IDD_CUSTOM_DIALOG dialog box was closed with the OK button.

Exercise Answer

Add the following code in the OnExitButton() function (in the MyCusDlg.cpp file):

```
void CMyCusDlg::OnExitButton()
{
// TODO: Add your control notification handler code here

//////////////////////////
// MY CODE STARTS HERE
//////////////////////////

int iResult =
MessageBox ( "Exit?",
             "Are you sure you want to exit?",
             MB_YESNO+MB_ICONQUESTION);

if (iResult == IDYES)
   {
   OnOK();
   }

//////////////////////////
// MY CODE ENDS HERE
//////////////////////////

}
```

The code you typed displays a message box whenever the user clicks the Exit button. The message box includes a Yes button and No button. If the user clicks the No button, the code under the if statement is not executed. If the user clicks the Yes button, the code under the if statement is executed. This code terminates the program.

Graphics and Drawings

In this chapter, you'll learn how to create programs that draw graphics and how to install and use a timer.

The Graph Program

The Graph program illustrates how to use graphics drawing in your Visual C++ programs. Before creating the Graph program yourself, review its specifications:

- When you execute the Graph program, the window shown in Figure 7.1 appears.

Figure 7.1.
The window of the Graph program.

- As you can see, the Graph program continuously draws a circle with a varying radius. The radius of the circle increases, reaches its maximum, and then decreases. When the radius of the circle reaches its minimum value, the whole process starts over again.
- When you click the Draw Graphics button, the dialog box shown in Figure 7.2 is displayed.

Figure 7.2.
The Set Graph dialog box.

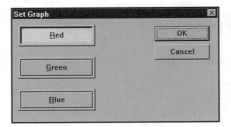

- You can then select a color from the dialog box. For example, if you select the Blue button and then click the OK button, the circle will be drawn in blue.
- While the Set Graph dialog box is displayed, the circle in the main window of the program should keep changing its radius. (See Figure 7.3.) However, the new color you select should be applied only after you click the OK button.

Figure 7.3.
While the Set Graph dialog box is displayed, the Graph program keeps animating the circle.

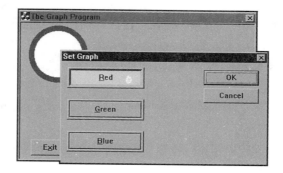

Now that you know what the Graph program should do, start by creating the program's project.

Creating the Project of the Graph Program

Follow these steps to create the project of the Graph program:

☐ Create the C:\TYVCProg\Programs\CH07 directory, start Visual C++, select New from the File menu, then select Project Workspace from the New dialog box.

☐ Select MFC AppWizard (exe) from the Type list, set the program name to Graph, click the Browse button, and select the C:\TYVCProg\Programs\Ch07 directory.

☐ Click the Create button of the New Project Workspace dialog box.

   Visual C++ responds by displaying the MFC ClassWizard Step 1 window.

☐ In the Step 1 window, choose the option to create a dialog-based application, then click the Next button.

☐ In the Step 2 window, use the default settings and enter Graph as the title for the dialog box. When you're done, click the Next button.

☐ In the Step 3 window, use the default settings, then click the Next button.

☐ In the Step 4 window, notice that AppWizard has created the CGraphApp and CGraphDlg classes for you. Click the Finish button to display the New Project Information window, then click the OK button of the New Project Information window.

   Visual C++ responds by creating the Graph project and all its skeleton files.

☐ Select Set Default Configuration from the Build menu and Graph - Win32 Release item from the Default Project Configuration dialog box. Finally, click the OK button of the Default Project Configuration dialog box.

That's it—Visual C++ has created the project of the Graph program.

The Visual Design of the Graph Program

You'll now visually design the main window of the Graph program:

☐ In the Project Workspace, click the ResourceView tab, expand the Graph resources item, and expand the Dialog item. Finally, double-click the IDD_GRAPH_DIALOG item.

Visual C++ responds by displaying the IDD_GRAPH_DIALOG dialog box in design mode.

☐ Delete the OK button, Cancel button, and TODO text in the IDD_GRAPH_DIALOG dialog box.

☐ Set up the IDD_GRAPH_DIALOG dialog box according to Table 7.1. When you finish, it should look like the one in Figure 7.4.

Table 7.1. The properties table of the IDD_GRAPH_DIALOG dialog box.

Object	Property	Setting
Dialog Box	**ID**	**IDD_GRAPH_DIALOG**
	Caption	The Graph Program
	Font	System, Size 10
	Client edge	Checked (Extended Styles tab)
	Static edge	Checked (Extended Styles tab)
Push Button	**ID**	**IDC_EXIT_BUTTON**
	Caption	E&xit
Push Button	**ID**	**IDC_DRAWGRAPHICS_BUTTON**
	Caption	&Draw Graphics…
	Client edge	Checked (Extended Styles tab)
	Static edge	Checked (Extended Styles tab)
	Modal frame	Checked (Extended Styles tab)

Figure 7.4.
*IDD_GRAPH_DIALOG
in design mode.*

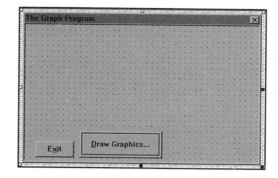

Attaching Code to the *BN_CLICKED* Event of the Exit Button

You'll now attach code to the BN_CLICKED event of the Exit button:

☐ Select ClassWizard from the View menu. In the Message Maps tab of ClassWizard, select the following event:

Class name:	CGraphDlg
Object ID:	IDC_EXIT_BUTTON
Message:	BN_CLICKED

☐ Click the Add Function button of ClassWizard, name the new function OnExitButton, then click the Edit Code button.

Visual C++ responds by opening the file GraphDlg.cpp with the function OnExitButton() ready for you to edit.

☐ Write the following code in the OnExitButton() function:

```
void CGraphDlg::OnExitButton()
{
// TODO: Add your control notification handler code here

///////////////////////////
// MY CODE STARTS HERE
///////////////////////////

OnOK();

///////////////////////////
// MY CODE ENDS HERE
///////////////////////////

}
```

The code you typed terminates the program whenever you click the Exit button.

Installing a Timer

The Graph program uses a *timer,* which is a software mechanism that generates the WM_TIMER event at regular time intervals. Your program's code will set the frequency at which the WM_TIMER event will occur. For example, if you set the interval of the timer to 500 milliseconds (0.5 seconds), the WM_TIMER event will occur every 500 milliseconds, as will the the code you attach to the WM_TIMER event.

Here is how you install a timer:

☐ In the Message Maps tab of the ClassWizard window, select the following event:

Class name:	CGraphDlg
Object ID:	CGraphDlg
Message:	WM_INITDIALOG

☐ Click ClassWizard's Edit Code button.

> *Visual C++ responds by opening the file GraphDlg.cpp with the function* OnInitDialog() *ready for you to edit.*

☐ Write the following code in the OnInitDialog() function:

```
BOOL CGraphDlg::OnInitDialog()
{

…
…
…

// TODO: Add extra initialization here

/////////////////////////
// MY CODE STARTS HERE
/////////////////////////

// Install a system timer.
int iInstallResult;

iInstallResult = SetTimer(1,
                          500,
                          NULL);

if (iInstallResult == 0 )
{

MessageBox ("cannot install timer!");

}

/////////////////////////
// MY CODE ENDS HERE
/////////////////////////
```

```
    return TRUE;
    // return TRUE   unless you set the focus to a control
    }
```

The `OnInitDialog()` function is automatically executed when you start the program.

The code you typed first declares a variable:

```
int iInstallResult;
```

Then the `SetTimer()` function is executed:

```
iInstallResult = SetTimer(1,
                          500,
                          NULL);
```

The `SetTimer()` function has three parameters. The first parameter is the ID of the timer, which you declared as `Timer 1`. The second parameter indicates the interval at which the `WM_TIMER` event will occur; you specified every 500 milliseconds. The third parameter specifies the address of a function that will be executed every 500 milliseconds. Because you supplied `NULL` as the third parameter, this means you didn't specify a function; therefore, the `WM_TIMER` event will be executed every 500 milliseconds. (You'll attach code to the `WM_TIMER` event later in this chapter.)

An `if` statement is then executed to examine the returned value of `SetTimer()`:

```
if (iInstallResult == 0 )
{

MessageBox ("cannot install timer!");

}
```

If the returned value of `SetTimer()` is equal to `0`, it means that the timer was not installed.

Note: It's very important to use an `if` statement to examine the returned value of `SetTimer()`. Why? Because depending on the particular system you are using, you can install only a finite number of timers on your PC. Suppose that before executing the Graph program, the user already executed several other programs that use a timer, and the PC had exceeded the number of timers that can be installed. In that case, the Graph program's `SetTimer()` function will fail to install an additional timer.

In that situation, you should display a message box to your user, telling him or her that the Graph program cannot be executed because other programs are using the timers. Your message box should suggest closing some of the programs that are running, then starting the Graph program again.

7.

Note: Once a timer is installed, you can remove it by executing the `KillTimer()` function as follows:

☐ In the Message Maps tab of the ClassWizard window, select the following event:

Class name:	CGraphDlg
Object ID:	CGraphDlg
Message:	WM_DESTROY

☐ Add the `OnDestroy()` function, then edit it in the GraphDlg.cpp file as follows:

```
void CGraphDlg::OnDestroy()
{
    CDialog::OnDestroy();

// TODO: Add your message handler code here

/////////////////////////
// MY CODE STARTS HERE
/////////////////////////

KillTimer(1);

/////////////////////////
// MY CODE ENDS HERE
/////////////////////////

}
```

Note that the parameter of the `KillTimer()` function is the ID of the timer you installed.

The `OnDestroy()` function is executed when the IDD_GRAPH_DIALOG dialog box is about to be destroyed in one of three ways. First, if the user clicks the Exit button, the program terminates, but the `KillTimer()` function kills the timer before terminating the program. Second, if the user clicks the × icon on the upper-right corner of the window, the program terminates. However, before terminating, the WM_DESTROY event occurs, and the `KillTimer()` function in the `OnDestroy()` function is executed. Third, if the user right-clicks the caption of the IDD_GRAPH_DIALOG dialog box (or clicks the icon on the upper-left corner), then selects Close from the system menu that pops up, the WM_DESTROY event occurs.

Testing the Timer

Before proceeding with the Graph program, make sure the timer has been installed and is working as expected:

☐ In the Message Maps tab of the ClassWizard window, select the following event:

Class name:	CGraphDlg
Object ID:	CGraphDlg
Message:	WM_TIMER

☐ Click the Add Function button, create the new function OnTimer, then click the Edit Code button.

> *Visual C++ responds by opening the file GraphDlg.cpp with the function* OnTimer() *ready for you to edit.*

☐ Write the following code in the OnTimer() function:

```
void CGraphDlg::OnTimer(UINT nIDEvent)
{
// TODO: Add your message handler code
// here and/or call default

/////////////////////////
// MY CODE STARTS HERE
/////////////////////////

MessageBeep((WORD)-1);


/////////////////////////
// MY CODE ENDS HERE
/////////////////////////


CDialog::OnTimer(nIDEvent);
}
```

The code you typed causes the PC to beep every 500 milliseconds.

☐ Compile, link, and execute the Graph program to make sure the PC beeps every 500 milliseconds.

☐ Terminate the Graph program by clicking its Exit button.

Before proceeding with the Graph program, remove the code that causes the PC to beep every 500 milliseconds:

7

☐ Comment out the `MessageBeep()` statement in the `OnTimer()` function (in the GraphDlg.cpp file) as follows:

```
void CGraphDlg::OnTimer(UINT nIDEvent)
{
// TODO: Add your message handler code here
// and/or call default

///////////////////////////
// MY CODE STARTS HERE
///////////////////////////

//// MessageBeep((WORD)-1);


///////////////////////////
// MY CODE ENDS HERE
///////////////////////////

CDialog::OnTimer(nIDEvent);
}
```

Later in this chapter, you'll add additional code to the `OnTimer()` function.

☐ Compile, link, and execute the Graph program to make sure the PC does not beep every 500 milliseconds.

The *WM_PAINT* Event

What is the `WM_PAINT` event? Suppose you are covering the window of the Graph program with another window. Then you expose the Graph program's window by removing the other application's window, which means the area that was covered by the other application has to be "repainted." What does Windows do about this? Instead of repainting the area, Windows generates the `WM_PAINT` event. It is your job to repaint the window whenever the `WM_PAINT` event occurs. Windows also generates the `WM_PAINT` event whenever the window of the Graph program needs to be repainted. For example, suppose you drag Graph's window so that half the window is outside the screen, then drag it back into the screen again. In such a case, the window of the Graph program has to be repainted. Again, Windows will not repaint Graph's window, but Windows will generate the `WM_PAINT` event so that the code you attached to the `WM_PAINT` event will be executed.

You'll now type code that demonstrates the need for `WM_PAINT`:

☐ In the Message Maps tab of the ClassWizard window, select the following event:

Class name:	CGraphDlg
Object ID:	IDC_DRAWGRAPHICS_BUTTON
Message:	BN_CLICKED

☐ Click the Add Function button, name the new function OnDrawgraphicsButton, and click the Edit Code button.

Visual C++ responds by opening the file GraphDlg.cpp with the function OnDrawgraphicsButton() *ready for you to edit.*

☐ Write the following code in the OnDrawgraphicsButton() function:

```
void CGraphDlg::OnDrawgraphicsButton()
{
// TODO: Add your control notification handler code here

/////////////////////////
// MY CODE STARTS HERE
/////////////////////////

// Create a DC object
CClientDC dc(this);

// Create a new pen
CPen MyNewPen;

MyNewPen.CreatePen (PS_SOLID,
                    10,
                    RGB(255,0,0) );


// Select the new pen.
CPen*  pOriginalPen;
pOriginalPen = dc.SelectObject(&MyNewPen);


CRect MyRectangle (20,
                   10,
                   120,
                   110);

// Draw the circle
dc.Ellipse (&MyRectangle);

// Return the original pen
dc.SelectObject(pOriginalPen);

/////////////////////////
// MY CODE ENDS HERE
/////////////////////////

}
```

The code you typed is executed whenever you click the Draw Graphics button.

First, a device context is created:

```
// Create a DC object
CClientDC dc(this);
```

7

197

Next, a new pen is created that's solid red and 10 pixels wide:

```
// Create a new pen
CPen MyNewPen;

MyNewPen.CreatePen (PS_SOLID,
                    10,
                    RGB(255,0,0) );
```

The new pen is selected:

```
// Select the new pen.
CPen*  pOriginalPen;
pOriginalPen = dc.SelectObject(&MyNewPen);
```

Note that once the new pen is selected, it replaces the current pen. The returned value of `SelectObject()` is a pointer to the original pen.

Next, a rectangle object is created:

```
CRect MyRectangle (20,
                   10,
                   120,
                   110);
```

The rectangle is declared so that its upper-left corner is 20 pixels to the right of the window's left edge and 10 pixels below the window's upper edge. The rectangle's lower-right corner is 120 pixels to the right of the window's left edge and 110 pixels below the window's upper edge.

An ellipse is then drawn:

```
// Draw the circle
dc.Ellipse (&MyRectangle);
```

The parameter of the `Ellipse()` function is the rectangle you declared. Therefore, the ellipse is drawn so that the rectangle encloses the ellipse. Because the rectangle you declared is a square, the ellipse is a circle.

Finally, the original pen is selected:

```
// Return the original pen
dc.SelectObject(pOriginalPen);
```

The first question in this chapter's "Q&A" section discusses the parameter and returned value of `SelectObject()`. You may want to read that section now.

☐ Compile, link, and execute the Graph program.

   The window of the Graph program appears, as shown in Figure 7.5.

Figure 7.5.

When you start the Graph program now, no circle is drawn.

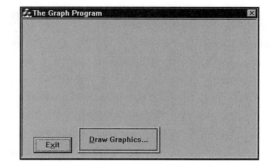

☐ Click the Draw Graphics button.

> *Graph responds by drawing a circle so it's enclosed by an imaginary rectangle with the coordinates specified by the* MyRectangle *object you created and supplied as the parameter of the* Ellipse() *function. (See Figure 7.6.)*

Figure 7.6.

After you click the Draw Graphics button, a circle is drawn.

This point is 20 pixels from the left and 10 pixels from the top

This point is 120 pixels from the left and 110 pixels from the top

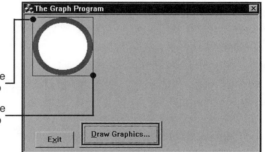

Follow these steps to demonstrate why you need the WM_PAINT event:

☐ Drag the Graph program's window to the left so that half the circle is outside the screen. (See Figure 7.7.)

☐ Drag the Graph program's window to the right so you can see the entire window again.

As shown in Figure 7.8, now only half the circle is shown. The half that was outside the screen has not been redrawn.

7

Figure 7.7.
Dragging the Graph program's window to the left so that half the circle is outside the screen.

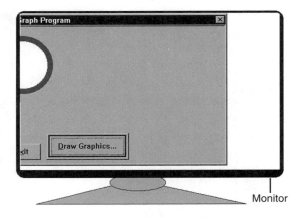

Monitor

Figure 7.8.
After returning the window to its original position, the section of the circle that was outside the screen is not redrawn.

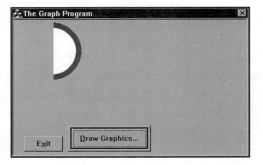

Naturally, your first impression is that something is wrong with Windows! But actually, there is nothing wrong with Windows. Windows did notice that the window of Graph needs to be repainted and generated the WM_PAINT message. Here's how you verify that happened:

☐ Select ClassWizard from the View menu. In the Message Maps tab of the ClassWizard window, select the following event:

Class name:	CGraphDlg
Object ID:	CGraphDlg
Message:	WM_PAINT

☐ Click ClassWizard's Edit Code button.

Visual C++ responds by opening the file GraphDlg.cpp with the function OnPaint() *ready for you to edit.*

☐ Write the following code in the `OnPaint()` function:

```
void CGraphDlg::OnPaint()
{
    if (IsIconic())
    {
    …
    …
    …
    else
    {
/////////////////////////
// MY CODE STARTS HERE
/////////////////////////

MessageBeep((WORD)-1);

/////////////////////////
// MY CODE ENDS HERE
/////////////////////////
    …
    …
    …
    }
}
```

> **Note:** Typically, Visual C++ inserts the following text so you'll know where to type your own code:
>
> `// TODO: Add your control notification handler code here`
>
> In the current version of Visual C++ 4.0, the TODO text does not appear in the `OnPaint()` function, so make sure you type the preceding code as instructed under the `else` statement.

The code you typed makes the PC beep whenever Windows generates the WM_PAINT event.

☐ Compile, link, and execute the Graph program.

☐ Drag Graph's window to the left, then back to its original location.

As you can hear, Windows noticed that Graph's window needed to be repainted, and the WM_PAINT event occurred.

☐ Experiment with the Graph program, then click its Exit button to terminate the program.

Writing Repainting Code

Now that you're convinced the window needs to be redrawn in the OnPaint() function, add the repaint code:

☐ Modify the code of the OnPaint() function:

```
void CGraphDlg::OnPaint()
{
     if (IsIconic())
     {
     …
     …
     …
     else
     {
/////////////////////////
// MY CODE STARTS HERE
/////////////////////////

/// MessageBeep((WORD)-1);

OnDrawgraphicsButton();

/////////////////////////
// MY CODE ENDS HERE
/////////////////////////
     …
     …
     …
     }
}
```

The code you added comments out the MessageBeep() function:

```
/// MessageBeep((WORD)-1);
```

Then the OnDrawgraphicsButton() function is executed:

```
OnDrawgraphicsButton();
```

Now, whenever Graph's window needs to be repainted, Windows will generate the WM_PAINT event. The code you typed in the OnPaint() function is the same code executed when you click the Draw Graphics button; therefore, the circle is redrawn.

☐ Compile, link, and execute the Graph program to make sure that the window is repainted when needed and that the full circle is drawn.

☐ Click the Exit button of the Graph program to terminate the program.

Modifying the *OnPaint()* Function

You did the redrawing in `OnPaint()` by executing the `OnDrawgraphicsButton()` function in the previous section. However, later in this chapter you'll add additional code in the `OnDrawgraphicsButton()` function that you won't want to be executed every time the `WM_PAINT` event occurs, so modify the code in the `OnPaint()` function:

☐ Modify the code in the `OnPaint()` function (in the GraphDlg.cpp file) as follows:

```
void CGraphDlg::OnPaint()
{
    if (IsIconic())
    {
    …
    …
    …
    else
    {
//////////////////////////
// MY CODE STARTS HERE
//////////////////////////

//// MessageBeep((WORD)-1);

//// OnDrawgraphicsButton();


// Create a DC object
CPaintDC dc(this);

// Create a new pen
CPen MyNewPen;

MyNewPen.CreatePen (PS_SOLID,
                    10,
                    RGB(255,0,0) );


// Select the new pen.
CPen*  pOriginalPen;
pOriginalPen = dc.SelectObject(&MyNewPen);


CRect MyRectangle (20,
                   10,
                   120,
                   110);


dc.Ellipse (&MyRectangle);

// Return the original pen
dc.SelectObject(pOriginalPen);
```

```
/////////////////////////
// MY CODE ENDS HERE
/////////////////////////
...
...
...
        }
}
```

The code you typed comments out the execution of `OnDrawgraphicsButton()`:

```
//// OnDrawgraphicsButton();
```

You then created a `dc` object as follows:

```
// Create a DC object
CPaintDC dc(this);
```

The rest of the code is identical to the code in the `OnDrawgraphicsButton()` function:

```
// Create a new pen
CPen MyNewPen;

MyNewPen.CreatePen (PS_SOLID,
                    10,
                    RGB(255,0,0) );


// Select the new pen.
CPen*  pOriginalPen;
pOriginalPen = dc.SelectObject(&MyNewPen);

CRect MyRectangle (20,
                   10,
                   120,
                   110);

dc.Ellipse (&MyRectangle);

// Return the original pen
dc.SelectObject(pOriginalPen);
```

☐ Compile, link, and execute the Graph program.

☐ Drag the window of the Graph program and verify that the code in the `OnPaint()` function repaints the window properly.

The Visual Design of the IDD_CUSTOM_DIALOG Dialog Box

You'll now design the IDD_CUSTOM_DIALOG dialog box, which will be displayed when you click the Draw Graphics button:

☐ In the Project Workspace, click the Resource View tab, expand the Graph resources item, then expand the Dialog item.

As you can see, the Graph program currently has two dialog boxes: IDD_GRAPH_DIALOG (the main window of the Graph program) and IDD_ABOUTBOX (the About dialog box).

☐ Right-click the Dialog item.

   Visual C++ responds by displaying a menu.

☐ Select Insert Dialog from the menu.

   Visual C++ responds by inserting a dialog box to the project with the default ID of IDD_DIALOG1.

☐ Set the ID property of the new dialog box to `IDD_CUSTOM_DIALOG`.

☐ Set its properties according to Table 7.2. When you finish designing the dialog box, it should look like the one shown back in Figure 7.2.

Table 7.2. The properties table of the IDD_CUSTOM_DIALOG dialog box.

Object	Property	Setting
Dialog Box	**ID**	**IDD_CUSTOM_DIALOG**
	Caption	Set Graph
	Font	System, Size 10
Radio Button	**ID**	**IDC_RED_RADIO**
	Caption	&Red
	Group	Checked (General tab)
	Push-like	Checked (Styles tab)
	Client edge	Checked (Extended Styles tab)
	Static edge	Checked (Extended Styles tab)
	Modal frame	Checked (Extended Styles tab)
Radio Button	**ID**	**IDC_GREEN_RADIO**
	Caption	&Green
	Group	Not Checked (General tab)
	Push-like	Checked (Styles tab)
	Client edge	Checked (Extended Styles tab)
	Static edge	Checked (Extended Styles tab)

continues

Table 7.2. continued

Object	Property	Setting
	Modal frame	Checked (Extended Styles tab)
Radio Button	**ID**	**IDC_BLUE_RADIO**
	Caption	&Blue
	Group	Not Checked (General tab)
	Push-like	Checked (Styles tab)
	Client edge	Checked (Extended Styles tab)
	Static edge	Checked (Extended Styles tab)
	Modal frame	Checked (Extended Styles tab)

Keep the following points in mind while you're designing the IDD_CUSTOM_DIALOG dialog box:

- When designing the IDD_CUSTOM_DIALOG dialog box, do NOT delete the OK and Cancel buttons, as you usually do.
- Table 7.2 instructs you place three radio buttons in the IDD_CUSTOM_DIALOG dialog box. Make sure you place them in sequential order: first the IDC_RED_RADIO radio button, then the IDC_GREEN_RADIO radio button, and finally the IDC_BLUE_RADIO radio button. When you finish placing the three radio buttons, select Resource Symbols from the View menu and make sure the ID numbers of the radio buttons are sequential numbers.
- Checking the Push-like property of the radio buttons makes them look like pushbuttons. However, because the three radio buttons belong to the same group, only one radio button can be pushed down at any given time. Consequently, these three controls are still "regular" radio buttons, except that they look different from conventional radio buttons. This was done for cosmetic reasons and to demonstrate the Push-like property of the radio buttons in Visual C++.

☐ Select Save All from the File menu to save your work.

Attaching a Variable to the Radio Buttons

You'll now attach a variable to the radio buttons you placed in the IDD_CUSTOM_DIALOG dialog box.

☐ Right-click the IDD_CUSTOM_DIALOG dialog box to display a menu, then select the ClassWizard item.

Visual C++ responds by displaying the Adding a Class dialog box since IDD_CUSTOM_DIALOG does not have a class of its own yet.

☐ Make sure the "Create a new class" radio button is selected, then click the OK button of the Adding a Class dialog box.

Visual C++ responds by displaying the Create New Class dialog box.

☐ Set the Name box to `CSetDlg` and the base class to `CDialog`.

☐ Click the Change button to display the Change Files dialog box. Notice that the name of the files associated with the new `CSetDlg` class you are creating are SetDlg.cpp and SetDlg.h.

☐ Close the Change Files dialog box, then click the Create button of the Create New Class dialog box.

Visual C++ responds by creating the CSetDlg class of the IDD_CUSTOM_DIALOG dialog box, and the MFC ClassWizard window appears.

☐ Make sure the Class name box of the MFC ClassWizard window is set to `CSetDlg`. Then click the Member Variables tab of the MFC ClassWizard window, select the IDC_RED_RADIO item, and click the Add Variable button.

Visual C++ responds by displaying the Add Member Variable dialog box.

☐ Set the options listed below:

Variable name:	`m_RedRadio`
Category:	`Value`
Variable type:	`int`

☐ Click the OK button of the Add Member Variable dialog box.

Visual C++ responds by adding a member variable to the radio buttons.

Therefore, when `m_RedRadio` is equal to `0`, the Red radio button is selected; when it's equal to `1`, the Green radio button is selected; and when it's equal to `2`, the Blue radio button is selected.

Creating an Object of Class *CSetDlg*

In the previous sections, you created the class `CSetDlg`. This class is derived from `CDialog`, and the IDD_CUSTOM_DIALOG dialog box is associated with the `CSetDlg` class. The two files associated with the `CSetDlg` class are SetDlg.cpp and SetDlg.h. You'll now create an object `m_dlg` of class `CSetDlg`:

☐ In the constructor function of the `CGraphDlg` class (in the GraphDlg.h file), add code that creates an object called `m_dlg` of class `CSetDlg` as follows: (Note: To open the GraphDlg.h file, display the Project Workspace window, click the FileView tab, expand the Graph files item, expand the Dependencies item, and finally, double-click the GraphDlg.h item.)

```
class CGraphDlg : public CDialog
{
// Construction
public:
CGraphDlg(CWnd* pParent = NULL);
// standard constructor

////////////////////////
// MY CODE STARTS HERE
////////////////////////

CSetDlg m_dlg;

////////////////////////
// MY CODE ENDS HERE
////////////////////////

...
...
...
};
```

The code you typed creates an object m_dlg of class CSetDlg. However, when the compiler compiles the GraphDlg.h file, it won't know the meaning of CSetDlg. You need to use the #include statement in the declaration of the CSetDlg class, which is in the file SetDlg.h.

☐ At the beginning of the GraphDlg.h file, add the #include statement as follows:

```
// GraphDlg.h : header file
//

//////////////////////////////////////////////////////
// CGraphDlg dialog


////////////////////////
// MY CODE STARTS HERE
////////////////////////

#include "SetDlg.h"

////////////////////////
// MY CODE ENDS HERE
////////////////////////
...
...
...
```

Modifying the Code of the *BN_CLICKED* Event of the Draw Graphics Button

You'll now modify the code in the BN_CLICKED event of the Draw Graphics button:

☐ In the Message Maps tab of the ClassWizard window, select the following event:

Class name:	CGraphDlg
Object ID:	IDC_DRAWGRAPHICS_BUTTON
Message:	BN_CLICKED

☐ Click the Edit Code button of ClassWizard.

Visual C++ responds by opening the file GraphDlg.cpp with the function OnDrawgraphicsButton() *ready for you to edit.*

☐ Modify the code in the OnDrawgraphicsButton() function as follows:

```
void CGraphDlg::OnDrawgraphicsButton()
{
// TODO: Add your control notification handler code here

/////////////////////////
// MY CODE STARTS HERE
/////////////////////////

m_dlg.DoModal();

/////////////////////////
// MY CODE ENDS HERE
/////////////////////////

}
```

After deleting the code you previously typed in this function, you typed the following statement, which displays the m_dlg object (the IDD_CUSTOM_DIALOG dialog box):

```
m_dlg.DoModal();
```

Although you haven't finished the Graph program, see some of the code you typed in action:

☐ Select Save All from the File menu to save your work.

☐ Compile, link, and execute the Graph program.

☐ Click the Draw Graph button.

Graph responds by displaying the IDD_CUSTOM_DIALOG dialog box. Note that initially, none of the radio buttons is selected.

7

☐ Experiment with the radio buttons of the IDD_CUSTOM_DIALOG dialog box. Notice that only one pushbutton-like radio button can be selected at any given time. When you're done, terminate the Graph program.

Initializing the Radio Buttons

As you saw in the previous section, when you start the Graph program, none of the radio buttons is selected. You'll now add code that makes the Red radio button the selected button:

☐ In the Message Maps tab of the ClassWizard window, select the following event:

Class name:	CGraphDlg
Object ID:	CGraphDlg
Message:	WM_INITDIALOG

☐ Click the Edit Code button of ClassWizard.

Visual C++ responds by opening the file GraphDlg.cpp file with the function OnInitDialog() *ready for you to edit.*

☐ Write the following code in the OnInitDialog() function:

```
BOOL CGraphDlg::OnInitDialog()
{
…
…
…

// TODO: Add extra initialization here

///////////////////////////
// MY CODE STARTS HERE
///////////////////////////

// Install a system timer.
int iInstallResult;

iInstallResult = SetTimer(1,
                          500,
                          NULL);

if (iInstallResult == 0 )
{

MessageBox ("cannot install timer!");

}

// Select the Red radio button
m_dlg.m_RedRadio = 0;
```

```
/////////////////////////
// MY CODE ENDS HERE
/////////////////////////

return TRUE;
// return TRUE  unless you set the focus to a control
}
```

The code you added makes the Red radio button the selected button:

```
// Select the Red radio button
m_dlg.m_RedRadio = 0;
```

☐ Select Save All from the File menu.

☐ Compile, link, and execute the Graph program.

☐ Click the Draw Graphics button.

> *Graph responds by displaying the IDD_CUSTOM_DIALOG dialog box with the Red radio button selected.*

☐ Experiment with the Graph program, then click the Exit button to terminate it.

Adding Member Variables to the *CGraphDlg* Class

You'll now add two member variables to the CGraphDlg class so they will be visible from any of the class's member functions:

☐ In the constructor function of the CGraphDlg class, add the declarations of the m_Radius and m_Direction member variables as follows:

```
class CGraphDlg : public CDialog
{
// Construction
public:
CGraphDlg(CWnd* pParent = NULL);
// standard constructor

/////////////////////////
// MY CODE STARTS HERE
/////////////////////////

CSetDlg m_dlg;

int m_Radius;
int m_Direction;

/////////////////////////
// MY CODE ENDS HERE
/////////////////////////
```

```
...
...
...

};
```

The code you typed declares two member variables as follows:

```
int m_Radius;
int m_Direction;
```

Initializing the Values of *m_Radius* and *m_Direction*

You'll now write code that initializes the values of m_Radius and m_Direction:

☐ In the Message Maps tab of the ClassWizard window, select the following event:

Class name:	CGraphDlg
Object ID:	CGraphDlg
Message:	WM_INITDIALOG

☐ Click the Edit Code button of ClassWizard.

Visual C++ responds by opening the file GraphDlg.cpp file with the function OnInitDialog() ready for you to edit.

☐ Write the following code in the OnInitDialog() function:

```
BOOL CGraphDlg::OnInitDialog()
{
...
...
...

// TODO: Add extra initialization here

////////////////////////
// MY CODE STARTS HERE
////////////////////////

// Install a system timer.
int iInstallResult;

iInstallResult = SetTimer(1,
                          500,
                          NULL);

if (iInstallResult == 0 )
{

MessageBox ("cannot install timer!");

}
```

```
// Select the Red radio button
m_dlg.m_RedRadio = 0;

m_Radius = 50;
m_Direction = 1;

/////////////////////////
// MY CODE ENDS HERE
/////////////////////////

return TRUE;
// return TRUE  unless you set the focus to a control
}
```

The code you added initializes the m_Radius and m_Direction variables as follows:

```
m_Radius = 50;
m_Direction = 1;
```

Attaching Code to the *Timer* Event

At the beginning of this chapter, you installed a timer and verified that the OnTimer() function was executed every 500 milliseconds. You'll now add code to the OnTimer() function:

☐ Add the following code to the OnTimer() function in the GraphDlg.cpp file:

```
void CGraphDlg::OnTimer(UINT nIDEvent)
{
// TODO: Add your message handler code here
// and/or call default

/////////////////////////
// MY CODE STARTS HERE
/////////////////////////

//// MessageBeep((WORD)-1);


m_Radius = m_Radius + m_Direction;

if (m_Radius >= 100 )
{
m_Direction = -1;
}


if (m_Radius <=10
{
m_Direction = 1;
}

// Cause the execution of the OnPaint() function
Invalidate();
```

```
/////////////////////////
// MY CODE ENDS HERE
/////////////////////////

    ...
    ...
    ...
}
```

The m_Direction variable can be 1 or -1. m_Radius is then increased or decreased by 1:

```
m_Radius = m_Radius + m_Direction;
```

A series of two if statements are then executed to determine the value of m_Radius. If m_Radius exceeds 100, the value of m_Direction is set to -1:

```
if (m_Radius >= 100 )
{
m_Direction = -1;
}
```

If m_Radius is less than or equal to 10, the value of m_Direction is set to 1:

```
if (m_Radius <=10)
{
m_Direction = 1;
}
```

Because the OnTimer() function is executed every 500 milliseconds, the values of m_Radius and m_Direction are as follows:

m_Direction	m_Radius
1	50
1	51
1	52
...	...
...	...
...	...
1	100
-1	99
-1	98
-1	97
...	...
...	...
...	...
-1	11
-1	10
1	11

1	12
...	...
...	...
...	...

The last statement you typed in the `OnTimer()` function executes the `Invalidate()` function:

```
// Cause the execution of the OnPaint() function
Invalidate();
```

The `Invalidate()` function causes `WM_PAINT` to occur—every 500 milliseconds, the `WM_PAINT` event occurs, which causes the `OnPaint()` function to be executed.

> **Note:** The `WM_PAINT` event occurs automatically whenever Windows discovers the window needs to be repainted. You can force the generation of the `WM_PAINT` event by executing the `Invalidate()` function as follows:
>
> ```
> // Cause the execution of the OnPaint() function
> Invalidate();
> ```

Modifying the Code Attached to the *WM_PAINT* Event

You attached code to the `WM_PAINT` event of the IDD_GRAPH_DIALOG dialog box earlier in this chapter; follow these steps to modify it:

☐ In the Message Maps tab of the ClassWizard window, select the following event:

Class name:	CGraphDlg
Object ID:	CGraphDlg
Message:	WM_PAINT

☐ Click the Edit Code button of ClassWizard.

Visual C++ responds by opening the file GraphDlg.cpp with the function `OnPaint()` *(in the GraphDlg.cpp file) ready for you to edit.*

☐ Modify the code in the `OnPaint()` function as follows:

```
void CGraphDlg::OnPaint()
{
    if (IsIconic())
        {
        ...
        ...
        ...
        }
```

```
    else
     {

//////////////////////////
// MY CODE STARTS HERE
//////////////////////////


//// MessageBeep((WORD)-1);

//// OnDrawgraphicsButton();


// Create a DC object
CPaintDC dc(this);

// Create a new pen
CPen MyNewPen;

MyNewPen.CreatePen (PS_SOLID,
                    10,
                    RGB(255,0,0) );


// Select the new pen.
CPen*  pOriginalPen;
pOriginalPen = dc.SelectObject(&MyNewPen);


// CRect MyRectangle (20,
//                    10,
//                    120,
//                    110);


CRect MyRectangle (20,
                   10,
                   20+m_Radius*2,
                   10+m_Radius*2);


dc.Ellipse (&MyRectangle);

// Return the original pen
dc.SelectObject(pOriginalPen);


//////////////////////////
// MY CODE ENDS HERE
//////////////////////////
...
...
...
     }
...
...
...
}
```

The code you typed comments out the statement that defines the rectangle:

```
// CRect MyRectangle (20,
//                     10,
//                     120,
//                     110);
```

New coordinates are defined for the rectangle that will enclose the circle:

```
CRect MyRectangle (20,
                    10,
                    20+m_Radius*2,
                    10+m_Radius*2);
```

The lower-right corner of the rectangle is at 20 + m_Radius * 2 pixels to the right of the window's left edge and 10 + m_Radius * 2 pixels below the top of the window.

Recall that the OnTimer() function changes the value of m_Radius. For example, when m_Radius is equal to 50, the lower-right corner of the rectangle is 20+50*2=120 pixels to the right of the window's left edge and 10+50*2=110 pixels below the window's top edge. Then OnTimer() changes the value of m_Radius to 51, which makes the lower-right corner of the rectangle enclosing the circle 20+51*2=122 pixels to the right of the window's left edge and 10+51*2=112 pixels below the window's top edge. In other words, the circle will be drawn with a different radius every time the OnTimer() function is executed.

Modifying the Installation Setting of the Timer

You'll now change the timer's setting. When you installed the timer, you set the second parameter of the SetTimer() function to 500, which means that the OnTimer() function is executed every 500 milliseconds. To see "fast action" in the Graph program, set the second parameter of SetTimer() to 50 to execute the OnTimer() function every 50 milliseconds:

☐ In the Message Maps tab of the ClassWizard window, select the following event:

Class name:	CGraphDlg
Object ID:	CGraphDlg
Message:	WM_INITDIALOG

☐ Click the Edit Code button of ClassWizard.

Visual C++ responds by opening the file GraphDlg.cpp with the function OnInitDialog() ready for you to edit.

☐ Modify the code in the OnInitDialog() function as follows:

```
BOOL CGraphDlg::OnInitDialog()
{
...
```

7

```
...
// TODO: Add extra initialization here

////////////////////////
// MY CODE STARTS HERE
////////////////////////

// Install a system timer.
int iInstallResult;

iInstallResult = SetTimer(1,
                          50,
                          NULL);

if (iInstallResult == 0 )
{

MessageBox ("cannot install timer!");

}


// Select the Red radio button
m_dlg.m_RedRadio = 0;


m_Radius = 50;
m_Direction = 1;

////////////////////////
// MY CODE ENDS HERE
////////////////////////

return TRUE;
// return TRUE  unless you set the focus to a control
}
```

As you can see, now the second parameter of SetTimer() is 50:

```
iInstallResult = SetTimer(1,
                          50,
                          NULL);
```

☐ Select Save All from the File menu.

☐ Compile, link, and execute the Graph program.

Notice that the radius of the circle changes every 50 milliseconds.

Flickering? Avoid Flickering with WinG

No matter how fast your PC is, chances are that while the circle is being redrawn every 50 milliseconds, you'll see annoying flickering on your screen. Why? Because Windows was not

designed to perform operations like fast drawing. Windows is sometimes referred to as a *graphical operating system,* but *graphical* means that this operating system was designed to draw static, not dynamic, graphic objects. For example, a pushbutton is used in almost every Windows program. When you click the button, it's displayed in its pushed-down position, but this is the limit of the graphical aspect of Windows. When it comes to drawing fast graphics in Windows, you'll find it's very slow—in fact, much slower than DOS. DOS is faster when it comes to drawing graphics because it enables the user to directly access the memory cells corresponding to the monitor. In DOS, changing a memory cell that corresponds to a pixel onscreen almost immediately changes the onscreen pixel.

In Windows, on the other hand, the programmer doesn't have direct access to the memory cells corresponding to the onscreen pixels. Once you issue statements from within your program to change pixels onscreen (as you did in the Graph program when you drew the circle), Windows processes the statements through many layers of software; eventually, the onscreen pixels are changed. However, this process takes a long time and results in the annoying flickering you see onscreen.

Is there a solution to the flickering? Sure there is! Microsoft realized the drawing limitations of Windows, so it released the WinG library to help you develop fast graphics operations with Windows. When you're using WinG, you won't notice any flickering on your screen, and you'll be able to perform fast graphics operations in Windows. The subject of WinG is beyond the scope of this book, but applying WinG technology is actually very easy. It's not much different from the code you used in this chapter when you created the Graph program. The easiest way to apply WinG is to use a WinG OLE control. The TegoSoft WinG OLE control lets you perform very fast operations from within your Visual C++ programs (see disk offer at the end of this book).

Drawing Circles with Different Colors

The Graph program currently draws the circles with a red pen, but the IDD_CUSTOM_DIALOG dialog box was designed so that you can select different colors for the pen that draws the circles. Once you select a radio button, the m_RedRadio variable changes accordingly (m_RedRadio=0 for red, m_RedRadio=1 for green, and m_RedRadio=2 for blue). To change colors according to the value of m_RedRadio, you have to modify the code in the OnPaint() function (in the GraphDlg.cpp file).

Exercise 1 at the end of this chapter instructs you to modify the OnPaint() program so that the circles will be drawn according to the selected color.

Summary

This chapter has shown how drawing programs are created. You have learned about the WM_PAINT event and how to attach drawing code to the OnPaint() function. Various drawing functions have been used in this chapter—Ellipse(), CreatePen(), SelectObject(), and so on. You have also learned how to install a timer and attach code to the WM_TIMER event, which is executed periodically.

This chapter also discusses the powerful WinG technology that enables you to design fast graphics programs in Windows.

Q&A

Q **I'm confused! I created the new pen as follows:**

```
CClientDC dc(this);
CPen MyNewPen;
MyNewPen.CreatePen (PS_SOLID,
                    10,
                    RGB(255,0,0) );
```

Then I selected it with these statements:

```
CPen*  pOriginalPen;
pOriginalPen = dc.SelectObject(&MyNewPen);
```

But when I selected the original pen, I used SelectObject() as follows:

```
dc.SelectObject(pOriginalPen);
```

Why not use &OriginalPen?

A When you created the new pen, you used the following statement, which created an object of class CPen:

```
CPen MyNewPen;
```

You then selected the new pen as follows:

```
pOriginalPen = dc.SelectObject(&MyNewPen);
```

The parameter of SelectObject() is &MyNewPen because SelectObject() expects the address of the new pen as its parameter. The returned value of SelectObject() is the address of the original pen. This is why you declare pOriginalPen as a pointer to CPen:

```
CPen*  pOriginalPen;
```

When you execute SelectObject() as follows, the returned value of SelectObject() (which is a pointer to CPen) matches pOriginalPen:

```
pOriginalPen = dc.SelectObject(&MyNewPen);
```

Finally, when you return the original pen as follows, you supply pOriginalPen as the parameter of SelectObject() because SelectObject() expects the address of the pen as its parameter:

```
dc.SelectObject(pOriginalPen);
```

Q I drew the ellipse with the following statements, but the result is a circle, not an ellipse. Why?

```
// Draw the circle
dc.Ellipse (&MyRectangle);
```

A Before executing the Ellipse() function, you declared MyRectangle as follows:

```
CRect MyRectangle (20,
                   10,
                   120,
                   110);
```

The rectangle is a square with each side being 100 pixels long, so the ellipse enclosed by this rectangle must be a circle. A circle is a special case of an ellipse.

Q Before adding the code in the OnPaint() function, the Graph program did not repaint the window when needed, as shown in Figure 7.8. But guess what? I dragged the Graph window just a little bit on the screen (without hiding any part of the circle), and Windows repainted it. So it looks to me as though Windows does repaint the window sometimes.

A Good observation. When Windows can take care of the required repainting, it does it automatically for you.

Quiz

1. Why is Windows referred to as a *graphical operating system*?

2. WinG is a technology that enables you to _____.

Exercises

1. Modify the OnPaint() function (in the GraphDlg.cpp file) so that the circles of the Graph program will be drawn in the selected color.

2. After finishing Exercise 1, you will have to perform the following steps to change the circle's color:

☐ Click the Draw Graphics button.

☐ Select a color from the IDD_CUSTOM_DIALOG dialog box.

☐ Click the OK button of the IDD_CUSTOM_DIALOG dialog box to draw the circle in the selected color.

Add code so that the program immediately draws the circle with the selected color (without clicking the OK button) once you choose it from the IDD_CUSTOM_DIALOG dialog box.

Quiz Answers

1. Windows is also called a graphical operating system because it uses static graphical controls such as pushbuttons, radio buttons, scrollbars, and so on.

2. WinG enables you to develop fast drawing graphics in Windows.

Exercise Answers

1. Follow these steps to modify the Graph program so that the circles will be drawn in the selected color:

☐ Modify the OnPaint() function (in the GraphDlg.cpp file) as follows:

```
void CGraphDlg::OnPaint()
{
    if (IsIconic())
     {
       …
       …
       …
     else
     {

/////////////////////////
// MY CODE STARTS HERE
/////////////////////////

//// MessageBeep((WORD)-1);

//// OnDrawgraphicsButton();


// Create a DC object
CPaintDC dc(this);

// Create a new pen
CPen MyNewPen;

//MyNewPen.CreatePen (PS_SOLID,
//                    10,
//                    RGB(255,0,0) );

switch (m_dlg.m_RedRadio)
{
case 0:
MyNewPen.CreatePen (PS_SOLID,
                    10,
```

SAMS
Sams
Learning
Center
SAMS
PUBLISHING

```
                        RGB(255,0,0) );
break;

case 1:
MyNewPen.CreatePen (PS_SOLID,
                    10,
                    RGB(0,255,0) );
break;

case 2:
MyNewPen.CreatePen (PS_SOLID,
                    10,
                    RGB(0,0,255) );
break;
}


// Select the new pen.
CPen*  pOriginalPen;
pOriginalPen = dc.SelectObject(&MyNewPen);


// CRect MyRectangle (20,
//                    10,
//                    120,
//                    110);


CRect MyRectangle (20,
                   10,
                   20+m_Radius*2,
                   10+m_Radius*2);


dc.Ellipse (&MyRectangle);

// Return the original pen
dc.SelectObject(pOriginalPen);


/////////////////////////
// MY CODE ENDS HERE
/////////////////////////
...
...
...
}
```

A switch is created that examines the value of m_RedRadio; accordingly, the pen is created with the proper color:

```
switch (m_dlg.m_RedRadio)
{
case 0:
MyNewPen.CreatePen (PS_SOLID,
                    10,
                    RGB(255,0,0) );
```

7

```
break;

case 1:
MyNewPen.CreatePen (PS_SOLID,
                    10,
                    RGB(0,255,0) );
break;

case 2:
MyNewPen.CreatePen (PS_SOLID,
                    10,
                    RGB(0,0,255) );
break;
}
```

Note that the `m_RedRadio` variable is referred to in the `OnPaint()` function as follows:

```
switch (m_dlg.m_RedRadio)
{

}
```

The `m_dlg` object is a data member of the `CGraphDlg` class, so it's accessible from within the member functions of the `CGraphDlg` class. `m_RedRadio` is a member variable of `m_dlg`, so from within the `OnPaint()` function, you refer to this variable as

`m_dlg.m_RedRadio`.

☐ Compile, link, and execute the Graph program.

☐ Click the Draw Graphics button, select a color from the IDD_CUSTOM_DIALOG dialog box, and notice that the circle is drawn in the selected color.

Again, flickering occurs! To avoid flickering, use WinG technology.

2. To modify the Graph program again so that the circle is drawn in the selected color without clicking IDD_CUSTOM_DIALOG's OK button, follow these steps:

☐ Use ClassWizard to attach code to the BN_CLICKED event of the IDC_RED_RADIO radio button.

☐ Name the function OnRedRadio().

☐ Edit the code of the OnRedRadio() function in the SetDlg.cpp file as follows:

```
void CSetDlg::OnRedRadio()
{
// TODO: Add your control notification handler code here

//////////////////////////
// MY CODE STARTS HERE
//////////////////////////

UpdateData(TRUE);
```

```
/////////////////////////
// MY CODE ENDS HERE
/////////////////////////

}
```

As soon as you select the Red radio button, the m_RedRadio variable is updated, and the circle is drawn with a red pen.

Now you need to attach code to the BN_CLICKED event of the other radio buttons in a similar manner. Here is the code for the other radio buttons:

```
void CSetDlg::OnBlueRadio()
{
// TODO: Add your control notification handler code here

/////////////////////////
// MY CODE STARTS HERE
/////////////////////////

UpdateData(TRUE);

/////////////////////////
// MY CODE ENDS HERE
/////////////////////////

}

void CSetDlg::OnGreenRadio()
{
// TODO: Add your control notification handler code here

/////////////////////////
// MY CODE STARTS HERE
/////////////////////////

UpdateData(TRUE);

/////////////////////////
// MY CODE ENDS HERE
/////////////////////////

}
```

Once you click any radio button, the circle will be drawn in the selected color, without needing to click the OK button first.

7

On the first day of Week 2, you'll learn how to display bitmaps from within your Visual C++ programs.

On the second day, you'll learn how to create programs that use different fonts and font sizes.

On the third day, you'll learn how to load and display BMP files during runtime. While you're creating today's program, you'll also learn how to display the common Open dialog box, a standard dialog box used for selecting a file from the hard drive.

On the fourth day, you'll learn what a single-document interface (SDI) application is and how to create one with Visual C++.

On the fifth day, you'll learn how to write a Visual C++ program that performs background tasks.

On the sixth day, you'll learn what a multiple-document interface (MDI) application is and how to create one with Visual C++.

On the seventh day, you'll learn how to write code that writes and reads data to and from files by using serialization.

Displaying Bitmaps

In this chapter, you'll learn how to display bitmaps from within your Visual C++ programs.

The MyBMP Program

The MyBMP program demonstrates how you can display bitmap files from within your Visual C++ programs. Before creating the MyBMP program, review its specifications.

- When you start the MyBMP program, the window shown in Figure 8.1 appears. As you can see, a BMP picture is displayed in the window.

Figure 8.1.
The window of the MyBMP program.

- You can now resize the window of the MyBMP program, and the BMP picture displayed in the window is resized accordingly. Figure 8.2 shows the window of the MyBMP program at a smaller size.

Figure 8.2.
The BMP picture is resized as you shrink the MyBMP window.

Now that you know what the MyBMP program is supposed to do, you can start creating the project.

Creating the Project of the MyBMP Program

To create the project of the MyBMP program, follow these steps:

☐ Create the C:\TYVCProg\Programs\CH08 directory, start Visual C++, and select New from the File menu to open the New dialog box.

☐ Select Project Workspace from the New dialog box and click the OK button.

☐ In the New Project Workspace dialog box, enter MyBMP in the Name box.

☐ Click the Browse button, select the C:\TYVCProg\Programs\CH08 directory, and click the Create button.

Visual C++ responds by displaying the MFC AppWizard Step 1 window.

☐ Set the Step 1 window to create a dialog-based application, then click the Next button.

☐ In the Step 2 window, use the default settings and enter the title MyBMP, then click the Next button.

☐ In the Step 3 window, use the default settings and click the Next button.

☐ In the Step 4 window, use the default settings, then click the Finish button.

Visual C++ responds by displaying the New Project Information window.

☐ Click the OK button of the New Project Information window.

Visual C++ responds by creating the project of the MyBMP program and all its associated files.

☐ Select Set Default Configuration from the Build menu, select MyBMP - Win32 Release from the Project Default Configuration dialog box, then click the OK button.

That's it—you're ready to start creating the program.

The Visual Design of MyBMP's Main Window

You'll now visually design the main window of the MyBMP program:

☐ In the Project Workspace, click the ResourceView tab and expand the MyBMP resources item, then the Dialog item. Finally, double-click the IDD_MYBMP_DIALOG item.

Visual C++ responds by displaying the IDD_MYBMP_DIALOG dialog box in design mode. IDD_MYBMP_DIALOG serves as the main window of the MyBMP program.

☐ Design the IDD_MYBMP_DIALOG dialog box according to Table 8.1.

Table 8.1. The properties table of the IDD_MYBMP_DIALOG dialog box.

Object	Property	Setting
Dialog Box	**ID**	**IDD_MYBMP_DIALOG**
	Caption	The MyBMP Program
	Font	System, Size 10
	Border	Resizing (Styles tab)

Note: In Table 8.1, you set the Border property of the dialog box to Resizing in the Styles tab, which enables you to enlarge or shrink the area of the MyBMP window by dragging its edges during runtime.

The Visual Design of the Menu

You'll now visually design the menu of the MyBMP program:

☐ In the Project Workspace, select the ResourceView tab and right-click the MyBMP resources item.

Visual C++ responds by displaying a pop-up menu.

☐ Select Insert from the menu, then the Menu item from the Insert Resource dialog box that opens. Next, click Insert Resource's OK button.

Visual C++ responds by displaying an empty menu in design mode.

☐ Customize the menu so that the File menu has an Exit item and the Help menu has an About item. (See Figures 8.3 and 8.4.)

Figure 8.3.
The File menu of the MyBMP program.

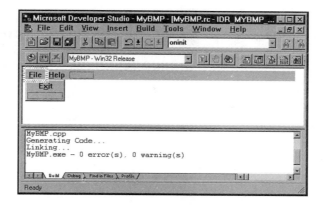

Figure 8.4.
The Help menu of the MyBMP program.

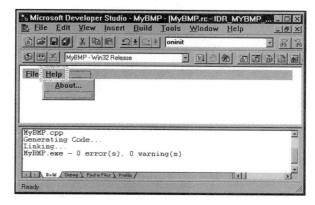

Visual C++ assigns IDR_MENU1 as the default ID for the new menu. Change the ID to IDR_MYBMP_MENU:

☐ Set the ID property of the menu to IDR_MYBMP_MENU by right-clicking IDR_MENU1 in the Project Workspace, selecting Properties, then setting the ID property in the Properties window that pops up.

Next, associate the menu with the CMyBMPDlg class. Here is how you do that:

☐ While the menu window is selected, select ClassWizard from the View menu.

Visual C++ responds by displaying the Adding a Class dialog box.

☐ Make sure the "Select an existing class" radio button is selected, then click the OK button.

Visual C++ responds by displaying the Select Class dialog box.

☐ Select the CMyBMPDlg item, then click the Select button.

Visual C++ responds by displaying the MFC ClassWizard dialog box.

☐ Click the OK button of the MFC ClassWizard dialog box.

Attaching the Menu to the Dialog Box

You'll now attach the IDR_MYBMP_MENU menu to the IDD_MYBMP_DIALOG dialog box:

☐ Double-click the IDD_MYBMP_DIALOG item in the Project Workspace window.

Visual C++ responds by displaying the IDD_MYBMP_DIALOG dialog box in design mode.

☐ Set the Menu property (in the General tab) of IDD_MYBMP_DIALOG to IDR_MYBMP_MENU. (See Figure 8.5.)

Figure 8.5.
Setting the Menu property to IDR_MYBMP_MENU.

Attaching Code to the Exit Menu Item

You'll now attach code to the COMMAND event of the Exit menu item:

☐ Highlight the IDR_MYBMP_MENU item in the Project Workspace window, then select ClassWizard from the View menu.

Visual C++ responds by displaying the MFC ClassWizard dialog box.

☐ Select ID_FILE_EXIT in the Object IDs list, select COMMAND in the Message list, then click the Add Function button.

Visual C++ responds by suggesting you name the new function OnFileExit.

☐ Accept OnFileExit as the name of the new function, then click the Edit Code button.

☐ Enter the following code in the OnFileExit() function (in the MyBMPDlg.cpp file):

```
void CMyBMPDlg::OnFileExit()
{
// TODO: Add your command handler code here
```

8

```
//////////////////////////
// MY CODE STARTS HERE
//////////////////////////

OnOK();

//////////////////////////
// MY CODE STARTS HERE
//////////////////////////

}
```

The code you typed is executed when you select Exit from the File menu; it terminates the MyBMP program.

☐ Select Save All from the File menu to save your work.

☐ Compile, link, and execute the MyBMP program to make sure it works as expected.

Displaying the About Dialog Box

You'll now add the code that's executed when you select the About item from the Help menu:

☐ Double-click the IDR_MYBMP_MENU item to display the menu in design mode.

☐ Select ClassWizard from the View menu.

☐ Select the ID_HELP_ABOUT item from the Object IDs list, select COMMAND from the Messages list, then click the Add Function button.

> *Visual C++ responds by suggesting you name the function* OnHelpAbout.

☐ Click the Edit Code button, then add the following code in the OnHelpAbout() function:

```
void CMyBMPDlg::OnHelpAbout()
{
// TODO: Add your command handler code here

//////////////////////////
// MY CODE STARTS HERE
//////////////////////////

CAboutDlg dlg;
dlg.DoModal();

//////////////////////////
// MY CODE ENDS HERE
//////////////////////////

}
```

☐ Save your work, then compile and link the program.

☐ Execute the program to make sure the About dialog box is displayed when you click the About item from the Help menu.

☐ Select Exit from the File menu to terminate the MyBMP program.

Inserting a BMP Picture in Your Project

You'll now draw the BMP picture:

☐ Execute the Paint program that comes with Windows 95 (usually in the Accessories folder).

☐ Select Attributes from Paint's Image menu.

Paint responds by displaying the Attributes dialog box.

☐ Set the Width box to 250 pixels and the Height box to 250 pixels. Finally, click the OK button of the Attributes dialog box.

Paint responds by displaying an empty area (250 pixels × 250 pixels) ready for you to paint. (See Figure 8.6.)

Figure 8.6.
Ready to paint with Paint.

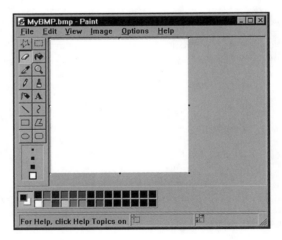

☐ Draw something with Paint. Figure 8.7 shows how you can import clip art to enhance your program.

☐ Select Save As from Paint's File menu and save your drawing as a BMP file with the filename MyBMP.BMP in the C:\TYVCProg\Programs\CH08\MyBMP\Res directory.

☐ Terminate the Paint program.

Figure 8.7.
Importing clip art into Paint.

Now add the MyBMP.BMP file to the MyBMP project:

☐ In the Project Workspace, click the ResourceView tab and right-click the MyBMP resources item.

☐ Click the Import item from the pop-up menu that Visual C++ displays.

   Visual C++ responds by displaying the Import Resource dialog box.

☐ Select the C:\TYVCProg\Programs\CH08\MyBMP\Res\MyBMP.BMP file, then click the Import button.

   Visual C++ responds by adding the MyBMP.BMP picture to the project.

The ID that Visual C++ assigned to the new picture is IDB_BITMAP1. Change this ID to IDB_MYBMP:

☐ Right-click the IDB_BITMAP1 item in the Project Workspace window, then select Properties from the pop-up menu.

☐ Set the ID to IDB_MYBMP.

The Bitmap Properties window should now look like the one in Figure 8.8.

☐ Select Save All from the File menu to save your work.

☐ You can compile, link, and execute the MyBMP program to make sure everything is OK. Of course, you won't see your picture because you haven't added the code for displaying the MyBMP.BMP pictures.

Figure 8.8.
The Bitmap Properties window.

Accessing the *m_hInstance* Variable

Later in this chapter, you'll write code that displays the MyBMP.BMP picture. This code requires the m_hInstance variable. What is the m_hInstance variable? It contains the instance of the application. Whenever Windows executes an application, it generates a unique ID. This ID is associated with the application and stored in the m_hInstance variable.

The code you add later uses the m_hInstance variable as one of the parameters of a function you'll execute. However, the m_hInstance variable isn't "known" in the MyBMPDlg.cpp file, so how can you use it? You'll have to make m_hInstance accessible to MyBMPDlg.cpp by following these steps:

☐ In the Project Workspace, click the FileView tab and expand the MyBMP Files item. Finally, double-click the MyBMP.cpp item. (Make sure you double-click MyBMP.cpp, not MyBMPDlg.cpp.)

   Visual C++ responds by displaying the MyBMP.cpp file ready for you to edit.

☐ Scroll down through the file to find the InitInstance() function.

☐ Add the following code to the InitInstance() function:

```
BOOL CMyBMPApp::InitInstance()
{
// Standard initialization

...
...
...

CMyBMPDlg dlg;

/////////////////////////
// MY CODE STARTS HERE
/////////////////////////

dlg.m_hInstance = m_hInstance;
```

```
//////////////////////////
// MY CODE ENDS HERE
//////////////////////////

  ...
  ...
  ...
}
```

As you can see, Visual C++ has already written the code that creates an object called dlg of class CMyBMPDlg:

```
CMyBMPDlg dlg;
```

The preceding statement creates the dlg dialog box, which is the IDD_MYBMP_DIALOG dialog box.

The code you typed sets the m_hInstance data member of the dlg object to m_hInstance:

```
dlg.m_hInstance = m_hInstance;
```

In other words, the CMyBMPApp class has a data member called m_hInstance that is updated with the instance of the application. In the preceding statement, you set the m_hInstance data member of dlg to the value of m_hInstance of the CMyBMPApp class. However, the dlg object doesn't have a data member called m_hInstance yet, so now you'll add the m_hInstance data member to the CMyBMPDlg class:

☐ Select Save All from the File menu to save your work.

☐ In the Project Workspace, click the FileView tab, expand the Dependencies item, and double-click the MyBMPDlg.h item.

Visual C++ responds by displaying the MyBMPDlg.h file ready for you to edit.

☐ Add the m_hInstance data member to the class declaration:

```
/////////////////////////////////////////////////////
// CMyBMPDlg dialog

class CMyBMPDlg : public CDialog
{
// Construction
public:
CMyBMPDlg(CWnd* pParent = NULL);
// standard constructor


//////////////////////////////
// MY CODE STARTS HERE
//////////////////////////////

HINSTANCE m_hInstance;
```

```
/////////////////////////////
// MY CODE ENDS HERE
/////////////////////////////

...
...
...
};
```

The code you typed declares a data member called m_hInstance of type HINSTANCE in the CMyBMPDlg class.

Displaying the Bitmap Picture

You'll now write code that displays the bitmap:

☐ In the Message Maps tab of the ClassWizard window, select the following event:

Class name: CMyBMPDlg
Object ID: CMyBMPDlg
Message: WM_PAINT

☐ Click the Edit Code button of ClassWizard.

Visual C++ responds by opening the file MyBMPDlg.cpp with the function OnPaint() ready for you to edit.

☐ Write the following code in the OnPaint() function:

```
void CMyBMPDlg::OnPaint()
{
  if (IsIconic())
    {
...
...
...
    }
    else
    {

///////////////////////
// MY CODE STARTS HERE
///////////////////////

CPaintDC dc(this);

HBITMAP hbitmap =
   ::LoadBitmap( m_hInstance,
                 MAKEINTRESOURCE(IDB_BITMAP1) );

// Create a memory DC
HDC hMemDC = ::CreateCompatibleDC(NULL);
```

```
// Select the bitmap in the memory dc.
SelectObject(hMemDC,hbitmap);


// Copy the memory dc into the screen dc
::StretchBlt(dc.m_hDC,    //destination
             50,
             50,
             100,
             100,
             hMemDC,    // Source
             0,
             0,
             250,
             250,
             SRCCOPY);

// Delete the memory DC and the bitmap
::DeleteDC(hMemDC);
::DeleteObject(hbitmap);


//////////////////////
// MY CODE ENDS HERE
//////////////////////

CDialog::OnPaint();
    }
}
```

The code you typed creates a device context (dc):

```
CPaintDC dc(this);
```

Then a variable of type HBITMAP is created:

```
HBITMAP hbitmap;
```

The hbitmap variable is assigned the returned value of the LoadBitmap() function:

```
hbitmap =
    ::LoadBitmap( m_hInstance,
                  MAKEINTRESOURCE(IDB_MYBMP) );
```

The preceding statement supplies the m_hInstance data member of the CMyBMPDlg class as the first parameter of the LoadBitmap() function. This is the second parameter:

```
MAKEINTRESOURCE(IDB_MYBMP)
```

During the visual design of the project, you set MyBMP.BMP's ID to IDB_MYBMP. MAKEINTRESOURCE() is a macro that converts IDB_MYBMP to a value as required by the second parameter of LoadBitmap(). Therefore, the LoadBitmap() function loads the picture of MyBMP.BMP.

Note: The contents of the MyBMP.BMP file are stored in the MyBMP.rc file. After you compile and link the MyBMP program, its contents become an integral part of the MyBMP.EXE program file, so the `LoadBitmap()` function "loads" the BMP picture from the MyBMP.EXE file.

Note: In this chapter, you're creating a program that has the BMP file embedded in the EXE program, so you have to incorporate the BMP file into the projects during design time. This technique does not let the user select an arbitrary BMP file from the hard drive. In Chapter 10, "Loading and Displaying Picture Files," you'll learn how to create a program that uses a different technique for loading and displaying BMP files, one that lets the user load and display any BMP file.

Next, you created a memory device context as follows:

```
HDC hMemDC = ::CreateCompatibleDC(NULL);
```

What is a *memory device context?* It is a section in memory that's an exact replica of your screen. In Windows you can't display bitmaps directly in the screen; you have to place them in a memory device context (dc). When everything is ready to be displayed, you transfer the contents of the memory dc to the screen dc.

The :: operator is used in the preceding statement because the Windows `CreateCompatibleDC()` SDK function is used. You're indicating to the compiler that you want to use the SDK function (not a member function of the `CMyBMPDlg` class).

Now that the `hMemDC` has been created, you can select the bitmap into the memory dc (in plain English, it means "place the BMP picture in the memory device context"):

```
SelectObject(hMemDC,hbitmap);
```

Now that everything is ready, you can transfer the contents of the memory dc into the screen as follows:

```
// Copy the memory dc into the screen dc
::StretchBlt(dc.m_hDC,   //destination
             50,
             50,
             100,
             100,
             hMemDC,  //Source
             0,
             0,
```

```
250,
250,
SRCCOPY);
```

The first parameter of the SDK function `StretchBlt()` is `dc.m_hDC`, which is the device context of the destination—the screen. The second and third parameters are the x- and y-coordinates in the IDD_MYBMP_DIALOG dialog box where the upper-left corner of the BMP picture will be displayed.

The fourth and fifth parameters of the `StretchBlt()` function are the width and height of the area where the BMP picture will be displayed. During the visual design, you set the width and height of the picture to 250 pixels for each. Now you've specified that the BMP picture should be enclosed in a rectangle with its upper-left corner at coordinates 50,50. Furthermore, you specified that the width and height of the rectangle holding the BMP picture should be 100 pixels wide and 100 pixels high. This means that the `StretchBlt()` function will have to shrink the original large BMP picture to fit in the smaller rectangle.

The sixth parameter in the preceding statement is `hMemDC`, which specifies the source `dc`. The seventh and eighth parameters of `StretchBlt()` indicate the upper-left corner of the rectangle at coordinates 0,0 in the source picture; the ninth and tenth parameters indicate the width and height of the rectangle. This rectangle defines the area in the source BMP picture that will be transferred to the destination. The values you supplied mean that the entire BMP picture will be transferred.

The last parameter specifies the operation you want to be performed by the `StretchBlt()` function. You specified `SRCCOPY` to copy the picture from the memory `dc` to the screen `dc` in the IDD_MYBMP_DIALOG dialog box.

The last two statements added in the `OnPaint()` function delete the memory `dc` and screen `dc` you created:

```
// Delete the memory DC and the bitmap
::DeleteDC(hMemDC);
::DeleteObject(hbitmap);
```

☐ Select Save All from the File menu to save your work.

☐ Compile, link, and execute the MyBMP program to see your code in action.

The window of the MyBMP program should display the MyBMP.BMP picture as specified by the parameters of the `StretchBlt()` function. (See Figure 8.9.)

☐ Select Exit from the File menu to terminate the MyBMP program.

Figure 8.9.
The window of the MyBMP program.

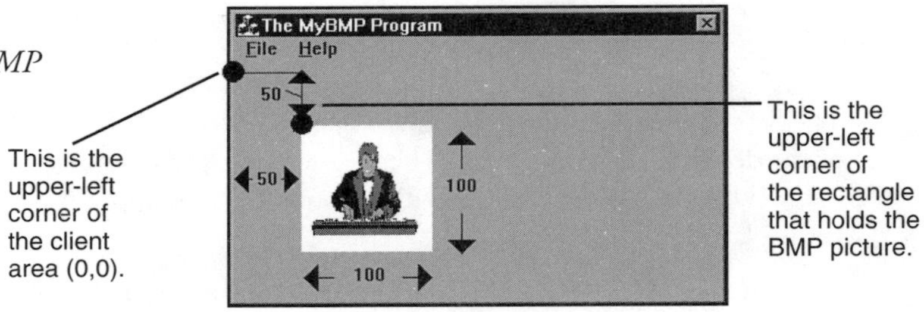

The MyBMP Program
File Help
50
50
100
100
This is the upper-left corner of the client area (0,0).
This is the upper-left corner of the rectangle that holds the BMP picture.

Enlarging the BMP Picture

In the previous section, you shrank the picture from 250 pixels × 250 pixels to 100 pixels × 100 pixels. For practice, try enlarging the BMP picture:

☐ Modify the parameters of the `StretchBlt()` function in the `OnPaint()` function:

```
::StretchBlt(dc.m_hDC,    //destination
             50,
             50,
             300,
             300,
             hMemDC,  // Source
             0,
             0,
             250,
             250,
             SRCCOPY);
```

As you can see, the width and height of the destination picture is now 300 pixels × 300 pixels.

☐ Compile, link, and execute the MyBMP program.

The MyBMP.BMP picture is so large now that it can't fit in the MyBMP window. (See Figure 8.10.)

Figure 8.10.
Enlarging the MyBMP.BMP picture.

The MyBMP Program
File Help

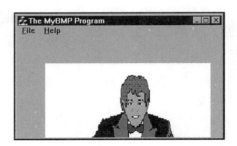

☐ Size the window of the MyBMP program so that it's large enough to contain the picture. The result is shown in Figure 8.11.

Figure 8.11.
*After enlarging the window
of the MyBMP program.*

☐ Select Exit from MyBMP's File menu to terminate the program.

Adding Two Data Member Variables to the *CMyBMPDlg* Class

You'll now add two data members to the CMyBMPDlg class:

☐ In the Project Workspace, click the FileView tab and expand the MyBMP Files item,
then the Dependencies item. Finally, double-click the MyBMPDlg.h item to display that
file.

☐ Add the m_Width and m_Height data members to the CMyBMPDlg class (in the
MyBMPDlg.h file). After adding these data members, the constructor function of the
CMyBMPDlg class should look like the following:

```
class CMyBMPDlg : public CDialog
{
// Construction
public:
CMyBMPDlg(CWnd* pParent = NULL);   // standard constructor


/////////////////////////////
// MY CODE STARTS HERE
/////////////////////////////

HINSTANCE m_hInstance;
int m_Width;
int m_Height;
```

245

```
/////////////////////////////
// MY CODE ENDS HERE
/////////////////////////////

...
...
...
};
```

Why did you add the m_Width and m_Height data members? Because you want to update these data members with the width and height of the IDD_MYBMP_DIALOG dialog box, and you want every member function of the CMyBMPDlg class to be able to access these variables.

Extracting the Width and Height of the Window

You declared the m_Width and m_Height data members in the previous section; now you'll update them with the width and height of the IDD_MYBMP_DIALOG dialog box:

☐ In the Message Maps tab of ClassWizard, select the following event:

Class name:	CMyBMPDlg
Object ID:	CMyBMPDlg
Message:	WM_SIZE

☐ Click the Edit Code button of ClassWizard.

Visual C++ responds by opening the file MyBMPDlg.cpp with the function OnSize() *ready for you to edit.*

☐ Write the following code in the OnSize() function:

```
void CMyBMPDlg::OnSize(UINT nType, int cx, int cy)
{
CDialog::OnSize(nType, cx, cy);

// TODO: Add your message handler code here

/////////////////////////
// MY CODE STARTS HERE
/////////////////////////

m_Width = cx;
m_Height = cy;

Invalidate();

/////////////////////////
// MY CODE ENDS HERE
/////////////////////////

}
```

This `OnSize()` function is automatically executed whenever the size of the IDD_MYBMP_DIALOG dialog box changes, such as when you drag the edges of the MyBMP window. The `OnSize()` function is also executed when you display the IDD_MYBMP_DIALOG dialog for the first time.

The second and third parameters of the `OnSize()` function are cx, the new width of the window, and cy, the new height of the window. Therefore, `m_Width` and `m_Height` are updated with values representing the width and height of the IDD_MYBMP_DIALOG window.

The `Invalidate()` function is executed to force the execution of the `OnPaint()` function:

```
Invalidate();
```

Resizing the BMP Picture

You'll now change the size of the BMP picture to the exact size of the client area of the IDD_MYBMP_DIALOG dialog box. (The *client area* is the window area available for displaying a picture.)

☐ Modify the `OnPaint()` function (in the MyBMPDlg.cpp file) as follows:

```
void CMyBMPDlg::OnPaint()
{
    if (IsIconic())
        {
...
...
...
        }
        else
        {

/////////////////////////
// MY CODE STARTS HERE
/////////////////////////

CPaintDC dc(this);

HBITMAP hbitmap;

hbitmap =
    ::LoadBitmap( m_hInstance,
                  MAKEINTRESOURCE(IDB_MYBMP) );

// Create a new memory DC
HDC hMemDC = ::CreateCompatibleDC(NULL);

SelectObject(hMemDC,hbitmap);
```

```
// Copy the memory dc into the screen dc
::StretchBlt(dc.m_hDC,     //destination
            0,
            0,
            m_Width,
            m_Height,
            hMemDC,  // Source
            0,
            0,
            250,
            250,
            SRCCOPY);

// Delete the memory DC and the bitmap
::DeleteDC(hMemDC);
::DeleteObject(hbitmap);


/////////////////////////
// MY CODE ENDS HERE
/////////////////////////

    CDialog::OnPaint();
    }
}
```

In the preceding code, you modified the parameters of the StretchBlt() function:

```
::StretchBlt(dc.m_hDC,     //destination
            0,
            0,
            m_Width,
            m_Height,
            hMemDC,  // Source
            0,
            0,
            250,
            250,
            SRCCOPY);
```

Now the fourth and fifth parameters of the StretchBlt() function are m_Width and m_Height. This means that the BMP picture will be stretched to fit the entire client area of the IDD_MYBMP_DIALOG dialog box.

☐ Select Save All from the File menu to save your work.

☐ Compile, link, and execute the MyBMP program so you can experiment by dragging the window's edges. Notice that as you change the size of the MyBMP's window, the picture shrinks or enlarges to fit the entire size of the dialog box. (See Figures 8.12 and 8.13.)

Figure 8.12.
A smaller window results in a smaller picture.

Figure 8.13.
A larger window results in a larger picture.

Summary

In this chapter, you have learned how to display BMP pictures and stretch them to any size you want. When you create the MyBMP program, you extract the m_hInstance variable of the application so you can use it from within the MyBMPDlg.cpp file.

Q&A

Q Suppose I want to distribute the MyBMP.EXE program. Should I include the MyBMP.BMP file with the distribution disk?

A No. The MyBMP.BMP file is an integral part of the MyBMP.EXE file.

Q Where can I learn to design programs that let the user load and display any BMP file?

A The technique described in Chapter 10 lets the user load and display any BMP file from the hard drive.

Q The code I typed in the OnSize() function of the MyBMP program uses the cx and cy parameters of the OnSize() function. I noticed that the OnSize() function also has the nType parameter as its first parameter. What is this parameter used for?

A The `nType` parameter specifies that the window was resized in some way. For example, if `nType` is equal to `SIZE_MAXIMIZED`, it means the window was maximized. The following `if` statement can be used to detect whether the window was maximized:

```
if ( nType == SIZE_MAXIMIZED )
{

// Write code here that is executed whenever the
// window is maximized.
…
…
…

}
```

Similarly, you can detect whether the window was minimized by using the following `if` statement:

```
if ( nType == SIZE_MIMIMIZED )
{

// Write here code that is executed whenever the
// window was maximized.
…
…
…

}
```

Quiz

1. What do the `cx` and `cy` parameters of the `OnSize()` function specify?
2. The `StretchBlt()` function does which of the following?
   a. There is no such function.
   b. Stretches the window as specified in the function's parameters.
   c. Stretches the picture as specified in the function's parameters.

Exercise

Modify the MyBMP program so that the PC beeps when the user maximizes the window of the MyBMP program.

Quiz Answers

1. The `cx` and `cy` parameters of the `OnSize()` function specify the new size of the window.
2. c.

Exercise Answer

Use these steps to modify the MyBMP program:

☐ Display the IDD_MYBMP_DIALOG dialog box in design mode.

☐ Check the Maximize check box.

☐ Check the Minimize check box.

Figure 8.14 shows the Properties dialog box with its Styles tab displayed. As you can see, the Maximize and Minimize check boxes are checked.

Figure 8.14.

Selecting the Maximize and Minimize check boxes for the IDD_MYBMP_DIALOG dialog box.

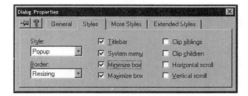

Now that you've checked the Maximize and Minimize check boxes, the MyBMP window will have maximize and minimize icons on its upper-right corner. Also, the program's system menu will include Maximize and Minimize menu items. (The user can display the system menu of the program by clicking the icon on the upper-left corner of the window.)

☐ Modify the OnSize() function (in the MyBMPDlg.cpp file) as follows:

```
void CMyBMPDlg::OnSize(UINT nType, int cx, int cy)
{
  CDialog::OnSize(nType, cx, cy);

// TODO: Add your message handler code here

//////////////////////////
// MY CODE STARTS HERE
//////////////////////////

if (nType == SIZE_MAXIMIZED)
{
MessageBeep((WORD)-1);
}

m_Width = cx;
m_Height = cy;

Invalidate();

//////////////////////////
// MY CODE ENDS HERE
//////////////////////////

}
```

The code you typed examines the value of nType:

```
if (nType == SIZE_MAXIMIZED)
{
MessageBeep((WORD)-1);
}
```

The code under the if statement is executed if the user maximizes the window. This code causes the PC to beep.

☐ Save your work, then compile and link the MyBMP program.

☐ Execute the MyBMP program and make sure the PC beeps when you maximize the MyBMP window.

9

Displaying Text in Different Fonts

In this chapter, you'll learn how to create programs that use different fonts and font sizes.

The MyFnt Program

The MyFnt program illustrates how you can create programs that use different fonts and different font sizes, but before creating it yourself, review its specifications:

- When you start the MyFnt program, the window shown in Figure 9.1 appears.

Figure 9.1.
The window of the MyFnt program.

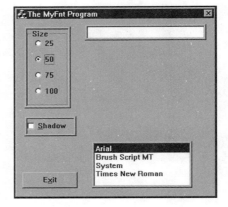

- You can then type text in the edit box. Whatever you type in the edit box appears in the window of the MyFnt program with the selected font, size, and shadowing style.

Figures 9.2 and 9.3 show some samples of text created with the MyFnt program.

Figure 9.2.
Sample text in Arial font.

Figure 9.3.
Sample text in Brush Script MT font.

9

Creating the Project of the MyFnt Program

To create the project of the MyFnt program, follow these steps:

☐ Create the C:\TYVCProg\Programs\CH09 directory, then select New from the File menu of Visual C++.

☐ In the New Project Workspace dialog box, select MFC AppWizard (exe) and enter MyFnt in the Name box.

☐ Click the Browse button, select the C:\TYVCProg\Programs\CH09 directory, and click the Create button.

Visual C++ responds by displaying the MFC AppWizard Step 1 window.

☐ Set the Step 1 window to create a dialog-based application, then click the Next button.

☐ In the Step 2 window, use the default settings and enter MyFnt as the dialog box title. When you're done, click the Next button.

☐ In the Step 3 window, accept the default settings and click the Next button.

☐ In the Step 4 window, notice that AppWizard has created the CMyFntApp and CMyFntDlg classes. Click the Finish button, then click the OK button of the New Project Information window.

Visual C++ responds by creating the project and all its associated files.

☐ Select Set Default Configuration from the Build menu and MyFnt - Win32 Release from the Default Project Configuration dialog box.

The Visual Design of the MyFnt Program

You'll now visually design the IDD_MYFNT_DIALOG dialog box that serves as the main window of the MyFnt program:

☐ In the Project Workspace, click the ResourceView tab, expand the MyFnt resources item, expand the Dialog item, and double-click the IDD_MYFNT_DIALOG dialog box.

> *Visual C++ responds by displaying the IDD_MYFNT_DIALOG dialog box in design mode.*

☐ Delete the OK button, Cancel button, and TODO text of the IDD_MYFNT_DIALOG dialog box.

☐ Design the IDD_MYFNT_DIALOG dialog box according to Table 9.1. When you finish, it should look like the one in Figure 9.4.

Table 9.1. The properties table of the IDD_MYFNT_DIALOG dialog box.

Object	Property	Setting
Dialog Box	ID	**IDD_MYFNT_DIALOG**
	Caption	The MyFnt Program
	Font	System, Size 10
Push Button	ID	**IDC_EXIT_BUTTON**
	Caption	E&xit
Edit Box	ID	**IDC_DATA_EDIT**
	Client edge	Checked (Extended Styles tab)
	Static edge	Checked (Extended Styles tab)
	Modal frame	Checked (Extended Styles tab)

Figure 9.4.
IDD_MYFNT_DIALOG in design mode.

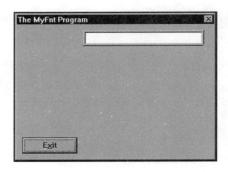

Attaching a Variable to the Edit Box

To attach a variable to the IDC_DATA_EDIT edit box control, follow these steps:

☐ In the Member Variables tab of ClassWizard, make the following selections:

Class name:	CMyFntDlg
Control ID:	IDC_DATA_EDIT

☐ Click the Add Variable button and set the variable as follows:

Variable name:	m_DataEdit
Category:	Value
Variable type:	CString

☐ Click the OK button, then click ClassWizard's OK button.

Attaching Code to the *BN_CLICKED* Event of the Exit Button

You'll now attach code to the BN_CLICKED event of the Exit button:

☐ In the Message Maps tab of ClassWizard, select the following event:

Class name:	CMyFntDlg
Object ID:	IDC_EXIT_BUTTON
Message:	BN_CLICKED

☐ Click the Add Function button, name the new function OnExitButton, and click the Edit Code button.

Visual C++ responds by opening the file MyFntDlg.cpp with the function OnExitButton() ready for you to edit.

☐ Write the following code in the OnExitButton() function:

```
void CMyFntDlg::OnExitButton()
{
// TODO: Add your control notification handler code here

/////////////////////////
// MY CODE STARTS HERE
/////////////////////////

OnOK();

/////////////////////////
// MY CODE ENDS HERE
/////////////////////////

}
```

The code you entered, which is executed when you click the Exit button, terminates the MyFnt program.

Attaching Code to the *EN_CHANGE* Event of the Edit Box

You'll now attach code to the EN_CHANGE event of the edit box, which occurs when you change the edit box's contents:

☐ In the Message Maps tab of the ClassWizard window, select the following event:

Class name:	CMyFntDlg
Object ID:	IDC_DATA_EDIT
Message:	EN_CHANGE

☐ Click the Add Function button, name the new function OnChangeDataEdit, and click the Edit Code button.

Visual C++ responds by opening the file MyFntDlg.cpp with the function OnChangeDataEdit() ready for you to edit.

☐ Write the following code in the OnChangeDataEdit() function:

```
void CMyFntDlg::OnChangeDataEdit()
{
// TODO: Add your control notification handler code here

/////////////////////////
// MY CODE STARTS HERE
/////////////////////////

Invalidate();


/////////////////////////
// MY CODE ENDS HERE
/////////////////////////

}
```

The following statement causes the WM_PAINT event to occur:

```
Invalidate();
```

When you change the contents of the edit box, the OnPaint() function is executed, which you'll verify in the following section.

Attaching Code to the *WM_PAINT* Event

You'll now attach code to the WM_PAINT event:

☐ In the Message Maps tab of ClassWizard, select the following event:

Class name:	CMyFntDlg
Object ID:	CMyFntDlg
Message:	WM_PAINT

☐ Click the Edit Code button of ClassWizard.

Visual C++ responds by opening the file MyFntDlg.cpp with the function OnPaint() *ready for you to edit.*

☐ Modify the following code in the OnPaint() function:

```
void CMyFntDlg::OnPaint()
{
    if (IsIconic())
        {
….
….
….
        }
    else
        {
////////////////////////
// MY CODE STARTS HERE
////////////////////////

MessageBeep((WORD)-1);

////////////////////////
// MY CODE ENDS HERE
////////////////////////

CDialog::OnPaint();
    }
}
```

The code you typed causes the PC to beep whenever you change the contents of the edit box.

☐ Select Save All from the File menu.

☐ Compile, link, and execute the MyFnt program to make sure the PC beeps whenever you change the contents of the edit box.

☐ Click the Exit button to terminate the program.

Displaying Text

The experiment in the previous section has proved that the OnPaint() function is executed when you change the contents of the edit box. Now try modifying the OnPaint() function to display the contents of the edit box:

☐ Modify the OnPaint() function (in the MyFntDlg.cpp file) as follows:

```cpp
void CMyFntDlg::OnPaint()
{
   if (IsIconic())
      {
…
…
…
      }
      else
      {
/////////////////////
// MY CODE STARTS HERE
/////////////////////

/// MessageBeep((WORD)-1);

CPaintDC dc(this); // device context for painting

// Update control's variables
UpdateData(TRUE);


// Create a font object
CFont MyFont;

MyFont.CreateFont (25,
                   0,
                   0,
                   0,
                   400,
                   FALSE,
                   FALSE,
                   0,
                   ANSI_CHARSET,
                   OUT_DEFAULT_PRECIS,
                   CLIP_DEFAULT_PRECIS,
                   DEFAULT_QUALITY,
                   DEFAULT_PITCH | FF_SWISS,
                   "Arial");


// Select the new font object
CFont* pOldFont = dc.SelectObject(&MyFont);


// Draw the text
dc.TextOut (100,
```

```
          120,
          m_DataEdit);

// Select the old font
dc.SelectObject(pOldFont);

/////////////////////////
// MY CODE ENDS HERE
/////////////////////////

CDialog::OnPaint();

}
```

The code you typed comments out the beeping:

```
/// MessageBeep((WORD)-1);
```

Then a device context (dc) is created:

```
CPaintDC dc(this); // device context for painting
```

The control variables are then updated:

```
UpdateData(TRUE);
```

In other words, the OnPaint() function is executed because you changed the contents of the edit box. Earlier, you attached the m_DataEdit variable to the edit box. Therefore, after executing the UpdateData() function with TRUE as its parameter, the m_DataEdit variable is updated with the new contents of the edit box.

You then created an object called MyFont of class CFont:

```
CFont MyFont;
```

The CreateFont() function sets its characteristics:

```
MyFont.CreateFont (25,
                   0,
                   0,
                   0,
                   400,
                   FALSE,
                   FALSE,
                   0,
                   ANSI_CHARSET,
                   OUT_DEFAULT_PRECIS,
                   CLIP_DEFAULT_PRECIS,
                   DEFAULT_QUALITY,
                   DEFAULT_PITCH | FF_SWISS,
                   "Arial");
```

There are 14 parameters to the CreateFont() function; they specify how to create the font.

> **Note:** One of the nice things about Visual C++ is its ability to give you instant help. No one expects you to remember the meaning of the 14 parameters of the `CreateFont()` function. You can immediately discover the meaning of each parameter by highlighting the text `CreateFont`, then pressing F1 on the keyboard.

You've created a font; now you apply this font by executing the `SelectObject()` function as follows:

```
// Select the new font object
CFont* pOldFont = dc.SelectObject(&MyFont);
```

Note that the returned value of the `SelectObject()` function is a pointer to the original font (the font replaced by the new `MyFont` object).

Now that the `m_DataEdit` variable is updated and the new `MyFont` is selected, you can finally draw the text:

```
// Draw the text
dc.TextOut (100,
            120,
            m_DataEdit);
```

The first and second parameters specify the location of the upper-left corner of the cell displaying the first character. The first character will be displayed 100 units to the right of the MyFnt window's left edge and 120 units below the window's top edge.

The third parameter of the `TextOut()` function is the string that will be displayed. You supplied `m_DataEdit` as the third parameter, so the contents of the edit box will be displayed.

The last statement you executed returns the original font:

```
// Select the old font
dc.SelectObject(pOldFont);
```

☐ Select Save All from the File menu.

☐ Compile, link, and execute the MyFnt program.

☐ Type something in the edit box.

The window of the MyFnt program displays the text you typed in the edit box, using the font you set in the `OnPaint()` function. (See Figure 9.5.)

☐ Experiment with the MyFnt program, then click its Exit button to terminate the program.

Figure 9.5.
Displaying the text in the edit box.

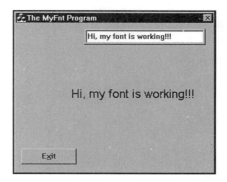

Changing the Font During Runtime

You can now add code that lets you change the font during runtime by changing the first parameter of the `CreateFont()` function in the `OnPaint()` function:

☐ In the Project Workspace, click the ResourceView tab and expand the MyFnt resources item, then the Dialog item. Finally, double-click the IDD_MYFNT_DIALOG item.

   Visual C++ responds by displaying the IDD_MYFNT_DIALOG dialog box in design mode.

☐ Place a group box in the IDD_MYFNT_DIALOG dialog box and set its properties as follows:

ID:	`IDC_SIZE_STATIC`
Caption:	`Size`
Client edge:	Checked (Extended Styles tab)
Static edge:	Checked (Extended Styles tab)
Modal frame:	Checked (Extended Styles tab)

☐ Place four radio buttons in the group box and set their properties according to Table 9.2. When you finish, the IDD_MYFNT_DIALOG dialog box should look like the one in Figure 9.6. Place the radio buttons one after the other so that their ID numbers will be in sequential order.

Table 9.2. The properties table for the four radio buttons.

Object	Property	Setting
Radio Button	**ID**	**IDC_25_RADIO**
	Caption	25
	Group	Checked (General tab)

continues

Table 9.2. continued

Object	Property	Setting
Radio Button	**ID**	**IDC_50_RADIO**
	Caption	50
	Group	Not Checked (General tab)
Radio Button	**ID**	**IDC_75_RADIO**
	Caption	75
	Group	Not Checked (General tab)
Radio Button	**ID**	**IDC_100_RADIO**
	Caption	100
	Group	Not Checked (General tab)

Figure 9.6.

The four radio buttons in design mode.

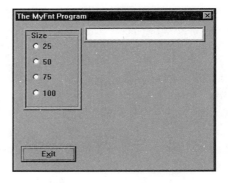

Note: Follow these steps to make sure the radio buttons' ID numbers are in sequential order:

☐ Select Resource Symbols from the View menu.

> *Visual C++ responds by displaying the Resource Symbol dialog box.*

☐ Browse through the IDs in the Resource Symbol dialog box and verify that the radio buttons' IDs have sequential numbers in the following order:

```
IDC_25_RADIO
IDC_50_RADIO
IDC_75_RADIO
IDC_100_RADIO
```

Attaching a Variable to the Radio Buttons

During the visual design of the radio buttons, you checked the Group property for the IDC_25_RADIO radio button, but not for the rest of the radio buttons. This means that the four radio buttons belong to the same group; therefore, a single variable is used to note the status of any of the radio buttons. Here is how you attach a variable to the four radio buttons:

☐ In the Member Variables tab of ClassWizard, make the following selections:

Class name:	CMyFntDlg
Control ID:	IDC_25_RADIO

☐ Click the Add Variable button and set the variable as follows:

Variable name:	m_SizeRadio
Category:	Value
Variable type:	int

☐ Click the OK button of the Add Member Variable dialog box, then click ClassWizard's OK button.

So when m_SizeRadio is equal to 0, the IDC_25_RADIO radio button is selected. When m_SizeRadio is equal to 1, the IDC_50_RADIO radio button is selected, and so on.

Initializing the Radio Buttons

If you compile, link, and execute the MyFnt program now, you'll realize that none of the radio buttons is selected when you start the program. To make the IDC_25_RADIO radio button the selected radio button when the program starts, you need to write code in the OnInitDialog() function as follows:

☐ In the Message Maps tab of ClassWizard, select the following event:

Class name:	CMyFntDlg
Object ID:	MyFntDlg
Message:	WM_INITDIALOG

☐ Click the Edit Code button of ClassWizard.

Visual C++ responds by opening the file MyFntDlg.cpp with the function OnInitDialog() ready for you to edit.

☐ Write the following code in the OnInitDialog() function:

```
BOOL CMyFntDlg::OnInitDialog()
{
...
...
...
```

```
/////////////////////////
// MY CODE STARTS HERE
/////////////////////////

m_SizeRadio = 0;
UpdateData(FALSE);

/////////////////////////
// MY CODE ENDS HERE
/////////////////////////

return TRUE;
// return TRUE   unless you set the focus to a control
}
```

The code you typed sets the m_SizeRadio variable to 0, then the UpdateData() function with FALSE as a parameter is executed:

```
UpdateData(FALSE);
```

This means that the IDC_25_RADIO radio button will be selected.

> **Note:** Previously, you typed code in the OnPaint() function (in the MyFntDlg.cpp file) that draws the text as follows:
>
> ```
> // Draw the text
> dc.TextOut (100,
>             120,
>             m_DataEdit);
> ```
>
> Text is displayed in imaginary rectangles. The preceding statement means that the first character will be drawn with the upper-left corner of its imaginary rectangle 100 units to the right of the window's left edge and 120 units below the window's top edge.
>
> Depending on the placement of the four radio buttons, you may have to start drawing the text a little bit more to the right. When the program executes, if you see that the first character is drawn in the area of the four radio buttons, then change the first parameter of TextOut(). For example, to draw the first character 150 units to the right of the left edge, use the following statement:
>
> ```
> // Draw the text
> dc.TextOut (150,
>             120,
>             m_DataEdit);
> ```

Changing the Font with the Size Radio Buttons

You'll now set the font according to the radio buttons' settings:

☐ Modify the OnPaint() function (in the MyFntDlg.cpp file) as follows:

```
void CMyFntDlg::OnPaint()
{
  if (IsIconic())
    {
…
…
…
    }
  else
    {
//////////////////////////
// MY CODE STARTS HERE
//////////////////////////

/// MessageBeep((WORD)-1);

CPaintDC dc(this); // device context for painting

// Update the variables of the controls
UpdateData(TRUE);


// Create a font object
CFont MyFont;

MyFont.CreateFont (25+25*m_SizeRadio,
                   0,
                   0,
                   0,
                   400,
                   FALSE,
                   FALSE,
                   0,
                   ANSI_CHARSET,
                   OUT_DEFAULT_PRECIS,
                   CLIP_DEFAULT_PRECIS,
                   DEFAULT_QUALITY,
                   DEFAULT_PITCH | FF_SWISS,
                   "Arial");


// Select the new font object
CFont* pOldFont = dc.SelectObject(&MyFont);



// Draw the text
dc.TextOut (150,
            120,
            m_DataEdit);
```

```
// Select the old font
dc.SelectObject(pOldFont);

//////////////////////////
// MY CODE ENDS HERE
//////////////////////////

CDialog::OnPaint();
        }
    }
```

You modified the first parameter of the `CreateFont()` function as follows:

```
MyFont.CreateFont (25+25*m_SizeRadio,
                   0,
                   0,
                   0,
                   400,
                   FALSE,
                   FALSE,
                   0,
                   ANSI_CHARSET,
                   OUT_DEFAULT_PRECIS,
                   CLIP_DEFAULT_PRECIS,
                   DEFAULT_QUALITY,
                   DEFAULT_PITCH | FF_SWISS,
                   "Arial");
```

If `m_SizeRadio` is equal to `0`, the first parameter of `CreateFont()` is 25+25*0=25. If `m_SizeRadio` is equal to 1, the first parameter is 25+25*1=50, and so on. Therefore, the first parameter of the `CreateFont()` function is set according to the selected radio button:

Selected Button	First Parameter of `CreateFont()`
IDC_25_RADIO	25
IDC_50_RADIO	50
IDC_75_RADIO	75
IDC_100_RADIO	100

Attaching Code to the *BN_CLICKED* Event of the Radio Buttons

You'll now attach code to the `BN_CLICKED` event of the IDC_25_RADIO radio button:

☐ In the Message Maps tab of ClassWizard, select the following event:

Class name:	CMyFntDlg
Object ID:	IDC_25_RADIO
Message:	BN_CLICKED

☐ Click the Add Function button, name the new function `On25Radio`, and click the Edit Code button.

Visual C++ responds by opening the file MyFntDlg.cpp with the function On25Radio() *ready for you to edit.*

☐ Write the following code in the On25Radio() function:

```
void CMyFntDlg::On25Radio()
{
// TODO: Add your control notification handler code here

/////////////////////////
// MY CODE STARTS HERE
/////////////////////////

Invalidate();

/////////////////////////
// MY CODE ENDS HERE
/////////////////////////

}
```

The code you typed executes the Invalidate() function:

```
Invalidate();
```

This means that when you click the IDC_25_RADIO radio button, the OnPaint() function is executed. For example, if the MyFnt program displays text with its font at size 75, after you click the IDC_25_RADIO radio button, the text will be displayed at size 25.

☐ Use ClassWizard again to attach code to the BN_CLICKED event of the IDC_50_RADIO radio button and name the function On50Radio. Edit the On50Radio() function (in the MyFntDlg.cpp file) as follows:

```
void CMyFntDlg::On50Radio()
{
// TODO: Add your control notification handler code here

/////////////////////////
// MY CODE STARTS HERE
/////////////////////////

Invalidate();

/////////////////////////
// MY CODE ENDS HERE
/////////////////////////

}
```

☐ Follow the same procedure for the IDC_75_RADIO and IDC_100_RADIO radio buttons, substituting the correct object IDs and function names (use the procedure for IDC_50_RADIO if you need help).

As a result of adding this code for the radio buttons, the `OnPaint()` function is executed whenever you select any of the radio buttons.

☐ Select Save All from the File menu to save your work.

☐ Compile, link, and execute the MyFnt program.

☐ Type something in the edit box, then click the radio buttons.

MyFnt responds by displaying the text at the size corresponding to the radio button you selected. Figures 9.7 and 9.8 show the text displayed at different sizes.

Figure 9.7.
The font size displayed when the 25 radio button is selected.

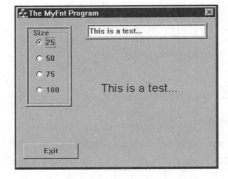

Figure 9.8.
The font size displayed when the 100 radio button is selected.

☐ Experiment with the MyFnt program, then click the Exit button to terminate the program.

Displaying Shadowed Text

Displaying shadowed text from within your Visual C++ program is easy. *Shadowed text* is composed of two separate texts overlapping each other. For example, the top of Figure 9.9 shows two *A* characters: the dark red *A* on the left and the light red *A* on the right.

Figure 9.9.
Displaying shadowed text.

Dark red ——**A** **A**—— Light red

Light red over dark
red with horizontal ——**A**
and vertical offset.

A—— Dark red over light
red with horizontal
and vertical offset.

The middle *A* in Figure 9.9 is constructed with an *offset*. The light red *A* is placed over the dark red *A* slightly below and to the right. The result is an *A* that looks as though it has a shadow. The bottom *A* is composed by overlapping the dark red *A* over the light red *A* and offsetting the dark red *A* slightly.

Other shadow combinations can be generated. For example, you can place the dark red *A* over the light red *A,* but offset the dark red *A* slightly above and to the left.

You'll now add code to the MyFnt program that displays the text in the edit box as shadowed text.

Placing a Shadow Check Box in the MyFnt Window

First, add a check box to the IDD_MYFNT_DIALOG dialog box:

☐ Place a check box in the IDD_MYFNT_DIALOG dialog box and set its properties as follows:

ID:	IDC_SHADOW_CHECK
Caption:	&Shadow
Client edge:	Checked (Extended Styles tab)
Static edge:	Checked (Extended Styles tab)
Modal frame:	Checked (Extended Styles tab)

Attaching a Variable to the Shadow Check Box

You'll now attach a variable to the Shadow check box:

☐ In the Member Variables tab of ClassWizard, make the following selection:

Class name:	CMyFntDlg
Control ID:	IDC_SHADOW_CONTROL

☐ Click the Add Variable button and set the variable as follows:

Variable name:	`m_ShadowCheck`
Category:	`Value`
Variable type:	`BOOL`

☐ Click the OK button of the Add Member Variable dialog box, then click ClassWizard's OK button.

Attaching Code to the Shadow Check Box

You'll now add code that displays the text as a shadowed text:

☐ In the Message Maps tab of ClassWizard, select the following event:

Class name:	`CMyFntDlg`
Object ID:	`IDC_SHADOW_CHECK`
Message:	`BN_CLICKED`

☐ Click the Add Function button, name the new function `OnShadowCheck`, and click the Edit Code button.

> *Visual C++ responds by opening the file MyFntDlg.cpp with the function* `OnShadowCheck()` *ready for you to edit.*

☐ Write the following code in the `OnShadowCheck()` function:

```
void CMyFntDlg::OnShadowCheck()
{
// TODO: Add your control notification handler code here

/////////////////////////
// MY CODE STARTS HERE
/////////////////////////

Invalidate();

/////////////////////////
// MY CODE ENDS HERE
/////////////////////////

}
```

The code you typed causes the execution of the `OnPaint()` function whenever you click the Shadow check box. Checking the Shadow check box causes the `OnPaint()` function to draw shadowed text; unchecking it causes the `OnPaint()` function to draw non-shadowed text. Now add the code in the `OnPaint()` function that draws shadowed text:

☐ Edit the `OnPaint()` function (in the MyFntDlg.cpp file) as follows:

```
void CMyFntDlg::OnPaint()
{
    if (IsIconic())
```

9

```
        {
...
...
...
        }
    else
        {

/////////////////////
// MY CODE STARTS HERE
/////////////////////


/// MessageBeep((WORD)-1);

CPaintDC dc(this); // device context for painting

// Update the variables of the controls
UpdateData(TRUE);


// Create a font object
CFont MyFont;

MyFont.CreateFont (25+25*m_SizeRadio,
                   0,
                   0,
                   0,
                   400,
                   FALSE,
                   FALSE,
                   0,
                   ANSI_CHARSET,
                   OUT_DEFAULT_PRECIS,
                   CLIP_DEFAULT_PRECIS,
                   DEFAULT_QUALITY,
                   DEFAULT_PITCH | FF_SWISS,
                   "Arial");


// Select the new font object
CFont* pOldFont = dc.SelectObject(&MyFont);


if (m_ShadowCheck == TRUE )
{

/// MessageBeep((WORD)-1);

// Set the color of the text
dc.SetTextColor( RGB(255,0,0) );


// Draw the text
dc.TextOut (150,
            120,
```

```
                m_DataEdit);


    }

    // Set the color of the text
    dc.SetTextColor( RGB(0, 255, 0) );

    // Draw the text
    dc.TextOut (150 + 25,
                120 + 25,
                m_DataEdit);


    // Select the old font
    dc.SelectObject(pOldFont);


    ////////////////////////
    // MY CODE ENDS HERE
    ////////////////////////

        CDialog::OnPaint();
    }
}
```

The code in the OnPaint() function first creates the device context:

```
CPaintDC dc(this); // device context for painting
```

Then the variables of the controls are updated:

```
// Update variables of controls
UpdateData(TRUE);
```

An object of class CFont is created:

```
CFont MyFont;
MyFont.CreateFont (25+25*m_SizeRadio,
                   0,
                   0,
                   0,
                   400,
                   FALSE,
                   FALSE,
                   0,
                   ANSI_CHARSET,
                   OUT_DEFAULT_PRECIS,
                   CLIP_DEFAULT_PRECIS,
                   DEFAULT_QUALITY,
                   DEFAULT_PITCH | FF_SWISS,
                   "Arial");
```

Then the new font object is selected:

```
CFont* pOldFont = dc.SelectObject(&MyFont);
```

An `if` statement is then executed to examine the status of the Shadow check box:

```
if (m_ShadowCheck == TRUE )
{
…
…
…
}
```

If the Shadow check box is checked, the code under the `if` statement is executed. When drawing shadowed text, the contents of the edit box are drawn twice. The code under the `if` statement draws the text in red by setting the color as follows:

```
dc.SetTextColor( RGB(255,0,0) );
```

From now on, whenever the `TextOut()` function is executed, the text is drawn with a red pen.

The last statement under the `if` statement draws the text:

```
dc.TextOut (150,
            120,
            m_DataEdit);
```

The statements following the `if` block are executed no matter what the status of the Shadow check box is. However, now the text is drawn with a green pen because the `SetTextColor()` function is executed with `RGB(0,255,0)` as its parameter:

```
dc.SetTextColor( RGB(0, 255, 0) );
```

Then the `TextOut()` function is executed to draw the text:

```
dc.TextOut (150 + 25,
            120 + 25,
            m_DataEdit);
```

Note that when text is drawn for the second time, the first and second parameters of the `TextOut()` function are 150+25 and 120+25; the first time `TextOut()` was executed, they were 150 and 120. Therefore, the second text is drawn with the offset specified by the first and second parameters of `TextOut()`, which specify the upper-left corner of the imaginary rectangle enclosing the characters. (See Figure 9.10.)

As shown in Figure 9.10, the green text is offset from the red text by 25 horizontal units and 25 vertical units. Actually, 25 units is too much! In shadowed text, the offset is typically 3 horizontal and 3 vertical units. For demonstration purposes, however, 25 units is used, as explained in the following steps:

☐ Select Save All from the File menu.

☐ Compile, link, and execute the MyFnt program.

☐ Type something in the edit box, click the 100 radio button, then check the Shadow check box.

Figure 9.10.

Offsetting the second text.

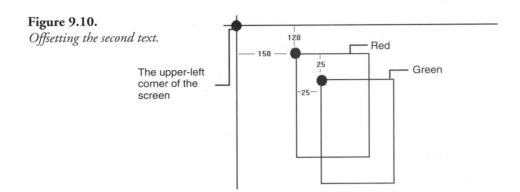

The window of MyFnt now looks like Figure 9.11. The bad news is that this is NOT what you wanted to draw!

Figure 9.11.

Offsetting text by 25 horizontal units and 25 vertical units.

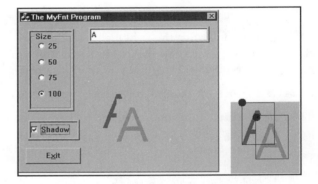

The green *A* was drawn first. When the red *A* was drawn, part of its imaginary rectangle covered part of the green *A*'s rectangle. You can see the result in Figure 9.11. What caused this problem? Background sections of the second *A* are opaque where they should be transparent. You'll take care of this in the next section.

Drawing Text with a Transparent Background

You'll now modify the OnPaint() function so that the text will be drawn with a transparent background:

☐ Modify the OnPaint() function (in the MyFntDlg.cpp file) as follows:

```
void CMyFntDlg::OnPaint()
{
   if (IsIconic())
      {
...
...
...
      }
   else
      {

//////////////////////
// MY CODE STARTS HERE
//////////////////////

/// MessageBeep((WORD)-1);

CPaintDC dc(this); // device context for painting

// Update m_DataEdit
UpdateData(TRUE);


// Create a font object
CFont MyFont;

MyFont.CreateFont (25+25*m_SizeRadio,
                   0,
                   0,
                   0,
                   400,
                   FALSE,
                   FALSE,
                   0,
                   ANSI_CHARSET,
                   OUT_DEFAULT_PRECIS,
                   CLIP_DEFAULT_PRECIS,
                   DEFAULT_QUALITY,
                   DEFAULT_PITCH | FF_SWISS,
                   "Arial");


// Select the new font object
CFont* pOldFont = dc.SelectObject(&MyFont);


if (m_ShadowCheck == TRUE )
{

/// MessageBeep((WORD)-1);

// Set the color of the text
dc.SetTextColor( RGB(255,0,0) );


// Make the background color transparent
```

```
dc.SetBkMode(TRANSPARENT);

// Draw the text
dc.TextOut (150,
            120,
            m_DataEdit);


}

// Set the color of the text
dc.SetTextColor( RGB(0, 255, 0) );


// Draw the text
dc.TextOut (150 + 25,
            120 + 25,
            m_DataEdit);


// Select the old font
dc.SelectObject(pOldFont);


/////////////////////////
// MY CODE ENDS HERE
/////////////////////////

    CDialog::OnPaint();
      }
}
```

Now the code under the `if` statement includes this statement:

```
// Make the background color transparent
dc.SetBkMode(TRANSPARENT);
```

You execute the `SetBkMode()` function with `TRANSPARENT` as its parameter. To see the effect of the preceding statement, execute the MyFnt program.

☐ Select Save All from the File menu.

☐ Compile, link, and execute the MyFnt program.

☐ Type the character A in the edit box, select the 100 radio button, and check the Shadow check box.

   MyFnt responds by displaying the text with a transparent background, as shown in Figure 9.12.

☐ Experiment with the MyFnt program, then click the Exit button to terminate the program.

Figure 9.12.
Displaying the text with a transparent background.

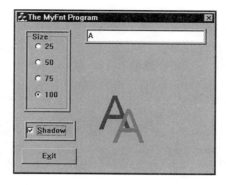

The MyFnt program is almost ready to display shadowed text; just add a few more modifications:

☐ Modify the second `TextOut()` function of the `OnPaint()` function as follows:

```
// Draw the text
dc.TextOut (150 + 3,
            120 + 3;
            m_DataEdit);
```

The offset has been changed to 3 horizontal units and 3 vertical units.

☐ Select Save All from the File menu.

☐ Compile, link, and execute the MyFnt program.

☐ Type A in the edit box, select the 100 radio button, and check the Shadow check box.

    MyFnt responds by displaying the A character as shadowed text. (See Figure 9.13.)

Figure 9.13.
Displaying shadowed text with the MyFnt program.

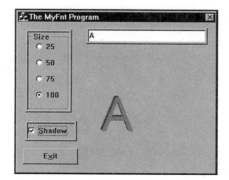

☐ Experiment with the MyFnt program, then click its Exit button to terminate the program.

Using Other Fonts

So far, you have drawn text by setting the last parameter of the CreateFont() function to Arial. What will happen if the PC on which the MyFnt program is executed doesn't have the Arial font installed? If your program includes a font that wasn't installed, Windows will try to substitute a close match for the font you supplied as the last parameter of the CreateFont() function.

> **Note:** In the exercise at the end of this chapter, you'll experiment by supplying other values for the last parameter of the CreateFont() function. You'll do this by adding a list box to the MyFnt program that lets the user select various fonts.

Summary

In this chapter, you have learned how to draw text and how to select its font and other characteristics with the CreateFont() function. You have also learned how to create shadowed text (also called *3-D text*), set different colors for the text foreground, and make the background of the text transparent.

Q&A

Q **What are raised fonts and inset fonts, and how can I generate them?**

A The *raised font* looks as though it's raised above the display surface, and the *inset font* looks as though it's embedded in the display surface. You generate them the same way you generate the shadowed font. In fact, you could consider raised and inset fonts as special cases of shadowed fonts.

Although the shadowed font is usually constructed by using two different colors, the raised and inset fonts are typically displayed on a light gray surface. The raised or inset character is then drawn on the light gray surface as follows:

☐ The background character is displayed.

☐ Next, the foreground character is displayed with a horizontal and vertical offset in relation to the background character. The character's foreground color is black and its background color is white, or vice versa.

The top of Figure 9.14 shows a black *A* and a white *A* on a light gray background, then several possibilities for placing one *A* over the other are shown.

Figure 9.14.

Raised and inset fonts.

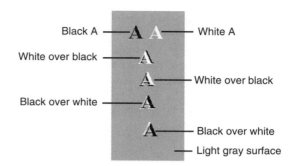

Black A ——— White A

White over black ———

——— White over black

Black over white ———

——— Black over white

——— Light gray surface

Q I have some ideas for creating attractive-looking fonts, but it takes too long to create these fonts from within my Visual C++ program. By the time I add the code, I forget my "creative" ideas. Any suggestions?

A There are many combinations and possibilities for creating attractive fonts—use different sizes, fonts, and colors; offset in different directions; use different surface colors. Before creating a particular font in your Visual C++ program, try using the Paint program that comes with Windows 95. Draw a character, draw another character, and then drag the first character over the second using Paint's tools. When you're satisfied with the font, create it from within your Visual C++ program.

Quiz

1. The `EN_CHANGE` event of the edit box control occurs when?
    a. Whenever the edit box is enabled.
    b. Whenever the edit box is disabled.
    c. Whenever the user changes the contents of the edit box.

2. What is the `CreateFont()` function's job?

3. What is the `TextOut()` function's job?

Exercise

Currently, the MyFnt program draws the font as Arial font (see the last parameter of the `CreateFont()` function). Modify the MyFnt program so that various fonts can be selected by the user. In particular, let the user select the font from a list box. (To perform this exercise, follow the steps in the solution to this exercise.)

Quiz Answers

1. c.

2. The CreateFont() function defines the font that will be used when drawing the text with the TextOut() function.

3. The TextOut() function draws text. The text that's drawn is specified as the third parameter of the TextOut() function.

Exercise Answer

Follow these steps to modify the MyFnt program:

☐ Place a list box control in the IDD_MYFNT_DIALOG dialog box.

☐ Set the properties of the list box as follows:

ID:	IDC_FONT_LIST
Client edge:	Checked (Extended Styles tab)
Static edge:	Checked (Extended Styles tab)
Modal frame:	Checked (Extended Styles tab)

The IDD_MYFNT_DIALOG dialog box should now look like the one in Figure 9.15. You enlarge the IDD_MYFNT_DIALOG dialog box vertically.

Figure 9.15.
IDD_MYFNT_DIALOG
with its list box in design
mode.

☐ Attach the m_FontList variable to the IDC_FONT_LIST list box as follows:

Member variable:	m_FontList
Category:	Control
Variable type:	CListBox

☐ Use ClassWizard to edit the `OnInitDialog()` function (in the MyFntDlg.cpp file) as follows:

```
BOOL CMyFntDlg::OnInitDialog()
{
….
….
….

// TODO: Add extra initialization here

/////////////////////////
// MY CODE STARTS HERE
/////////////////////////

m_SizeRadio = 0;
UpdateData(FALSE);


m_FontList.AddString("Arial");
m_FontList.AddString("System");
m_FontList.AddString("Times New Roman");
m_FontList.AddString("Brush Script MT");

m_FontList.SelectString(0, "Arial");


/////////////////////////
// MY CODE ENDS HERE
/////////////////////////

return TRUE;
// return TRUE  unless you set the focus to a control
}
```

The code you added to the `OnInitDialog()` function adds three items to the list box:

```
m_FontList.AddString("Arial");
m_FontList.AddString("System");
m_FontList.AddString("Times New Roman");
m_FontList.AddString("Brush Script MT");
```

The list box will have the `Arial` string as its first item, `System` as the second item, `Times New Roman` as the third item, and `Brush Script MT` as the fourth item.

When you start the program, the list box will highlight the Arial item in the list:

```
m_FontList.SelectString(0, "Arial");
```

☐ Use ClassWizard to create a function for the `LBN_SELCHANGE` event of the IDC_FONT_LIST list box. Name the function `OnSelchangeFontList`.

☐ Edit the OnSelchangeFontList() function (in the MyFntDlg.cpp file) as follows:

```
void CMyFntDlg::OnSelchangeFontList()
{
// TODO: Add your control notification handler code here

/////////////////////////
// MY CODE STARTS HERE
/////////////////////////

Invalidate();

/////////////////////////
// MY CODE ENDS HERE
/////////////////////////

}
```

The OnSelchangeFontList() function is executed whenever the user makes a selection from the IDC_FONT_LIST list box.

The code you typed causes the execution of the OnPaint() function:

```
Invalidate();
```

☐ Modify the OnPaint() function (in the MyFntDlg.cpp file) as follows:

```
void CMyFntDlg::OnPaint()
{
  if (IsIconic())
      {
....
....
....
      }
    else
      {

/////////////////////////
// MY CODE STARTS HERE
/////////////////////////


/// MessageBeep((WORD)-1);

CPaintDC dc(this); // device context for painting

// Update m_DataEdit
UpdateData(TRUE);

CString CurrentSelectedText;
m_FontList.GetText(m_FontList.GetCurSel(),
                   CurrentSelectedText);

// Create a font object
CFont MyFont;
```

```
MyFont.CreateFont (25+25*m_SizeRadio,
                   0,
                   0,
                   0,
                   400,
                   FALSE,
                   FALSE,
                   0,
                   ANSI_CHARSET,
                   OUT_DEFAULT_PRECIS,
                   CLIP_DEFAULT_PRECIS,
                   DEFAULT_QUALITY,
                   DEFAULT_PITCH | FF_SWISS,
                   CurrentSelectedText);


// Select the new font object
CFont* pOldFont = dc.SelectObject(&MyFont);


if (m_ShadowCheck == TRUE )
{

/// MessageBeep((WORD)-1);

// Set the color of the text
dc.SetTextColor( RGB(255,0,0) );


// Make the background color transparent
dc.SetBkMode(TRANSPARENT);

// Draw the text
dc.TextOut (150,
            120,
            m_DataEdit);


}

// Set the color of the text
dc.SetTextColor( RGB(0, 255, 0) );


// Draw the text
dc.TextOut (150 + 3,
            120 + 3,
            m_DataEdit);


// Select the old font
dc.SelectObject(pOldFont);
```

```
///////////////////////
// MY CODE ENDS HERE
///////////////////////

CDialog::OnPaint();
    }
}
```

You added the statement that declares the `CurrentSelectedText` variable:

```
CString CurrentSelectedText;
```

The `CurrentSelectedText` variable will hold the text selected from the list box. You assign the selected text from the list box to the `CurrentSelectedText` variable as follows:

```
m_FontList.GetText(m_FontList.GetCurSel(),
                   CurrentSelectedText);
```

The `GetText()` function fills the second parameter of `GetText()` with the text mentioned in the first parameter of the `GetText()` function. This is the first parameter:

```
m_FontList.GetCurSel()
```

`GetCurSel()` returns the index number representing the item currently selected in the list box. For example, if the first item in the list is selected, the `GetCurSel()` function returns 0. If the second item is currently selected, `GetCurSel()` returns 1, and so on.

When 0 is supplied as the first parameter of the `GetText()` function, the second parameter of `GetText()` is filled with the first item of the list box. When 1 is supplied as the second parameter of the `GetText()` function, the second parameter of `GetText()` is filled with the second item of the list box, and so on.

Therefore, the `CurrentSelectedText` variable is filled with the text selected in the list box.

You also changed the last parameter of the `CreateFont()` function:

```
MyFont.CreateFont (25+25*m_SizeRadio,
                   0,
                   0,
                   0,
                   400,
                   FALSE,
                   FALSE,
                   0,
                   ANSI_CHARSET,
                   OUT_DEFAULT_PRECIS,
                   CLIP_DEFAULT_PRECIS,
                   DEFAULT_QUALITY,
                   DEFAULT_PITCH | FF_SWISS,
                   CurrentSelectedText);
```

The last parameter of the `CreateFont()` function is now the selected font from the list box.

☐ Select Save All from the File menu.

☐ Compile, link, and execute the MyFnt program.

☐ Experiment with the MyFnt program, then click the Exit button to terminate the program.

Figures 9.16 through 9.18 show some of the text fonts drawn with the MyFnt program.

Figure 9.16.
Drawing Arial shadowed text.

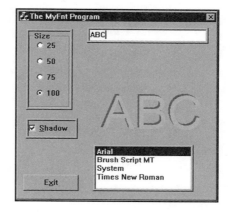

Figure 9.17.
Drawing Brush Script MT shadowed text.

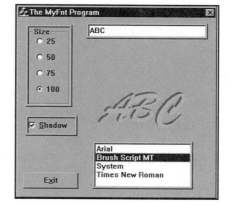

Figure 9.18.
Drawing Brush Script MT non-shadowed text.

Loading and Displaying Picture Files

In this chapter, you'll learn how to load BMP files during runtime and display the loaded BMP files. While you're creating this chapter's program, you'll learn how to display the common Open dialog box, a standard dialog box used for selecting a file from the hard drive.

> **Note:** In Chapter 8, "Displaying Bitmaps," you learned how to display BMP pictures embedded in the program's EXE file. The MyBMP.EXE program in Chapter 8 lets you display only BMP pictures incorporated into the project during its visual design. In this chapter, you'll create a program that lets the user load any BMP file from the hard drive during runtime, then display that BMP picture.

The MyPic Program

Before creating the MyPic program yourself, review its specifications:

- When you start the MyPic program, the window shown in Figure 10.1 appears.

Figure 10.1.
The window of the MyPic program.

- You can then select Open from MyPic's File menu to display the Open BMP File dialog box shown in Figure 10.2.

Figure 10.2.
The Open BMP File dialog box.

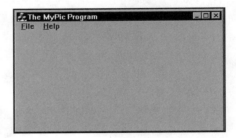

- Once you select a BMP file, the MyPic program displays its picture, and the window's caption displays the name of the BMP file.
- You can drag the edges of the window to shrink or enlarge its size; the picture displayed in the window shrinks or increases accordingly. The BMP picture is always displayed over the entire client area of the program's window. (See Figures 10.3 and 10.4, which show an example of importing clip art.)

Figure 10.3.
Enlarging the window size increases the picture's size.

Figure 10.4.
Shrinking the window size shrinks the picture's size.

Creating the Project of the MyPic Program

To create the project of the MyPic program, follow these steps:

☐ Create the C:\TYVCProg\Programs\CH10 directory and start Visual C++.

☐ Select New from the File menu, select Project Workspace from the New dialog box, then select the MFC AppWizard (exe) item from the New Project Workspace dialog box.

☐ Set the Name box in the New Project Workspace dialog box to MyPic.

☐ Click the Browse button, select the C:\TYVCProg\Programs\CH10 directory, then click the Create button.

> *Visual C++ responds by displaying the MFC AppWizard Step 1 window.*

☐ In Step 1, use the default setting to create a dialog-based application, then click the Next button.

☐ In Step 2, use the default settings and enter MyPic for the dialog box's title. When you're done, click the Next button.

☐ In Step 3, use the default settings, then click Next.

☐ In Step 4, use the default settings and notice that AppWizard has created the CMyPicApp and CMyPicDlg classes. Click the Finish button.

   Visual C++ responds by displaying the New Project Information window.

☐ Click the OK button of the New Project Information window.

   Visual C++ responds by creating the project of the MyPic program and all its associated files.

☐ Select Set Default Configuration from the Build menu, then select MyBMP - Win32 Release and click the OK button.

That's it—you're ready to start designing the program.

The Visual Design of MyPic's Main Window

You'll now visually design the IDD_MYPIC_DIALOG dialog box that serves as the main window of the MyPic program:

☐ In the Project Workspace, click the ResourceView tab and expand the MyPic resources item, then the Dialog item. Finally, double-click the IDD_MYPIC_DIALOG item.

   Visual C++ responds by displaying the IDD_MYPIC_DIALOG dialog box in design mode.

☐ Delete the TODO text, OK button, and Cancel button of the IDD_MYPIC_DIALOG dialog box.

☐ Design the IDD_MYPIC_DIALOG dialog box according to Table 10.1. When you finish, it should look like the one in Figure 10.5.

Table 10.1. The properties table of the IDD_MYPIC_DIALOG dialog box.

Object	Property	Setting
Dialog Box	ID	**IDD_MYPIC_DIALOG**
	Caption	The MyPic Program

Object	Property	Setting
	Font	System, size 10
	Border	Resizing (Styles tab)
	Minimize box	Checked (Styles tab)
	Maximize box	Checked (Styles tab)

Figure 10.5.
IDD_MYPIC_DIALOG in
design mode.

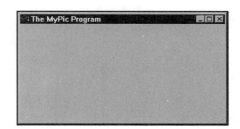

> **Note:** Table 10.1 specifies setting the Border property of the dialog box to Resizing. The Border list box is in the Styles tab of IDD_MYPIC_DIALOG's Properties window. Setting the Border property to Resizing enables you to enlarge or shrink MyBMP's window by dragging its edges during runtime.
>
> The Maximize and Minimize check boxes in the Styles tab should also be checked so that the IDD_MYPIC_DIALOG dialog box can be maximized and minimized during runtime.

The Visual Design of the Menu

You'll now visually design the menu of the MyPic program:

☐ In the Project Workspace, select the ResourceView tab and right-click the MyPic resources item.

Visual C++ responds by displaying a pop-up menu.

☐ Select Insert from the menu.

Visual C++ responds by displaying the Insert Resource dialog box.

☐ Select the Menu item from the Insert Resource dialog box, then click the OK button.

Visual C++ responds by displaying an empty menu in design mode.

☐ Customize the menu as shown in Figures 10.6 and 10.7. You will add the Open BMP and Exit items to the File menu and the About item to the Help menu.

Figure 10.6.

The File menu of the MyBMP program.

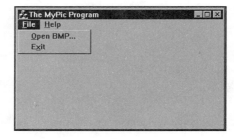

Figure 10.7.

The Help menu of the MyBMP program.

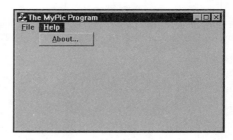

The default ID that Visual C++ assigns to the new menu is IDR_MENU1. Change the ID to IDR_MYPIC_MENU:

☐ Set the ID property of the menu to IDR_MYPIC_MENU by right-clicking the IDR_MENU1 item in the Project Workspace window, selecting Properties, then setting the ID property in the Properties window that pops up.

Next, you have to associate the menu with the CMyPicDlg class. Here is how you do that:

☐ While the menu window is selected, select ClassWizard from the View menu.

Visual C++ responds by displaying the Adding a Class dialog box.

☐ Make sure that the "Select an existing class" radio button is selected, then click the OK button.

Visual C++ responds by displaying the Select Class dialog box.

☐ Select the CMyPicDlg item, then click the Select button.

Visual C++ responds by displaying the MFC ClassWizard dialog box.

☐ Click the OK button of the MFC ClassWizard dialog box.

Attaching the Menu to the Dialog Box

You'll now attach the IDR_MYPIC_MENU menu to the IDD_MYPIC_DIALOG dialog box:

☐ Double-click the IDD_MYPIC_DIALOG item in the Project Workspace window.

Visual C++ responds by displaying IDD_MYPIC_DIALOG in design mode.

☐ Set the Menu property (in the General tab) of IDD_MYPIC_DIALOG to IDR_MYPIC_MENU. (To display the Properties window, double-click in a free area of the dialog box.)

Attaching Code to the Exit Menu Item

You'll now attach code to the COMMAND event of the Exit menu item:

☐ Highlight the IDR_MYPIC_MENU item in the Project Workspace window, then select ClassWizard from the View menu.

Visual C++ responds by displaying the MFC ClassWizard dialog box.

☐ Select ID_FILE_EXIT in the Object IDs list, select COMMAND in the Message list, then click the Add Function button.

Visual C++ responds by suggesting OnFileExit as the new function's name.

☐ Accept OnFileExit as the name of the new function, then click the Edit Code button.

☐ Enter code in the OnFileExit() function (in the MyPicDlg.cpp file) as follows:

```
void CMyPicDlg::OnFileExit()
{
// TODO: Add your command handler code here

/////////////////////////
// MY CODE STARTS HERE
/////////////////////////

OnOK();

/////////////////////////
// MY CODE ENDS HERE
/////////////////////////


}
```

This code, which terminates the MyBMP program, is executed when you select Exit from the File menu.

☐ Save your work.

☐ Compile, link, and execute MyPic.EXE to make sure the Exit menu item works as expected.

Attaching Code to the About Menu Item

You'll now add the code that's executed when you select the About item from the Help menu:

☐ Double-click the IDR_MYPIC_MENU item to display the menu in design mode.

☐ Select ClassWizard from the View menu.

☐ Select the ID_HELP_ABOUT item from the Object IDs list, select COMMAND in the Messages list, then click the Add Function button.

> *Visual C++ responds by suggesting* OnHelpAbout *as the new function's name.*

☐ Accept the function name that Visual C++ suggests, then click the Edit Code button.

☐ Enter code in the OnHelpAbout() function as follows:

```
void CMyPicDlg::OnHelpAbout()
{
// TODO: Add your command handler code here

/////////////////////////
// MY CODE STARTS HERE
/////////////////////////

CAboutDlg dlg;
dlg.DoModal();

/////////////////////////
// MY CODE ENDS HERE
/////////////////////////

}
```

This code creates an object dlg of class CAboutDlg, the class associated with the About dialog box IDD_ABOUTBOX:

```
CAboutDlg dlg;
```

Then the About dialog box is displayed as a modal dialog box:

```
dlg.DoModal();
```

☐ Save your work.

☐ Compile, link, and execute the program to make sure the About dialog box is displayed when you select the About item from the Help menu.

☐ Experiment with the program, then select Exit from the File menu to terminate the MyPic program.

Overhead, Overhead, Overhead...

The StretchBlt() function you used in Chapter 8 to display BMP pictures contains a lot of code and uses a variety of other functions. As a Visual C++ programmer, you don't really need to know exactly how the StretchBlt() function was created by the Visual C++ designers. All you want to know is what parameters should be supplied. Suppose the StretchBlt() function was composed of 20 functions, and Microsoft supplied these 20 functions instead of the StretchBlt() function. You would have to re-create the StretchBlt() function each time by using those 20 functions! Thanks to Microsoft, your job is easier because the StretchBlt() function is supplied with Visual C++.

However, there's no function supplied by Visual C++ that lets you load an arbitrary BMP file from the hard drive. It would be nice if Visual C++ were equipped with a function like the following:

```
// Wishful thinking
OpenBMPFile(FileName);
```

Instead of supplying a convenient function like OpenBMPFile(), Visual C++ is equipped with functions that let you create such a function.

Use the steps in this section to create a function that serves as the "missing" OpenBMPFile() function. Rather than try to understand the exact nature of the code you add to this function, you should think of the code that loads BMP files as overhead code. You'll be concentrating on the objective of loading BMP files and displaying BMP pictures. Unfortunately, the code is not short (and as you know, even the slightest typing mistake causes a compiling error). However, once you type this code, you can reuse it in future projects. It's worthwhile to have this code at your disposal because loading BMP files is a useful feature.

☐ In the Project Workspace, click the FileView tab, expand the Dependencies item, and finally double-click the MyPicDlg.h file.

> *Visual C++ responds by displaying the MyPicDlg.h file, ready for you to edit.*

Note: As you type the code, you'll encounter the word *DIB,* which stands for *device-independent bitmap. Bitmap* refers to a file that contains data; the bytes of the data represent a picture by specifying the location and colors of pixels.

Windows is a device-independent operating system. This means that to display a certain BMP file, your program doesn't have to specify things like your end-user's screen resolution, the type of VGA/EGA card used, and so on. No matter what hardware your user has, your program should work without problems (hence the name *device-independent bitmap*).

☐ Add the following code to the beginning of the MyPicDlg.h file:

```
// MyPicDlg.h : header file
//

/////////////////////////////////////////////////////
// CMyPicDlg dialog


/////////////////////////
// MY CODE STARTS HERE
/////////////////////////


// Overhead declarations for DIB manipulations.
typedef    LPBITMAPINFOHEADER PDIB;

#define DibWidth(lpbi) \
(UINT)(((LPBITMAPINFOHEADER)(lpbi))->biWidth)

#define DibHeight(lpbi) \
(UINT)(((LPBITMAPINFOHEADER)(lpbi))->biHeight)

#define DibColors(lpbi) \
((RGBQUAD FAR *)((LPBYTE)(lpbi) + (int)(lpbi)->biSize))

#ifdef WIN32
#define DibPtr(lpbi) \
((lpbi)->biCompression == BI_BITFIELDS \
? (LPVOID)(DibColors(lpbi) + 3) \
: (LPVOID)(DibColors(lpbi) + (UINT)(lpbi)->biClrUsed))
#else
#define DibPtr(lpbi) \
(LPVOID)(DibColors(lpbi) + (UINT)(lpbi)->biClrUsed)
#endif

#define DibInfo(pDIB) \
((BITMAPINFO FAR *)(pDIB))

#define DibNumColors(lpbi) \
((lpbi)->biClrUsed == 0 && (lpbi)->biBitCount <= 8 \
? (int)(1 << (int)(lpbi)->biBitCount) \
: (int)(lpbi)->biClrUsed)

#define DibPaletteSize(lpbi) \
(DibNumColors(lpbi) * sizeof(RGBQUAD))

#define BFT_BITMAP 0x4d42

#define WIDTHBYTES(i)  \
((unsigned)((i+31)&(~31))/8)

#define DibWidthBytesN(lpbi, n) \
(UINT)WIDTHBYTES((UINT)(lpbi)->biWidth * (UINT)(n))

#define DibWidthBytes(lpbi) \
DibWidthBytesN(lpbi, (lpbi)->biBitCount)
```

```
#define DibSizeImage(lpbi)  \
((lpbi)->biSizeImage == 0 \
? ((DWORD)(UINT)DibWidthBytes(lpbi) * (DWORD)(UINT)(lpbi)->biHeight) \
: (lpbi)->biSizeImage)
#ifndef BI_BITFIELDS
#define BI_BITFIELDS 3
#endif
#define FixBitmapInfo(lpbi) \
if ((lpbi)->biSizeImage == 0) \
(lpbi)->biSizeImage = DibSizeImage(lpbi); \
if ((lpbi)->biClrUsed == 0)   \
(lpbi)->biClrUsed = DibNumColors(lpbi); \
if ((lpbi)->biCompression == BI_BITFIELDS && (lpbi)->biClrUsed == 0)

//////////////////////////
// MY CODE ENDS HERE
//////////////////////////
```

☐ Save your work.

☐ Select Build MyPic.EXE from the Build menu.

☐ Make sure there are no compiling/linking errors at this point in your program's development. If you receive compiling/linking errors, go over the code and make sure you typed it correctly.

Attaching Code to the Open Menu Item

You'll now attach code to the Open menu item of the File menu:

☐ Highlight the IDR_MYPIC_MENU item in the Project Workspace window, then select ClassWizard from the View menu.

Visual C++ responds by displaying the MFC ClassWizard dialog box.

☐ Select ID_FILE_OPENBMP in the Object IDs list, select COMMAND in the Message list, then click the Add Function button.

Visual C++ responds by suggesting OnFileOpenbmp *as the new function's name.*

☐ Accept OnFileOpenbmp as the name of the new function, then click the Edit Code button.

☐ Enter code in the OnFileOpenbmp() function as follows:

```
void CMyPicDlg::OnFileOpenbmp()
{
// TODO: Add your command handler code here

//////////////////////////
// MY CODE STARTS HERE
//////////////////////////
```

```
m_pdibPicture =
DibOpenFile("C:\\Movie.BMP");

Invalidate();

/////////////////////////
// MY CODE ENDS HERE
/////////////////////////

}
```

The code you typed uses the `DibOpenFile()` function:

```
m_pdibPicture =
DibOpenFile("C:\\Movie.BMP");
```

The `DibOpenFile()` function is responsible for loading the BMP file from the hard drive. It has a single parameter that contains the name and path of the BMP file you want to load. As you can see, the parameter you supplied specifies the Movie.BMP file from the root directory of your C: drive, so in the following steps you'll use Paint to draw a picture and save it as Movie.BMP in the C:\ directory.

> **Note:** Don't forget to use the two backslash characters (\\) required by C/C++ when specifying the path of the BMP file:
>
> ```
> m_pdibPicture =
> DibOpenFile("C:\\Movie.BMP");
> ```
>
> The `DibOpenFile()` function returns a value and assigns it to the `m_pdibPicture` data member, which you'll declare in the next section. `m_pdibPicture` is a pointer to an address. Which address? The address where the loaded BMP pictures is stored in memory.

Follow these steps to draw the Movie.BMP picture:

☐ Execute the Windows 95 Paint program in the Accessories folder.

☐ Select Attributes from Paint's Image menu.

Paint responds by displaying the Attributes dialog box.

☐ Set the Width box to 250 pixels and the Height box to 90 pixels. Finally, click the OK button of the Attributes dialog box.

Paint responds by displaying an empty area (250 pixels × 90 pixels) ready for you to paint.

☐ Draw something with Paint. (See Figure 10.8 for an example; this image shows how you can import clip art to enhance your program.)

Figure 10.8.
Using the Paint program.

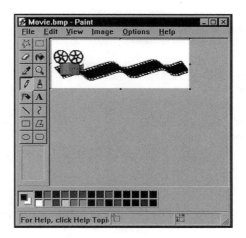

☐ Select Save As from Paint's File menu and save your drawing as a BMP file with the filename Movie.BMP in the C:\ directory.

☐ Terminate the Paint program.

The last statement in the OnFileOpenbmp() function causes the OnPaint() function to be executed:

```
Invalidate();
```

As you'll soon see, you actually display the loaded BMP file in the OnPaint() function.

Declaring the *m_pdibPicture* Data Member

In the previous section, you executed the DibOpenFile() function as follows:

```
m_pdibPicture =
DibOpenFile("C:\\Movie.BMP");
```

The returned value of DibOpenFile() is assigned to the m_pdibPicture data member of the CMyPicDlg class. You'll now declare the m_pdibPicture data member:

☐ In the Project Workspace, click the FileView tab, expand the Dependencies item, and double-click the MyPicDlg.h file.

Visual C++ responds by displaying the MyPicDlg.h file, ready for you to edit.

☐ Add the declaration of the m_pdibPicture data member as follows:

```
class CMyPicDlg : public CDialog
{
// Construction
public:
CMyPicDlg(CWnd* pParent = NULL); // standard constructor
```

301

```
///////////////////////////
// MY CODE STARTS HERE
///////////////////////////

// Data members.
PDIB m_pdibPicture;

///////////////////////////
// MY CODE ENDS HERE
///////////////////////////

...
...
...
};
```

The code you typed declares the m_pdibPicture data member as PDIB, which is a pointer to a DIB picture:

```
PDIB m_pdibPicture;
```

Creating the *DibOpenFile()* Function

Now it's time to create the DibOpenFile() function. The first step is to add the function prototypes with the following steps:

☐ Open the MyPicDlg.h file. At the beginning, add the prototypes of the DibOpenFile() function and another function called DibReadBitmapInfo() (which you'll write later in this chapter):

```
class CMyPicDlg : public CDialog
{
// Construction
public:
CMyPicDlg(CWnd* pParent = NULL);   // standard constructor


// Data members.
PDIB m_pdibPicture;

...
...
...

// Dialog Data
...
...
...
// Implementation
protected:
    HICON m_hIcon;
```

```
/////////////////////////
// MY CODE STARTS HERE
/////////////////////////

// Member functions.
PDIB      DibOpenFile(LPSTR szFile);
PDIB      DibReadBitmapInfo(HFILE fh);

/////////////////////////
// MY CODE ENDS HERE
/////////////////////////
...
...
...

};
```

In the preceding code you added the prototypes of two functions:

```
PDIB      DibOpenFile(LPSTR szFile);
PDIB      DibReadBitmapInfo(HFILE fh);
```

Attaching Code to *DibOpenFile()* and *DibReadBitmapInfo()*

You'll now add the code of the DibOpenFile() function (consider this overhead code you can reuse in future projects):

☐ In the Project Workspace, click the FileView tab, then open the MyPicDlg.cpp file. Add the DibOpenFile() function by inserting the following code to the end of the MyPicDlg.cpp file:

```
/////////////////////////
// MY CODE STARTS HERE
/////////////////////////

PDIB CMyPicDlg::DibOpenFile(LPSTR szFile)
{
    HFILE           fh;
    DWORD           dwLen;
    DWORD           dwBits;
    PDIB            pdib;
    LPVOID          p;
    OFSTRUCT        of;

#if defined(WIN32) || defined(_WIN32)
    #define GetCurrentInstance()    GetModuleHandle(NULL)
#else
#define GetCurrentInstance()   (HINSTANCE)SELECTOROF((LPVOID)&of)
#endif

fh = OpenFile(szFile, &of, OF_READ);

    if (fh == -1)
    {
    HRSRC h;
```

```
h = FindResource(GetCurrentInstance(), szFile, RT_BITMAP);

#if defined(WIN32) ¦¦ defined(_WIN32)
if (h)
return (PDIB)LockResource(LoadResource(GetCurrentInstance(), h));
#else
if (h)
fh = AccessResource(GetCurrentInstance(), h);
#endif
}

if (fh == -1)
   return NULL;

pdib = DibReadBitmapInfo(fh);

if (!pdib)
   return NULL;


dwBits = pdib->biSizeImage;
dwLen  = pdib->biSize + DibPaletteSize(pdib) + dwBits;

p = GlobalReAllocPtr(pdib,dwLen,0);

if (!p)
   {
   GlobalFreePtr(pdib);
   pdib = NULL;
   }
else
   {
   pdib = (PDIB)p;
   }

if (pdib)
   {
_hread(fh,
(LPBYTE)pdib + (UINT)pdib->biSize + DibPaletteSize(pdib), dwBits);
   }

   _lclose(fh);

   return pdib;
}

//////////////////////////
// MY CODE ENDS HERE
//////////////////////////
```

Some of the code you typed in the DibOpenFile() function requires you to use an #include statement in the Windowsx.h file:

☐ Add an #include statement to the beginning of the MyPicDlg.cpp file as follows:

```
// MyPicDlg.cpp : implementation file
//

#include "stdafx.h"
#include "MyPic.h"
#include "MyPicDlg.h"

/////////////////////////
// MY CODE STARTS HERE
/////////////////////////

#include <windowsx.h>

/////////////////////////
// MY CODE ENDS HERE
/////////////////////////
...
...
...
```

The code of the `DibOpenFile()` function executes the `DibReadBitmapInfo()` function. You already typed the prototype of the `DibReadBitmapInfo()` function, so now add the code:

☐ Type the code of the `DibReadBitmapInfo()` function at the end of the MyPicDlg.cpp file:

```
/////////////////////////
// MY CODE STARTS HERE
/////////////////////////

PDIB CMyPicDlg::DibReadBitmapInfo(HFILE fh)
{
    DWORD      off;
    HANDLE     hbi = NULL;
    int        size;
    int        i;
    int        nNumColors;

    RGBQUAD FAR       *pRgb;
    BITMAPINFOHEADER  bi;
    BITMAPCOREHEADER  bc;
    BITMAPFILEHEADER  bf;
    PDIB              pdib;

    if (fh == -1)
        return NULL;

    off = _llseek(fh,0L,SEEK_CUR);

if (sizeof(bf) != _lread(fh,(LPSTR)&bf,sizeof(bf)))
    return FALSE;

if (bf.bfType != BFT_BITMAP)
    {
     bf.bfOffBits = 0L;
     _llseek(fh,off,SEEK_SET);
    }
```

```
if (sizeof(bi) != _lread(fh,(LPSTR)&bi,sizeof(bi)))
   return FALSE;

switch (size = (int)bi.biSize)
{
 default:
     case sizeof(BITMAPINFOHEADER):
      break;

case sizeof(BITMAPCOREHEADER):
    bc = *(BITMAPCOREHEADER*)&bi;
    bi.biSize              = sizeof(BITMAPINFOHEADER);
    bi.biWidth             = (DWORD)bc.bcWidth;
    bi.biHeight            = (DWORD)bc.bcHeight;
    bi.biPlanes            =  (UINT)bc.bcPlanes;
    bi.biBitCount          =  (UINT)bc.bcBitCount;
    bi.biCompression       = BI_RGB;
    bi.biSizeImage         = 0;
    bi.biXPelsPerMeter     = 0;
    bi.biYPelsPerMeter     = 0;
    bi.biClrUsed           = 0;
    bi.biClrImportant      = 0;

_llseek(fh,(LONG)sizeof(BITMAPCOREHEADER)-sizeof(BITMAPINFOHEADER),SEEK_CUR);

    break;
}

nNumColors = DibNumColors(&bi);

#if 0
if (bi.biSizeImage == 0)
   bi.biSizeImage = DibSizeImage(&bi);

if (bi.biClrUsed == 0)
   bi.biClrUsed = DibNumColors(&bi);
#else
   FixBitmapInfo(&bi);
#endif

pdib = (PDIB)GlobalAllocPtr(GMEM_MOVEABLE,
    (LONG)bi.biSize + nNumColors * sizeof(RGBQUAD));

if (!pdib)
   return NULL;

*pdib = bi;

pRgb = DibColors(pdib);

if (nNumColors)
   {
    if (size == sizeof(BITMAPCOREHEADER))
       {
_lread(fh,(LPVOID)pRgb,nNumColors * sizeof(RGBTRIPLE));
```

```
for (i=nNumColors-1; i>=0; i-- )
    {
    RGBQUAD rgb;

    rgb.rgbRed      = ((RGBTRIPLE FAR *)pRgb)[i].rgbtRed;
    rgb.rgbBlue     = ((RGBTRIPLE FAR *)pRgb)[i].rgbtBlue;
    rgb.rgbGreen    = ((RGBTRIPLE FAR *)pRgb)[i].rgbtGreen;
    rgb.rgbReserved = (BYTE)0;

    pRgb[i] = rgb;
    }
  }
  else
  {
  _lread(fh,(LPVOID)pRgb,nNumColors * sizeof(RGBQUAD));
  }
 }

if (bf.bfOffBits != 0L)
  _llseek(fh,off + bf.bfOffBits,SEEK_SET);

return pdib;
}

/////////////////////////
// MY CODE ENDS HERE
/////////////////////////
```

The details of the DibOpenFile() and the DibReadBitmapInfo() functions aren't necessary for the purposes of this chapter—just think of the DibOpenFile() function as a function that came with Visual C++ ready to be used.

To make sure you typed the preceding code without any errors, compile and link the program:

☐ Save your work.

☐ Select Build MyPic.EXE from the Build menu.

☐ Make sure you get no errors during the compiling/linking process.

Of course, the Movie.BMP picture isn't displayed in the MyPic window because you haven't added the OnPaint() function's code yet.

The *OnPaint()* Function

You're ready to enter the code of the OnPaint() function, since all the required overhead code is ready for displaying the BMP picture from within the OnPaint() function:

☐ In the Message Maps tab of ClassWizard, select the following event:

Class name:	CMyPicDlg
Object ID:	CMyPicDlg
Message:	WM_PAINT

☐ Click the Edit Code button of ClassWizard.

Visual C++ responds by opening the file MyPicDlg.cpp with the function OnPaint() *ready for you to edit.*

☐ Write the following code in the OnPaint() function:

```
void CMyPicDlg::OnPaint()
{
…
…
…
   if (IsIconic())
    {
…
…
…
    }

    else
    {

/////////////////////////
// MY CODE STARTS HERE
/////////////////////////

if (m_pdibPicture!=NULL)
{

CPaintDC dc(this);  // device context for painting

::StretchDIBits(dc.m_hDC, // Destination
               50,
               50,
               250,
               90,
               0,           //Source
               0,
               DibWidth(m_pdibPicture),
               DibHeight(m_pdibPicture),
               DibPtr(m_pdibPicture),
               DibInfo(m_pdibPicture),
               DIB_RGB_COLORS,
               SRCCOPY);
}

/////////////////////////
// MY CODE ENDS HERE
/////////////////////////

        CDialog::OnPaint();
    }
}
```

The code you typed creates a device context (dc):

```
CPaintDC dc(this);  // device context for painting
```

Then the StretchDIBits() function is executed:

```
::StretchDIBits(dc.m_hDC, // Destination
                50,
                50,
                90,
                200,
                0,          //Source
                0,
                DibWidth(m_pdibPicture),
                DibHeight(m_pdibPicture),
                DibPtr(m_pdibPicture),
                DibInfo(m_pdibPicture),
                DIB_RGB_COLORS,
                SRCCOPY);
}
```

The StretchDIBits() function is similar to the StretchBlt() function you used in Chapter 8. Its first parameter is the dc of the destination, which is the screen.

The second and third parameters specify the x- and y-coordinates of the destination rectangle's upper-left corner where the BMP picture will be displayed.

The fourth and fifth parameters specify the width and height of the destination rectangle where the BMP will be displayed.

The loaded BMP picture (Movie.BMP) is currently stored in memory. The StretchDIBits() function copies a rectangle area of the loaded BMP into the screen. The sixth and seventh parameters specify the coordinates of the upper-left corner of the source rectangle. Since you specified (0,0), the upper-left corner of the rectangle copied into the destination is at the upper-left corner of the loaded BMP picture.

The eighth and ninth parameters specify the width and height of the source. You specified DibWidth(m_pdibPicture) as the width of the rectangle area copied from the source to the destination and DibHeight(m_pdibPicture) as the height of the rectangle area copied from the source to the destination. These two values represent the width and height of the loaded BMP picture.

The tenth parameter represents the address of the loaded BMP picture. You supplied m_pdibPicture as the tenth parameter of the StretchDIBits() function. Recall that in the OnFileOpenbmp() function you loaded the BMP picture with the DibOpenFile() function as follows:

```
m_pdibPicture =
DibOpenFile("C:\\Movie.BMP");
```

Therefore, the loaded BMP is stored in memory at the address m_pdibPicture.

When you load a BMP picture, it has two sections: the bitmap bits representing the picture's pixels and the bitmap data representing information about the loaded BMP picture. The eleventh parameter of the StretchDIBits() function is the address of the bitmap data. You supplied DibInfo(m_pdibPicture) as the eleventh parameter. As you can see, the DibInfo() function is used to extract the address of the bitmap data by supplying m_pdibPicture as the parameter of the DibInfo() function.

The twelfth parameter specifies the color table that should be used for displaying the BMP picture. It can be either DIB_PAL_COLORS or DIB_RGB_COLORS.

The thirteenth parameter function specifies SRCCOPY, so that a straight copy operation will be performed from the source to the destination.

Initializing the Pointer

If you compile and link the program now, you won't get compiling/linking errors, but if you execute the program, you'll get a runtime error! Why? Because you haven't initialized the m_pdibPicture pointer.

In the OnPaint() function you used an if statement, as follows:

```
if (m_pdibPicture!=NULL)
{

// Statement that draw the BMP picture

}
```

That is, m_pdibPicture is a pointer to the address of the loaded BMP file. For example, suppose the value of m_pdibPicture is 1000. The loaded BMP file will be stored, therefore, starting at address 1000. The StretchDIBits() function uses values for some of its parameters assumed to be in the memory area starting at address 1000. If, for some reason, a valid BMP picture is NOT stored in that memory area, a runtime error will occur when the OnPaint() function is executed because there's no valid data starting at address 1000.

Therefore, next you'll set the value of m_pdibPicture to NULL in the OnInitDialog() function. The DibOpenFile() function in the OnFileOpenbmp() function sets the value of m_pdibPicture to the address of the loaded BMP picture. If you haven't loaded a BMP file yet, m_pdibPicture will still be equal to NULL, and the code under the if statement in the OnPaint() function won't be executed. Setting m_pdibPicture to NULL serves as a flag: When m_pdibPicture is equal to NULL, no BMP picture has been loaded; therefore, the code under the if statement in the OnPaint() function is not executed.

Here is how you initialize the m_pdibPicture pointer to NULL:

☐ In the Message Maps tab of ClassWizard, select the following event:

Class name:	CMyPicDlg
Object ID:	CMyPicDlg
Message:	WM_INITDIALOG

☐ Click the Edit Code button of ClassWizard.

Visual C++ responds by opening the file MyPicDlg.cpp with the function OnInitDialog()
ready for you to edit.

☐ Write the following code in the OnInitDialog() function:

```
BOOL CMyPicDlg::OnInitDialog()
{
    CDialog::OnInitDialog();
…
…
…


    // TODO: Add extra initialization here

    /////////////////////////////
    // MY CODE STARTS HERE
    /////////////////////////////

    // Set m_pdibPicture to NULL
    m_pdibPicture    = NULL;

    /////////////////////////////
    // MY CODE ENDS HERE
    /////////////////////////////


    return TRUE;
    // return TRUE  unless you set the focus to a control
}
```

The code you typed sets the m_pdibPicture pointer as follows:

```
// Initialize m_pdibPicture
m_pdibPicture    = NULL;
```

Freeing the Memory Used for the Loaded BMP Picture

As stated, m_pdibPicture is a pointer to the address containing the loaded BMP picture. When you terminate the MyPic program, the memory used by the loaded BMP picture is still occupied by that picture. If you execute the MyPic program again, the program will load the BMP picture into memory, but will use a different address to store the loaded BMP picture. Therefore, if you execute the MyPic program many times, sooner or later your PC will run out of memory. The solution is to free the area in memory occupied by the loaded BMP picture when you terminate the MyPic program. Here is how you do that:

☐ In the Message Maps tab of ClassWizard, select the following event:

Class name:	CMyPicDlg
Object ID:	CMyPicDlg
Message:	WM_DESTROY

☐ Click the Add Function button, name the new function OnDestroy, then click the Edit Code button.

Visual C++ responds by opening the file MyPicDlg.cpp with the function OnDestroy() *ready for you to edit.*

☐ Write the following code in the OnDestroy() function:

```
void CMyPicDlg::OnDestroy()
{
    CDialog::OnDestroy();

// TODO: Add your message handler code here

//////////////////////////
// MY CODE STARTS HERE
//////////////////////////

GlobalFreePtr(m_pdibPicture);

//////////////////////////
// MY CODE ENDS HERE
//////////////////////////

}
```

This code is executed whenever the IDD_MYPIC_DIALOG dialog box is destroyed. As you know, there are several ways to terminate the program—select Exit from the File menu, display the system menu and select Close, and so forth. No matter how you terminate the MyPic program, the WM_DESTROY event occurs and the OnDestroy() function is executed.

The code in the OnDestroy() function uses the GlobalFreePtr() function to free the memory:

```
GlobalFreePtr(m_pdibPicture);
```

As you can see, m_pdibPicture is supplied as the parameter of the GlobalFreePtr() function. Therefore, when you terminate the MyPic program, the memory used for storing the BMP picture is freed.

☐ Save your work.

☐ Compile, link, and execute the MyPic.EXE program.

☐ Select Open from the File menu.

The window of the MyPic program should look like the one in Figure 10.9.

Figure 10.9.
The Movie.BMP picture displayed according to the parameters of StretchDIBits().

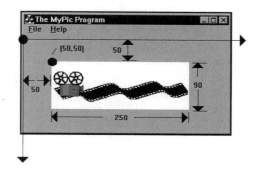

10

☐ Select Exit from the File menu to terminate the MyPic program.

Displaying BMP Pictures over the Entire MyPic Window

You'll now add code that causes the MyPic program to display the BMP picture over MyPic's entire client area. Start by adding two data members to the CMyPicDlg class:

☐ Open the MyPicDlg.h file and add two data members (m_WindowWidth and m_WindowHeight) to the declaration of the CMyPicDlg class. After adding the two data members, the CMyPicDlg class declaration should look like the following:

```
class CMyPicDlg : public CDialog
{
// Construction
public:
CMyPicDlg(CWnd* pParent = NULL);
// standard constructor

/////////////////////////
// MY CODE STARTS HERE
/////////////////////////

// Data members.
PDIB m_pdibPicture;

int m_WindowWidth;
int m_WindowHeight;

/////////////////////////
// MY CODE ENDS HERE
/////////////////////////
```

```
...
...
...

// Implementation
protected:
    HICON m_hIcon;

/////////////////////////////
// MY CODE STARTS HERE
/////////////////////////////

// Member functions.
PDIB     DibOpenFile(LPSTR szFile);
PDIB     DibReadBitmapInfo(HFILE fh);

/////////////////////////////
// MY CODE ENDS HERE
/////////////////////////////

...
...
...
};
```

Sizing the BMP Picture According to the Window's Size

You'll now write the code that updates m_WindowWidth and m_WindowHeight with the width and height of the MyPic window.

☐ In the Message Maps tab of ClassWizard, select the following event:

Class name:	CMyPicDlg
Object ID:	CMyPicDlg
Message:	WM_SIZE

☐ Click the Add Function button, name the new function OnSize, then click the Edit Code button.

Visual C++ responds by opening the file MyPicDlg.cpp with the function OnSize() ready for you to edit.

☐ Write the following code in the OnSize() function:

```
void CMyPicDlg::OnSize(UINT nType, int cx, int cy)
{
CDialog::OnSize(nType, cx, cy);

// TODO: Add your message handler code here
```

```
/////////////////////////
// MY CODE STARTS HERE
/////////////////////////

m_WindowWidth = cx;
m_WindowHeight = cy;

Invalidate();

/////////////////////////
// MY CODE ENDS HERE
/////////////////////////

}
```

The OnSize() function is executed whenever you change the size of the program's window by dragging its edges or whenever you start the MyPic program.

The second and third parameters of the OnSize() function are cx and cy, which represent the new width and height of the window. The code you typed updates m_WindowWidth and m_WindowHeight with these parameters:

```
m_WindowWidth = cx;
m_WindowHeight = cy;
```

The Invalidate() function is then executed to force the execution of the OnPaint() function:

```
Invalidate(();
```

Stretching the Picture After Resizing the Window

OK, m_WindowWidth and m_WindowHeight have been updated with the new width and height of the window. You can now update the parameters of the StretchDIBits() of the OnPaint() function, so that the BMP picture will fit the new width and height of the window:

☐ Modify the code of the OnPaint() function (in the MyPicDlg.cpp file) as follows:

```
void CMyPicDlg::OnPaint()
{
    if (IsIconic())
    {
...
...
...
    }
    else
    {
/////////////////////////
// MY CODE STARTS HERE
/////////////////////////

if (m_pdibPicture!=NULL)
{
```

```
CPaintDC dc(this);   // device context for painting

::StretchDIBits(dc.m_hDC, // Destination
                0,
                0,
                m_WindowWidth,
                m_WindowHeight,
                0,          //Source
                0,
                DibWidth(m_pdibPicture),
                DibHeight(m_pdibPicture),
                DibPtr(m_pdibPicture),
                DibInfo(m_pdibPicture),
                DIB_RGB_COLORS,
                SRCCOPY);
}

/////////////////////////
// MY CODE ENDS HERE
/////////////////////////

    CDialog::OnPaint();
  }
}
```

The code you typed modifies the second, third, fourth, and fifth parameters of the StretchDIBits() function:

```
::StretchDIBits(dc.m_hDC, // Destination
                0,
                0,
                m_WindowWidth,
                m_WindowHeight,
                0,          //Source
                0,
                DibWidth(m_pdibPicture),
                DibHeight(m_pdibPicture),
                DibPtr(m_pdibPicture),
                DibInfo(m_pdibPicture),
                DIB_RGB_COLORS,
                SRCCOPY);
```

The new second and third parameters specify that the rectangle the BMP picture is copied into is at coordinates (0,0). This rectangle has m_WindowWidth as its width and m_WindowHeight as its height, so the BMP picture is stretched to cover the entire client area of the window.

☐ Save your work.

☐ Compile, link, and execute the MyPic.EXE program.

☐ Select Open BMP from the File menu of MyPic.

MyPic responds by displaying the Movie.BMP file to cover the entire client area of the window. (See Figure 10.10.)

Figure 10.10.

The BMP picture covers the window's entire client area.

☐ Use the mouse to enlarge MyPic's window by dragging its edges.

As you enlarge MyPic's window, the BMP picture is enlarged accordingly. (See Figures 10.11 and 10.12.)

Figure 10.11.

Enlarging MyPic's window to enlarge the BMP picture.

Figure 10.12.

Shrinking MyPic's window to shrink the BMP picture.

☐ Experiment with the MyPic program, then select Exit from the File menu to terminate the program.

Loading and Displaying a BMP Picture During Runtime

The code you typed in the `OnFileOpenbmp()` function loads the C:\Movie.BMP file as follows:

```
m_pdibPicture =
DibOpenFile("C:\\Movie.bmp");
```

The BMP filename is *hard-coded* (specified in the program's code). You'll now add code that does the following: When you select Open BMP from MyPic's File menu, an Open BMP File dialog box appears. You can then select the BMP picture from the hard drive, and the MyPic program will display it.

☐ Modify the code in the `OnFileOpenbmp()` function (in the MyPicDlg.cpp file):

```
void CMyPicDlg::OnFileOpenbmp()
{
// TODO: Add your command handler code here

/////////////////////////////
// MY CODE STARTS HERE
/////////////////////////////

char FileName[500];
char FileTitle[100];


OPENFILENAME ofn;
_fmemset(&ofn, 0, sizeof(ofn));
ofn.lStructSize = sizeof(OPENFILENAME);
ofn.hwndOwner=NULL;
ofn.hInstance =NULL;

ofn.lpstrFilter  =
TEXT("Bitmap picture files *.bmp\0*.bmp\0All Files *.*\0*.*\0\0");

ofn.lpstrCustomFilter = NULL;
ofn.nMaxCustFilter = 0;
ofn.nFilterIndex = 1;
ofn.lpstrFile = FileName;
ofn.nMaxFile = 500;
ofn.lpstrFileTitle = FileTitle;
ofn.nMaxFileTitle = 99;
ofn.lpstrInitialDir = NULL;
ofn.lpstrTitle = "Open BMP File";
ofn.Flags = OFN_FILEMUSTEXIST;
ofn.lpstrDefExt = "BMP";
ofn.lCustData =NULL;
ofn.lpfnHook = NULL;
ofn.lpTemplateName =NULL;

FileName[0]='\0';

GetOpenFileName(&ofn);
```

```
if (FileName[0]=='\0')
{
return;
}

m_pdibPicture = DibOpenFile(FileName);

Invalidate();

////////////////////////////
// MY CODE ENDS HERE
////////////////////////////

}
```

The code you typed declares two variables:

```
char FileName[500];
char FileTitle[100];
```

The FileName variable is a string that can contain a maximum of 500 characters; FileTitle is a string that can contain a maximum of 100 characters. FileName will store the filename and path of the selected BMP file, and FileTitle will store the filename of the loaded BMP file without the path.

Next, the ofn structure of type OPENFILENAME is declared:

```
OPENFILENAME ofn;
```

The OPENFILENAME structure has various structure members. The next block of code sets the values of the data members of the ofn structure.

The FileName string is set to null:

```
FileName[0]='\0';
```

Then the GetOpenFileName() function is executed:

```
GetOpenFileName(&ofn);
```

GetOpenFileName() displays a common dialog box. Note that it has a single parameter. Previously, you set the values of the data members of the ofn structure, so the GetOpenFileName() function will display the common dialog box according to the setting of the ofn structure.

When you set the values of the data members of the ofn structure, you set the lpstrFile data member to FileName as follows:

```
ofn.lpstrFile = FileName;
```

The preceding statement means that GetOpenFileName() will fill the FileName string with the path and filename of the selected file.

An `if` statement is then executed to examine the value of `FileName`:

```
if (FileName[0]=='\0')
{
return;
}
```

If you don't select a file when the common dialog box is displayed, the `FileName` variable is not modified by the `GetOpenFileName()` function. In this case, the code under the `if` statement will be executed, which terminates the `OnFileOpenbmp()` function. If you do select a file, the `FileName` variable is updated with the path and filename of the selected file, and the code under the `if` statement is not executed.

At this point in the program, the `FileName` variable stores the filename and path of the BMP file you selected. So you can actually load the selected file as follows:

```
m_pdibPicture = DibOpenFile(FileName);
```

`m_pdibPicture` is therefore updated with the address pointing to the area in memory that stores the loaded BMP file.

Note: The `GetOpenFileName()` function simply lets you select a file from the hard drive; it doesn't actually load the selected file. To load the selected file, use the `DibOpenFile()` function as follows:

```
m_pdibPicture = DibOpenFile(FileName);
```

Remember that you created the `DibOpenFile()` function with overhead code.

Finally, the `Invalidate()` function is executed to force the execution of the `OnPaint()` function:

```
Invalidate();
```

☐ Save your work, then compile, link, and execute the MyPic program.

☐ Select Open BMP from the File menu.

MyPic responds by displaying the common dialog box shown in Figure 10.13.

The dialog box shown in Figure 10.13 is displayed according to the parameter you supplied to the `GetOpenFileName()` function—namely, the setting of the `ofn` data structure.

☐ Select a BMP file with the common dialog box, then click the Open button.

MyPic responds by loading and displaying the selected BMP file.

☐ Experiment with the MyPic program, then terminate it.

Figure 10.13.
*The Open BMP File
dialog box.*

Note: There's something wrong with the MyPic program! Can you tell what it is?
Try the following:

☐ Select Open BMP from the File menu of MyPic.

MyPic responds by displaying the Open BMP File dialog box.

☐ While the dialog box is displayed, select Open BMP from the File menu again.

Oops! Another Open BMP File dialog box appears! Exercise 2 at the end of this
chapter shows how this problem can be easily fixed.

Changing the Window's Caption

Currently, the caption of the MyPic window is The MyPic Program. (See, for example, Figure
10.11.) You'll now add code that displays the name of the loaded file in the window's caption:

☐ Modify the code of the OnFileOpenbmp() function (in the MyPicDlg.cpp file) as follows:

```
void CMyPicDlg::OnFileOpenbmp()
{
// TODO: Add your command handler code here

/////////////////////////////
// MY CODE STARTS HERE
/////////////////////////////

...
...
...

m_pdibPicture = DibOpenFile(FileName);


SetWindowText(FileTitle);
```

```
Invalidate();

/////////////////////////
// MY CODE ENDS HERE
/////////////////////////

}
```

You set the caption of the window as follows:

```
SetWindowText(FileTitle);
```

The `GetOpenFileName()` function updates the `FileTitle` variable with the filename (without the path) of the selected file. You supplied `FileTitle` as the parameter of the `SetWindowText()` function.

☐ Save your work, then compile, link, and execute the MyPic program.

☐ Select Open BMP from the File menu.

MyPic responds by displaying the common dialog box that lets you select a file.

☐ Select a BMP file with the common dialog box, then click the Open button.

MyPic responds by loading and displaying the selected BMP file. However, now the caption of MyPic's window shows the name of the loaded file. (See Figure 10.14.)

Figure 10.14.
The window's caption displays the name of the selected file.

☐ Experiment with the MyPic program, then terminate it.

Summary

In this chapter, you have learned how to load and display BMP pictures during runtime. You can select any file from the hard drive and display the picture during the program's execution.

While creating the MyPic program, you have learned how to use the `GetOpenFileName()` function to set up a common dialog box for selecting a file from the hard drive. You have also learned how to set the caption of the window to the name of the selected file.

SAMS

Sams
Learning
Center

SAMS
PUBLISHING

Q&A

Q **Writing a program as described in this chapter means I supply the program file as well as the BMP files to my end-user. Can I create a program with the BMP file embedded in the EXE program file?**

A Yes. The MyBMP.EXE program you created in Chapter 8 is an example of a program in which the BMP file is an integral part of the EXE program file.

Q **In Chapter 8, I learned how to create a program with an embedded BMP file. In this chapter, the BMP file wasn't embedded in the EXE file. Which method is better?**

A It depends on the particular application you're developing. Naturally, if you embed the BMP file in your EXE file, then the user can't load whatever file he or she wants. Also, the EXE file is larger because the BMP file is added.

If you want your user to be able to load any file he or she wants, then the technique described in this chapter is suitable.

In general, if you want to display a certain BMP picture in your application without letting the user choose the BMP file, then it is better to embed the BMP file into the EXE file. Why? Because the BMP file will never be separated from the EXE file. If you use the technique in this chapter, you'll have to give your user the BMP file as well as the EXE file. You then run the risk of the user losing the BMP file or accidentally deleting or altering it.

Q **When I change the size of MyPic's window, the BMP picture changes its size accordingly. However, when the BMP picture is stretched over a large area, I see a lot of flickering (and I own a very fast computer!). Can I do something to avoid the flickering?**

A Yes, you can. You can use WinG technology, which will enable you to move graphical objects without flickering.

10

Quiz

1. When specifying a path of a file in C/C++, you must use two backslash characters (\\), as in the following statement:

```
C:\\MyDir\\MyFile.TXT
```

   a. True
   b. False

Exercises

1. The `OnDestroy()` function (in the MyPicDlg.cpp file) has the following code:

```
void CMyPicDlg::OnDestroy()
{
    CDialog::OnDestroy();

// TODO: Add your message handler code here

/////////////////////////////
// MY CODE STARTS HERE
/////////////////////////////

GlobalFreePtr(m_pdibPicture);

/////////////////////////////
// MY CODE ENDS HERE
/////////////////////////////

}
```

The code in the `OnDestroy()` function frees the memory used to store the loaded BMP file.

There are several ways to terminate the MyPic program. Create one that lets you verify that the `OnDestroy()` function is executed no matter how the user terminates the MyPic program.

2. Currently, if the user selects Open BMP from MyPic's File menu, the Open BMP File dialog box is displayed. If the user again selects Open BMP from the File menu, another Open BMP File dialog box is displayed. Now there are two dialog boxes onscreen.

Modify the program so that the user can't open more than one dialog box at any given time. To perform this exercise, follow the steps outlined in the solution.

Quiz Answer

1. a.

Exercise Answers

1. The good old `MessageBeep()` function can be used to verify that the `OnDestroy()` function is executed no matter what method is used to terminate the program.

☐ Add the `MessageBeep()` statement to the `OnDestroy()` function (in the MyPicDlg.cpp file):

```
void CMyPicDlg::OnDestroy()
{
     CDialog::OnDestroy();

// TODO: Add your message handler code here

//////////////////////////
// MY CODE STARTS HERE
//////////////////////////

MessageBeep((WORD)-1);
GlobalFreePtr(m_pdibPicture);

//////////////////////////
// MY CODE ENDS HERE
//////////////////////////

}
```

☐ Save your work, then compile and link the MyPic program.

☐ Execute the MyPic program, then terminate it by selecting Exit from MyPic's File menu.

> *As you can hear, the PC beeps when the MyPic program is terminated.*

☐ Execute the MyPic program again, but now terminate it by right-clicking the caption of MyPic's window, then selecting Close from the system menu that pops up. Make sure the PC beeps before the MyPic program terminates.

☐ Repeat the preceding step by terminating the program another way (for example, click the × icon on the upper-right corner of the window; click the icon on the upper-left corner of MyPic's window, then select Close from the system menu that pops up; double-click the icon on the upper-left corner of MyPic's window).

Note: Remember that you must release the memory used by the loaded BMP picture. If you don't, your PC can't use this memory even after the MyPic program is terminated.

If you develop programs that don't release occupied memory, sooner or later your user will notice that when your programs are used, there are some memory problems with the PC.

2. Follow these steps to solve Exercise 2:

☐ Modify the OnFileOpenbmp() function (in the MyPicDlg.cpp file) as follows:

```
void CMyPicDlg::OnFileOpenbmp()
{
// TODO: Add your command handler code here

////////////////////////////
// MY CODE STARTS HERE
////////////////////////////

char FileName[500];
char FileTitle[100];


OPENFILENAME ofn;
_fmemset(&ofn, 0, sizeof(ofn));
ofn.lStructSize = sizeof(OPENFILENAME);

//ofn.hwndOwner=NULL;

ofn.hwndOwner=m_hWnd;

ofn.hInstance =NULL;

ofn.lpstrFilter  =
TEXT("Bitmap picture files *.bmp\0*.bmp\0All Files *.*\0*.*\0\0");

ofn.lpstrCustomFilter = NULL;
ofn.nMaxCustFilter = 0;
ofn.nFilterIndex = 1;
ofn.lpstrFile = FileName;
ofn.nMaxFile = 500;
ofn.lpstrFileTitle = FileTitle;
ofn.nMaxFileTitle = 99;
ofn.lpstrInitialDir = NULL;
ofn.lpstrTitle = "Open BMP File";
ofn.Flags = OFN_FILEMUSTEXIST;
ofn.lpstrDefExt = "BMP";
ofn.lCustData =NULL;
ofn.lpfnHook = NULL;
ofn.lpTemplateName =NULL;

FileName[0]='\0';

GetOpenFileName(&ofn);

if (FileName[0]=='\0')
{
return;
}

m_pdibPicture = DibOpenFile(FileName);
```

```
SetWindowText(FileTitle);

Invalidate();

/////////////////////////
// MY CODE ENDS HERE
/////////////////////////

}
```

The code you typed comments out this statement:

`//ofn.hwndOwner=NULL;`

Instead, the following statement is used:

`ofn.hwndOwner=m_hWnd;`

In other words, the structure member hwndOwner of the ofn structure is updated with the value of the m_hWnd data member of the CMyPicDlg class. Therefore, the dialog box displayed by GetOpenFileName() is displayed so that the IDD_MYPIC_DIALOG dialog box is the "owner" of the common dialog box.

☐ Save your work, compile and link the MyPic program, then execute it.

☐ Select Open BMP from MyPic's File menu. While the Open BMP File dialog box is displayed, try to click in the main window of the MyPic program.

As you can see, you cannot switch to the main window of the MyPic program while the dialog box is displayed.

11

Writing Single-Document Interface (SDI) Applications

In this chapter, you'll learn what a single-document interface application is and how to create one with Visual C++.

What Is an SDI Application?

As its name implies, a *single-document interface* (SDI) application lets you work with a single document. The document is where the program's data is stored. The program allows you to save the document into a file and open previously saved documents from files. For example, in a text editor SDI program, the document you work on is text. You can save text into text files and load text from previously saved text files. Similarly, in a sound editor SDI program, you can save sound into sound files and load sound from previously saved sound files.

In an SDI program, you can work on only one document at any time; you can't open several documents simultaneously. An example of an SDI program is the Notepad program shipped with Windows. You can view and edit text files with Notepad. However, you can view and edit only one file at a time, not several files simultaneously. Figure 11.1 shows the Notepad program with an open file.

Figure 11.1.
The Windows Notepad program (an SDI program).

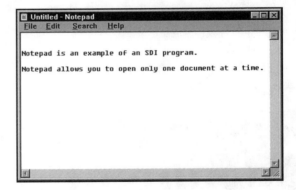

A multiple-document interface (MDI) program also works with documents, but you can work on several documents simultaneously. An example of an MDI program is the Word for Windows program. Chapter 13, "Writing Multiple-Document Interface (MDI) Applications," will cover this topic in more detail.

The Circle.EXE Program

In this chapter, you'll write a Visual C++ program called Circle.EXE, an example of an SDI program. Before you start writing the Circle program, first specify what it should look like and what it should do.

- When you start the Circle program, its window should display a circle in the middle. (See Figure 11.2.)

Figure 11.2.
The main window of the Circle program.

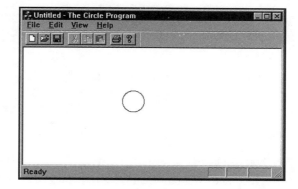

- The Circle program is a simple SDI program; its document is a circle. You can place the circle anywhere in the window and then save the circle into a file. Later, you can open the previously saved file, and the circle will appear onscreen.
- You can draw a circle anywhere in Circle's window by simply clicking the mouse at the desired point. Figure 11.3 shows the window of the Circle program after clicking the mouse at the upper-right corner of the program's window.

Figure 11.3.
Drawing a circle at the upper-right corner of the window.

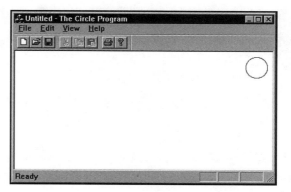

- You can save the circle into a file by selecting Save (or Save As) from the File menu of the Circle program. (See Figure 11.4.)
- You can load a previously saved circle by selecting Open from the File menu of the Circle program. Once you select Open from the File menu, the Circle program displays an Open dialog box for selecting the saved file.

Figure 11.4.
The File menu of the Circle program.

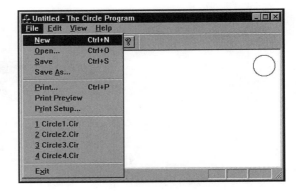

- You can print the currently displayed circle by selecting Print from the File menu.
- The Circle program includes a toolbar displayed at the top of the program's window. Click the desired tool on the toolbar to perform the operation you want. For example, clicking the Save tool (the one with a disk icon) is equivalent to selecting Save from the File menu.

Now you know what the Circle program should do, start by creating the project of the Circle program.

> **Note:** The Circle program you create in this chapter uses basically the same code and functions as the MCircle program in Chapter 13 and the Circle.LIB library in Chapter 16, "Creating Your Own Classes and Modules." This is done so you can see how different types of programs and component modules can use the same code; it is hoped that this repetition will help you understand the various ways code can be used.

Creating the Project of the Circle Program

Follow these steps to create the project and skeleton files of the Circle program:

☐ As in previous chapters, create the directory C:\TYVCProg\Programs\CH11 and then open a new project workspace by selecting New from the File menu of Visual C++.

Visual C++ responds by displaying the New Project Workspace dialog box.

☐ Select MFC AppWizard (exe) from the Type list and enter Circle in the Name box.

☐ Click the Browse button, select the C:\TYVCProg\Programs\CH11 directory, then click the Create button.

   Visual C++ responds by displaying the MFC AppWizard - Step 1 window.

☐ Set the Step 1 window as shown in Figure 11.5 to create a single-document–type application, then click the Next button. Note that the "Single document" radio button is selected.

Figure 11.5.
Creating an SDI application.

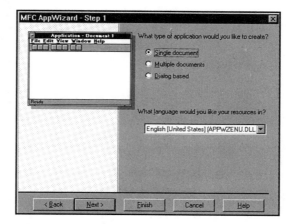

   Visual C++ responds by displaying the MFC AppWizard - Step 2 of 6 window.

☐ Set the Step 2 window as shown in Figure 11.6, then click the Next button.

Figure 11.6.
Choosing the option for no database support.

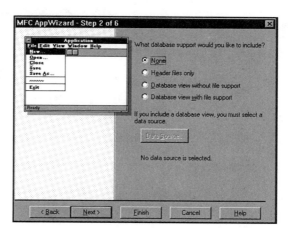

Visual C++ responds by displaying the MFC AppWizard - Step 3 of 6 window.

☐ Set the Step 3 window as shown in Figure 11.7, then click the Next button.

Figure 11.7.
Choosing not to include OLE features.

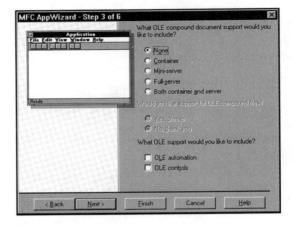

Visual C++ responds by displaying the MFC AppWizard - Step 4 of 6 window.

☐ Set the Step 4 window as shown in Figure 11.8. You want the program to support these features: docking toolbar, initial toolbar, printing and print preview, and 3-D controls. Leave the combo box specifying the number of files on the recent file list at the default setting of 4. When you're done, click the Next button.

Figure 11.8.
Selecting which features to include.

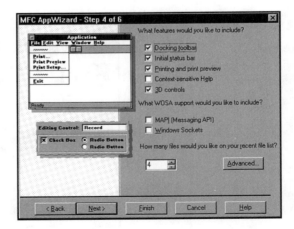

Visual C++ responds by displaying the MFC AppWizard - Step 5 of 6 window.

☐ In the Step 5 window, use the default settings and click the Next button. (See Figure 11.9.)

Figure 11.9.
Using the default settings.

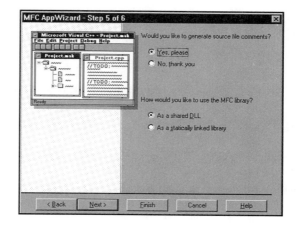

Visual C++ responds by displaying the MFC AppWizard - Step 6 of 6 window.

In the Step 6 window, notice that AppWizard has created the following classes for you: `CCircleApp`, `CMainFrame`, `CCircleDoc`, `CCircleView`. (See Figure 11.10.)

Figure 11.10.
Checking the classes created by AppWizard.

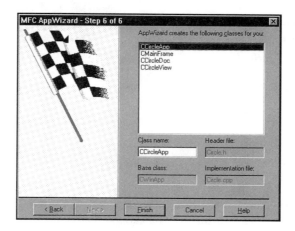

The two most important classes are `CCircleView` and `CCircleDoc`. In the following sections, you will write code in the member functions of these two classes only. The `CCircleView` class is the Circle program's *view class*, which is responsible for what you see onscreen. The `CCircleDoc` class is the Circle program's *document class*, which is responsible for storing the document (the data) of the program. The code you write in the document class will be responsible for saving your circle drawing into a file and loading previously saved files.

☐ Click the Finish button of the Step 6 of 6 window.

Visual C++ responds by displaying the New Project Information window.

☐ Click the OK button of the New Project Information window.

☐ Select Set Default Configuration from the Build menu.

Visual C++ responds by displaying the Default Project Configuration dialog box.

☐ Select Circle - Win32 Release in the Default Project Configuration dialog box, then click the OK button.

That's it! You've finished creating the project and skeleton files of the Circle program.

Running the Circle Program Before Customization

Before you start customizing the Circle program, first compile, link, and execute it. You'll see that the skeleton files Visual C++ created for you yield an SDI program that already performs some functions.

☐ Compile, link, and execute the Circle.EXE program.

The main window of the Circle program appears, as shown in Figure 11.11.

Figure 11.11.
The main window of the Circle program before customization.

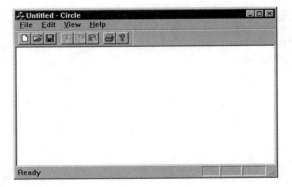

As you can see, the skeleton code yielded a nice-looking SDI program. The program includes a standard SDI menu system and toolbar. Of course, at this point the Circle program won't do what you want it to do. In the following sections, you'll write code that customizes the Circle program so you can draw a circle, save the circle drawing into a file, and load previously saved files.

☐ Terminate the Circle program by selecting Exit from its File menu.

As you can see, although you haven't written a single line of code yet, the Exit menu item does what it's supposed to do—terminate the program.

Declaring the Data Members of the Document Class

As discussed earlier, the code you write in the document class is responsible for storing the document (the program's data). This code will enable you to save the program's data into a file and to load data from previously saved files. You'll now add data members to CCircleDoc, the document class of the Circle program, for storing Circle's document data:

☐ Select Project Workspace from the View menu.

> *Visual C++ responds by displaying the Project Workspace window of the Circle program.*

☐ Open the file CircleDoc.h, where the document class of the Circle program is declared. You'll now declare two data members in the CCircleDoc class:

☐ Modify the declaration of the CCircleDoc class as follows:

```
class CCircleDoc : public CDocument
{
protected: // create from serialization only
    CCircleDoc();
    DECLARE_DYNCREATE(CCircleDoc)

// Attributes
public:

//////////////////////////
// MY CODE STARTS HERE
//////////////////////////

int m_PosX;
int m_PosY;

//////////////////////////
// MY CODE ENDS HERE
//////////////////////////

// Operations
public:

..
..
};
```

☐ Save your work.

The code you added to the declaration of the CCircleDoc class declares two int data members, m_PosX and m_PosY:

```
int m_PosX;
int m_PosY;
```

The m_PosX data member will be used for storing the x-coordinate of the circle you draw, and the m_PosY data member will be used for storing the y-coordinate of the circle.

If you wish, you can add additional data members that define the drawn circle, such as the radius or color of the circle. However, for simplicity's sake, in the Circle program you can specify only the x-y coordinate of the circle, the point at which the circle will be drawn. All other aspects of the circle will be fixed.

The document class of the Circle program now has two data members: m_PosX and m_PosY. These data members make up the document of the Circle program. Later, you will write code for saving m_PosX and m_PosY into a file and loading data from previously saved files into m_PosX and m_PosY.

Declaring the Data Members of the View Class

As discussed earlier, the code you write in the view class is responsible for what you see onscreen. The data members you're adding to the view class are a mirror image of the data members you declared in the document class because the code of the view class is supposed to display onscreen whatever the document specifies. For example, if the document specifies that the circle should be displayed at a certain x-y coordinate, the code of the view class will display the circle at the specified coordinate. You'll now add data members to CCircleView, the view class of the Circle program, for drawing a circle in the program's window:

☐ Open the file CircleView.h, where the view class of the Circle program is declared. You'll now declare two data members in the CCircleView class:

☐ Modify the declaration of the CCircleView class as follows:

```
class CCircleView : public CView
{
protected: // create from serialization only
     CCircleView();
     DECLARE_DYNCREATE(CCircleView)

// Attributes
public:
     CCircleDoc* GetDocument();

///////////////////////////
// MY CODE STARTS HERE
///////////////////////////

int m_PosX;
int m_PosY;

///////////////////////////
// MY CODE ENDS HERE
///////////////////////////
```

```
// Operations
public:

    ..
    ..
};
```

☐ Save your work.

The code you added to the declaration of the `CCircleView` class is identical to the code you added for the `CCircleDoc` class. This code declares two `int` data members, `m_PosX` and `m_PosY`, used for holding the x-y coordinates of the circle:

```
int m_PosX;
int m_PosY;
```

At this point, the document class and the view class have the same two data members: `m_PosX` and `m_PosY`. The values of these data members should always be the same in each class, so that the values stored in the document are the same as the values you see onscreen. Therefore, the code you write in the following sections will ensure that the document class data members always have the same values as their corresponding view class data members.

Initializing the Data Members of the Document Class

You'll now write the code that initializes the data members of the document class in the `OnNewDocument()` member function of the `CCircleDoc` class.

☐ Open the file CircleDoc.cpp and locate the `OnNewDocument()` function.

☐ Write the following code in the `OnNewDocument()` function:

```
BOOL CCircleDoc::OnNewDocument()
{
if (!CDocument::OnNewDocument())
    return FALSE;

// TODO: add reinitialization code here
// (SDI documents will reuse this document)

/////////////////////////
// MY CODE STARTS HERE
/////////////////////////

// Initialize the data members of the document.
m_PosX = 200;
m_PosY = 100;
```

```
/////////////////////////
// MY CODE ENDS HERE
/////////////////////////

return TRUE;

}
```

☐ Save your work.

As its name implies, the OnNewDocument() member function of the document class is automatically executed whenever a new document is created—when you start the program and when you select New from the File menu.

The code you wrote in the OnNewDocument() function initializes the value of the m_PosX data member to 200 and the m_PosY data member to 100:

```
m_PosX = 200;
m_PosY = 100;
```

Whenever a new document is created, the m_PosX document data member will be set to a value of 200 and the m_PosY document data member will be set to a value of 100.

Initializing the Data Members of the View Class

In the preceding section, you initialized the data members of the document class. They represent the values that will be stored in a document file. You'll now write the code that initializes the data members of the view class, which are just as important as the data members of the document class. They represent what you see onscreen.

Follow these steps to write the code that initializes the view class data members in the OnInitialUpdate() member function of the CCircleView class:

☐ In the Message Maps tab of ClassWizard, select the following event:

Class name:	CCircleView
Object ID:	CCircleView
Message:	OnInitialUpdate

☐ Click the Add Function button.

Visual C++ responds by adding the OnInitialUpdate() function.

☐ Click the Edit Code button.

Visual C++ responds by opening the file CircleView.cpp with the function OnInitialUpdate() ready for you to edit.

☐ Write the following code in the `OnInitialUpdate()` function:

```
void CCircleView::OnInitialUpdate()
{
CView::OnInitialUpdate();

// TODO: Add your specialized code here and/or call
//       the base class

/////////////////////////
// MY CODE STARTS HERE
/////////////////////////

// Get a pointer to the document
CCircleDoc* pDoc = GetDocument();

// Update data members of the view with the
// corresponding document values.
m_PosX  = pDoc->m_PosX;
m_PosY  = pDoc->m_PosY;

/////////////////////////
// MY CODE ENDS HERE
/////////////////////////

}
```

☐ Save your work.

As its name implies, the `OnInitialUpdate()` member function of the `CCircleView` class is responsible for initializing the data members of the view class. The code you just attached to the `OnInitalUpdate()` function updates the view class data members with the current values of the document class data members.

The first statement you typed uses the `GetDocument()` function to extract a pointer, `pDoc`, to the document:

```
CCircleDoc* pDoc = GetDocument();
```

The remaining statements you typed use the `pDoc` pointer to initialize the view class data members with the current values of the document class data members:

```
m_PosX  = pDoc->m_PosX;
m_PosY  = pDoc->m_PosY;
```

These statements update the `m_PosX` and `m_PosY` data members of the view class with the corresponding document data members.

Writing the Code That Displays the Circle

You'll now write the code that displays the circle onscreen. In which class will you write this code? You guessed it! In the view class, because it's responsible for what you see onscreen. You'll write

the drawing code in the OnDraw() member function of the CCircleView class. The OnDraw() function of the view class is automatically executed whenever the program's window needs to be drawn.

☐ Open the file CircleView.cpp and locate the OnDraw() function.

☐ Write the following code in the OnDraw() function:

```
void CCircleView::OnDraw(CDC* pDC)
{
CCircleDoc* pDoc = GetDocument();
ASSERT_VALID(pDoc);

// TODO: add draw code for native data here

/////////////////////////
// MY CODE STARTS HERE
/////////////////////////

// Define the rectangular boundaries of the
// circle to be drawn.
RECT  rect;
rect.left = m_PosX - 20;
rect.top = m_PosY -20;
rect.bottom = m_PosY + 20;
rect.right = m_PosX +20;

// Draw the circle.
pDC->Ellipse(&rect);

/////////////////////////
// MY CODE ENDS HERE
/////////////////////////

}
```

☐ Save your work.

The code you typed in the OnDraw() function draws a circle in the program's window at the position specified by the m_PosX and m_PosY data members of the view class.

The first five statements you typed define the coordinates and dimensions of a rectangle called rect:

```
RECT  rect;
rect.left = m_PosX - 20;
rect.top = m_PosY -20;
rect.bottom = m_PosY + 20;
rect.right = m_PosX +20;
```

These statements define the rectangle so that its center is at the x-y coordinate specified by the m_PosX and m_PosY data members. The width of the rectangle is 40 pixels and the height is also 40 pixels, so rect is defined as a square.

The last statement you typed uses the Ellipse() function to draw an ellipse:

```
pDC->Ellipse(&rect);
```

pDC, the parameter of the OnDraw() function, is the pointer to the dc (device context). By executing the Ellipse() function on the pDC pointer, you are drawing an ellipse in the program's window.

As you can see, the parameter of the Ellipse() function in the preceding statement is &rect. Therefore, the ellipse will be drawn within the boundaries of the rectangle you defined. Since rect is a square, the ellipse will be drawn as a circle.

Putting it all together, the code you wrote in the OnDraw() function draws a circle in the program's window at the x-y coordinate specified by the m_PosX and m_PosY data members of the view class.

☐ Compile, link, and execute the Circle program to see your code in action.

Visual C++ responds by executing the Circle program. The main window of the Circle program appears, as shown in Figure 11.12.

Figure 11.12.
The main window of the Circle program after customization.

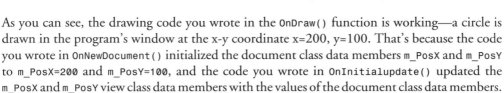

As you can see, the drawing code you wrote in the OnDraw() function is working—a circle is drawn in the program's window at the x-y coordinate x=200, y=100. That's because the code you wrote in OnNewDocument() initialized the document class data members m_PosX and m_PosY to m_PosX=200 and m_PosY=100, and the code you wrote in OnInitialupdate() updated the m_PosX and m_PosY view class data members with the values of document class data members.

The drawing code you wrote in the OnDraw() member function of the view class is executed whenever the screen needs to be redrawn and whenever you select Print from the File menu. The code in OnDraw() is responsible for both what you see onscreen and what is printed when you select Print from the File menu. To see the Print menu item in action, do the following:

☐ Select Print from the File menu of the Circle program.

The Circle program responds by displaying the Print dialog box. (See Figure 11.13.)

Figure 11.13.
The Print dialog box.

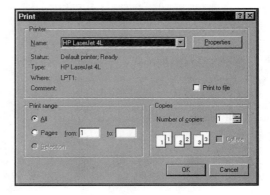

☐ Click the OK button.

The Circle program responds by printing a page with a circle drawn on it.

☐ Terminate the Circle program by selecting Exit from its File menu.

Writing Code to Draw the Circle at Any Point Onscreen

At this point, when you start the Circle program, it displays a circle at the x-y coordinate x=200, y=100. You'll now write code that enables you to draw the circle anywhere in the program's window by simply clicking the mouse at the desired point. Since this code involves what you see onscreen, you'll write it in the view class.

☐ In the Message Maps tab of ClassWizard, select the following event:

Class name:	`CCircleView`
Object ID:	`CCircleView`
Message:	`WM_LBUTTONDOWN`

☐ Click the Add Function button.

Visual C++ responds by adding the `OnLButtonDown()` function.

☐ Click the Edit Code button.

Visual C++ responds by opening the file CircleView.cpp with the function `OnLButtonDown()` ready for you to edit.

☐ Write the following code in the OnLButtonDown() function:

```
void CCircleView::OnLButtonDown(UINT nFlags, CPoint point)
{

// TODO: Add your message handler code here
// and/or call default

/////////////////////////
// MY CODE STARTS HERE
/////////////////////////

// Update the m_PosX and m_PosY data members of
// the view class with the x-y coordinate of the
// point where the mouse was clicked.
m_PosX = point.x;
m_PosY = point.y;

// Trigger a call to the OnDraw() function.
Invalidate();

// Get a pointer to the document
CCircleDoc* pDoc = GetDocument();

// Update data members of the document with the
// new values of the view class data members.
pDoc->m_PosX = m_PosX;
pDoc->m_PosY = m_PosY ;

// Signal that the document has been modified.
pDoc->SetModifiedFlag(TRUE);

/////////////////////////
// MY CODE ENDS HERE
/////////////////////////

CView::OnLButtonDown(nFlags, point);

}
```

☐ Save your work.

The OnLButtonDown() member function of the view class is automatically executed whenever you click the left mouse button on the program's window.

The second parameter of the OnLButtonDown() function, point, specifies the point onscreen where you click the mouse button: point.x holds the x-coordinate of the point and point.y holds the y-coordinate.

The first two statements you typed update the m_PosX and m_PosY data members of the view class with the x-y coordinates of the point where you clicked the mouse:

```
m_PosX = point.x;
m_PosY = point.y;
```

The next statement calls the `Invalidate()` function to execute the `OnDraw()` function:

```
Invalidate();
```

Recall that the code you wrote in the `OnDraw()` function draws a circle at the point specified by `m_PosX` and `m_PosY`. Therefore, the preceding statements will draw a circle at the point where you clicked the mouse.

The next statement uses the `GetDocument()` function to extract a pointer, pDoc, to the document:

```
CCircleDoc* pDoc = GetDocument();
```

The next two statements use the pDoc pointer to update the data members of the document class with the new values of the view class data members:

```
pDoc->m_PosX = m_PosX;
pDoc->m_PosY = m_PosY ;
```

Now the data members of the document class have the same values as their corresponding data members in the view class. Whenever you change the values of data members in the view class, you should change the corresponding data members in the document class to the same values. This is necessary because you always want the data stored in the program's document to be the same as the data viewed onscreen.

The last statement you typed calls the `SetModifiedFlag()` function:

```
pDoc->SetModifiedFlag();
```

Note that the `SetModified()` function is executed on the pDoc document pointer because it's a member function of the document class (not the view class). What does the `SetModifiedFlag()` function do? It raises a flag in the document to indicate that the data has been changed. If you try to exit the program without first saving the currently open document, the program will display a warning message box to give you a chance to save the changes made in the document. You should always call the `SetModifiedFlag()` function after changing the values of the document class data members.

☐ Compile, link, and execute the Circle program to see the code you wrote in the `OnLButtonDown()` function in action.

Visual C++ responds by executing the Circle program. The main window of the Circle program appears, as shown back in Figure 11.12.

☐ Click the mouse at the upper-right corner of the program's window.

The Circle program responds by drawing a circle at the point where you clicked the mouse. (See Figure 11.14.)

Figure 11.14.
Drawing a circle at the upper-right corner of the program's window.

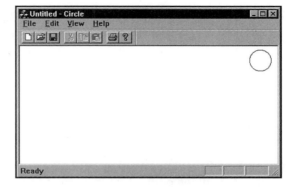

☐ Try clicking the mouse at various points in the program's window to see how the circle is drawn.

☐ Terminate the Circle program by selecting Exit from its File menu.

Writing Code That Saves and Loads Files

You'll now write the code responsible for saving the document into a file and loading previously saved files. You'll write this code in the document class.

☐ Open the file CircleDoc.cpp and locate the Serialize() function.

The Serialize() function is automatically executed when you select Save, Save As, or Open from the File menu of the program:

```
void CCircleDoc::Serialize(CArchive& ar)
{
if (ar.IsStoring())
    {
    // TODO: add storing code here

    }
    else
    {
    // TODO: add loading code here

    }
}
```

The code in the Serialize() function is made up of a simple if…else statement:

```
if (ar.IsStoring())
    {
    // TODO: add storing code here
    ........................................
    ... This code is automatically executed ...
```

```
... whenever the user selects Save or   ...
... Save As from the File menu.          ...
.........................................
}
else
{
// TODO: add loading code here
.........................................
... This code is automatically executed ...
... whenever the user selects Open       ...
... from the File menu.                  ...
.........................................

}
```

This is the if condition of the if...else statement:

```
if (ar.IsStoring())
```

In this code, ar is the parameter of the Serialize() function and represents the archive (the file) you're trying to read or write. If you select Save or Save As from the File menu, then the condition of the preceding if statement is satisfied and the code under the if is executed. If you select Open from the File menu, then the code under the else is executed.

Therefore, your job is to do the following:

1. Write code under the if statement that writes data to the file.
2. Write code under the else statement that reads data from the file.

The code for writing and reading data to and from the file is easy. Follow these steps:

☐ Write the following code in the Serialize() function:

```
void CCircleDoc::Serialize(CArchive& ar)
{
if (ar.IsStoring())
    {
    // TODO: add storing code here

    ////////////////////////
    // MY CODE STARTS HERE
    ////////////////////////

    // Save m_PosX and m_PosY into the file.
    ar << m_PosX;
    ar << m_PosY;

    ////////////////////////
    // MY CODE ENDS HERE
    ////////////////////////

    }
else
    {
```

```
    // TODO: add loading code here

    /////////////////////////
    // MY CODE STARTS HERE
    /////////////////////////

    // Fill m_PosX and m_PosY with data from the file.
    ar >> m_PosX;
    ar >> m_PosY;

    /////////////////////////
    // MY CODE ENDS HERE
    /////////////////////////

    }
}
```

☐ Save your work.

The code responsible for saving data into the file (the code under the `if` statement) is this:

```
ar << m_PosX;
ar << m_PosY;
```

The insertion operator (<<) indicates that you want to save data into the file. For example, this statement stores the data member `m_PosX` of the document class into the file:

```
ar << m_PosX;
```

Into what file? It depends on whether you selected Open, Save, or Save As from the File menu. If you selected Save As, for example, and selected the file MyFile.TRY from the Save As dialog box, then the statement `ar<<m_PosX` will store the `m_PosX` variable in the MyFile.TRY file. You can think of `ar` as the file you selected.

> **Note:** `ar` is the archive object (an object of class `CArchive`) corresponding to the file you selected. Therefore, the following statement literally means "Save the variable `m_PosX` into the file that the user selected":
>
> ```
> ar << m_PosX;
> ```
>
> The `CArchive` class is discussed in Chapter 14, "File Access and Serialization."

The code responsible for loading the data from the file into the variables (the code under the `else` statement in the `Serialize()` function) is this:

```
ar >> m_PosX;
ar >> m_PosY;
```

The extractor operator (>>) indicates that you want to load data from the file into the variable. For example, the following statement fills the data member m_PosX with data from the file:

```
ar >> m_PosX;
```

From which file? Again, it depends on what you did. If, for example, you selected Open from the File menu, then selected the file MyFile.TRY from the Open File dialog box, then the statement ar>>m_PosX will fill the m_PosX variable with data from the MyFile.TRY file.

The order in which you extract the data must be the same order used for saving the data. For example, if you save data to the file with these statements:

```
ar << Var1;
ar << Var2;
ar << Var3;
```

then when you extract the data from the file into the variables, you must use the same order:

```
ar >> Var1;
ar >> Var2;
ar >> Var3;
```

> **Note:** In the previous code, you used the insertion (<<) and extractor (>>) operators on several lines. You can also use these operators on a single line. For example, these three statements,
>
> ```
> ar << Var1;
> ar << Var2;
> ar << Var3;
> ```
>
> are equivalent to this single statement:
>
> ```
> ar << Var1 << Var2 << Var3;
> ```
>
> Similarly, these three statements,
>
> ```
> ar >> Var1;
> ar >> Var2;
> ar >> Var3;
> ```
>
> are equivalent to this single statement:
>
> ```
> ar >> Var1 >> Var2 >> Var3;
> ```

You have finished writing the code for the Circle program!

☐ Compile, link, and execute the Circle program to see your code in action.

Visual C++ responds by executing the Circle program. The main window of the Circle program appears, as shown back in Figure 11.12.

The title of the program's window is currently Untitled - Circle. The "Untitled" means you just started the program and haven't saved the document into a file.

To test the saving and loading code you wrote in the Serialize() function of the document class, do the following:

☐ Click the mouse at the lower-left corner of the program's window.

The Circle program responds by drawing the circle at the lower-left corner of the program's window. (See Figure 11.15.)

Figure 11.15.
Drawing a circle at the lower-left corner of the window.

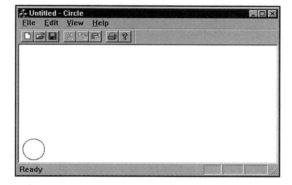

Now save the document into a file as follows:

☐ Select Save As from the File menu of the Circle program.

The Circle program responds by displaying the Save As dialog box. (See Figure 11.16.)

Figure 11.16.
The Save As dialog box.

☐ Type MyCircle.Cir in the File name edit box, then click the Save button.

The Circle program responds by creating the MyCircle.Cir file and saving the document into this file.

Because you saved the document in the file MyCircle.Cir, the title of the program's window is now `MyCircle.Cir - Circle`. (See Figure 11.17.)

Figure 11.17.
Changing the title of the program's window.

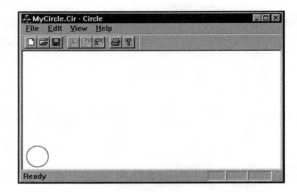

To make sure your document is saved in the MyCircle.Cir file, do the following:

☐ Select New from the File menu of the Circle program.

> *The Circle program responds by closing the MyCircle.Cir document and opening a new document.*

The window of your Circle program should now look like the one back in Figure 11.12—the title of the program's window is `Untitled - Circle`, and there is a circle in the center of the window.

Now open the MyCircle.Cir document as follows:

☐ Select Open from the File menu of the Circle program.

> *The Circle program responds by displaying the Open dialog box. (See Figure 11.18.)*

Figure 11.18.
The Open dialog box.

☐ Use the Open dialog box to select the MyCircle.Cir file you saved earlier, then click the Open button.

The Circle program responds by opening the MyCircle.Cir file.

The window of your Circle program should now look like the one back in Figure 11.17—the title of the program's window is `MyCircle.Cir - Circle`, and the circle is drawn in the lower-left corner.

The code you wrote in the `Serialize()` member function of the document class is working! You can save documents into files and load previously saved files.

☐ Keep experimenting with the Circle program. For example, place the circle at different places in the window and save the document under different filenames.

As you experiment with the Circle program, notice that the File menu of the program maintains a most recently used (MRU) file list. (See Figure 11.19.)

Figure 11.19.
The MRU file list of Circle's File menu.

The MRU list in the File menu lists the last four files you've worked with. When you click one of the files in the MRU list, the file is opened. Why four? Recall that when you created the project of the Circle program, in Step 4 of the AppWizard you accepted the default setting of 4 for the number of files in your MRU list. (Refer back to Figure 11.8.)

Note: The Circle program includes a toolbar displayed at the top of the window. You can perform operations by clicking the tool you want on the toolbar. For example, clicking the Save tool on the toolbar (the one with a disk icon) is equivalent to selecting Save from the File menu; clicking the About tool (the one with a question mark icon) is the same as selecting About from the Help menu.

The tools were created for you by Visual C++ when you created the project and skeleton files of the program. In Chapter 15, "Toolbars and Status Bars," you'll learn how to create your own custom tools in the program's toolbar.

☐ Terminate the Circle program by selecting Exit from its File menu.

Enhancing the Circle Program

You will now enhance the Circle program in two ways:

- Change the caption in the title of the application's window from Circle to Circle for Windows.
- Change the default file type displayed in the Save As and Open dialog boxes from *.* to *.cir. This means that whenever you select Open or Save As from the dialog box, the default files displayed in the File list box will have a .cir file extension.

Follow these steps to perform the enhancements:

☐ In the Project Workspace, select the ResourceView tab and expand the Circle resources item, then the String Table item.

> *After you expand the String Table item, a second String Table item appears underneath it. (See Figure 11.20.)*

Figure 11.20.
Expanding the String Table item in the Project Workspace window.

☐ Double-click the second String Table item in the Project Workspace window.

> *Visual C++ responds by displaying the String Table dialog box of the Circle project. (See Figure 11.21.)*

You use the String Table dialog box to view and edit various strings used by the program. As you can see in Figure 11.21, the string whose ID is IDR_MAINFRAME is currently highlighted. This is the current value of the string:

```
Circle\n\nCircle\n\n\nCircle.Document\nCircle Document
```

Figure 11.21.
The String Table dialog box.

ID	Value	Caption
IDR_MAINFRAME	128	Circle\n\nCircle\n\n\nCircle.Document
AFX_IDS_APP_TITLE	57344	Circle
AFX_IDS_IDLEMESSAGE	57345	Ready
ID_FILE_NEW	57600	Create a new document\nNew
ID_FILE_OPEN	57601	Open an existing document\nOpen
ID_FILE_CLOSE	57602	Close the active document\nClose
ID_FILE_SAVE	57603	Save the active document\nSave
ID_FILE_SAVE_AS	57604	Save the active document with a new r
ID_FILE_PAGE_SETUP	57605	Change the printing options\nPage Seti
ID_FILE_PRINT_SETUP	57606	Change the printer and printing options\
ID_FILE_PRINT	57607	Print the active document\nPrint
ID_FILE_PRINT_PREVIEW	57609	Display full pages\nPrint Preview
ID_FILE_MRU_FILE1	57616	Open this document
ID_FILE_MRU_FILE2	57617	Open this document
ID_FILE_MRU_FILE3	57618	Open this document
ID_FILE_MRU_FILE4	57619	Open this document

The \n serves as a separator between substrings. Therefore, the preceding string is made of the following seven substrings:

```
Circle
Null
Circle
Null
Null
Circle.Document
Circle Document
```

The substrings you need to work with are the first, fourth, and fifth substrings. The first substring specifies the title in the program's main window. Your objective is to make the program's main window title `Circle for Windows`. Therefore, you need to change the first substring from `Circle` to `Circle for Windows`.

The fourth and fifth substrings specify the default document type displayed in the Save As dialog box and Open dialog box. For example, if you set the fourth substring to

`CIR Files (*.cir)`

and the fifth substring to

`.cir`

then when you select Save As or Open from the File menu, the files listed in the File list box will have the .cir file extension, and the text in the file type box will be `CIR Files (*.cir)`.

Figure 11.22 shows the Open dialog box, listing files with the extension .cir. The text `CIR Files (*.cir)` appears in the file type box.

Now change the IDR_MAINFRAME string so that the first substring will be `Circle for Windows`, the fourth substring will be `CIR Files (*.cir)`, and the fifth substring will be `.cir`. All the rest of the substrings will remain the same. Here is how you do that:

☐ Double-click the IDR_MAINFRAME string.

Visual C++ responds by displaying the String Properties window for the IDR_MAINFRAME string. (See Figure 11.23.)

Figure 11.22.
The Open dialog box, listing files with the .cir extension.

Figure 11.23.
The String Properties window for the IDR_MAINFRAME string.

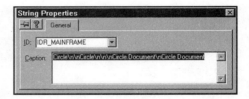

The value of the string is displayed in the Caption box.

☐ Change the value of the string to this:

```
Circle for Windows\n\nCircle\nCIR Files (*.

cir)\n.cir\nCircle.Document\nCircle Document
```

Note: The preceding text should be typed on a single line; don't press the Enter key. Visual C++ will wrap the line when it's too long.

Your String Properties window for the IDR_MAINFRAME string should now look like the one shown in Figure 11.24.

☐ Save your work.

☐ Compile, link, and execute the Circle.EXE program to see the effects of the changes you made to the IDR_MAINFRAME string.

Visual C++ responds by executing the Circle program. The main window of the Circle program appears, as shown in Figure 11.25.

Figure 11.24.
Changing the string value in the String Properties window.

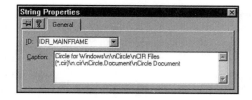

Figure 11.25.
Changing the main window of the Circle program.

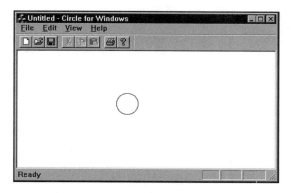

As shown in Figure 11.25, the title of the program's window includes the text Circle for Windows because you set the first substring of the IDR_MAINFRAME string to Circle for Windows.

☐ Select Save As from the File menu of the Circle program.

The Circle program responds by displaying the Save As dialog box. (See Figure 11.26.)

Figure 11.26.
The Save As dialog box listing files with the .cir extension.

As shown in Figure 11.26, now the Save As dialog box lists files with the .cir file extension and the text in the file type box is CIR Files (*.cir). That's because you set the fourth substring of the IDR_MAINFRAME string to CIR Files (*.cir), and the fifth substring to .cir.

Summary

In this chapter, you have written an SDI (single-document interface) program called Circle.EXE that behaves like a standard Windows SDI program—it lets you view a document, store the document in a file, and load previously saved files. The steps you take to create the Circle program are the same steps you'll take when you design other SDI programs.

Q&A

Q In this chapter, I learned how to write an SDI program. How do I write a multiple-document interface (MDI) program?

A In Chapter 13, "Writing Multiple-Document Interface (MDI) Applications," you'll learn how to create MDI programs.

Quiz

1. What does SDI stand for?
2. What is the purpose of the code you write in the view class of an SDI program?
3. What is the purpose of the code you write in the document class of an SDI program?
4. What code do you write in the Serialize() member function of the document class?

Exercise

The title of the Circle program's window currently displays the text Circle for Windows. Enhance the Circle program so that the title will include the text The Circle Program instead of Circle for Windows.

Quiz Answers

1. SDI stands for *single-document interface*. The word "single" in single-document interface means that you can work on only one document at a time (unlike multiple-document interface, in which multiple documents are used).

2. The code you write in the member functions of the view class is responsible for what you see onscreen.

3. The code you write in the member functions of the document class is responsible for maintaining the program's data, particularly saving documents and loading previously saved files.

4. The code you write in the Serialize() member function of the document class is responsible for saving data into files and loading previously saved files.

Exercise Answer

To make the title of the program's window display the text The Circle Program, you have to change the IDR_MAINFRAME string so that its first substring will be The Circle Program. The rest of the substrings remain the same. Here is how you do that:

☐ In the Project Workspace, select the ResourceView tab and expand the Circle resources item and the String Table item. Finally, double-click the second String Table item.

Visual C++ responds by displaying the String Table dialog box of the Circle project.

☐ Double-click the IDR_MAINFRAME string.

Visual C++ responds by displaying the String Properties window for the IDR_MAINFRAME string.

☐ Change the value of the string to this (remember to type this code on a single line):

```
The Circle Program\n\nCircle\nCIR Files (*.

cir)\n.cir\nCircle.Document\nCircle Document
```

☐ Save your work.

That's it! If you compile, link, and execute the Circle program, you'll see that the text The Circle Program appears in the title of the program's window, as it did in Figure 11.2.

Multitasking

In this chapter, you'll learn how to create a Visual C++ program that performs background tasks. *Multitasking* is the ability to work on other tasks within the same program or run other programs while your program performs background tasks.

The Tasks Program

To illustrate how to write a Visual C++ program that performs several background tasks, you'll write a program called Tasks. Before you start writing the program, first review what it should look like and what it should do.

- When you start the Tasks program, the program's window contains two Task edit boxes: Task 1 (50 ms) and Task 2 (500 ms). (See Figure 12.1.)

Figure 12.1.
The window of the Tasks program.

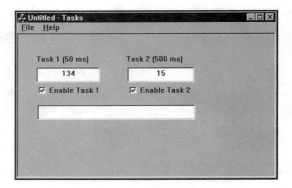

- The Tasks program performs two background tasks. The first increments the number in the Task 1 edit box every 50 milliseconds, and the second increments the number in the Task 2 edit box every 500 milliseconds.

- The two tasks are performed in the background. For example, while you type in the edit box at the bottom of the program's window, the two tasks will keep running. You can also switch to another Windows program, and the two tasks will keep on running.

> **Note:** The two background tasks of the Tasks program are performed only when Windows is idle—when all the currently running applications aren't receiving any messages from Windows.
>
> Because a typical Windows program has a lot of idle time, from your point of view it seems as though the tasks are running simultaneously with other programs. However, in reality, the Tasks program performs its tasks only when the system is idle.

- Each of the two Task edit boxes has a check box below it. You can disable a task by removing the check mark from its corresponding check box. For example, to disable Task 1, remove the check mark from the Enable Task 1 check box.

- To terminate the Tasks program, select Exit from the program's File menu.

Now that you know what the Tasks program should do, you can start by creating the project.

Creating the Project of the Tasks Program

The Tasks program is an SDI-type (single-document interface) program, like the one you created in Chapter 11, "Writing Single-Document Interface (SDI) Applications." Follow these steps to create the project and skeleton files of the Tasks program:

☐ Create the directory C:\TYVCProg\Programs\CH12, start Visual C++, select New from the File menu, then select Project Workspace from the New dialog box.

☐ Select MFC AppWizard (exe) from the Type list and enter Tasks in the Name box.

☐ Click the Browse button, select the C:\TYVCProg\Programs\CH12 directory, then click the Create button.

Visual C++ responds by displaying the MFC AppWizard - Step 1 window.

☐ Set the Step 1 window as you did in Chapter 11 by choosing the "Single document" radio button to create an SDI program. When you're done, click the Next button.

☐ In the Step 2 window, choose "None" because you don't want the program to support any database features. Click the Next button.

☐ In the Step 3 window, choose "None" because you don't want the program to support any OLE features. Click the Next button.

☐ In the Step 4 window, choose only the option to include 3-D controls. (See Figure 12.2.) Leave the number of files on the MRU (most recently used) list at its default setting of 4. When you're done, click the Next button.

☐ In the Step 5 window, select the "Yes, please" and "As a shared DLL" radio buttons, as you've done in previous chapters, then click the Next button.

☐ Set the Step 6 window as follows: Select the CTasksView class in the list box at the top and set the Base class drop-down list to CFormView. (See Figure 12.3.) When you're done, click the Finish button.

Visual C++ responds by displaying the New Project Information window.

12

Figure 12.2.

Including 3-D controls in the Tasks program.

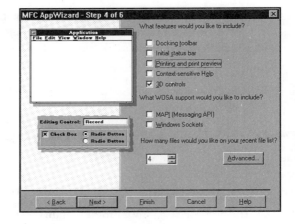

Figure 12.3.

Specifying the base class for the Tasks program's view class.

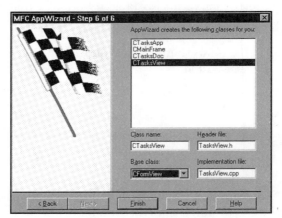

☐ Click the OK button, then select Set Default Configuration from the Build menu.

Visual C++ responds by displaying the Default Project Configuration dialog box.

☐ Select Tasks - Win32 Release, then click the OK button.

That's it! You've finished creating the project and skeleton files of the Tasks program.

Customizing the Menu of the Tasks Program

You'll now customize the menu of the Tasks program:

☐ In the Project Workspace, select the ResourceView tab and expand the Tasks resources item, then the Menu item. Finally, double-click the IDR_MAINFRAME item under the Menu item.

> *Visual C++ responds by displaying the IDR_MAINFRAME menu in design mode ready for you to customize.*

☐ Open the File pop-up menu of the IDR_MAINFRAME menu (by clicking the File menu title) and delete all its menu items except Exit. (To delete a menu item, select it, then press the Delete key.)

☐ Delete the entire Edit pop-up menu of the IDR_MAINFRAME menu by clicking the Edit menu title, then pressing the Delete key.

☐ Do not customize the Help pop-up menu.

☐ Compile, link, and execute the Tasks.EXE program to see your customization of the IDR_MAINFRAME menu in action.

☐ Make sure the menu looks just as you customized it—the File menu has only one menu item (Exit), there is no Edit menu, and the Help menu has the About Tasks menu item. (See Figures 12.4 and 12.5.)

Figure 12.4.
The File menu of the Tasks program.

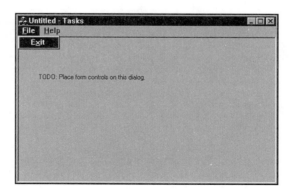

Figure 12.5.
The Help menu of the Tasks program.

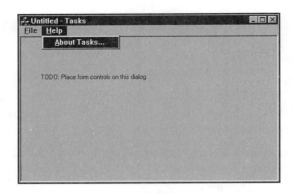

Although you removed the Open, Save, and Save As menu items of the File menu, their accelerator keys still work. To verify this, do the following:

☐ Press Ctrl+O on the keyboard.

> *The Tasks program responds by displaying the Open dialog box, just as though you selected Open from the File menu.*

☐ Close the Open dialog box by clicking its Cancel button.

☐ Press Ctrl+S on the keyboard.

> *The Tasks program responds by displaying the Save As dialog box, just as though you selected Save As from the File menu.*

☐ Close the Save As dialog box by clicking its Cancel button.

☐ Terminate the Tasks program by selecting Exit from its File menu.

To remove the accelerator keys, follow these steps:

☐ Select the ResourceView tab in the Project Workspace, expand the Accelerator item, and double-click the IDR_MAINFRAME item.

> *Visual C++ responds by displaying a list of all the accelerators in the Tasks program. (See Figure 12.6.)*

☐ Delete all the accelerators by pressing the Delete key.

☐ Save your work.

☐ Now compile, link, and execute the Tasks.EXE program to make sure the accelerators are no longer working.

☐ Press Ctrl+O and Ctrl+S and make sure nothing happens.

☐ Terminate the Tasks program by selecting Exit from its File menu.

Figure 12.6.
Listing the program's accelerator keys.

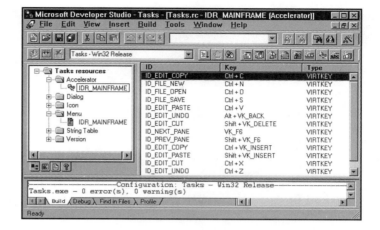

The Visual Design of the Program's Form

When you created the project of the Tasks program, you specified CFormView as the base class of the program's view class. (Refer back to Figure 12.3.) Visual C++ created a form (a dialog box) that's attached to the program's view class. This dialog box serves as the main window of the program. Visual C++ named this dialog box IDD_TASKS_FORM. You'll now customize the IDD_TASKS_FORM dialog box until it looks like the window shown back in Figure 12.1:

☐ In the Project Workspace, select the ResourceView tab, expand the Dialog item, and double-click the IDD_TASKS_FORM item.

Visual C++ responds by displaying the IDD_TASKS_FORM dialog box in design mode.

☐ Delete the static text control displaying the text TODO: Place form controls on this dialog.

☐ Set up the IDD_TASKS_FORM dialog box according to Table 12.1. When you finish, it should look like Figure 12.7.

Table 12.1. The properties table of the IDD_TASKS_FORM dialog box.

Object	Property	Setting
Dialog Box	**ID**	**IDD_TASKS_FORM**
	Font	System, Size 10
Static Text	**ID**	**IDC_STATIC**
	Caption	Task 1 (50 ms)

continues

Table 12.1. continued

Object	Property	Setting
Edit Box	ID	IDC_TASK1_EDIT
	Multi-line	Checked (Styles tab)
	Align text	Center (Styles tab)
Check Box	ID	IDC_ENABLE_TASK1_CHECK
	Caption	Enable Task 1
Static Text	ID	IDC_STATIC
	Caption	Task 2 (500 ms)
Edit Box	ID	IDC_TASK2_EDIT
	Multi-line	Checked (Styles tab)
	Align text	Center (Styles tab)
Check Box	ID	IDC_ENABLE_TASK2_CHECK
	Caption	Enable Task 1
Edit Box	ID	IDC_TEST_EDIT

Figure 12.7.
The IDD_TASKS_FORM dialog box in design mode.

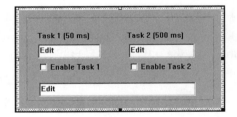

Note: It's OK to assign the same ID to more than one control if your code won't be using those controls. For example, in Table 12.1, the two static text controls have the same IDs because the ID IDC_STATIC is never used from within the code.

☐ Save your work, then compile, link, and execute the program to see your visual design in action.

Visual C++ responds by executing the Tasks program. The main window of the Tasks program looks like Figure 12.8, just as you designed it.

☐ Terminate the Tasks program by selecting Exit from its File menu.

Figure 12.8.
The main window of the Tasks program.

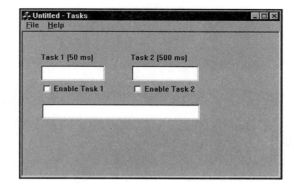

Attaching Variables to Controls in IDD_TASKS_FORM

You'll now attach variables to the Task 1 edit box, Enable Task 1 check box, Task 2 edit box, and Enable Task 2 check box. When you write the program's code, you'll use these variables to access the controls.

☐ In the Member Variables tab of ClassWizard, make sure that the Class name is set to CTasksView and attach variables to the controls as follows:

Object ID	Variable Name	Variable Type
IDC_ENABLE_TASK1_CHECK	m_EnableTask1Check	BOOL
IDC_ENABLE_TASK2_CHECK	m_EnableTask2Check	BOOL
IDC_TASK1_EDIT	m_Task1Edit	long
IDC_TASK2_EDIT	m_Task2Edit	long

You set the variables of the IDC_TASK1_EDIT and IDC_TASK2_EDIT edit boxes to type long because your code will display numbers in these dialog boxes. You don't have to attach a variable to the IDC_TEST_EDIT edit box because the code you write won't have to access this edit box. It's included in the Tasks program only to illustrate that you can type in it while the two tasks are running in the background.

Initializing the Two Check Box Controls

You now write code that initializes the two check box controls (Enable Task 1 and Enable Task 2) so that when you start the program, they will have check marks in them. You'll write this initialization code in the OnInitialUpdate() member function of the program's view class:

☐ In the Message Maps tab of ClassWizard, select the following event:

Class name:	CTasksView
Object ID:	CTasksView
Message:	OnInitialUpdate

☐ Click the Add Function button.

Visual C++ responds by adding the function OnInitialUpdate().

☐ Click the Edit Code button.

Visual C++ responds by opening the file TasksView.cpp with the function OnInitialUpdate() *ready for you to edit.*

☐ Write the following code in the OnInitialUpdate() function:

```
void CTasksView::OnInitialUpdate()
{

CFormView::OnInitialUpdate();

// TODO: Add your specialized code here and/or call the
//       base class

//////////////////////////
// MY CODE STARTS HERE
//////////////////////////

// Place check marks in the IDC_ENABLE_TASK1_CHECK
// and IDC_ENABLE_TASK2_CHECK check boxes.
m_EnableTask1Check = TRUE;
m_EnableTask2Check = TRUE;
UpdateData(FALSE);

//////////////////////////
// MY CODE ENDS HERE
//////////////////////////

}
```

☐ Save your work.

The first two statements you wrote in the OnInitialUpdate() function set the variables of the two check box controls to values of TRUE:

```
m_EnableTask1Check = TRUE;
m_EnableTask2Check = TRUE;
```

The third statement transfers the new values of the variables to the screen:

```
UpdateData(FALSE);
```

Therefore, when you start the program, the two check box controls will have check marks in them.

☐ Compile, link, and execute the program to see your initialization code in action.

Visual C++ responds by executing the Tasks program. The main window of the Tasks program appears with check marks in the two check box controls. (See Figure 12.9.)

☐ Terminate the Tasks program.

Figure 12.9.
The main window of the Tasks program.

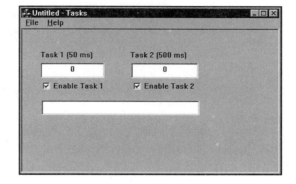

Writing the Code That Performs the Background Tasks

Recall that the Tasks program should perform two background tasks: incrementing a counter in the Task 1 edit box and incrementing another counter in the Task 2 edit box. To write code that accomplishes these background tasks, you need to attach code to the OnIdle event of the program's application class (CTasksApp). This event occurs whenever the system is idle and no other tasks are being performed.

Follow these steps to attach code to the OnIdle event of the program's application class:

☐ In the Message Maps tab of ClassWizard, select the following event:

Class name:	CTasksApp
Object ID:	CTasksApp
Message:	OnIdle

Note: In the preceding step, you are instructed to attach code to the program's application class (CTasksApp), not to the program's view class. Make sure the correct class is entered in ClassWizard's Class name box.

After selecting the OnIdle event of the CTasksApp class, your ClassWizard window should look like Figure 12.10.

Figure 12.10.

Selecting the OnIdle *event with ClassWizard.*

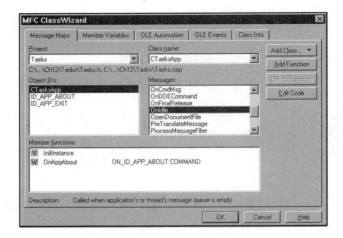

☐ Click the Add Function button of ClassWizard.

> *Visual C++ responds by adding the* OnIdle() *member function to the CTasksApp class.*

☐ Click the Edit Code button.

> *Visual C++ responds by opening the file Tasks.cpp with the function* OnIdle() *ready for you to edit.*

The code you write in the OnIdle() function will be automatically executed whenever the system is idle (no other tasks are being performed). To verify this, first write some simple code in the OnIdle() function that causes the PC to beep:

☐ Write the following code in the OnIdle() function:

```
BOOL CTasksApp::OnIdle(LONG lCount)
{

// TODO: Add your specialized code here and/or call the
// base class

///////////////////////////
// MY CODE STARTS HERE
///////////////////////////

// Call the base class CWinApp::OnIdle() function to
// finish its overhead tasks.
CWinApp::OnIdle(lCount);

// Beep.
MessageBeep((WORD)-1);

// Return TRUE so that OnIdle() will be called again.
return TRUE;
```

```
/////////////////////////
// MY CODE ENDS HERE
/////////////////////////

   }
```

☐ Save your work.

The first statement you typed calls the OnIdle() member function of the base class CWinApp:

`CWinApp::OnIdle(lCount);`

CWinApp is the base class of the CTasksApp class (the application class of the Tasks program). It's necessary to call the OnIdle() member function of the base class because it performs overhead tasks needed for the normal operation of the program.

The next statement you typed in the OnIdle() function causes the PC to beep:

`MessageBeep((WORD)-1);`

The last statement terminates the OnIdle() function and returns a value of TRUE:

`return TRUE;`

When you terminate the OnIdle() function by returning a value of TRUE, the OnIdle() function will be executed again and again for as long as the system is idle.

☐ Compile, link, and execute the program to see (or rather, hear) the code you wrote in the OnIdle() function in action.

As you can hear, the code you wrote causes continuous beeping through the PC speaker. The code you typed in the OnIdle() function is being executed again and again for as long as the system is idle.

☐ Try to type something in the edit boxes of the Tasks program.

As you can hear, even while you are typing in the edit boxes, your PC keeps on beeping. That's because when you type characters in an edit box, there is some idle time between typing each character. During the idle time, the OnIdle() function is automatically executed and the code you wrote causes the PC to beep.

The OnIdle() function is executed even when other programs are currently active. To verify this, do the following:

☐ Leave the Tasks program running and start another Windows program, such as Paint.

As you can hear, the PC keeps beeping even while the other program is active. As long as the system is idle, the OnIdle() function of the Tasks program is executed.

☐ Switch back to the Tasks program.

12

☐ Open the File menu of the Tasks program.

The PC stops beeping because the OnIdle() function stops executing when you open a menu of the Tasks program. However, when you open a menu of another program, the OnIdle() function of the Tasks program will keep on executing.

☐ Terminate the Tasks program.

Now that you've verified the OnIdle() function is executed whenever the system is idle, change the code in the OnIdle() function so that it will perform two tasks (instead of beeping): the first to increment a counter in the Task 1 edit box and the second to increment a counter in the Task 2 edit box. You will write the code so that the first task will be executed every 50 milliseconds and the second task will be executed every 500 milliseconds.

☐ Change the code of the OnIdle() function in the Tasks.cpp file:

```
BOOL CTasksApp::OnIdle(LONG lCount)
{

// TODO: Add your specialized code here and/or call the
// base class

////////////////////////
// MY CODE STARTS HERE
////////////////////////

// Call the base class CWinApp::OnIdle() function to
// finish its overhead tasks.
CWinApp::OnIdle(lCount);

// Get a pointer to the document template.
POSITION pos = GetFirstDocTemplatePosition();
CDocTemplate* pDocTemplate = GetNextDocTemplate(pos);

// Get a pointer to the document.
pos = pDocTemplate->GetFirstDocPosition();
CDocument* pDoc = pDocTemplate->GetNextDoc(pos);

// Get a pointer to the view.
pos = pDoc->GetFirstViewPosition();
CTasksView* pView =(CTasksView*) pDoc->GetNextView(pos);

// Declare and initialize two static
// variables: PrevTimeTask1 and PrevTimeTask2.
static DWORD PrevTimeTask1 = 0;
static DWORD PrevTimeTask2 = 0;

// Get the current time.
DWORD CurrentTime = GetTickCount();

// Update the variables of the controls.
pView->UpdateData(TRUE);
```

```
// If more than 50 milliseconds have elapsed since task 1
// was last performed and the Enable Task 1 check box is
// checked, perform task 1.
if (CurrentTime > PrevTimeTask1+50 &&
    pView->m_EnableTask1Check )
   {
   pView->m_Task1Edit = pView->m_Task1Edit+1;
   pView->UpdateData(FALSE);
   PrevTimeTask1 = CurrentTime;
   }

// If more than 500 milliseconds have elapsed since task 2
// was last performed and the Enable Task 2 check box is
// checked, perform task 2.
if (CurrentTime > PrevTimeTask2+500 &&
pView->m_EnableTask2Check )
   {
   pView->m_Task2Edit = pView->m_Task2Edit+1;
   pView->UpdateData(FALSE);
   PrevTimeTask2 = CurrentTime;
   }

// Return TRUE so that OnIdle() will be called again.
return TRUE;

/////////////////////////
// MY CODE ENDS HERE
/////////////////////////

}
```

☐ Save your work.

12

The first statement you wrote calls the OnIdle() member function of the base class CWinApp:

```
CWinApp::OnIdle(lCount);
```

Remember that this is necessary because the OnIdle() member function of the base class performs overhead tasks needed for the program's normal operation.

The next six statements extract a pointer to the view of the program:

```
// Get a pointer to the document template.
POSITION pos = GetFirstDocTemplatePosition();
CDocTemplate* pDocTemplate = GetNextDocTemplate(pos);

// Get a pointer to the document.
pos = pDocTemplate->GetFirstDocPosition();
CDocument* pDoc = pDocTemplate->GetNextDoc(pos);

// Get a pointer to the view.
pos = pDoc->GetFirstViewPosition();
CTasksView* pView =(CTasksView*) pDoc->GetNextView(pos);
```

You do this because subsequent statements in the OnIdle() function need to access data members and member functions of the view class. Since the OnIdle() function is not a member of the program's view class, the preceding statements extract a pointer to the view of the program.

After the preceding six statements are executed, the pointer pView points to the view of the program. Subsequent statements in the OnIdle() function will use the pView pointer to access data members and member functions of the program's view class.

The next two statements declare and initialize two numeric static variables, PrevTimeTask1 and PrevTimeTask2, to 0:

```
static DWORD PrevTimeTask1 = 0;
static DWORD PrevTimeTask2 = 0;
```

Because you are declaring these variables as static, they won't lose their values once the OnIdle() function is terminated. On the next execution of the OnIdle() function, PrevTimeTask1 and PrevTimeTask2 will hold the same values they had when the previous iteration of OnIdle() terminated.

In the preceding statements, PrevTimeTask1 and PrevTimeTask2 are initialized to 0 so that on the first execution of the OnIdle() function, each of these variables will have a value of 0. The PrevTimeTask1 variable holds a number indicating the last time Task 1 was executed, and the PrevTimeTask2 variable holds a number indicating the last time Task 2 was executed.

The next statement fills the variable CurrentTime with the returned value of the GetTickCount() function:

```
DWORD CurrentTime = GetTickCount();
```

The GetTickCount() function returns the number of milliseconds that have elapsed since Windows was started. The variable CurrentTime now holds the number of milliseconds elapsed since you started Windows.

The next statement updates the data members of the view class with the current contents of the controls onscreen:

```
pView->UpdateData(TRUE);
```

Recall that earlier statements in the OnIdle() function extracted pView—a pointer to the program's view. Therefore, after the preceding statement is executed, the two variables attached to the Enable Task 1 and Enable Task 2 check boxes are updated according to their states.

The next block of code uses an if statement to determine whether more than 50 milliseconds have elapsed since Task 1 was executed and whether the Enable Task 1 check box is checked:

```
if (CurrentTime > PrevTimeTask1+50 &&
    pView->m_EnableTask1Check )
  {
  pView->m_Task1Edit = pView->m_Task1Edit+1;
```

```
pView->UpdateData(FALSE);
PrevTimeTask1 = CurrentTime;
}
```

If this is the case, the preceding `if` condition is satisfied, and these three statements under the `if` are executed:

```
pView->m_Task1Edit = pView->m_Task1Edit+1;
pView->UpdateData(FALSE);
PrevTimeTask1 = CurrentTime;
```

These statements increment the value in the Task 1 edit box and update the `PrevTimeTask1` static variable with the value of `CurrentTime`.

The next block of code uses an `if` statement to determine whether more than 500 milliseconds have elapsed since Task 2 was executed and whether the Enable Task 2 check box is checked:

```
if (CurrentTime > PrevTimeTask2+500 &&
pView->m_EnableTask2Check )
    {
    pView->m_Task2Edit = pView->m_Task2Edit+1;
    pView->UpdateData(FALSE);
    PrevTimeTask2 = CurrentTime;
    }
```

If this is the case, the preceding `if` condition is satisfied, and these three statements under the `if` are executed:

```
pView->m_Task2Edit = pView->m_Task2Edit+1;
pView->UpdateData(FALSE);
PrevTimeTask2 = CurrentTime;
```

These statements increment the value in the Task 2 edit box and update the `PrevTimeTask2` static variable with the value of `CurrentTime`.

The last statement terminates the `OnIdle()` function and returns a value of `TRUE`:

```
return TRUE;
```

As discussed earlier, if you terminate the `OnIdle()` function by returning a value of `TRUE`, the `OnIdle()` function will be executed again and again for as long as the system is idle.

The Tasks program is now finished. To see the code you wrote in the `OnIdle()` function in action, do the following:

☐ Compile, link, and execute the Tasks.EXE program.

   Visual C++ responds by executing the Tasks program.

As expected, the code you attached to the `OnIdle()` function performs two tasks. One task keeps incrementing a counter in the IDC_TASK1_EDIT edit box every 50 milliseconds and the second task keeps incrementing a counter in the IDC_TASK2_EDIT box every 500 milliseconds.

☐ Leave the Tasks program running, start another Windows program, make the window of the other program the active window, and verify that the Tasks program keeps performing the two tasks.

☐ Terminate the Tasks program.

Summary

In this chapter, you have learned how to write code that performs background tasks; this ability to perform background tasks while working on other tasks is called *multitasking*. As you have seen, adding a background task to your Visual C++ program is quite simple—just attach code to the OnIdle event of the program's application class. The code you attach to the OnIdle event will be automatically executed whenever the system is idle.

Q&A

Q **In the code I wrote in the OnIdle() function of the Tasks program, the Task 1 edit box is updated as follows:**

```
pView->m_Task1Edit = pView->m_Task1Edit + 1;
pView->UpdateData(FALSE);
```

Why can't I use simpler code (without using the pView pointer), like the following?

```
m_Task1Edit = m_Task1Edit + 1;
UpdateData(FALSE);
```

A The variable m_Task1Edit and the function UpdateData() are both members of the program's view class (CTasksView). The OnIdle() function is a member function of the program's application class (CTasksApp). Therefore, to access m_Task1Edit and UpdateData() from the OnIdle() function, you first have to extract a pointer to the program's view (pView), then use this pointer to access m_Task1Edit and UpdateData().

Quiz

1. When does the OnIdle event occur?
2. The OnIdle() function is a member function of which class?

Exercise

Enhance the Tasks program as follows:

Add an additional edit box to the program's main window and add a third background task that keeps on incrementing a counter in this edit box every 1000 milliseconds, or every second.

Quiz Answers

1. The OnIdle event occurs when the system is idle.
2. The OnIdle() function is a member function of the program's application class.

Exercise Answer

To add a third edit box and a task that increments a counter every 1000 milliseconds, follow these steps:

☐ Add a third edit box to the IDD_TASKS_FORM dialog box. Set the ID of this edit box to IDC_TASK3_EDIT.

☐ Attach a variable of type long to the IDC_TASK3_EDIT edit box and name this variable m_Task3Edit.

☐ Modify the code of the OnIdle() function as follows:

```
BOOL CTasksApp::OnIdle(LONG lCount)
{

// TODO: Add your specialized code here and/or call the
// base class

/////////////////////////
// MY CODE STARTS HERE
/////////////////////////

// Call the base class CWinApp::OnIdle() function to
// finish its overhead tasks.
CWinApp::OnIdle(lCount);

// Get a pointer to the document template.
POSITION pos = GetFirstDocTemplatePosition();
CDocTemplate* pDocTemplate = GetNextDocTemplate(pos);

// Get a pointer to the document.
pos = pDocTemplate->GetFirstDocPosition();
CDocument* pDoc = pDocTemplate->GetNextDoc(pos);

// Get a pointer to the view.
pos = pDoc->GetFirstViewPosition();
CTasksView* pView =(CTasksView*) pDoc->GetNextView(pos);
```

12

```
// Declare and initialize three static
// variables: PrevTimeTask1, PrevTimeTask2, and PrevTimeTask3.
static DWORD PrevTimeTask1 = 0;
static DWORD PrevTimeTask2 = 0;
static DWORD PrevTimeTask3 = 0;


// Get the current time.
DWORD CurrentTime = GetTickCount();

// Update the variables of the controls.
pView->UpdateData(TRUE);

// If more than 50 milliseconds have elapsed since task 1
// was last performed and the Enable Task 1 check box is
// checked, perform task 1.
if (CurrentTime > PrevTimeTask1+50 &&
pView->m_EnableTask1Check )
   {
   pView->m_Task1Edit = pView->m_Task1Edit+1;
   pView->UpdateData(FALSE);
   PrevTimeTask1 = CurrentTime;
   }

// If more than 500 milliseconds have elapsed since task 2
// was last performed and the Enable Task 2 check box is
// checked, perform task 2.
if (CurrentTime > PrevTimeTask2+500 &&
pView->m_EnableTask2Check )
   {
   pView->m_Task2Edit = pView->m_Task2Edit+1;
   pView->UpdateData(FALSE);
   PrevTimeTask2 = CurrentTime;
   }

// If more than 1000 milliseconds have elapsed since task 3
// was last performed, perform task 3.
if (CurrentTime > PrevTimeTask3+1000)
{
   pView->m_Task3Edit = pView->m_Task3Edit+1;
   pView->UpdateData(FALSE);
   PrevTimeTask3 = CurrentTime;
   }

// Return TRUE so that OnIdle() will be called again.
return TRUE;

////////////////////////
// MY CODE ENDS HERE
////////////////////////

}
```

WEEK
2

Writing Multiple-Document Interface (MDI) Applications

In this chapter, you'll learn what a multiple-document interface (MDI) application is and how to create one with Visual C++.

What Is a Multiple-Document Interface (MDI) Application?

Recall from Chapter 11, "Writing Single-Document Interface (SDI) Applications," that an SDI program lets you work with documents, but only one document at a time. You can create a document, save the document into a file, and load previously saved files.

A multiple-document interface program (an MDI program) also enables you to work with documents. However, an MDI program lets you work on and open several documents simultaneously. Word for Windows is an example of an MDI program. Figure 13.1 shows Word for Windows with several documents open.

Figure 13.1.

An example of an MDI program.

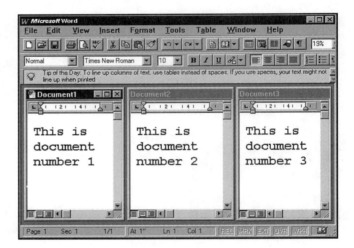

Note: In this chapter, you'll learn how to write a multiple-document interface program. As you'll soon see, the steps you need to take to create a multiple-document interface program are not much different than the steps you took when you created a single-document interface program in Chapter 11. However, an MDI program is much more powerful and impressive than an SDI program.

Even if you haven't read Chapter 11, or haven't read it recently, you can still follow this chapter's material. This chapter does not assume any know-how from Chapter 11.

The MCircle.EXE Program

In this chapter, you'll write a Visual C++ program called MCircle.EXE, an example of an MDI program. Before you start writing the MCircle program, first review what it should look like and what it should do.

The MCircle.EXE program is very similar to the Circle.EXE program you wrote in Chapter 11. The only difference is that the MCircle.EXE program will be an MDI program, so you can open several documents simultaneously.

- When you start the MCircle program, the window of the program should look like Figure 13.2.

Figure 13.2.
The window of the MCircle program at startup.

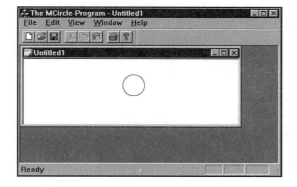

- When you start the MCircle program, it creates a new circle document and displays the window (or view) of this document. As shown in Figure 13.2, the title of the new document is Untitled1. It contains the word "Untitled" because the document has just been created and hasn't been saved into a file. When you save it, the title Untitled1 will be replaced with the name of the saved file.
- The MCircle program is a simple MDI program in which the document is a circle. You can place the circle anywhere in the window by simply clicking the mouse at the desired point, then save the circle into a file. At a later time, you can open a previously saved file, and the saved circle will appear onscreen.
- You can save the drawn circle into a file by selecting Save (or Save As) from the File menu of the MCircle program. (See Figure 13.3.)

  You can load a previously saved circle by selecting Open from the File menu of the MCircle program. Once you select Open from the File menu, the MCircle program displays an Open dialog box for selecting the previously saved circle file.

- You can print the currently displayed document by selecting Print from the File menu.

Figure 13.3.
The File menu of the
MCircle program.

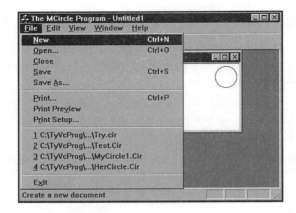

- In the MCircle program, you can open several documents simultaneously because it's an MDI program. Figure 13.4 shows the desktop of the MCircle program with three circle documents open.

Figure 13.4.
Opening three circle
documents simultaneously.

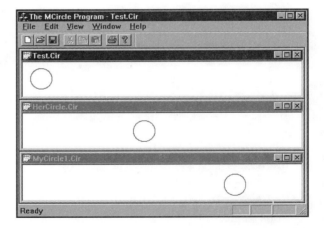

You can minimize any of the windows of the currently open documents. Figure 13.5 shows the desktop of the MCircle program with three windows minimized.

- You can use the Window menu of the MCircle program to move from one window to another. At any given time, the Window menu lists the names of all the currently open windows on the desktop. (See Figure 13.6.)

Figure 13.5.
Minimizing the windows of three circle documents.

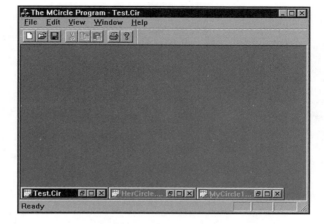

Figure 13.6.
The Window menu of the MCircle program.

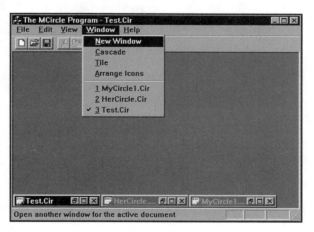

The New Window item of the Window menu enables you to display several views (windows) of the same document. When you select New Window, the MCircle program responds by opening another window for the current document. For example, Figure 13.7 shows two windows for the same document—both of these windows display the circle of the Test.Cir document. When you change one view of the document, the other view is automatically updated.

Why is seeing several views of the same document useful? If you have an MDI program with an extremely long document, such as a long text document or a large picture, you may need to work on several sections at a time of the same document. In such cases, you can open several views (windows) of the same document and display a different section of the document in each window. When you change one view of the document, all the other views of the document are automatically updated.

• The MCircle program includes a toolbar displayed at the top of the program's window. You can perform various operations by clicking the tool you need. For example, clicking the Save tool on the toolbar (the one with a disk icon) is equivalent to selecting Save from the File menu; clicking the About tool (the one with the question mark icon) is the same as selecting About from the Help menu.

Figure 13.7.

Opening two views of the same document.

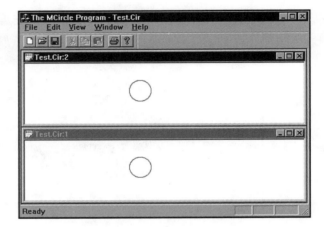

Now that you know what the MCircle program should do, start creating this program.

Creating the Project of the MCircle Program

Follow these steps to create the project and skeleton files of the MCircle program:

☐ Create the directory C:\TYVCProg\Programs\CH13 and start Visual C++.

☐ Select New from the File menu.

Visual C++ responds by displaying the New dialog box.

☐ Select Project Workspace from the New dialog box, then click the OK button.

Visual C++ responds by displaying the New Project Workspace dialog box.

☐ Select MFC AppWizard (exe) from the Type list and enter MCircle in the Name box.

☐ Click the Browse button, select the C:\TYVCProg\Programs\CH13 directory, and click the Create button.

Visual C++ responds by displaying the MFC AppWizard - Step 1 window.

☐ In the Step 1 window, choose the "Multiple documents" radio button to create an MDI program. (See Figure 13.8.) When you're done, click the Next button.

Figure 13.8.
Creating an MDI program.

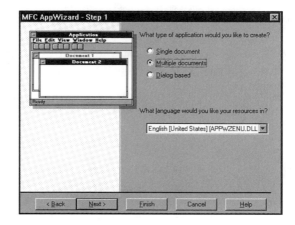

☐ In the Step 2 window, select the "None" option because you don't want the program to support any database features. Click the Next button.

☐ In the Step 3 window, select the "None" option because you don't want the program to support any OLE features. Click the Next button.

☐ Set the Step 4 window as shown in Figure 13.9. You want the program to support these features: docking toolbar, initial toolbar, printing and print preview, and 3-D controls. Leave the number of files for the MRU (most recently used) list at the default setting of 4. When you're done, click the Next button.

Figure 13.9.
Choosing features to include in your MDI program.

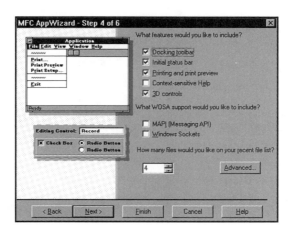

☐ In the Step 5 window, use the default settings and click the Next button.

☐ In the Step 6 window, notice that Visual C++ has created the following classes for you: CMCircleApp, CMainFrame, CChildFrame, CMCircleDoc, and CMCircleView. (See Figure 13.10.) Remember from Chapter 11 that the document class, CMCircleDoc, is where you write code for maintaining the program's data and the view class, CMCircleView, is where you write code concerning what you see onscreen. You'll write code in the member functions of these two classes only. When you're done reviewing the classes, click the Finish button.

Visual C++ responds by displaying the New Project Information window.

Figure 13.10.
The classes created for the MCircle program.

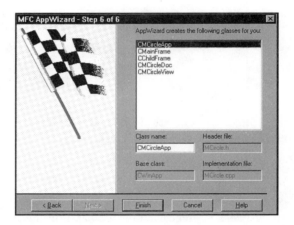

☐ Click the OK button of the New Project Information window, then select Set Default Configuration from the Build menu.

Visual C++ responds by displaying the Default Project Configuration dialog box.

☐ Select MCircle - Win32 Release in the Default Project Configuration dialog box, then click the OK button.

That's it! You've finished creating the project file and skeleton files of the MCircle program.

Running the MCircle Program Before Customization

Before you start customizing the MCircle program, first compile, link, and execute it at this stage. As you'll see, the skeleton files Visual C++ created for you yield an MDI program that already performs some functions.

☐ Compile, link, and execute the MCircle.EXE program.

Visual C++ responds by executing the MCircle.EXE program. The main window of the MCircle program appears, as shown in Figure 13.11.

Figure 13.11.
The main window of the MCircle program.

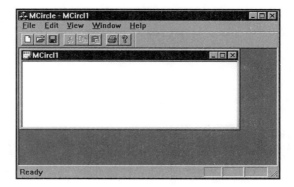

At this early stage, you already have a working MDI program! The skeleton code that Visual C++ wrote for you yielded an impressive MDI program that includes a standard MDI menu system and toolbar.

Of course, at this point the MCircle program doesn't do what you want it to, so in the following sections, you'll write code to customize the MCircle project. The code will enable you to create circle documents, save circle documents, and load previously saved documents. You will also be able to work on multiple circle documents simultaneously.

☐ Terminate the MCircle program by selecting Exit from its File menu.

Declaring the Data Members of the Document Class

The code you'll write in the document class, `CMCircleDoc`, of the MCircle program is responsible for storing the document (the program's data). This code will enable you to save the program's data into a file and load data from previously saved files. You'll now add data members to the document class that will be used for storing MCircle's document data:

☐ Select Project Workspace from the View menu.

Visual C++ responds by displaying the Project Workspace window of the MCircle project.

☐ Open the file MCircleDoc.h, where the document class, `CMCircleDoc`, of the MCircle program is declared. (Select the FileView tab of the Project Workspace window, expand the MCircle Files item, expand the Dependencies item, and double-click the MCircleDoc.h item.)

You'll now declare two data members in the CMCircleDoc class:

☐ Modify the declaration of the CMCircleDoc class as follows:

```
class CMCircleDoc : public CDocument
{
protected: // create from serialization only
    CMCircleDoc();
    DECLARE_DYNCREATE(CMCircleDoc)

// Attributes
public:

/////////////////////////
// MY CODE STARTS HERE
/////////////////////////

int m_PosX;
int m_PosY;

/////////////////////////
// MY CODE ENDS HERE
/////////////////////////

// Operations
...
...
...

};
```

☐ Save your work.

The code you added to the declaration of the CMCircleDoc class declares two int data members, m_PosX and m_PosY:

```
int m_PosX;
int m_PosY;
```

The m_PosX data member will be used for storing the x-coordinate of the circle you draw, and the m_PosY data member will be used for storing the y-coordinate of the circle. You can add other data members that define the drawn circle, such as its radius or color. However, to keep it simple, in the MCircle program you'll specify only the x-y coordinate of the circle—the point where the circle will be drawn. All other aspects will be fixed.

The document class of the MCircle program now has two data members: m_PosX and m_PosY. These data members are the data composing the document of the MCircle program. Later you will write code for saving m_PosX and m_PosY into a file and loading data from previously saved files into the m_PosX and m_PosY data members.

Declaring the Data Members of the View Class

The code you write in the view class, CMCircleView, of the MCircle program is responsible for what you see onscreen. You'll now add data members to the view class so that when you write code later, you can use these data members to draw a circle in the documents' windows.

The view class data members are a mirror image of the data members you added to the document class. This is necessary because the code of the view class is supposed to display onscreen whatever the document specifies. For example, if the document specifies that the circle should be displayed at a certain x-y coordinate, the code of the view class will display the circle at the specified coordinate.

☐ Open the file MCircleView.h, where the view class, CMCircleView, is declared. (Select the FileView tab of the Project Workspace window, expand the MCircle Files item, expand the Dependencies item, and double-click the MCircleView.h item.)

You'll now declare two data members (with the same names as the document class data members) in the CMCircleView class:

☐ Modify the declaration of the CMCircleView class as follows:

```
class CMCircleView : public CView
{
protected: // create from serialization only
    CMCircleView();
    DECLARE_DYNCREATE(CMCircleView)

// Attributes
public:
    CMCircleDoc* GetDocument();

/////////////////////////
// MY CODE STARTS HERE
/////////////////////////

int m_PosX;
int m_PosY;

/////////////////////////
// MY CODE ENDS HERE
/////////////////////////

// Operations
...
...
...

};
```

☐ Save your work.

The code you added to the declaration of the CMCircleView class is identical to the code you added for the CMCircleDoc class. This code declares two int data members, m_PosX and m_PosY:

```
int m_PosX;
int m_PosY;
```

The m_PosX data member will hold the x-coordinate of the circle, and the m_PosY data member will hold the y-coordinate of the circle. Now the document class and the view class have the same two data members: m_PosX and m_PosY.

The code you write later to draw the circle will be written in the view class of the program. This code will draw the circle according to the values of the m_PosX and m_PosY view class data members. The code you write later for saving and loading circles will be written in the document class of the program. This code will use the m_PosX and m_PosY document class data members.

As you will see in the following sections, the values of the view class data members should always be the same as the values of the document class data members. You want the values stored in the document to be the same as the values that you see onscreen. Therefore, the code you write in the following sections will ensure that the data members of these two classes always have the same values.

Initializing the Data Members of the Document Class

You'll now write the code that initializes the data members of the document class in the OnNewDocument() member function of the document class:

☐ Open the file MCircleDoc.cpp and locate the OnNewDocument() function.

☐ Write the following code in the OnNewDocument() function:

```
BOOL CMCircleDoc::OnNewDocument()
{
if (!CDocument::OnNewDocument())
    return FALSE;

// TODO: add reinitialization code here
// (SDI documents will reuse this document)

/////////////////////////
// MY CODE STARTS HERE
/////////////////////////

// Initialize the data members of the document.
m_PosX = 200;
m_PosY = 50;
```

```
/////////////////////////
// MY CODE ENDS HERE
/////////////////////////

return TRUE;
}
```

☐ Save your work.

The `OnNewDocument()` member function of the document class is automatically executed whenever a new document is created by starting the program or selecting New from the File menu.

The code you wrote in the `OnNewDocument()` function initializes the value of the `m_PosX` data member to `200` and initializes the `m_PosY` data member to `50`:

```
m_PosX = 200;
m_PosY = 50;
```

Therefore, whenever a new document is created, the `m_PosX` document data member will be set to a value of `200` and the `m_PosY` document data member will be set to a value of `50`.

Initializing the Data Members of the View Class

In the preceding section, you initialized the data members of the document class, which represent the values stored into a document file. You'll now write the code that initializes the data members of the view class, which represent what you see onscreen. This code is written in the `OnInitialUpdate()` member function of the view class.

☐ Select ClassWizard from the View menu. In the Message Maps tab of the ClassWizard window, select the following event:

Class name:	CMCircleView
Object ID:	CMCircleView
Message:	OnInitialUpdate

☐ Click the Add Function button of ClassWizard.

Visual C++ responds by adding the `OnInitialUpdate()` function.

☐ Click the Edit Code button of ClassWizard.

Visual C++ responds by opening the file MCircleView.cpp with the function `OnInitialUpdate()` ready for you to edit.

☐ Write the following code in the `OnInitialUpdate()` function:

13

```
void CMCircleView::OnInitialUpdate()
{
CView::OnInitialUpdate();

// TODO: Add your specialized code here and/or call the base
//       class

/////////////////////////
// MY CODE STARTS HERE
/////////////////////////

// Get a pointer to the  document
CMCircleDoc* pDoc = GetDocument();

// Update data members of the view with the
// corresponding document values.
m_PosX  = pDoc->m_PosX;
m_PosY  = pDoc->m_PosY;

/////////////////////////
// MY CODE ENDS HERE
/////////////////////////

}
```

☐ Save your work.

The OnInitialUpdate() member function of the view class initializes the view class data members. The code you just attached to the OnInitialUpdate() function updates the view class data members with the current values of the document class data members.

The first statement you typed uses the GetDocument() function to extract a pointer, pDoc, to the document:

```
CMCircleDoc* pDoc = GetDocument();
```

The remaining statements use the pDoc pointer to initialize the view class data members with the current values of the document data members:

```
m_PosX  = pDoc->m_PosX;
m_PosY  = pDoc->m_PosY;
```

These statements update the m_PosX and m_PosY data members of the view class with the corresponding document class data members.

Writing the Code That Displays the Circle

You'll now write the code in the view class that displays the circle onscreen. As discussed earlier, the view class is responsible for whatever you see onscreen, so you'll write the drawing code in the OnDraw() member function of the CMCircleView class. The OnDraw() function of the view class is automatically executed whenever there is a need to draw the document's window.

☐ Open the file MCircleView.cpp and locate the OnDraw() function.

☐ Write the following code in the OnDraw() function:

```cpp
void CMCircleView::OnDraw(CDC* pDC)
{
CMCircleDoc* pDoc = GetDocument();
ASSERT_VALID(pDoc);

// TODO: add draw code for native data here

///////////////////////////
// MY CODE STARTS HERE
///////////////////////////

// Define the rectangular boundaries of the
// circle to be drawn.
RECT  rect;
rect.left = m_PosX - 20;
rect.top = m_PosY -20;
rect.bottom = m_PosY + 20;
rect.right = m_PosX +20;

// Draw the circle.
pDC->Ellipse(&rect);

///////////////////////////
// MY CODE ENDS HERE
///////////////////////////

}
```

☐ Save your work.

The code you typed in the OnDraw() function draws a circle at the position specified by the m_PosX and m_PosY data members of the view class.

The first five statements you typed define the coordinates and dimensions of a rectangle called rect:

```cpp
RECT  rect;
rect.left = m_PosX - 20;
rect.top = m_PosY -20;
rect.bottom = m_PosY + 20;
rect.right = m_PosX +20;
```

These statements define the rectangle's center at the x-y coordinate specified by the m_PosX and m_PosY data members. The width and height of the rectangle are both 40 pixels, so the rect rectangle is defined as a square.

The last statement you typed uses the Ellipse() function to draw an ellipse:

```cpp
pDC->Ellipse(&rect);
```

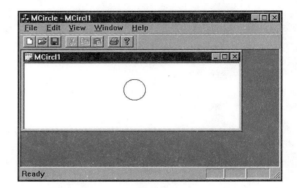
pDC, the parameter of the OnDraw() function, is the pointer to the dc (device context). By executing the Ellipse() function on the pDC pointer, you are drawing an ellipse in the window. The parameter of the Ellipse() function in the preceding statement is &rect. Therefore, the ellipse will be drawn within the boundaries of the rectangle you defined. Because the rect rectangle is a square, the ellipse will be drawn as a circle.

Putting it all together, the code you wrote in the OnDraw() function draws a circle at the x-y coordinate specified by the m_PosX and m_PosY view class data members.

☐ Compile, link, and execute the MCircle.EXE program to see your drawing code in action.

> *Visual C++ responds by executing the MCircle program. The main window of the MCircle program appears, as shown in Figure 13.12.*

Figure 13.12.
The main window of the MCircle program with a Circle document.

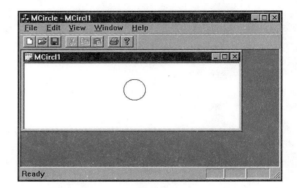

As you can see, the drawing code you wrote in the OnDraw() function is working—when you start the MCircle program, a new document called MCircl1 is created and a circle is drawn at the x-y coordinate x=200, y=50. That's because the code you wrote in the OnNewDocument() member function of the document class initialized the document class data members m_PosX and m_PosY to m_PosX=200 and m_PosY=50, and the code you wrote in the OnInitialUpdate() member function of the view class updated the m_PosX and m_PosY view class data members with the values of the document class data members.

Exploring the MDI Features of the MCircle Program

As you can see, the SDI Circle program in Chapter 11 and the MDI MCircle program in this chapter are very similar. However, the MCircle is an MDI program, so the focus of this chapter is on exploring the MDI features of the program that let you create and work on several

documents simultaneously. To see some of the MDI features of the MCircle program, create two additional documents:

☐ Select New from the File menu of the MCircle program.

The MCircle program responds by creating a second new document called MCircl2 and displaying the window (view) of this document on the desktop.

☐ Select New from the File menu of the MCircle program again.

The MCircle program responds by creating a new document called MCircl3 and displaying the window (view) of this document on the desktop.

The desktop of your MCircle program should now look like the one shown in Figure 13.13—three windows (views) of three documents are open on the desktop.

Figure 13.13.
Opening three windows (views) of three documents.

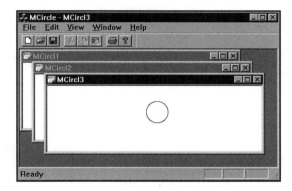

The MCircle program automatically assigns these names to the three documents: MCircl1, MCircl2, and MCircl3. If you create a fourth document, the MCircle program will automatically assign the name MCircl4 to it. Later in the chapter, you'll write code that enables you to save a document into a file. When you save a document, the name of the document will be the filename under which you saved the document.

13

Note: In the "Exercise" section at the end of this chapter, you'll learn how to enhance the MCircle program so that the default names of new documents will be Untitled1, Untitled2, Untitled3, and so on.

Now experiment with some of the MDI features of the MCircle program:

☐ Select Tile from the Window menu of the MCircle program.

The MCircle program responds by displaying the three windows of the documents in tile format. (See Figure 13.14.)

Figure 13.14.

Viewing the documents in tile format.

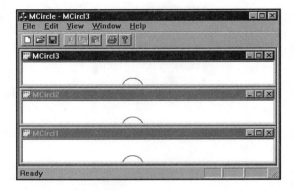

As shown in Figure 13.14, you can see only half a circle in each of the three windows because the main window is too small. Increase the height of the window as follows:

☐ Increase the height of the MCircle program's main window by dragging the bottom edge of the main window downward.

☐ Select Tile from the Window menu of the MCircle program.

The desktop of your MCircle program should now look like Figure 13.15—you can see a whole circle in each of the windows.

Figure 13.15.

Increasing the height of the main window for viewing tiled documents.

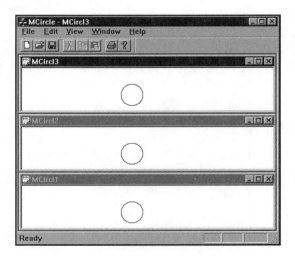

To view the windows of the three documents in cascading format, do the following:

☐ Select Cascade from the Window menu of the MCircle program.

The MCircle program responds by displaying the three documents in cascading format. (See Figure 13.16.)

Figure 13.16.
Viewing the documents in cascading format.

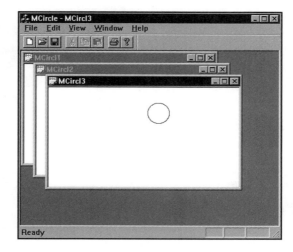

You can minimize the windows of the three documents as follows:

☐ Minimize the MCircl1 window by clicking its Minimize button, the small icon with an underscore mark (_) at the upper-right corner.

☐ Minimize the MCircl2 window.

☐ Minimize the MCircl3 window.

The desktop of the MCircle program with the windows of the three documents minimized is shown in Figure 13.17.

You can move any minimized window to any location on the desktop by dragging it.

☐ Move the three minimized windows to different locations in the desktop.

You can now arrange the three minimized windows in an orderly manner:

☐ Select Arrange Icons from the Window menu of the MCircle program.

The MCircle program responds by rearranging the minimized windows as shown in Figure 13.17.

Figure 13.17.
Minimizing the windows of the three cascaded documents.

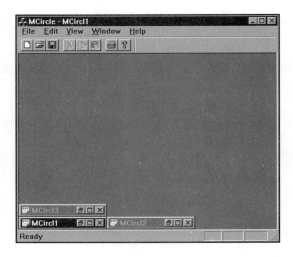

The Window menu of the MCircle program has one additional menu item you have not experimented with yet—the New Window menu item. You'll get a chance to experiment with this menu item later in the chapter.

The Window menu of the MCircle program also lists all the windows' names of the currently open documents. You currently have three open windows on the desktop—MCircl1, MCircl2, and MCircl3—so their names are listed in the Window menu. (See Figure 13.18.)

Figure 13.18.
Listing currently open documents in the Window menu.

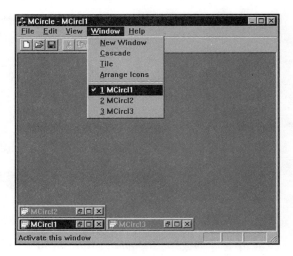

The drawing code you wrote in the OnDraw() member function of the view class is executed whenever there is a need to redraw the screen and whenever you select Print from the File menu. The code you wrote is responsible for both what you see onscreen as well as what is printed when you select Print from the File menu. To see the Print menu item of the MCircle program in action, print the MCircl1 document:

☐ Select MCircl1 from the Window menu of the MCircle program.

☐ Select Print from the File menu of the MCircle program.

The MCircle program responds by displaying the Print dialog box. (See Figure 13.19.)

Figure 13.19.
The Print dialog box.

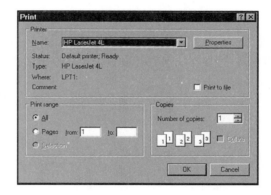

☐ Click the OK button of the Print dialog box.

The MCircle program responds by printing the MCircl1 document on your printer.

☐ Terminate the MCircle program by selecting Exit from its File menu.

Writing Code That Draws the Circle at Any Location

At this point, when you create a new document, the window displays a circle at the x-y coordinate x=200, y=50. You'll now write code that enables you to draw the circle anywhere in the document's window by simply clicking the mouse at the desired point. You'll write this code in the view class because it concerns what you see onscreen.

☐ Select ClassWizard from the View menu. In the Message Maps tab of the ClassWizard window, select the following event:

Class name:	CMCircleView
Object ID:	CMCircleView
Message:	WM_LBUTTONDOWN

☐ Click the Add Function button of ClassWizard.

Visual C++ responds by adding the OnLButtonDown() *function.*

☐ Click the Edit Code button of ClassWizard.

Visual C++ responds by opening the file MCircleView.cpp with the function OnLButtonDown() *ready for you to edit.*

☐ Write the following code in the OnLButtonDown() function:

```
void CMCircleView::OnLButtonDown(UINT nFlags, CPoint point)
{
// TODO: Add your message handler code here and/or call
//       default

//////////////////////////
// MY CODE STARTS HERE
//////////////////////////

// Update the m_PosX and m_PosY data members of
// the view class with the x-y coordinate of the
// point where the mouse was clicked.
m_PosX = point.x;
m_PosY = point.y;

// Trigger a call to the OnDraw() function.
Invalidate();

// Get a pointer to the document
CMCircleDoc* pDoc = GetDocument();

// Update data members of the document with the
// new values of the view class data members.
pDoc->m_PosX = m_PosX;
pDoc->m_PosY = m_PosY;

// Signal that the document has been modified.
pDoc->SetModifiedFlag(TRUE);

//////////////////////////
// MY CODE ENDS HERE
//////////////////////////

CView::OnLButtonDown(nFlags, point);

}
```

☐ Save your work.

The OnLButtonDown() member function of the view class is automatically executed whenever you press the left mouse button down over the document's window.

The second parameter of the OnLButtonDown() function, point, specifies the point onscreen where you pressed the mouse button; point.x holds the x-coordinate and point.y holds the y-coordinate of the point.

The first two statements you typed update the m_PosX and m_PosY view class data members with the x- and y-coordinates of the point where you clicked the mouse:

```
m_PosX = point.x;
m_PosY = point.y;
```

The next statement calls the Invalidate() function, which causes the execution of the OnDraw() function:

```
Invalidate();
```

Recall that the code you wrote in the OnDraw() function draws a circle at the point specified by m_PosX and m_PosY, so the preceding statements will draw a circle at the point where you clicked the mouse.

The next statement uses the GetDocument() function to extract a pointer, pDoc, to the document:

```
CMCircleDoc* pDoc = GetDocument();
```

The next two statements use the pDoc pointer to update the document class data members with the new values of the view class data members:

```
pDoc->m_PosX = m_PosX;
pDoc->m_PosY = m_PosY;
```

Now the document class data members have the same values as their corresponding data members in the view class. Whenever you change the values of data members in the view class, you should change the corresponding data members in the document class to the same values so that the data stored in the document of the program is the same as the data you view onscreen.

The last statement you typed calls the SetModifiedFlag() function:

```
pDoc->SetModifiedFlag();
```

In the preceding statement, the SetModified() function is executed on the pDoc document pointer because SetModifiedFlag() is a member function of the document class (not the view class). As its name implies, the SetModifiedFlag() function raises a flag in the document to indicate that the document's data has been changed. If you try to exit the program without saving the modified document first, the program will display a warning message box to give you a chance to save the changes made in the document. You should always call the SetModifiedFlag() function after changing the values of the document class data members.

☐ Compile, link, and execute the MCircle.EXE program to see the code you wrote in the OnLButtonDown() function in action.

> *Visual C++ responds by executing the MCircle program. The desktop of the MCircle program appears with a new document titled MCircl1. (Refer back to Figure 13.12.)*

☐ Click the mouse at the upper-right corner of the program's window.

> *The MCircle program responds by drawing a circle at the point where you clicked the mouse.*

403

☐ Try clicking the mouse at various points in the document's window and notice how a circle is drawn at each point where you click the mouse.

☐ Create new documents (by selecting New from the File menu) and verify that clicking the mouse produces the same results.

☐ Terminate the MCircle program by selecting Exit from its File menu.

When you terminate the program, the MCircle program displays a message box asking if you would like to save changes you have made to the documents. Click the No button of the message box because you don't want to save any changes. In the following section, you'll write the code responsible for saving the documents into files.

Writing Code That Saves and Loads Documents

You'll now write the code responsible for saving the documents into files and loading previously saved document files. You'll write this code in the document class.

☐ Open the file MCircleDoc.cpp and locate the `Serialize()` function. It should look like this:

```
void CMCircleDoc::Serialize(CArchive& ar)
{
if (ar.IsStoring())
    {
    // TODO: add storing code here
    }
else
    {
    // TODO: add loading code here
    }
}
```

The `Serialize()` function is automatically executed when you select Save, Save As, or Open from the File menu of the program. As you can see, the code in the `Serialize()` function is made up of a simple `if...else` statement:

```
if (ar.IsStoring())
    {
    // TODO: add storing code here
    ........................................
    ... This code is automatically executed ...
    ... whenever the user selects Save or   ...
    ... Save As from the File menu.         ...
    ........................................
    }
else
    {
    // TODO: add loading code here
```

```
.........................................
... This code is automatically executed ...
... whenever the user selects Open      ...
... from the File menu.                  ...
.........................................

   }
```

This is the if condition of the if...else statement:

```
if (ar.IsStoring())
```

In this code, the parameter of the Serialize() function, ar, represents the archive (the file) you are trying to read or write. If you select Save or Save As from the File menu, then the condition of the preceding if statement is satisfied and the code under the if is executed. If you select Open from the File menu, then the code under the else is executed.

Therefore, your job is to do the following:

1. Write code under the if statement that writes data to the file.
2. Write code under the else statement that reads data from the file.

Follow these steps to write this code:

☐ Write the following code in the Serialize() function:

```
void CMCircleDoc::Serialize(CArchive& ar)
{
if (ar.IsStoring())
   {
   // TODO: add storing code here

   ///////////////////////
   // MY CODE STARTS HERE
   ///////////////////////

   // Save m_PosX and m_PosY into the file.
   ar << m_PosX;
   ar << m_PosY;

   ///////////////////////
   // MY CODE ENDS HERE
   ///////////////////////

   }
   else
   {
   // TODO: add loading code here

   ///////////////////////
   // MY CODE STARTS HERE
   ///////////////////////
```

```
// Fill m_PosX and m_PosY with data from the file.
ar >> m_PosX;
ar >> m_PosY;

//////////////////////
// MY CODE ENDS HERE
//////////////////////

   }
}
```

☐ Save your work.

The code you wrote under the `if` statement is responsible for saving data into the file:

```
ar << m_PosX;
ar << m_PosY;
```

The insertion operator (`<<`) indicates you want to save data into the file. For example, this statement stores the data member `m_PosX` of the document class into the file:

```
ar << m_PosX;
```

Into what file? It depends on what you did. If you select Save As, then select the file MyFile.TRY from the Save As dialog box, the statement `ar << m_PosX` will store the `m_PosX` variable in the MyFile.TRY file. You can think of `ar` as the file that you selected.

Note: `ar` is the archive object (an object of class `CArchive`) that corresponds to the file you selected. Therefore, the statement `ar << m_PosX` literally means "save the variable `m_PosX` into the file you selected."

The `CArchive` class is discussed in Chapter 14, "File Access and Serialization."

The code you wrote under the `else` statement in the `Serialize()` function is responsible for loading the data from the file into the variables:

```
ar >> m_PosX;
ar >> m_PosY;
```

The extractor operator (`>>`) indicates you want to load data from the file into the variable. For example, this statement fills the data member `m_PosX` with data from the file:

```
ar >> m_PosX;
```

Again, the file depends on what you did. If you select Open from the File menu, then select the file MyFile.TRY from the Open File dialog box, the statement `ar >> m_PosX` will fill the `m_PosX` variable with data from MyFile.TRY.

Note that the order in which you extract the data must be the same order used for saving the data. For example, if you save data to the file with these statements,

```
ar << Var1;
ar << Var2;
ar << Var3;
```

then when you extract the data from the file into the variables, you must use the same order:

```
ar >> Var1;
ar >> Var2;
ar >> Var3;
```

In the previous code you used the insertion (<<) and extractor (>>) operators on several lines. You can also use these operators on a single line. For example, these three statements:

```
ar << Var1;
ar << Var2;
ar << Var3;
```

are equivalent to this single statement:

```
ar << Var1 << Var2 << Var3;
```

☐ Compile, link, and execute the MCircle.EXE program to see your code in action.

Visual C++ responds by executing the MCircle program, which creates a new document called MCircl1. The main window of the MCircle program looks like the one shown back in Figure 13.12.

To test the saving and loading code you wrote in the `Serialize()` function of the document class, do the following:

☐ Click the mouse at the lower-left corner of the MCircl1 window.

The MCircle program responds by drawing the circle at the lower-left corner of the MCircl1 window.

Now, save the document into a file as follows:

☐ Select Save As from the File menu of the MCircle program.

The MCircle program responds by displaying the Save As dialog box. (See Figure 13.20.)

☐ Delete the name `MCircl1` in the File name edit box and enter `MyCircle.Cir`, then click the Save button.

The MCircle program responds by creating the MyCircle.Cir file and saving the document into this file.

Because you saved the document in the file MyCircle.Cir, the title of the document's window is now `MyCircle`. (See Figure 13.21.)

13

Figure 13.20.
The Save As dialog box.

Figure 13.21.
The window's title changes to the filename of the saved document.

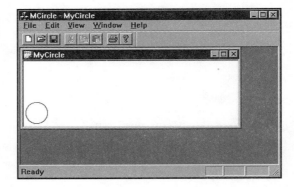

To verify your document is indeed saved in the MyCircle.Cir file, do the following:

☐ Select Close from the File menu of the MCircle program.

    The MCircle program responds by closing the MyCircle document.

☐ Select Open from the File menu of the MCircle program.

    The MCircle program responds by displaying the Open dialog box. (See Figure 13.22.)

☐ Use the Open dialog box to select the MyCircle.Cir file you saved earlier, then click the Open button.

    The MCircle program responds by opening the MyCircle.Cir file.

The window of your MCircle program should now look like the one shown back in Figure 13.21—the window of the MyCircle.Cir document is open on the desktop with a circle drawn in the lower-left corner.

You have just verified that the code you wrote in the Serialize() member function of the document class is working! You are able to save documents into files and load previously saved files.

Figure 13.22.
The Open dialog box.

☐ Keep experimenting with the MCircle program. For example, create new documents (by selecting New from the File menu), place the circle at different places in their windows, and save the documents under different filenames.

As you experiment with the MCircle program, notice that the File menu of the program maintains a most recently used file list—an MRU list. (See Figure 13.23.)

Figure 13.23.
*The MRU list in MCircle's
File menu.*

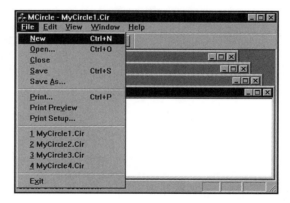

The MRU list of the MCircle program lists the four most recent files you've worked on. When you click one of the files in the list, the file is opened. Recall that when you created the project of the MCircle program, you accepted the default setting of 4 for the MRU list in Step 4 of the AppWizard. (Refer back to Figure 13.9.)

Note: The tools on the toolbar of the MCircle program were created for you by Visual C++ when you created the project and skeleton files of the project. In Chapter 15, "Toolbars and Status Bars," you'll learn how to create your own custom tools in the program's toolbar.

Notice that the main window of the MCircle program displays the title:

```
MCircle - filename
```

where *filename* is the name of the currently active window. For example, in Figure 13.24, the title of the program's main window is `MCircle - MyCircle1.Cir` because the MyCircle1.Cir document is the currently active window.

Figure 13.24.
The title of the program's main window reflects the filename of the open document.

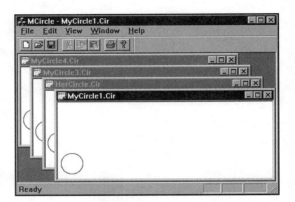

☐ Terminate the MCircle program by selecting Exit from its File menu.

Multiple Views of the Same Document

The MCircle program doesn't currently support multiple views of the same document—being able to open several windows for the same document. When you change the data in one of the windows, the data in the rest of the windows (of the same document) is updated automatically. To verify that the MCircle program does not support multiple views, try the following experiment:

☐ Execute the MCircle program by selecting Execute MCircle.EXE from the Build menu.

> *The main window of the MCircle program appears with a new document called MCircl1 (its default name).*

☐ Select Save from the File menu and save the new document as Test.Cir.

☐ Select New Window from the Window menu.

> *The MCircle program responds by opening another view (another window) for the Test.Cir document.*

☐ Select Tile from the Window menu.

Your MCircle program should now look like Figure 13.25.

Figure 13.25.
Two views of the Test.Cir document.

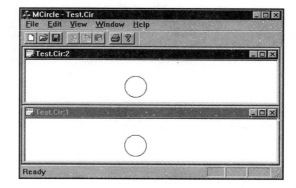

As you can see, the Test.Cir document has two views (windows): one with the title `Test.Cir:1` and the other with the title `Test.Cir:2`.

☐ Click the mouse at the upper-right corner of the Test.Cir:2 window.

> *The MCircle program responds by drawing the circle at the point where you clicked the mouse. However, the Test.Cir:1 window is not updated. (See Figure 13.26.)*

Figure 13.26.
After changing the Test.Cir:2 window, the Test.Cir:1 window is not updated.

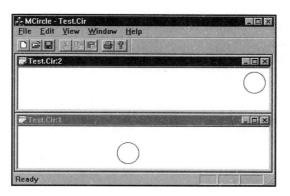

When you change one view of a document, the other view of the same document is not updated! This means that the MCircle program does not currently support multiple views of the same document.

In the following sections, you'll add code to the MCircle program so that when you change one view of a document, all the other views of the same document will be updated automatically.

☐ Terminate the MCircle program by selecting Exit from its File menu.

The *UpdateAllViews( )* and *OnUpdate( )* Functions

When you change a certain view by drawing the circle at a new point, you want to update all the views of the particular document you're changing. You do that by calling the UpdateAllViews() member function of the document class, which notifies all the views of the modified document that they need to be updated. The UpdateAllViews() function does this by calling the OnUpdate() member function of the view class for each view that should be updated.

So your job is this:

1. To write the code that calls UpdateAllViews() whenever a view is changed by drawing a circle.

2. To write the OnUpdate() member function of the view class.

Calling the *UpdateAllViews( )* Function

As stated, when you change a view by drawing a circle, you need to call the UpdateAllViews() member function of the document class. Follow these steps to add the statement that calls this function:

☐ Open the file MCircleView.cpp and locate the OnLButtonDown() function. (You wrote the code of the OnLButtonDown() function earlier; it draws a circle at the point where you clicked the mouse.)

☐ Add the following statement to the end of the OnLButtonDown() function:

```
// Update all the other views of the same document.
pDoc->UpdateAllViews(this);
```

After you add this statement, your OnLButtonDown() function should look like this:

```
void CMCircleView::OnLButtonDown(UINT nFlags, CPoint point)
{
// TODO: Add your message handler code here and/or call
//       default

////////////////////////////
// MY CODE STARTS HERE
////////////////////////////

// Update the m_PosX and m_PosY data members of
// the view class with the x-y coordinate of the
// point where the mouse was clicked.
m_PosX = point.x;
m_PosY = point.y;

// Trigger a call to the OnDraw() function.
Invalidate();

// Get a pointer to the document
```

```
CMCircleDoc* pDoc = GetDocument();

// Update data members of the document with the
// new values of the view class data members.
pDoc->m_PosX = m_PosX;
pDoc->m_PosY = m_PosY ;

// Signal that the document has been modified.
pDoc->SetModifiedFlag(TRUE);

// Update all the other views of the same document.
pDoc->UpdateAllViews(this);

//////////////////////////
// MY CODE ENDS HERE
//////////////////////////

CView::OnLButtonDown(nFlags, point);

}
```

The statement you just added to the OnLButtonDown() function calls the UpdateAllViews() member function of the document class:

```
pDoc->UpdateAllViews(this);
```

The parameter this is passed to tell UpdateAllViews() which is the current view (the this keyword is a pointer to the current view object). This way, UpdateAllViews() will update all the views of the current document except the current view.

For example, if you clicked the mouse at the upper-right corner in a certain view (window) of the document Test.Cir, UpdateAllViews() will update all the other views of Test.Cir. There is no need for UpdateAllViews() to update the current view because it's already been updated.

The *OnUpdate()* Member Function of the View Class

At this point, whenever you draw a circle in any view of a particular document, the UpdateAllViews() member function of the document class is executed. The UpdateAllViews() function will update the contents of the other views of the same document by calling the OnUpdate() member function of the view class. Therefore, you need to write the OnUpdate() function. Here is how you do that:

☐ Select ClassWizard from the View menu. In the Message Maps tab of ClassWizard, select the following event:

Class name:	CMCircleView
Object ID:	CMCircleView
Message:	OnUpdate

☐ Click the Add Function button of ClassWizard.

Visual C++ responds by adding the OnUpdate() *function.*

☐ Click the Edit Code button of ClassWizard.

Visual C++ responds by opening the file MCircleView.cpp with the function OnUpdate() *ready for you to edit.*

☐ Write the following code in the OnUpdate() function:

```
void CMCircleView::OnUpdate(CView* pSender, LPARAM lHint,
                           CObject* pHint)
{

// TODO: Add your specialized code here and/or call the base
//       class

////////////////////////////
// MY CODE STARTS HERE
////////////////////////////

// Get a pointer to the document
CMCircleDoc* pDoc = GetDocument();

// Update the view with the current document values.
m_PosX = pDoc->m_PosX;
m_PosY = pDoc->m_PosY;

// Trigger a call to the OnDraw() function.
Invalidate();

////////////////////////////
// MY CODE ENDS HERE
////////////////////////////

}
```

☐ Save your work.

The first statement you typed in the OnUpdate() function extracts pDoc (the pointer for the document class):

```
CMCircleDoc* pDoc = GetDocument();
```

Then the data members of the view class are updated with the current values of the document:

```
m_PosX = pDoc->m_PosX;
m_PosY = pDoc->m_PosY;
```

Finally, the Invalidate() function is used to trigger a call to the OnDraw() function so that the circle will be drawn at the new location specified by m_PosX and m_PosY:

```
Invalidate();
```

That's it! You have finished writing all the necessary code for multiple viewing of the same document.

To verify that the MCircle program supports multiple viewing of the same document, do the following:

☐ Execute the MCircle program by selecting Execute MCircle.EXE from the Build menu.

> *The main window of the MCircle program appears with a new document.*

☐ Select Save from the File menu and save the new document as `Try.cir`.

☐ Select New Window from the Window menu.

> *The MCircle program responds by opening another view (another window) for the Try.cir document.*

☐ Select Tile from the Window menu.

As you can see, the document Try.cir has two views (windows): one with the title `Try.cir:1` and the other with the title `Try.cir:2`.

☐ Click the mouse at the upper-right corner of the Try.cir:2 window.

> *The MCircle program responds by drawing the circle at the point where you clicked the mouse in the Try.cir:2 window; the Try.cir:1 window is automatically updated. (See Figure 13.27.)*

Figure 13.27.
After changing the Try.cir:2 window, the Try.cir:1 window is automatically updated.

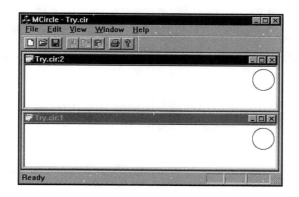

13

☐ Keep drawing the circle in one window of the Try.cir document at different locations, and notice how the other window of the Try.cir document is automatically updated.

You can now add as many views as you wish for the Try.cir document by selecting New Window from the Window menu. You'll see that when you change one view of Try.cir, all the other views are updated automatically.

☐ Terminate the MCircle program by selecting Exit from its File menu.

Enhancing the MCircle Program

You will now enhance the MCircle program in two ways:

1. Change the caption in the title of the program's main window from

   `MCircle - filename`

   to

   `The MCircle Program - filename`

   (where *filename* is the name of the currently active window).
2. Change the default file type displayed in the Save As and Open dialog boxes from *.*
   to *.cir. Whenever you select Open or Save As from the File menu, the default files
   displayed in the Files of type list box will have a .cir file extension.

Follow these steps to perform these enhancements:

☐ Select Project Workspace from the View menu. Select the ResourceView tab, expand the
MCircle resources item, then expand the String Table item.

> *After you expand the String Table item, a second String Table item appears under the first.
> (See Figure 13.28.)*

Figure 13.28.
*Expanding the String Table
item in the Project
Workspace window.*

☐ Double-click the second String Table item in the Project Workspace window.

> *Visual C++ responds by displaying the String Table dialog box of the MCircle project. (See
> Figure 13.29.)*

The String Table dialog box lets you view and edit various strings used by the program. As you
can see from Figure 13.29, the string whose ID is IDR_MAINFRAME is currently highlighted.
The current value of this string is `MCircle`. In an MDI program, the IDR_MAINFRAME string

specifies the text in the title of the program's main window. You'll now change the value of the IDR_MAINFRAME string from MCircle to The MCircle Program. Here is how you do that:

☐ Double-click the IDR_MAINFRAME string.

Visual C++ responds by displaying the String Properties window for the IDR_MAINFRAME string.

Figure 13.29.
The String Table dialog box.

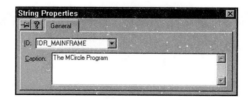

The value of the string is displayed in the Caption box.

☐ Change the value of the string to The MCircle Program.

Your String Properties window for the IDR_MAINFRAME string should now look like Figure 13.30.

Figure 13.30.
Entering a new string value for the IDR_MAINFRAME string.

The string listed below the IDR_MAINFRAME string in the String Table dialog box (refer back to Figure 13.29) is the IDR_MCIRCLTYPE string. The current value of the IDR_MCIRCLTYPE string is this:

```
\nMCircl\nMCircl\n\n\nMCircle.Document\nMCircl Document
```

The \n in the string serves as a separator between substrings. Therefore, the preceding string is made of the following seven substrings:

    Null
    MCircl
    MCircl

```
Null
Null
MCircle.Document
MCircl Document
```

The fourth and fifth substrings specify the default document type displayed in the Save As dialog box and Open dialog box of the program. For example, if you set the fourth substring to CIR Files (*.cir) and the fifth substring to .cir, then when you select Save As or Open from the File menu, the files listed in the File name list box will have the .cir file extension and the text in the Files of type box will be CIR Files (*.cir). (See Figure 13.31.)

Figure 13.31.
The Open dialog box, listing files with the .cir extension.

You'll now change the IDR_MCIRCLTYPE string so that the fourth substring will be CIR Files (*.cir), and the fifth substring will be .cir. All the rest of the substrings will remain as they are now. Here is how you do that:

☐ Double-click the IDR_MCIRCLTYPE string in the String Table dialog box.

   Visual C++ responds by displaying the String Properties window for the IDR_MCIRCLTYPE string.

The value of the string is displayed in the Caption box.

☐ Change the value of the string to this:

```
\nMCircl\nMCircl\nCIR Files (*.cir)\n.cir\nMCircle.Document\nMCircl Document
```

Note: The preceding text should be typed on a single line without pressing the Enter key. Visual C++ will wrap the line when it's too long.

Your String Properties window for the IDR_MCIRCLTYPE string should now look like the one shown in Figure 13.32.

Figure 13.32.

Entering a new string value for the IDR_MCIRCLTYPE string.

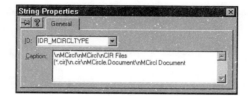

☐ Save your work.

☐ Compile, link, and execute the MCircle.EXE program to see the effects of the changes you made to the IDR_MAINFRAME and IDR_MCIRCLTYPE strings.

Visual C++ responds by executing the MCircle program. The main window of the MCircle program appears, as shown in Figure 13.33.

Figure 13.33.

The title of the program's main window now includes the text The MCircle Program.

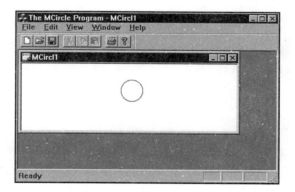

As shown in Figure 13.33, the title of the program's main window now includes the text The MCircle Program because you set the value of the IDR_MAINFRAME string to The MCircle Program.

☐ Select Save As from the File menu of the MCircle program.

The MCircle program responds by displaying the Save As dialog box. (See Figure 13.34.)

As shown in Figure 13.34, now the Save As dialog box lists files with the .cir file extension and the text in the Save as type box as CIR Files (*.cir) because you set the fourth substring of the IDR_MCIRCLTYPE string to CIR Files (*.cir) and the fifth substring to .cir.

Figure 13.34.
The Save As dialog box, listing files with the .cir file extension.

Summary

In this chapter, you have written an MDI program called MCircle.EXE that behaves like a standard Windows MDI program—it lets you view several documents, save the documents into files, and load previously saved files. The steps you took to create the MCircle program are the same steps for designing other MDI programs. You can use these steps as template steps for your future MDI projects.

Q&A

Q The steps I took in this chapter to create the MCircle MDI program are not much different from the steps I took in Chapter 11 to create the Circle SDI program, yet the MCircle MDI program is much more impressive. So why would I ever want to write an SDI program when writing the MDI version of the same program doesn't require much more effort?

A In most cases, you'll probably find it best to write MDI programs. However, sometimes you may find it useful to write SDI programs, in which the user is forced to work on only one document at a time, to save space, resources, or time.

Quiz

1. What is the purpose of the code you write in the view class of an MDI program?
2. What is the purpose of the code you write in the document class of an MDI program?
3. What code do you write in the `Serialize()` member function of the document class of an MDI program?
4. What does the `UpdateAllViews()` member function of the document class do?
5. How does the `UpdateAllViews()` member function of the document class notify all the views of the document that they need to be updated?

Exercise

Currently, whenever you create a new document, the default name assigned to the new document is MCirclX (where X is an integer). For example, the default name of the first new document is MCircl1, the next will be MCircl2, and so on.

Modify the MCircle program so that the default name assigned to the new document is UntitledX (where X is an integer). For example, the default name of the first new document will be Untitled1, the next will be Untitled2, and so on.

Hint: To set the default name that MCircle assigns to new documents, change the value of the second substring of the IDR_MCIRCLTYPE from MCircl to Untitled.

Quiz Answers

1. The code you write in the member functions of the view class of an MDI program is responsible for what you see onscreen.

2. The code you write in the member functions of the document class of an MDI program is responsible for maintaining the program's data. In particular, this code is responsible for saving documents into files and loading previously saved files.

3. The code you write in the `Serialize()` member function of the document class is responsible for saving data into files and loading previously saved files.

4. The `UpdateAllViews()` member function of the document class notifies all the views of the document that they need to be updated.

5. The `UpdateAllViews()` function notifies all the views of the document that they need to be updated by calling the `OnUpdate()` member function of the view class for each view that should be updated.

Exercise Answer

To make the default name that the MCircle program assigns to new documents UntitledX (where X is an integer), change the value of the second substring of the IDR_MCIRCLTYPE from MCircl to Untitled. All the rest of the substrings will remain as they are now. Here is how you do that:

☐ Select Project Workspace from the View menu. In the ResourceView tab of the Project Workspace window, expand the MCircle resources item, then expand the String Table item.

After you expand the String Table item, a second String Table item appears under the first.

☐ Double-click the second String Table item in the Project Workspace window.

Visual C++ responds by displaying the String Table dialog box of the MCircle project.

☐ Double-click the IDR_MCIRCLTYPE string.

Visual C++ responds by displaying the String Properties window for the IDR_MCIRCLTYPE string.

☐ Change the value of the string to the following (remember to type this on a single line without pressing Enter):

```
\nUntitled\nMCircl\nCIR Files (*.cir)\n.cir\nMCircle.Document\nMCircl Document
```

☐ Save your work.

That's it! If you compile, link, and execute the MCircle program now, you'll see that whenever it creates a new document, the default name assigned to the new document is Untitled*X* (for example, Untitled1, Untitled2, and so on).

14

File Access and
Serialization

In this chapter, you'll learn how to write code that writes and reads data to and from files by using *serialization,* which is the process that lets you save data to the hard drive.

The *CArchive* Class

Recall from Chapter 11, "Writing Single-Document Interface (SDI) Applications," and from Chapter 13, "Writing Multiple-Document Interface (MDI) Applications," that the parameter of the Serialize() member function of the document class is an object of class CArchive. For example, a typical Serialize() function of the document class looks like this:

```
void CTryDoc::Serialize(CArchive& ar)
{

if (ar.IsStoring())
    {

    /////////////////////////
    // MY CODE STARTS HERE
    /////////////////////////

    ar << m_Var1 << m_Var2 << m_Var3;

    /////////////////////////
    // MY CODE ENDS HERE
    /////////////////////////

    }
    else
    {

    /////////////////////////
    // MY CODE STARTS HERE
    /////////////////////////

    ar >> m_Var1 >> m_Var2 >> m_Var3;

    /////////////////////////
    // MY CODE ENDS HERE
    /////////////////////////

    }

}
```

The parameter of the Serialize() function (ar) is an archive object (an object of class CArchive) and corresponds to a file. In the case of the Serialize() function of the document class, ar corresponds to the file you select from the File menu. For example, if you select Open from the File menu and then select the file MyFile.TXT, then the Serialize() function is automatically executed and the parameter ar corresponds to the file MyFile.TXT.

Sometimes you'll find it useful to create and customize a CArchive object yourself, such as when you don't want the user to select the file, but you want to serialize data to or from a specific file. In the following sections, you'll learn how to write code that serializes data to and from a file. This code uses the CArchive class to save data into a particular file and load data from a previously saved file.

The Arch Program

You'll now write the Arch program. The code you'll write creates an object of class CArchive and uses this object to write and read data to and from a file. Before you start writing the Arch program, first review what the program should look like and what it should do.

- When you start the Arch program, the main window of the program appears, as shown in Figure 14.1.

Figure 14.1.
The main window of the Arch program.

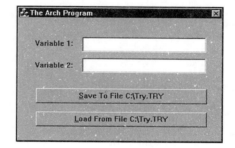

As you can see from Figure 14.1, the main window of the program displays a blank form with two fields, Variable 1 and Variable 2 and two pushbuttons, Save To File C:\Try.TRY and Load From File C:\Try.TRY.

- You can set the Variable 1 and Variable 2 fields to any string value and then click the Save To File C:\Try.TRY button. The Arch program will respond by saving the two string values into the file C:\Try.TRY.

- You can then type different values in the fields and click the Load From File C:\Try.TRY button. The Arch program will respond by loading the values previously stored in the C:\Try.TRY file and displaying them in the Variable 1 and Variable 2 fields.

Now that you know what the Arch program is supposed to do, you can start writing it.

Creating the Project of the Arch Program

Follow these steps to create the project and skeleton files of the Arch program:

☐ Create the directory C:\TYVCProg\Programs\CH14 and start Visual C++.

☐ Select New from the File menu, select Project Workspace, then click the OK button.

> *Visual C++ responds by displaying the New Project Workspace dialog box.*

☐ Select MFC AppWizard (exe) from the Type list and enter Arch in the Name box.

☐ Click the Browse button, select the C:\TYVCProg\Programs\CH14 directory, and click the Create button.

> *Visual C++ responds by displaying the MFC AppWizard - Step 1 window.*

☐ In the Step 1 window, select the "Dialog based" radio button to create a dialog-based program, then click the Next button.

☐ Set the Step 2 window as follows, then click the Next button:

About Box:	Checked
Context-sensitive Help:	Not Checked
3D Controls:	Checked
OLE Automation:	Not Checked
OLE Controls:	Not Checked
Windows Sockets:	Not Checked
Dialog title:	The Arch Program

☐ In the Step 3 window, use the default settings and click the Next button.

☐ Click the Finish button of the Step 4 window.

> *Visual C++ responds by displaying the New Project Information window.*

☐ Click the OK button of the New Project Information window and select Set Default Configuration from the Build menu.

> *Visual C++ responds by displaying the Default Project Configuration dialog box.*

☐ Select Arch - Win32 Release in the Default Project Configuration dialog box, then click the OK button.

That's it! You've finished creating the project file and skeleton files of the Arch program.

The Visual Design of the Arch Program

You'll now visually design the dialog box that serves as the main window of the Arch program (the IDD_ARCH_DIALOG dialog box):

☐ Select Project Workspace from the View menu. In the ResourceView tab, expand the Arch resources item, expand the Dialog item, and double-click the IDD_ARCH_DIALOG item.

Visual C++ responds by displaying the IDD_ARCH_DIALOG dialog box in design mode.

☐ Delete the OK button, Cancel button, and text in the IDD_ARCH_DIALOG dialog box.

☐ Set up the IDD_ARCH_DIALOG dialog box according to Table 14.1. When you finish, it should look like Figure 14.2.

Table 14.1. The properties table of the IDD_ARCH_DIALOG dialog box.

Object	Property	Setting
Dialog Box	**ID**	**IDD_ARCH_DIALOG**
	Caption	The Arch Program
	Font	System, Size 10
Static Text	**ID**	**IDC_STATIC**
	Caption	Variable 1:
Edit Box	**ID**	**IDC_VAR1_EDIT**
Static Text	**ID**	**IDC_STATIC**
	Caption	Variable 2:
Edit Box	**ID**	**IDC_VAR2_EDIT**
Push Button	**ID**	**IDC_SAVE_BUTTON**
	Caption	&Save To File C:\\Try.TRY
Push Button	**ID**	**IDC_LOAD_BUTTON**
	Caption	&Load From File C:\\Try.TRY

Note: Note that in Table 14.1, these are the captions of the pushbuttons:
```
&Save To File C:\\Try.TRY
&Load From File C:\\Try.TRY
```
You typed a double-backslash (\\) because in Visual C/C++, when you want to use the \ character in a string, you have to precede it with another \ character.

Figure 14.2.
*The IDD_ARCH_DIALOG
dialog box in design mode
(after customization).*

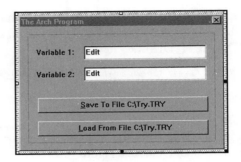

☐ Compile, link, and execute the Arch.EXE program to see your visual design in action.

> *Visual C++ responds by executing the Arch.EXE program. The main window of Arch.EXE
> appears, as shown back in Figure 14.1.*

As you can see, the main window of the Arch.EXE program (the IDD_ARCH_DIALOG dialog
box) appears just as you designed it.

☐ Terminate the Arch.EXE program by clicking the × icon.

Attaching Variables to the Two Edit Boxes

You'll now attach variables to the two edit box controls of the IDD_ARCH_DIALOG dialog
box because when you write the program's code, you'll use these variables to read the contents
of the edit box controls.

Follow these steps to attach a variable to the IDC_VAR1_EDIT edit box control:

☐ Select ClassWizard from the View menu. In the Member Variables tab, make the
following selection:

Class name:	CArchDlg
Control ID:	IDC_VAR1_EDIT

☐ Click the Add Variable button of ClassWizard, and set the variable as follows:

Variable name:	m_Var1Edit
Category:	Value
Variable type:	CString

☐ Click the OK button of the Add Member Variable dialog box.

Next, attach a variable to the IDC_VAR2_EDIT edit box control:

☐ Use the ClassWizard dialog box to make the following selection:

           Class name: CArchDlg
           Control ID: IDC_VAR2_EDIT

☐ Click the Add Variable button of ClassWizard, and set the variable as follows:

           Variable name: m_Var2Edit
           Category: Value
           Variable type: CString

☐ Click the OK button of the Add Member Variable dialog box.

☐ Click the OK button of ClassWizard.

Attaching Code to the Save Button

Whenever you click the Save To File C:\Try.TRY button, the contents of the two edit boxes (IDC_VAR1_EDIT and IDC_VAR2_EDIT) should be serialized into the file C:\Try.TRY.

Follow these steps to attach code to the Save button:

☐ Select ClassWizard from the View menu. In the Message Maps tab of ClassWizard, select the following event:

           Class name: CArchDlg
           Object ID: IDC_SAVE_BUTTON
           Message: BN_CLICKED

☐ Click the Add Function button, name the new function OnSaveButton, then click the Edit Code button.

    Visual C++ responds by opening the file ArchDlg.cpp with the function OnSaveButton() *ready for you to edit.*

☐ Write the following code in the OnSaveButton() function:

```
void CArchDlg::OnSaveButton()
{

// TODO: Add your control notification handler code here

/////////////////////////
// MY CODE STARTS HERE
/////////////////////////

// Update m_Var1Edit and m_Var2Edit with the
// screen contents.
UpdateData(TRUE);
```

14

```
// Create the file C:\Try.TRY.
CFile f;
f.Open("C:\\Try.TRY",
        CFile::modeCreate | CFile::modeWrite );

// Create an archive object.
CArchive ar( &f, CArchive::store );

// Serialize m_Var1Edit and m_Var2Edit into the archive.
ar << m_Var1Edit << m_Var2Edit;

// Close the archive
ar.Close();

// Close the file.
f.Close();

/////////////////////
// MY CODE ENDS HERE
/////////////////////

}
```

☐ Save your work.

The first statement you typed updates the variables of the edit boxes (m_Var1Edit and m_Var2Edit) with the current values displayed in the edit boxes:

```
UpdateData(TRUE);
```

The next two statements create the file C:\\Try.TRY:

```
CFile f;
f.Open("C:\\Try.TRY",
        CFile::modeCreate | CFile::modeWrite );
```

The first statement creates an object of class CFile, called f, and the second statement uses the Open() member function of the CFile class to create the C:\Try.TRY file.

The next statement creates an object, called ar, of class CArchive:

```
CArchive ar( &f, CArchive::store );
```

As you can see, this statement passes two parameters to the constructor function of CArchive. The first parameter is the address of the CFile object associated with the archive. In this statement, the first parameter is &f, the address of the CFile object of the C:\Try.TRY file. Therefore, the archive object ar will be associated with the file C:\Try.TRY.

The second parameter in this statement specifies the mode of the archive object. An archive object can be created for storage purposes (to save variables into the archive) or for loading purposes (to load data from the archive into variables). This is the second parameter:

```
CArchive::store
```

Therefore, the archive object ar will be used for storage purposes because you want the m_Var1Edit and m_Var2Edit variables to be saved into the archive whenever you click the Save button.

Now that you have an archive object associated with the file C:\Try.TRY, and this archive object is in a storage mode, you can serialize variables into the file Try.TRY. The next statement in the function serializes the two data members, m_Var1Edit and m_Var2Edit, into Try.TRY:

```
ar << m_Var1Edit << m_Var2Edit;
```

The next statement uses the Close() member function of the CArchive class to close the ar archive:

```
ar.Close();
```

The last statement uses the Close() member function of the CFile class to close the file associated with the f object (Try.TRY):

```
f.Close();
```

Attaching Code to the Load Button

Whenever you click the Load From File C:\Try.TRY button, the contents of the two edit boxes (IDC_VAR1_EDIT and IDC_VAR2_EDIT) should be filled with the values stored in the file Try.TRY.

Follow these steps to attach code to the Load button:

☐ Select ClassWizard from the View menu. In the Message Maps tab of ClassWizard, select the following event:

Class name:	CArchDlg
Object ID:	IDC_LOAD_BUTTON
Message:	BN_CLICKED

☐ Click the Add Function button, name the new function OnLoadButton, then click the Edit Code button.

Visual C++ responds by opening the file ArchDlg.cpp with the function OnLoadButton() ready for you to edit.

☐ Write the following code in the OnLoadButton() function:

```
void CArchDlg::OnLoadButton()
{

// TODO: Add your control notification handler code here
```

14

431

```
/////////////////////////
// MY CODE STARTS HERE
/////////////////////////

// Open the file C:\Try.TRY.
CFile f;
if ( f.Open("C:\\Try.TRY", CFile::modeRead)== FALSE )
   return;

// Create an archive object.
CArchive ar( &f, CArchive::load );

// Serialize data from the archive into m_Var1Edit and
// m_Var2Edit.
ar >> m_Var1Edit >> m_Var2Edit;

// Close the archive
ar.Close();

// Close the file.
f.Close();

// Update screen with the new values of m_Var1Edit and
// m_Var2Edit.
UpdateData(FALSE);

/////////////////////////
// MY CODE ENDS HERE
/////////////////////////

}
```

☐ Save your work.

The first two statements you typed open the file C:\Try.TRY in read mode:

```
CFile f;
if ( f.Open("C:\\Try.TRY", CFile::modeRead)== FALSE )
   return;
```

The first statement creates an object of class CFile, called f:

```
CFile f;
```

The second statement is an if statement that uses the Open() member function of the CFile class to open the C:\Try.TRY file in read mode:

```
if ( f.Open("C:\\Try.TRY", CFile::modeRead)== FALSE )
   return;
```

If the returned value of the Open() function is FALSE, you know that the file cannot be opened, in which case the if condition is satisfied and the function is terminated with the return statement.

The next statement creates an object of class CArchive called ar:

```
CArchive ar( &f, CArchive::load );
```

432

As you can see, this statement passes two parameters to the constructor function of CArchive. The first parameter is the address of the CFile object associated with the archive. In this statement, the first parameter is &f, the address of the CFile object of the C:\Try.TRY file. Therefore, the archive object ar will be associated with the file Try.TRY.

The second parameter specifies the mode of the archive object. As stated before, an archive object can be created for storage purposes or for loading purposes. This is the second parameter, so the archive object ar will be used for loading purposes:

```
CArchive::load
```

You want to use ar for loading purposes because you want to load data from the archive into the m_Var1Edit and m_Var2Edit variables whenever you click the Load button.

Now that you have an archive object associated with the file Try.TRY, and this archive object is in a loading mode, you can serialize data from Try.TRY into variables.

The next statement in the function serializes data from Try.TRY into the two data members, m_Var1Edit and m_Var2Edit:

```
ar >> m_Var1Edit >> m_Var2Edit;
```

The next statement uses the Close() member function of the CArchive class to close the ar archive:

```
ar.Close();
```

The next statement uses the Close() member function of the CFile class to close the file associated with the f object (Try.TRY):

```
f.Close();
```

The last statement in the OnLoadButton() function updates the screen (the two edit boxes) with the new values of m_Var1Edit and m_Var2Edit:

```
UpdateData(FALSE);
```

You've finished writing the code for the Arch program!

☐ Compile, link, and execute the Arch.EXE program to test your code.

Visual C++ responds by executing the program.

Experiment with the Save and Load buttons as follows:

☐ Type something in the two edit boxes.

☐ Click the Save button.

The Arch program responds by saving the contents of the two edit boxes into the C:\Try.TRY file.

☐ Change the contents of the two edit boxes.

☐ Click the Load button.

The Arch program responds by loading the contents of the C:\Try.TRY file. The two edit box controls now display the original text you typed.

As you can see, when you click the Save button, the contents of the two edit boxes are saved; when you click the Load button, the edit boxes are filled with the saved data.

Summary

In this chapter, you have learned how to serialize data to and from a file, which requires very little code. You can use this code in all your future programs when you need to save and load data to and from files.

Q&A

Q In the Arch.EXE program I wrote in this chapter, I serialized string variables to and from a file. Can I serialize other types of variables?

A Yes. You can serialize other types of variables (just as you serialized the CString variables of the Arch.EXE program).

Quiz

1. Describe what the following code does:

```
CFile f;
f.Open( "C:\\Try.TRY",
        CFile::modeCreate | CFile::modeWrite );

CArchive ar( &f, CArchive::store );

long MyNumber = 100;
CString MyString = "Test";

ar << MyNumber << MyString;

ar.Close();

f.Close();
```

2. Describe what the following code does:

```
// Open the file C:\Try.TRY.
CFile f;
f.Open("C:\\Try.TRY", CFile::modeRead);
```

```
// Create an archive object.
CArchive ar( &f, CArchive::load );

// Declare two variables.
long MyNumber;
CString MyString;

// Serialize data from the archive into the MyNumber
// and MyString variables.
ar >> MyNumber >> MyString;

// Close the archive
ar.Close();

// Close the file.
f.Close();
```

Exercise

Write code that serializes the text THIS IS A TEST into the file C:\Test.TRY.

Quiz Answers

1. Here is the code for Question 1 with explanatory comments:

```
// Create the file C:\Try.TRY.
CFile f;
f.Open("C:\\Try.TRY",
       CFile::modeCreate | CFile::modeWrite );

// Create an archive object.
CArchive ar( &f, CArchive::store );

// Declare and initialize two variables.
long MyNumber = 100;
CString MyString = "Test";

// Serialize the two variables MyNumber and MyString into
// the archive.
ar << MyNumber << MyString;

// Close the archive
ar.Close();

// Close the file.
f.Close();
```

2. Here is the code for Question 2 with explanatory comments:

```
// Open the file C:\Try.TRY.
CFile f;
f.Open("C:\\Try.TRY", CFile::modeRead);

// Create an archive object.
CArchive ar( &f, CArchive::load );
```

14

```
// Declare two variables.
long MyNumber;
CString MyString;

// Serialize data from the archive into the MyNumber
// and MyString variables.
ar >> MyNumber >> MyString;

// Close the archive
ar.Close();

// Close the file.
f.Close();
```

Exercise Answer

The following code serializes the string THIS IS A TEST into the file C:\Test.TRY:

```
// Create the file C:\Test.TRY.
CFile f;
f.Open("C:\\Test.TRY",
        CFile::modeCreate | CFile::modeWrite );

// Create an archive object.
CArchive ar( &f, CArchive::store );

// Declare and initialize a string variable.
CString MyString = "THIS IS A TEST";

// Serialize the variable MyString into the archive.
ar << MyString;

// Close the archive
ar.Close();

// Close the file.
f.Close();
```

This is the third and final week! On the first day of this week, you'll learn how to incorporate toolbars and status bars into your Visual C++ programs. As you'll see, with Visual C++ it is very easy.

On the second day, you'll learn how to write your own software library that contains your own classes. Typically, you design your own software libraries to distribute and sell or to distribute within your organization.

On the third day, you'll learn about DLLs. You'll learn what a DLL is, how to create one with Visual C++, and how to use one in Visual C++.

On the fourth day, you'll learn how to create an OLE control with Visual C++.

On the fifth day, you'll learn how to customize the OLE control you created the day before.

The sixth and seventh days are all fun and games! On the sixth day, you'll learn about the fascinating field of multimedia technology. You'll learn to incorporate playback of WAV sound files, MIDI sound files, movie AVI files, and audio CD. What a day!

On the seventh day, you'll learn how to create a 3-D virtual reality program with Visual C++. You'll learn how to make a 2-D drawing with a regular text editor, such as Wordpad. You'll then "plug" an OLE control into your program that converts the 2-D drawing to a 3-D picture and write your own code that lets your user "travel" inside the 3-D picture! You'll also place sprite objects in the 3-D picture and animate them; as your user travels inside the 3-D picture, he or she will encounter these animated sprite objects.

Toolbars and
Status Bars

In this chapter, you'll learn how to incorporate toolbars and status bars into your Visual C++ programs. As you'll see, it's very easy with Visual C++.

The Shp Program

You'll now create the Shp program, a program that illustrates how the toolbar and status bar are incorporated into a Visual C++ program.

The Shp program has a Circle icon and a Rectangle icon on its toolbar. When you click the Circle icon on the toolbar, you can then click the mouse in the window of the Shp program to draw a circle. The circle will be drawn with its center at the point where the mouse was clicked. When you click the Rectangle icon on the toolbar, you can then click the mouse in the window of the Shp program to draw a rectangle. The rectangle will be drawn at the point where the mouse was clicked. (See Figure 15.1.)

Figure 15.1.
Drawing a rectangle with the Shp program.

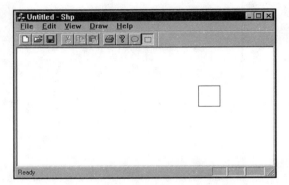

Creating the Project of the Shp Program

You'll now create the project of the Shp program:

☐ Create the C:\TYVCProg\Programs\CH15 directory and start Visual C++.

☐ Select New from the File menu to display the New dialog box, select the Project Workspace item from the New dialog box, then click the OK button of the New dialog box.

    Visual C++ responds by displaying the New Project Workspace dialog box.

☐ Set the Name box to Shp.

☐ Click the Browse button of the New Project Workspace dialog box, select the C:\TYVCProg\Programs\CH15 directory, then click the Create button.

Visual C++ responds by displaying the MFC AppWizard Step 1 window.

☐ In the Step 1 window, select the "Single document" radio button, then click the Next button.

☐ In the Step 2 window, leave the default setting at None, then click the Next button.

☐ In the Step 3 window, leave the default setting at None, then click the Next button.

☐ Set the Step 4 window to include a docking toolbar, an initial status bar, printing and print preview, and 3-D controls. (See Figure 15.2.) When you're done, click the Next button.

Figure 15.2.

Selecting features to include in the Shp program.

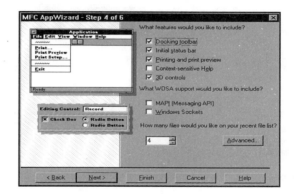

☐ In the Step 5 window, use the default settings, then click the Next button.

☐ Leave the default settings as they are in the Step 6 window, then click the Finish button.

Visual C++ responds by displaying the New Project Information window.

☐ Click the OK button of the New Project Information window.

Visual C++ responds by creating the project of the Shp program and all its associated files.

☐ Select Set Default Configuration from the Build menu, then select Shp - Win32 Release from the Project Default Configuration dialog box and click the OK button.

That's it—you are now ready to start designing the Shp program.

The Default Toolbar

Before you start writing the code of the Shp program, review what the Shp program can do at this point in developing the program. The Shp program already has several features—consider them gifts from Microsoft.

☐ Compile, link, and execute the Shp.EXE program to see what features it already has.

Visual C++ responds by executing the Shp.EXE program, and the window shown in Figure 15.3 appears. The toolbar is magnified.

Figure 15.3.
The window of the Shp program with a magnified toolbar.

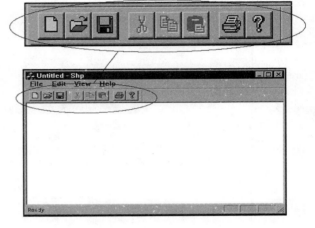

The toolbar serves as a visual menu. Try displaying the About dialog box:

☐ Select About Shp from the Help menu.

The Shp program responds by displaying the About dialog box.

☐ Click the OK button to close the About dialog box.

Instead of using the menu to display the About dialog box, you can use the toolbar:

☐ Click the Help tool, the rightmost icon on the toolbar (the one with a question mark icon). Note that you can program the tool names to be anything you want; in Chapter 13, "Writing Multiple-Document Interface (MDI) Applications," this tool was referred to as the About tool.

Shp responds by displaying the About dialog box.

The Help tool serves the same purpose as the About item of the Help menu.

The Print Tool

To the left of the Help tool, you see the Print tool, which serves the same purpose as the Print item of the File menu.

☐ Prepare your printer for printing.

☐ Click the Print tool on the toolbar.

The Shp program responds by letting you print the contents of its window. If you send the contents of Shp's window to the printer, a blank page will be printed at this point in the program's development.

Later in this chapter, you'll write code that displays a circle and a rectangle in Shp's window. You'll then be able to click the Print tool to send the contents of Shp's window to the printer.

The Save Tool

The third tool from the left is the Save tool (the one with a disk icon), which serves the same purpose as the Save item of the File menu.

☐ Click the Save tool.

Shp responds by displaying the Save As dialog box.

☐ Click the Cancel button of the Save As dialog box.

For now, you have nothing to save, but later you'll add code to the Shp program that saves files to the hard drive.

The New and Open Tools

The first and second tools from the left on the toolbar are the New and Open tools. The New tool looks like a blank page and the Open tool looks like an open folder. These tools serve the same purpose as the New and Open items of the File menu. Later you'll add code to the Shp program that makes use of the New and Open tools.

Note: As you have just seen, the toolbar of the Shp program has several useful tools, a gift from Microsoft. You'll enhance the Shp program so that the toolbar will include your own custom-made tools. In particular, you'll add the Circle tool and the Rectangle tool.

The Default Status Bar

The Shp program includes a status bar that displays various status messages to the user.

☐ Place (but do not click) the mouse cursor on the Help tool.

As shown in Figure 15.4, the status bar displays text to describe the purpose of the Help tool. In a similar manner, the status bar displays descriptions of other tools on the toolbar.

Figure 15.4.

The status bar message for the Help tool.

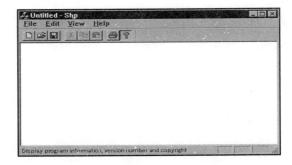

☐ Place the mouse cursor on other tools and observe the messages that the status bar displays.

The status bar also displays messages corresponding to the menu items. To see this in action, do the following:

☐ Open the File menu, then use the arrow keys to highlight the Exit menu item.

As shown in Figure 15.5, the status bar displays a message describing the action of the Exit menu item.

Figure 15.5.

The status bar's message about the Exit menu item.

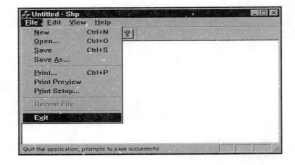

The View Menu

The View menu of the Shp program, shown in Figure 15.6, has two menu items: Toolbar and Status Bar. Currently, both these menu items have check marks in them, which means the Shp program is displaying the toolbar and status bar.

☐ Select the Toolbar item from the View menu to remove the check mark.

Shp responds by removing the toolbar. (See Figure 15.7.)

☐ Open the View menu of the Shp program; notice that the Toolbar item of the View menu does not have a check mark.

Figure 15.6.
*The View menu of the
Shp program.*

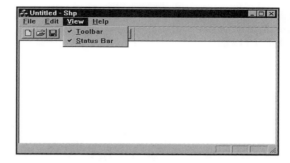

Figure 15.7.
*The Shp program without
its toolbar.*

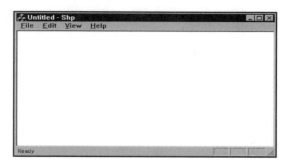

☐ Select the Toolbar item from the View menu to place a check mark next to it.

> *Shp responds by including the toolbar in Shp's window; now a check mark appears in the
> Toolbar menu item.*

The Toolbar menu item toggles; selecting it places or removes the check mark from the menu
item. The Status Bar menu item of the View menu also toggles. When there's a check mark next
to the Status Bar menu item, the status bar appears in Shp's window; no check mark means
there's no status bar in Shp's window. (See Figure 15.8.)

Figure 15.8.
*The window of the Shp
program without its
status bar.*

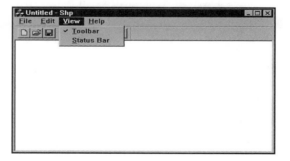

Displaying the Toolbar in Different Formats

So far, you have displayed the toolbar horizontally below the menu bar, as shown in Figure 15.3. However, the Shp program lets you display the toolbar in other locations and other formats.

☐ Double-click the space to the left of the Print tool on the toolbar.

Shp responds by displaying the toolbar as a floating toolbar. (See Figure 15.9.)

Figure 15.9.
The floating toolbar.

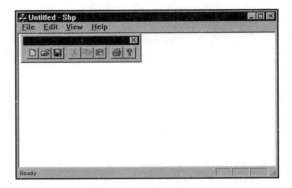

You can now drag the caption of the floating toolbar to any location onscreen. You can move the toolbar both within and outside the window of the Shp program.

☐ Drag the toolbar (by dragging its caption) to a different location on the screen.

You can place the toolbar as a fixed (non-floating) vertical toolbar as follows:

☐ Drag the toolbar toward the left edge of Shp's window. While you drag the toolbar, you'll see a rectangle the size of the toolbar following the mouse movements. When the mouse cursor is near the inner-left edge of the window, you'll see that the rectangle becomes a vertical rectangle. At that point, release the mouse.

Shp responds by displaying the toolbar as a fixed vertical toolbar. (See Figure 15.10).

The toolbar can also be placed on the right edge of the screen or even horizontally along the bottom of the window above the status bar.

☐ Double-click the space underneath the Save tool on the toolbar.

Shp responds by displaying the toolbar as a floating toolbar.

☐ Drag the edges of the floating toolbar to decrease its width.

As shown in Figure 15.11, you can also display the toolbar with more than one row of icons.

15

Figure 15.10.
*Displaying the toolbar as
a fixed vertical toolbar.*

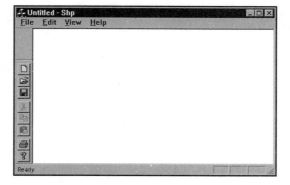

Figure 15.11.
*Displaying the toolbar with
two rows of icons.*

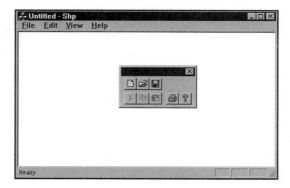

☐ Drag the toolbar upward. When the rectangle representing the toolbar becomes a narrow horizontal rectangle, release the mouse.

The toolbar is now attached to the upper edge of the window (below the menu bar).

Status Keys on the Status Bar

Look at the status bar again. The right side includes space for displaying the status of the Caps Lock, Num Lock, and Scroll Lock keys.

☐ Press the Num Lock key several times. As you can see, the status bar displays the text Num whenever the Num Lock key is on.

☐ Experiment with the Caps Lock, Num Lock, and Scroll Lock keys. Figure 15.12 shows the status bar when these keys are on.

Figure 15.12.
Indicating the status of the Caps Lock, Num Lock, and Scroll Lock keys.

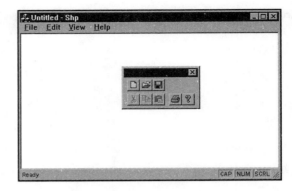

 Note: As you have seen, all the toolbar and status bar features that the Shp program includes are incorporated without having to write any code.

☐ Experiment with the Shp program, then select Exit from the File menu to terminate the program.

Adding the Circle Tool

You'll now add the Circle tool to the toolbar:

☐ Select Project Workspace from the View menu. In the ResourceView tab, expand the Shp resources item, then expand the Toolbar item.

The Project Workspace should now look like Figure 15.13. As you can see, the ID of the toolbar is IDR_MAINFRAME.

Figure 15.13.
The ID of the toolbar is IDR_MAINFRAME.

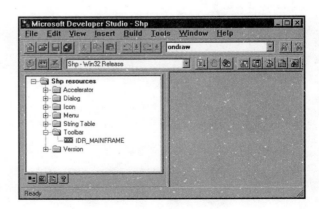

□ Double-click the IDR_MAINFRAME item.

Visual C++ responds by displaying the toolbar in design mode. (See Figure 15.14.)

Figure 15.14.
The icon of the New tool in design mode.

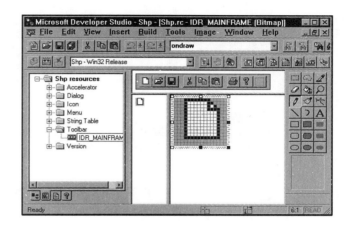

If you click the New tool (the leftmost icon) on the toolbar shown in Figure 15.14, the New icon (the one that looks like a blank page) is displayed in design mode. Similarly, if you click the Open tool, the Open icon is displayed in design mode. (See Figure 15.15.)

Figure 15.15.
The icon of the Open tool in design mode.

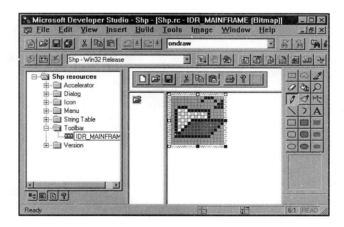

The toolbar has an empty icon to the right of the question mark icon. This is where you'll add the new icon.

□ Click the rightmost icon on the toolbar.

Visual C++ responds by displaying the new empty icon ready for you to design. (See Figure 15.16.)

Figure 15.16.
The new icon of the toolbar ready for you to design.

Click this empty icon to display it in design mode.

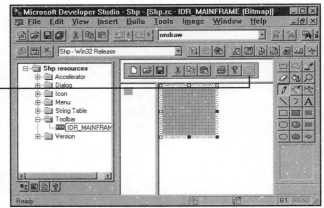

You'll now draw in the new empty icon with a red drawing pen:

☐ Select Toolbars from the View menu.

Visual C++ responds by displaying the Toolbars dialog box.

☐ Place a check mark in the Colors check box, then click the Close button. (Depending on the setting of your Visual C++, you may already have a check mark in the Colors check box.)

Visual C++ responds by displaying the Colors palette shown in Figure 15.17.

Figure 15.17.
The Colors palette.

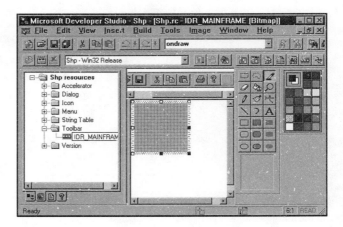

☐ Click the Select Color tool in the rightmost column on the first row.

☐ Click the Red palette to draw in the empty icon with a red pen.

☐ Click the Ellipse tool in the leftmost column on the last row.

Note: To examine the nature and purpose of each tool in the Tools window, hold the mouse cursor without clicking over the tool you want to examine. Visual C++ responds by displaying a yellow rectangle—called a *tool tip*—showing the tool's name.

Now you are ready to draw a red circle.

☐ Click in the new icon and drag the mouse while holding the left mouse button down.

Visual C++ responds by drawing a circle, as shown in Figure 15.18.

Figure 15.18.
Drawing a circle in the new icon.

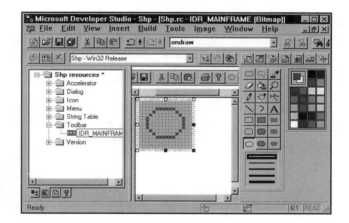

☐ Although you haven't finished designing the Shp program, compile, link, and execute it to check your progress.

Visual C++ responds by executing the Shp.EXE program, and the window shown in Figure 15.19 appears.

Figure 15.19.
The window of the Shp program with its new Circle tool.

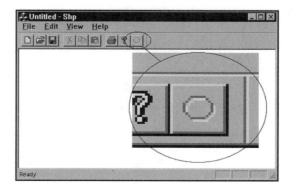

Of course, the Circle tool isn't working yet because you haven't added code for it. Furthermore, the Circle tool is disabled (dimmed).

☐ Select Exit from the File menu of the Shp program to terminate the program.

Adding the Rectangle Tool

You'll now add the Rectangle tool to the toolbar:

☐ Display the IDR_MAINFRAME toolbar in design mode, and click the empty icon to the right of the Circle tool. Visual C++ placed an new empty icon on the toolbar after the icon you drew for the Circle tool.

Visual C++ responds by displaying the new empty icon, ready for you to design.

☐ Repeat the same steps you used to draw the Circle icon, but now draw a rectangle instead of a circle. In Figure 15.20, the Rectangle tool is shown two rows above the Circle tool.

After you draw the new icon, it should look like Figure 15.20.

Figure 15.20.

The new icon for the Rectangle tool.

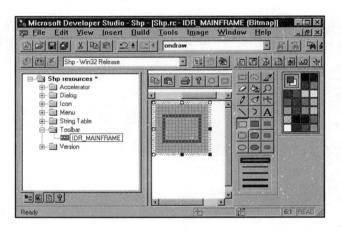

☐ Save your work.

☐ Compile, link, and execute the Shp.EXE program to check your progress.

The window of the Shp program appears, as shown in Figure 15.21. The toolbar now contains the Circle tool and the Rectangle tool; both are disabled (dimmed) at this stage.

☐ Select Exit from the File menu of the Shp program to terminate the program.

Figure 15.21.
The Circle tool and the
Rectangle tool in Shp's
toolbar.

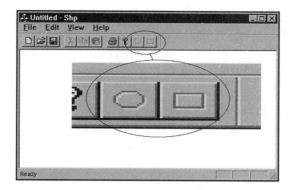

Creating the Menu of the Shp Program

You'll now create the Draw menu of the Shp program:

☐ Select Project Workspace from the View menu. In the ResourceView tab, expand the Shp resources item, expand the Menu item, and then double-click the IDR_MAINFRAME item.

> *Visual C++ responds by displaying the menu of the Shp program in design mode.*

☐ Drag the title of the Help menu to the right to make space for a new menu between the Help menu and the View menu.

☐ Create the Draw menu, shown in Figure 15.22, with two items in it: the Circle item and the Rectangle item.

Figure 15.22.
The Draw menu of the
Shp program.

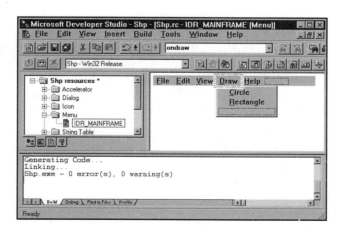

☐ Make sure the ID of the Circle menu item is ID_DRAW_CIRCLE and the ID of the Rectangle menu item is ID_DRAW_RECTANGLE. To do this, double-click the Circle or Rectangle menu item to display its Properties window and examine the ID box in the General tab.

Assigning an ID to the New Tools

As stated, the toolbar serves as a visual menu. For example, the Print tool serves the same purpose as the Print menu item of the File menu. Likewise, you want the Circle tool to have the same function as the Circle item of the Draw menu and the Rectangle tool to have the same function as the Rectangle item of the Draw menu. Here is how you accomplish this:

☐ Display the toolbar in design mode (double-click the IDR_MAINFRAME item under the Toolbar item in the Project Workspace window).

☐ Double-click the Circle icon of the toolbar in the window of the IDR_MAINFRAME toolbar window. Do not double-click the big Circle icon in the window; instead, double-click the small icon on the toolbar.

   Visual C++ responds by displaying the Toolbar Button Properties window of the Circle tool.

☐ Set the ID box in the Toolbar Button Properties window of the Circle icon to ID_DRAW_CIRCLE.

In the preceding step, you set the ID of the Circle tool to the same ID used by the Circle menu item of the Draw menu; therefore, the Circle tool will perform the same function as the Circle menu item.

☐ Set the Prompt box in the Toolbar Button Properties window to Draw circle with the mouse.

During the execution of the Shp program, when the Circle menu item is highlighted, the text Draw circle with the mouse will be displayed in the status bar. This text will also be displayed on the status bar when the mouse cursor is placed on the Circle tool of the toolbar.

☐ Double-click the small Rectangle tool of the toolbar (not the big Rectangle icon in the window) in the window of the IDR_MAINFRAME toolbar window.

   Visual C++ responds by displaying the Toolbar Button Properties window of the Rectangle tool.

☐ Set the ID box in the Properties window of the Rectangle tool to ID_DRAW_RECTANGLE.

In the preceding step, you set the ID of the Rectangle tool to the same ID used by the Rectangle menu item of the Draw menu. From now on, the Rectangle tool will perform the same function as the Rectangle menu item.

☐ Set the Prompt box in the Toolbar Button Properties window to `Draw rectangle with the mouse`.

Now the text `Draw rectangle with the mouse` will be displayed in the status bar when the Rectangle item is highlighted in the Draw menu. This text will also be displayed in the status bar when the mouse cursor is placed on the Rectangle tool!.

☐ Save your work.

☐ Compile, link, and execute the Shp.EXE program to make sure you performed the preceding steps correctly.

The Circle and Rectangle tools are currently disabled. Now check to see whether the corresponding menu items for the Circle and Rectangle tools are disabled, too:

☐ Open the Draw menu.

Yes, the Circle and Rectangle menu items are disabled because you haven't attached any code to them yet.

☐ Select Exit from the File menu of the Shp program to terminate the program.

Attaching Code to the Circle Menu Item

You'll now attach code to the Circle menu item of the Draw menu:

☐ Select Project Workspace from the View menu, click the ResourceView tab, expand the Shp resources item, expand the Menu item, highlight the IDR_MAINFRAME item, then select ClassWizard from the View menu.

   Visual C++ responds by displaying the MFC ClassWizard dialog box.

☐ In the Message Maps tab of ClassWizard, make sure the Class name box is set to `CShpView` and select the following event:

Class name:	`CShpView`
Object ID:	`IDC_DRAW_CIRCLE`
Message:	`COMMAND`

> **Note:** You must set the Class name box in the preceding step to `CShpView`. (The default setting that ClassWizard set for the Class name is `CMainFrame`.) If you are new to Visual C++, probably the most common error you'll make while creating this book's programs is not setting the Class name box of the MFC ClassWizard window as instructed.

☐ Click the Add Function button, name the new function `OnDrawCircle`, and click the Edit Code button.

Visual C++ responds by opening the file ShpView.cpp with the function `OnDrawCircle()` ready for you to edit.

☐ Write the following code in the `OnDrawCircle()` function:

```
void CShpView::OnDrawCircle()
{
// TODO: Add your command handler code here

/////////////////////////
// MY CODE STARTS HERE
/////////////////////////

// Good old MessageBeep()
::MessageBeep((WORD)-1);

/////////////////////////
// MY CODE ENDS HERE
/////////////////////////


}
```

The code you typed is executed whenever you click the Circle tool or select Circle from the Draw menu.

The code you typed causes the PC to beep:

```
// Good old MessageBeep()
::MessageBeep((WORD)-1);
```

Yes, the good old `MessageBeep()` function is used to verify that the code is executed when you click the Circle tool or select Circle from the Draw menu.

☐ Save your work.

☐ Compile, link, and execute the Shp.EXE program.

The window of the Shp program appears, as shown in Figure 15.23.

As you can see, now the Circle tool is enabled. The Rectangle tool is still disabled because you haven't attached code for it yet.

☐ Click the Circle tool on the toolbar.

The Shp program responds by causing the PC to beep.

☐ Select the Circle item of the Draw menu.

The Shp program responds by causing the PC to beep.

Figure 15.23.
*The toolbar of the Shp
program with its Circle
tool enabled.*

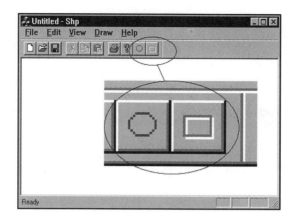

☐ Place the mouse cursor (without clicking) on the Circle tool.

The status bar displays the text Draw circle with the mouse.

☐ Highlight the Circle menu item of the Draw menu.

The status bar displays the text Draw circle with the mouse.

☐ Experiment with the Shp program, then select Exit from the File menu to terminate the
program.

Declaring the Data Members of the View Class

You'll now declare four data members in the view class (CShpView): m_XPos, m_YPos, m_Shape, and
m_SelectedShapeOnToolbar.

☐ Select Project Workspace from the View menu, click the FileView tab, expand the Shp
files item, expand the Dependencies item, and then double-click the ShpView.h item.

Visual C++ responds by opening the ShpView.h file.

☐ Declare m_XPos, m_YPos, m_Shape, and m_Selected ShapeOnToolbar as data members of the
CShpView class. After declaring these four data members, the CShpView class declaration (in
the ShpView.h file) should look like the following:

```
class CShpView : public CView
{
protected: // create from serialization only
CShpView();
DECLARE_DYNCREATE(CShpView)

// Attributes
public:
  CShpDoc* GetDocument();
```

```
/////////////////////////
// MY CODE STARTS HERE
/////////////////////////

int        m_XPos;
int        m_YPos;
CString    m_Shape;
CString    m_SelectedShapeOnToolbar;

/////////////////////////
// MY CODE ENDS HERE
/////////////////////////
...
...
...
};
```

Now the `CShpView` class has the `m_XPos`, `m_YPos`, `m_Shape`, and `m_SelectedShapeOnToolbar` data members. The data members `m_XPos` and `m_YPos` will store the x-y coordinates of the currently displayed shape (a circle or a rectangle). `m_Shape` will store the string indicating which shape is currently being displayed (`CIRCLE` or `RECTANGLE`). `m_Selected ShapeOnToolbar` will store the currently selected icon on the toolbar (`CIRCLE` or `RECTANGLE`).

Declaring the Data Members of the Document Class

In the previous section, you declared four data members in the view class (`CShpView`): `m_XPos`, `m_YPos`, `m_Shape`, and `m_SelectedShapeOnToolbar`. The document class (`CShpDoc`) should have a mirror image of three of these view class data members. You'll now declare the following three data members in the document class: `m_XPos`, `m_YPos`, and `m_Shape`.

☐ Open the ShpDoc.h file and add the declarations of these data members as follows:

```
class CShpDoc : public CDocument
{
protected: // create from serialization only
CShpDoc();
DECLARE_DYNCREATE(CShpDoc)

// Attributes
public:

/////////////////////////
// MY CODE STARTS HERE
/////////////////////////

int     m_XPos;
int     m_YPos;
CString m_Shape;
```

```
/////////////////////////
// MY CODE ENDS HERE
/////////////////////////
...
...
...
};
```

Now the view class (CShpView) has four data members: m_XPos, m_YPos, m_Shape, and m_SelectedShapeOnToolbar, and the document class (CShpDoc) has three data members: m_XPos, m_YPos, and m_Shape. You'll set the data members of the document class to be mirror images of the view class data members.

During the execution of the Shp program, you can change the view. For example, when you select a certain shape from the toolbar (Circle or Rectangle) and then click the mouse to draw the shape, the code you write will update the m_XPos, m_YPos, and m_Shape view class data members. You will also write code that updates the m_XPos, m_YPos, and m_Shape data members of the document class with the same values as the view class data members.

These values must be the same because you want to save the drawing into a file, and the file you'll save will contain the values of m_XPos, m_YPos, and m_Shape. There is no reason to have the m_Selected ShapeOnToolbar as a data member of the document class, because when you save the file to the hard drive, there is no need to save the status of the Circle and Rectangle icons of the toolbar.

Attaching Code to the *UPDATE_COMMAND_UI* Message of the Circle Menu Item

You'll now attach code to the UPDATE_COMMAND_UI message of the Circle menu item:

☐ Highlight the IDR_MAINFRAME item in the Project Workspace window, then select ClassWizard from the View menu.

Visual C++ responds by displaying the MFC ClassWizard dialog box.

☐ In the Message Maps tab of ClassWizard, make sure the Class name box is set to CShpView and select the following event:

Class name:	CShpView
Object ID:	IDC_DRAW_CIRCLE
Message:	UPDATE_COMMAND_UI

☐ Click the Add Function button, name the new function OnUpdateDrawCircle, then click the Edit Code button.

Visual C++ responds by opening the file ShpView.cpp with the function `OnUpdateDrawCircle()` *ready for you to edit.*

☐ Write the following code in the `OnUpdateDrawCircle()` function:

```
void CShpView::OnUpdateDrawCircle(CCmdUI* pCmdUI)
{
// TODO: Add your command update UI handler code here

//////////////////////////
// MY CODE STARTS HERE
//////////////////////////

if (m_SelectedShapeOnToolbar == "CIRCLE" )
{
    // Place check mark to the left of the menu item
    pCmdUI->SetCheck(1);
}
else
{
    // Remove check mark from menu item
    pCmdUI->SetCheck(0);
}

//////////////////////////
// MY CODE ENDS HERE
//////////////////////////

}
```

The UPDATE_COMMAND_UI event occurs before the Draw menu is displayed. As you know, the Draw menu contains two items: Circle and Rectangle. When you open the Draw menu, the menu items will be displayed. Before the menu is opened, however, the UPDATE_COMMAND_UI event occurs. This is your chance to have code executed before displaying the menu.

What code would you want to execute before displaying the items of the Draw menu? You want to place a check mark next to the item selected last; in other words, you want to maintain the m_SelectedShapeOnToolbar data member with data containing either the string "CIRCLE" or the string "RECTANGLE". When you select the Circle tool or the Circle item from the Draw menu, the m_SelectedShapeOnToolbar string should be filled with the string "CIRCLE". When you select the Rectangle tool or the Rectangle item from the Draw menu, the m_SelectedShapeOnToolbar string should be filled with the string "RECTANGLE".

Now when you open the Draw menu, the UPDATE_COMMAND_UI event occurs. The code you typed examines the value of the m_SelectedShapeOnToolbar data member, and accordingly, a check mark is placed or removed from the Circle menu item.

The code you typed in the `OnUpdateDrawCircle()` function takes care of the Circle menu item. The parameter of the `OnUpdateDrawCircle()` function is pCmdUI:

```
void CMainFrame::OnUpdateDrawCircle(CCmdUI* pCmdUI)
{
...
...
...
}
```

pCmdUI is a pointer that represents the Circle menu item.

The code under the if statement is executed whenever m_SelectedShapeOnToolbar is equal to "CIRCLE":

```
if (m_SelectedShapeOnToolbar == "CIRCLE" )
{
    // Place check mark to the left of menu item
    pCmdUI->SetCheck(1);
}
else
{
    // Remove check mark from menu item
    pCmdUI->SetCheck(0);
}
```

The code under the if statement places a check mark next to the Circle menu item:

```
pCmdUI->SetCheck(1);
```

The code under the else is executed if m_SelectedShapeOnToolbar is not equal to "CIRCLE". This code removes the check mark from the Circle menu item:

```
pCmdUI->SetCheck(0);
```

Note: To place a check mark next to a menu item, use the SetCheck() function as follows:

```
pCmdUI->SetCheck(1);
```

The preceding statement assumes that pCmdUI is a pointer to the menu item.

To remove a check mark from a menu item, use the SetCheck() function as follows:

```
pCmdUI->SetCheck(0);
```

The preceding statement again assumes that pCmdUI is a pointer to the menu item.

There's no harm done if you try to place a check mark next to a menu item that's already checked or try to remove a check mark from a menu item with no check mark.

461

Attaching Code to the *UPDATE_COMMAND_UI* Message of the Rectangle Menu item

You'll now attach code to the UPDATE_COMMAND_UI message of the Rectangle menu item:

☐ Highlight the IDR_MAINFRAME item under the Menu item of the Project Workspace window, then select ClassWizard from the View menu.

Visual C++ responds by displaying the MFC ClassWizard dialog box.

☐ In the Message Maps tab of ClassWizard, select the following event:

Class name:	CShpView
Object ID:	IDC_DRAW_RECTANGLE
Message:	UPDATE_COMMAND_UI

☐ Click the Add Function button, name the new function OnUpdateDrawRectangle, then click the Edit Code button.

Visual C++ responds by opening the file ShpView.cpp with the function OnUpdateDrawRectangle() ready for you to edit.

☐ Write the following code in the OnUpdateDrawRectangle() function:

```
void CShpView::OnUpdateDrawRectangle(CCmdUI* pCmdUI)
{
// TODO: Add your command update UI handler code here

/////////////////////////
// MY CODE STARTS HERE
/////////////////////////

if (m_SelectedShapeOnToolbar == "RECTANGLE" )
{
    // Place check mark to the left of menu item
    pCmdUI->SetCheck(1);
}
else
{
    // Remove check mark from menu item
    pCmdUI->SetCheck(0);
}

/////////////////////////
// MY CODE ENDS HERE
/////////////////////////


}
```

The code you typed in the `OnUpdateDrawRectangle()` function is very similar to the code in the `OnUpdateDrawCircle()` function. However, now `pCmdUI` represents the pointer to the Rectangle menu item because you attached code to the `UPDATE_COMMAND_UI` event of the Rectangle menu item.

☐ Save your work.

☐ Compile, link, and execute the Shp program.

☐ Open the Draw menu.

As you can see, the Rectangle menu item is still disabled because you haven't attached code to it yet. Also, note that the Circle menu item does not have a check mark next to it. Why? Because you haven't set the value of `m_SelectedShapeOnToolbar` to either `CIRCLE` or `RECTANGLE`. In the next section, you'll initialize the value of `m_SelectedShapeOnToolbar` to `CIRCLE` so that the Circle menu item will have a check mark next to it.

☐ Terminate the Shp program.

Initializing the *m_SelectedShapeOnToolbar* Data Member

You'll now write code that initializes the `m_SelectedShapeOnToolbar` data member of the view class:

☐ Add code in the constructor function of the `CShpView` class (in the ShpView.cpp file) as follows:

```
/////////////////////////////////////////////////////////
// CShpView construction/destruction

CShpView::CShpView()
{
// TODO: add construction code here

/////////////////////////
/// MY CODE STARTS HERE
/////////////////////////

m_SelectedShapeOnToolbar = "CIRCLE";

/////////////////////////
/// MY CODE ENDS HERE
/////////////////////////

}
```

The code you typed sets the value of the `m_SelectedShapeOnToolbar` data member to `CIRCLE`:

`m_SelectedShapeOnToolbar ="CIRCLE";`

When you start the Shp program, an object of class `CShpView` is created, which means that the constructor function of the `CShpView` class is executed. This causes the `m_SelectedShapeOnToolbar` data variable to be equal to `CIRCLE`.

☐ Save your work.

☐ Compile, link, and execute the Shp program.

☐ Open the Draw menu of the Shp program.

As you can see in Figure 15.24, the Circle menu item of the Draw item has a check mark.

Figure 15.24.

The Circle menu item with a check mark.

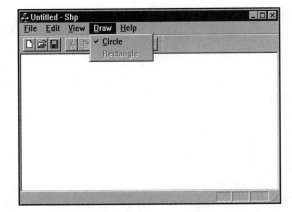

> **Note:** The check mark next to the Circle item, shown in Figure 15.24, also tells you that Circle was the last menu item selected from the Draw menu. Since the toolbar is the visual representation of the menu, how does it indicate that the Circle menu item was the last item selected from the Draw menu?
>
> Figure 15.25 shows the icon of the Circle tool in its "pushed-down" position. The beauty of this feature is that you do not have to write any code or draw the icon to display it in this pushed-down position. All you have to do is set the ID of the Circle tool to the ID of the Circle menu item.

☐ Terminate the Shp program.

Figure 15.25.
The icon of the Circle tool in its pushed-down position.

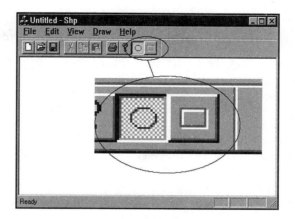

Attaching Code to the Circle and Rectangle Menu Items

You'll now attach code to the Circle and Rectangle menu items of the Draw menu:

☐ Display the menu in design mode.

☐ Select ClassWizard from the View menu.

Visual C++ responds by displaying the MFC ClassWizard dialog box.

☐ In the Message Maps tab of ClassWizard, select the following event (remember to check the class name carefully):

Class name:	CShpView
Object ID:	ID_DRAW_CIRCLE
Message:	COMMAND

☐ Click the Edit Code button of ClassWizard.

Visual C++ responds by opening the file ShpView.cpp with the function OnDrawCircle() *ready for you to edit.*

☐ Edit the code in the OnDrawCircle() function (in the ShpView.cpp file) as follows:

```
void CShpView::OnDrawCircle()
{
// TODO: Add your command handler code here

/////////////////////////
// MY CODE STARTS HERE
/////////////////////////
```

```
// Good old MessageBeep()
//::MessageBeep((WORD)-1);

m_SelectedShapeOnToolbar = "CIRCLE";

///////////////////////
// MY CODE ENDS HERE
///////////////////////

}
```

The code you typed is executed when you select Circle from the Draw menu or click the Circle tool. This code sets the m_SelectedShapeOnToolbar data member to CIRCLE:

```
m_SelectedShapeOnToolbar = "CIRCLE";
```

☐ Display the menu in design mode.

☐ Select ClassWizard from the View menu.

> *Visual C++ responds by displaying the MFC ClassWizard dialog box.*

☐ In the Message Maps tab of ClassWizard, select the following event:

Class name:	CShpView
Object ID:	ID_DRAW_RECTANGLE
Message:	COMMAND

☐ Click the Add Function button, name the new function OnDrawRectangle, then click the Edit Code button.

> *Visual C++ responds by opening the file ShpView.cpp with the function OnDrawRectangle() ready for you to edit.*

☐ Edit the code in the OnDrawRectangle() function (in the ShpView.cpp file) as follows:

```
void CShpView::OnDrawRectangle()
{
// TODO: Add your command handler code here

///////////////////////
// MY CODE STARTS HERE
///////////////////////

m_SelectedShapeOnToolbar = "RECTANGLE";

///////////////////////
// MY CODE ENDS HERE
///////////////////////

}
```

The code you typed is executed whenever you select Rectangle from the Draw menu or click the Rectangle tool. This code sets the `m_SelectedShapeOnToolbar` data member to `RECTANGLE`:

```
m_SelectedShapeOnToolbar = "RECTANGLE";
```

☐ Save your work.

☐ Compile, link, and execute the Shp.EXE program.

   Visual C++ responds by executing the Shp.EXE program.

☐ Click the Rectangle tool.

   Visual C++ responds by displaying the Rectangle tool in its pushed-down position.

☐ Open the Draw menu.

As you can see, the Rectangle menu item has a check mark.

☐ Experiment with the Shp program, and note that whenever the Circle menu item has a check mark, the Circle tool is displayed in its pushed-down state. Likewise, whenever the Rectangle menu item has a check mark, the Rectangle tool is displayed in its pushed-down state.

☐ Terminate the program.

Attaching Code to the *WM_LBUTTONDOWN* Event of the View Class

Whenever you press the mouse's left button, the `WM_LBUTTONDOWN` event of the view class occurs. You'll now attach code to the `WM_LBUTTONDOWN` event of the view class:

☐ Select ClassWizard from the View menu.

   Visual C++ responds by displaying the MFC ClassWizard dialog box.

☐ In the Message Maps tab of ClassWizard, select the following event:

Class name:	CShpView
Object ID:	CShpView
Message:	WM_LBUTTONDOWN

☐ Click the Add Function button, then click the Edit Code button.

   Visual C++ responds by opening the file ShpView.cpp with the function OnLButtonDown() function ready for you to edit.

☐ Write the following code in the OnLButtonDown() function:

```
void CShpView::OnLButtonDown(UINT nFlags, CPoint point)
{
// TODO: Add your message handler code here and/or call default

/////////////////////////
// MY CODE STARTS HERE
/////////////////////////

// Update the data members of the view
m_XPos     = point.x;
m_YPos     = point.y;
m_Shape    = m_SelectedShapeOnToolbar;


// Update the data member of the document
// with the new value of the view.

CShpDoc* pDoc = GetDocument();

pDoc->m_Shape = m_Shape;
pDoc->m_XPos  = m_XPos;
pDoc->m_YPos  = m_YPos;

// Trigger a call to the OnDraw function.
Invalidate();

/////////////////////////
// MY CODE ENDS HERE
/////////////////////////

CView::OnLButtonDown(nFlags, point);
}
```

The second parameter of the OnLButtonDown() function is point:

```
void CShpView::OnLButtonDown(UINT nFlags, CPoint point)
{
...
...
...
}
```

point represents the coordinates of the mouse at the time the left mouse button was pressed.

The code you typed sets the value of the two view class data members to the x-y coordinates of the mouse at the time you pressed the left mouse button:

```
m_XPos     = point.x;
m_YPos     = point.y;
```

Then the m_Shape data member is updated with the current selected tool on the toolbar:

```
m_Shape    = m_SelectedShapeOnToolbar;
```

So what have you accomplished so far? You've updated the view class data members with the data of the shape that will be drawn. To draw the shape, you have to know where to draw the shape (m_XPos and m_YPos), and you need to know what to draw (m_Shape can be CIRCLE or RECTANGLE). Next you are going to update the corresponding data members of the document class.

You extract a pointer to the document:

```
CShpDoc* pDoc = GetDocument();
```

Then you update the data members of the document with the new values of the view:

```
pDoc->m_Shape = m_Shape;
pDoc->m_XPos  = m_XPos;
pDoc->m_YPos  = m_YPos;
```

Again, you update the data members of the document because later you'll write code that saves to the hard drive a file containing the data members m_XPos, m_YPos, and m_Shape of the document class.

Then the Invalidate() function is executed to cause the execution of the OnDraw() function:

```
Invalidate();
```

The actual drawing of the shape will be accomplished in the OnDraw() function. The shape will be drawn based on the values of m_XPos, m_YPos, and m_Shape.

Drawing the Circle and the Rectangle

You'll now type the code that causes the Shp program to draw a circle or a rectangle at the point where you click the mouse:

☐ Open the ShpView.cpp file and modify the OnDraw() function as follows:

```
void CShpView::OnDraw(CDC* pDC)
{
    CShpDoc* pDoc = GetDocument();
    ASSERT_VALID(pDoc);

// TODO: add draw code for native data here

//////////////////////////////
// MY CODE STARTS HERE
//////////////////////////////

RECT  MyRect;
MyRect.left = m_XPos - 20;
MyRect.top = m_YPos -20;
MyRect.bottom = m_YPos + 20;
MyRect.right = m_XPos +20;
```

```
if (m_Shape == "CIRCLE")
{
pDC->Ellipse(&MyRect);
}

if (m_Shape == "RECTANGLE")
{

pDC->Rectangle(&MyRect);

}

/////////////////////////
// MY CODE ENDS HERE
/////////////////////////

}
```

The code you typed declares a rectangle:

```
RECT   MyRect;
MyRect.left = m_XPos - 20;
MyRect.top = m_YPos -20;
MyRect.bottom = m_YPos + 20;
MyRect.right = m_XPos +20;
```

Note that the circle you'll draw is enclosed by this rectangle. The center of the rectangle serves as the center of the circle. (See Figure 15.26.)

Figure 15.26.
Declaring the rectangle to enclose a circle with a radius of 20.

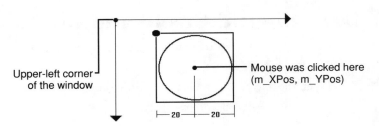

An `if` statement is then executed to examine the value of `m_Shape`:

```
if (m_Shape == "CIRCLE")
{

pDC->Ellipse(&MyRect);

}
```

If `m_Shape` is equal to `CIRCLE`, a circle is drawn.

The second `if` statement examines the value of `m_Shape`; if `m_Shape` is equal to `RECTANGLE`, a rectangle is drawn:

```
if (m_Shape == "RECTANGLE")
{

pDC->Rectangle(&MyRect);

}
```

☐ Save your work.

☐ Compile, link, and execute the Shp.EXE program.

☐ Click the Circle tool, then click in the window of the Shp program.

Shp responds by drawing a circle. (See Figure 15.27.)

Figure 15.27.
Drawing a circle with the Shp program.

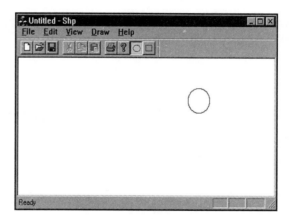

☐ Click the Rectangle tool, then click in the window of the Shp program.

Shp responds by drawing a rectangle, as shown back in Figure 15.1.

☐ Experiment with the Shp program, then terminate the program.

Initializing the Data Members of the Document Class

Whenever a new document is created by starting the program or selecting New from the File menu, the data members of the document class should be initialized to some value. You'll now write the code that does this:

☐ Open the ShpDoc.cpp file, search for the `OnNewDocument()` function in the ShpDoc.cpp file, then add code to the `OnNewDocument()` function as follows:

```
BOOL CShpDoc::OnNewDocument()
{
    if (!CDocument::OnNewDocument())
        return FALSE;

    // TODO: add reinitialization code here
    // (SDI documents will reuse this document)

///////////////////////////
// MY CODE STARTS HERE
///////////////////////////

m_XPos  = 10;
m_YPos  = 10;
m_Shape = "CIRCLE";

///////////////////////////
// MY CODE ENDS HERE
///////////////////////////

    return TRUE;
}
```

The `OnNewDocument()` function is executed whenever you start the Shp program or select New from the File menu of the Shp program.

The code you typed sets the values of the data members of the document class:

```
m_XPos  = 10;
m_YPos  = 10;
m_Shape = "CIRCLE";
```

☐ Save your work.

☐ Compile, link, and execute the Shp.EXE program.

The window of the Shp program appears without any circle or rectangle. In the `OnNewDocument()` function, you initialized the data members as follows:

```
m_XPos  = 10;
m_YPos  = 10;
m_Shape = "CIRCLE";
```

So why doesn't the window of the Shp program have a circle according to the preceding data? Because the `OnDraw()` function (in the ShpView.cpp file) draws the shape according to the data members of the view class (not the data members of the document class). This means you have to initialize the data members of the view class according to the data members of the document class. You'll accomplish this in the next section.

Initializing the Data Members of the View Class

You'll now initialize the data members of the view class to the values of the document class data members:

☐ Select ClassWizard from the View menu. In the Message Maps tab of ClassWizard, select the following event:

Class name:	CShpView
Object ID:	CShpView
Message:	OnInitialUpdate

☐ Click the Add Function button, then click the Edit Code button.

Visual C++ responds by opening the file ShpView.cpp with the function OnInitialUpdate() *ready for you to edit.*

☐ Write the following code in the OnInitialUpdate() function (in the ShpView.cpp file) as follows:

```
void CShpView::OnInitialUpdate()
{
    CView::OnInitialUpdate();

// TODO: Add your specialized code here and/or
// call the base class

////////////////////////////
// MY CODE STARTS HERE
////////////////////////////

// get a pointer to the document
CShpDoc* pDoc = GetDocument();

// update data members of view with the
// corresponding document values
m_XPos  = pDoc->m_XPos;
m_YPos  = pDoc->m_YPos;
m_Shape = pDoc->m_Shape;

////////////////////////////
// MY CODE ENDS HERE
////////////////////////////

}
```

The OnInitialUpdate() function is automatically executed whenever you start the Shp program or select New from the File menu. The OnInitialUpdate() function is executed after the document has already been created and initialized.

A pointer to the document is extracted:

```
CShpDoc* pView = GetDocument();
```

Then the data members of the view class are updated with the values of the data members of the document:

```
m_XPos  = pDoc->m_XPos;
m_YPos  = pDoc->m_YPos;
m_Shape = pDoc->m_Shape;
```

☐ Save your work.

☐ Compile, link, and execute the Shp.EXE program.

The window of the Shp program appears with a circle in it. (See Figure 15.28.)

Figure 15.28.

The circle in the Shp window when you start the Shp program.

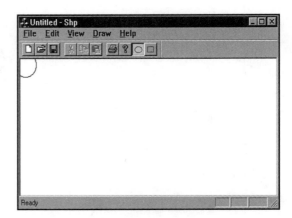

As you can see in Figure 15.28, the shape is a circle whose center is 10 units to the right of the window's left edge and 10 units below the window's top edge.

☐ Click in the window of the Shp program.

Shp responds by drawing a circle at the point where you clicked.

☐ Select New from the File menu of the Shp program.

Shp responds by opening a new document, and a circle at point x=10, y=10 appears in the window.

☐ Experiment with the Shp program, then terminate the program.

The Preparing to Save Flag

In the OnLButtonDown() function of the view class (in the ShpView.cpp file), you wrote code that sets the document class data members to the values of the view class data members. Later, you'll write code that saves the document class data members to the hard drive.

When you terminate the Shp program, it should display a message box asking whether the document should be saved. Also, when you select New from the File menu of the Shp program, the program should display a message asking whether the data of the previous document should be saved. To accomplish this, you have to call the SetModifiedFlag() function whenever the document is modified.

☐ Open the ShpView.cpp file and search for the OnLButtonDown() function.

☐ Modify the OnLButtonDown() function (in the ShpView.cpp file) as follows:

```
void CShpView::OnLButtonDown(UINT nFlags, CPoint point)
{
// TODO: Add your message handler code here and/or call default

/////////////////////////
// MY CODE STARTS HERE
/////////////////////////

m_XPos      = point.x;
m_YPos      = point.y;
m_Shape     = m_SelectedShapeOnToolbar;


// Update the data member of the document
// with the new value of the view.
CShpDoc* pDoc = GetDocument();

pDoc->m_Shape = m_Shape;
pDoc->m_XPos  = m_XPos;
pDoc->m_YPos  = m_YPos;

// Set the Modify flag of the document class to TRUE
pDoc->SetModifiedFlag();


Invalidate();

/////////////////////////
// MY CODE ENDS HERE
/////////////////////////

CView::OnLButtonDown(nFlags, point);
}
```

The statement you added to the OnLButtonDown() function calls the SetModifiedFlag() member function of the document class:

```
// Set the Modify flag of the document class to TRUE
pDoc->SetModifiedFlag();
```

☐ Save your work.

☐ Select Build Shp.EXE from the Build menu.

☐ Execute the Shp.EXE program.

☐ Click in the window of the Shp program.

Shp responds by drawing the shape at the point where you clicked.

☐ Select New from the File menu of the Shp program.

Shp responds by displaying a message box asking if you want to save the document.

☐ Click the Cancel button (at this point, you don't want to save the document).

☐ Experiment with the Shp program, then select Exit from its File menu.

Shp responds by displaying a message box asking if you want to save the document.

☐ Click the Cancel button (at this point, you don't want to save the document).

Writing and Reading Data to a File

The last thing to add to the Shp program is the code that saves the data members of the document to a file and loads previously saved files:

☐ Open the ShpDoc.cpp file, search for the Serialize() function, then add code to the Serialize() function (in the ShpDoc.cpp file) as follows:

```
/////////////////////////////////////////////////////////
// CShpDoc serialization

void CShpDoc::Serialize(CArchive& ar)
{
  if (ar.IsStoring())
     {
     // TODO: add storing code here

/////////////////////////
// MY CODE STARTS HERE
/////////////////////////

ar<<m_XPos;
ar<<m_YPos;
ar<<m_Shape;
```

```
///////////////////////
// MY CODE ENDS HERE
///////////////////////


    }
    else
    {
    // TODO: add loading code here

///////////////////////
// MY CODE STARTS HERE
///////////////////////

ar>>m_XPos;
ar>>m_YPos;
ar>>m_Shape;

///////////////////////
// MY CODE ENDS HERE
///////////////////////

        }
}
```

The code you typed under the `if` statement saves the data members of the document to the file. The code you typed under the `else` statement updates the data members of the document from a previously saved file.

☐ Save your work.

☐ Compile, link, and execute the Shp.EXE program.

   The window of the Shp program appears with a circle in its upper-left corner.

☐ Click the mouse in the upper-right corner of the Shp program.

   Shp responds by displaying a circle at the point where you clicked.

☐ Select Save As from the File menu of the Shp program and save the file as `MyCircle.Shp`.

Now the MyCircle.Shp file contains the data members `m_XPos`, `m_YPos`, and `m_Shape` of the document class. The values of these data members correspond to the circle you drew in the upper-right corner of the window.

☐ Select New from the File menu of the Shp program.

   A new document is created, and the Shp program displays the initial circle in the upper-left corner of the window.

☐ Select Open from the File menu of the Shp program and select the MyCircle.Shp file you previously saved.

Shp responds by displaying the circle you previously saved. The circle will appear in the upper-right corner of the window.

☐ Click the Rectangle tool and draw a rectangle by clicking the mouse.

☐ Select Save as from the File menu of the Shp program and save the file as `MyRect.Shp`.

☐ Select New from the File menu of the Shp program.

The initial circle in the upper-left corner of Shp's program appears.

☐ Select Open from the File menu of the Shp program and load the MyRect.Shp file.

The rectangle you previously saved appears.

☐ Experiment with the Shp program by saving additional files and make sure the Save As and Open features work as expected.

☐ Select Exit from the File menu of the Shp program to terminate the program.

Note: Experiment with the other features of the Shp program, such as the Print tool, Help tool, Print Preview, and so on. These features were created for you by Visual C++ without your having to write any code.

Summary

In this chapter, you have learned how to create and use a toolbar and a status bar. As you've seen, the toolbar serves as a visual menu.

Typically, you do not place icons for each of the menu items because too many icons on the toolbar make it difficult to locate a tool during runtime. Instead, place icons on the toolbar that correspond to the most frequently used menu items.

Q&A

Q When I place the mouse cursor on the icons of the toolbar, a tool tip is displayed. For example, when I place the mouse cursor on the New icon, the tool tip displays the text New. I would like to add tool tips for the Circle and Rectangle icons as well. Can it be done?

A Yes, it can be done. In the "Exercise" section of this chapter, you'll learn how to do this.

Q I saved the `m_XPos`, `m_YPos`, and `m_Shape` data members to a file, but the data member `m_SelectedShapeOnToolbar` of the view class was not saved. I did not declare the data member `m_SelectedShapeOnToolbar` in the document class. Why?

A The `m_SelectedShapeOnToolbar` data member indicates which icon (Circle or Rectangle) is currently selected on the toolbar. However, to draw a shape, you don't need to know which icon is currently selected. All that's needed to draw the shape is its location (`m_XPos` and `m_YPos`) and shape (`m_Shape`, which can be CIRCLE or RECTANGLE).

Q During the course of this chapter, I was instructed to save the data files of the Shp program with the file extension `*.shp` (for example, MyCircle.Shp). Does the file extension have to be Shp?

A No. You can save the data files by any name and any file extension (for example, OurDrawing.drw).

Quiz

1. The IDs of the icons on the toolbar are set to the IDs of what?
2. What is the reason for setting the IDs of the toolbar's icons to the IDs of the menu items?
3. When a menu item has a check mark next to it, how will the corresponding icon on the toolbar be shown?
4. When a menu item is disabled, how will the corresponding icon on the toolbar be shown?

Exercise

Add tool tips to the Circle and Rectangle tools of the toolbar.

Quiz Answers

1. The IDs of the icons on the toolbar are set to the IDs of the corresponding menu items.
2. You want the effects of clicking the toolbar's icons to be identical to the effects of selecting the corresponding menu items.
3. When a menu item has a check mark next to it, the corresponding icon on the toolbar is shown in its pushed-down state.
4. When a menu item is disabled, the corresponding icon on the toolbar will be shown dimmed.

Exercise Answer

Follow these steps to add tool tips to the Circle and Rectangle tools:

☐ Display the toolbar in design mode (select Project Workspace from the View menu, click the ResourceView tab, expand the Shp resources item, expand the Toolbar item, and finally double-click the IDR_MAINFRAME item.)

Visual C++ responds by displaying the toolbar in design mode.

☐ Double-click the Circle icon on the toolbar.

Visual C++ responds by displaying the Toolbar Button Properties window.

☐ Modify the contents of the Set the Prompt box as follows:

`Draw circle with the mouse\nDraw Circle`

During runtime, when you place the mouse cursor on the Circle icon, the text `Draw circle with the mouse` *will appear in the status bar. The text* `Draw Circle` *will appear in a tool tip next to the Circle icon.*

☐ Double-click the Rectangle icon on the toolbar.

Visual C++ responds by displaying the Toolbar Button Properties window.

☐ Modify the contents of the Set the Prompt box as follows:

`Draw rectangle with the mouse\nDraw Rectangle`

During runtime, when you place the mouse cursor on the Rectangle icon, the text `Draw rectangle with the mouse` will appear in the status bar. The text `Draw Rectangle` will appear in a tool tip next to the Rectangle icon.

16

Creating Your Own Classes and Modules

As you have probably noticed in this book, Visual C++ is a highly *modular* programming language. This means you create applications by "plugging in" software modules created by others. A classic example of such software modules are the Microsoft classes you have used throughout this book (the MFC).

In this chapter, you'll learn how to write your own software modules that contain your own classes. You can design your own software modules to distribute and sell them or to distribute them in your organization.

Why Create Professional Software Modules?

Typically, you design a *software module* to perform a task that's not otherwise available in Visual C++ and that's not easy to create. For example, you can design a software module that enables programmers to display 3-D graphs.

Sure, the programmer could probably design such a 3-D program by himself or herself, but most programmers prefer to purchase an off-the-shelf software module that performs the task. Therefore, the programmer can concentrate on his or her own program. When the application requires displaying 3-D graphs, the programmer can plug in your software module rather than spend time designing one.

Note: In this book, the term *programmer* usually means you, the reader, and the term *end-user* means the person who uses your application.

In this chapter, however, you'll learn how to write software modules and how to distribute them to other programmers. Therefore, the term *programmer* means another programmer who uses your software modules, and the term *end-user* means a person (a Visual C++ programmer) who purchases and uses your software modules.

Why not create a function or set of functions that perform the particular task, then distribute the C++ source code to your end-users? There are several reasons for not distributing your software as a set of C++ functions:

- The person who receives your code might accidentally (or even not accidentally) mess up the code.
- You don't want your end-user to know how you created the task; you only want your user to know how to use your software.

- Your end-user expects a "finished product" that can be easily plugged into his or her projects.

Different Formats for Software Modules

The current trend is to sell and distribute software in the form of software modules. Naturally, the format of the software module depends on the particular software package and programming language your user uses. For example, you can create OLE controls (OCX files) or DLL files. The advantage of creating an OLE control or a DLL file is that programmers of many different languages can use your software module because DLL files and OLE controls are supported by a variety of Windows programming languages. You'll learn how to create DLL files in Chapter 17, "Creating Your Own DLLs," and OLE controls in Chapter 18, "Creating Your Own OLE Control (Part I)," and Chapter 19, "Creating Your Own OLE Control (Part II)."

You can also distribute software modules exclusively to Visual C++ programmers by creating a Visual C++ library file (.LIB file). For example, you can create and distribute a file called Circle.LIB that lets your users perform operations related to a circle (for example, calculate the circle's area). Instead of writing functions that calculate the circle's area, your user simply plugs the Circle.LIB file into his or her application. Your responsibility is only to supply information to your users, telling them how they can apply your library to calculate circles' areas. In the following sections, you'll create the Circle.LIB library. Its code is simple; the point is to teach you how a library is prepared with Visual C++ and how to prepare the library for distribution.

Creating the Project of the Circle.LIB Library

Follow these steps to create the project for the Circle.LIB library:

☐ Create the directory C:\TYVCProg\Programs\CH16 and start Visual C++.

☐ Select New from the File menu.

   Visual C++ responds by displaying the New dialog box.

☐ Select Project Workspace from the New dialog box, then click the OK button.

   Visual C++ responds by displaying the New Project Workspace dialog box.

☐ Select Static Library from the Type list and enter Circle in the Name box. (See Figure 16.1.)

Figure 16.1.

Selecting Static Library in the New Project Workspace dialog box.

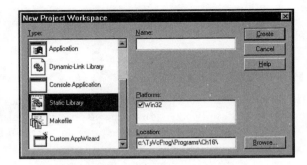

☐ Click the Browse button, select the C:\TYVCProg\Programs\CH16 directory, then click the Create button.

☐ Select Set Default Configuration from the Build menu, select Circle - Win32 Release in the Default Project Configuration dialog box, then click the OK button.

That's it! You've finished creating the project file of the Circle.LIB library.

Creating the Circle.cpp and Circle.h Files

The Circle.LIB file you create will be generated from the Circle.cpp and Circle.h files. You'll now create the Circle.cpp and Circle.h files:

☐ Select New from the File menu, select Text File from the New dialog box, then click the OK button.

Visual C++ responds by displaying a new window where you can type code.

☐ Type the following code in the new window:

```
/////////////////////
// Circle.CPP
/////////////////////

// Copyright (C) 1995

// This file is used for generating the Circle.LIB file

#include "Circle.h"
```

☐ Save the text file as Circle.cpp in the \TYVCProg\Programs\CH16\Circle directory.

☐ Select New from the File menu, select Text File from the New dialog box, then click the OK button.

Visual C++ responds by displaying a new window.

☐ Type the following code in the new window:

```
////////////////
// Circle.H
////////////////

// Copyright (C) 1994
```

☐ Save the text file as `Circle.h` in the \TYVCProg\Programs\CH16\Circle directory.

You now have the Circle.cpp and Circle.h files used for generating the Circle.LIB library. (Of course, later you'll write more code in these files.)

Next, you need to add the Circle.cpp file to the project of the Circle.LIB library. Here is how you do that:

☐ Select Files Into Project from the Insert menu.

Visual C++ responds by displaying the Insert Files into Project dialog box.

☐ Use the Insert Files into Project dialog box to select the file
C:\TYVCProg\Programs\CH16\Circle\Circle.cpp, then click the Add button.

Visual C++ responds by adding the Circle.cpp file and Circle.h file to the project.

Note: Notice that you did not have to add the Circle.h file to the project. You had to add only the file Circle.cpp to the project. Visual C++ automatically added the Circle.h file to the project because the code you wrote in the Circle.cpp file includes this statement:

```
#include "Circle.h"
```

That's it—the Circle.cpp and Circle.h files are now part of the project.

To make sure you've successfully added the Circle.cpp and Circle.h files to the project, do the following:

☐ Select Project Workspace from the View menu.

☐ Select the FileView tab of the Project Workspace window.

☐ Expand the Circle files item, then expand the Dependencies item.

Your Project Workspace window should now look like Figure 16.2. As shown, the Circle.cpp file and the Circle.h file are part of the project.

Figure 16.2.
Listing the files of the Circle project.

You have performed all the overhead tasks needed for telling Visual C++ to generate the Circle.LIB library. It's now time to start writing the code of the project.

Declaring the *CCircle* Class

You'll now write the code that declares a class called CCircle:

☐ Select Open from the File menu and select the Circle.h file.

Visual C++ responds by opening the Circle.h file.

☐ Add code to the Circle.h file as follows:

```
//////////////////
// Circle.h
//////////////////

// Copyright (C) 1995

// Class declaration

class CCircle
{
public:

 CCircle();  // Constructor

 void  SetRadius   ( int r );
 int   GetRadius   ( void );
 void  DisplayArea ( void );

 ~CCircle();  // Destructor

private:
 int m_radius;
 float CalcArea    ( void );

};
```

The code you typed in Circle.h declares the CCircle class:

```
class CCircle
{
...
...
...
};
```

The public section of the class contains the constructor, destructor, and three member functions:

```
public:

 CCircle();  // Constructor

 void  SetRadius   ( int r );
 int   GetRadius   ( void  );
 void  DisplayArea ( void  );

~CCircle();  // Destructor
```

The private section of the class contains one data member and one member function:

```
private:
 int m_radius;
 float CalcArea    ( void  );
```

☐ Select Save from the File menu to save the Circle.h file.

Writing Code in the Circle.cpp File

You'll now write code in the Circle.cpp file:

☐ Select Open from the File menu and open the Circle.cpp file.

☐ Add code to the Circle.cpp file as follows:

```
///////////////////
// Circle.cpp
///////////////////

// Copyright (C) 1995

// This file is used for generating the Circle.LIB file

#include "Circle.h"

#include <windows.h>

#include <stdio.h>
#include <stdlib.h>
#include <string.h>
```

```cpp
////////////////////////////
// The constructor function
////////////////////////////
CCircle::CCircle()
{


}

////////////////////////////
// The destructor function
////////////////////////////
CCircle::~CCircle()
{


}

////////////////////////////
// The SetRadius() function
////////////////////////////
void  CCircle::SetRadius   ( int r )
{

m_radius = r;

}

////////////////////////////
// The GetRadius() function
////////////////////////////
int   CCircle::GetRadius   ( void  )
{

return m_radius;

}


////////////////////////////
// The CalcArea() function
////////////////////////////
float CCircle::CalcArea ( void )
{

return float(3.14 * m_radius * m_radius);

}


////////////////////////////
// The DisplayArea() function
////////////////////////////
void  CCircle::DisplayArea ( void  )
{
```

```
    float   fArea;
    char    sArea[100];

    fArea = CalcArea ();


    sprintf ( sArea, "Area is:%f", fArea );


    MessageBox ( NULL,
                 sArea,
                 "Circle Area",
                 0 );

}
```

The code you typed starts with several #include statements:

```
#include "Circle.h"

#include <windows.h>

#include <stdio.h>
#include <stdlib.h>
#include <string.h>
```

The constructor and destructor functions of CCircle have no code:

```
/////////////////////////////
// The constructor function
/////////////////////////////
CCircle::CCircle()
{


}

/////////////////////////////
// The destructor function
/////////////////////////////
CCircle::~CCircle()
{


}
```

The SetRadius() member function sets the m_radius data member:

```
/////////////////////////////
// The SetRadius() function
/////////////////////////////
void  CCircle::SetRadius    ( int r )
{

m_radius = r;

}
```

The GetRadius() member function returns the m_radius data member:

```
/////////////////////////////
// The GetRadius() function
/////////////////////////////
int    CCircle::GetRadius   ( void   )
{

return m_radius;

}
```

The CalcArea() member function calculates the circle's area:

```
/////////////////////////////
// The CalcArea() function
/////////////////////////////
float CCircle::CalcArea ( void )
{

return float(3.14 * m_radius * m_radius);

}
```

The DisplayArea() function displays the calculated area:

```
/////////////////////////////
// The DisplayArea() function
/////////////////////////////
void  CCircle::DisplayArea ( void   )
{

float  fArea;
char   sArea[100];

fArea = CalcArea ();

sprintf ( sArea, "Area is:%f", fArea );

MessageBox ( NULL,
             sArea,
             "Circle Area",
             0 );

}
```

☐ Select Save from the File menu to save the Circle.cpp file.

Making the Circle.LIB Library

You are now ready to generate the Circle.LIB file:

☐ Select Build Circle.LIB from the Project menu.

Visual C++ responds by creating the Circle.LIB file.

Take a look in your \TYVCProg\Programs\CH16\Circle\Release directory. This directory now contains the Circle.LIB file!

Testing the Library: The Test1.EXE Program

You'll now write a program called Test1.EXE that uses the Circle.LIB library:

☐ Close the Circle project and all its associated files by selecting Close Workspace from the File menu.

☐ Select New from the File menu.

Visual C++ responds by displaying the New dialog box.

☐ Select Project Workspace from the New dialog box, then click the OK button.

Visual C++ responds by displaying the New Project Workspace dialog box.

☐ Select MFC AppWizard (exe) from the Type list and enter Test1 in the Name box.

☐ Click the Browse button, select the C:\TYVCProg\Programs\CH16 directory, then click the Create button.

Visual C++ responds by displaying the MFC AppWizard - Step 1 window.

☐ In the Step 1 window, select the option to create a dialog-based application, then click the Next button.

☐ In the Step 2 window, include the features "About box" and "3D controls" and set the title of the dialog to The Test1 Program. When you're done, click the Next button.

☐ In the Step 3 window, use the default settings and click the Next button.

☐ In the Step 4 window, notice that AppWizard has created the classes CTest1App and CTest1Dlg. Click the Finish button.

Visual C++ responds by displaying the New Project Information window.

☐ Click the OK button of the New Project Information window, then select Set Default Configuration from the Build menu.

Visual C++ responds by displaying the Default Project Configuration dialog box.

☐ Select Test1 - Win32 Release in the Default Project Configuration dialog box, then click the OK button.

That's it! You've finished creating the project file and skeleton files of the Test1 program.

The Visual Design of the Test1 Program's Main Window

You'll now visually design the main window of the Test1 program:

☐ Select Project Workspace from the View menu. In the ResourceView tab, expand the Test1 resources item, expand the Dialog item, then double-click the IDD_TEST1_DIALOG item.

> *Visual C++ responds by displaying the IDD_TEST1_DIALOG dialog box in design mode.*

☐ Delete the OK button, Cancel button, and text in the IDD_TEST1_DIALOG dialog box.

☐ Set up the IDD_TEST1_DIALOG dialog box according to Table 16.1. When you finish, it should look like Figure 16.3.

Table 16.1. The properties table of the IDD_TEST1_DIALOG dialog box.

Object	Property	Setting
Dialog Box	**ID**	**IDD_TEST1_DIALOG**
	Caption	The Test1 Program
	Font	System, Size 10
Static Text	**ID**	**IDC_STATIC**
	Caption	Testing the Circle.LIB Library
Push Button	**ID**	**IDC_MYCIRCLE_BUTTON**
	Caption	&My Circle
	Client edge	Checked (Extended Styles tab)
	Static edge	Checked (Extended Styles tab)
	Modal frame	Checked (Extended Styles tab)
Push Button	**ID**	**IDC_HERCIRCLE_BUTTON**
	Caption	He&r Circle
	Client edge	Checked (Extended Styles tab)
	Static edge	Checked (Extended Styles tab)
	Modal frame	Checked (Extended Styles tab)
Push Button	**ID**	**IDC_HISCIRCLE_BUTTON**
	Caption	&His Circle

Object	Property	Setting
	Client edge	Checked (Extended Styles tab)
	Static edge	Checked (Extended Styles tab)
	Modal frame	Checked (Extended Styles tab)
Push Button	**ID**	**IDC_OURCIRCLE_BUTTON**
	Caption	&Our Circle
	Client edge	Checked (Extended Styles tab)
	Static edge	Checked (Extended Styles tab)
	Modal frame	Checked (Extended Styles tab)

Figure 16.3.
*IDD_TEST1_DIALOG
in design mode (after
customization).*

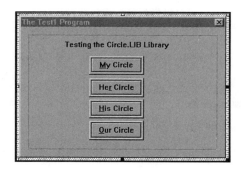

Attaching Code to the My Circle Button

You'll now attach code to the My Circle button of the IDD_TEST1_DIALOG dialog box:

☐ Select ClassWizard from the View menu. In the Message Maps tab of ClassWizard, select
the following event:

Class name:	CTest1Dlg
Object ID:	IDC_MYCIRCLE_BUTTON
Message:	BN_CLICKED

☐ Click the Add Function button, name the new function OnMycircleButton, then click the
Edit Code button.

*Visual C++ responds by opening the file Test1Dlg.cpp with the function
OnMycircleButton() ready for you to edit.*

☐ Write the following code in the OnMycircleButton() function:

```
void CTest1Dlg::OnMycircleButton()
{
```

```
// TODO: Add your control notification handler code here

/////////////////////////
// MY CODE STARTS HERE
/////////////////////////

// Create the object
CCircle MyCircle;

// Set the radius of the circle
MyCircle.SetRadius(1);

// Display the area
MyCircle.DisplayArea();

/////////////////////////
// MY CODE ENDS HERE
/////////////////////////

}
```

The code you typed creates the `MyCircle` object of class `CCircle`:

```
CCircle MyCircle;
```

The radius of `MyCircle` is set to 1:

```
MyCircle.SetRadius(1);
```

Finally, the area of `MyCircle` is displayed:

```
MyCircle.DisplayArea();
```

Attaching Code to the His Circle Button

You'll now attach code to the His Circle button of the IDD_TEST1_DIALOG dialog box:

☐ Select ClassWizard from the View menu. In the Message Maps tab of ClassWizard, select the following event:

Class name:	CTest1Dlg
Object ID:	IDC_HISCIRCLE_BUTTON
Message:	BN_CLICKED

☐ Click the Add Function button, name the new function `OnHiscircleButton`, then click the Edit Code button.

Visual C++ responds by opening the file Test1Dlg.cpp with the function `OnHiscircleButton()` ready for you to edit.

☐ Write the following code in the `OnHiscircleButton()` function:

```
void CTest1Dlg::OnHiscircleButton()
{

// TODO: Add your control notification handler code here

///////////////////////
// MY CODE STARTS HERE
///////////////////////

// Create the object
CCircle HisCircle;

// Set the radius of the circle
HisCircle.SetRadius(2);

// Display the area
HisCircle.DisplayArea();

///////////////////////
// MY CODE ENDS HERE
///////////////////////

}
```

The code you typed is similar to the code you typed in the `OnMycircleButton()` function, except that now you have created the `HisCircle` object and set the radius to 2.

Attaching Code to the Her Circle Button

You'll now attach code to the Her Circle button of the IDD_TEST1_DIALOG dialog box:

☐ Select ClassWizard from the View menu. In the Message Maps tab of ClassWizard, select the following event:

Class name:	CTest1Dlg
Object ID:	IDC_HERCIRCLE_BUTTON
Message:	BN_CLICKED

☐ Click the Add Function button, name the new function `OnHercircleButton`, then click the Edit Code button.

> *Visual C++ responds by opening the file Test1Dlg.cpp with the function* `OnHercircleButton()` *ready for you to edit.*

☐ Write the following code in the `OnHercircleButton()` function:

```
void CTest1Dlg::OnHercircleButton()
{
```

```
// TODO: Add your control notification handler code here

////////////////////////
// MY CODE STARTS HERE
////////////////////////

// Create the object
CCircle HerCircle;

// Set the radius of the circle
HerCircle.SetRadius(3);

// Display the area
HerCircle.DisplayArea();

////////////////////////
// MY CODE ENDS HERE
////////////////////////

}
```

The code you typed is similar to the code you typed in the `OnMycircleButton()` and the `OnHiscircleButton()` functions, except that now you have created the `HerCircle` object and set the radius to 3.

Attaching Code to the Our Circle Button

You'll now attach code to the Our Circle button of the IDD_TEST1_DIALOG dialog box:

☐ Select ClassWizard from the View menu. In the Message Maps tab of ClassWizard, select the following event:

Class name:	CTest1Dlg
Object ID:	IDC_OURCIRCLE_BUTTON
Message:	BN_CLICKED

☐ Click the Add Function button, name the new function `OnOurcircleButton`, then click the Edit Code button.

Visual C++ responds by opening the file Test1Dlg.cpp with the function OnOurcircleButton() ready for you to edit.

☐ Write the following code in the `OnOurcircleButton()` function:

```
void CTest1Dlg::OnOurcircleButton()
{

// TODO: Add your control notification handler code here

////////////////////////
// MY CODE STARTS HERE
////////////////////////
```

```
// Create the object
CCircle OurCircle;

// Set the radius of the circle
OurCircle.SetRadius(4);

// Display the area
OurCircle.DisplayArea();

////////////////////////
// MY CODE ENDS HERE
////////////////////////

}
```

☐ Save your work.

The code you typed is similar to the code you attached to the other buttons of the IDD_TEST1_DIALOG dialog box, except that now you have created the OurCircle object and set the radius to 4.

Plugging In the Circle.LIB Library

If you try to compile and link the Test1 project now, you'll get plenty of errors! Why? Because the Test1 project knows nothing about the CCircle class. Therefore, you must use the #include statement on the Circle.h file at the beginning of the Test1Dlg.h file:

☐ Open the Test1Dlg.h file and use an #include statement on the Circle.h file as follows:

```
// Test1Dlg.h : header file
//

/////////////////////////////////////////////////////
// CTest1Dlg dialog

////////////////////////
// MY CODE STARTS HERE
////////////////////////

#include "C:\TyVcProg\Programs\Ch16\Circle\Circle.H"

////////////////////////
// MY CODE ENDS HERE
////////////////////////
....
....
....
```

Because you used the #include statement on the Circle.h file, the prototypes of the CCircle class member function will be known to the compiler. However, the linker needs to use the actual code of these member functions, which is in the Circle.LIB file. In the following steps, you'll plug the Circle.LIB file into the Test1 project:

☐ Select Files into Project from the Insert menu.

Visual C++ responds by displaying the Insert Files into Project dialog box. (See Figure 16.4.)

Figure 16.4.
The Insert Files into Project dialog box.

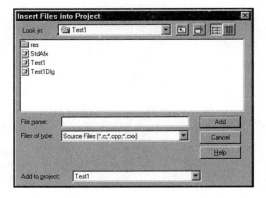

You'll now add the \TYVCProg\Programs\CH16\Circle\Release\Circle.LIB file to the project:

☐ Set the Files of Type drop-down list to `Library files (*.lib)`.

☐ Select the \TYVCProg\Programs\CH16\Circle\Release\Circle.LIB file, then click the Add button.

Visual C++ responds by adding the \TYVCProg\Programs\CH16\Circle\Release\Circle.LIB file to the Test1 project.

☐ Save your work.

Compiling, Linking, and Executing the Test1 Program

You'll now compile, link, and execute the Test1 program:

☐ Select Build Test1.EXE from the Project menu.

Visual C++ responds by compiling and linking the Test1 program.

☐ Select Execute Test1.EXE from the Project menu.

Visual C++ responds by executing the Test1.EXE program and displaying the window shown in Figure 16.5.

Figure 16.5.

The window of the Test1.EXE program.

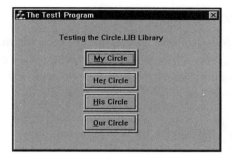

16

☐ Experiment with the four buttons of the Test1 program and verify that the program operates properly.

☐ Terminate the Test1 program by clicking the × icon at the upper-right corner of the program's window.

Distributing Your Software Modules

In the preceding section you proved that the Circle.LIB library works as expected. So what will you distribute to your users? You have to distribute the following:

• The Circle.LIB file.

• The Circle.h file.

• Documentation showing how to use Circle.LIB. (It is a good idea to distribute the Test1 program as part of your documentation because your user can see how the Circle.LIB library is used.)

> **Note:** Note that your CCircle class calculates the area of the circle by using the formula Area=3.14*radius*radius, but because you did not supply the source code, the "secret" of calculating the circle's area remains with you. Your user doesn't know how you performed the calculations! Of course, this is more relevant when you write code that accomplishes a more complicated task.

Summary

In this chapter, you have learned how to create a library file (.LIB file) that contains your own class. As you have seen, creating a library file with Visual C++ is quite simple. Once you finish your library file, you can distribute it to other Visual C++ programmers who can incorporate it into their projects.

Q&A

Q Why do I have to distribute the .h file that declares my class with my .LIB file?

A You must distribute the .h file that declares your class with your .LIB file so that your end-user's project will know about your class (the names and types of your class data members and the prototypes of your class member functions).

Quiz

1. When you distribute your library file to your end-user, you have to distribute the source code of your library.
    a. True.
    b. False.

2. To use your library file, your end-user needs to add your .LIB file to his or her project and then build the project.
    a. True.
    b. False.

Exercise

Describe the steps needed to create a project for a library file.

Quiz Answers

1. b. False.
2. a. True.

Exercise Answer

To create a project for a library file, use the following steps:

☐ Select New from the File menu.

☐ Select Project Workspace from the New dialog box, then click the OK button.

   Visual C++ responds by displaying the New Project Workspace dialog box.

☐ Select Static Library from the Type list and enter the project name in the Name box.

☐ Click the Browse button, select the directory where you want to create the project, then click the Create button.

Creating Your
Own DLLs

In this chapter you'll learn what a *DLL* (dynamic link library) is, how to create a DLL with Visual C++, and how to use a DLL in Visual C++.

What Is a DLL?

A DLL is a library file that contains functions. A programmer can integrate a DLL file into his or her program and use the DLL's functions. For example, you can create a DLL called CIRCLE.DLL containing functions that pertain to circles, such as `DrawCircle()`, `CalculateCircleArea()`, and so on. You can then distribute the CIRCLE.DLL file to other programmers, and they can use these functions in their programs.

As its name implies, a DLL is a library linked dynamically to the program that uses it. This means that when you create the EXE file of your program, you don't link the DLL file to your program. The DLL file will be dynamically linked to your program during runtime. So when you write a program that uses a DLL, you must distribute the DLL file with the EXE file of your program.

> **Note:** For a program that uses a DLL file to work, the DLL file must reside in any of the following directories:
>
> - The \WINDOWS\SYSTEM directory
> - Any directory within the DOS path
> - The directory where the program resides
>
> Typically, the INSTALL program copies the DLL file into the user's \WINDOWS\SYSTEM directory so that other programs can use the DLL file and your program won't depend on the current setting of the user's DOS path.

A DLL file can be used by any programming language that supports DLLs (for example, Visual C++ and Visual Basic for Windows). In the following sections, you'll create a simple DLL file and write a Visual C++ program that uses this file.

Creating a DLL

In the following sections, you'll create a DLL file called MyDLL.DLL and you'll write a program that uses its functions.

Creating the Project of MyDLL.DLL

Follow these steps to create the project for MyDLL.DLL:

☐ Create the directory C:\TYVCProg\Programs\CH17 and start Visual C++.

☐ Select New from the File menu, then select Project Workspace from the New dialog box and click the OK button.

Visual C++ responds by displaying the New Project Workspace dialog box.

☐ Select Dynamic-Link Library from the Type list (see Figure 17.1) and enter MyDLL in the Name box.

Figure 17.1.
Selecting Dynamic-Link Library in the New Project Workspace window.

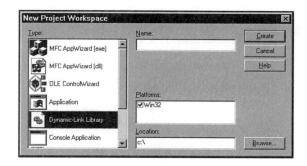

☐ Click the Browse button, select the C:\TYVCProg\Programs\CH17 directory, then click the Create button.

☐ Select Set Default Configuration from the Build menu, select MyDLL - Win32 Release in the Default Project Configuration dialog box, then click the OK button.

That's it! You've finished creating the project file of MyDLL.DLL.

Writing the Overhead Code of the DLL

Writing the code of a DLL involves writing some overhead code that's the same for all DLLs. In the following steps, you'll write this overhead code in two files: MyDLL.cpp and MyDLL.def.

Follow these steps to create the MyDLL.cpp file:

☐ Select New from the File menu, select Text File from the New dialog box, then click the OK button.

Visual C++ responds by displaying a new window where you can type code.

☐ Type the following in the new window:

```
//////////////////////////////////////////////
// MyDLL.cpp
//
// A sample DLL.
//
//////////////////////////////////////////////
```

```
#include <windows.h>

//////////////////////////////////////////////
// DllEntryPoint(): The entry point of the DLL
//
//////////////////////////////////////////////
BOOL WINAPI DllEntryPoint (HINSTANCE hDLL, DWORD dwReason,
                           LPVOID Reserved)
{

switch (dwReason)
   {

   case DLL_PROCESS_ATTACH:
       {


       break;
       }


   case DLL_PROCESS_DETACH:
       {

       break;
       }
   }

return TRUE;

}
```

☐ Select Save from the File menu and save the text file as MyDLL.cpp in the \TYVCProg\Programs\CH17\MyDLL directory.

Follow these steps to create the MyDLL.def file:

☐ Select New from the File menu, select Text File from the New dialog box, then click the OK button.

Visual C++ responds by displaying a new window.

☐ Type the following in the new window (note that in .def files, the semicolon is used for indicating a comment):

```
;;;;;;;;;;;;;;;;;;;;;;;;;;;;;;;;;;;;;
; MyDLL.def
;
; The DEF file for the MyDLL.DLL DLL.
;

LIBRARY    mydll
```

```
CODE       PRELOAD MOVEABLE DISCARDABLE
DATA       PRELOAD SINGLE

EXPORTS
    ; The names of the DLL functions
```

☐ Select Save from the File menu and save the text file as MyDLL.def in the \TYVCProg\Programs\CH17\MyDLL directory.

You now have the MyDLL.cpp and MyDLL.def files used for generating MyDLL.DLL. (Of course, later you'll write more code in these files.) Next, you need to add the MyDLL.cpp and MyDLL.def files to the project of MyDLL.DLL. Here is how you do that:

☐ Select Files into Project from the Insert menu.

Visual C++ responds by displaying the Insert Files into Project dialog box.

☐ Use the Insert Files into Project dialog box to select the file C:\TYVCProg\Programs\CH17\MyDLL\MyDLL.cpp, then click the Add button.

Visual C++ responds by adding the MyDLL.cpp file to the project.

To add the MyDLL.def file to the project, do the following:

☐ Select Files Into Project from the Insert menu.

Visual C++ responds by displaying the Insert Files Into Project dialog box.

☐ Set the Files of Type drop-down list to Definition Files (*.def).

☐ Use the Insert Files Into Project dialog box to select the file C:\TYVCProg\Programs\CH17\MyDLL\MyDLL.def, then click the Add button.

Visual C++ responds by adding the MyDLL.def file into the project.

To make sure you've successfully added the MyDLL.cpp and MyDLL.def files to the project, do the following:

☐ Select Project Workspace from the View menu. Select the FileView tab and expand the MyDLL files item in the Project Workspace window.

Your Project Workspace window should now look like Figure 17.2—the MyDLL.cpp and MyDLL.def files are part of the project.

You have performed all the overhead tasks needed for telling Visual C++ to generate MyDLL.DLL. It's now time to start writing the code.

Figure 17.2.
*Listing the files of the
MyDLL project.*

Customizing the MyDLL.cpp File

First, you'll customize the MyDLL.cpp file, which currently looks like this:

```cpp
/////////////////////////////////////////////
// MyDLL.cpp
//
// A sample DLL.
//
/////////////////////////////////////////////

#include <windows.h>

/////////////////////////////////////////////////
// DllEntryPoint(): The entry point of the DLL
//
/////////////////////////////////////////////////
BOOL WINAPI DllEntryPoint (HINSTANCE hDLL, DWORD dwReason,
                           LPVOID Reserved)
{

switch (dwReason)
   {

   case DLL_PROCESS_ATTACH:
       {


       break;
       }


   case DLL_PROCESS_DETACH:
       {

       break;
       }
   }

return TRUE;

}
```

As you can see, the code you wrote earlier in the MyDLL.cpp file has one function: `DllEntryPoint()`, which is the entry point of the DLL. When an EXE program that uses a DLL loads the DLL, the `DllEntryPoint()` function is automatically executed. (You'll write an EXE program that loads MyDLL.DLL and uses its functions later in this chapter.)

As you can see, the `DllEntryPoint()` function is made up of a `switch` statement:

```
BOOL WINAPI DllEntryPoint (HINSTANCE hDLL, DWORD dwReason,
                           LPVOID Reserved)
{

switch (dwReason)
   {

   case DLL_PROCESS_ATTACH:
       {

       break;
       }


   case DLL_PROCESS_DETACH:
       {

       break;
       }
   }

return TRUE;

}
```

The `switch` statement evaluates `dwReason` (the second parameter of the `DllEntryPoint()` function).

The code under the `DLL_PROCESS_ATTACH` case is executed when the DLL is attached to the EXE file (when the EXE file loads the DLL). Therefore, you can write initialization code under the `DLL_PROCESS_ATTACH` case. The code under the `DLL_PROCESS_DETACH` case is executed when the DLL is detached from the EXE file. For example, when the EXE that uses the DLL terminates, the code under the `DLL_PROCESS_DETACH` case is executed. Therefore, you can write clean-up code under the `DLL_PROCESS_DETACH` case.

Now you'll add two simple functions to the MyDll.cpp file. Later in the chapter you will create an EXE file that will use these functions:

☐ Add a function called `MyBeep()` to the end of the MyDLL.cpp file as follows:

```
int MyBeep(void)
{
```

```
// Beep
MessageBeep( (WORD) -1 );

return 1;

}
```

☐ Add another function called MyDelay() to the end of the MyDLL.cpp file as follows:

```
int MyDelay( long wait )
{

// Delay.
Sleep(wait);

return 1;

}
```

Note: As you can see, the two functions you added to MyDLL.DLL are very simple; their only purpose is to illustrate how to add functions to a DLL. Later in the chapter you'll write an EXE program that loads MyDLL.DLL and uses the MyBeep() and MyDelay() functions.

You now have to declare the prototypes of the MyBeep() and MyDelay() functions:

☐ Add the prototype declarations of these functions to the beginning of the MyDLL.cpp file as follows:

```
/////////////////////////////////////////////
// MyDLL.cpp
//
// A sample DLL.
//
/////////////////////////////////////////////

#include <windows.h>

// Declare the DLL functions prototypes.
int MyBeep  ( void );
int MyDelay ( long wait );
```

☐ Save your work.

The code in your MyDLL.cpp file should now look like this:

```
/////////////////////////////////////////
// MyDLL.cpp
//
// A sample DLL.
//
/////////////////////////////////////////

#include <windows.h>

// Declare the DLL functions prototypes.
int MyBeep  ( void );
int MyDelay ( long wait );


/////////////////////////////////////////////
// DllEntryPoint(): The entry point of the DLL
//
/////////////////////////////////////////////
BOOL WINAPI DllEntryPoint (HINSTANCE hDLL, DWORD dwReason,
                              LPVOID Reserved)
{
switch (dwReason)
    {
    case DLL_PROCESS_ATTACH:
        {
        break;
        }
    case DLL_PROCESS_DETACH:
        {
        break;
        }
    }

return TRUE;
}

int MyBeep(void)
{
// Beep
MessageBeep( (WORD) -1 );
return 1;
}

int MyDelay( long wait )
{
// Delay.
Sleep(wait);
return 1;
}
```

Customizing the MyDLL.def File

The last thing you have to do is customize the MyDLL.def file:

☐ Open the MyDLL.def file and modify it as follows:

```
;;;;;;;;;;;;;;;;;;;;;;;;;;;;;;;;;;;;;;;;
; MyDLL.def
;
; The DEF file for the MyDLL.DLL DLL.
;

LIBRARY    mydll

CODE       PRELOAD MOVEABLE DISCARDABLE
DATA       PRELOAD SINGLE

EXPORTS
   ; The names of the DLL functions
   MyBeep
   MyDelay
```

☐ Save your work.

The def file defines various characteristics of the DLL. Notice that the comment lines are preceded with the semicolon (;) character (not the / / characters).

In the preceding code, you set the library name with the LIBRARY statement because you're creating MyDLL.DLL:

```
LIBRARY    mydll
```

In the preceding code you also added the two function names MyBeep and MyDelay under the EXPORTS statement:

```
EXPORTS
   ; The names of the DLL functions
   MyBeep
   MyDelay
```

Therefore, an EXE program that loads MyDLL.DLL will be able to use the two functions MyBeep() and MyDelay().

That's it! You have finished writing all the necessary code for creating MyDLL.DLL. To create the MyDLL.DLL file, do the following:

☐ Select Build MyDLL.DLL from the Build menu.

Visual C++ responds by creating the MyDLL.DLL file.

You can verify that Visual C++ created the MYDLL.DLL file by examining your C:\TYVCProg\Programs\CH17\MyDLL\Release directory.

> **Note:** Visual C++ created the MyDLL.DLL file in the C:\TYVCProg\Programs\
> CH17\MyDLL\Release directory because when you created the project of
> MyDLL.DLL, you set the Default Project Configuration to `MyDLL - Win32`
> `Release`.
>
> Had you left the Default Project Configuration at the default setting `MyDLL - Win32`
> `Debug`, Visual C++ would have created the MyDLL.DLL file in the C:\TYVCProg\
> Programs\CH17\MyDLL\Debug directory.

You now have a DLL file called MyDLL.DLL with two functions: `MyBeep()` and `MyDelay()`. You can now distribute this DLL file to any programmer of a language that supports DLLs (for example, Visual C++ or Visual Basic); he or she will be able to use the functions of your DLL.

When you distribute the DLL, you should also supply documentation that specifies the prototypes of the `MyBeep()` and `MyDelay()` functions.

In the following section, you'll write a Visual C++ program that loads MyDLL.DLL and uses its two functions.

Writing a Visual C++ Program That Uses MyDLL.DLL

In the following sections, you'll write a Visual C++ program called Test2.EXE that uses the DLL you created. The Test2.EXE program will load MyDLL.DLL and use its two functions, `MyBeep()` and `MyDelay()`.

Creating the Project of the Test2 Program

To create the project of the Test2 program, do the following:

☐ Close the MyDLL project and all its associated files by selecting Close Workspace from the File menu.

☐ Select New from the File menu, then select Project Workspace from the New dialog box and click the OK button.

Visual C++ responds by displaying the New Project Workspace dialog box.

☐ Select MFC AppWizard (exe) from the Type list and enter `Test2` in the Name box.

☐ Click the Browse button, select the C:\TYVCProg\Programs\CH17 directory, then click the Create button.

> *Visual C++ responds by displaying the MFC AppWizard - Step 1 window.*

☐ Set the Step 1 window to create a dialog-based application, then click the Next button.

☐ In the Step 2 window, select the options "About box" and "3D controls" and enter The Test2 Program for the title of the dialog box. When you're done, click the Next button.

☐ In the Step 3 window, use the default settings and click the Next button.

☐ Notice that AppWizard has created the CTest2App and CTest2Dlg classes, then click the Finish button of the Step 4 window.

> *Visual C++ responds by displaying the New Project Information window.*

☐ Click the OK button of the New Project Information window, then select Set Default Configuration from the Build menu.

> *Visual C++ responds by displaying the Default Project Configuration dialog box.*

☐ Select Test2 - Win32 Release in the Default Project Configuration dialog box, then click the OK button.

You've finished creating the project file and skeleton files of the Test2 program.

The Visual Design of the Test2 Main Window

You'll now visually design the main window of the Test2 program:

☐ Select Project Workspace from the View menu. In the ResourceView tab of the Project Workspace window, expand the Test2 resources item, expand the Dialog item, and double-click the IDD_TEST2_DIALOG item.

> *Visual C++ responds by displaying the IDD_TEST2_DIALOG dialog box in design mode.*

☐ Delete the OK button, Cancel button, and text in the IDD_TEST2_DIALOG dialog box.

☐ Set up the IDD_TEST2_DIALOG dialog box according to Table 17.1. When you finish, the dialog box should look like Figure 17.3.

Table 17.1. The properties table of the IDD_TEST2_DIALOG dialog box.

Object	Property	Setting
Dialog Box	**ID**	**IDD_TEST2_DIALOG**
	Caption	The Test2 Program
	Font	System, Size 10
Static Text	**ID**	**IDC_STATIC**
	Caption	Testing the MyDLL.DLL DLL
Push Button	**ID**	**IDC_LOAD_BUTTON**
	Caption	&Load MyDLL.DLL
Push Button	**ID**	**IDC_TEST_BUTTON**
	Caption	&Test MyDLL.DLL

Figure 17.3.
IDD_TEST2_DIALOG in design mode (after customization).

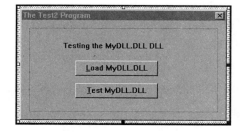

Declaring Global Variables

As you'll soon see, the code that loads and uses MyDLL.DLL uses global variables. You'll now declare these global variables.

☐ Open the file Test2Dlg.cpp and add code to its beginning, as follows:

```
// Test2Dlg.cpp : implementation file
//

#include "stdafx.h"
#include "Test2.h"
#include "Test2Dlg.h"

#ifdef _DEBUG
#define new DEBUG_NEW
#undef THIS_FILE
static char THIS_FILE[] = __FILE__;
#endif
```

DAY
17

```
////////////////////////
// MY CODE STARTS HERE
////////////////////////

// The instance of the MyDLL.DLL library.
HINSTANCE gLibMyDLL = NULL;

// Declare the MyBeep() function of the MyDLL.DLL library.
typedef int (*MYBEEP)(void);
MYBEEP MyBeep;

// Declare the MyDelay() function of
// the MyDLL.DLL library.
typedef int (*MYDELAY)(long);
MYDELAY MyDelay;

////////////////////////
// MY CODE ENDS HERE
////////////////////////
```

☐ Save your work.

The statements you've just added to the beginning of the Test2Dlg.cpp file declare several global variables.

The first statement declares the gLibMyDLL variable and initializes it to NULL:

```
HINSTANCE gLibMyDLL = NULL;
```

The code that loads MyDLL.DLL uses gLibMyDLL for storing the handle of the DLL.

The next two statements declare the MyBeep() function of the MyDLL.DLL library. The first statement declares a variable type called MYBEEP that holds a pointer (address) of a function that returns int and takes no parameters:

```
typedef int (*MYBEEP)(void);
```

The second statement declares a variable MyBeep of type MYBEEP:

```
MYBEEP MyBeep;
```

From now on, the variable MyBeep can be considered a regular function that returns an int and takes no parameters.

Similarly, the last two statements you typed declare the MyDelay() function of MyDLL.DLL:

```
typedef int (*MYDELAY)(long);
MYDELAY MyDelay;
```

Notice that these statements declare MyDelay() as a function that returns an int type and takes one parameter of type long.

Loading MyDLL.DLL

Before you can use the functions of MyDLL.DLL, you must first load MyDLL.DLL. You'll attach the code that accomplishes this to the Load pushbutton so that the DLL will be loaded when the user clicks the Load button. Normally, you would want the DLL to be loaded automatically without the user having to click anything, so you would write the code that loads a DLL library at the entry point of the program. For example, in the Test2.EXE program, you could attach the code that loads a DLL to the OnInitDialog() member function of the CTest2Dlg class (in the Test2Dlg.cpp file).

Follow these steps to attach code to the Load button:

☐ Select ClassWizard from the View menu. In the Message Maps tab of ClassWizard, select the following event:

Class name:	CTest2Dlg
Object ID:	IDC_LOAD_BUTTON
Message:	BN_CLICKED

☐ Click the Add Function button, name the new function OnLoadButton, and click the Edit Code button.

Visual C++ responds by opening the file Test2Dlg.cpp with the function OnLoadButton() *ready for you to edit.*

☐ Write the following code in the OnLoadButton() function:

```
void CTest2Dlg::OnLoadButton()
{

// TODO: Add your control notification handler code here

/////////////////////////
// MY CODE STARTS HERE
/////////////////////////

// If the MyDLL.DLL has already been loaded,
// tell the user and terminate this function.
if ( gLibMyDLL != NULL )
    {
    MessageBox("The MyDLL.DLL DLL has already been loaded.");
    return;
    }

// Load the MyDLL.DLL DLL.
gLibMyDLL = LoadLibrary("MYDLL.DLL");

// If the DLL was not loaded successfully, display
// an error message box.
if ( gLibMyDLL == NULL )
    {
```

```
        char msg[300];
        strcpy (msg, "Cannot load the MYDLL.DLL DLL. ");
        strcat (msg, "Make sure that the file MYDLL.DLL ");
        strcat (msg, "is in your \\WINDOWS\\SYSTEM directory.");
        MessageBox( msg );
        }

// Get the address of the MyBeep() function
// of the MyDLL.DLL library.
MyBeep = (MYBEEP)GetProcAddress(gLibMyDLL, "MyBeep");

// Get the address of the MyDelay() function
// of the MyDLL.DLL library.
MyDelay = (MYDELAY)GetProcAddress(gLibMyDLL, "MyDelay");

/////////////////////////
// MY CODE ENDS HERE
/////////////////////////

}
```

☐ Save your work.

The first statement you typed in the OnLoadButton() function is an if statement:

```
if ( gLibMyDLL != NULL )
    {
    MessageBox("The MyDLL.DLL DLL has already been loaded.");
    return;
    }
```

This if statement determines whether MyDLL.DLL has already been loaded by evaluating the gLibMyDLL global variable. If gLibMyDLL is not equal to NULL, MyDLL.DLL has already been loaded (the user clicked the Load button). If this is the case, the if condition is satisfied and the code under the if displays a message box telling the user that MyDLL.DLL has already been loaded; the function is terminated with the return statement.

If, however, gLibMyDLL is equal to NULL, the MyDLL.DLL has not been loaded yet, and the rest of the statements in the function are executed. (Recall that when you declared the global variable gLibMyDLL you initialized it to NULL. Therefore, when the user clicks the Load button for the first time, gLibMyDLL is NULL.)

The next statement uses the LoadLibrary() function to load MyDLL.DLL and assign the handle of the DLL to the gLibMyDLL variable:

```
gLibMyDLL = LoadLibrary("MYDLL.DLL");
```

Note that the name of the DLL file—MYDLL.DLL—is specified without the full pathname. The LoadLibrary() function will search for the DLL file in the current directory, in all the directories within the DOS path, and in the \WINDOWS\SYSTEM directory. If the LoadLibrary() function fails in loading the DLL, LoadLibrary() will return NULL.

The next statement is an `if` statement that evaluates the returned value of the `LoadLibrary()` function:

```
if ( gLibMyDLL == NULL )
   {
   char msg[300];
   strcpy (msg, "Cannot load the MYDLL.DLL DLL. ");
   strcat (msg, "Make sure that the file MYDLL.DLL ");
   strcat (msg, "is in your \\WINDOWS\\SYSTEM directory.");
   MessageBox( msg );
   }
```

If the returned value of `LoadLibrary()` was `NULL`, the DLL was not loaded successfully. If this is the case, the statements under the `if` display a message box telling the user that MYDLL.DLL cannot be loaded. The message box also tells the user to make sure that MYDLL.DLL is in the \WINDOWS\SYSTEM directory.

The next statement uses the `GetProcAddress()` function to fill the variable `MyBeep` with the address of the `MyBeep()` function of MyDLL.DLL:

```
MyBeep = (MYBEEP)GetProcAddress(gLibMyDLL, "MyBeep");
```

As you can see, the first parameter of the `GetProcAddress()` function is the handle of the DLL, and the second parameter is the name of the function whose address you want to retrieve.

At this point, the global variable `MyBeep` is filled with the address of the `MyBeep()` function of MyDLL.DLL. This means that from now on you can use the `MyBeep` variable as if it were the `MyBeep()` function. You can call the `MyBeep()` function just the way you call any other function.

Similarly, the last statement in the `OnLoadButton()` function fills the `MyDelay` global variable with the address of the `MyDelay()` function of MyDLL.DLL:

```
MyDelay = (MYDELAY)GetProcAddress(gLibMyDLL, "MyDelay");
```

From now on, you can call the `MyDelay()` function of MyDLL.DLL just as you call any other function.

Attaching Code to the Test MyDLL.DLL Button

You'll now attach code to the Test MyDLL.DLL button. This code will test MyDLL.DLL by calling its two functions `MyBeep()` and `MyDelay()`.

Follow these steps to attach code to the Test MyDLL.DLL button:

☐ Select ClassWizard from the View menu. In the Message Maps tab of ClassWizard, select the following event:

Class name:	CTest2Dlg
Object ID:	IDC_TEST_BUTTON
Message:	BN_CLICKED

☐ Click the Add Function button, name the new function OnTestButton, then click the Edit Code button.

Visual C++ responds by opening the file Test2Dlg.cpp with the function OnTestButton() ready for you to edit.

☐ Write the following code in the OnTestButton() function:

```
void CTest2Dlg::OnTestButton()
{

// TODO: Add your control notification handler code here

/////////////////////////
// MY CODE STARTS HERE
/////////////////////////

// If the MyDLL.DLL has not been loaded yet, tell
// the user and terminate this function.
if ( gLibMyDLL == NULL )
    {
    MessageBox ("You must first load the MyDLL.DLL DLL.");
    return;
    }

// Call the MyBeep() function of the MyDLL.DLL DLL.
MyBeep();

// Call the MyDelay() function of the MyDLL.DLL DLL.
MyDelay(500);

// Call the MyBeep() function of the MyDLL.DLL DLL.
MyBeep();

/////////////////////
// MY CODE ENDS HERE
/////////////////////

}
```

☐ Save your work.

The first statement you typed in the OnTestButton() function is an if statement:

```
if ( gLibMyDLL == NULL )
    {
```

```
MessageBox ("You must first load the MyDLL.DLL DLL.");
return;
}
```

This `if` statement checks whether the `gLibMyDLL` variable is NULL. If it is, MyDLL.DLL has not been loaded yet. If this is the case, the code under the `if` displays a message box telling the user that MyDLL.DLL must be loaded, and the function is terminated with the `return` statement.

If, however, the `gLibMyDLL` variable is not NULL because MyDLL.DLL has been loaded, the rest of the statements in the function are executed:

```
// Call the MyBeep() function of the MyDLL.DLL DLL.
MyBeep();

// Call the MyDelay() function of the MyDLL.DLL DLL.
MyDelay(500);

// Call the MyBeep() function of the MyDLL.DLL DLL.
MyBeep();
```

These statements simply call the `MyBeep()` and `MyDelay()` functions of MyDLL.DLL. Therefore, whenever the user clicks the Test MyDLL.DLL button, the program will beep once, delay for 500 milliseconds (half a second), then beep again.

To see the code you wrote in action do the following:

☐ Compile, link, and execute the Test2.EXE program to see your code in action.

Visual C++ responds by executing the Test2.EXE program and displaying the window shown in Figure 17.4.

Figure 17.4.
The window of the Test2.EXE program.

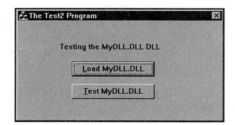

☐ Click the Load MyDLL.DLL button.

The Test2.EXE program responds by displaying a message box telling you that MyDLL.DLL could not be loaded.

Test2.EXE could not load the MyDLL.DLL library because you haven't copied the MyDLL.DLL file to any directory within the DOS path, the directory where the Test2.EXE file resides, or the \WINDOWS\SYSTEM directory.

☐ Use the Windows Explorer to copy the MyDLL.DLL file you created earlier from the \TYVCProg\Programs\CH17\MyDLL\Release directory to your \WINDOWS\ SYSTEM directory.

☐ Switch back to the Test2.EXE program and click the Load MyDLL.DLL button again.

This time, the Test2.EXE program loads MyDLL.DLL successfully (no error message is displayed).

☐ Click the Test MyDLL.DLL button.

As expected, the Test2.EXE program responds by beeping twice, with a 500-millisecond delay between the beeps.

> **Note:** If for some reason your PC speaker (or sound card) does not beep, you can modify the code of MyDLL.DLL so that the MyBeep() function of MyDLL.DLL displays a message box instead of beeping. After you modify and build the project of MyDLL.DLL, don't forget to copy the new version of the MyDLL.DLL file to your \WINDOWS\SYSTEM directory.

☐ Terminate the Test2.EXE program by clicking the × icon.

As you have just seen, the Test2.EXE program successfully loads the MyDLL.DLL file and uses its functions.

Summary

In this chapter, you have learned how to create a dynamic link library (a DLL file) that contains your own functions. As you have seen, creating a DLL file with Visual C++ is quite simple.

Once you finish your DLL file, you can distribute it to other Visual C++ programmers who can incorporate it into their projects. Your DLL could also be used by programmers of any programming language that supports DLLs (for example, Visual Basic).

Q&A

Q The Test2.EXE program I wrote in this chapter uses the MyDLL.DLL file I created in this chapter, but I didn't have to add the MyDLL.DLL file to the project of the Test2.EXE program. Why?

A You did not have to add MyDLL.DLL to the project of the Test2.EXE program because the Test2.EXE program loads MyDLL.DLL in runtime—the MyDLL.DLL file is a dynamic link library so it's linked to the program that uses it during runtime.

Quiz

1. When you distribute your DLL file to your end-user, you must distribute the source code of your library.

   a. True.
   b. False.

2. To use your DLL file, your end-user needs to add your DLL file to his or her project and then build the project.

   a. True.
   b. False.

Exercise

Describe the steps you take to create a project for a DLL file.

Quiz Answers

1. b. False.
2. b. False.

Exercise Answer

To create a project for a DLL file, use the following steps:

☐ Select New from the File menu.

☐ Select Project Workspace from the New dialog box, then click the OK button.

   Visual C++ responds by displaying the New Project Workspace dialog box.

☐ Select Dynamic-Link Library from the Type list and enter the name of the project in the Name box.

☐ Click the Browse button, select the directory where you want to create the project, and click the Create button.

Creating Your Own OLE Control (Part I)

In this chapter and the following chapter, you'll learn how to create your own OLE (object linking and embedding) control by using Visual C++.

Reviewing OLE Controls

Before you start learning how to create an OLE control, first review what an OLE control is. In Chapter 3, "Using OLE Controls and the Component Gallery," you learned that an OLE control is a file with an OCX extension (for example, MyButton.OCX) used for object linking and embedding. Visual C++ and other visual programming languages enable you to incorporate an OLE control into your program and use it just as you use standard Visual C++ controls. You place an OLE control in a dialog box, set its properties, and attach code to its events. Once you complete your OLE control, you can distribute it to other programmers who can plug your OLE control into their programs.

Because the file extension of OLE controls is .OCX, OLE controls are sometimes referred to as OCX controls. In this chapter and the next, the term *OLE control* is used.

The MyClock OLE Control

In this chapter and the following two chapters, you'll develop and test your own OLE control, called MyClock.OCX. As its name implies, the MyClock.OCX control will be used for displaying the current time. When a programmer places a MyClock.OCX control in a form or dialog box, the MyClock.OCX control will keep displaying the current time.

Creating the Project of the MyClock.OCX Control

Follow these steps to create the project for the MyClock.OCX control:

☐ Create the directory C:\TYVCProg\Programs\CH18 and start Visual C++.

☐ Select New from the File menu, then select Project Workspace from the New dialog box and click the OK button.

Visual C++ responds by displaying the New Project Workspace dialog box.

☐ Select OLE ControlWizard from the Type list (see Figure 18.1) and enter MyClock in the Name box.

☐ Click the Browse button, select the C:\TYVCProg\Programs\CH18 directory, then click the Create button.

Visual C++ responds by displaying the OLE ControlWizard - Step 1 of 2 dialog box. (See Figure 18.2.)

Figure 18.1.
Selecting OLE ControlWizard in the New Project Workspace dialog box.

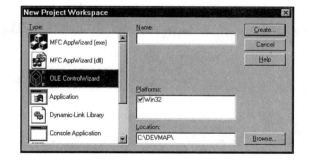

Figure 18.2.
Step 1 of the OLE ControlWizard.

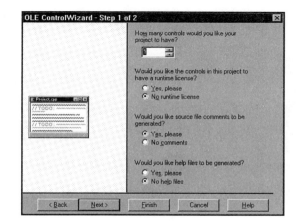

☐ Leave the OLE ControlWizard Step 1 window at its default settings, as shown in Figure 18.2, then click the Next button.

Visual C++ responds by displaying the OLE ControlWizard - Step 2 of 2 dialog box. (See Figure 18.3.)

☐ Leave the OLE ControlWizard Step 2 window at its default settings, as shown in Figure 18.3, then click the Finish button.

Visual C++ responds by displaying the New Project Information dialog box.

☐ Click the OK button of the New Project Information dialog box, then select Set Default Configuration from the Build menu.

Visual C++ responds by displaying the Default Project Configuration dialog box.

☐ Select MyClock - Win32 Release in the Default Project Configuration dialog box, then click the OK button.

Figure 18.3.
Step 2 of the OLE ControlWizard.

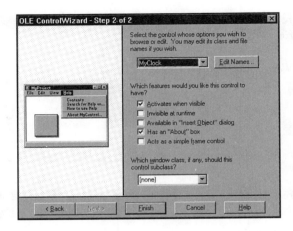

That's it! You've finished creating the project file and skeleton files of the MyClock.OCX OLE control.

Checking the MyClock Control Before Customization

In the preceding section, you created the project and skeleton files of the MyClock control. Your job, with the help of Visual C++, is to customize these files so that the MyClock control will look and behave the way you want it to.

Before you start customizing the files of the MyClock control, first compile, link, and test the MyClock control in its current state. As you'll see, the skeleton files you created in the preceding section already have code that actually produces a working OLE control.

To compile and link the MyClock control, do the following:

☐ Select Build MyClock.OCX from the Build menu.

Visual C++ responds by compiling and linking the files of the MyClock control and creating the file MyClock.OCX.

Although you haven't written a single line of code, you have a working OLE control in your hands—MyClock.OCX. In the following section, you'll test the MyClock.OCX control.

Testing the MyClock Control with Test Container

The ultimate way to test an OLE control is to use a visual programming language that lets the programmer add the OLE control to the Tools window. Once you add the OLE control to the Tools window, you can test it by placing it in forms (dialog boxes), by changing its properties,

and by attaching code to its events. For example, to test the MyClock.OCX control, you can write a Visual C++ program that uses the MyClock.OCX control. (You learned how to write a Visual C++ program that uses an OLE control in Chapter 3.)

Another way to test an OLE control is to use the Test Container program that comes with Visual C++, which lets you test an OLE control by placing it in the window of the Test Container program.

Follow these steps to test the MyClock control with the Test Container program:

☐ Select OLE Control Test Container from the Tools menu.

Visual C++ responds by executing the Test Container program. (See Figure 18.4.)

Figure 18.4.
The Test Container program.

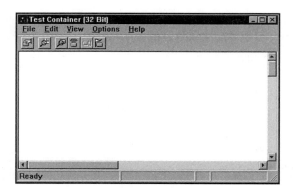

☐ Select Insert OLE Control from Test Container's Edit menu.

Test Container responds by displaying the Insert OLE Control dialog box.

☐ Select MyClock Control from the list displayed in the dialog box, then click the OK button.

Test Container responds by inserting the MyClock control. (See Figure 18.5.)

As shown in Figure 18.5, the MyClock control now appears in the window of Test Container, and its tool icon appears in the toolbar of Test Container. Notice that the tool icon of the MyClock control displays the letters *OCX*. Later, you'll customize the MyClock control so that the tool icon will display a more appropriate picture of a clock.

Notice also that the MyClock control displays an ellipse. The skeleton code that Visual C++ wrote for you is displaying this ellipse. Later, you'll customize the code of the MyClock control so that it will do what it's supposed to—display the current time.

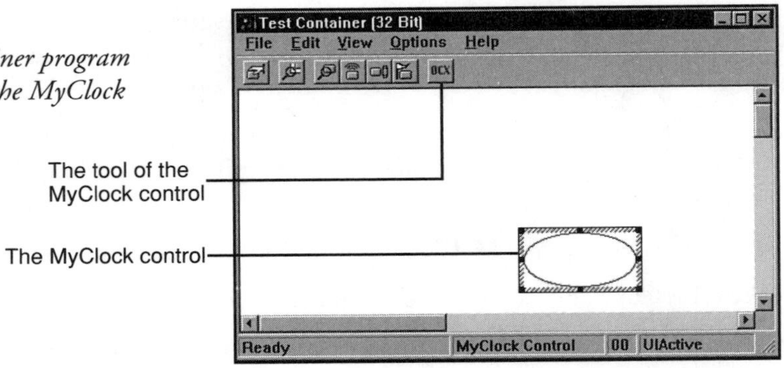

Figure 18.5.
The Test Container program after you insert the MyClock control.

The tool of the MyClock control

The MyClock control

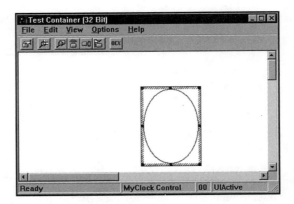

The MyClock control is surrounded by a frame with handles you can use to size the MyClock control. For example, to make the control taller, do the following:

☐ Drag any of the handles at the bottom of the control's frame downward, then release the mouse.

> *Once you release the mouse, the control changes its size, and the size of the ellipse in the control changes accordingly. (See Figure 18.6.)*

Figure 18.6.
Increasing the size of the MyClock control.

Besides sizing the control, Test Container also allows you to move the control:

☐ Drag the frame of the control to the point where you want to place the control. Drag any point of the control's frame except the where the handles are.

Once you release the mouse, the control moves to that point. Figure 18.7 shows the window of Test Container after you move the MyClock control to the upper-left corner.

Figure 18.7.

Moving the MyClock control to the upper-left corner of the window.

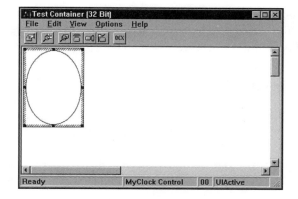

You can also place several MyClock controls in the window of Test Container:

☐ Click the tool of the MyClock control on Test Container's toolbar, shown in Figure 18.5.

> *Test Container responds by placing another MyClock control in its window. (See Figure 18.8.)*

Figure 18.8.

Placing another MyClock control in the window of Test Container.

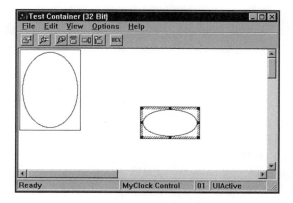

☐ Place several more MyClock controls by clicking the tool of the MyClock control.

In the preceding steps, you used Test Container to test the visual aspects of the MyClock control: placing the control in the window of Test Container, sizing the control, moving the control, and placing several controls in the window.

Test Container also lets you test the events and properties of the control. However, at this point the MyClock control does not have any events or properties because Visual C++ couldn't guess which ones you wanted. Later when you add properties and events to the MyClock control, you'll use Test Container to test them.

You have just verified, with Test Container's help, that the skeleton code Visual C++ wrote for you produces a functional OLE control. Of course, the code doesn't make the MyClock control behave and look the way you want it to, so you'll customize its files throughout this chapter and the next.

☐ Terminate Test Container by selecting Exit from the File menu.

Customizing the Picture of the MyClock Control Tool

As shown in Figure 18.5, the icon of the MyClock control tool displays a picture of the letters *OCX*. You'll now customize the MyClock control so that its tool will display a picture of a clock.

To customize the icon of the MyClock control tool, you need to work on the bitmap IDB_MYCLOCK. This bitmap was created by Visual C++.

To display the IDB_MYCLOCK bitmap in design mode, do the following:

☐ Select Project Workspace from the View menu. Select the ResourceView tab, expand the MyClock resources item, expand the Bitmap item, then double-click the IDB_MYCLOCK item.

   Visual C++ responds by displaying the IDB_MYCLOCK bitmap in design mode.

☐ Use the visual tools of Visual C++ to change the picture of the IDB_MYCLOCK bitmap from the letters *OCX* to a picture of a simple clock—a circle with two lines, the clock's hands, in it.

Figure 18.9 shows the IDB_MYCLOCK bitmap before customization, and Figure 18.10 shows the IDB_MYCLOCK bitmap after customization.

Figure 18.9.
The IDB_MYCLOCK bitmap before customization.

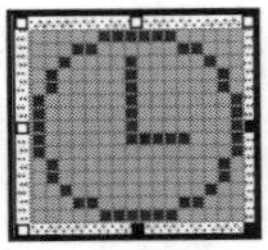

Figure 18.10.
The IDB_MYCLOCK bitmap after customization.

☐ Save your work.

To see your work in action, do the following:

☐ Select Build MyClock.OCX from the Project menu.

Visual C++ responds by compiling and linking the MyClock control.

☐ Select OLE Control Test Container from the Tools menu.

Visual C++ responds by running the Test Container program.

☐ Select Insert OLE Control from Test Container's Edit menu.

Test Container responds by displaying the Insert OLE Control dialog box.

☐ Select MyClock Control from the list displayed in the dialog box, then click the OK button.

Test Container responds by inserting the MyClock control and displaying its tool on Test Container's toolbar. (See Figure 18.11.)

Figure 18.11.
The new tool icon of the MyClock control.

The tool of the MyClock control——

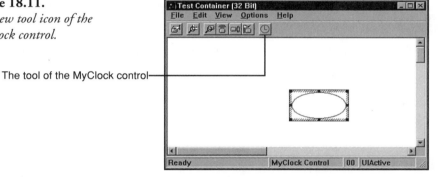

The tool icon of the MyClock tool now displays your picture of a clock!

☐ Terminate Test Container by selecting Exit from the File menu.

Summary

In this chapter, you have used Visual C++ to create the skeleton files for the MyClock.OCX OLE control. As you have seen, even though you haven't written any code yet, the skeleton code Visual C++ writes for you produces a working control that displays an ellipse in it. You have also customized the icon of the MyClock control tool to display a picture of a clock.

In the next chapter, you will further customize the MyClock control by writing the code responsible for displaying the current time, adding properties to the MyClock control, and adding events to the MyClock control.

Q&A

Q **Can I test the MyClock OLE control with Visual Basic?**

A Yes. Just like Visual C++, Visual Basic supports OLE controls, so you can use the MyClock.OCX control in your Visual Basic programs just as you can use other OLE controls.

Q **Suppose I write a Visual C++ program called MyProg.EXE that uses the MyClock.OCX control. Do I have to distribute the MyClock.OCX file with the MyProg.EXE file to my users?**

A Yes. You have to distribute both the MyProg.EXE file and the MyClock.OCX file to your user. You have to instruct your user to copy the MyClock.OCX file to his or her \WINDOWS\SYSTEM directory (or you can write an Install program that will automatically copy the MyClock.OCX to the user's \WINDOWS\SYSTEM directory).

Quiz

1. When you distribute your .OCX file to your end-user, you have to distribute the source code of your OLE control.

    a. True.
    b. False.

2. How can you test your OLE control?

Exercise

Describe the steps you take to create a project for an OLE control.

Quiz Answers

1. b. False.

2. You can test your OLE control by writing a program that uses it (using Visual C++, Visual Basic, or any other programming language that supports OLE controls) or by using the Test Container program of Visual C++.

Exercise Answer

To create a project for an OLE control, take the following steps:

☐ Select New from the File menu.

☐ Select Project Workspace from the New dialog box, then click the OK button.

Visual C++ responds by displaying the New Project Workspace dialog box.

☐ Select OLE ControlWizard from the Type list and type the name of the project in the Name box.

☐ Click the Browse button, select the directory where you want to create the project, then click the Create button.

☐ Click the Next button in the OLE ControlWizard Step 1 dialog box, click the Finish button in the OLE ControlWizard Step 2 dialog box, and finally click the OK button of the New Project Information dialog box.

18

19

Creating Your
Own OLE Control
(Part II)

Creating Your Own OLE Control (Part II)

In this chapter, you'll continue developing the MyClock control that you created in the previous chapter—you'll write the code that makes the control continuously display the current time, you'll add properties to the control, you'll write the code that sets the control's initial size, and you'll add events and methods to the control.

> **Note:** Since you'll continue working on the previous chapter's project, this chapter assumes that you have read and performed all the steps in Chapter 18, "Creating Your Own OLE Control (Part I)."

Drawing in the MyClock Control

Currently, the MyClock control displays an ellipse according to code that Visual C++ wrote for you. However, you want the MyClock control to display the current time, so you need to write code that does this. First, you'll write code that draws text in the MyClock control:

☐ Start Visual C++.

☐ Open the project workspace file (.MDP file) of the MyClock control you created in the previous chapter (if it's not already open) by selecting Open Workspace from the File menu, then selecting the C:\TYVCProg\Programs\CH18\MyClock\MyClock.MDP file.

☐ Open the file MyClockCtl.cpp in the directory C:\TYVCProg\Programs\CH18\MyClock.

MyClockCtl.cpp is the implementation file of the MyClock control created for you by Visual C++; it's where you'll write your own code for customizing the MyClock control.

☐ Locate the function OnDraw() in the MyClockCtl.cpp file.

The OnDraw() function currently looks like this:

```
/////////////////////////////////////////////////////
// CMyClockCtrl::OnDraw - Drawing function

void CMyClockCtrl::OnDraw(
    CDC* pdc, const CRect& rcBounds, const CRect& rcInvalid)
{

// TODO: Replace the following code with your own drawing code.
pdc->FillRect(rcBounds,
    CBrush::FromHandle((HBRUSH)GetStockObject(WHITE_BRUSH)));
pdc->Ellipse(rcBounds);

}
```

The OnDraw() function is automatically executed whenever there is a need to draw the control (for example, when the control is placed in a dialog box for the first time). The code currently in the OnDraw() function draws an ellipse in the control. Change the code in the OnDraw() function so that the control will display your own text:

☐ Delete the code currently in the OnDraw() function and replace it with your own custom code as follows:

```
void CMyClockCtrl::OnDraw(
    CDC* pdc, const CRect& rcBounds, const CRect& rcInvalid)
{

/////////////////////////
// MY CODE STARTS HERE
/////////////////////////

// Draw text in the control.
pdc->ExtTextOut(rcBounds.left,
                rcBounds.top,
                ETO_CLIPPED,
                rcBounds,
                "This is my first OCX control",
                28,
                NULL);

/////////////////////////
// MY CODE ENDS HERE
/////////////////////////

}
```

☐ Save your work.

The code you typed in the OnDraw() function is made up of one statement:

```
pdc->ExtTextOut(rcBounds.left,
                rcBounds.top,
                ETO_CLIPPED,
                rcBounds,
                "This is my first OCX control",
                28,
                NULL);
```

This statement executes the ExtTextOut() function on the pdc object to display text in the control. pdc (the first parameter of the OnDraw() function) is a pointer to an object of class CDC and holds the dc (device context) of the control. Therefore, after the preceding statement is executed, the text This is my first OCX control will be displayed in the MyClock control.

Notice that the preceding statement uses the variable rcBounds (an object of class CRect), which is the second parameter of the OnDraw() function. It specifies the rectangular dimensions (boundaries) of the control. For example, rcBounds.left is the x-coordinate of the upper-left corner of the control.

19

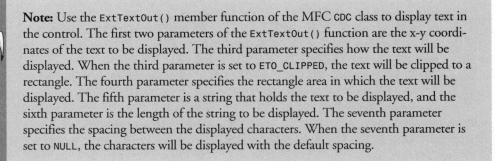

Note: Use the ExtTextOut() member function of the MFC CDC class to display text in the control. The first two parameters of the ExtTextOut() function are the x-y coordinates of the text to be displayed. The third parameter specifies how the text will be displayed. When the third parameter is set to ETO_CLIPPED, the text will be clipped to a rectangle. The fourth parameter specifies the rectangle area in which the text will be displayed. The fifth parameter is a string that holds the text to be displayed, and the sixth parameter is the length of the string to be displayed. The seventh parameter specifies the spacing between the displayed characters. When the seventh parameter is set to NULL, the characters will be displayed with the default spacing.

☐ Compile and link MyClock.OCX to see your drawing code in action.

Visual C++ responds by compiling and linking the files of the MyClock control.

☐ Select OLE Control Test Container from the Tools menu.

Visual C++ responds by running the Test Container program.

☐ Select Insert OLE Control from Test Container's Edit menu.

Test Container responds by displaying the Insert OLE Control dialog box.

☐ Select MyClock Control from the list displayed in the dialog box, then click the OK button.

Test Container responds by inserting the MyClock control. As shown in Figure 19.1, the text This is my first *is displayed in the control.*

Figure 19.1.

The MyClock control displaying the text This is my first.

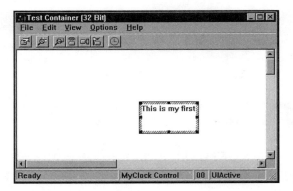

☐ Increase the width of the MyClock control by dragging the handle on the control's right edge to the right. (See Figure 19.2.)

Figure 19.2.
The MyClock control after increasing its width.

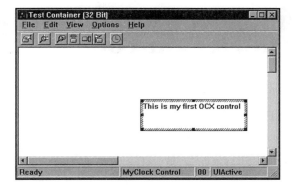

The code that you wrote in the OnDraw() function is working! Whenever the MyClock control needs to be redrawn, such as when you resize the control, the OnDraw() function is automatically executed and the code you wrote displays the text This is my first OCX control in the control.

☐ Place several more controls in the window of Test Container by clicking the tool of the MyClock control in the Test Container toolbar. Each control displays the text This is my first OCX control. (See Figure 19.3.)

Figure 19.3.
Displaying several MyClock controls.

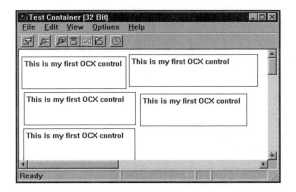

19

After you place a control in the window, you can move it by dragging any point on the control's frame except the points where the control's handles are located.

☐ Terminate Test Container by selecting Exit from the File menu.

Note: It's necessary to terminate the Test Container program because the Visual C++ linker will fail to link the MyClock project if any program is using the MyClock.OCX control.

Displaying the Current Time in the MyClock Control

The code of the MyClock control currently displays the text This is my first OCX control. You'll now change the code so that it will display the current time:

☐ Open the file MYCLOCTL.cpp (if it's not open already).

☐ Modify the OnDraw() function as follows:

```
void CMyClockCtrl::OnDraw(
    CDC* pdc, const CRect& rcBounds, const CRect& rcInvalid)
{

// TODO: Replace the following code with your own drawing
//       code.

/////////////////////////
// MY CODE STARTS HERE
/////////////////////////

char CurrentTime[30];
struct tm *newtime;
long lTime;

// Get the current time
time(&lTime);
newtime=localtime(&lTime);

// Convert the time into a string.
strcpy(CurrentTime, asctime(newtime));

// Pad the string with 1 blank.
CurrentTime[24]=' ';

// Terminate the string.
CurrentTime[25] = 0;

// Display the current time
pdc->ExtTextOut(rcBounds.left,
                rcBounds.top,
                ETO_CLIPPED,
                rcBounds,
                CurrentTime,
                strlen(CurrentTime),
                NULL);

/////////////////////////
// MY CODE ENDS HERE
/////////////////////////

}
```

☐ Save your work.

The first three statements you typed in the OnDraw() function declare three local variables:

```
char CurrentTime[30];
struct tm *newtime;
long lTime;
```

The rest of the code uses these three variables to get the current time and display it.

This statement uses the time() function to store in the variable lTime the number of seconds elapsed since midnight of January 1, 1970:

```
time(&lTime);
```

Of course, this number is not "friendly" enough, so you use the next statement to convert the number stored in lTime into a friendlier representation of time:

```
newtime=localtime(&lTime);
```

This statement uses the localtime() function to convert lTime into a structure of type tm and assigns the result to the structure newtime. Now the fields of the structure newtime store the current time.

The next statement uses the asctime() function to convert the current time stored in newtime into a string:

```
strcpy(CurrentTime, asctime(newtime));
```

The resulting string is assigned to the CurrentTime string, which now contains a string with 24 characters representing the current time. This string includes the day of the week, month, time, and year.

The next statement fills the 24th character at the end of the CurrentTime string with a blank for cosmetic reasons:

```
CurrentTime[24]=' ';
```

The next statement terminates the CurrentTime string:

```
CurrentTime[25]=0;
```

Finally, the last statement you typed in the OnDraw() function uses the ExtTextOut() function to display the CurrentTime string in the control:

```
pdc->ExtTextOut(rcBounds.left,
                rcBounds.top,
                ETO_CLIPPED,
                rcBounds,
                CurrentTime,
                strlen(CurrentTime),
                NULL);
```

☐ Compile and link MyClock.OCX to see the code you added to OnDraw() in action.

Visual C++ responds by compiling and linking the files of the MyClock control.

☐ Select OLE Control Test Container from the Tools menu.

Visual C++ responds by running the Test Container program.

☐ Select Insert OLE Control from Test Container's Edit menu.

Test Container responds by displaying the Insert OLE Control dialog box.

☐ Select the MyClock control, then click the OK button.

Test Container responds by inserting the MyClock control.

☐ Increase the width of the MyClock control. (See Figure 19.4.)

Figure 19.4.
The MyClock control displaying the current time.

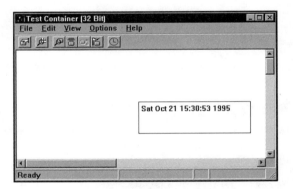

As you can see, the code you wrote in the OnDraw() function displays the current time in the control. However, the time is not updated continuously. In the following section, you will enhance the code so that the control will keep displaying the current time continuously.

☐ Terminate Test Container by selecting Exit from the File menu.

Displaying the Current Time Continuously

To display the time continuously, you need to do the following:

- Write code that installs a timer for the MyClock control with a 1000-millisecond interval.
- Attach code to the WM_TIMER event of the MyClock control.

After you install such a timer, Windows sends a WM_TIMER message every 1000 milliseconds (every second) to the MyClock control, and the code you attach to the WM_TIMER event of the MyClock control is executed. The code you attach to the WM_TIMER event will simply display the current time, so the current time will be displayed continuously.

You want to install the timer when the control is first created, so you need to attach the code that installs the timer to the WM_CREATE event of the control:

☐ Display the ClassWizard dialog box by selecting ClassWizard from the View menu. In the Message Maps tab of ClassWizard, select the following event:

Class name:	CMyClockCtrl
Object ID:	CMyClockCtrl
Message:	WM_CREATE

Your ClassWizard dialog box should now look like the one shown in Figure 19.5.

Figure 19.5.
Selecting the WM_CREATE event in ClassWizard.

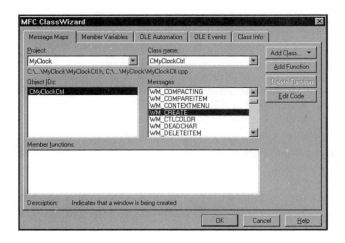

☐ Click the Add Function button.

Visual C++ responds by adding the OnCreate() member function to the CMyClockCtrl class.

☐ Click the Edit Code button of ClassWizard.

ClassWizard responds by opening the file MyClockCtrl.cpp, with the function OnCreate() ready for you to edit.

☐ Write the following code in the OnCreate() function:

```
int CMyClockCtrl::OnCreate(LPCREATESTRUCT lpCreateStruct)
{

if (COleControl::OnCreate(lpCreateStruct) == -1)
   return -1;

// TODO: Add your specialized creation code here

////////////////////////////
// MY CODE STARTS HERE
////////////////////////////

// Install a timer.
SetTimer(1, 1000, NULL);

///////////////////////////
// MY CODE ENDS HERE
///////////////////////////

return 0;

}
```

☐ Save your work.

The code you wrote is composed of one statement that uses the SetTimer() function to install a timer with a 1000-millisecond interval:

```
SetTimer(1, 1000, NULL);
```

From now on, Windows will send a WM_TIMER message to the control every 1000 milliseconds.

Now you need to attach code to the WM_TIMER event of the control:

☐ Select ClassWizard from the View menu. In the Message Maps tab of ClassWizard, select the following event:

Class name:	CMyClockCtrl
Object ID:	CMyClockCtrl
Message:	WM_TIMER

☐ Click the Add Function button.

Visual C++ responds by adding the OnTimer() *member function to the* CMyClockCtrl *class.*

☐ Click the Edit Code button of ClassWizard.

ClassWizard responds by opening the file MyClockCtl.cpp, with the function OnTimer() *ready for you to edit.*

☐ Write the following code in the OnTimer() function:

```
void CMyClockCtrl::OnTimer(UINT nIDEvent)
{

// TODO: Add your message handler code here and/or call
//       default

/////////////////////////
// MY CODE STARTS HERE
/////////////////////////

// Trigger a call to the OnDraw() function.
InvalidateControl();

/////////////////////////
// MY CODE ENDS HERE
/////////////////////////

COleControl::OnTimer(nIDEvent);


}
```

☐ Save your work.

The code you wrote has one statement that uses the `InvalidateControl()` function to trigger a call to the `OnDraw()` function you wrote earlier:

`InvalidateControl();`

Calling the `InvalidateControl()` function causes the control to redraw itself.

The code you wrote in the `OnCreate()` function installs a timer with a 1000-millisecond interval. As a result, the code you wrote in the `OnTimer()` function is automatically executed every 1000 milliseconds. This code causes the execution of the `OnDraw()` function by calling the `InvalidateControl()` function. The code you wrote in the `OnDraw()` function displays the current time; therefore, every 1000 milliseconds the displayed time is updated.

☐ Increase the width of the MyClock control so you can see the seconds portion of the time.

Now the MyClock control displays the current time continuously—the seconds portion of the time keeps changing.

☐ Terminate Test Container by selecting Exit from the File menu.

Adding Stock Properties to the MyClock Control

Stock properties (or standard properties) are predefined. As you'll see, adding a stock property to a control is very easy. Table 19.1 lists all the stock properties you can add to an OLE control.

Table 19.1. Stock properties.

Property	Stored Value
Appearance	The control's appearance (for example, 3-D or flat)
BackColor	The control's background color
BorderStyle	The control's border style
Caption	The control's caption
Enabled	The control's enabled/disabled status
Font	The control's font for drawing text
ForeColor	The control's foreground color
hWnd	The control's window handle
Text	The control's text

For practice, you'll now add two stock properties to the MyClock control, BackColor and ForeColor, to determine the background and foreground colors of the control. Follow these steps to add the BackColor property to the MyClock control:

☐ Select ClassWizard from the View menu. In the OLE Automation tab of ClassWizard, make sure the Class name list box is set to `CMyClockCtrl`. (See Figure 19.6.)

Figure 19.6.
Selecting the OLE Automation tab of ClassWizard.

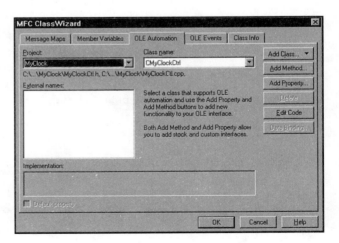

☐ Click the Add Property button.

Visual C++ responds by displaying the Add Property dialog box.

☐ Click the down arrow of the External names combo box and select BackColor from the list.

Your Add Property dialog box should now look like the one shown in Figure 19.7.

Figure 19.7.
Selecting BackColor in the
Add Property dialog box.

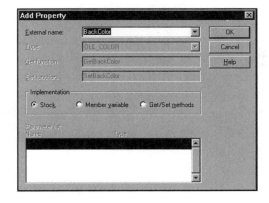

☐ Click the OK button of the Add Property dialog box.

The ClassWizard dialog box reappears, as shown in Figure 19.8.

Figure 19.8.
The ClassWizard dialog box
after you add the BackColor
stock property.

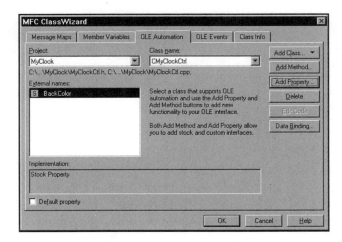

As shown in Figure 19.8, the External names list now contains the property BackColor preceded by the letter *S*, which indicates that BackColor is a stock property.

Now add the ForeColor property:

☐ Click the Add Property button.

Visual C++ responds by displaying the Add Property dialog box.

☐ Click the down arrow of the External names combo box and select ForeColor from the list.

☐ Click the OK button of the Add Property dialog box.

The ClassWizard dialog box reappears, as shown in Figure 19.9.

Figure 19.9.
The ClassWizard dialog box after you add the ForeColor stock property.

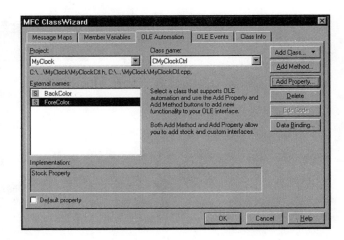

As shown in Figure 19.9, the External names list now contains both the BackColor property and ForeColor property preceded by the letter *S* because both are stock properties.

☐ Click the OK button of ClassWizard.

That's it! You have finished adding the BackColor and ForeColor properties to the MyClock control.

To verify that the MyClock control now has the BackColor and ForeColor properties, do the following:

☐ Compile and link MyClock.OCX.

Visual C++ responds by compiling and linking the files of the MyClock control.

☐ Select OLE Control Test Container from the Tools menu.

Visual C++ responds by running the Test Container program.

☐ Select Insert OLE Control from Test Container's Edit menu.

Test Container responds by displaying the Insert OLE Control dialog box.

☐ Select the MyClock control, then click the OK button.

Test Container responds by inserting the MyClock control.

☐ Increase the width of the MyClock control so you can see the entire text of the current time.

☐ Select Properties from the View menu of Test Container.

Test Container responds by displaying the Properties dialog box. (See Figure 19.10.)

Figure 19.10.
The Properties dialog box of
Test Container.

☐ Click the down arrow of the Property combo box.

Test Container responds by popping up a list with the properties of the MyClock control.
(See Figure 19.11.) The only properties listed are the BackColor and ForeColor properties.

Figure 19.11.
Listing the properties of the
MyClock control.

19

☐ Select the BackColor property.

Your Properties dialog box should now look like Figure 19.12.

Figure 19.12.
Selecting the BackColor
property.

The Properties dialog box displays the current value of the BackColor property and enables you to change this value. You can specify a color by typing its corresponding value or you can select the color visually by clicking the three-dots button to the right of the Value edit box.

☐ Click the three-dots button to the right of the Value edit box.

The Colors tab appears. (See Figure 19.13.)

Figure 19.13.
The Colors tab.

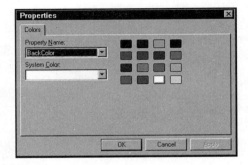

If you try to set the BackColor property of the MyClock control to any color, you'll see that the background color of the control doesn't change to the color you selected. Why not? Because you've only added the BackColor property to the MyClock control—you haven't written the code that makes the BackColor property functional.

In the following section, you'll write code that makes the BackColor and ForeColor properties functional. When you set the BackColor or ForeColor property to a certain value, your code will change the background or foreground color of the control to the color you selected.

☐ Terminate Test Container by selecting Exit from the File menu.

Making the BackColor and ForeColor Properties Functional

The MyClock control currently has the BackColor and ForeColor properties, but does not make use of the values stored in these properties. You'll now write the code that accomplishes that in the OnDraw() function:

☐ Open the file MyClockCtl.cpp (if it's not open already) and add code at the beginning of the OnDraw() function so it looks like the following:

```
void CMyClockCtrl::OnDraw(
  CDC* pdc, const CRect& rcBounds, const CRect& rcInvalid)
{

// TODO: Replace the following code with your own drawing
//       code.
```

```
/////////////////////////
// MY CODE STARTS HERE
/////////////////////////

// Set the foreground color (i.e. the text color)
// according to the ForeColor property.
pdc->SetTextColor(TranslateColor(GetForeColor()));

// Set the background mode to transparent mode.
pdc->SetBkMode(TRANSPARENT);

// Create a brush based on the BackColor property.
CBrush bkBrush(TranslateColor(GetBackColor()));

// Paint the background using the BackColor property
pdc->FillRect(rcBounds, &bkBrush);

char CurrentTime[30];
struct tm *newtime;
long lTime;

// Get the current time
time(&lTime);
newtime=localtime(&lTime);

// Convert the time into a string.
strcpy(CurrentTime, asctime(newtime));

// Pad the string with 1 blank.
CurrentTime[24]=' ';

// Terminate the string.
CurrentTime[25] = 0;

// Display the current time
pdc->ExtTextOut(rcBounds.left,
                rcBounds.top,
                ETO_CLIPPED,
                rcBounds,
                CurrentTime,
                strlen(CurrentTime),
                NULL);

/////////////////////
// MY CODE ENDS HERE
/////////////////////

    }
```

☐ Save your work.

The statements you added to the beginning of the OnDraw() function change the background color and foreground color of the MyClock control according to the current values of the BackColor and ForeColor properties. Therefore, whenever there is a need to redraw the control (whenever the OnDraw() function is executed), the control will be painted with the background and foreground colors currently stored in the BackColor and ForeColor properties.

19

The first statement you added to the the OnDraw() function sets the text color (the foreground color) of the control according to the current value of the ForeColor property:

```
pdc->SetTextColor(TranslateColor(GetForeColor()));
```

Notice that the value of the ForeColor property is retrieved with the GetForeColor() function.

The next statement sets the background mode to transparent mode:

```
pdc->SetBkMode(TRANSPARENT);
```

The next statement creates a brush (bkBrush) based on the current value of the BackColor property:

```
// Create a brush based on the BackColor property.
CBrush bkBrush(TranslateColor(GetBackColor()));
```

Notice that you retrieve the BackColor property by using the GetBackColor() function.

The last statement you added fills the control with the color of the bkBrush brush (the color of the BackColor property):

```
// Paint the background using the BackColor property
pdc->FillRect(rcBounds, &bkBrush);
```

Notice that the first parameter of the FillRect() function is rcBounds. rcBounds (an object of class CRect) is the second parameter of the OnDraw() function. It specifies the rectangular dimensions (boundaries) of the control.

To see the code that you added to the OnDraw() function in action, do the following:

☐ Select Build MyClock.OCX from the Build menu.

    Visual C++ responds by compiling and linking the files of the MyClock control.

☐ Start Test Container, select Insert OLE Control from its Edit menu, select the MyClock control, then click the OK button.

    Test Container responds by inserting the MyClock control.

☐ Increase the width of the MyClock control so that you can see the entire text of the current time.

☐ Select Properties from the View menu of Test Container.

    Test Container responds by displaying the Properties dialog box.

☐ Click the down arrow of the Property combo box.

    Test Container responds by popping up a list with the properties of the MyClock control.

☐ Select the BackColor property.

☐ Click the three-dots button to the right of the Value edit box.

   A Colors tab appears, shown back in Figure 19.13.

☐ Select the red color by clicking the rectangle painted red, then click the Apply button.

☐ Click the OK button of the Colors dialog box, then click the Close button of the Properties dialog box.

   As you can see, the control changed its background color to red. The code you added to the OnDraw() *function is working!*

Similarly, you can experiment with the ForeColor property. You will see that after you set the ForeColor property to a certain color, the foreground color of the control (the color of the text) changes accordingly. When you select a color in the Colors tab, don't forget to first click the Apply button of the Colors tab, then the OK button of the Colors tab, and finally the Close button of the Properties dialog box.

☐ Terminate Test Container by selecting Exit from the File menu.

Setting the Initial Size of the MyClock Control

As you have seen in the preceding steps, when you place the MyClock control in the window of Test Container, its initial size is not wide enough. To see the seconds portion of the displayed time, you have to make the control wider.

You'll now add code that sets the initial size of the MyClock control so that the control will be wide enough when you place it in a window.

☐ Open the file MyClockCtl.cpp (if it's not open already).

☐ Locate the constructor function of the CMyClockCtrl class in the MyClockCtl.cpp file and add the following code:

```
CMyClockCtrl::CMyClockCtrl()
{
InitializeIIDs(&IID_DMyClock, &IID_DMyClockEvents);

// TODO: Initialize your control's instance data here.

/////////////////////////
// MY CODE STARTS HERE
/////////////////////////

// Set initial size of control to width=200, height=15.
SetInitialSize(200, 15);
```

19

```
/////////////////////
// MY CODE ENDS HERE
/////////////////////

}
```

☐ Save your work.

The code you typed in the constructor function has one statement that uses the `SetInitialSize()` function to set the initial width of the control to `200` and the initial height to `15`:

```
SetInitialSize(200, 15);
```

To see your code in action, do the following:

☐ Compile and link the MyClock control's files.

☐ Start Test Container, select Insert OLE Control from its Edit menu, select the MyClock control, then click the OK button.

Test Container responds by inserting the MyClock control.

As you can see, the MyClock control is now wide enough! You don't have to widen it to see the seconds portion of the time.

☐ Terminate Test Container by selecting Exit from the File menu.

Adding a Custom Property to the MyClock Control

In many cases, you will have to add a property to your OLE control that's not a standard property. Such a property is called a *custom property*—a property custom-made by you.

In the following steps, you'll add an additional property to the MyClock control called UpdateInterval, which is used for storing numbers. You will use this property later in the chapter, but now all you want to do is add it to the MyClock control:

☐ Select ClassWizard from the View menu. In the OLE Automation tab of ClassWizard, make sure the Class name box is set to `CMyClockCtrl`.

☐ Click the Add Property button.

Visual C++ responds by displaying the Add Property dialog box.

☐ Type `UpdateInterval` in the External name combo box and set the Type list box to `long`.

☐ Make sure the Member variable radio button is selected in the Implementation frame.

Your Add Property dialog box should now look like Figure 19.14.

Figure 19.14.
Adding the UpdateInterval property in the Add Property dialog box.

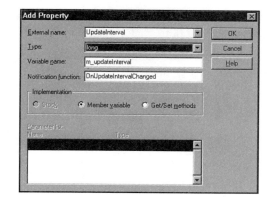

By setting the Add Property dialog box as shown in Figure 19.14, you are specifying that the name of the new property should be UpdateInterval and that this property will be used to hold numbers of type `long`. Figure 19.14 also shows the Variable name box set to `m_updateInterval`. This means that the variable associated with the UpdateInterval property will be `m_updateInterval`, a data member of the `CMyClockCtrl` class.

In Figure 19.14, the Notification function box is set to `OnUpdateIntervalChange`. Whenever the value of the UpdateInterval property is changed, the function `OnUpdateIntervalChange()` will be executed automatically. You'll write the code of the `OnUpdateIntervalChange()` function later.

☐ Click the OK button of the Add Property dialog box.

The ClassWizard dialog box reappears, as shown in Figure 19.15.

Figure 19.15.
Listing the UpdateInterval custom property in ClassWizard.

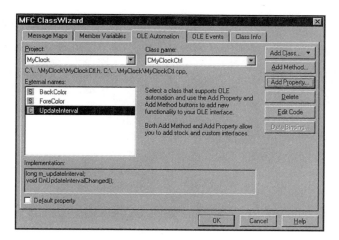

As shown in Figure 19.15, the Name list now contains the property UpdateInterval preceded by the letter *C* to indicate that UpdateInterval is a custom property.

That's it! You've finished adding the UpdateInterval custom property to the MyClock control. To verify that the MyClock control now has the UpdateInterval property, do the following:

☐ Compile and link the MyClock control's files.

☐ Start Test Container, select Insert OLE Control from its Edit menu, select the MyClock control, then click the OK button.

   Test Container responds by inserting the MyClock control.

☐ Select Properties from the View menu of Test Container.

☐ Click the down arrow of the Property combo box.

   Test Container responds by popping up a list with the properties of the MyClock control. (See Figure 19.16.) The UpdateInterval property you added to the control is in the list.

Figure 19.16.
Checking listed properties in the Properties dialog box.

☐ Select the UpdateInterval property.

Your Properties dialog box should now look like Figure 19.17.

Figure 19.17.
The Properties dialog box after you select the UpdateInterval property.

As you can see from Figure 19.17, the Properties dialog box displays the current value of the UpdateInterval property and enables you to change this value. You can specify a new value for the UpdateInterval property by entering it in the Value edit box, then clicking the Apply button.

If you try to set the UpdateInterval property of the MyClock control to a value, the UpdateInterval property will be changed to the new value, but nothing will happen to the control. Why not? Because you haven't written the code that makes the UpdateInterval property functional. You'll do that later in this chapter.

☐ Terminate Test Container by selecting Exit from the File menu.

Initializing the UpdateInterval Property

At this point, when you place the MyClock control in a dialog box or form, the UpdateInterval property is not initialized to any specific value. You'll now write code that initializes the UpdateInterval property to 1000. The UpdateInterval property will be used for setting the timer interval of the MyClock control.

To write code that initializes the UpdateInterval property to 1000, do the following:

☐ Open the file MyClockCtl.cpp (if it's not open already).

☐ Locate the function DoPropExchange() in the MyClockCtl.cpp file and add code as follows:

```
void CMyClockCtrl::DoPropExchange(CPropExchange* pPX)
{
ExchangeVersion(pPX, MAKELONG(_wVerMinor, _wVerMajor));
COleControl::DoPropExchange(pPX);

// TODO: Call PX_ functions for each persistent custom
//       property.

//////////////////////////
// MY CODE STARTS HERE
//////////////////////////

// Initialize the UpdateInterval property to 1000.
PX_Long(pPX, _T("UpdateInterval"), m_updateInterval, 1000);

//////////////////////////
// MY CODE ENDS HERE
//////////////////////////

}
```

☐ Save your work.

The code you wrote in the DoPropExchange() has one statement that uses the PX_Long() function to initialize the value of the UpdateInterval property to 1000:

```
PX_Long(pPX, _T("UpdateInterval"), m_updateInterval, 1000);
```

The PX_Long() function is used because the UpdateInterval property is of type long. To initialize other types of properties you can use other PX_ functions such as PX_Bool(), PX_Short, and PX_String().

> **Note:** Be careful when you type this statement:
>
> `PX_Long(pPX,_T("UpdateInterval"),m_updateInterval,1000);`
>
> The second parameter is `_T("UpdateInterval")` because UpdateInterval is the property you are initializing.
>
> The third parameter is `m_updateInterval` (with a lowercase *u* in "update") because `m_updateInterval` is the variable associated with the UpdateInterval property. As you saw in Figure 19.14, when you added the UpdateInterval property, you specified the name of the variable as `m_updateInterval` (not `m_UpdateInterval`).

To see your initialization code in action, do the following:

☐ Compile and link the files of the MyClock control.

☐ Start Test Container, select Insert OLE Control from its Edit menu, select the MyClock control, then click the OK button.

☐ Select Properties from Test Container's View menu, click the down arrow of the Property combo box and select the UpdateInterval property.

Your Properties dialog box should now look like the one shown in Figure 19.18. As expected, the initial value of the UpdateInterval property is 1000. The code you wrote in the DoPropExchange() function is working!

Figure 19.18.
The Properties dialog box after you select the UpdateInterval property.

Properties	☒
Property: UpdateInterval ▾	Apply
Value: 1000	Close
Invoke Properties Verb...	Multiple Selection Props...

☐ Terminate Test Container by selecting Exit from the File menu.

Making the UpdateInterval Property Functional

At this point, the MyClock control has the UpdateInterval property, which has been initialized to 1000. You'll now add code to the MyClock control that makes the UpdateInterval property functional.

What should the UpdateInterval property do? This property should determine the interval at which the MyClock control updates itself. Currently, the MyClock control updates the

displayed time every 1000 milliseconds because you installed the timer of the control in the OnCreate() function with a 1000-millisecond interval. You'll now enhance the code of the MyClock control, so that it will update the displayed time every X milliseconds, where X is the current value of the UpdateInterval property. Here is how you do that:

☐ Open the file MyClockCtl.cpp (if it's not open already).

☐ Locate the function OnUpdateIntervalChanged() in the MyClockCtl.cpp file. ClassWizard wrote this function for you when you added the UpdateInterval property; it's automatically executed when the value of the UpdateInterval property is changed.

☐ Add code to the OnUpdateIntervalChanged() function as follows:

```
void CMyClockCtrl::OnUpdateIntervalChanged()
{

// TODO: Add notification handler code

//////////////////////////
// MY CODE STARTS HERE
//////////////////////////

// Reinstall the timer with interval set
// to the current value of the UpdateInterval
// property.
SetTimer(1, (UINT)m_updateInterval, NULL);

//////////////////////////
// MY CODE ENDS HERE
//////////////////////////

SetModifiedFlag();

}
```

☐ Save your work.

The code you added is a single statement that reinstalls the timer and sets the timer's interval to the value of the variable m_updateInterval:

```
SetTimer(1, (UINT)m_updateInterval, NULL);
```

Recall that m_updateInterval is the variable of the UpdateInterval property. Therefore, whenever someone changes the value of the UpdateInterval property, the interval of the timer changes accordingly. Note that in the preceding statement the cast (UINT) is used, because the SetTimer() function expects its second parameter to be of type UINT, and the UpdateInterval property is defined as type long.

> **Note:** Be careful when you type this statement:
>
> SetTimer(1, (UINT)m_updateInterval, NULL);
>
> The second parameter is m_updateInterval, not m_UpdateInterval.

Recall that in the OnCreate() function you set the interval of the timer to 1000 milliseconds with this statement:

```
SetTimer(1, 1000, NULL);
```

Now change the OnCreate() function so that it will use the current value of the UpdateInterval property, not the hard-coded value of 1000. This way, whenever a MyClock control is created, the initial value of the timer interval will be the same as the current value of the UpdateInterval property.

☐ Locate the OnCreate() function in the MyClockCtl.cpp file and change it as follows:

```
int CMyClockCtrl::OnCreate(LPCREATESTRUCT lpCreateStruct)
{

if (COleControl::OnCreate(lpCreateStruct) == -1)
   return -1;

// TODO: Add your specialized creation code here

/////////////////////////
// MY CODE STARTS HERE
/////////////////////////

// Install a timer.
SetTimer(1, (UINT)m_updateInterval, NULL);

/////////////////////////
// MY CODE ENDS HERE
/////////////////////////

return 0;

}
```

Again, when you type the preceding code, make sure you type m_updateInterval (not m_UpdateInterval).

☐ Save your work.

To see the code you attached to the OnUpdateIntervalChanged() function in action, do the following:

☐ Compile and link the files of the MyClock control.

☐ Start Test Container, select Insert OLE Control from its Edit menu, select the MyClock control, then click the OK button.

☐ Select Properties from Test Container's View menu, click the down arrow of the Property combo box, and select the UpdateInterval property.

As you can see, the initial value of the UpdateInterval property is 1000 because earlier you wrote code in the DoPropExchange() function that initializes the UpdateInterval property to 1000.

☐ Observe the seconds portion of the displayed time in the MyClock control and make sure the time is updated every 1000 milliseconds.

☐ Change the value of the UpdateInterval property to 5000 and click the Apply button.

☐ Observe the MyClock control again, and notice that now the time is updated every 5000 milliseconds.

As soon as you changed the UpdateInterval property to 5000, the code you wrote in the OnUpdateIntervalChanged() function was automatically executed; this code set the timer's interval to the new value of the UpdateInterval property.

☐ Terminate Test Container by selecting Exit from the File menu.

Validating the Value of the UpdateInterval Property

You can write code that validates the value entered for the UpdateInterval property. Suppose, for example, that you don't want the user to enter negative values for the UpdateInterval property. Your validation code will prompt the user with a message box and set the UpdateInterval property to a valid value. To write this validation code, follow these steps:

☐ Open the file MyClockCtl.cpp (if it's not open already).

☐ Locate the function OnUpdateIntervalChanged() in the MyClockCtl.cpp file and add code as follows:

```
void CMyClockCtrl::OnUpdateIntervalChanged()
{

// TODO: Add notification handler code

/////////////////////////
// MY CODE STARTS HERE
/////////////////////////

// Make sure the user did not set the property to a
// negative value.
if (m_updateInterval < 0)
    {
    MessageBox("This property cannot be negative!");
    m_updateInterval = 1000;
    }
```

19

```
// Reinstall the timer with interval set
// to the current value of the UpdateInterval
// property.
SetTimer(1, (UINT)m_updateInterval, NULL);

////////////////////////
// MY CODE ENDS HERE
////////////////////////

SetModifiedFlag();

}
```

☐ Save your work.

The validation code you added to the OnUpdateIntervalChanged() function is made up of a single if statement:

```
if (m_updateInterval < 0)
    {
    MessageBox("This property cannot be negative!");
    m_updateInterval = 1000;
    }
```

This if statement evaluates the value of the UpdateInterval property (m_updateInterval) to see whether it's less than 0. If m_updateInterval is less than 0, the code under the if displays an error message box and sets the value of m_updateInterval to a valid value (1000).

To see your validation code in action, follow these steps:

☐ Compile and link the files of the MyClock control.

☐ Start Test Container, select Insert OLE Control from its Edit menu, select the MyClock control, then click the OK button.

☐ Select Properties from Test Container's View menu and set the Property combo box to UpdateInterval.

☐ Change the value of the UpdateInterval property to a negative value (for example, -1000) and click the Apply button.

As expected, the message box shown in Figure 19.19 appears.

Figure 19.19.
The message box that appears after you set the UpdateInterval property to a negative value.

562

☐ Click the OK button of the message box.

☐ Observe the value of the UpdateInterval property. It should be 1000.

The validation code that you wrote in the OnUpdateIntervalChanged() function is working. When someone tries to set the UpdateInterval property to a negative value, your validation code displays a message box and sets the UpdateInterval property to 1000.

☐ Terminate Test Container by selecting Exit from the File menu.

Adding a Properties Page to the MyClock Control

So far, you have accessed the properties of the MyClock control by selecting Properties from Test Container's View menu and then using the Properties dialog box to view and set values of properties.

Another way to view or set properties during design time is with *properties pages,* which let you view or change properties in a friendly visual manner. Each properties page lets you view or set related properties. For example, you can view or select color properties in the Colors properties page and font properties in the Fonts properties page.

To illustrate what a properties page is and how to add it to a control, you'll add a Colors properties page to the MyClock control for viewing or setting the BackColor and ForeColor properties.

Before you write the code that adds the Colors properties page, first run the Test Container program and verify that the MyClock control does not have the Colors properties page:

☐ Start Test Container, select Insert OLE Control from its Edit menu, select the MyClock control, then click the OK button.

> *Test Container responds by inserting the MyClock control.*

☐ Double-click the thin frame surrounding the MyClock control.

> *The MyClock Control Properties dialog box appears, as shown in Figure 19.20.*

Figure 19.20.
The MyClock Control Properties dialog box.

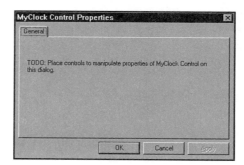

Note: The preceding step instructs you to display the MyClock Control Properties dialog box by double-clicking the frame surrounding the MyClock control. You can also click the MyClock control, then select Properties MyClock Control Object from Test Container's Edit menu.

As shown in Figure 19.20, the MyClock Control Properties dialog box includes only one tab—the General tab—because the MyClock control has only the General properties page. After you write code adding the Colors properties page, the Myclock Properties dialog box will have another tab called Colors.

The General tab (the General properties page) currently includes this text:

```
TODO: Place controls to manipulate properties of MyClock Control on this dialog.
```

The General properties page should contain general properties that don't belong to any other properties page. Later in this chapter, you'll customize the General properties page.

☐ Close the MyClock Control Properties dialog box by clicking its OK button.

☐ Terminate the Test Container program by selecting Exit from the File menu.

To write the code that adds the Colors properties page to the MyClock control, follow these steps:

☐ Open the file MyClockCtl.cpp (if it's not open already) and locate the Property Pages table in the MyClockCtl.cpp file.

☐ Modify the Property Pages table as follows (the statements you change or add are shown in boldface type):

```
/////////////////////////////////////////////////
// Property pages

// TODO: Add more property pages as needed.
//       Remember to increase the count!
BEGIN_PROPPAGEIDS(CMyClockCtrl, 2)
    PROPPAGEID(CMyClockPropPage::guid)
    PROPPAGEID(CLSID_CColorPropPage)
END_PROPPAGEIDS(CMyClockCtrl)
```

First, you modified the second parameter in this statement from 1 to 2:

```
BEGIN_PROPPAGEIDS(CMyClockCtrl, 2)
```

You also added this statement:

```
PROPPAGEID(CLSID_CColorPropPage)
```

☐ Save your work.

Now take a close look at how the Property Pages table is constructed. The first statement begins the table:

```
BEGIN_PROPPAGEIDS(CMyClockCtrl, 2)
```

The first parameter, CMyClockCtrl, is the class name of the MyClock control. The second parameter, 2, specifies the total number of property pages. As you add more property pages to the control, you have to change this parameter accordingly.

The next two statements list the IDs of the property pages. The first statement lists the ID of the General properties page:

```
PROPPAGEID(CMyClockPropPage::guid)
```

This statement was written for you by Visual C++ when you created the project of the MyClock project. That's why the MyClock control already has a General properties page.

The second ID statement lists the ID of the Colors properties page:

```
PROPPAGEID(CLSID_CColorPropPage)
```

The last statement of the Property Pages table ends the table:

```
END_PROPPAGEIDS(CMyClockCtrl)
```

By adding the ID of the Colors properties page to the Property Pages table, you added the Colors properties page to the MyClock control. You don't have to write any additional code!

To make sure the MyClock control now has the Colors properties page, follow these steps:

☐ Compile and link the files of the MyClock control.

☐ Start Test Container, select Insert OLE Control from its Edit menu, select the MyClock control, then click the OK button.

☐ Double-click the frame of the MyClock control (or click the MyClock control and select Properties MyClock Control Object from the Edit menu of Test Container).

The MyClock Control Properties dialog box appears, as shown in Figure 19.21.

Figure 19.21.

*The MyClock Control
Properties dialog box with
the Colors properties page.*

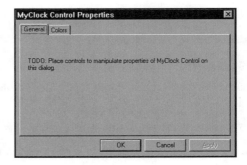

The MyClock Control Properties dialog box now includes two property pages: General and Colors.

☐ Select the Colors Properties page. (See Figure 19.22.)

Figure 19.22.

*The Colors Properties page
of the MyClock Control.*

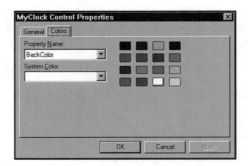

As you can see, the Colors Properties page gives you an easy and user-friendly interface to view and set the color properties of the MyClock control. You can select the desired Color property from the Property Name combo box and set its value by clicking the desired color.

After you click the down arrow of the Property Name combo box, it lists only the color properties of the MyClock control so you can concentrate on the color aspect of the control. (See Figure 19.23.)

☐ Experiment with the Colors properties page and notice how easy it is use. Make sure the MyClock control changes its foreground and background colors according to your selections after you click the OK button of the dialog box.

☐ Close the MyClock Control Properties dialog box by clicking its OK button.

☐ Terminate the Test Container program by selecting Exit from the File menu.

Figure 19.23.
The Property Name combo box lists only the Colors properties.

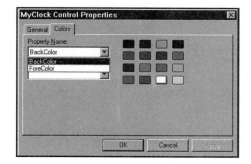

Customizing the General Properties Page

As you have seen in the previous steps, the MyClock control now has two properties pages: General and Colors. The Colors properties page is fully functional. However, the General properties page does not include any properties. You'll now customize the General properties page so that you can view and set the value of the UpdateInterval property.

To customize the General properties page, you need to work on the IDD_PROPPAGE_MyClock dialog box, created for you by Visual C++. To display the IDD_PROPPAGE_MyClock dialog box, do the following:

☐ Select Project Workspace from the View menu. In the ResourceView tab, expand the MyClock resources item, expand the Dialog item, and double-click the IDD_PROPPAGE_MyClock item.

Visual C++ responds by displaying the IDD_PROPPAGE_MyClock dialog box in design mode ready for you to edit. (See Figure 19.24.)

Figure 19.24.
IDD_PROPPAGE_MyClock dialog box before customization.

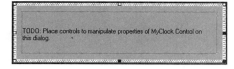

☐ Delete the TODO text in the IDD_PROPPAGE_MyClock dialog box.

☐ Place a static text control in the dialog box, double-click it, and set its Caption property to UpdateInterval:.

☐ Place an edit box control in the dialog box, double-click it, and set its ID property to IDC_UPDATE_INTERVAL.

☐ Save your work.

Your IDD_PROPPAGE_MyClock dialog box should now look like the one shown in Figure 19.25.

Figure 19.25.
IDD_PROPPAGE_MyClock
after customization.

Now you have to attach a variable to the IDC_UPDATE_INTERVAL edit box and associate this variable with the UpdateInterval property. Here is how you do that:

☐ Select ClassWizard from the View menu. In the Member Variables tab, set the Class Name combo box to CMyClockPropPage.

Your ClassWizard dialog box should now look like Figure 19.26.

Figure 19.26.
The Member Variables tab
after you select the
CMyClockPropPage class.

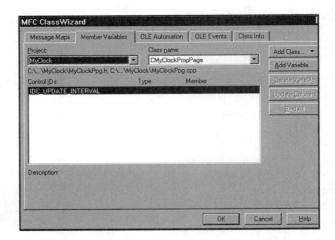

☐ Make sure that IDC_UPDATE_INTERVAL is selected in the Control IDs list, then click the Add Variable button and make the following selections in the Add Member Variable dialog box:

Variable name:	m_updateInterval
Category:	Value
Variable type:	long
Optional OLE property name:	UpdateInterval

Your Add Member Variable dialog box should now look like Figure 19.27.

Figure 19.27.
Attaching a variable to the
IDC_UPDATE_INTERVAL
edit box.

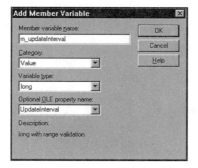

☐ Click the OK button of the Add Member Variable dialog box, then click the OK button of ClassWizard.

☐ Save your work.

That's it! You have finished customizing the General properties page. To make sure the General properties page is no longer blank and it enables the user to view and set the UpdateInterval property, follow these steps:

☐ Compile and link the files of the MyClock control.

☐ Start Test Container, select Insert OLE Control from its Edit menu, select the MyClock control, then click the OK button.

☐ Double-click the frame of the MyClock control (or click the MyClock control and select Properties MyClock Control Object from the Edit menu of Test Container).

The MyClock Control Properties dialog box appears, as shown in Figure 19.28.

Figure 19.28.
The General properties page
now includes the
UpdateInterval property.

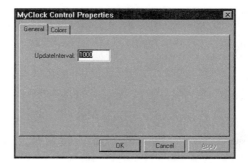

As shown in Figure 19.28, the General properties page looks just the way you designed it. The edit box contains the value 1000 because this is the current value of the UpdateInterval property. The edit box contains the value of the UpdateInterval property because when you created it with ClassWizard, you set the Optional OLE Property Name combo box to UpdateInterval.

☐ Try to set the UpdateInterval property to various values, then click the OK button and make sure the MyClock control updates itself. For example, if you set the UpdateInterval to 5000, then the seconds portion of the clock should change once every 5 seconds.

☐ Terminate the Test Container program by selecting Exit from the File menu.

What Have You Accomplished So Far?

So far, you have written the code that makes the MyClock control display the current time, added two stock properties (BackColor and ForeColor) and one custom property (UpdateInterval), written validation code for the UpdateInterval property, added a Colors properties page to the MyClock control, and customized the General properties page of the MyClock control.

In the following sections, you'll further customize the MyClock control by adding a stock event, a custom event, and a method.

Adding Stock Events to the MyClock Control

Now you'll learn how to add a stock event to the control. As you'll see, the steps to add a stock event are as easy as the steps you took when you added a stock property. *Stock events,* such as Click (mouse click) and DblClick (mouse double-click), are predefined. You can add any of the following stock events to an OLE control:

```
Click
DblClick
Error
KeyDown
KeyPress
KeyUp
MouseDown
MouseMove
MouseUp
```

The names of these events are self-explanatory: The Click event occurs when you click the control; the DblClick event occurs when you double-click the control; the Error event occurs when there's an error within the control; the KeyDown event occurs when you press a key while the control has the keyboard focus; and so on. The mouse events apply to any of the mouse buttons: left, middle, or right. For practice, add two stock events to the MyClock control: Click and DblClick.

Follow these steps to add the Click event to the MyClock control:

☐ Select ClassWizard from the View menu. In the OLE Events tab of ClassWizard, set the Class name box to `CMyClockCtrl`.

Your ClassWizard dialog box should now look like Figure 19.29.

Figure 19.29.
Setting the class name to
`CMyClockCtrl` *in the OLE Events tab.*

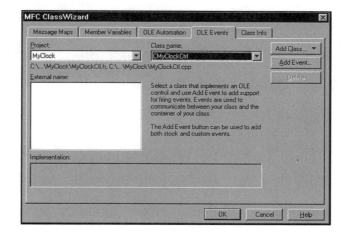

☐ Click the Add Event button.

> *Visual C++ responds by displaying the Add Event dialog box.*

☐ Click the down arrow of the External name combo box and select Click from the list that pops up.

Your Add Event dialog box should now look like Figure 19.30.

Figure 19.30.
Setting the External name combo box to Click.

☐ Click the OK button of the Add Event dialog box.

The ClassWizard dialog box reappears, as shown in Figure 19.31.

Figure 19.31.
The ClassWizard dialog box after you add the Click *stock event.*

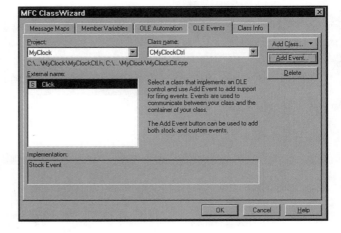

As shown in Figure 19.31, the External name list now contains the event Click preceded by the letter *S* to indicate that this is a stock event.

Now use the same steps to add the DblClick event:

☐ Click the Add Event button, click the down arrow of the External name combo box, select DblClick from the pop-up list, and click the OK button of the Add Event dialog box.

The ClassWizard dialog box reappears, as shown in Figure 19.32.

Figure 19.32.
The ClassWizard dialog box after adding the DblClick *stock event.*

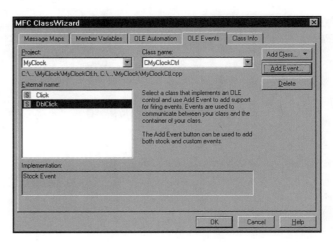

Now the External name list contains both the Click event and DblClick event preceded by the letter *S* to indicate they're stock events.

☐ Click the OK button of ClassWizard.

That's it! You've finished adding the Click and DblClick events to the MyClock control. This means that programmers who use your MyClock control in their programs will be able to attach code to these events.

To make sure the MyClock control now has the Click and DblClick events, do the following:

☐ Compile and link the files of the MyClock control.

☐ Start Test Container, select Insert OLE Control from its Edit menu, select the MyClock control, then click the OK button.

☐ Select Event Log from the View menu of Test Container.

Test Container responds by displaying the Event Log dialog box. (See Figure 19.33.)

Figure 19.33.
The Event Log dialog box of Test Container.

The Event Log dialog box displays a log of events as they occur. To verify that the MyClock control has a Click event, do the following:

☐ Leave the Event Log dialog box open.

☐ Click in the MyClock control. (Don't click on the frame of the control; click inside the control.)

The Event Log dialog box logs a Click event. (See Figure 19.34.)

Figure 19.34.
Logging a Click event in the Event Log dialog box.

☐ Click the MyClock control several more times, and notice how the Event Log dialog box logs a `Click` event each time you click the MyClock control. (See Figure 19.35.) Notice that it doesn't matter which mouse button you use to click the MyClock control.

Figure 19.35.
Logging four `Click` events.

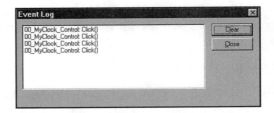

To verify that the MyClock control has a `DblClick` event, do the following:

☐ Double-click inside the MyClock control.

    The Event Log dialog box logs a `DblClick` event. (See Figure 19.36.)

Figure 19.36.
Logging a `DblClick` event in the Event Log dialog box.

☐ Double-click the MyClock control several more times, and notice how the Event Log dialog box logs a DblClick event and a Click event each time you click the MyClock control. That's because every time you double-click the control, two events occur: a regular click and a double-click. The first click of a double-click is a regular click. Notice, too, that the DblClick event occurs whether you use the left, middle, or right mouse button.

☐ Terminate Test Container by selecting Exit from the File menu.

Adding a Custom Event to the MyClock Control

In many cases, you'll have to add a custom-made event to your OLE control, called a *custom event.* You'll now add a custom event to the MyClock control called `NewMinute`. Later you will make this event functional, but now all you want to do is add it to the MyClock control.

Follow these steps to add the `NewMinute` custom event to the MyClock control:

☐ Select ClassWizard from the View menu. In the OLE Events tab of ClassWizard, make sure that the Class name box is set to CMyClockCtrl.

Your ClassWizard dialog box should now look like Figure 19.37.

Figure 19.37.
The OLE Events tab.

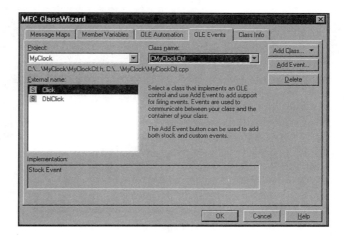

☐ Click the Add Event button.

> *Visual C++ responds by displaying the Add Event dialog box.*

☐ Enter NewMinute in the External name combo box.

Notice that as you type NewMinute in the External name combo box, Visual C++ automatically fills the Internal name edit box with the text FireNewMinute.

Your Add Event dialog box should now look like Figure 19.38.

Figure 19.38.
Entering NewMinute in the Add Event dialog box.

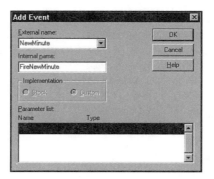

☐ Click the OK button of the Add Event dialog box.

The ClassWizard dialog box reappears, as shown in Figure 19.39.

Figure 19.39.
The ClassWizard dialog box after you add the NewMinute *custom event.*

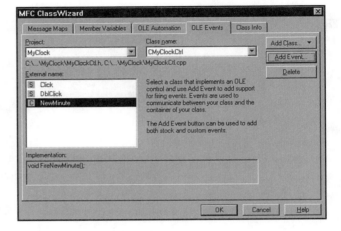

As shown in Figure 19.39, the External name list now contains the event NewMinute preceded by the letter *C* to indicate that this is a custom event.

☐ Close the ClassWizard dialog box by clicking its OK button.

> **Note:** When you add a custom event to a control, you can add parameters to the event by clicking the empty item in the Parameters list. (Refer to Figure 19.38.) In the preceding steps, you were not instructed to add a parameter in the Add Event dialog box because you don't want the NewMinute event to have any parameters.
>
> In your future OLE control projects, you may need to add parameters to a certain event. When an event has parameters, whoever receives the event can make use of these parameters to get more information about the event.

That's it! You have finished adding the NewMinute custom event to the MyClock control. To verify that the MyClock control now has the NewMinute event, do the following:

☐ Compile and link the files of the MyClock control.

☐ Start Test Container, select Insert OLE Control from its Edit menu, select the MyClock control, then click the OK button.

To see a list of all the events of the MyClock control, do the following:

☐ Select View Event List from the Edit menu of Test Container.

> *Test Container responds by displaying the Events for MyClock Control dialog box. (See Figure 19.40.)*

Figure 19.40.
The Events for MyClock Control dialog box.

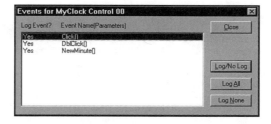

As you can see, the NewMinute event is listed! The MyClock control has three events: Click, DblClick, and NewMinute.

☐ Close the dialog box by clicking its Close button.

☐ Terminate Test Container by selecting Exit from the File menu.

Firing the *NewMinute* Event

As you have just verified, the MyClock control has the NewMinute event you added. However, to make the NewMinute event occur, you need to write some code.

When you add a stock event to a control, such as the DblClick event you added earlier, it already includes built-in code that makes the event happen. In the case of the DblClick event, it occurs automatically whenever you double-click the MyClock control.

However, when you add a custom event to a control, you need to write code that makes the event happen. Your code needs to recognize that the event has occurred and then use the Fire function of the event to fire the event—to make the event happen. The Fire function of the NewMinute event is FireNewMinute(). To make the NewMinute event happen, your code needs to detect when it occurs, then call the FireNewMinute() function.

When should the NewMinute event occur? Whenever a new minute begins. Follow these steps to write the code that fires the NewMinute event:

☐ Open the file MyClockCtl.cpp (if it's not open already).

☐ Locate the function OnDraw() in the MyClockCtl.cpp file and add an if statement to the end of the OnDraw() function as follows:

19

```
void CMyClockCtrl::OnDraw(
  CDC* pdc,const CRect& rcBounds,const CRect& rcInvalid)
{
// TODO: Replace the following code with your own drawing
//       code.

////////////////////////////
// MY CODE STARTS HERE //
////////////////////////////

// Set the foreground color (i.e. the text color)
// according to the ForeColor property.
pdc->SetTextColor(TranslateColor(GetForeColor()));

// Set the background mode to transparent mode.
pdc->SetBkMode(TRANSPARENT);

// Create a brush based on the BackColor property.
CBrush bkBrush(TranslateColor(GetBackColor()));

// Paint the background using the BackColor property
pdc->FillRect(rcBounds, &bkBrush);

char CurrentTime[30];
struct tm *newtime;
long lTime;

// Get the current time
time(&lTime);
newtime=localtime(&lTime);

// Convert the time into a string.
strcpy(CurrentTime, asctime(newtime));

// Pad the string with 1 blank.
CurrentTime[24]=' ';

// Terminate the string.
CurrentTime[25] = 0;

// Display the current time
pdc->ExtTextOut(rcBounds.left,
                rcBounds.top,
                ETO_CLIPPED,
                rcBounds,
                CurrentTime,
                strlen(CurrentTime),
                NULL);

// If new minute has just begun, fire a NewMinute event.
if (newtime->tm_sec==0)
   FireNewMinute();

////////////////////////////
// MY CODE ENDS HERE //
////////////////////////////

}
```

The code you just added to the OnDraw() function is one if statement:

```
if (newtime->tm_sec==0)
   FireNewMinute();
```

This if statement checks whether the tm_sec field of the newtime structure is currently 0. If it is, a new minute has just begun, and the FireNewMinute() function is executed to fire the NewMinute event:

```
FireNewMinute();
```

Note that the FireNewMinute() event is called without any parameters because you didn't specify any when you added the NewMinute event to the control.

You have finished writing the code that fires the NewMinute event! Now whenever a new minute begins, the code you wrote will fire a NewMinute event, and the code attached to the NewMinute event will be executed automatically.

The code you wrote for detecting the NewMinute event is not perfect. This code is executed whenever the OnDraw() function is executed, which is determined by the value of the UpdateInterval property. If the UpdateInterval property is ever set to a value greater than 1000 milliseconds, a new minute might begin without your code detecting it.

To verify that the code you wrote actually fires the NewMinute event, do the following:

☐ Compile and link the files of the MyClock control.

☐ Start Test Container, select Insert OLE Control from its Edit menu, select the MyClock control, then click the OK button.

☐ Select Event Log from the View menu of Test Container.

   Test Container responds by displaying the Event Log dialog box.

☐ Leave the Event Log dialog box open.

☐ Observe the time that the MyClock control displays, and wait for a new minute to begin.

As expected, as soon as a new minute begins, the Event Log dialog box logs the NewMinute event! (See Figure 19.41.)

Figure 19.41.
The Event Log dialog box after a new minute has begun.

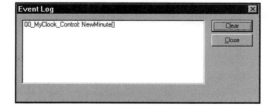

You have just verified that the NewMinute event is working. Whenever a new minute begins, the code you wrote in the OnDraw() function detects that a new minute has begun, and your code fires the NewMinute event by calling the FireNewMinute() function.

☐ Terminate Test Container by selecting Exit from the File menu.

Adding Methods to the MyClock Control

Besides adding properties and events to an OLE control, you can also add *methods*, which are like C++ member functions. After you add a method to your control, programmers who use your control can use your method in their programs. For example, suppose you add a method called MyMethod() to the MyClock control. Then, if a programmer adds a MyClock control in his or her program and names it Clock1, the programmer can use a statement such as the following:

```
Clock1.MyMethod()
```

This statement would execute the MyMethod() method on the Clock1 control.

The *AboutBox()* Method: A Gift from Visual C++

Although you haven't written any code to add a method to the MyClock control, it already has a method called AboutBox() created by Visual C++ when you created the MyClock's project. As its name implies, the AboutBox() method displays an About dialog box for the MyClock control. When programmers who use your MyClock control call the AboutBox() method from their programs, an About dialog box appears.

Before you add your own methods to the MyClock control, test the AboutBox() method that Visual C++ created for you:

☐ Start Test Container, select Insert OLE Control from its Edit menu, select the MyClock control, then click the OK button.

☐ Select Invoke Methods from the Edit menu of Test Container.

Test Container responds by displaying the Invoke Control Method dialog box. (See Figure 19.42.)

As shown in Figure 19.42, the Name list box of the Invoke Control Method dialog box is set to AboutBox. If you click the Invoke button, Test Container will execute the AboutBox() method of the MyClock control.

☐ Click the Invoke button.

Test Container responds by executing the AboutBox() *method of the MyClock control. The* AboutBox() *method displays an About dialog box, shown in Figure 19.43.*

Figure 19.42.
The Invoke Control Method dialog box.

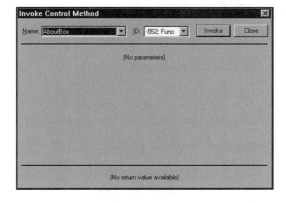

Figure 19.43.
The About dialog box displayed by the AboutBox() *method.*

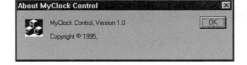

☐ Close the About dialog box by clicking its OK button.

☐ Close the Invoke Control Method dialog box by clicking its Close button.

☐ Terminate Test Container by selecting Exit from the File menu.

In the following sections, you'll add more methods to the MyClock control.

Note: If you wish, you can customize the About dialog box shown in Figure 19.43. To customize it, you need to work on the IDD_ABOUTBOX_MYCLOCK dialog box created by Visual C++.

To display the IDD_ABOUTBOX_MYCLOCK dialog box, do the following:

☐ Select Project Workspace from the View menu. In the ResourceView tab, expand the MyClock resources item, then expand the Dialog item.

☐ Double-click the IDD_ABOUTBOX_MYCLOCK item.

Adding a Stock Method to the MyClock Control

Stock methods are predefined. The current version of Visual C++ (4.0) supports two stock methods: `DoClick()` and `Refresh()`. The `DoClick()` method simulates a clicking of the control. In other words, executing the `DoClick()` method has the same effect as clicking the control. The `Refresh()` method causes the control to redraw itself by triggering a call to the `OnDraw()` function of the control.

For practice, add the `Refresh()` stock method to the MyClock control by following these steps:

☐ Select ClassWizard from the View menu. In the OLE Automation tab of ClassWizard, make sure the Class name box is set to `CMyClockCtrl`.

☐ Click the Add Method button.

    Visual C++ responds by displaying the Add Method dialog box.

☐ Click the down arrow of the External name combo box and select Refresh from the list that pops up.

Your Add Method dialog box should now look like Figure 19.44.

Figure 19.44.
The Add Method dialog box after setting the External name combo box to `Refresh`.

☐ Click the OK button of the Add Method dialog box.

    The ClassWizard dialog box reappears, as shown in Figure 19.45.

As shown in Figure 19.45, the External names list now contains the method `Refresh` preceded by the letter *M* to indicate that `Refresh` is a method.

☐ Close the ClassWizard dialog box by clicking its OK button.

Figure 19.45.

The ClassWizard dialog box after you add the Refresh() *stock method.*

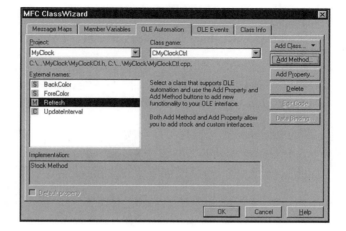

That's it! You have finished adding the Refresh() stock method to the MyClock control. To verify that the MyClock control now has the Refresh() method and to see it in action, do the following:

☐ Compile and link the files of the MyClock control.

☐ Start Test Container, select Insert OLE Control from its Edit menu, select the MyClock control, then click the OK button.

To see the Refresh() method in action, you first have to increase the value of the UpdateInterval property. Currently, the UpdateInterval property is set to 1000 milliseconds (1 second), so the MyClock control keeps updating itself every second. Therefore, when you invoke the Refresh() method, you can't see its effects.

Increase the value of the UpdateInterval property as follows:

☐ Select Properties from Test Container's View menu, click the down arrow of the Property combo box, and select the UpdateInterval property.

☐ Change the value of the UpdateInterval property to 15000, click the Apply button, then click the Close button.

☐ Observe the MyClock control and verify that the displayed time is refreshed every 15000 milliseconds (15 seconds).

Note: In the preceding steps, you changed the UpdateInterval property of the MyClock control by selecting Properties from the View menu of Test Container. You can also double-click the frame of the MyClock control, then set the UpdateInterval property in the General properties page.

Now test the Refresh() method as follows:

☐ Select Invoke Methods from the Edit menu of Test Container.

   Test Container responds by displaying the Invoke Control Method dialog box.

☐ Make sure the Name list box of the Invoke Control Method dialog box is set to Refresh, as shown in Figure 19.46, because you want to test the Refresh() method.

Figure 19.46.
The Invoke Control Method dialog box.

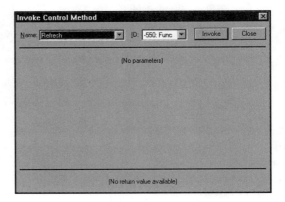

☐ Move the Invoke Control Method dialog box by dragging its title so that you can see the MyClock control.

☐ Click the Invoke button.

   Test Container responds by executing the Refresh() method of the MyClock control. As soon as you click the Invoke button, the MyClock control redraws itself. The Refresh() method you added to the MyClock control is working!

☐ Click the Invoke button several more times, and notice that after each click, the MyClock control redraws itself.

☐ Close the Invoke Control Method dialog box by clicking its Close button.

☐ Terminate Test Container by selecting Exit from the File menu.

Adding a Custom Method to the MyClock Control

In many cases, you'll want to add your own method, which isn't a standard method, to your OLE control. Such a method is called a *custom method*. In this section, you'll add a simple custom method, called Beep(), to the MyClock control. Calling this method will generate a beep.

Follow these steps to add the Beep() custom method to the MyClock control:

☐ Select ClassWizard from the View menu. In the OLE Automation tab of ClassWizard, make sure the Class name box is set to CMyClockCtrl.

☐ Click the Add Method button.

> *Visual C++ responds by displaying the Add Method dialog box.*

☐ Type Beep in the External name combo box.

As you type Beep in the External name combo box, Visual C++ automatically fills the Internal name edit box with the text Beep. The Internal name edit box specifies the function name of the MyClock control that will be executed when anyone executes the Beep() method. You'll write the code of the Beep() function soon.

☐ Set the Return type list box to void because you don't want the Beep() method to return any value.

Your Add Method dialog box should now look like Figure 19.47.

Figure 19.47.
Adding the Beep() method to the MyClock control.

☐ Click the OK button of the Add Method dialog box.

> *The ClassWizard dialog box reappears, as shown in Figure 19.48.*

As shown in Figure 19.48, the External names list now contains the method Beep preceded by the letter *M* to indicate that Beep is a method.

Figure 19.48.

The ClassWizard dialog box after you add the Beep() *custom method.*

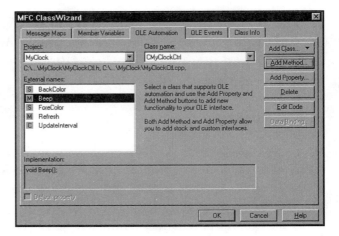

Note: When you add a custom method to a control, you can add parameters by clicking the empty item in the Parameters list of the Add Method dialog box. (Refer to Figure 19.47.)

In the preceding steps, you weren't instructed to add any parameters, but you might want to do this in future OLE projects. When a method has parameters, whoever calls the method needs to pass these parameters to the method.

☐ Close the ClassWizard dialog box by clicking its OK button.

To write the code of the Beep() method, do the following:

☐ Open the file MyClockCtl.cpp (if it's not open already) and locate the function Beep(). (Visual C++ wrote the skeleton of this function when you added the Beep() method.)

☐ Write the following code in the Beep() function:

```
void CMyClockCtrl::Beep()
{
// TODO: Add your dispatch handler code here

////////////////////////
// MY CODE STARTS HERE
////////////////////////

MessageBeep((WORD)-1);

////////////////////////
// MY CODE ENDS HERE
////////////////////////

}
```

☐ Save your work.

The code you just typed in the `Beep()` function uses the `MessageBeep()` function to beep:

```
MessageBeep((WORD)-1);
```

That's it! You have finished adding the `Beep()` custom method to the MyClock control. To verify that the MyClock control now has the `Beep()` method and to see (or rather, hear) the `Beep()` method in action, do the following:

☐ Compile and link the files of the MyClock control.

☐ Start Test Container, select Insert OLE Control from its Edit menu, select the MyClock control, then click the OK button.

Now test the `Beep()` method as follows:

☐ Select Invoke Methods from the Edit menu of Test Container.

Test Container responds by displaying the Invoke Control Method dialog box.

☐ Set the Name list box of the Invoke Control Method dialog box to `Beep`, as shown in Figure 19.49, because you want to test the `Beep()` method.

Figure 19.49.

Testing the `Beep()` *method with the Invoke Control Method dialog box.*

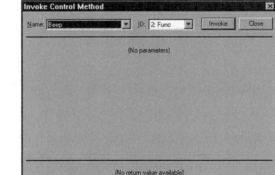

☐ Click the Invoke button several times.

As you can hear, each time you click the Invoke button, your PC beeps. The `Beep()` custom method you added to the MyClock control is working!

☐ Close the Invoke Control Method dialog box by clicking its Close button.

☐ Terminate Test Container by selecting Exit from the File menu.

Summary

In this chapter, you have customized the MyClock OLE control you created in the previous chapter. You have added stock properties, a custom property, a stock event, a custom event, a stock method, and a custom method. As you have seen, developing an OLE control with Visual C++ is easy.

Once you finish developing an OLE control, programmers of all languages that support OLE controls, such as Visual C++ and Visual Basic, can use your OLE control.

Q&A

Q **In this chapter and the previous chapter, I tested the MyClock.OCX control by using the Test Container program that comes with Visual C++. How else can I test the MyClock.OCX control?**

A You can test the MyClock.OCX control by writing a Visual C++ program that uses it. Refer to Chapter 3, "Using OLE Controls and the Component Gallery," to review how to write a Visual C++ program that uses an OLE control.

Quiz

1. What is a stock property?
2. Give an example of a stock property.
3. After adding a stock property to an OLE control, you need to write the code that makes the stock property functional.

    a. True.
    b. False.

4. What is a custom property?
5. What is a stock event?
6. After adding a stock event to an OLE control, you need to write the code that makes the stock event occur.

    a. True.
    b. False.

7. What is a custom event?
8. After adding a custom event to an OLE control, you need to write the code that makes the custom event occur.

    a. True.
    b. False.

Exercise

Add a new method to the MyClock.OCX control called SayHello() that will display a Hello message box.

Quiz Answers

1. Stock properties (or standard properties) are predefined by Visual C++. Table 19.1 lists all the stock properties you can add to an OLE control.

2. Any of the properties listed in Table 19.1, such as BackColor, is a stock property.

3. a. True.

   After you add a stock property to an OLE control, you need to write code that makes it functional. For example, after you added the two stock properties BackColor and ForeColor to the MyClock control, you wrote code in the OnDraw() function that uses these properties.

4. A custom property is a property custom-made by you. Any property that's not a stock property is a custom property. For example, the UpdateInterval property of the MyClock.OCX control is a custom property.

5. Stock events (or standard events) are predefined by Visual C++. For example, the Click event is a stock event.

6. b. False.

   After you add a stock event to an OLE control, you do NOT need to write code that makes the event occur. For example, after you added the two stock events Click and DblClick to the MyClock control, you did not have to write any code to make these events occur.

7. A custom event is an event custom-made by you. Any event that's not a stock event is a custom event. For example, the NewMinute event of the MyClock.OCX control is a custom event.

8. a. True.

   After you add a custom event to an OLE control, you need to write code that makes the event occur. You do that by calling the Fire() function of the event. For example, after you added the custom event NewMinute, you had to write code that detects when it occurs. This code fired the NewMinute event by calling the FireNewMinute() function.

19

Exercise Answer

To add the SayHello() method to the MyClock OLE control, follow these steps:

☐ Open the project workspace file (.MDP file) of the MyClock control (if it's not already open) by selecting Open Workspace from the File menu, then selecting the C:\TYVCProg\Programs\CH18\MyClock\MyClock.MDP file.

☐ Select ClassWizard from the View menu. In the OLE Automation tab of ClassWizard, make sure the Class name box is set to CMyClockCtrl and click the Add Method button.

Visual C++ responds by displaying the Add Method dialog box.

☐ Type SayHello in the External name combo box. Visual C++ automatically fills the Internal name edit box with the text SayHello.

☐ Set the Return type list box to void because you don't want the SayHello() method to return any value.

☐ Click the OK button of the Add Method dialog box.

☐ Close the ClassWizard dialog box by clicking its OK button.

To write the code of the SayHello() method, do the following:

☐ Open the file MyClockCtl.cpp and locate the function SayHello(). (Visual C++ wrote the skeleton of this function when you added the SayHello() method.)

☐ Write the following code in the SayHello() function :

```
    void CMyClockCtrl::SayHello()
{
// TODO: Add your dispatch handler code here

//////////////////////
// MY CODE STARTS HERE
//////////////////////

MessageBox("Hello!");

//////////////////////
// MY CODE ENDS HERE
//////////////////////

}
```

☐ Save your work.

That's it! You have finished adding the SayHello() custom method to the MyClock control.

To verify that the MyClock control now has the SayHello() method and to see the SayHello() method in action, do the following:

☐ Compile and link the files of the MyClock control.

☐ Start Test Container, select Insert OLE Control from its Edit menu, select the MyClock control, then click the OK button.

    Test Container responds by inserting the MyClock control.

Now test the SayHello() method as follows:

☐ Select Invoke Methods from the Edit menu of Test Container.

    Test Container responds by displaying the Invoke Control Method dialog box.

☐ Set the Name list box of the Invoke Control Method dialog box to SayHello and click the Invoke button.

As you can see, a Hello message box is displayed. The SayHello() custom method you added to the MyClock control is working!

19

20

Using the
Multimedia OLE
Control

In this chapter, you'll learn how to incorporate multimedia into your Visual C++ applications. Multimedia technology has become very popular, so most PC vendors ship their PCs with multimedia hardware, such as sound cards and speakers, already installed.

What Is Multimedia?

As its name implies, *multimedia* is a technology that lets your PC use various media. For example, a sound card is used to play and record *WAV files*, which contain bytes representing a sound recording. Typically, a sound card is also capable of playing *MIDI files,* which contain bytes representing instructions to the sound card. The sound card has special electronic circuits that interpret these instructions to produce sound. A sound card capable of playing MIDI files can emulate the sound of pianos, guitars, horns, drums, and other musical instruments. A MIDI file usually has instructions that tell the sound card to play several instruments simultaneously. In fact, a MIDI file can contain music that sounds as though a whole orchestra is playing.

Movies are another multimedia function that's frequently used. Your PC is capable of playing movies by displaying the film on the monitor and playing the movie's sound track through the sound card.

You will often find CD audio included as a multimedia feature. Most PC vendors ship their PCs with a CD-ROM drive already installed. The CD-ROM drive is used for reading *data CDs,* which contain data such as EXE files, WAV files, MIDI files, OLE files, and so on. However, most CD-ROM drives can also play *audio CDs,* like the ones you purchase in music stores. Your PC cannot read the contents of the audio CD; it can only instruct the CD-ROM drive to play the audio CD.

Note: When you're using the PC and the CD-ROM drive for playing CD audio, the PC is used as a controller—it sends instructions to the CD-ROM drive to start playing, stop playing, go forward, go backward, and so on. The PC itself has absolutely nothing to do with the playback of the CD audio. It merely serves as a controller, just as you use your TV remote control to change channels on your TV, turn the TV on and off, and so on.

Recording WAV Files

A WAV file contains a recording of sound, which can be the human voice, music, or any other type of sound recorded by the microphone. Figure 20.1 illustrates a PC with a sound card installed in it.

Figure 20.1.
Recording WAV files.

The sound is introduced to the microphone, which then converts the sound's air waves to an *analog signal,* a continuous electronic signal that represents the sound. PCs cannot deal with analog signals; they work with bytes. To accommodate this, the sound card *samples* the incoming analog signal at regular time intervals. For example, the sound card may discover that at time 0, the incoming analog signal is at a certain level. After a set time interval, the sound card again "takes a look" at the incoming analog signal and records the signal's level at that time. These samples are collected by the sound card, converted to bytes, and stored as a WAV file on the hard drive.

As you can see, it's important that the sound card takes samples frequently. If the sound card samples the analog signal every 5 minutes, for example, the resulting WAV file is useless because most of the sound information wasn't read. The frequency at which the sound card takes samples is called the *sampling rate,* measured in units of hertz (Hz). For example, a sampling rate of 11,025Hz means the sound card took samples of the incoming analog signal every 0.0000907 seconds:

```
1/11,025 = 0.000090703 seconds = 90.703 microseconds
```

Similarly, a sampling rate of 22,050Hz means the sound card took samples every 0.0000453 seconds:

```
1/22,050 = 0.000045351 seconds = 45.351 Microseconds
```

20

In Windows, typical sampling rates of WAV files are 11,025Hz, 22,050Hz, and 44,100Hz. As you might guess, the higher the sampling rate, the better the recording quality. However, the WAV file is larger when a higher sampling rate is used. For example, when recording at a sampling rate of 44,100Hz, there will be 44,100 samples saved to the WAV file each second; a sampling rate of 11,025Hz saves only 11,025 samples each second to the WAV file.

> **Note:** A sampling rate of 11,025Hz is referred to in Windows as 11 kilohertz or 11KHz (not 11.025 kilohertz); a sampling rate of 22,050Hz is 22KHz, and a sampling rate of 44,100Hz is 44KHz.

Recording Methods

There are two methods of recording: 8-bit recording and 16-bit recording. When each sample is saved as one byte (which equals 8 bits), it's called an *8-bit recording.* Some sound cards are capable of recording WAV files as *16-bit recordings,* which means each sample is saved as two bytes. When you're recording with 16-bit recordings, the sample's resolution is better because it's represented by two bytes. So naturally, 16-bit recordings produce far better quality than 8-bit recordings. However, the size of a WAV file recorded as a 16-bit recording (two-byte samples) is twice the size of an 8-bit recording (one-byte samples).

Mono and Stereo Recording

Some sound cards are capable of recording in *stereo,* as though the sound card is recording two separate WAV files. Sounds picked up by the microphone from both the left side and right side of the room are sampled. Suppose that the following samples were picked up from the left side of the room:

```
1, 15, -32, ...
```

The following samples were generated by sampling the sound from the right side of the room:

```
-4, 16, 221, ...
```

The resulting WAV file has the following samples:

```
1, -4, 15, 16, -32, 221, ......
```

Therefore, a stereo WAV file is composed of two *mono* WAV files integrated into one WAV file, making a stereo WAV file double the size of a mono WAV file.

The first few bytes of a WAV file are called the *header file.* These bytes represent information about how the WAV file was recorded (8-bit or 16-bit recording, mono or stereo recording,

sampling rate used for the recording). When playing WAV files, the sound card first reads the header file to determine how the WAV file was recorded; the samples are then sent to the speakers attached to the sound card.

Note: So which sampling rate should you use? And which recording technique should you use: 8-bit or 16-bit? And should you record mono or stereo WAV files? It all depends on your application. Just remember, the better the quality of the WAV file, the larger the file.

As a comparison, the telephone company uses technology that makes the audio quality of a regular phone conversation equivalent to an 8-bit mono recording sampled at 8,000Hz. A tape recorder's quality is equivalent to an 8-bit mono recording sampled at 22,050Hz, and a CD recording is equivalent to a 16-bit stereo WAV file sampled at 44,100Hz.

If you want to impress somebody with your singing, then use a 16-bit stereo recording sampled at 44,100Hz. But if your recording is used in a game program for producing fire noise, then an 8-bit mono recording sampled at 11,025Hz should be good enough.

Recording MIDI Files

And how do you record MIDI files? You have to connect special MIDI equipment that looks like a musical keyboard. The MIDI keyboard is attached to the MIDI port of your sound card. Most sound cards have a joystick port, and some will allow you to connect MIDI equipment to the joystick port. Figure 20.2 illustrates a MIDI keyboard connected to a sound card.

As you play the musical keyboard, the music is stored as bytes in a MIDI file, such as MyMIDI.MID. You'll then use special MIDI software that lets you edit the MIDI recording by changing the tempo, assigning different instruments to the music, increasing or decreasing the volume, and so forth. As you can see, recording MIDI files is a little more complicated than recording WAV files because it requires special MIDI hardware, MIDI software, and, most important, musical talent. It would be very interesting to hear MIDI music created by a musical genius like Mozart, had this technology been available in his time.

Movie (AVI) Files

Multimedia technology includes the playback of video files, also known as *AVI movie files*. A video file, such as MyMovie.AVI, contains the pictures (frames) and the sound track of the movie. Therefore, your PC is capable of displaying real movies, just as your TV and VCR do.

Figure 20.2.
Connecting a MIDI keyboard to the sound card.

To record a video file, you need a video capture card. (See Figure 20.3.) You can connect the video capture card to your camcorder or your VCR.

Figure 20.3.
Capturing a movie into an AVI file.

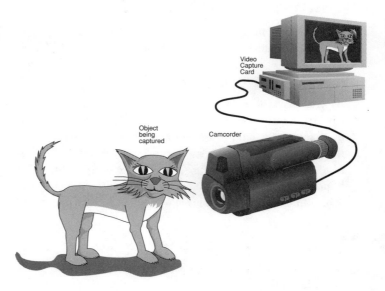

 Note: To play a movie AVI file on your PC, you don't need any special hardware—just a VGA monitor or better and an 80386 CPU or better.

Testing Your PC's Multimedia Capabilities

At the time the multimedia hardware was installed in your PC, several drivers were also installed into the hard drive. You can easily determine your PC's multimedia capabilities with the following steps:

☐ Execute the Media Player program. (The Media Player program comes with Windows 95, Windows NT, and Windows 3.1x.) In Windows 95, select Run from the Start menu and execute the C:\Windows\MPlayer.EXE program.

Windows responds by executing Media Player, and the window shown in Figure 2.4 appears.

Figure 20.4.
The window of the Media Player (MPlayer.EXE) program.

☐ Select the Device menu of Media Player.

The Device menu shown in Figure 20.5 appears.

Figure 20.5.
Media Player's Device menu.

Depending on the multimedia hardware and software installed in your PC, your Device menu may contain more or fewer items than the one in Figure 20.5. The PC on which this Media Player was executed can play Video for Windows (movie files), Sound (WAV files), MIDI Sequencer (MIDI files), and CD Audio.

> **Note:** The beauty of Windows is that it's device independent. Your Visual C++ program doesn't care what the sound card's part number or manufacturer is. As long as Windows accepted the sound card during the installation, every Windows application will be able to use this sound card. The same applies for other hardware installed on your PC.
>
> The Media Player program is provided as part of Windows so you can test your PC's multimedia capabilities. Any Windows program will be able to play the devices listed in the Media Player's Device menu.

The JukeW Program

You'll now design and execute the JukeW program, a Jukebox program that lets you select and play WAV files. Before you design the JukeW program, look at its specifications.

>
>
> **Note:** The OLE controls needed to create this chapter's programs can be downloaded from CompuServe or the Internet. See the instructions under "Free Online Code Offer" at the back of this book.

>
>
> **Note:** One of the main advantages of using Visual C++ 4.0 is that it enables you to use OLE controls, which can enhance the capabilities of your Visual C++ package.
>
> The trend in modern modular programming (such as Visual C++, Visual Basic, and other object-oriented programming languages) is to use OLE controls developed by third-party software vendors. This way, you can get an OLE control inexpensively that does the job you want. Instead of spending time developing software that's available off-the-shelf, you can concentrate your programming efforts on developing sophisticated, state-of-the-art applications quickly.
>
> In this chapter, you'll enhance the capability of Visual C++ by using various OLE controls. However, even if you don't have these OLE controls, continue reading this chapter because you'll learn what it takes to develop sophisticated Visual C++ programs.
>
> The OLE controls used in this chapter are from the TegoSoft OLE Control kit, a collection of OLE controls for Visual C++ (see the disk offer at the end of this book).

☐ When you execute the JukeW.EXE program, the window shown in Figure 20.6 is displayed.

Figure 20.6.
The window of the JukeW.EXE program.

The nine buttons above the picture of the cassette are the Multimedia control. (The cassette picture is included just to make the program look better.) Click the Play button (the third button from the left) to play the WAV file corresponding to the selected radio button.

For example, in Figure 20.6, the Reagan radio button is selected. When you click the Play button, a speech by former President Reagan is played. In Figure 20.7, the Nixon radio button is selected, so you'll hear a speech by former President Nixon when you click the Play button of the Multimedia control.

Figure 20.7.
Selecting the Nixon radio button.

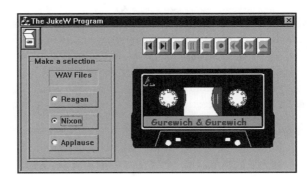

☐ You can click the Exit switch in the upper-left corner of the window to display the message box shown in Figure 20.8. If you click the message box's Yes button, the program terminates.

Figure 20.8.
The JukeW message box.

Using "Primitive" Tools in Windows 95

PC technology represents one of the most impressive advances of this century and is now used in almost every type of industry. The PC's reliability is one of the main reasons for its widespread use. The PC's main component is the *CPU integrated circuit* (also known as the CPU chip) made of millions of *transistors,* electronic components that process bits. Everything inside the CPU chip is accomplished electronically. There aren't any turning wheels or rotating motors inside the CPU chip. In fact, most PC parts are nonmoving parts—the serial port, the parallel port, the memory (RAM chips)—which is why the PC is so reliable. However, the PC isn't completely made up of nonmoving parts. For example, the hard drive is a machine with moving parts; when the CPU extracts data from the hard drive, a rotating motor positions the hard drive in the proper place. Similarly, the CD-ROM drive, the floppy drives, and the PC fan have motors and the keyboard has springs. Moving parts have a finite lifetime, and this is why PCs are not 100 percent reliable.

So why does Windows use "moving parts" as part of its graphical user interface? For example, Windows programs ask you to click a "mechanical" pushbutton and drag the thumb of a "mechanical" scrollbar; you also see the ancient hourglass used to represent the mouse's cursor when you're waiting for the PC to perform a task. These mechanical look-alike devices are used in Windows to give you the feeling that you're operating in a real environment. For example, clicking a "mechanical" pushbutton is more tangible than simply clicking on a flat square. Therefore, linking "primitive" technology, such as pushbuttons, switches, scrollbars, and hourglasses, in Windows is actually a good idea. The JukeW program illustrates such a "mechanical" device: the Exit switch on the upper-left corner of the application window shown in Figures 20.6 and 20.7.

Creating the Project of the JukeW Program

You'll now create the project of the JukeW program:

☐ Create the directory C:\TYVCProg\Programs\CH20, start Visual C++, then choose New from the File menu.

> *Visual C++ responds by displaying the New dialog box.*

☐ Select Project Workspace from the New dialog box, then click the OK button.

Visual C++ responds by displaying the New Project Workspace dialog box.

☐ Select the MFC AppWizard (exe) item from the Type list.

☐ Click the Browse button and select the C:\TYVCProg\Programs\CH20 directory.

☐ In the Name box, type JukeW, then click the Create button.

Visual C++ responds by displaying the MFC AppWizard - Step 1 dialog box.

☐ In the Step 1 window, choose the option to make the JukeW program a dialog-based application, then click the Next button.

☐ In the Step 2 window, select the About box, 3-D controls, and OLE controls, then click the Next button.

☐ In the Step 3 window, use the default settings and click the Next button.

☐ In the Step 4 window, accept the default settings. Notice that the entry in the Class name box should be CJukeWApp, then click the Finish button.

☐ In the New Project Information dialog box, click the OK button, then select Set Default Configuration from the Build menu. Select JukeW - Win32 Release in the Default Project Configuration dialog box, then click the OK button.

That's it! Visual C++ has created the JukeW project and all its associated files.

Registering the OLE Controls for the JukeW Program

Before you can use an OLE control in a program, you must first register it with Windows. First, you'll register the Switch control (TegoSW32.OCX):

☐ Make sure the TegoSW32.OCX file, part of the TegoSoft OLE Control Kit, is in your C:\Windows\System directory. You can load the TegoSW32.OCX file from CompuServe or the Internet (see "Free Online Code Offer" on the last page of this book).

☐ Select OLE Control Test Container from the Tools menu of Visual C++.

Visual C++ responds by displaying the Test Container window. (See Figure 20.9.)

☐ Select Register Controls from the File menu of the Test Container window.

Visual C++ responds by displaying the Controls Registry window. (See Figure 20.10.)

☐ Click the Register button of the Controls Registry window.

Visual C++ responds by displaying the Register Control window.

20

Figure 20.9.

The Test Container window.

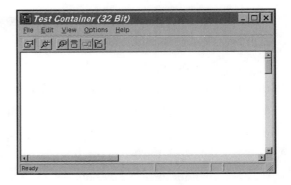

Figure 20.10.

The Controls Registry window.

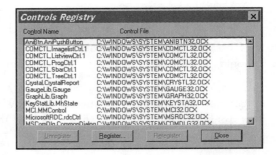

☐ Use the Register Control window to select the TegoSW32.OCX file in the C:\Windows\System directory.

> *Visual C++ responds by registering the TegoSW32.OCX control. You can scroll down the list of registered controls in the Controls Registry window and verify that the TegoSW32.OCX control is registered. (See Figure 20.11.)*

You'll now register the Multimedia control used in the JukeW program:

☐ Make sure the TegoMM32.OCX file, part of the TegoSoft OLE Control Kit, is in your C:\Windows\System directory. You can load the TegoMM32.OCX file from CompuServe or the Internet (see "Free Online Code Offer" on the back of this book).

☐ Use the same steps you did above to register the TegoMM32.OCX control.

> *Visual C++ responds by registering the TegoMM32.OCX control. You can scroll down the list of registered controls in the Controls Registry window and verify that the TegoMM32.OCX control is registered. (See Figure 20.12.)*

Figure 20.11.
*The TegoSW32.OCX
control is registered.*

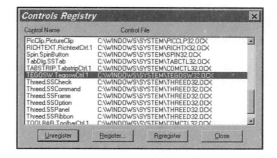

Figure 20.12.
*The TegoMM32.OCX
control is registered.*

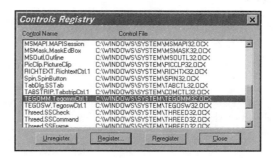

There is one more control to register, the TegoSoft Transparent Picture control:

☐ Load the TegoPic3.OCX file into your C:\Windows\System directory. (See "Free Online Code Offer" at the back of this book for instructions on loading this file.)

☐ Follow the same steps listed above to register the TegoPic3.OCX control.

> *Visual C++ responds by registering the TegoPic3.OCX control. You can scroll down the list of registered controls in the Controls Registry window and verify that the TegoPic3.OCX control is registered. (See Figure 20.13.)*

Figure 20.13.
*The TegoPic3.OCX control
is registered.*

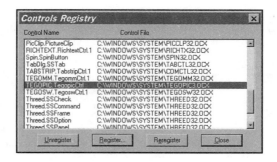

☐ Click the Close button of the Controls Registry window.

☐ Close the Test Container window.

The Visual Design of the JukeW Program

You'll now visually design the JukeW program:

☐ Select Project Workspace from the View menu, click the ResourceView tab, expand the JukeW resources item, expand the Dialog item, then double-click the IDD_JUKEW_DIALOG item.

> *Visual C++ responds by displaying the IDD_JUKEW_DIALOG dialog box in design mode.*

☐ Delete the OK button, Cancel button, and text in the IDD_JUKEW_DIALOG dialog box.

☐ Design the IDD_JUKEW_DIALOG dialog box according to Table 20.1. When you finish, it should look like the one in Figure 20.14.

Note: To place an OLE control in the dialog box you're designing, right-click the mouse on a free area in the dialog box, then select the OLE control from the Insert OLE Control dialog box that Visual C++ displays. The Insert OLE Control dialog box lists all the registered OLE controls.

Table 20.1 instructs you to set the ImagePicture and MaskPicture properties of the Transparent Picture control to Tape00.BMP and MTape00.BMP. These BMP files are included as sample BMP files with the Picture Transparent OLE control. However, you can use your own BMP pictures.

Table 20.1. The properties table of the IDD_JUKEW_DIALOG dialog box.

Object	Property	Setting
Dialog Box	**ID**	**IDD_JUKEW_DIALOG**
	Caption	The JukeW Program
	Font	System, Size 10 (General tab)
	Client edge	Checked (Extended Styles tab)
	Static edge	Checked (Extended Styles tab)

Object	Property	Setting
Switch	**ID**	**IDC_EXIT_SWITCH**
	Value	Checked (Control tab)
	Align text	Center (Styles tab)
Static Text	**ID**	**IDC_WAV_STATIC**
	Caption	WAV Files
	Sunken	Checked (Styles tab)
Radio Button	**ID**	**IDC_REAGAN_RADIO**
	Caption	Reagan
	Group	Checked
	Modal frame	Checked (Extended Styles tab)
Radio Button	**ID**	**IDC_NIXON_RADIO**
	Caption	Nixon
	Group	Not Checked
	Modal frame	Checked (Extended Styles tab)
Radio Button	**ID**	**IDC_APPLAUSE_RADIO**
	Caption	Applause
	Group	Not Checked
	Modal frame	Checked (Extended Styles tab)
Multimedia	**ID**	**IDC_MM_TEGO**
	BevelWidth	5 (Control tab)
Static Text	**ID**	**IDC_SELECT_STATIC**
	Caption	Make a selection
	Client edge	Checked (Extended Styles tab)
	Static edge	Checked (Extended Styles tab)
	Modal frame	Checked (Extended Styles tab)
Transparent Picture	**ID**	**IDC_PIC_TEGO**
	ImagePicture	Tape00.BMP (Pictures tab)
	MaskPicture	MTape00.BMP (Pictures tab)
	AutoSize	Checked (Control tab)

□ Select Test from the Layout menu to test your visual design, then click the × icon on the upper-right corner to terminate the test.

Figure 20.14.
IDD_JUKEW_DIALOG
in design mode.

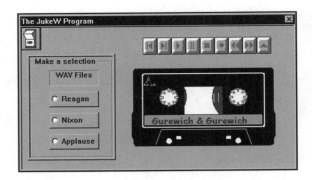

Attaching Member Variables to Controls

You'll now attach member variables to some of the controls you placed in the IDD_JUKEW_DIALOG window.

Attaching a Member Variable to the Switch OLE Control

You'll use Class Wizard to attach a member variable to the Exit Switch control you placed in the IDD_JUKEW_DIALOG dialog box.

☐ Right-click the Switch control.

Visual C++ responds by displaying a pop-up menu.

☐ Select Class Wizard from the pop-up menu.

Visual C++ responds by displaying the MFC ClassWizard dialog box. (See Figure 20.15.)

Figure 20.15.
The MFC ClassWizard
dialog box.

☐ Select the Member Variables tab, select IDC_EXIT_SWITCH from the Control IDs list, and click the Add Variable button.

Visual C++ responds by displaying the message box shown in Figure 20.16.

Figure 20.16.
Trying to add a member variable to an OLE control not yet used by the program.

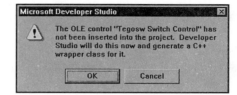

☐ Click the message box's OK button.

Visual C++ responds by displaying the Confirm Classes dialog box shown in Figure 20.17.

Figure 20.17.
The Confirm Classes dialog box.

☐ Click the OK button of the Confirm Classes dialog box.

Visual C++ responds by displaying the Add Member Variable dialog box.

Note: When you attach a member variable to a control, such as the scrollbar, pushbutton, radio button, and other standard controls in the Tools window of Visual C++, the sequence of windows shown in Figures 20.16 and 20.17 isn't displayed. These windows appear only when you add the first member variable of an OLE control.

☐ Set the Add Member Variable dialog box as follows:

Variable name:	m_ExitButton
Category:	Control
Variable type:	CTegosw

☐ Click the OK button.

Visual C++ responds by displaying the MFC ClassWizard dialog box.

☐ Click the OK button of the MFC ClassWizard dialog box.

That's it! The m_ExitButton variable is associated with the IDC_EXITSWITCH control.

Attaching a Member Variable to the Multimedia Control

Use ClassWizard to attach the following member variable to the Multimedia control you placed in the IDD_JUKEW_DIALOG dialog box:

☐ Set the Add Member Variable dialog box as follows:

Variable name:	m_TegoMM
Category:	Control
Variable type:	CTegomm

Attaching a Member Variable to the Radio Buttons

You'll now use ClassWizard to attach a member variable to the radio buttons. During the visual design, you checked the Group property of the Reagan radio button, but not for the rest of the radio buttons. This means you attach a member variable to the Reagan radio button only.

☐ Set the Add Member Variable dialog box as follows:

Variable name:	m_WAVSelected
Category:	Value
Variable type:	int

Now the m_WAVSelected variable is a member variable associated with the three radio buttons you placed in the IDD_JUKEW_DIALOG window. This finishes the visual design of the JukeW program.

☐ Compile, link, and execute the JukeW program to check your progress at this point.

Visual C++ responds by executing JukeW.EXE.

Notice that the Exit switch has its red lamp ON because you checked its Value property during design time. (Refer back to Table 20.1.) Naturally, the Exit switch isn't functional because you

haven't attached any code yet. To terminate the JukeW program so you can start attaching code, click the × icon.

Attaching Code to the *Click* Event of the Exit Switch

You'll now attach code to the Click event of the Exit switch.

☐ Use ClassWizard to create the OnClickExitSwitch() function for the Click event of IDC_EXIT_SWITCH.

☐ Edit the code in the OnClickExitSwitch() function. When you finish, the function should look like the following:

```
void CJukeWDlg::OnClickExitButton()
{
// TODO: Add your control notification handler code here

/////////////////////////
// MY CODE STARTS HERE
/////////////////////////

if (m_ExitButton.GetValue() == FALSE)
    {
    int Answer =
        MessageBox("Are you sure you want to quit?",
                   "Exit Jukebox",
                    MB_ICONQUESTION+MB_YESNO);

    if (Answer == IDYES)
        {
        OnOK();
        }
    else
        {
        m_ExitButton.SetValue(TRUE);
        }

    }


/////////////////////////
// MY CODE ENDS HERE
/////////////////////////

}
```

The code you typed is executed whenever you click the Exit switch. An if statement is used to determine the current Value property of the switch:

```
if (m_ExitButton.GetValue() == FALSE)
    {
```

```
//// This code is executed if the Value
//// property of the switch is FALSE

}
```

The Value property of the switch has two settings. When the Value property of the switch is TRUE, the switch's red lamp is ON. When the Value property of the switch is FALSE, the switch's red lamp is OFF. The Value property of the switch toggles between TRUE and FALSE whenever you click the switch.

The code under the preceding if statement will be executed if the Value property of the switch is FALSE—that is, you've clicked the switch from ON to OFF. When you turn the switch OFF, a message box is displayed:

```
int Answer =
   MessageBox("Are you sure you want to quit?",
            "Exit Jukebox",
            MB_ICONQUESTION+MB_YESNO);
```

The message box asks if you want to quit. It has two buttons: Yes and No. The returned value from the MessageBox() function is stored in the Answer variable. If you click the Yes button of the message box, Answer is updated with IDYES; if you click the No button, Answer is updated with IDNO.

An if…else statement is then executed to examine the Answer variable:

```
if (Answer == IDYES)
   {
   OnOK();
   }
else
   {
   m_ExitButton.SetValue(TRUE);
   }
```

If Answer is equal to IDYES (you clicked the Yes button), the OnOK() function is executed, which terminates the program. If Answer is not equal to IDYES (you clicked the No button), the code under the else is executed:

```
m_ExitButton.SetValue(TRUE);
```

This code sets the Value property of the switch to TRUE, which turns the switch ON.

☐ Compile, link, and execute the JukeW program.

☐ Click the Exit switch and verify that a message box is displayed.

☐ Click the No button of the message box and make sure the program does not terminate and the Exit switch returns to its ON state.

☐ Click the Exit switch again, then click the Yes button of the message box to terminate the program.

Editing the *OnInitDialog()* Function

You'll now write the code that's executed when you start the program.

☐ Use ClassWizard to access the OnInitDialog() function. (See Figure 20.18.)

Figure 20.18.
*Using ClassWizard to access
the* OnInitDialog()
function.

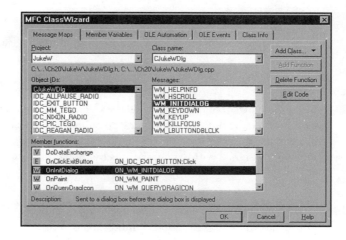

☐ Add code to the OnInitDialog() function as follows:

```
BOOL CJukeWDlg::OnInitDialog()
{

    ...
    ...
    ...

    // TODO: Add extra initialization here

    /////////////////////////
    // MY CODE STARTS HERE
    /////////////////////////

    // Make the Reagan option button selected.
    m_WAVSelected = 0;
    UpdateData(FALSE);

    // Open a session for 8Reagan.WAV.
    m_TegoMM.SetDeviceType("WaveAudio");
    m_TegoMM.SetFileName("8Reagan.WAV");
    m_TegoMM.SetCommand("Open");

    /////////////////////////
    // MY CODE ENDS HERE
    /////////////////////////
```

```
    return TRUE;
    // return TRUE  unless you set the focus to a control
    }
```

The code you added selects the Reagan radio button:

```
// Make the Reagan option button selected.
m_WAVSelected = 0;
UpdateData(FALSE);
```

The three radio buttons should be placed in the following sequence:

```
Reagan
Nixon
Applause
```

During the visual design, you checked the Group property of the Reagan radio button, but not the other two radio buttons. So the Reagan radio button is considered radio button 0, the Nixon radio button is 1, and the Applause radio button is 2. You may want to check that the radio buttons are assigned with sequential IDs by following these steps:

☐ Select Resource Symbols from the View menu.

   Visual C++ responds by displaying the Resource Symbols dialog box.

☐ Browse through the Resource Symbols dialog box and make sure the values for the radio buttons' IDs are sequential. For example, if the value of the Reagan radio button's ID is 1002, then the value of the Nixon radio button's ID should be 1003, and the value of the Applause radio button's ID should be 1004.

Therefore, the code you typed in the `OnInitDialog()` function causes the Reagan radio button to be selected when you start the JukeW program.

Opening a WAV Session

You then open a WAV session as follows:

```
// Open a session for 8Reagan.WAV.
m_TegoMM.SetDeviceType("WaveAudio");
m_TegoMM.SetFileName("8Reagan.WAV");
m_TegoMM.SetCommand("Open");
```

Assign the `WaveAudio` string to the DeviceType property of the Multimedia control:

```
m_TegoMM.SetDeviceType("WaveAudio");
```

The preceding statement means that the Multimedia control will play WAV files.

> **Note:** To play WAV files with the Multimedia control, set the DeviceType
> property as follows:
>
> ```
> m_TegoMM.SetDeviceType("WaveAudio");
> ```
>
> The Multimedia control is capable of playing other types of multimedia files. For
> example, to play MIDI files, set the DeviceType property as follows:
>
> ```
> m_TegoMM.SetDeviceType("Sequencer");
> ```
>
> To play AVI movie files, set the DeviceType property as follows:
>
> ```
> m_TegoMM.SetDeviceType("AVIVideo");
> ```
>
> To play audio CD, set the DeviceType property as follows:
>
> ```
> m_TegoMM.SetDeviceType("CDAudio");
> ```

You then tell the Multimedia control the name of the multimedia file:

```
m_TegoMM.SetFileName("8Reagan.WAV");
```

This statement will cause the Multimedia control to play the 8Reagan.WAV file. Since you
didn't specify the directory for the 8Reagan.WAV file, the program assumes it's in the same
directory the JukeW program is executed from. Therefore, you must copy the 8Reagan.WAV
file to the directory the program is executed from:

☐ Make sure the 8Reagan.WAV file is in the C:\TYVCProg\Programs\CH20\JukeW
   directory, which is the directory the JukeW program is executed from when you choose
   Execute JukeW from the Build menu.

Once you finish designing the JukeW program, you won't need Visual C++ any more. The
JukeW.EXE program will be generated in the C:\TYVCProg\Programs\CH20\JukeW\Release
directory. If you use the Windows Explorer or choose Run from Windows to execute the
JukeW.EXE program, the program is executed from that directory. Therefore, to execute the
JukeW program with these methods, you must copy the WAV file into that same directory.

☐ Make sure the 8Reagan.WAV file is in the C:\TYVCProg\Programs\CH20\JukeW\
   Release directory.

If you decide later to move the JukeW program to another directory, don't forget to copy the
WAV files into the same directory as the JukeW.EXE program.

Note: The FileName property holds the name of the multimedia file that will be played. For example, to play the 8Reagan.WAV file, use the following statement:

```
m_TegoMM.SetFileName("8Reagan.WAV");
```

To play the MyMIDI.MID file, use the following statement:

```
m_TegoMM.SetFileName("MyMIDI.MID");
```

To play the MyMovie.AVI file, use the following statement:

```
m_TegoMM.SetFileName("MyMovie.AVI");
```

When playing audio CD, there's no need to set the FileName property of the Multimedia control.

The next statement opens the WAV session:

```
m_TegoMM.SetCommand("Open");
```

If the WAV session was opened successfully, some of the buttons of the Multimedia control become available (are not dimmed). The Play button is the third from the left. If the WAV session was opened successfully, the Play button becomes available, and you can click it to play the WAV file.

Note: There are several reasons why a WAV session would not open successfully. It may be that the WAV file was not found or that a sound card is not installed. You could check whether the WAV session was opened successfully by examining the Error property of the Multimedia control as follows:

```
m_TegoMM.SetCommand("Open");
short OpenResult = GetError();
```

If OpenResult is equal to 0, it means that the Open command was executed successfully.

Note that by examining the Error property, you can determine whether the PC has a sound card installed.

Even though you haven't finished writing the JukeW program, take a look at your code in action:

☐ Select Build JukeW.EXE from the Build menu.

Visual C++ responds by compiling and linking the JukeW program.

☐ Make sure the 8Reagan.WAV file is in the directory the JukeW.EXE program is executed from.

☐ Select Execute JukeW.EXE from the Build menu.

The window of the JukeW.EXE program appears with the buttons of the Multimedia control available.

☐ Click the Play button to play the WAV file.

☐ Click the Rewind button (the leftmost button) to rewind the WAV file.

☐ Click the Play button again to play the WAV file.

☐ Experiment with the JukeW program, then click the Exit switch to terminate the program.

Automatic Rewinding of the WAV File

In the previous section, you were instructed to click the Rewind button. Can you write code that automatically senses the entire WAV file was played, then rewinds the WAV file? Sure you can! Here is how you do that:

☐ Use ClassWizard to create the `OnDoneMmTego()` function associated with the `Done` message of the IDC_MM_TEGO Multimedia control. (See Figure 20.19.)

Figure 20.19.
Using ClassWizard to create the `OnDoneMmTego()` function.

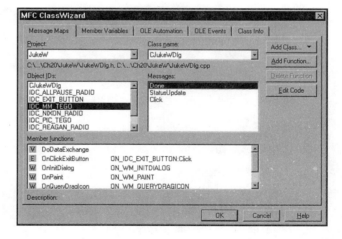

20

☐ Enter the following code to edit the `OnDoneMmTego()` function:

```
void CJukeWDlg::OnDoneMmTego()
{
// TODO: Add your control notification handler code here

//////////////////////////
// MY CODE STARTS HERE
//////////////////////////
```

```
if (m_TegoMM.GetPosition() == m_TegoMM.GetLength() )
   {
   m_TegoMM.SetCommand("Prev");
   }

////////////////////////
// MY CODE ENDS HERE
////////////////////////

}
```

After issuing the Play command, a playback is in progress. The playback can be stopped for several reasons, such as a Stop command being issued or the WAV file reaching its end. The code you typed uses an if statement to examine the reason for the Done event. The if statement checks to see whether the current position of the WAV file is equal to the length of the file:

```
if (m_TegoMM.GetPosition() == m_TegoMM.GetLength() )
   {

   ////The entire WAV file was played

   }
```

If the entire WAV file was played, the code under the if statement is executed:

```
m_TegoMM.SetCommand("Prev");
```

The Prev command rewinds the WAV file to the beginning of the file.

Note: You can make the Multimedia control invisible (typically in the OnInitDialog() function) as follows:

```
m_TegoMM.ShowWindow(SW_HIDE);
```

Instead of using the Multimedia control's buttons, you can use your own buttons. During design time, you'll place several buttons, such as the Rewind button, that will control the multimedia file with the following code:

```
m_TegoMM.SetCommand("Prev");
```

Every time you click the Rewind button, the WAV file will be rewound.

Similarly, when you place the Play button, you'll attach the following code to the Click event of the Play button:

```
m_TegoMM.SetCommand("Play");
```

Your Stop button will execute the following statement when its Click event occurs:

```
m_TegoMM.SetCommand("Stop");
```

SAMS
Sams
Learning
Center
SAMS
PUBLISHING

The advantage of using your own buttons is that you can make the program more attractive and easier to use. For example, you can attach pictures to the surface of the Teg3DP32.OCX button control, which also makes your pushbutton look three-dimensional.

Although you haven't finished writing the JukeW program, use the following steps to check how the Rewind button is working:

☐ Compile, link, and execute the JukeW.EXE program.

Visual C++ responds by executing the JukeW program.

☐ Click the Play button to play the WAV file.

☐ Wait until the entire WAV file is played, then click the Play button again.

As you can see, the program automatically rewinds the WAV file.

☐ Experiment with the JukeW program, then click the Exit switch to terminate the program.

Attaching Code to the Radio Buttons

You'll now attach code to the Click events of the radio buttons so that you'll hear the corresponding WAV file when you select a radio button. When you select the Reagan radio button, you'll hear a speech by former President Reagan; when the Nixon radio button is selected, you'll hear a speech by former President Nixon; and when the Applause radio button is selected, you'll hear applause.

☐ Use ClassWizard to create the OnReaganRadio() function for the Click event of the Reagan radio button.

☐ Edit the OnReaganRadio() function so that it looks like this:

```
void CJukeWDlg::OnReaganRadio()
{
// TODO: Add your control notification handler code here


/////////////////////////
// MY CODE STARTS HERE
/////////////////////////

// Make the Reagan option button selected.
m_WAVSelected = 0;
UpdateData(FALSE);
```

20

```
// Open a session for 8Reagan.WAV.
m_TegoMM.SetDeviceType("WaveAudio");
m_TegoMM.SetFileName("8Reagan.WAV");
m_TegoMM.SetCommand("Open");


////////////////////////
// MY CODE ENDS HERE
////////////////////////

}
```

The code you typed is executed whenever you click the Reagan radio button. This code prepares the Multimedia control for playing the 8Reagan.WAV file.

☐ Use ClassWizard to create the OnNixonRadio() function for the Click event of the Nixon radio button.

☐ Edit the code in the OnNixonRadio() function:

```
void CJukeWDlg::OnNixonRadio()
{
// TODO: Add your control notification handler code here

////////////////////////
// MY CODE STARTS HERE
////////////////////////


// Make the Nixon option button selected.
m_WAVSelected = 1;
UpdateData(FALSE);

// Open a session for 8Nixon.WAV.
m_TegoMM.SetDeviceType("WaveAudio");
m_TegoMM.SetFileName("8Nixon.WAV");
m_TegoMM.SetCommand("Open");


////////////////////////
// MY CODE ENDS HERE
////////////////////////

}
```

The code you typed is similar to the code you typed in the OnReaganRadio() function, except that now you open the 8Nixon.WAV file. It assumes that the 8Nixon.WAV file is in the directory the JukeW.EXE program is executed from, so copy the 8Nixon.WAV file to the following directories:

☐ Copy the 8Nixon.WAV file to the C:\TYVCProg\Programs\CH20\JukeW directory.

☐ Copy the 8Nixon.WAV file to the C:\TYVCProg\Programs\CH20\JukeW\Release directory.

You'll now attach code to the Click event of the Applause radio button:

☐ Use ClassWizard to create the OnApplauseRadio() function for the Click event of the Applause radio button.

☐ Edit the code of the OnApplauseRadio() function:

```
void CJukeWDlg::OnAllpauseRadio()
{
// TODO: Add your control notification handler code here

/////////////////////////
// MY CODE STARTS HERE
/////////////////////////


// Make the Applause option button selected.
m_WAVSelected = 2;
UpdateData(FALSE);

// Open a session for Applaus2.WAV.
m_TegoMM.SetDeviceType("WaveAudio");
m_TegoMM.SetFileName("Applaus2.WAV");
m_TegoMM.SetCommand("Open");


/////////////////////////
// MY CODE ENDS HERE
/////////////////////////

}
```

The code you typed is similar to the code in the OnReaganRadio() function, but now you're opening the Applaus2.WAV file. The code assumes that the Applaus2.WAV file is in the directory the JukeW.EXE program is executed from, so copy the Applaus2.WAV file to the following directories:

☐ Copy the Applaus2.WAV file to the C:\TYVCProg\Programs\CH20\JukeW directory.

☐ Copy the Applaus2.WAV file to the C:\TYVCProg\Programs\CH20\JukeW\Release directory.

☐ Compile, link, and execute the JukeW.EXE program.

Visual C++ responds by executing the JukeW.EXE program.

☐ Experiment with the JukeW.EXE program. In particular, make sure the correct WAV file is played when you click the radio buttons. For example, when you click the Reagan radio button, then click the Play button, you should hear the Reagan speech.

☐ Click the Exit switch to terminate the JukeW program.

20

Summary

In this chapter, you have learned that multimedia technology lets you incorporate various media into your Visual C++ programs.

In the Q&A, Quiz, and Exercises of this chapter, you'll learn about producing CDs, manipulating WAV files, playing through the PC speaker, and other multimedia-related topics.

Q&A

Q I installed a sound card that came with software for playing WAV files. This software works well. However, I don't see the Sound item in Media Player's Device menu. Should I insist on seeing Sound as a menu item?

A Yes. The only way you can make sure that every Windows program will be capable of using your multimedia program is by making sure that particular multimedia device appears in the Device menu of Media player.

Q How can I record WAV files?

A You can record into the WAV file with the JukeW.EXE program. The fourth button from the right on the Multimedia control is the Record button. You can also place a button in the window, set the Caption to Record, and attach the following code to the Click event of the Record button:

```
m_TegoMM.SetCommand("Record");
```

When you're recording with the JukeW program, the sampling rate used for the recording is the same sampling rate used to record the currently loaded WAV file (8Reagan.WAV, 8Nixon.WAV, or Applaus2.WAV). Additional code is needed to actually save the WAV file with the new recording into the hard drive.

Q Can I write code to play back only a section of a WAV file?

A Sure you can! Set the From property of the Multimedia control to the byte location at the beginning of the section you want to play. Set the To property to the byte location at the end of the section you want to play. Then issue the Play command. The WAV file will be played from the location indicated by the From property to the location indicated by the To property. You can indicate the From and To properties in units of bytes as well as milliseconds. (You set the units by setting the TimeFormat property of the Multimedia control to Samples or Milliseconds.)

Quiz

1. A sampling rate of 44,100Hz means that the WAV file was recorded with a sample taken every _____ seconds.

2. Before you play a multimedia file, what steps must you perform?

3. To play MIDI files, you must have the musical talent that Mozart had and you must install other MIDI equipment.

    a. True
    b. False

4. To record MIDI files, you must have musical talent and special MIDI equipment.

    a. True
    b. False

5. What do you need to create a data CD?

6. What do you need to record an audio CD?

Exercises

1. Create the JukeM.EXE program (a MIDI Jukebox program). It should be similar to the JukeW program, except it plays MIDI files instead of WAV files.

2. Create the JukeA.EXE program (an AVI Jukebox program). It should be similar to the JukeW program, but it will play movie files instead of WAV files.

3. Create the JukeC.EXE program, a CD Audio Jukebox program that plays audio CDs.

Quiz Answers

1. 1/44,100 = 0.0000226757 seconds = 22.6757 microseconds.

2. Before playing a multimedia file, perform the following steps:

    ☐ Set the DeviceType property of the Multimedia control.

    ☐ Set the FileName property of the Multimedia control.

    ☐ Issue the Open command to the Multimedia control.

3. b. All you need is a sound card capable of playing MIDI files. (Most sound cards are capable of playing MIDI files).

4. a. To record MIDI files, you need special MIDI equipment (and of course, you need to have musical talent).

5. To produce your own data CD, you need a special CD-ROM drive capable of writing into a *recordable CD,* a special CD that you can write data into. These recordable CDs cost about $10.00 each. The special CD-ROM drive you need costs anywhere between $1,200 to $7,000. There are currently two types of recordable CDs:

    • Write-once recordable CD. You can write only once into this type of CD. If you make a mistake, you have to throw away the CD. Also, you have to write

the data into the CD in "one shot." You cannot write data, then stop the process, and add data later.

- Multisession CD. You can write data into the CD several times.

Recordable CD technology is still evolving; currently, only the more expensive equipment can generate a reliable CD. Keep in mind that a multisession CD can be read only by CD-ROM drives designed to read multisession CDs.

Since recordable CDs are so expensive, you should use them only for generating the master CD. Once you've tested the master CD, send it to production where mass CDs are produced from your master recordable CD. Typically, the vendor who produces the mass CDs for you will charge you a one-time setup charge of about $500.00, and each CD will cost you about $1.50. It is important to note that the vendor producing the CDs doesn't require you to submit a master CD; he or she will accept backup tapes and even disks to make a master CD. A word of advice: Ask your vendor to submit one CD for testing before going ahead with mass production.

6. Basically, the same answer as the one for Question 5. With most of these special CD-ROM drives capable of writing into recordable CDs, you can plug in a recorded audio signal into the recordable CD.

Exercise Answers

1. Basically, the JukeM program is the same as the JukeW program. When you're designing the JukeM program, make sure to set the DeviceType to Sequencer, as follows:

```
m_TegoMM.SetDeviceType("Sequencer");
```

Set the FileName property of the Multimedia control to play the MIDI file. For example, to play the MySong.MID file, use the following statement:

```
m_TegoMM.SetFileName("MySong.MID");
```

Naturally, the radio buttons' captions should contain the names of the MIDI songs. Also, you can set a new picture for the window of the JukeM program, such as the one shown in Figure 20.20.

2. The JukeA program is basically the same as the JukeW program. When you're designing the JukeA program, make sure to set the DeviceType to AVIVideo:

```
m_TegoMM.SetDeviceType("AVIVideo");
```

Set the FileName property of the Multimedia control to play the AVI file. For example, use the following statement to play the MyMovie file:

```
m_TegoMM.SetFileName("MyMovie.AVI");
```

Figure 20.20.
The window of the JukeM program.

The radio buttons' captions should display the names of the AVI movies. You can also use a new picture for the window of the JukeA program, like the one shown in Figure 20.21.

Figure 20.21.
The window of the JukeA program.

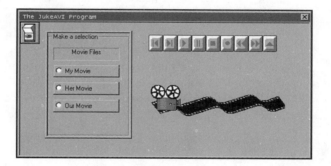

The Multimedia control has the hWndDisplay property, which contains the hWnd of the window you want the movie to be displayed in (hWnd is the window's handle assigned by Windows assigned). If you don't set the hWndDisplay property, the movie will be displayed in the window where the Multimedia control is placed. However, displaying the movie in another window means you can move and size the window any way you want.

3. The JukeC program is the same as the JukeW program, except that the DeviceType property is set to CDAudio:

```
m_TegoMM.SetDeviceType("CDAudio");
```

There's no need to set the FileName property when you're playing Audio CD. You also don't need radio buttons, but you can add a new picture for the program's window. (See Figure 20.22 for an example.)

Figure 20.22.
The window of the JukeC program.

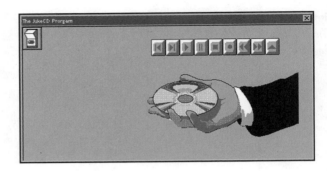

Some of the Multimedia controls are available only when a certain media is used. For example, the rightmost button is the Eject button, which is available only when you play audio CDs. Clicking the Eject button causes the CD-ROM drive to eject the audio CD. However, when you're playing WAV files, it doesn't make sense to eject the WAV file, so the Eject button is automatically dimmed.

The second and third buttons from the right are the Forward and Backward buttons. These buttons serve different functions when different media are used. When you're playing audio CDs, the Forward and Backward buttons move the current position of the audio CD from track to track. When you're playing AVI movie files, each click on the Backward or Forward button displays the next or previous frame of the movie. When you're playing WAV files, the Backward and Forward buttons are dimmed.

Note: Here are a few ideas for further practicing with multimedia technology:

☐ Use the common dialog box OLE control to let the user select any file (WAV, MIDI, AVI).

☐ Depending on the particular file the user selected, set the DeviceType property of the Multimedia control and issue the Open command.

This program will serve as a general jukebox that lets the user play any multimedia file.

☐ To make the program more interesting, display animation during the playback. For example, use the TegoAnim3.OCX control (see "Free Online Code Offer" at the back of this book) to display a cassette rotating the magnetic tape during the playback of the WAV files. Try another type of animation during the playback of the MIDI file.

☐ Create other "gadgets" in your multimedia applications. Users expect multimedia applications to be clever, easy to use, and attractive. In short, multimedia technology is a lot of fun!

21

Games and 3-D
Virtual Reality

In this chapter, you'll learn about the fascinating subject of 3-D virtual reality. In particular, you'll learn how to design and create a 3-D virtual reality program (a DOOM-like program) with Visual C++.

What Is Virtual Reality?

Virtual reality technology enables you to interact with a virtual environment. Unlike a regular program that reacts to simple user actions such as clicking buttons, scrolling scroll bars, and so on, a virtual reality program makes you feel as though you're in a real-world environment.

How does the virtual reality program let you feel as though you're working in a real-world environment? By letting you "travel" in 3-D pictures. The virtual reality program displays a 3-D picture, and you can use the mouse (or the keyboard) to travel in the 3-D picture. To add a feeling of reality to the program, the virtual reality program also typically plays sound through an installed sound card. A typical virtual reality program also moves *sprites* in the 3-D world. So as you travel in the 3-D picture, you meet other people, animals, monsters, machines, and so on.

Virtual reality can be used for serious applications, such as flight simulation. The Air Force and the airline companies train pilots, navigators, and flight engineers by having students practice on a virtual reality flight-simulation program. A professional flight-simulation program displays an exact replica of the aircraft instruments. The student takes off, lands, and flies the aircraft by setting the virtual instruments. The program "flies" the plane according to the student's actions. Naturally, using a virtual plane for practicing has a great advantage over practicing with a real plane because the mistakes the student makes during training don't cause fatal accidents. Also, flying a virtual plane means there's no need to spend money on fuel and replacement parts. The instructor can program the virtual reality program to simulate various weather conditions, mechanical and electrical faults, and so on.

Virtual reality technology is used in many other industries. For example, a real estate agency in California can sell a house to a person in New York by sending the potential client the virtual representation of the house. The client in New York can "travel" in the house, "look" through the windows, and get a sense of what the house is like. Virtual reality technology is also used in the medical industry, where surgeries are performed on virtual "patients."

One of the most popular applications of virtual reality is 3-D PC games. You can construct a 3-D virtual reality game where your user travels in buildings, floors, halls, and fields. During the traveling, you can see monsters, UFOs, and other good and bad creatures. You can shoot at the enemies (and the enemies can shoot at you).

In this chapter, you'll learn how to create a 2-D drawing of a floor. Your program will convert the 2-D drawing to a 3-D picture, then let you use the mouse and keyboard to travel in your 3-D floor.

Note: One of the main advantages of using Visual C++ 4 is that it enables you to use OLE controls to enhance the capabilities of your off-the-shelf Visual C++ package.

The trend in modern modular programming (such as Visual C++, Visual Basic, and other object-oriented programming languages) is to use OLE controls developed by third-party software vendors. For an inexpensive price, you can get an OLE control that does the job you are trying to accomplish. Instead of spending time on developing software that's available off-the-shelf, you concentrate your programming efforts on your specific application. This way, you can develop sophisticated state-of-the-art technology applications in a short time.

In this chapter, you'll enhance the capability of Visual C++ by using a sophisticated OLE control from the TegoSoft OLE Control Kit, a collection of OLE controls for Visual C++ (see disk offer at the end of this book). The OLE control used in this chapter can be downloaded from CompuServe or the Internet (see "Free Online Code Offer" on the last page of this book).

What Is the 3-D Floor OLE Control?

The 3-D Floor OLE control enables you to write a 3-D virtual reality program that displays a three-dimensional environment and lets you move around in this environment. As you move in the 3-D environment, depending on your movements, the 3-D Floor OLE control displays the appropriate 3-D views.

This OLE control is called the 3-D Floor control because it enables you to design 3-D floors with walls and rooms. First, you design a two-dimensional representation of the 3-D floor. The control then uses your 2-D design to display the corresponding 3-D floor.

The 3-D Floor OLE control includes a sprite mechanism that enables you to add stationary objects, such as chairs and tables, as well as moving objects, such as dogs, cats, and monsters, to the 3-D environment. Your program enables you to interact with the sprites. For example, if you bump into a chair, the program can move the chair.

The 3-D Floor OLE control uses WinG technology. WinG (pronounced "win-gee") enhances the standard graphics capabilities of Windows. Because the 3-D Floor OLE control uses WinG technology, you must first install WinG in your Windows system before you can execute and write programs that use the 3-D Floor OLE control. To install WinG in your Windows system, do the following.

21

☐ Copy all the files from the \TYVCProg\WinG directory from the online code into your \WINDOWS\SYSTEM directory.

The VR (3-D Virtual Reality) Program

In the following sections, you'll write a program called VR that illustrates how to use the 3-D Floor OLE control. Before you start writing the VR program, execute a copy of the program from the online code for this chapter, which you downloaded from the Internet or Compuserve (see the back of this book).

☐ If you haven't installed WinG in your Windows operating system, do so now. Copy all the files \TYVCProg\WinG directory to your \WINDOWS\SYSTEM directory.

☐ Execute the VR.EXE program from the \TYVCProg\CH21\Release directory.

The main window of the VR program appears, as shown in Figure 21.1.

Figure 21.1.
The main window of the VR program.

The VR program places you in a virtual 3-D room. You are currently facing the room's exit door. You can use the right-arrow key and the left-arrow key to rotate your view of the room. When you press the right-arrow key, you rotate clockwise; when you press the left-arrow key, you rotate counterclockwise. To see the right-arrow and left-arrow keys in action, do the following:

☐ Make sure the Num Lock key on your keyboard is on.

☐ Press the left-arrow key several times.

Every time you press the left-arrow key, you rotate counterclockwise about 6 degrees. Figure 21.2 shows a snapshot of your 3-D view as you rotate counterclockwise.

Figure 21.2.
The view after rotating counterclockwise.

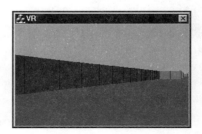

Note: The left-arrow and right-arrow keys enable you to rotate your view of the room from the point where you're standing. You don't move forward or backward—you simply rotate.

☐ Now press the left-arrow key and hold it down for several seconds.

As you can see, you rotate counterclockwise continuously. After rotating in a counterclockwise direction, you might feel a little dizzy, so now rotate in a clockwise direction.

☐ Press the right-arrow key several times or press and hold down the right-arrow key to rotate clockwise.

So far, you have only rotated around the point where you're standing. To move forward or backward in the same direction you're facing, use the up-arrow and down-arrow keys. The up-arrow key moves you forward and the down-arrow key moves you backward in your current viewing direction. To see the up-arrow and down-arrow keys in action, do the following:

☐ Use the left-arrow key to change your direction until you are facing a corner of the room.

☐ Press the up-arrow key several times to move closer to the corner.

Every time you press the up-arrow key, you move closer to the corner. Figure 21.3 shows the view as you move closer to the corner.

Figure 21.3.
Moving closer to the corner.

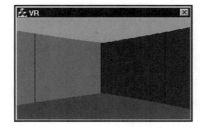

In a similar manner, you can use the down-arrow key to move backward in your current viewing direction.

Note: You can move forward and backward by pressing the up-arrow and down-arrow keys. Of course, when you reach an obstacle like a wall, you cannot "get into" the wall.

> **Note:** In the preceding steps, you moved around by using the four arrow keys. Another way to move around is by dragging the mouse. Dragging the mouse to the left and right is the equivalent of pressing the left-arrow and right-arrow keys; dragging the mouse up and down is the equivalent of pressing the up-arrow and down-arrow keys.
>
> Using the mouse to move around is not as easy as using the arrow keys because the mouse is more sensitive than the keyboard. However, when you use the mouse, you can move faster.

You should know you are not alone on this floor. There are two other objects here. One object is a robot—the jogging robot—who runs around the main hall of this floor, and the other object is another robot—the exercising robot—who is preparing for a battle in another room on this floor.

You'll soon have a chance to meet these robots. Before you move to another room, take a look at Figure 21.4. This figure shows a two-dimensional map of this floor.

Figure 21.4.

A two-dimensional map of the floor in the VR program.

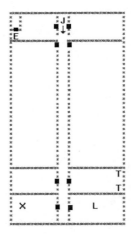

As shown in Figure 21.4, the VR program's floor is made up of several rooms. The exit door for each of these rooms connects to the main hall. Each exit door is marked as a black square. As you can see, the room at the upper-left corner of the floor has a small sub-room.

Figure 21.4 shows several uppercase letters on the map that represent various points on the floor that have objects (moving objects and stationary objects). Point X is the point you're standing at when the program starts. Point E represents the exercising robot. Point J (with the down-arrow next to it) represents the jogging robot who runs up and down the hall. The two T points represent two trees. Point L represents a light fixture (a chandelier) attached to the ceiling.

 **Note:** When you write your own 3-D virtual reality program, designing the program's floor (or floors) is an important part of the program's development. For example, you can develop a 3-D virtual reality game in which the objective—the secret of the game—is to map the floor. Once you map the floor by traveling through it, you can score more points.

Now that you are familiar with the VR program's map, you can travel throughout the floor:

☐ Use the arrow keys (or the mouse) to move toward the exit door of the room.

As you move closer to the exit door, you can see the inside of the room on the other side of the hall more clearly. You can see that this new room has a chandelier attached to the ceiling.

☐ Exit to the hall and turn left so that you are facing the far end of the hall. (See Figure 21.5.)

Figure 21.5.
Facing the far end of the hall.

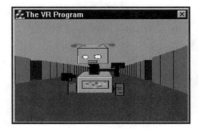

As mentioned earlier, a jogging robot runs up and down the main hall from the far end to the point where you are now standing. Once the jogging robot reaches the other side of the hall, the program places him back at the far end of the hall and he runs toward you again.

In Figure 21.6, you can see a small image of the jogging robot running in your direction from far away.

Figure 21.6.
The jogging robot running toward you from far away.

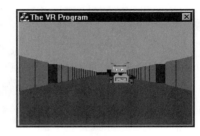

21

Once the jogging robot is close to you (as in Figure 21.5), you can see the details of his appearance. Notice that the jogging robot is a sprite picture—it has transparent regions. For example, the area around the robot's neck is a transparent region, so you can see behind the jogging robot in this area.

Also notice that the program uses two-frame animation for the robot's movements. In each frame, the robot's feet and hands are in different positions. The two pictures (frames) that make up the animation of the jogging robot are shown in Figure 21.7.

Figure 21.7.
The two frames that animate the robot moving toward you.

Frame 1 of the robot animation when the robot moves toward you

Frame 2 of the robot animation when the robot moves toward you

☐ Once the jogging robot passes you, make a 180-degree turn (by pressing the left-arrow or right-arrow key) so you can see the back of the robot as he is running away from you. (See Figure 21.8.)

Figure 21.8.
The robot running away from you.

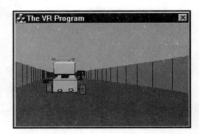

The animation for the robot as he moves away from you is also made up of two frames, shown in Figure 21.9.

As shown in the two-dimensional map of the floor, the upper-left room of the floor has an *E* representing the point where the exercising robot is. Figure 21.10 shows the exercising robot as you move closer to it.

The animation for the exercising robot consists of the same two frames shown back in Figure 21.7.

The two robots look innocent and harmless, but they are really evil and must be destroyed!

Figure 21.9.

The two frames that animate the robot moving away from you.

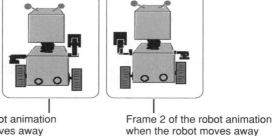

Frame 1 of the robot animation
when the robot moves away

Frame 2 of the robot animation
when the robot moves away

Figure 21.10.

Moving toward the exercising robot.

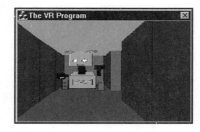

☐ Move to the room where the exercising robot is. Consult Figure 21.4 to locate the upper-left room where the E is placed, then move to this room.

☐ Press the spacebar to shoot the exercising robot.

The VR program responds by destroying the robot. (See Figure 21.11.) The robot is on fire!

Figure 21.11.

The destroyed robot.

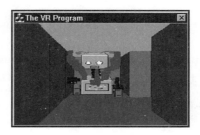

☐ To restore the robot, press the spacebar again.

You can enhance the animation of the jogging robot, the exercising robot, and the exploding robot by adding more frames to make the action more smooth and realistic. However, for the sake of simplicity, only two frames for each animation have been included.

So far you've seen the jogging robot and the exercising robot, but there are still three more sprites for you to inspect: two trees and a chandelier.

☐ Move into the room that contains the two trees. As shown back in Figure 21.4, the second room from the lower-right corner has two points marked T to represent where the trees are. Figure 21.12 shows these two trees as you move toward them.

Figure 21.12.
Moving toward the two trees.

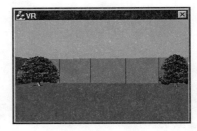

The last sprite on this floor is the light fixture (a chandelier). As shown in Figure 21.4, the lower-right room has a point marked L to represent the light fixture.

☐ Move into the room where the light fixture is located.

Figure 21.13 shows a snapshot of the 3-D view as you move toward the light fixture.

Figure 21.13.
Moving toward the light fixture.

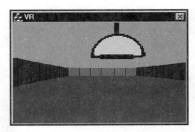

The light fixture is an example of a *soft sprite,* which means you can walk through it. On the other hand, the jogging robot sprite, the exercising robot sprite, and the tree sprites are *hard sprites.* You cannot walk through hard sprites; you have to walk around them. The light fixture sprite is a soft sprite because you should be able to walk through it. Once you are exactly under the light fixture, you do not see it. As you'll see when you write the code for the VR program, making a sprite either soft or hard is easy.

☐ Keep experimenting with the VR program by moving to the various rooms.

☐ Terminate the VR program by clicking the × icon.

Registering the TegFlr32.OCX Control

The VR program uses the TegFlr32.OCX control. Follow these steps to add this control to the project:

☐ Create the C:\TYVCProg\Programs\CH21 directory and start Visual C++.

Note: In the following steps you'll register the TegFlr32.OCX control. Before performing the following steps, make sure the TegFlr32.OCX file is in the \WINDOWS\SYSTEM directory. You can copy the TegFlr32.OCX file from the \TYVCProg\OCX32 directory to your \WINDOWS\SYSTEM directory.

☐ Select OLE Control Test Container from the Tools menu.

   Visual C++ responds by displaying the Test Container window.

☐ Select Register Controls from the File menu of the Test Container window.

   Visual C++ responds by displaying the Control Registry window, where all the currently registered controls are listed.

☐ Search for the FLOOR.FloorCtrl item in the list of registered controls. If it isn't in the list, click the Register button, then select the TegFlr32.OCX file from the \WINDOWS\SYSTEM directory.

Figure 21.14 shows the Controls Registry window with the FLOOR.FloorCtrl OLE control listed as a registered control.

Figure 21.14.
The Controls Registry window.

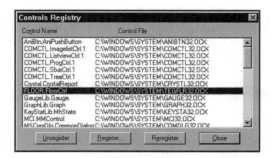

☐ Click the Close button of the Controls Registry window.

   Visual C++ responds by displaying the Test Container window.

☐ Select Exit from the File menu of the Test Container window.

21

The Visual Design of the VR Program

You'll now visually design the window of the VR program:

☐ Start Visual C++, then select New from the File menu. Select the Project Workspace item, then click the OK button.

Visual C++ responds by displaying the New Project Workspace window.

☐ Make sure the Type is set to MFC AppWizard (exe) and set the Name box to VR.

☐ Click the Browse button, select the C:\TYVCProg\CH21 directory, then click the Create button.

Visual C++ responds by displaying the MFC AppWizard - Step 1 window.

☐ In the Step 1 window, select the "Dialog based" radio button, then click the Next button.

☐ In the Step 2 window, select the OLE Controls check box because the 3-D VR program uses an OLE control. Click the Next button.

☐ In the Step 3 window, accept the default settings and click the Next button.

☐ In the Step 4 window, click the Finish button.

Visual C++ responds by displaying the New Project Information window.

☐ Click the OK button of the New Project Information window.

Visual C++ responds by creating the project and all of its associated files.

☐ Select Set Default Configuration from the View menu, then select the VR - Win32 Release item from the Default Project Configuration dialog box.

Adding the 3-D Floor Control to the Tools Window

You've already registered the 3-D Floor control (TegFlr32.OCX). You'll now add this OLE control to the Tools window of the project:

☐ Select Project Workspace from the View menu. Click the ResourceView tab, expand the VR resources item, expand the Dialog item, and finally double click the IDD_VR_DIALOG item.

Visual C++ responds by displaying the IDD_VR_DIALOG dialog box in design mode.

The 3-D Floor control is not in the Controls window that's used for placing controls in the IDD_VR_DIALOG dialog box.

☐ Select Component from the Insert menu.

Visual C++ responds by displaying the Component Gallery window.

☐ Click the OLE Controls tab of the Component Gallery window.

☐ Use the scrollbar of the Component Gallery window to search for the TegoSoft 3-D Floor Control icon, then click it. (See Figure 21.15.)

Figure 21.15.
The Component Gallery window.

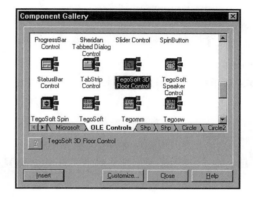

☐ Click the Insert button of the Component Gallery window.

Visual C++ responds by displaying the Confirm Classes window.

☐ Click the OK button of the Confirm Classes window.

☐ Click the Close button of the Component Gallery window.

The Controls window now contains the tool icon of the 3-D Floor control. (See Figure 21.16).

☐ Save your work.

Figure 21.16.
The Controls window with the 3-D Floor control.

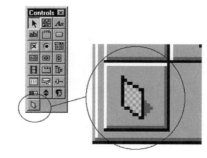

The Visual Design of the VR Program's Main Window

You'll now design the main window of the VR program, the IDD_VR_DIALOG dialog box:

☐ Delete the OK button, Cancel button, and TODO text.

☐ Set up the IDD_VR_DIALOG dialog box according to Table 21.1. When you finish, it should look like Figure 21.17.

Table 21.1. The properties table of the IDD_VR_DIALOG dialog box.

Object	Property	Setting
Dialog Box	**ID**	**IDD_VR_DIALOG**
	Caption	The VR Program
	Client edge	Checked (Extended Styles tab)
	Static edge	Checked (Extended Styles tab)
3-D Floor	**ID**	**IDC_FLOORCTRL1**

Figure 21.17.
The IDD_VR_DIALOG dialog box in design mode.

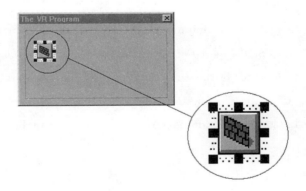

Follow these steps to test your visual design:

☐ Select Test from the Layout menu.

> *Visual C++ responds by displaying the IDD_VR_DIALOG dialog box as it will appear during runtime. The 3-D Floor control is invisible during runtime.*

In the following sections, you'll write code that makes the 3-D Floor control visible, displays a 3-D picture in the room, and lets you travel in the 3-D picture.

☐ Click the × icon on the upper-right corner of the dialog box.

Visual C++ responds by closing the dialog box.

☐ Compile, link, and execute VR.EXE to make sure you performed the steps correctly.

Visual C++ responds by executing the VR program. Again, the 3-D Floor is invisible at this point.

☐ Click the × icon of the VR program's window to terminate the program.

Preparing a Floor File for the VR Program

Before you start writing the code for the VR program, you first have to prepare a floor file. A *floor file* is a text file containing a 2-D representation of a floor. Once you have prepared the floor file, you can use the 3-D Floor control to write a program that displays the floor file in three dimensions and enables you to move around in it.

A floor file typically has the file extension .FLR (for example, MyFloor.FLR). Because a floor file is a regular text file, you can use any text editor to create and edit it, such as WordPad in Windows 95. To see what a floor file looks like, do the following:

☐ The online code contains the Floor50.FLR file in the \TYVCProg\CH21\VR\Release directory.

☐ Use any text editor to open the Floor50.FLR file.

Figures 21.18 and 21.19 show the WordPad program with the Floor50.FLR file open. The Floor50.FLR file is displayed in two figures because its contents do not fit in one WordPad screen. To see the bottom section of the Floor50.FLR file in WordPad, you have to scroll through the file's contents.

Figure 21.18.

Viewing the Floor50.FLR file in WordPad (upper section).

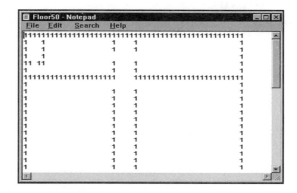

Figure 21.19.
Viewing the Floor50.FLR file in WordPad (lower section).

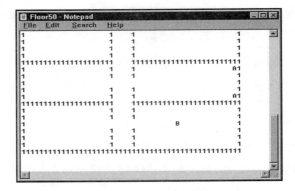

As you can see, a floor file is very simple. The 1 character represents a solid cell in the floor, and the space character (blank) represents an empty cell. Other characters in the floor files (for example, A, B) represent sprites.

**Note:** When you view a floor file with a word processor such as Word for Windows, you should set the font to Courier or Courier New so that all the characters of the FLR file are the same size.

When creating your own FLR file, save the file as a text file.

The following examples illustrate how to create floor files:

To create a floor file representing a floor with only one room 15 cells wide and 10 cells high, type the following text in the floor file:

```
111111111111111
1             1
1             1
1             1
1             1
1             1
1             1
1             1
1             1
111111111111111
```

The following text represents a floor with two rooms. The floor is 20 cells wide and 10 cells high.

```
111111111111111111111
1                    1
1                    1
1                    1
1                    1
11111111 1111111111
1                    1
1                    1
1                    1
111111111111111111111
```

As you can see, there is an opening between the two rooms because you want to be able to move from one room to the other. Of course, the preceding text is not the only way to create two rooms. You can rearrange the locations and sizes of the rooms in any way you wish.

> **Note:** The 3-D Floor OLE control enables you to place new cells in the floor or remove cells from the floor during runtime. This feature enables you to write game programs that contain secret openings. When you hit a secret cell, your program can remove the cell so you can move into the secret room.

The following text represents a floor 18 cells wide and 10 cells high. The floor contains four rooms:

```
111111111111111111
1       1        1
1       1        1
1       1        1
1       1        1
1111 11111111 1111
1       1        1
1                1
1       1        1
111111111111111111
```

In addition to 1s and spaces, a floor file may also contain nonnumeric characters (for example, A, a, B, b, C, c, and so on). These characters represent sprites. The pictures of these sprites are set during runtime from within your program. For example, your program can set the A sprite to a picture of a chair. Therefore, all cells in the FLR file that contain the letter *A* display a chair.

Now that you know how a floor file is constructed, inspect the Floor50.FLR file with your text editor. (See Figures 21.18 and 21.19.) When you inspect the Floor50.FLR file, notice the following items:

- The floor in the Floor50.FLR file is 50 cells wide and 50 cells high.

- The floor file contains several rooms. Each of these rooms is connected to the main hall of the floor.

21

- The upper-left room contains a small sub-room in it.
- The lower-right room contains the letter B in the middle. (Refer to Figure 21.19.) The B represents a sprite. As you will see later in this chapter, the code you write will define Sprite B as a picture of a light fixture. When you move into the lower-right room, you will see a light fixture in the middle of the room.
- The room above the lower-right room contains the letter A in two of its corners. (Refer to Figure 21.19.) The A represents a sprite. As you will see, the code you write will define Sprite A as a picture of a tree. When you move into the room with the two A sprites, you will see two trees.

Entering the Code of the VR Program

In the following sections, you'll write code for the VR program by using the Floor50.FLR floor file.

Attaching a Variable to the 3-D Floor Control

During the visual design, you placed a 3-D Floor control in the dialog box. You'll now attach a variable to this control, IDC_FLOORCTRL1:

☐ Select ClassWizard from the View menu. In the Member Variables tab of ClassWizard, make the following selection:

Class name:	CVRDlg
Control ID:	IDC_FLOORCTRL

☐ Click the Add Variable button and set the variable as follows:

Variable name:	m_vr
Category:	Control
Variable type:	CFloor

☐ Click the OK button of the Add Member Variable dialog box, then click the OK button of ClassWizard.

In the following sections you'll use the m_vr variable you attached to the IDC_FLOORCTRL control to write code that accesses the properties of the control.

Attaching Code to the *WM_INITDIALOG* Event

The WM_INITDIALOG event occurs whenever the IDD_VR_DIALOG dialog box is created—when the VR program starts. The code you'll attach to the WM_INITDIALOG event opens the Floor50.FLR floor file.

☐ Select ClassWizard from the View menu. In the Message Maps tab of ClassWizard, select the following event:

Class name:	CVRDlg
Object ID:	CVRDlg
Message:	WM_INITDIALOG

☐ Click the Edit Code button of ClassWizard.

Visual C++ responds by opening the file VRDlg.cpp with the function OnInitDialog() *ready for you to edit.*

☐ Write the following code in the OnInitDialog() function:

```
BOOL CVRDlg::OnInitDialog()
{
...
...
...

// TODO: Add extra initialization here

////////////////////////
// MY CODE STARTS HERE
////////////////////////

int iOpenResult;
CString Message;

// Open the Floor50.FLR file.
m_vr.SetFileName ("Floor50.FLR");
m_vr.SetHWndDisplay((long)m_hWnd);
m_vr.SetNumOfRows  (50);
m_vr.SetNumOfCols  (50);

iOpenResult = m_vr.Open();

// If FLR file could not be opened,
// terminate the program.
if (iOpenResult != 0)
   {

   Message = "Unable to open file: " + m_vr.GetFileName();

   Message = Message +"\n";
   char ErrorNumber[10];
   Message = Message + "Error Code: " +
             itoa(iOpenResult,ErrorNumber,10);
   MessageBox (Message);

   OnOK();

   }
```

21

```
// Set the initial user's position and viewing angle.
m_vr.SetX(4 * m_vr.GetCellWidth() );
m_vr.SetY(4 * m_vr.GetCellWidth() );
m_vr.SetAngle(0);

// Set the colors of the walls, ceiling, and floor.
m_vr.SetWallColorA (7);     // White
m_vr.SetWallColorB (4);     // Red
m_vr.SetCeilingColor (11);  // Light Cyan
m_vr.SetFloorColor (2);     // Green
m_vr.SetStripeColor (0);    // Black

/////////////////////////
// MY CODE ENDS HERE
/////////////////////////

return TRUE;
// return TRUE  unless you set the focus to a control
}
```

☐ Save your work.

The first two statements you typed declare two local variables:

```
int iOpenResult;
CString Message;
```

iOpenResult serves as a variable that will hold the result of success or failure in opening the FLR file. Message is a string that will hold the error message displayed if an error occurs during the opening of the FLR file.

The next five statements are responsible for opening the Floor50.FLR floor file. The first statement sets the FileName property of the 3-D Floor control to the name of the Floor50.FLR file:

```
m_vr.SetFileName ("Floor50.FLR");
```

The FileName property specifies which floor file you want to open.

Note: You set the FileName property of the 3-D Floor control to Floor50.FLR. This means that it's assumed that the Floor50.FLR file is in the same directory the VR.EXE program is executed from. For example, if the VR.EXE file is in the C:\TYVCProg\Programs\CH21\VR\Release directory, then the Floor50.FLR file must reside in this directory.

When executing the VR program from within Visual C++ (by selecting Execute VR.EXE from the Build menu), the C:\TYVCProg\Programs\CH21\VR\Release

The second statement you typed in the OnInitDialog() function sets the HWndDisplay property of the 3-D Floor control to the window handle of the IDD_VR_DIALOG dialog:

```
m_vr.SetHWndDisplay((long)m_hWnd);
```

The HWndDisplay property specifies the handle of the window where the 3-D graphics are displayed. Because you want the 3-D graphics to be displayed in the IDD_VR_DIALOG dialog box, you set the HWndDisplay property to IDD_VR_DIALOG's window handle.

The next two statements set the NumOfRows and NumOfCols properties of the 3-D Floor control to 50:

```
m_vr.SetNumOfRows  (50);
m_vr.SetNumOfCols  (50);
```

The NumOfRows property specifies the height of the floor file in units of cells, and the NumOfCols property specifies the width.

Finally, the Floor50.FLR file is opened by using the 3-D Floor control's Open() method:

```
iOpenResult = m_vr.Open();
```

The Open() method opens the floor file specified by the 3-D Floor control's FileName property. The returned value of the Open() method specifies whether the 3-D Floor control was able to open the floor file. If the floor file was opened successfully, then the returned value of the Open() method is 0. Otherwise, the returned value is a nonzero integer that specifies an error code. Notice that in the preceding statement, the returned value of the Open() method is assigned to the local variable iOpenResult.

An if statement is then executed to examine the value of iOpenResult:

```
// If FLR file could not be opened,
// terminate the program.
if (iOpenResult != 0)
   {
   Message = "Unable to open file: " + m_vr.GetFileName();

   Message = Message +"\n";
   char ErrorNumber[10];
```

21

```
Message = Message + "Error Code: " +
          itoa(iOpenResult,ErrorNumber,10);
MessageBox (Message);

OnOK();

}
```

So if the FLR file was not opened successfully, the `Message` string is constructed and the `MessageBox()` function is executed to display the message. The message tells you that the floor file could not be opened, and the error number (as reported by `iOpenResult`) is displayed.

Note: `GetFileName()` returns the current setting of the FileName property. For example, if you set the FileName property to `MyFloor.FLR`, `GetFileName()` returns `MyFloor.FLR`.

Note: To open a floor file, you first have to set the FileName, HWndDisplay, NumOfRows, and NumOfCols properties of the 3-D Floor control and then use the `Open()` method.

The NumOfRows and NumOfCols properties must be set to the correct height and width of the floor file. If you do not set the NumOfCols and NumOfRows properties to the correct values, the `Open()` method will fail.

The returned value of the `Open()` method specifies whether the `Open()` method was successful. If the returned value is equal to `0`, the floor file was successfully opened. If the returned value is not `0`, the `Open()` method failed.

The next three statements set your initial position and viewing direction:

```
// Set the initial user's position and viewing angle.
m_vr.SetX(4 * m_vr.GetCellWidth() );
m_vr.SetY(4 * m_vr.GetCellWidth() );
m_vr.SetAngle(0);
```

Your position is set by setting the 3-D Floor control's X and Y properties, which determine the x-y coordinate of your position in units of pixels. The coordinate for the lower-left corner is x=0, y=0. In the preceding code, both the X property and Y property are set to the following:

```
4 * m_vr.GetCellWidth()
```

The `GetCellWidth()` method returns the CellWidth property of a cell in units of pixels. Therefore, the preceding code places you at the cell fourth from the bottom and fourth from the left side of the floor. If you inspect the bottom section of the Floor50.FLR file (see Figure 21.19), you'll see that this cell is in the floor's lower-left room. Therefore, when you start the program, you will be in the floor's lower-left room.

The 3-D Floor control's Angle property specifies your viewing direction in units of degrees. The Angle property can be set to an integer in the range of 0 through 359. When you want to face the right side of the floor, set the Angle property to 0. In the preceding code you set the Angle property to 0 because when you start the program, you want to face the exit door in the lower-left room.

Note: When the program starts, you have to be placed somewhere in the floor. To do this, set the 3-D Floor control's X and Y properties.

Make sure to place yourself in an empty cell. You don't want to be placed inside a solid wall!

The last five statements in the `Form_Load()` procedure set the colors for the walls, the ceiling, and the floor:

```
// Set the colors of the walls, ceiling, and floor.
m_vr.SetWallColorA (7);    // White
m_vr.SetWallColorB (4);    // Red
m_vr.SetCeilingColor (11); // Light Cyan
m_vr.SetFloorColor (2);    // Green
m_vr.SetStripeColor (0);   // Black
```

The WallColorA property specifies the color of the vertical walls; the WallColorB property specifies the color of the horizontal walls; the CeilingColor property specifies the color of the ceiling; the FloorColor property specifies the color of the floor, and the StripeColor property specifies the color of the vertical stripes that separate cells. Table 21.2 lists all the possible values you can specify for the 3-D Floor control's color properties.

Table 21.2. The values assigned to the 3-D Floor control's color properties.

Value	Color
0	Black
1	Blue
2	Green

continues

Table 21.2. continued

Value	Color
3	Cyan
4	Red
5	Magenta
6	Yellow
7	White
8	Gray
9	Light blue
10	Light green
11	Light cyan
12	Light red
13	Light magenta
14	Light yellow
15	Bright white

The code you just wrote in the OnInitDialog() function is responsible for opening the floor file. In the following section, you'll write the code that actually displays the 3-D floor.

Attaching Code to the *WM_PAINT* Event

The WM_PAINT event occurs whenever there is a need to redraw the program's window (for example, when the program starts). Whenever there's a need to redraw the window, the program should draw the current 3-D view of the floor. You'll now write the code that accomplishes this task:

☐ Select ClassWizard from the View menu. In the Message Maps tab of ClassWizard, select the following event:

Class name:	CVRDlg
Object ID:	CVRDlg
Message:	WM_PAINT

☐ Click the Edit Code button of ClassWizard.

Visual C++ responds by opening the file VRDlg.cpp with the function OnPaint() *ready for you to edit.*

☐ Write the following code in the `OnPaint()` function:

```
void CVRDlg::OnPaint()
{
  if (IsIconic())
      {
      ...
      ...
      ...
      }
  else
      {

//////////////////////////
// MY CODE STARTS HERE
//////////////////////////

// Display the 3-D view.
m_vr.Display3D();

//////////////////////////
// MY CODE ENDS HERE
//////////////////////////

    CDialog::OnPaint();
    }
}
```

☐ Save your work.

The code you typed is made up of a single statement that displays the current 3-D view of the floor by using the 3-D Floor control's `Display3D()` method:

```
m_vr.Display3D();
```

The `Display3D()` method displays the current 3-D view of the floor based on the values of the X, Y, and Angle properties. (Recall you initialized the floor control's X, Y, and Angle properties in the `OnInitDialog()` function.)

To see the code you have written in action, follow these steps:

☐ Select Build VR.EXE from the Build menu.

Visual C++ responds by compiling and linking the VR program.

☐ Execute the VR program. However, do not execute the program by selecting Execute VR.EXE from the Build menu. Instead, use Windows Explorer to double-click the VR.EXE file in the C:\TYVCProg\CH21\VR\Release directory, or use the Run feature of Windows 95 to execute the VR.EXE program from the C:\TYVCProg\CH21\ VR\Release directory. (Remember that you can't use Execute VR.EXE from the Build menu because the Floor50.FLR file must be in the same directory the VR.EXE program is executed from.)

21

As you can see, the program displays a 3-D view of the floor. (See Figure 21.20.) The program places you in the floor's lower-left room facing the exit door.

Figure 21.20.

The initial 3-D view displayed by the VR program.

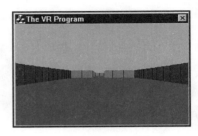

Of course, if you try to move around the floor by pressing the arrow keys or using the mouse, nothing happens because you haven't written the code that accomplishes this task.

☐ Terminate the VR program by clicking the × icon.

In the following section, you'll write the code that enables you to move around the floor.

Attaching Code to the *WM_KEYDOWN* Event

You'll now attach code to the WM_KEYDOWN event of the program's window. This code enables you to move around the floor by using the arrow keys.

☐ Select ClassWizard from the View menu. In the Message Maps tab of ClassWizard, select the following event:

> Class name: CVRDlg
> Object ID: CVRDlg
> Message: WM_KEYDOWN

☐ Click the Add Function button, then click the Edit Code button.

> *Visual C++ responds by opening the file CVRDlg.cpp with the function* OnKeyDown() *ready for you to edit.*

☐ Write the following code in the OnKeyDown() function:

```
void CVRDlg::OnKeyDown(UINT nChar, UINT nRepCnt,
    UINT nFlags)
{
// TODO: Add your message handler code here and/or call default

/////////////////////////
// MY CODE STARTS HERE
/////////////////////////
```

```
switch (nChar)
    {

    case 39:
        // Right key (39) was pressed.
        m_vr.SetAngle (m_vr.GetAngle() - 6);
        break;

    case 102:
        // 6 key (102) was pressed.
        m_vr.SetAngle (m_vr.GetAngle() - 6);
        break;

    case 37:
        // Left key (37) was pressed.
        m_vr.SetAngle (m_vr.GetAngle() + 6);
        break;

    case 100:
        // 4 key (100) was pressed.
        m_vr.SetAngle (m_vr.GetAngle() + 6);
        break;

    case 38:
        // Up key (38) was pressed.
        m_vr.Advance (40);
        break;

     case 104:
        // 8 key (104) was pressed.
        m_vr.Advance (40);
        break;

     case 40:
        // Down key (40) was pressed.
        m_vr.Advance (-40);
        break;

     case 98:
        // 2 key (98) was pressed.
        m_vr.Advance (-40);
        break;

    }

// Display the 3D view.
m_vr.Display3D();

////////////////////////
// MY CODE ENDS HERE
////////////////////////

CDialog::OnKeyDown(nChar, nRepCnt, nFlags);
}
```

☐ Save your work.

The OnKeyDown() function is automatically executed whenever you press a key while the window of the VR program is active. The nChar parameter of the OnKeyDown() function specifies which key you have pressed.

The code in the OnKeyDown() function uses a switch statement to evaluate the nChar parameter:

```
switch (nChar)
     {
      ...
      ...
      ...
     }
```

If you press the right-arrow key (or the 6 key), then the statement under the first case (or the second case) is executed. Here are the first and second case statements:

```
case 39:
     // Right key (39) was pressed.
     m_vr.SetAngle (m_vr.GetAngle() - 6);
     break;

case 102:
     // 6 key (102) was pressed.
     m_vr.SetAngle (m_vr.GetAngle() - 6);
     break;
```

Note: The numeric keypad can serve two purposes. For example, if the Num Lock key on your keyboard is on, the 6 key serves as the number 6. If the Num Lock key is off, the 6 key serves as the right-arrow key.

The statements under the case statements decrease the Angle property of the 3-D Floor control by 6 degrees. If the Angle property is set to a value less than 0, the 3-D Floor control automatically adjusts the value of the Angle property to a value from 0 to 359. For example, if the current value of the Angle property is 2, then the preceding statement sets the Angle property to 2-6=-4. Because -4 equates to 360-4=356, the Angle is set to 356 degrees. If the current angle is 30, then the statement under the case sets the Angle property to 30-6=24.

In a similar manner, if you press the left-arrow key (or the 4 key), the following case statements are executed:

```
case 37:
     // Left key (37) was pressed.
     m_vr.SetAngle (m_vr.GetAngle() + 6);
     break;

case 100:
     // 4 key (100) was pressed.
     m_vr.SetAngle (m_vr.GetAngle() + 6);
     break;
```

The Angle property is increased by 6 degrees. Again, because the Angle property can have a value from 0 to 359, the 3-D Floor control will automatically set the proper value for the Angle property. For example, if the current Angle is 30, GetAngle() will return 30. Increasing the Angle property by 6 degrees means that the angle is set to 30+6=36 degrees. If the Angle property is equal to 356, increasing the angle by 6 means that Angle is set to 2 (because 356+6=362, which is the same as 2 degrees).

If you press the up-arrow key (or the 8 key), then the following case statements are executed:

```
case 38:
    // Up key (38) was pressed.
    m_vr.Advance (40);
    break;

case 104:
    // 8 key (104) was pressed.
    m_vr.Advance (40);
    break;
```

These statements use the 3-D Floor control's Advance() method to advance your position by 40 pixels in the current viewing direction.

If you press the down-arrow key (or the 2 key), then the statement under the following case is executed:

```
case 40:
    // Down key (40) was pressed.
    m_vr.Advance (-40);
    break;

case 98:
    // 2 key (98) was pressed.
    m_vr.Advance (-40);
    break;
```

This statement uses the 3-D Floor control's Advance() method to advance you by -40 pixels in the current viewing direction; you're moved 40 pixels backward in the current viewing direction.

The last statement in the OnKeyDown() function uses the 3-D Floor control's Display3D() method to display the new 3-D view corresponding to your new position:

```
m_vr.Display3D ();
```

To see the code you attached to the WM_KEYDOWN event in action, follow these steps:

☐ Select Build VR.EXE from the Build menu.

☐ Use Windows Explorer or the Run feature of Windows 95 to execute the VR program (do not use the Build menu).

☐ Make sure that the Num Lock key on your keyboard is on.

☐ Use the arrow keys to move to various locations in the floor to make sure they work properly.

☐ Terminate the VR program by clicking the × icon.

> **Note:** As you move around the floor, notice that there aren't any sprites. Later in this chapter, you'll write the code that places sprites in the floor.

Attaching Code to the *WM_MOUSEMOVE* Event

At this point, you can use the arrow keys to move in the 3-D floor. You'll now attach code to the WM_MOUSEMOVE event so you can use the mouse to move in the 3-D floor.

Dragging the mouse to the right or left produces the same result as pressing the right-arrow or left-arrow key; dragging the mouse up or down produces the same result as pressing the up-arrow or down-arrow key.

☐ Select ClassWizard from the View menu. In the Message Maps tab of ClassWizard, select the following event:

Class name:	CVRDlg
Object ID:	CVRDlg
Message:	WM_MOUSEMOVE

☐ Click the Add Function button of ClassWizard, then click the Edit Code button.

> *Visual C++ responds by opening the file VRDlg.cpp with the function* OnMouseMove() *ready for you to edit.*

☐ Write the following code in the OnMouseMove() function:

```
void CVRDlg::OnMouseMove(UINT nFlags, CPoint point)
{
// TODO: Add your message handler code
// here and/or call default

/////////////////////////
// MY CODE STARTS HERE
/////////////////////////

static int PrevX, PrevY;


// If none of the mouse buttons is pressed down,
// terminate this procedure.
```

```
   if (!nFlags)
      {
      return;
      }

   // Change the user's position according to the
   // mouse movement.

   if (point.y < PrevY )
      m_vr.Advance (50);

   if (point.y > PrevY )
      m_vr.Advance (-50);

   if (point.x < PrevX )
       m_vr.SetAngle (m_vr.GetAngle() + 3);

   if (point.x > PrevX )
      m_vr.SetAngle (m_vr.GetAngle() - 3);

   // Display the 3D view.
   m_vr.Display3D();

   // Update PrevX and PrevY for next time.
   PrevX = point.x;
   PrevY = point.y;


   ///////////////////////
   // MY CODE ENDS HERE
   ///////////////////////

   CDialog::OnMouseMove(nFlags, point);
   }
```

☐ Save your work.

The first statement in the OnMouseMove() function declares two static variables:

```
static int PrevX, PrevY;
```

These variables are declared as static; therefore, they do not lose their values when the procedure terminates. As you'll soon see, PrevX and PrevY are used by the OnMouseMove() function to store the previous mouse position.

The next statement is an if statement that evaluates the value of the parameter nFlags of the OnMouseMove() function:

```
// If none of the mouse buttons is pressed down,
// terminate this procedure.

if (!nFlags)
   {
   return;
   }
```

21

The code under the `if` statement is executed if none of the mouse's buttons was pressed during the mouse movement; the `OnMouseMove()` procedure terminates.

If, however, a mouse button is currently pressed because you're dragging the mouse, then the remaining statements in the `OnMouseMove()` function are executed.

The next block of code is a series of four `if` statements:

```
// Change the user's position according to the
// mouse movement.

if (point.y < PrevY )
   m_vr.Advance (50);

if (point.y > PrevY )
   m_vr.Advance (-50);

if (point.x < PrevX )
   m_vr.SetAngle (m_vr.GetAngle() + 3);

if (point.x > PrevX )
   m_vr.SetAngle (m_vr.GetAngle() - 3);
```

These `if` statements change your position in the 3-D floor based on the new position of the mouse. If you drag the mouse upward, then `point.y` (the current y position of the mouse provided as one of the parameters of the `OnMouseMove()` function) is less than `PrevY` (the previous y-position of the mouse). If this is the case, the first `if` condition is satisfied and this statement is executed:

```
m_vr.Advance (50);
```

This statement uses the 3-D Floor control's `Advance()` method to move you 50 pixels forward in the current viewing direction.

If you drag the mouse downward, then `point.y` (the current y-position of the mouse) is greater than `PrevY` (the previous y-position of the mouse). If this is the case, the second `if` condition is satisfied and this statement is executed:

```
m_vr.Advance (-50);
```

This statement uses the 3-D Floor control's `Advance()` method to move you 50 pixels backward in the current viewing direction.

If you drag the mouse to the left, then `point.x` (the current x-position of the mouse) is less than `PrevX` (the previous x-position of the mouse). If this is the case, the third `if` condition is satisfied and this statement is executed:

```
m_vr.SetAngle (m_vr.GetAngle() + 3);
```

This statement increases the 3-D Floor control's Angle property by 3 degrees.

If you drag the mouse to the right, then `point.x` (the current x-position of the mouse) is greater than `PrevX` (the previous x-position of the mouse). If this is the case, the fourth `if` condition is satisfied and this statement is executed:

```
m_vr.SetAngle (m_vr.GetAngle() - 3);
```

This statement decreases the 3-D Floor control's Angle property by 3 degrees.

The next statement in the `OnMouseMove()` function uses the 3-D Floor control's `Display3D()` method to display the 3-D view corresponding to your new position:

```
m_vr.Display3D();
```

Finally, the last two statements update the `PrevX` and `PrevY` static variables:

```
PrevX = point.x;
PrevY = point.y;
```

Therefore, on the next mouse movement, the `OnMouseMove()` function knows the previous x-position and y-position of the mouse.

To see the code you attached to the `WM_MOUSEMOVE` event of the VR's window in action, follow these steps:

☐ Select Build VR.EXE from the Build menu.

☐ Use Windows Explorer or the Run feature of Windows 95 to execute the VR program.

☐ Use the mouse to move to various locations in the floor.

☐ Terminate the VR program by clicking the × icon.

Writing the Code That Loads the Sprites

Recall that you want the VR program to contain several sprites (two trees, a light fixture, a jogging robot, and an exercising robot). In this section, you'll write the code that loads these sprites.

Note: A sprite is a picture that has transparent sections. A sprite has two BMP files associated with it:

- The bitmap file
- The mask bitmap file

The sprite's *bitmap file* contains the picture of the sprite. The sprite's *mask bitmap file* specifies which sections of the sprite picture are transparent and which sections are opaque.

21

> The BMP files for the sprites in the 3-D Floor control must be 256-color BMP files. You can convert any other types of BMP files into 256-color BMP files by using the Paint (or Paintbrush) program, or a similar painting program.

Before you write the code that loads these sprites, copy the BMP files for these sprites to your hard drive:

Your C:\TYVCProg\CH21\VR\Release directory should now contain the following BMP files:

- TREE.BMP   The bitmap file for the tree sprite.
- MTREE.BMP   The mask bitmap file for the tree sprite.
- LIGHT.BMP   The bitmap file for the light fixture sprite.
- MLIGHT.BMP   The mask bitmap file for the light fixture sprite.
- JOG1.BMP   Frame 1 of the bitmap file for the jogging robot sprite running toward you.
- MJOG1.BMP   Frame 1 of the mask bitmap file for the jogging robot sprite running toward you.
- JOG2.BMP   Frame 2 of the bitmap file for the jogging robot sprite running toward you.
- MJOG2.BMP   Frame 2 of the mask bitmap file for the jogging robot sprite running toward you.
- JOG3.BMP   Frame 1 of the bitmap file for the jogging robot sprite running away from you.
- MJOG3.BMP   Frame 1 of the mask bitmap file for the jogging robot sprite running away from you.
- JOG4.BMP   Frame 2 of the bitmap file for the jogging robot sprite running away from you.
- MJOG4.BMP   Frame 2 of the mask bitmap file for the jogging robot sprite running away from you.
- JOG5.BMP   Frame 1 of the bitmap file for the robot sprite on fire.
- MJOG5.BMP   Frame 1 of the mask bitmap file for the robot sprite on fire.
- JOG6.BMP   Frame 2 of the bitmap file for the robot sprite on fire.
- MJOG6.BMP   Frame 2 of the mask bitmap file for the robot sprite on fire.

Now that you have all the necessary BMP files for the sprites, you can write the code that loads them in the `OnInitDialog()` function.

☐ Add the following statements to the end of the `OnInitDialog()` function (in the VRDlg.cpp file) as follows:

```
BOOL CVRDlg::OnInitDialog()
{
...
...
...
// TODO: Add extra initialization here

/////////////////////////
// MY CODE STARTS HERE
/////////////////////////

int iOpenResult;
CString Message;


// Open the Floor50.FLR file.
m_vr.SetFileName ("Floor50.FLR");
m_vr.SetHWndDisplay((long)m_hWnd);
m_vr.SetNumOfRows   (50);
m_vr.SetNumOfCols   (50);

iOpenResult = m_vr.Open();


// If FLR file could not be opened,
// terminate the program.
if (iOpenResult != 0)
   {

   Message = "Unable to open file: " + m_vr.GetFileName();

   Message = Message +"\n";
   char ErrorNumber[10];
   Message = Message + "Error Code: " +
            itoa(iOpenResult,ErrorNumber,10);
   MessageBox (Message);

   OnOK();

   }


// Set the initial user's position and viewing angle.
m_vr.SetX(4 * m_vr.GetCellWidth() );
m_vr.SetY(4 * m_vr.GetCellWidth() );
m_vr.SetAngle(0);
```

21

661

```
// Set the colors of the walls, ceiling, and floor.
m_vr.SetWallColorA (7);       // White
m_vr.SetWallColorB (4);       // Red
m_vr.SetCeilingColor (11);    // Light Cyan
m_vr.SetFloorColor (2);       // Green
m_vr.SetStripeColor (0);      // Black

// Load the sprites.

m_vr.SetSprite(65,"TREE.BMP");   // 65 = ASCII of "A"
m_vr.SetSprite(66,"LIGHT.BMP");  // 66 = ASCII of "B"
m_vr.SetSprite(67,"JOG1.BMP");   // 67 = ASCII of "C"
m_vr.SetSprite(68,"JOG2.BMP");   // 68 = ASCII of "D"

m_vr.SetSprite(69,"JOG1.BMP");   // 69 = ASCII of "E"
m_vr.SetSprite(70,"JOG2.BMP");   // 70 = ASCII of "F"
m_vr.SetSprite(71,"JOG3.BMP");   // 71 = ASCII of "G"
m_vr.SetSprite(72,"JOG4.BMP");   // 71 = ASCII of "H"

// The destroyed robot
m_vr.SetSprite(73,"JOG5.BMP");   // 73 = ASCII of "I"
m_vr.SetSprite(74,"JOG6.BMP");   // 73 = ASCII of "J"

/////////////////////////
// MY CODE ENDS HERE
/////////////////////////

return TRUE;
// return TRUE  unless you set the focus to a control
}
```

☐ Save your work.

The code you've just added to the Form_Load() procedure is responsible for loading the sprites.

The first statement defines the 3-D Floor control's Sprite 65 as the sprite whose BMP file is TREE.BMP and whose mask BMP file is MTREE.BMP:

```
m_vr.SetSprite(65,"TREE.BMP");  // 65 = ASCII of "A"
```

Notice that in the preceding statement the name MTREE.BMP is not specified. The 3-D Floor control knows that the mask BMP file is MTREE.BMP by simply prefixing the TREE.BMP with an *M*.

Note: When you define a sprite in the 3-D Floor control, you specify only the sprite's bitmap filename. The sprite's mask bitmap filename is always the bitmap filename prefixed with an *M*. For example, the following statement defines Sprite 65 of the 3-D Floor control as the sprite whose BMP file is DOG.BMP and whose mask BMP file is MDOG.BMP:

```
m_vr.SetSprite(65,"DOG.BMP");  // 65 = ASCII of "A"
```

The statement you used defines Sprite 65 as the tree sprite. Why use the number 65 for the tree sprite? The number 65 is the ASCII code for the letter *A*. Therefore, by defining Sprite 65 as the tree sprite, you are telling the floor control to display the tree sprite wherever the letter *A* appears in the floor file. One of the rooms in the Floor50.FLR file contains the letter *A* in two corners (refer back to Figure 21.19). Therefore, when you move into this room, you will see a tree in each of two corners.

The following statement defines Sprite 66 as the sprite whose BMP file is LIGHT.BMP and whose mask BMP file is MLIGHT.BMP:

```
Floor1.Sprite(66) = "LIGHT.BMP"   ' 66 = ASCII of "B"
```

The number 66 is the ASCII code for the letter *B*. Therefore, whenever the 3-D Floor control encounters the letter *B* in the Floor50.FLR floor file, the light fixture sprite is displayed.

The JOG1.BMP and JOG2.BMP were assigned as Sprites C and D as follows:

```
m_vr.SetSprite(67,"JOG1.BMP");   // 67 = ASCII of "C"
m_vr.SetSprite(68,"JOG2.BMP");   // 68 = ASCII of "D"
```

Then JOG1.BMP, JOG2.BMP, JOG3.BMP, and JOG4.BMP were assigned as the E, F, G, and H sprites:

```
m_vr.SetSprite(69,"JOG1.BMP");   // 69 = ASCII of "E"
m_vr.SetSprite(70,"JOG2.BMP");   // 70 = ASCII of "F"
m_vr.SetSprite(71,"JOG3.BMP");   // 71 = ASCII of "G"
m_vr.SetSprite(72,"JOG4.BMP");   // 71 = ASCII of "H"
```

But JOG1.BMP and JOG2.BMP were already assigned as the C and D sprites! Yes, you can assign the same BMP picture to different sprite letters. This is done here to demonstrate that it's possible to assign the same BMP picture to different sprite letters. Now Sprites C and D are used for the animation of the exercising robot, and Sprites E, F, G, and H are used for the animation of the forward- and backward-jogging robot animation.

Finally, Sprites I and J are assigned with the JOG5.BMP and JOG6.BMP pictures:

```
// The destroyed robot
m_vr.SetSprite(73,"JOG5.BMP");   // 73 = ASCII of "I"
m_vr.SetSprite(74,"JOG6.BMP");   // 73 = ASCII of "J"
```

JOG5.BMP and JOG6.BMP are used for the animation of the exercising robot when it is on fire.

☐ Save your work.

☐ Select Build VR.EXE from the Build menu.

Visual C++ responds by compiling and linking the VR program.

☐ Execute the VR.EXE program by using Windows Explorer or the Run feature of Windows 95.

21

☐ Travel in the 3-D picture and note the following:

- Directly across from the room in which you start your traveling, there is a room with a light fixture in it. This is the B sprite shown in Figure 21.19.

- The room adjacent to the room with the light has two trees in it. These are the two A sprites shown in Figure 21.19.

- At this point, you do not see the jogging robot sprites or the exercising robot sprites. Why? Because the Floor50.FLR file does not have the C, D, E, F, G, H, I, or J sprites. You will write code that places these sprites in the 3-D picture during runtime.

> **Note:** You can place sprites in the 3-D picture during design time by incorporating the sprites into the FLR file, or you can place sprites in the 3-D picture during runtime, as demonstrated later in this chapter.

Making a Soft Sprite

Did you notice something wrong with the light sprite? If you travel into the room where the light is located and you try to walk under it, you'll discover you can't. In other words, the light fixture is a hard sprite. It is appropriate for the tree sprites to be hard sprites, as well as other objects like chairs, tables, doors, monsters, and so on. But the light fixture should be a soft sprite, so you can go under it. Here is how you make the light fixture a soft sprite:

☐ Add a statement to the end of the `OnInitDialog()` function (in the VRDlg.cpp file) as follows:

```
BOOL CVRDlg::OnInitDialog()
{
…
…
…
// TODO: Add extra initialization here

/////////////////////////
// MY CODE STARTS HERE
/////////////////////////

int iOpenResult;
CString Message;

…
…
…

// Set sprite number 66 (the Light sprite)
// as a soft sprite.
```

```
// (that is the user can walk through this sprite).
m_vr.SetSpriteSoft (66);


/////////////////////////
// MY CODE ENDS HERE
/////////////////////////

return TRUE;
// return TRUE  unless you set the focus to a control
}
```

The statement you added makes the B sprite (ASCII 66) a soft sprite:

```
m_vr.SetSpriteSoft (66);
```

☐ Select Build VR.EXE from the Build menu.

   Visual C++ responds by compiling and linking the VR program.

☐ Execute the VR.EXE program by using the Windows Explorer or the Run feature of
   Windows 95.

☐ Travel in the 3-D picture to the room where the light fixture is located, and note that
   now you can pass under the light fixture.

☐ Experiment with the VR program and then click the × icon to terminate the program.

> **Note:** By default, a sprite is a hard sprite. To make a sprite a soft sprite, use the
> 3-D Floor control's SetSpriteSoft() method. For example, the following state-
> ment sets Sprite 65 to a soft sprite:
>
> ```
> m_vr.SetSpriteSoft (65);
> ```
>
> In some programs, you might find it useful to make a sprite soft in certain situa-
> tions and hard in other situations. To make a soft sprite hard, use the
> SetSpriteHard() method. For example, the following statement sets Sprite 65 to a
> hard sprite:
>
> ```
> m_vr.SetSpriteHard (65);
> ```

21

Notice that at this point, the jogging robot sprite and the exercising robot sprite do not appear
in the floor because the Floor50.FLR file doesn't have cells with letters representing these sprites.
(Also, the exploding robot sprites are not shown.) In the following section, you'll write code that
displays and animates the jogging and exercising robot sprites.

Writing Code That Animates the Jogging and Exercising Robot Sprites

Unlike the tree and light fixture sprites, the jogging robot and exercising robot sprites are moving (dynamic) sprites. The illusion of a moving sprite is accomplished by animating several frames—the program displays several frames one after the other. Each frame shows the character (for example, the jogging robot) in a slightly different position. For example, the two frames used to animate the jogging robot when he moves toward you are shown in Figure 21.7.

You'll now write the code that animates the jogging and exercising robot sprites. You'll first set a timer, then attach code that accomplishes these animation tasks to the WM_TIMER event.

Creating a Timer

You'll now write code that installs a timer:

☐ Add a statement to the end of the OnInitDialog() function (in the VRDlg.cpp file) as follows:

```
BOOL CVRDlg::OnInitDialog()
{
…
…
…
////////////////////////
// MY CODE STARTS HERE
////////////////////////
…
…
…

// Set a timer
SetTimer(1,500,NULL);

////////////////////////
// MY CODE ENDS HERE
////////////////////////

return TRUE;
// return TRUE  unless you set the focus to a control
}
```

The code you typed establishes a timer called Timer 1 that causes the WM_TIMER event to occur every 500 milliseconds:

```
SetTimer(1,500,NULL);
```

☐ Save your work.

Killing the Timer

Because the PC can have only a finite amount of timers, it is highly recommended that you kill the timer when you terminate the program. If you do not, the PC will eventually reach the maximum allowable number of timers, and no additional timers can be installed.

☐ Select ClassWizard from the View menu. In the Message Maps tab of ClassWizard, select the following event:

Class name:	CVRDlg
Object ID:	CVRDlg
Message:	WM_DESTROY

☐ Click the Add Function button of ClassWizard, then click the Edit Code button.

Visual C++ responds by opening the file VRDlg.cpp file with the function OnDestroy() *ready for you to edit.*

☐ Write the following code in the OnDestroy() function:

```
void CVRDlg::OnDestroy()
{
CDialog::OnDestroy();

// TODO: Add your message handler code here

////////////////////////
// MY CODE STARTS HERE
////////////////////////

KillTimer(1);

////////////////////////
// MY CODE ENDS HERE
////////////////////////

}
```

The code you typed releases the timer you established in the OnInitDialog() function. The timer is released when the OnDestroy() function is executed to terminate the program.

Attaching Code to the *WM_TIMER* Event

Earlier you set a timer with a frequency of 500 milliseconds, so the WM_TIMER event occurs automatically every 500 milliseconds. Follow these steps to add the animation code:

☐ Select ClassWizard from the View menu. In the Message Maps tab of ClassWizard, select the following event:

Class name:	CVRDlg
Object ID:	CVRDlg
Message:	WM_TIMER

☐ Click the Add Function button of ClassWizard, then click the Edit Code button.

Visual C++ responds by opening the file VRDlg.cpp with the function OnTimer() *ready for you to edit.*

☐ Write the following code in the OnTimer() function:

```
void CVRDlg::OnTimer(UINT nIDEvent)
{
// TODO: Add your message handler
// code here and/or call default

/////////////////////////
// MY CODE STARTS HERE
/////////////////////////

static int ExerciseFrame;
static int JoggerY;
static int JoggerFrame;


// Display the next frame of the exercising robot
// (inside the cell at coordinate x=1, y=5).
// Frame 0 of the exercising robot is sprite
// number 67. And frame 1 of the exercising robot is
// sprite number 68.
if (ExerciseFrame == 0)
   {
   ExerciseFrame = 1;
   m_vr.SetCell(1,5 ,67);
   }
else
   {
   ExerciseFrame = 0;
   m_vr.SetCell( 1, 5,68);
   }


// Set the cell of the previous jogging robot position
// to an empty cell.
if (JoggerY != 0 )
   m_vr.SetCell( 23, JoggerY, 0);


// If the jogging robot has reached the end of the hall,
// reset JoggerY to 0.
if (JoggerY == 48 )
   JoggerY = 0;


// Increment JoggerY.
JoggerY = JoggerY + 1;

// Set JoggerFrame to the next frame number.
if (JoggerFrame == 0)
   JoggerFrame = 1;
```

```
   else
      JoggerFrame = 0;


   // If the user is facing the jogging robot, show the front
   // of the jogging robot (sprites 69 and 70). Otherwise, show
   // the back of the jogging robot (sprites 71 and 72).
   if (m_vr.GetCellPosY() >= JoggerY)
      {
      if (JoggerFrame == 0)
         m_vr.SetCell( 23, JoggerY, 69);
      else
         m_vr.SetCell( 23, JoggerY, 70);

      }
   else
      {
      if (JoggerFrame == 0)
         m_vr.SetCell( 23, JoggerY, 71);
      else
         m_vr.SetCell( 23, JoggerY, 72);

      }

   // Display the 3D view.
   m_vr.Display3D();

   ////////////////////////
   // MY CODE ENDS HERE
   ////////////////////////

   CDialog::OnTimer(nIDEvent);
   }
```

☐ Save your work.

The first three statements in the OnTimer() function declare three static variables:

```
static int ExerciseFrame;
static int JoggerY;
static int JoggerFrame;
```

Since these variables are declared as static, they do not lose their values when the procedure terminates. As you'll soon see, ExerciseFrame stores the current frame number of the exercising robot. JoggerY stores the current y-position of the jogging robot as he moves in the floor's main hall, and JoggerFrame is used for storing the current frame number of the jogging robot.

The next block of code is an if...else statement:

```
if (ExerciseFrame == 0)
   {
   ExerciseFrame = 1;
   m_vr.SetCell(1, 5, 67);
   }
else
```

21

```
{
ExerciseFrame = 0;
m_vr.SetCell(1, 5, 68);
}
```

This if…else statement is responsible for animating the exercising robot sprite. In each iteration of the OnTimer() procedure (every 500 milliseconds), the preceding if…else statement changes the value of the ExerciseFrame static variable. One time ExerciseFrame is set to 0; the next time (500 milliseconds later) ExerciseFrame is set to 1; the next time ExerciseFrame is set back to 0, and so on.

Depending on the current value of ExerciseFrame, the preceding if…else statement displays a different sprite of the exercising robot. If ExerciseFrame is currently 0, then the code under the if displays Sprite 67 in the cell with the x-y coordinate of x=1,y=5:

```
m_vr.SetCell(1, 5, 67);
```

If, however, the current value of ExerciseFrame is 1, then the code under the else statement displays Sprite 68 in the cell with the x-y coordinate of x=1,y=5:

```
m_vr.SetCell( 1, 5, 68);
```

Therefore, in every execution of the OnTimer() function (every 500 milliseconds) a different frame of the exercising robot is displayed in the cell with the x-y coordinate of x=1,y=5. One time Sprite 67 is displayed, the next time Sprite 68 is displayed, the next time Sprite 67 is displayed, and so on.

Note: The upper-left 1 of the FLR file is at x=0,y=0. Therefore, the following statement places the 68 sprite at the second column from the left and the sixth row from the top:

```
m_vr.SetCell( 1, 5, 68);
```

Here is the code responsible for animating the jogging robot:

```
// Set the cell of the previous jogger position
// to an empty cell.
if (JoggerY != 0 )
   m_vr.SetCell( 23, JoggerY, 0);


// If the jogger has reached the end of the hall,
// reset JoggerY to 0.
if (JoggerY == 48 )
   JoggerY = 0;

// Increment JoggerY.
JoggerY = JoggerY + 1;
```

```
// Set JoggerFrame to the next frame number.
if (JoggerFrame == 0)
   JoggerFrame = 1;
else
   JoggerFrame = 0;

// If the user is facing the jogger, show the front
// of the jogger (sprites 69 and 70). Otherwise, show
// the back of the jogger (sprites 71 and 72).
if (m_vr.GetCellPosY() >= JoggerY)
   {
   if (JoggerFrame == 0)
      m_vr.SetCell( 23, JoggerY, 69);
   else
      m_vr.SetCell( 23, JoggerY, 70);
   }
else
   {
   if (JoggerFrame == 0)
      m_vr.SetCell( 23, JoggerY, 71);
   else
      m_vr.SetCell( 23, JoggerY, 72);

   }
```

As you can see, the animation code for the jogging robot sprite is more involved than for the exercising robot sprite because the jogging robot does not remain in the same cell. Therefore, in addition to using a static variable that holds the current frame number of the jogging robot (JoggerFrame), the preceding code also uses the static variable JoggerY, which is used for holding the current y-cell position of the jogging robot.

In each iteration of the OnTimer() function, the previous cell position of the jogging robot is set to an empty cell, then JoggerY is incremented, and the jogging robot sprite is displayed in the new y-cell position. The x-cell position of the jogging robot is always the same (23).

Depending on your new y-cell position, different jogging robot sprites are animated. If your y-cell position is greater than the y-cell position of the jogging robot, then Sprites 69 and 70, which show the jogging robot facing you, are used. If, however, your y-cell position is less than the y-cell position of the jogging robot, then Sprites 71 and 72, which show the jogging robot with his back to you, are used.

Here is the last statement in the OnTimer() function:

```
m_vr.Display3D();
```

This statement uses the 3-D Floor control's Display3D() method to display the new 3-D view corresponding to the new status of the exercising robot and jogging robot sprites.

☐ Execute the VR program and make sure the exercising robot and jogging robot sprites are working as expected.

Shooting the Exercising Robot

As discussed, JOG5.BMP (and MJOG5.BMP) and JOG6.BMP (and MJOG6.BMP) are the pictures used for showing the exercising robot on fire. In the `OnInitDialog()` function, you already loaded these BMP pictures:

```
// The destroyed robot
m_vr.SetSprite(73,"JOG5.BMP");   // 73 = ASCII of "I"
m_vr.SetSprite(74,"JOG6.BMP");   // 73 = ASCII of "J"
```

Declaring the *m_Destroyed* Data Member

You'll now declare a data member called m_Destroyed. This data member will indicate the status of the exercising robot. When m_Destroyed is equal to TRUE, it means this robot is on fire. When m_Destroyed is equal to FALSE, it means the exercising robot is not destroyed.

☐ Open the VRDlg.h file and add the m_Destroyed data member as a BOOL variable (a variable that can be either TRUE or FALSE) to the CVRDlg class declaration as follows:

```
class CVRDlg : public CDialog
{
// Construction
public:
CVRDlg(CWnd* pParent = NULL);// standard constructor

/////////////////////////////
// MY CODE STARTS HERE
/////////////////////////////

// Data Members
BOOL m_Destroyed;

/////////////////////////////
// MY CODE ENDS HERE
/////////////////////////////

...
...
...
};
```

The code you typed declared the m_Destroyed data member:

```
BOOL m_Destroyed;
```

Initializing the *m_Destroyed* Data Member

You'll now initialize the m_Destroyed data member, which can be TRUE or FALSE. When you start the program, you want m_Destroyed to be equal to FALSE because the exercising robot should be shown in its non-destroyed state.

☐ Add code to the `OnInitDialog()` function (in the VRDlg.cpp file) as follows:

```
BOOL CVRDlg::OnInitDialog()
{
    CDialog::OnInitDialog();
…
…
…

// TODO: Add extra initialization here

/////////////////////////
// MY CODE STARTS HERE
/////////////////////////

int iOpenResult;
CString Message;

m_Destroyed = FALSE;

…
…
…
/////////////////////////
// MY CODE ENDS HERE
/////////////////////////

…
…
…
};
```

The code you typed initializes m_Destroyed to FALSE:

```
m_Destroyed = FALSE;
```

Writing the Code That Performs the Shooting

You'll now write the code that performs the shooting:

☐ Add a case condition to the switch statement in the OnKeyDown() function (in the VRDlg.cpp file) as follows:

```
void CVRDlg::OnKeyDown(UINT nChar, UINT nRepCnt,
        UINT nFlags)
{
// TODO: Add your message handler code
// here and/or call default

/////////////////////////
// MY CODE STARTS HERE
/////////////////////////

switch (nChar)
    {
```

```
        case 32:
            // Destroy the robot
            if (m_Destroyed == TRUE)
                m_Destroyed = FALSE;
            else
                m_Destroyed = TRUE;
            break;
    ...
    ...
    ...


//////////////////////////
// MY CODE ENDS HERE
//////////////////////////

    ...
    ...
    ...

    }
```

The ASCII code of the spacebar key is 32. The case condition you added uses an `if…else` statement to toggle the value of `m_Destroyed` to either TRUE or FALSE:

```
case 32:
        // Destroy the robot
        if (m_Destroyed == TRUE)
            m_Destroyed = FALSE;
        else
            m_Destroyed = TRUE;
        break;
```

If the `m_Destroyed` data member is equal to TRUE, you set the value of this data member to FALSE by pressing the spacebar. Likewise, if the current value of the `m_Destroyed` data member is FALSE, you set the value of this data member to TRUE by pressing the spacebar.

Performing the Fire Animation

You'll now add the code that performs the fire animation:

☐ Add code in the `OnTimer()` function (in the VRDlg.cpp file) as follows:

```
void CVRDlg::OnTimer(UINT nIDEvent)
{
// TODO: Add your message handler code
// here and/or call default

//////////////////////////
// MY CODE STARTS HERE
//////////////////////////

static int ExerciseFrame;
static int JoggerY;
static int JoggerFrame;
```

```
// Display the next frame of the exercising robot
// (inside the cell at coordinate x=1, y=5).
// Frame 0 of the exercising robot is sprite
// number 67. And frame 1 of the exercising robot is
// sprite number 68.
if (m_Destroyed == FALSE)
   {
   if (ExerciseFrame == 0)
      {
      ExerciseFrame = 1;
      m_vr.SetCell(1,5 ,67);
      }
   else
      {
      ExerciseFrame = 0;
      m_vr.SetCell( 1, 5,68);
      }
   }

if (m_Destroyed == TRUE)
   {
   if (ExerciseFrame == 0)
      {
      ExerciseFrame = 1;
      m_vr.SetCell(1,5 ,73);
      }
   else
      {
      ExerciseFrame = 0;
      m_vr.SetCell( 1, 5,74);
      }
   }

...
...
...

/////////////////////////
// MY CODE ENDS HERE
/////////////////////////


CDialog::OnTimer(nIDEvent);
   }
```

The code you typed uses an if statement to examine whether m_Destroyed is equal to FALSE:

```
if (m_Destroyed == FALSE)
   {
   if (ExerciseFrame == 0)
      {
      ExerciseFrame = 1;
      m_vr.SetCell(1,5 ,67);
      }
   else
      {
```

21

```
ExerciseFrame = 0;
m_vr.SetCell( 1, 5,68);
}
}
```

Because m_Destroyed is equal to FALSE, the exercising robot is displayed (Sprites 67 and 68).

Another if statement is executed:

```
if (m_Destroyed == TRUE)
   {
   if (ExerciseFrame == 0)
      {
      ExerciseFrame = 1;
      m_vr.SetCell(1,5 ,73);
      }
   else
      {
      ExerciseFrame = 0;
      m_vr.SetCell( 1, 5,74);
      }
   }
```

When m_Destroyed is equal to FALSE, Sprites 73 and 74 (which represent the robot on fire) are displayed.

☐ Select Build VR.EXE from the Build menu to compile and link the VR program.

☐ Use the Windows Explorer of Windows 95 to execute the VR.EXE program.

☐ Move to the room where the exercising robot is located.

☐ Press the spacebar.

The VR.EXE program responds by setting the exercising robot on fire.

☐ Press the spacebar again.

The VR.EXE program responds by restoring the exercising robot.

Summary

In this chapter, you have written a 3-D virtual reality program, called VR, that uses the 3-D Floor OLE control. As you have seen, writing a program with the 3-D Floor OLE control is easy. Basically, all you have to do is design a 2-D floor file (FLR text file). The 3-D Floor control converts your 2-D FLR text file into a 3-D picture. This enables you to move around in the virtual environment.

As demonstrated by the VR program, you can add sprites (stationary sprites and moving sprites) to the 3-D picture. A sprite can be a hard sprite or a soft sprite. You can walk through a soft sprite (the light fixture sprite, for example) but cannot walk through a hard sprite, such as tree sprites.

You can add a further sense of reality to your virtual reality programs by using sound. You can add the Multimedia TegoSoft OLE control (discussed in Chapter 20, "Using the Multimedia OLE Control") to the dialog box and create various sound effects. For example, when you press the spacebar to shoot the robot, you could add a shooting noise.

Q&A

Q I would like to experiment on my own with the 3-D Floor OLE control. Any suggestions for project ideas?

A Yes, try to create a DOOM-like game. Or use your imagination to apply this technology to other programs. For example, you can create a program in which the user makes a selection when he or she enters different rooms. When the user enters a certain room, it is equivalent to making a selection from a menu.

Quiz

1. What is a soft sprite?

   a. A popular drink.
   b. A sprite you can pass through.
   c. There's no such thing.

2. Sprites can be placed in the 3-D picture during design time as well as runtime.

   a. True
   b. False

Exercise

Modify the VR program so that the first room where you find yourself when the program starts has some decorative trees.

Quiz Answers

1. b.
2. a. During design time, you place the sprites in the FLR floor. During runtime, you place the sprites as you placed the tree sprites and the exercising robot sprite in the VR program.

Exercise Answer

All you have to do is place several *A*'s in the Floor50.FLR file. Use a text editor program such as WordPad to place the *A* characters. Be careful not to place an *A* in the starting cell; you don't want to start the program with a tree on top of you!

21

Learning C/C++ Quickly (Part I)

Appendixes A, B, and C assume that you have no previous experience with the C/C++ programming language, but you'll learn C/C++ quickly in these appendixes. This book teaches you how to use Visual C++ 4.0 for designing and using Windows programs. Naturally, you need some knowledge of C/C++ programming to use the Visual C++ package. The appendixes teach you everything you need to know about C/C++ for this book. Here is the bottom line: If you have never used C/C++ before, these appendixes are for you. After reading Appendixes A, B, and C, you'll have all the know-how needed for this book's chapters.

Note: Additional C/C++ topics are presented during the course of this book on a need-to-know-basis as you work through the book's programs.

Creating Console Applications

Visual C++ has the capability to create *console applications,* which are basically DOS programs executed in a Windows shell. The objective of this book is to teach you how to write C++ Windows applications with the Visual C++ package. Why, then, does this tutorial cover console applications? As you know, PC vendors are shipping their PCs with Windows 95 already installed. So why would anybody want to learn about console applications?

To use Visual C++ to write Windows applications, you need to know some basic C/C++ topics. However, even the simplest Windows program is long and contains several overhead files. Therefore, it is much easier to learn the basics of C/C++ by writing simple console applications than by writing Windows programs.

Writing a Simple Console Application with Visual C++

In this tutorial, you'll write a simple C++ DOS (console) program with Visual C++. You'll save the program you develop in this tutorial in the C:\TYVCProg\Programs\AppendA directory. Follow these steps to begin:

☐ Create the C:\TYVCProg\Programs\AppendA directory.

☐ From within Windows 95, start Visual C++. (See Figure A.1.)

> *Windows responds by running the Visual C++ program, and the desktop of Visual C++ is displayed, as shown in Figure A.2.*

Figure A.1.
*The Visual C++
program icon.*

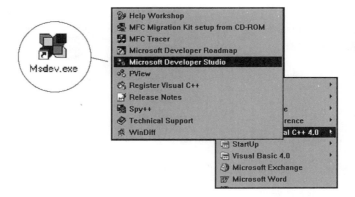

Figure A.2.
*The Microsoft Visual C++
window.*

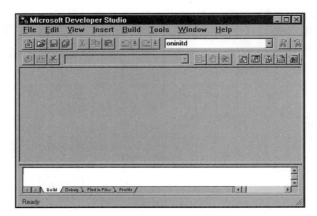

Depending on the setting of your Visual C++, the desktop you see on your PC may look a little different from the one shown in Figure A.2. For now, don't worry about this. The subject of setting and manipulating the Visual C++ desktop is discussed in detail during the course of this book.

Here is how you create a new project with Visual C++:

☐ Select New from the File menu of Visual C++.

> *Visual C++ responds by displaying the New dialog box.*

☐ Select the Text File item in the New dialog box, since you're creating a new text file. (See Figure A.3.)

Figure A.3.
Creating a new text file.

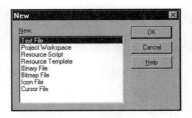

☐ Click the OK button of the New dialog box.

Visual C++ responds by creating the new Text1 window, as shown in Figure A.4.

Figure A.4.
The Text1 window in which you'll write your C/C++ code.

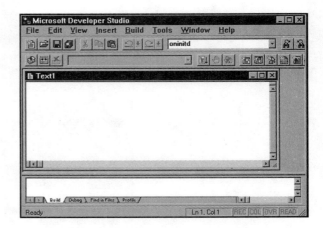

The new file you're creating is a regular text file. As shown in Figure A.4, the default name that Visual C++ assigns to the new text window is Text1. You'll now change the name of the Text1 window:

☐ Make sure the Text1 window is selected, then choose Save As from the File menu of Visual C++.

Visual C++ responds by displaying the Save As dialog box.

☐ Save the file as MyHello.cpp in the C:\TYVCProg\Programs\AppendA directory.

You'll write the code of the MyHello program in the MyHello.cpp text file. As you can see, it is customary to save the text file containing the program's code with the file extension *.cpp,* as in MyHello.cpp.

Writing the Code of the MyHello.cpp Program

Now you are ready to write the C++ code of the program, which you will type in the MyHello.cpp window.

☐ Type the code of the MyHello.cpp program:

```
// Program Name: MyHello.cpp

#include <iostream.h>

void main()
{

cout << "Hello, this is my first C++ program \n";

}
```

The MyHello.cpp window should now look like the one shown in Figure A.5.

Figure A.5.

The MyHello.cpp window with code in it.

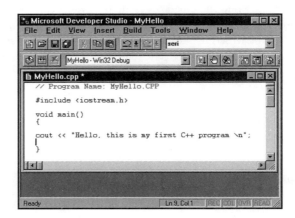

If you have never written C/C++ code before, the code you typed may look like it came from outer space. But don't worry; the code will be explained later in this chapter. For now, save your work:

☐ Make sure that MyHello.cpp window is selected and choose Save All from the File menu of Visual C++.

Compiling and Linking the MyHello.cpp Program

You'll now compile and link the MyHello program. What does it mean to compile and link? Take a look at Figure A.6, which is a pictorial representation of the compiling and linking process.

Figure A.6.
Compiling and linking the MyHello program.

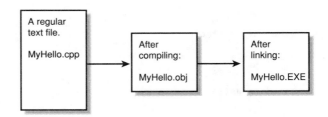

The compiler is a program that comes with Visual C++. It processes the MyHello.cpp text file to create a new file called MyHello.obj. What can you do with the MyHello.obj file? Practically nothing! The MyHello.obj file is an intermediate file used by another program called the linker program, which also comes with Visual C++. The linker program processes the MyHello.obj file to create a new file called MyHello.EXE—the final program file. You execute the MyHello.EXE program like any other program.

Try compiling and linking the MyHello program:

☐ Select Build MyHello.EXE from the Build menu of Visual C++.

Visual C++ responds by displaying the dialog box shown in Figure A.7.

Figure A.7.
The dialog box for generating a project workspace.

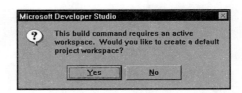

☐ Click the Yes button of the dialog box.

Visual C++ responds by compiling the MyHello.cpp file (to create the MyHello.obj file), then linking the MyHello program (to create the MyHello.EXE file).

If you typed the code of the MyHello.cpp file exactly as you were instructed, Visual C++ displays the following message (see Figure A.8):

```
MyHello.exe - 0 error(s). 0 warnings)
```

Figure A.8.
After compiling and linking the MyHello.EXE program.

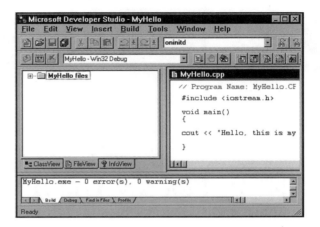

If you didn't type the code exactly as you were instructed, Visual C++ will tell you that errors occurred during the process of compiling and linking the program. In this case, make the appropriate corrections in the MyHello.cpp window, then select Build MyHello.EXE from the Build menu again.

Note: C/C++ is case sensitive. For example, you were instructed to type the following line in the MyHello.cpp file:

```
void main()
```

If you typed `void Main()` instead of `void main()`, or `Void main()` instead of `void main()`, you got errors.

Don't forget to type the semicolon (;) at the end of the line that starts with the word `cout`.

The window at the bottom of the desktop, shown in Figure A.8, is called the *output window*. This window displays the results of the compiling and linking process. When the output window contains the message `0 error(s), 0 warning(s)`, this window is referred to as the "happy window" because you are supposed to be happy when you receive 0 errors.

Note: Any time you want to display the output window, select Output from the View menu.

You can enlarge the output window by placing the mouse cursor on its upper edge and dragging the mouse upward. Notice that the output window has several tabs: Build, Debug, Find in Files, and Profile. To view the results of the compiling and linking, make sure that the Build tab is selected, as it is in Figure A.8.

If you did not get the 0 error(s) message, display the MyHello.cpp file and make sure you typed everything without any syntax errors:

☐ Select Windows from the Window menu to display the Windows dialog box, then select the MyHello.cpp item and click the Activate button.

Executing the MyHello.EXE Program

Once you compile and link the MyHello program without any errors, you can execute the MyHello.EXE program.

☐ Select Execute MyHello.EXE from the Build menu.

Visual C++ responds by executing the MyHello.EXE program, and the window shown in Figure A.9 appears.

Figure A.9.
Executing the MyHello.EXE program.

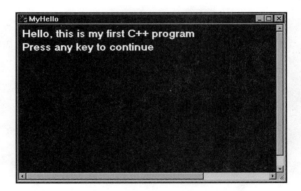

☐ Press any key on your keyboard to terminate the MyHello program.

As you can see from Figure A.9, the MyHello.EXE program displays the message:

```
Hello, this is my first C++ program.
```

In the previous step, you executed the MyHello.EXE program by selecting Execute MyHello.EXE from the Build menu. However, MyHello.EXE is a regular program file, so you can execute it just like any other EXE program:

☐ Use Windows to execute the MS-DOS program by clicking the Start button of Windows 95, selecting Programs, then selecting MS-DOS Prompt.

Windows responds by executing the MS-DOS program, and you'll see the DOS prompt.

☐ Log into the C:\TYVCProg\Programs\AppendA directory by typing the following at the DOS prompt:

```
CD C:\TYVCProg\Programs\AppendA  {Enter}
```

☐ Then enter this statement at the DOS prompt:

```
MyHello.exe  {Enter}
```

DOS responds by executing the MyHello.EXE program.

As you can see, the MyHello.EXE program displays this message:

```
Hello, this is my first C++ program.
```

☐ At the DOS prompt, type Exit, then press the Enter key.

Note: You should be aware that console EXE files generated by Visual C++ are not true DOS programs. In fact, if you can run MS-DOS as the true operating system of your PC, then exit to the DOS prompt, log in to the C:\TYVCProg\Programs\AppendA directory, and type the following text at the DOS prompt:

```
MyHello  {Enter}
```

You'll get this message:

```
This program cannot be run in DOS mode.
```

Examining the MyHello.cpp Program's Code

In reviewing the code of the MyHello.cpp program, you'll notice that the code contains // characters. Comments in C++ start with the // characters. For example, the following is a valid C++ comment:

```
// This is my comment.
```

When the compiler "works" on the MyHello.cpp text file, it ignores every line that starts with the // characters.

Here is another example of four comment lines in C++:

```
/////////////////////////////////////
//    This is my comment.
//    I can write whatever I want here.
/////////////////////////////////////
```

Why Use C/C++?

At the beginning, there was the C programming language, invented about two decades ago. It became the most popular programming language for generating professional applications; as a matter of fact, a big portion of the Windows operating system was written with the C programming language. So if Microsoft chose C to be the programming language for its major product, there must be something good about C. C is successful for several reasons:

☐ C generates stand-alone EXE files. Once you finish creating a program with a C compiler/linker, the result is a file with an .EXE file extension. The EXE file is the file you distribute to your users; you don't need to distribute any other file with your EXE file.

☐ The EXE file that C generates is a small file.

☐ C has proved to be a reliable, easy-to-use programming language.

☐ C compiler/linkers are available at reasonable prices from major software vendors (Microsoft and Borland are the most popular vendors of C compiler/linker packages).

☐ The EXE programs generated by a C compiler/linker are executed quickly by the computer.

☐ The processes of compiling a cpp file into an obj file and linking an obj file to an EXE file go very quickly.

OK, C is a successful product! But during the past two decades, C programmers accumulated much experience and started to demand more from C. Committees were established to consider suggestions, recommendations, and comments from C users. Eventually, a new programming language was conceived—the C++ programming language.

You could think of C++ as the second version of C. As you'll learn during the course of this tutorial, C++ lets you write *object-oriented programs,* which deal with classes and objects. You'll learn about these topics later in this tutorial.

The *#include* Statement

The first line you typed in the MyHello.cpp file is a comment line. This is the second line:

```
#include <iostream.h>
```

This statement tells the compiler to do the following:

```
"As you compile the MyHello.cpp file, make use of the iostream.h file."
```

The iostream.h file came with your Visual C++ program. (In the following section "The Code in the main() Function," you'll see why you need to tell the compiler to use the iostream.h file.) You then typed the following code:

```
void main()
{

cout << "Hello, this is my first C++ program \n";

}
```

The first line includes the main() function:

```
void main()
```

A *function* is a block of code enclosed by the curly brackets. The following is an example of a function called MyFunction():

```
void MyFunction()
{

// You type the code of the MyFunction() function here

}
```

Later in this tutorial (in the section "Scope of Variables"), you'll learn about the void word and the parentheses () that come after the function name.

Why did we choose to name the function main()? Because in C/C++ programs, you must include a function called main(). When you execute the MyHello.cpp program, the main() function is executed first.

The Code in the *main()* Function

A function's code is typed between the curly brackets. In the MyHello program, you typed the following statement in the main() function:

```
cout << "Hello, this is my first C++ program \n";
```

The most important thing you should know about the preceding statement is that it must end with the semicolon character (;). Every C++ statement must end with a semicolon.

The word cout causes the PC to display the text appearing after the << characters, so the preceding statement causes the PC to display this text:

```
Hello, this is my first C++ program
```

The \n characters are the carriage-return/line-feed characters. By including the \n characters, you are telling the PC to advance to the next line on the screen after displaying the text Hello, this is my first C++ program. Also, notice that the text you typed (including the \n characters) must be enclosed in double quotes (" ").

cout causes the PC to display characters on the screen, so you could think of cout as a function that performs something. But where is the code of cout? Who wrote the code that actually sends characters to the screen? Well, it all came with Visual C++, but you have to tell the compiler that cout is a preprepared function. In fact, all the information about the exact nature of cout is stored in a file called iostream.h. This is why you included the following statement at the beginning of the program:

```
#include <iostream.h>
```

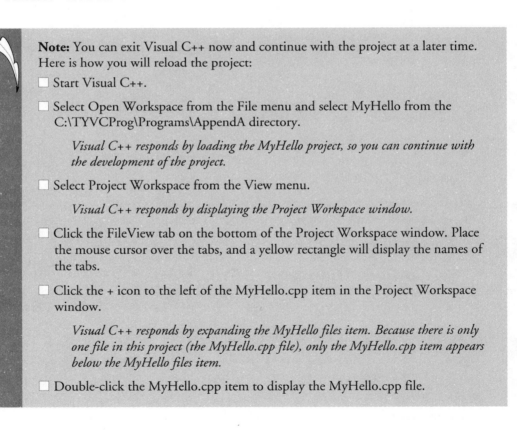

Note: You can exit Visual C++ now and continue with the project at a later time. Here is how you will reload the project:

☐ Start Visual C++.

☐ Select Open Workspace from the File menu and select MyHello from the C:\TYVCProg\Programs\AppendA directory.

Visual C++ responds by loading the MyHello project, so you can continue with the development of the project.

☐ Select Project Workspace from the View menu.

Visual C++ responds by displaying the Project Workspace window.

☐ Click the FileView tab on the bottom of the Project Workspace window. Place the mouse cursor over the tabs, and a yellow rectangle will display the names of the tabs.

☐ Click the + icon to the left of the MyHello.cpp item in the Project Workspace window.

Visual C++ responds by expanding the MyHello files item. Because there is only one file in this project (the MyHello.cpp file), only the MyHello.cpp item appears below the MyHello files item.

☐ Double-click the MyHello.cpp item to display the MyHello.cpp file.

Modifying the MyHello Program

You'll now modify the MyHello program so that it will display the following lines:

```
Hi, this is my first line!
Hi again, this is my second line!!
Hi again, this is my third line!!!
```

☐ Modify the code in the MyHello.cpp file as follows:

```
// Program Name: MyHello.cpp

#include <iostream.h>

void main()
{

//cout << "Hello, this is my first C++ program \n";

cout << "Hi, this is my first line! \n";
cout << "Hi again, this is my second line!! \n";
cout << "Hi again, this is my third line!!! \n";

}
```

You commented out the first cout statement:

```
//cout << "Hello, this is my first C++ program \n";
```

Then three cout statements are executed. Each cout statement displays a different message:

```
cout << "Hi, this is my first line! \n";
cout << "Hi again, this is my second line!! \n";
cout << "Hi again, this is my third line!!! \n";
```

Again, note that each statement is terminated with the semicolon character.

☐ Select Save All from the File menu to save your work.

☐ Select Build MyHello.EXE from the Build menu.

☐ If you got 0 errors, select Execute MyHello.EXE from the Build menu. (If you got errors in the previous step, make sure you typed the code exactly as you were instructed, and try to build the program again).

After executing the MyHello program, the window shown in Figure A.10 appears. As you can see, the three messages appear as dictated by the cout statements. Note that the last line, Press any key to continue, is inserted automatically for you; you didn't have to write any code to display that message.

Figure A.10.
The output window of the MyHello program.

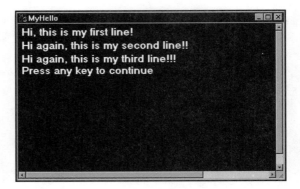

☐ Press any key to terminate the program.

Performing Addition with the MyHello Program

You'll now further modify the MyHello program. In particular, you'll type code that performs addition with two numbers.

☐ Modify the MyHello.cpp file so that it will look like the following:

```
// Program Name: MyHello.cpp

#include <iostream.h>

void main()
{

int iNum1;
int iNum2;
int iResult;

iNum1 = 2;
iNum2 = 3;
iResult = iNum1 + iNum2;

cout << "The result is: \n";
cout << iResult;
cout << "\n";

}
```

First, you deleted the previous code in the `main()` function, so now it starts with the following statement:

```
int iNum1;
```

The preceding statement defines a variable called `iNum1`. In C++, you must define the variables before using them. A *variable* contains data, and the `iNum1` variable is used for storing the number

2. When defining the variable, you must tell the compiler the name of the variable—iNum1—as well as the type of variable. That is, will the iNum1 variable store text? integers? floating numbers (numbers with fractions)? You preceded the name of the variable with the word int, which means you're telling the compiler that the iNum1 number is defined as an integer.

> **Note:** You defined the variable as int and named it iNum1. Another data type in C/C++ is char. A char variable stores a character. For example, the following statement defines the cMyCharacter variable:
>
> ```
> char cMyCharacter;
> ```
>
> Note that the name of the cMyCharacter variable is preceded with the letter *c* and the variable iNum1 is preceded with the letter *i.* Why? So that it will be easy to read the program. The prefix letters will tell you that iNum1 is a variable declared as int (integer) or that cMyCharacter is a variable declared as char (character).
>
> C++ doesn't require you to precede the names of the variables with letters, but it does make your program easier to read and understand.

You then declared two more variables, iNum2 and iResult:

```
int iNum2;
int iResult;
```

At this point in your program, you have declared three integer variables: iNum1, iNum2, and iResult. You then set the value of iNum1 as follows:

```
iNum1 = 2;
```

From now on, iNum1 is equal to 2.

> **Note:** You set the value of the iNum1 variable as follows:
>
> ```
> iNum1 = 2;
> ```
>
> C++ does not care if you use extra spaces or even spread the statements over two or more lines. Therefore, the following statements all have the same result:
>
> ```
> iNum1    = 2;
>
> iNum1=    2;
>
> iNum1 =
>          2;
> ```

However, you must not spread text that's enclosed in double quotation marks
(" "). For example, the following statement is not allowed:

```
// Never do this!!!
cout << " This is
            not allowed";
```

The next statement you typed sets the value of iNum2 to 3:

```
iNum2 = 3;
```

At this point in the program, iNum1 is equal to 2 and iNum2 is equal to 3. Then you set the value
of iResult as follows:

```
iResult = iNum1 + iNum2;
```

In essence, you set the value of iResult to 2+3=5.

You display the text The result is: as follows:

```
cout << "The result is: \n";
```

You then execute cout again to display the value of iResult:

```
cout << iResult;
```

Because iResult is not enclosed in double quotes, the cout statement won't display the text
iResult. Rather, the cout statement will display the value of iResult, which is 5.

☐ Select Build MyHello.EXE from the Build menu.

☐ Select Execute MyHello.EXE from the Build menu and verify that the MyHello program
   displays the expected results shown in Figure A.11.

Figure A.11.
*The MyHello program
displays the value of
iResult.*

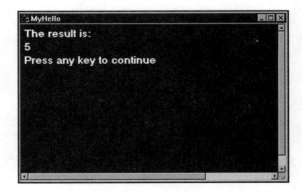

Functions in C++

The MyHello program currently has one function in it, the main() function. You'll now add a second function called AddIt():

☐ Modify the MyHello.cpp file so that it will look like the following:

```cpp
// Program Name: MyHello.cpp

#include <iostream.h>

void main()
{

int iNum1;
int iNum2;
int iResult;

iNum1 = 2;
iNum2 = 3;

iResult = AddIt(iNum1, iNum2);

cout << "The result is: \n";
cout << iResult;
cout << "\n";

}
```

You deleted the statement

```cpp
iResult = iNum1 + iNum2;
```

and replaced it with the following statement:

```cpp
iResult = AddIt(iNum1, iNum2);
```

AddIt() is the name of a function you'll write in the following sections. The text typed within the parentheses of the AddIt() function is called the *parameters* of the function. The parameters of the function are separated with commas. Therefore, you supplied two parameters to the AddIt() function: iNum1 and iNum2.

What will the AddIt() function do? AddIt() will perform an operation on the parameters iNum1 and iNum2: adding iNum1 to iNum2. Then AddIt() will return the value of the result of the addition. When you execute the statement

```cpp
iResult = AddIt(iNum1, iNum2);
```

you are telling the compiler to do the following:

```
"Set the value of iResult to the returned value of the AddIt() function".
```

695

Since you set the parameters of AddIt() to iNum1 and iNum2, the AddIt() function should return the value iNum1+iNum2=2+3=5.

Will the MyHello program work now? The answer is no! C++ is kind enough to supply you with the cout function as well as many other preprepared functions, but C++ does not come with a function called AddIt() that performs the task described in the preceding paragraphs. The bottom line is that you have to write the AddIt() function yourself.

Declaring the Prototype of the *AddIt()* Function

When the compiler encounters the words AddIt(iNum1,iNum2) in main(), it doesn't know what they mean. You have to tell the compiler that these words mean a function called AddIt. You also have to tell the compiler that AddIt() takes two parameters and that each of the parameters is a variable of the type integer. Furthermore, you have to tell the compiler that AddIt() returns an integer. Telling all these things to the compiler means that you have to write the prototype of the AddIt() function:

```
int AddIt( int, int);
```

The prototype declares the AddIt() function as one that returns an integer and takes two parameters, each of which is an integer.

☐ Type the prototype of the AddIt() function at the beginning of the MyHello.cpp file as follows:

```
// Program Name: MyHello.cpp

#include <iostream.h>

// Prototypes
int AddIt( int, int);

void main()
{

int iNum1;
int iNum2;
int iResult;

iNum1 = 2;
iNum2 = 3;

iResult = AddIt(iNum1, iNum2);

cout << "The result is: \n";
cout << iResult;
cout << "\n";

}
```

Now when the compiler encounters AddIt, it will know you're talking about a function called AddIt, and its description is declared in the prototype section at the beginning of the file. In the next section, you'll write the code of the AddIt() function.

Note: Every function must have a prototype, so where is the prototype of main()? As it turns out, main() is the only function that does not need a prototype.

Writing the Code of the *AddIt()* Function

You'll now write the code of the AddIt() function:

☐ In the MyHello.cpp file, add the code of the AddIt() function as follows:

```cpp
// Program Name: MyHello.cpp

#include <iostream.h>

// Prototypes
int AddIt( int, int);

void main()
{

int iNum1;
int iNum2;
int iResult;

iNum1 = 2;
iNum2 = 3;

iResult = AddIt(iNum1, iNum2);

cout << "The result is: \n";
cout << iResult;
cout << "\n";


}

int AddIt(int iNumber1, int iNumber2)
{

int iTheResult;

iTheResult = iNumber1 + iNumber2;

return iTheResult;

}
```

☐ Select Save All from the File menu to save your work.

The `AddIt()` function looks like this:

```
int AddIt(int iNumber1, int iNumber2)
{

// The code of the AddIt() function
// is typed here

}
```

The body of the function is enclosed in curly brackets. Take a look at the first line of the `AddIt()` function:

```
int AddIt(int iNumber1, int iNumber2)
```

It's almost the same as the statement of the `AddIt()` prototype, but the first line of the function doesn't have a semicolon at the end as the prototype does. Also, the prototype does not have to specify the names of the two integer parameters passed to the `AddIt()` function, but the first line of the function must include the variables' names.

Passing Parameters to a Function

As you saw in the previous section, the first line of the `AddIt()` function contains the names of the two integers that `main()` passes to `AddIt()`. Therefore, `main()` includes this statement:

```
iResult = AddIt( iNum1, iNum2);
```

The first line of the `AddIt()` function means that the code in `AddIt()` has two variables, `iNumber1` and `iNumber2`, that are integers:

```
int AddIt(int iNumber1, int iNumber2)
```

The value of `iNumber1` is the same as the value of `iNum1`, and the value of `iNumber2` is the same as the value of `iNum2`. This is because the parameters are passed to the `AddIt()` function in this order: `iNumber1`, then `iNumber2`.

Now the code in `AddIt()` has two variables: `iNumber1` and `iNumber2`. You can write code that performs addition with these two numbers, beginning with this statement:

```
int iTheResult;
```

You declared another variable called `iTheResult` as an integer. Now `AddIt()` has three variables: `iNumber1`, `iNumber2`, and `iTheResult`. The next statement sets the value of `iTheResult` to the result of adding `iNumber1` to `iNumber2`:

```
iTheResult = iNumber1 + iNumber2;
```

Now `iTheResult` is equal to `iNumber1+iNumber2`. Because `main()` executes `AddIt(iNum1, iNum2)` while `iNum1` is equal to 2 and `iNum2` is equal to 3, it is as though `main()` executed `AddIt(2,3)`. So when `AddIt()` is executed, `iNumber1` is assigned the number 2, and `iNumber2` is assigned the number 3. Now `iTheResult` is equal to 2+3=5.

The last statement in the `AddIt()` function returns the `iTheResult` variable:

```
return iTheResult;
```

This is the same as saying

```
return 5;
```

because `iTheResult` is currently equal to 5.

Now look back at this statement in `main()`:

```
iResult = AddIt (iNum1, iNum2);
```

This statement assigns the value 5 to `iResult`.

☐ Select Build MyHello.EXE from the Build menu.

☐ Select Execute MyHello.EXE from the Build menu and verify that the MyHello program is working as expected.

Scope of Variables

One of the most important things to know about C++ is the scope of the variables. `iNum1` is declared in `main()`, so only `main()` knows about this variable. If you try to use the `iNum1` variable from within `AddIt()`, you'll get a compiling error. Why? Because the `iNum1` variable was declared in `main()`; therefore, you can use `iNum1` only from within the code of `main()`. The same goes for `iNum2` and `iResult`.

The `AddIt()` function has three variables: `iNumber1`, `iNumber2`, and `iTheResult`. You can use these variables only from within the code of `AddIt()`. If you try to use any of these variables from within `main()`, you'll get a compiling error because `main()` doesn't know about these three variables.

Therefore, the scope of the `iNum1` variable, as well as `iNum2` and `iResult`, is in `main()`, but the scope of `iNumber1`, `iNumber2`, and `iTheResult` is in `AddIt()`.

Note: In the first line of `AddIt()`, the first word is `int`:

```
int AddIt(int iNumber1, int iNumber2)
```

This means that AddIt() returns an integer. Indeed, the last statement in AddIt() is the following:

```
return iTheResult;
```

iTheResult was defined as type integer, so you are indeed returning an integer.

Sometimes, a function doesn't return any value. In this case, the first word on the first line of the function is void. For example, in the MyHello program, main() does not return any value, so the first word on the first line is void:

```
void main()
```

Also, when a function does not have any parameters, you simply use parentheses with no text enclosed, as in the first line of main().

Performing Multiplication with the MyHello Program

Modify the MyHello program so that it will multiply two numbers, rather than add them:

☐ Add the prototype of the DoMultiplication() function to the beginning of the MyHello.cpp file:

```
// Program Name: MyHello.cpp

#include <iostream.h>

// Prototypes
int AddIt( int, int);
int DoMultiplication( int, int);
```

☐ Modify the main() function as follows:

```
void main()
{

int iNum1;
int iNum2;
int iResult;

iNum1 = 2;
iNum2 = 3;

/// iResult = AddIt(iNum1, iNum2);
iResult = DoMultiplication ( iNum1, iNum2 );

cout << "The result is: \n";
cout << iResult;
cout << "\n";

}
```

The code you typed comments out the statement that executes the AddIt() function:

```
/// iResult = AddIt(iNum1, iNum2);
```

Then iResult is set to the returned value of the DoMultiplication() function:

```
iResult = DoMultiplication ( iNum1, iNum2 );
```

In other words, you are passing two parameters, iNum1 and iNum2, to the DoMultiplication() function. Since iNum1 is equal to 2 and iNum2 is equal to 3, DoMultiplication will have to return the number 6 (2*3=6). In C/C++, the multiplication sign is the * character found on your keyboard's 8 key.

☐ Add the DoMultiplication() function to the MyHello.cpp file (after the last line of the AddIt() function). Here is the code of the complete MyHello.cpp file:

```cpp
// Program Name: MyHello.cpp

#include <iostream.h>

// Prototypes
int AddIt( int, int);
int DoMultiplication( int, int);

void main()
{

int iNum1;
int iNum2;
int iResult;

iNum1 = 2;
iNum2 = 3;

/// iResult = AddIt(iNum1, iNum2);
iResult = DoMultiplication ( iNum1, iNum2 );

cout << "The result is: \n";
cout << iResult;
cout << "\n";


}


int AddIt(int iNumber1, int iNumber2)
{

int iTheResult;

iTheResult = iNumber1 + iNumber2;

return iTheResult;

}
```

```
int DoMultiplication( int iNumber1, int iNumber2)
{

int iResultOfMultiply;

iResultOfMultiply = iNumber1 * iNumber2;

return iResultOfMultiply;

}
```

The first line of the DoMultiplication() function means that the function returns an integer and that two integers are passed to the function:

```
int DoMultiplication( int iNumber1, int iNumber2)
```

The two parameters that are passed are iNumber1 and iNumber2. It is important to understand that iNumber1 and iNumber2 of the DoMultiplication() function have absolutely nothing to do with the iNumber1 and iNumber2 variables of the AddIt() function. In the AddIt() function, the iNumber1 and iNumber2 variables have their scope in AddIt(). In DoMultiplication(), the scope of iNumber1 and iNumber2 is within the DoMultiplication() function.

☐ Select Save All from the File menu.

☐ Select Build MyHello.cpp from the Build menu.

☐ Select Execute MyHello.EXE from the Build menu and verify that the MyHello program works as expected—the program should report that 2*3 is 6.

Passing Parameters by Value

Take a look at how main() executes the AddIt() function:

```
iResult = AddIt( iNum1, iNum2)
```

Now take a look at the first line of the AddIt() function:

```
int AddIt( int iNumber1, int iNumber2 )
{

}
```

Every variable is stored in a memory cell in the PC's RAM. So iNum1 and iNum2 have their own memory cells. But what about iNumber1 and iNumber2 of the AddIt() function? Because of the way you wrote the AddIt() function, iNumber1 and iNumber2 have their own memory cells. The value 2 was copied from the memory cell of iNum1 to the memory cell of iNumber1, and the value 3 was copied from the memory cell of iNum2 to the memory cell of iNumber2. However, the important thing to note is that iNum1 uses a completely different memory cell than the one used

by `iNumber1`. The same goes for the variables of the `DoMultiplication()` function. This is illustrated in Figure A.12. Note that this method of passing variables is called *passing the variables by value.*

Figure A.12.
Passing variables by value.

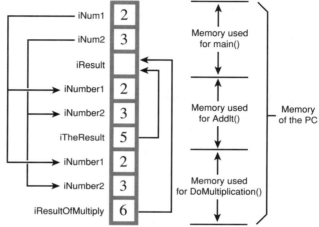

Note: A memory cell is called a *byte.* For simplicity, Figure A.12 (as well as subsequent figures) shows that `iNum1` occupies one memory cell and `iNum2` occupies one memory cell. However, the number of cells that a variable occupies depends on how the variable was defined. For example, when you declare a variable as `char`, the `cMyChar` variable occupies a single byte:

```
char cMyChar;
```

However, when a variable is declared as an integer, then `iNum1` uses four bytes of memory:

```
int iNum1;
```

Note: From the above discussion, you can see that instead of defining the `iResultOfMultiply` variable in the `DoMultiplication()` function, you could use a variable called `iResult`. The `DoMultiplication()` function could be written as follows:

```
int DoMultiplication( int iNumber1, int iNumber2)
{
```

```
int iResult;

iResultOfMultiply = iNumber1 * iNumber2;

return iResult;

}
```

The variable iResult in main() occupies completely different memory cells than the iResult variable in DoMultiplication(). Likewise, you can use iResult in the AddIt() function instead of the iTheResult variable.

You'll now prove that the names of the parameters of the AddIt() function could be changed from iNumber1 and iNumber2 to iX and iY:

☐ Modify the MyHello program so that instead of using iNumber1 and iNumber2 as the variables of AddIt(), the iX and iY variables are used:

```
int AddIt(int iX, int iY)
{

int iTheResult;

iTheResult = iX + iY;

return iTheResult;

}
```

The corresponding illustration of the memory cell map is shown in Figure A.13.

Figure A.13.
Using the iX and iY variables as the parameters of the AddIt() function.

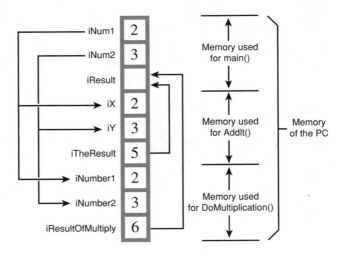

Using Global Variables

Take a look at Figure A.12. iNum1 is called a *local variable* of main() because its scope is only within main(). Likewise, iX and iY in Figure A.13 are local variables to AddIt().

In C, you can use *global variables,* which are variables whose memory cells are shared by all the functions of the program. You don't have to pass the variable to the function because the function can already use the variable. Follow these steps to see a global variable in action:

☐ At the beginning of the MyHello.cpp file, type the following statement:

```
int I_am_global;
```

The beginning of the MyHello.cpp file should now look like this:

```
// Program Name: MyHello.cpp

#include <iostream.h>

// Prototypes
int AddIt( int, int);
int DoMultiplication( int, int);

// Global variables
int I_am_global;
```

☐ Add the following prototype at the beginning of the MyHello.cpp file:

```
void SquareIt(int);
```

The beginning of the MyHello.cpp file should now look like the following:

```
// Program Name: MyHello.cpp

#include <iostream.h>

// Prototypes
int AddIt( int, int);
int DoMultiplication( int, int);
void SquareIt();

// Global variables
int I_am_global;
```

As you can see, you added the prototype of a function called SquareIt(). The SquareIt() function returns void, which means that the function doesn't return any value. The SquareIt() function has one parameter, which is an integer.

☐ Modify the code of the main() function:

```
void main()
{

int iNum1;
int iNum2;
int iResult;

iNum1 = 2;
iNum2 = 3;

//// iResult = AddIt(iNum1, iNum2);
//// iResult = DoMultiplication ( iNum1, iNum2 );
SquareIt(iNum1);
iResult = I_am_global;

cout << "The result is: \n";
cout << iResult;
cout << "\n";
}
```

The code you typed in `main()` executes the `SquareIt()` function:

```
SquareIt(iNum1);
```

`SquareIt()` multiplies `iNum1` by `iNum1` and assigns the result to `I_am_global`, the square of `iNum1`.

The next statement you typed sets the value of `iResult` to `I_am_global`:

```
iResult = I_am_global;
```

☐ Add the code of the `SquareIt()` function to the end of the MyHello.cpp file. When you finish, the complete MyHello.cpp file should look like the following:

```
// Program Name: MyHello.cpp

#include <iostream.h>

// Prototypes
int AddIt( int, int);
int DoMultiplication( int, int);
void SquareIt(int);

// Global variables
int I_am_global;


void main()
{

int iNum1;
int iNum2;
int iResult;

iNum1 = 2;
iNum2 = 3;
```

```
//// iResult = AddIt(iNum1, iNum2);
//// iResult = DoMultiplication ( iNum1, iNum2 );
SquareIt(iNum1);
iResult = I_am_global;

cout << "The result is: \n";
cout << iResult;
cout << "\n";

}


int AddIt(int iNumber1, int iNumber2)
{

int iTheResult;

iTheResult = iNumber1 + iNumber2;

return iTheResult;

}


int DoMultiplication( int iNumber1, int iNumber2)
{

int iResultOfMultiply;

iResultOfMultiply = iNumber1 * iNumber2;

return iResultOfMultiply;

}


void SquareIt( int iS )
{

I_am_global = iS * iS;

}
```

The code you typed in the SquareIt() function multiplies iS by iS, and the result is assigned to the I_am_global variable:

```
I_am_global = iS * iS;
```

Since iNum1 is equal to 2, then iS is equal to 2, and you set I_am_global to 2*2=4. The important thing to note is that every function has access to I_am_global because it was declared at the beginning of the MyHello.cpp file. Therefore, both main() and SquareIt() can use this variable.

☐ Select Save All from the File menu to save your work.

☐ Select Build MyHello.EXE from the Build menu.

☐ Select Execute MyHello.EXE from the Build menu and make sure the result is 4 (2*2=4).

Now here is the interesting part: Avoid using global variables as you avoid the plague! When your project becomes more complex, like including hundreds of functions in the program, it would be very easy to change the value of a global variable by mistake. In other words, it's too easy to change the value of a global variable because you can set its value from within any function of the program.

Take, for example, the iTheResult variable in the AddIt() function. This variable is known only in AddIt(); no other function can touch this variable. Even if your project contained hundreds of functions, you know that the AddIt() function is a completely independent module. No matter what your project does, the AddIt() function has a specific purpose (to add two numbers), and it does this regardless of what other functions in your project are doing.

From main(), you can execute the AddIt() function as follows:

```
iResult = AddIt(iNum1, iNum2);
```

Using the preceding function sets iResult to a number that's the result of adding iNum1 and iNum2. However, if you are updating a global variable in SquareIt(), and main() uses the SquareIt() function as follows,

```
SquareIt( iNum1);
```

```
iResult = I_am_global;
```

you are opening the door for the possibility of making silly mistakes. For example, suppose that after a year, you come back to the project and make some modifications to the code. As you are doing your modifications, you insert code between the statements, as follows:

```
SquareIt( iNum1);
….
…. // Additional code is inserted here
….
iResult = I_am_global;
```

Here is the problem: Suppose one of the statements you inserted executes another function that also makes use of the I_am_global variable. For example, some of the code you inserted between the two statements sets the value of I_am_global to 10. Now you have a bug in your program, because you expect iResult to be the square of iNum1.

You might say: Well, I'll be careful when inserting additional code. However, experience shows that no matter how careful you are, sooner or later you'll make the mistake of changing the value

of a global variable as described above. By the way, such mistakes are very difficult to debug when a program contains thousands of lines of code.

Addresses in C/C++

Take a look at Figure A.12. This figure shows that one of the memory cells is iNum1 and it contains the value 2. As a programmer, you call this memory cell iNum1, but the PC refers to this memory cell by a number. A PC's memory cells are numbered in sequential order: 1, 2, 3, 4, and so on. These numbers are called the *addresses* of the memory cells. As a programmer, you'll probably never need to know the address of the memory cell, which isn't always the same. Depending on what was executed first, what is already stored in memory, and other factors, the address used for storing iNum1 is different even on the same computer. Nevertheless, you can extract the address used for the cell by using the & operator. Follow these steps to see this in action:

☐ Modify the code in main():

```
void main()
{

int iNum1;
int iNum2;
int iResult;

iNum1 = 2;
iNum2 = 3;


cout << "Address of iNum1 is: \n";
cout <<   &iNum1;
cout << "\n";


cout << "Address of iNum2 is: \n";
cout <<   &iNum2;
cout << "\n";


//// iResult = AddIt(iNum1, iNum2);
//// iResult = DoMultiplication ( iNum1, iNum2 );
SquareIt(iNum1);
iResult = I_am_global;


cout << "The result is: \n";
cout << iResult;
cout << "\n";


}
```

The following block of code you added displays the address used for the memory cell of iNum1:

```
cout << "Address of iNum1 is: \n";
cout <<   &iNum1;
cout << "\n";
```

You then use the following code to display the address of the iNum2 variable:

```
cout << "Address of iNum2 is: \n";
cout <<   &iNum2;
cout << "\n";
```

☐ Save your work, compile and link the program, then execute the program.

As shown in Figure A.14, the MyHello program displays the addresses of the memory cells used by iNum1 and iNum2.

Figure A.14.

Displaying the addresses of
iNum1 and iNum2.

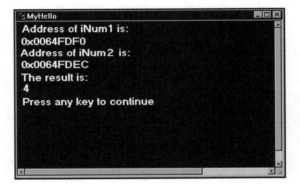

Note: In Figure A.14, the address of iNum1 is 0x0064FDF0, and the address of iNum2 is 0x0064FDEC. On your computer, you would probably see different values for the addresses, but the odd-looking number used for the address isn't important since you'll never use it in your programs. However, the discussion of addresses leads to the subject of pointers, which is what makes C famous. In fact, if C/C++ did not have the capability of using pointers, it would never have gained the popularity it has.

Figure A.15 shows a pictorial representation of the memory cells. As you can see, I_am_global can be accessed from any function of the program.

Figure A.15.
A pictorial representation of the memory cells.

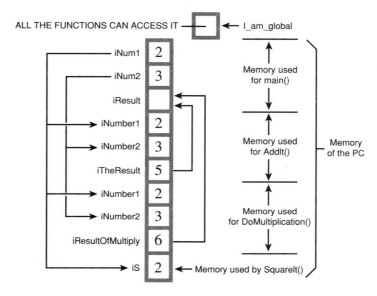

Using Pointers

An integer occupies four bytes in memory, so the left side of Figure A.16 is a more accurate representation of the memory map that shows iNum1 and iNum2.

Figure A.16.
Pointers to iNum1 and iNum2.

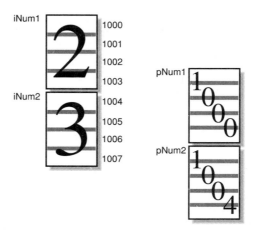

Suppose that iNum1 is equal to 2 and the address of iNum1 is 1000. iNum1 will occupy the bytes at locations 1000, 1001, 1002, and 1003. If iNum2 were equal to 3, then iNum2 would occupy the cells at addresses 1004, 1005, 1006, and 1007. Therefore, iNum1 starts at address 1000, and iNum2 starts at address 1004. However, even though iNum1 occupies four addresses, in C/C++ the address of iNum1 is called 1000 and the address of iNum2 is called 1004.

Now declare two variables, pNum1 and pNum2, as pointers. Your objective is to store the number 1000 (the address of iNum1) in pNum1 and the number 1004 (the address of iNum2) in pNum2. This is illustrated on the right side of Figure A.16.

☐ Modify main() so that it will look like the following:

```
void main()
{

int iNum1;
int iNum2;
int iResult;


int* pNum1;
int* pNum2;


iNum1 = 2;
iNum2 = 3;

pNum1 = &iNum1;
pNum2 = &iNum2;


iResult = *pNum1 + *pNum2;

cout << "The result is: \n";
cout << iResult;
cout << "\n";

}
```

The code you typed declares three integers:

```
int iNum1;
int iNum2;
int iResult;
```

Then two additional variables are declared:

```
int* pNum1;
int* pNum2;
```

Note that int* is used in the declarations. So what type of a variable is pNum1? Can you store integers in pNum1? The answer is no. You can store the address of a variable of type integer in

pNum1. According to Figure A.16, you should store 1000 in pNum1 because 1000 is the address of iNum1. Similarly, you want to store the address of an integer in pNum2. Then you set the values of iNum1 and iNum2:

```
iNum1 = 2;
iNum2 = 3;
```

Next, you update the values of pNum1 and pNum2 variables:

```
pNum1 = &iNum1;
pNum2 = &iNum2;
```

The preceding two statements store the address of iNum1 into pNum1 and the address of iNum2 into pNum2.

> **Note:** pNum1 is called the pointer of iNum1, and pNum2 is called the pointer of iNum2. Although it isn't a C/C++ requirement, pointer names have been preceded with the letter *p* so that it will be easy to tell that pNum1 is a pointer.

Next, you want to calculate the result of adding iNum1 to iNum2. You could easily use the following statement:

```
iResult = iNum1 + iNum2;
```

However, try performing the calculations by using pointers rather than variables. For example, you use the following statement to calculate the result of adding iNum1 and iNum2:

```
iResult = *pNum1 + *pNum2;
```

When you precede the pointer with the * character, you are extracting the value stored in the address. *pNum1 is the same as *1000 (because pNum1 is equal to 1000 in Figure A.16), so the program checks for the value stored in address 1000. Because pNum1 was declared as int*, (and the program knows that an integer occupies four memory cells), the program looks at addresses 1000, 1001, 1002, and 1003. The program finds the value 2 in these addresses, so *pNum1 is equal to 2. Similarly, *pNum2 is equal to 3 because pNum2 is equal to 1004, and memory cells 1003, 1004, 1005, and 1006 contain an integer with a value of 3.

Finally, cout is executed to display the value of iResult:

```
cout << "The result is: \n";
cout << iResult;
cout << "\n";
```

☐ Save your work, compile and link the MyHello program, then execute the program. Make sure that iResult is 5 (2+3=5).

It might seem as though pointers are a lot of trouble and were invented for the sole purpose of confusing a new C/C++ programmer, but this is not the case at all. To see why pointers are so important, suppose a certain function wants another function to be able to change its variable. For example, `main()` has a variable called `iToBeChanged`, and `main()` requires the `ChangeIt()` function to change the value of `iToBeChanged`. You could declare the `iToBeChanged` variable as a global variable, but if you do that, any function will be able to change `iToBeChanged`. You need to find a way to allow only the `ChangeIt()` function to change the `iToBeChanged` variable. You'll perform this task in the following steps:

☐ Declare the following prototype at the beginning of the MyHello.cpp file:

```
void ChangeIt(int*);
```

In other words, you are declaring a function that doesn't return anything. The parameter of the `ChangeIt()` function is a pointer to an integer.

☐ Modify the code of the `main()` function:

```
void main()
{

int iToBeChanged;

int* pToBeChanged;


iToBeChanged = 2;


pToBeChanged = &iToBeChanged;

ChangeIt( pToBeChanged);

cout << "iToBeChanged = \n";
cout << iToBeChanged;
cout << "\n";

}
```

The code you typed declares an integer variable:

```
int iToBeChanged;
```

Then the code declares a pointer to an integer variable:

```
int* pToBeChanged;
```

The `iToBeChanged` variable is then set to 2:

```
iToBeChanged = 2;
```

The pointer is then updated with the address of the iToBeChanged variable:

```
pToBeChanged = &iToBeChanged;
```

Next, the ChangeIt() function is executed:

```
ChangeIt( pToBeChanged);
```

You'll write the code of the ChangeIt() function later, but for now, assume that the ChangeIt() function changes the value of iToBeChanged.

Finally, the value of the iToBeChanged variable is displayed:

```
cout << "iToBeChanged = \n";
cout << iToBeChanged;
cout << "\n";
```

☐ Add the ChangeIt() function to the end of the MyHello.cpp file:

```
void ChangeIt(int* pMyVariable)
{

*pMyVariable = *pMyVariable + 1;

}
```

Recall that main() executes ChangeIt() as follows:

```
ChangeIt(pToBeChanged);
```

So the parameter of ChangeIt() is the address of the iToBeChanged integer. As you know by now, *pToBeChanged is the value stored in iToBeChanged (which is 2). The code in the ChangeIt() function changes the value of the parameter that was passed to it:

```
*iMyVariable = *iMyVariable + 1;
```

Therefore, if *iMyVariable was passed to ChangeIt() as 2, then the code in the ChangeIt() function changes 2 to 3 (2+1=3).

☐ Save your work.

☐ Compile and link the program.

☐ Execute the MyHello program and verify that the result is 3.

Keep in mind that main() enables the ChangeIt() function to touch the iToBeChanged variable. No other function in the program can touch the iToBeChanged variable, because main() passes the address of iToBeChanged to the ChangeIt() function.

if Statements

You'll now learn about the if statement in C/C++. An if statement examines the value of a variable. Based on the result, certain code is executed. To see the if statement in action, follow these steps:

☐ Modify the main() function:

```
void main()
{

int iMyVariable;
int iHerVariable;

iMyVariable = 20;
iHerVariable = 30;

if (iMyVariable == 20 )
   {
   cout << "Yes, it is 20! \n";
   }

if ( iHerVariable == 50 )
   {
   cout << "It's 50! \n";
   }
else
   {
   cout << "It's not 50! \n";
   }

}
```

The code you typed declares two variables:

```
int iMyVariable;
int iHerVariable;
```

Then you set the values of the two variables:

```
iMyVariable = 20;
iHerVariable = 30;
```

An if statement is then executed:

```
if (iMyVariable == 20 )
   {
   cout << "Yes, it is 20! \n";
   }
```

The code under the if is executed if iMyVariable is equal to 20. This code displays the following message:

```
Yes, it is 20!
```

Another if statement is then executed:

```
if ( iHerVariable == 50 )
    {
    cout << "It's 50! \n";
    }
else
    {
    cout << "It's not 50! \n";
    }
```

The code under the if statement is executed if iHerVariable is equal to 50. The code under the else is executed if iHerVariable is not equal to 50.

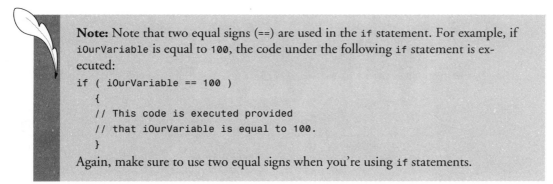

> **Note:** Note that two equal signs (==) are used in the if statement. For example, if iOurVariable is equal to 100, the code under the following if statement is executed:
>
> ```
> if ( iOurVariable == 100 )
>     {
>     // This code is executed provided
>     // that iOurVariable is equal to 100.
>     }
> ```
>
> Again, make sure to use two equal signs when you're using if statements.

☐ Save your work.

☐ Compile and link the program.

☐ Execute the program.

As shown in Figure A.17, the program displays the corresponding messages.

Figure A.17.
The messages displayed when the if and if...else statements are executed.

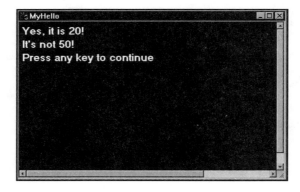

You can use other comparing statements with the `if` statement, as shown in the following example:

```
if ( i< 0 )
   {
   // This code is executed provided
   // that i is less than
   }


if ( i< = 0 )
   {
   // This code is executed provided
   // that i is less than or equal to 0
   }


if ( I > 0 )
   {
   // This code is executed provided
   // that i is greater than 0
   }


if ( I >=0 )
   {
   // This code is executed provided
   // that i is greater than or equal to 0
   }


if ( i != 3 )
   {
   // This code is executed provided
   // that i is not equal to 3
   }


if ( i == 3 && j == 4 )
   {
   // This code is executed provided
   // that i is equal to 3
   // and (&&) j is equal to 4
   }


if ( i == 3 ¦¦ j == 4 )
   {
   // This code is executed provided
   // that i is equal to 3
   // or (¦¦) j is equal to 4
   }
```

Strings

Strings are used to hold text. For example, `"This is my string"` is a string. C/C++ has a variety of data types: `int`, `long`, `char`, and so on. But in C/C++, there is no data type of the type `string`. So how do you handle strings? You actually build the string character-by-character, as demonstrated in the following steps:

☐ Modify `main()` so that it will look like the following:

```
void main()
{

char sMyString[100];

strcpy(sMyString, "ABC");

cout << sMyString;
cout << "\n";

}
```

The code you typed declares a variable called `sMyString` of type `char`:

```
char sMyString[100];
```

The square brackets are used to declare arrays in C/C++. `sMyString` is a variable capable of holding 100 characters. You then execute the `strcpy()` function:

```
strcpy(sMyString, "ABC");
```

The `strcpy()` function works as follows:

The first parameter of `strcpy()` is the destination string; the second parameter is the source string. The `strcpy()` function copies the contents of the source string to the destination string. In the preceding statement, the string `ABC` is copied into the `sMyString` string.

If you were able to examine the characters of the `sMyString` variable at this point, you'd see the following:

> The first character of `sMyString` is `A`.
> The second character of `sMyString` is `B`.
> The third character of `sMySTring` is `C`.

Also, the fourth character of `sMyString` contains the value `0`. The `strcpy()` function automatically inserts `0` for the fourth character of `sMyString`. In C/C++, when the last character of a string is `0`, it means this is the end of the string.

Finally, you display the contents of `sMyString`:

```
cout << sMyString;
cout << "\n";
```

As you have seen, `main()` uses the `strcpy()` function. However, you don't have to write the `strcpy()` function yourself. Why? Because C/C++ is good enough to include the `strcpy()` function. C/C++ comes with many useful functions you can use from within your programs. You don't have to write the code of the `strcpy()` function yourself, but you do have to include its prototype. As it turns out, the file string.h (a file that comes with the C/C++ compiler) has the prototype of the `strcpy()` function. So all you have to do is simply use the `#include` statement at the beginning if the MyHello.cpp file.

☐ Type the following statement at the beginning of the MyHello.cpp file:

```
#include <string.h>
```

Now the beginning of the MyHello.cpp file should look like this:

```
// Program Name: MyHello.cpp

#include <iostream.h>
#include <string.h>
```

☐ Save your work.

☐ Compile and link the program.

☐ Execute the MyHello program and verify that it displays the string ABC, as shown in Figure A.18.

Figure A.18.
Displaying strings.

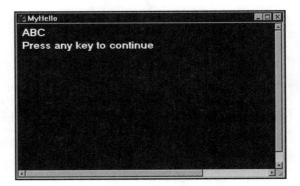

Summary

This is the end of Part I of the tutorial. Do you know the essentials of C/C++? To *really know* C/C++, you would have to program with it daily for at least several years. C/C++ is such a powerful, rich language that knowing everything about it is a long process requiring years of experience. However, since technology is changing so rapidly, you may often be asked to start writing sophisticated Windows programs in a very short time. Most programmers cannot afford to spend too long on the study of C/C++, and reality dictates that you'll start designing and developing Visual C++ Windows programs immediately. You'll learn about additional C/C++ topics during the course of this book, but on a need-to-know-basis. During the development of the programs, when a new C/C++ topic is used, it will be discussed at that point.

In Part II of this tutorial (Appendix B), you'll start learning about the C/C++ topics of classes and objects.

Learning C/C++
Quickly (Part II)

In this part of the tutorial, you'll learn about topics such as structures, classes, and objects.

C/C++ Structures

As you saw, in C/C++ you can declare variables as follows:

```
int iMyVariable;
```

In the preceding statement, you declared `iMyVariable` as an integer. Here is a declaration of a variable of type `char`:

```
char cMyCar;
```

Data types such as `int`, `float`, `char`, and `long` are an integral part of C/C++, so you don't have to write any code that tells the compiler what these words mean. However, C/C++ also lets you declare your own custom-made data types. In the following section, you'll learn how to declare *structures,* which can be considered custom-made data types.

The MyStruct Program

The MyStruct program illustrates the use of structures in C/C++. Follow these steps to create the program:

☐ Create the C:\TYVCProg\Programs\AppendB directory. You'll save all the programs of Appendix B into this directory.

☐ From within Windows 95, start Visual C++.

> *Windows responds by running the Visual C++ program, and the desktop of Visual C++ is displayed.*

☐ If you currently have an open project, select Close Project Workspace from the File menu of Visual C++.

☐ Select New from the File menu.

> *Visual C++ responds by displaying the New dialog box.*

☐ Select the Text File item in the New dialog box to create a new text file.

☐ Click the OK button of the New dialog box.

> *Visual C++ responds by creating the new Text1 window.*

The default name that Visual C++ assigned to the new Text window is Text1, so you need to change its name:

☐ Make sure the Text1 window is selected, then choose Save As from the File menu.

Visual C++ responds by displaying the Save As dialog box.

☐ Save the file as MyStruct.cpp in the C:\TYVCProg\Programs\AppendB\MyStruct directory.

The code of the MyStruct program is written in the MyStruct.cpp text file.

☐ Type the following code in the MyStruct.cpp file:

```
// The MyStruct.CPP Program

#include <iostream.h>
#include <string.h>

// Declaring the inside of a structure
struct MYSTRUCTURE
       {
       char sName[100];
       int  iAge;
       };


void main()
{

MYSTRUCTURE MyStructure;

strcpy( MyStructure.sName, "David" );
MyStructure.iAge = 13;

cout << "My name is ";
cout << MyStructure.sName;
cout << " and I am ";
cout << MyStructure.iAge;
cout << " years old.";
cout << "\n";

}
```

The code you typed uses two #include statements:

```
#include <iostream.h>
#include <string.h>
```

B

You include the file iostream.h because the code in main() uses cout, and the file string.h because the code in main() uses the strcpy() function (declared in the string.h file). You then declare the structure:

```
struct MYSTRUCTURE
       {
       char sName[100];
       int  iAge;
       };
```

Note the syntax for declaring a structure. The struct word appears first, followed by the name of the structure type. In this program, the structure type is called MYSTRUCTURE. Then the actual definition of the structure is declared in curly brackets. Don't forget to type the semicolon after the last curly bracket. Now take a look at the code in the curly brackets:

```
char sName[100];
int  iAge;
```

This means that MYSTRUCTURE is composed of a string called sName and an integer called iAge. sName and iAge are called the structure's *data members;* you've now declared the "inside" of the MYSTRUCTURE structure.

The code in main() declares a variable called MyStructure of type MYSTRUCTURE:

```
MYSTRUCTURE MyStructure;
```

Remember that in Appendix A you declared the iNum1 variable as follows:

```
int iNum1;
```

When you declare MyStructure to be a structure of type MYSTRUCTURE, think of MyStructure just as you think of iNum1. MyStructure is the name of the variable, and it's of type MYSTRUCTURE, just as iNum1 is of type int. (Note that, traditionally, the name of the structure is composed of lowercase or mixed-case characters, as in MyStructure, while the name of the structure type is all uppercase characters, as in MYSTRUCTURE.)

The next statement you typed in main() copies the string David into the MyStructure.sName data member:

```
strcpy ( MyStructure.sName, "David" );
```

The preceding statement refers to the sName data member as the following:

```
MyStructure.sName
```

The next statement updates the iAge data member of the structure:

```
MyStructure.iAge = 13;
```

Then a series of cout statements are executed:

```
cout << "My name is ";
cout << MyStructure.sName;
cout << " and I am ";
cout << MyStructure.iAge;
cout << " years old.";
cout << "\n";
```

To put it all together, the MyStruct program displays the message:

```
My name is David and I am 13 years old.
```

☐ Select Save All from the File menu to save your work.

☐ Select Build MyStruct.EXE from the Build menu. When Visual C++ asks if you want to create a project, click the Yes button.

☐ Select Execute MyStruct.EXE from the Build menu.

Visual C++ responds by executing the MyStruct program. As you can see, the MyStruct program displays this message:

```
My name is David and I am 13 years old.
```

Creating More Variables of Type *MYSTRUCTURE*

In the previous section, you created the variable MyStructure of type MYSTRUCTURE. You'll now create more variables of type MYSTRUCTURE:

☐ Modify the code in main() so that the MyStruct.cpp file will look like the following:

```
// The MyStruct.CPP Program

#include <iostream.h>
#include <string.h>

// Declaring the inside of a structure
struct MYSTRUCTURE
        {
        char sName[100];
        int  iAge;
        };


void main()
{

MYSTRUCTURE MyStructure;

MYSTRUCTURE HerStructure;
```

```
strcpy(MyStructure.sName,"David");
MyStructure.iAge = 13;

cout << "My name is ";
cout << MyStructure.sName;
cout << " and I am ";
cout << MyStructure.iAge;
cout << " years old.";
cout << "\n";

strcpy(HerStructure.sName,"Kim");
HerStructure.iAge = 12;

cout << "My name is ";
cout << HerStructure.sName;
cout << " and I am ";
cout << HerStructure.iAge;
cout << " years old.";
cout << "\n";

}
```

The main() function declares two variables, MyStructure and HerStructure:

```
MYSTRUCTURE MyStructure;
```

```
MYSTRUCTURE HerStructure;
```

MyStructure has two members: MyStructure.sName and MyStructure.iAge. HerStructure also has two members: HerStructure.sName and HerStructure.iAge.

You updated the MyStructure data members as you did in the previous version of the MyStruct program:

```
strcpy(MyStructure.sName,"David");
MyStructure.iAge = 13;
```

Then the message is displayed:

```
cout << "My name is ";
cout << MyStructure.sName;
cout << " and I am ";
cout << MyStructure.iAge;
cout << " years old.";
cout << "\n";
```

The preceding statements display this message:

```
My name is David and I am 13 years old.
```

Next, the data members of HerStructure are updated:

```
strcpy(HerStructure.sName,"Kim");
HerStructure.iAge = 12;
```

The sName data member of HerStructure is set to Kim, and the iAge data member is set to 12.

Then a message is displayed:

```
cout << "My name is ";
cout << HerStructure.sName;
cout << " and I am ";
cout << HerStructure.iAge;
cout << " years old.";
cout << "\n";
```

The preceding statements display this message:

```
My name is Kim and I am 12 years old.
```

☐ Select Save All from the File menu.

☐ Select Build MyStruct.EXE from the Build menu.

☐ Select Execute MyStruct.EXE from the Build menu.

> *The MyStruct program responds by displaying these messages:*
>
> ```
> My name is David and I am 13 years old.
> My name is Kim and I am 12 years old.
> ```

Classes

One of the main features of C++ that doesn't exist in C is the concept of *classes*. In fact, they're the most important concept in C++. C++ classes are similar to C structures. A C structure, however, defines only the data associated with the structure. The following example is a C structure:

```
struct CIRCLE
{
int radius;
int color;
};
```

After you declare the structure, you can use it from within your main() statement, as follows:

```
void main()
{
CIRCLE MyCircle;
...
...
...

MyCircle.radius = 10;
MyCircle.color = 255;   // 255 represents a color
...
...
...
}
```

The MyCircle structure has data associated with it (radius and color). A class in C++, on the other hand, has both data and functions associated with it. The data of the class is called *data members,* and the functions of the class are called *member functions.* In a program that uses classes, therefore, the following code is allowed:

```
MyCircle.radius = 20;
MyCircle.color = 255;
MyCircle.DisplayCircle();
```

The first two statements update the radius and color data members of MyCircle; the third statement uses the member function DisplayCircle() to display the MyCircle circle. MyCircle is called an *object* of class CIRCLE. Your program can declare another object called HerCircle of class CIRCLE as follows:

```
CIRCLE HerCircle;
```

The radius and color data members of HerCircle can be updated as follows:

```
HerCircle.radius = 30;
HerCircle.color = 0;
```

You can then use the DisplayCircle() member function to display the HerCircle circle:

```
HerCircle.DisplayCircle();
```

Declaring a Class

Before you can do anything with the class, your program must declare the class (just as before using the MYSTRUCTURE structure you had to declare its data members). In this section, you learn about the syntax used to declare a class. For practice, you'll declare a class called Circle:

```
class Circle
{
public:
    Circle();
    void SetRadius(void);
    void GetRadius(void);
    ~Circle();
private:
    void CalculateArea(void);
    int radius;
    int color;
};
```

The class declaration has the following skeleton:

```
class Circle
{
........
........
........
```

```
Here you type the declaration of the class
........
........
........
};
```

The `class` keyword is an indication to the compiler that whatever is typed between the curly brackets ({}) belongs to the class declaration. (Don't forget to include the semicolon at the end of the declaration.) The class declaration contains the declarations of data members (for example, `int radius`) and prototypes of the member functions of the class. In the `Circle` class declaration, there are two data members:

```
int radius;
int color;
```

The declaration also contains five prototypes of member functions:

```
Circle();
void SetRadius(void);
void GetRadius(void);
~CCircle();
void CalculateArea(void);
```

The first and third prototypes look strange. The first one is the prototype of the *constructor* function:

```
Circle();
```

You'll learn about the role of the constructor function later in this chapter; for now, examine the syntax that C++ uses for the prototype of the constructor function. When you write the prototype of the constructor function, you must follow these rules:

- Every class declaration must include the prototype of the constructor function.
- The name of the constructor function must be the same as the class name, followed by (). If you declare a class called `Rectangle`, for example, it must include the declaration of its constructor function, which must be `Rectangle()`. The declaration of the `Rectangle` class, therefore, looks like the following:

```
class Rectangle
{
public:
  Rectangle(); // The constructor
...
...
...
private:
...
...
...
};
```

- Don't mention any returned value for the constructor function. (The constructor function must be of type void, but do not mention it.)
- The constructor function must be under the public keyword.

> **Note:** At this point, you are probably asking yourself: What are the public and private keywords mentioned in the class declaration? These keywords indicate the visibility (accessibility) of the class's data members and member functions. You'll learn about these keywords later in the section "The *public* and *private* Keywords." For now, just remember that the constructor function must be under the public keyword.

The constructor function always has a return value of type void (even though you should not mention it in the prototype). As you'll soon see, the constructor function usually has one or more parameters.

The Destructor Function

The destructor function is mentioned in the class declaration as follows:

```
class Circle
{
public:
......
......
......
~Circle(); // The destructor
private:
......
......
......
};
```

Notice the tilde character [~] that precedes the prototype of the destructor function. (On most keyboards, you'll find the tilde character to the left of the 1 key.) When you write the prototype of the destructor function, observe the following rules:

- The name of the destructor function must be the same as the class name, preceded by the ~ character. If you declare a class called Rectangle, for example, the name of the destructor function must be ~Rectangle. The declaration of the Rectangle class, therefore, looks like this:

```
class Rectangle
{
public:
    Rectangle();  // The constructor
    .......
    .......
    .......
    ~Rectangle(); // The destructor
private:
    .......
    .......
    .......
};
```

- Don't mention any returned value for the destructor function. (The destructor function must be of type void, but do not mention it.)
- The destructor function does not have any parameters.

The *public* and *private* Keywords

You include the prototype of the functions and the declaration of the data members under the public or private section of the class declaration. The public and private keywords tell the compiler the accessibility of the functions and the data members. For example, the SetRadius() function is defined under the public section, which means that any function in the program can call the SetRadius() function. However, because the CalculateArea() function is declared under the private section, only code in the member functions of the Circle class can call the CalculateArea() function.

Similarly, because the radius data member is declared under the private section, only code in the member functions of the Circle class can update or read the value of this data member directly. Had you declared the radius data member under the public section, however, any function in the program could access (read and update) the radius data member.

Note: The class declaration defines the accessibility of its member functions and its data members with the public and private keywords.

The Circle Program

So far, you've learned about some important syntax topics in C++, such as the syntax of class declaration. Now you're ready to write a program that makes use of a class. The program you'll write is called Circle.cpp.

Writing the Code of the Circle.cpp Program

Follow these steps to write the Circle.cpp program:

☐ Select Close Project Workspace from the File menu to close any opened project.

☐ Select New from the File menu.

Visual C++ responds by displaying the New dialog box.

☐ Select the Text File item in the New dialog box to create a new text file.

☐ Click the OK button.

Visual C++ responds by creating the new Text1 window.

The default name that Visual C++ assigns to the new Text window is Text1. Follow these steps to change its name:

☐ Make sure the Text1 window is selected, then select Save As from the File menu.

Visual C++ responds by displaying the Save As dialog box.

☐ Save the file as Circle.cpp in the C:\TYVCProg\Programs\AppendB directory.

☐ Type the Circle program's code in Listing B.1 in the Circle.cpp file.

Listing B.1. The Circle.cpp program.

```
// Program Name: Circle.CPP

// #include files
#include <iostream.h>

// Declare the CCircle class
class CCircle
{
public:
CCircle( int r);      // Constructor
void    SetRadius(int r);
void    DisplayArea(void);
~CCircle();           // Destructor
private:
float CalculateArea(void);
int m_Radius;
int m_Color;
};
```

```cpp
// The constructor function
CCircle::CCircle ( int r )
{

// Set the radius
m_Radius = r;

}

// The destructor function
CCircle::~CCircle ()
{


}

// Function Name: DisplayArea()
void CCircle::DisplayArea ( void )
{

float fArea;

fArea = CalculateArea ( );

// Print the area
cout << "The area of the circle is: " << fArea;
cout << "\n";

}

// Function Name: CalculateArea()
float CCircle::CalculateArea ( void )
{

float f;

f = (float) (3.14 * m_Radius * m_Radius);

return f;

}

void main(void)
{
// Create an object of class Circle with
// radius equals to 10.
CCircle MyCircle ( 10 );

// Display the area of the circle
MyCircle.DisplayArea();

}
```

> **Note:** Class names usually start with the letter *C* (the CCircle class, the CRectangle class, and so on). Data-member names usually start with the characters m_ (m_Radius, m_Colors, and so on).
>
> These naming conventions aren't requirements in Visual C++, but they help you identify the names of classes and data members.

You haven't been instructed to type the code of the SetRadius() member function yet; you'll do that later in this appendix.

Examining the Circle Program's Code

In this section, you'll go over the code of the Circle.cpp program. First, the code must include the iostream.h file because the cout statement is used in this program:

```
#include <iostream.h>
```

The Circle.cpp program then declares the CCircle class:

```
class CCircle
{
public:
CCircle( int r);        // Constructor
void    SetRadius(int r);
void    DisplayArea(void);
~CCircle();             // Destructor
private:
float CalculateArea(void);
int m_Radius;
int m_Color;
};
```

The public section contains four prototypes. The first is the prototype of the constructor function:

```
CCircle( int r);        // Constructor
```

As always, the prototype of the constructor function doesn't mention that the function is of type void. Notice that the constructor function has the parameter int r.

Next are two more prototypes:

```
void    SetRadius(int r);
void    DisplayArea(void);
```

Remember, you'll be able to access these functions from any function in the program because they're public member functions. The fourth prototype under the public section is the prototype of the destructor function:

```
~CCircle();
```

Again, the prototype of the destructor function doesn't mention that this function is of type void. Notice that the ~ character precedes the name of the destructor function.

The `private` section of the `CCircle` class declaration contains the prototype of one function and the declaration of two data members:

```
private:
float CalculateArea(void);
int m_Radius;
int m_Color;
```

Since `CalculateArea()` is declared under the `private` section of the `CCircle` class declaration, you can call the `CalculateArea()` function only from within member functions of the `CCircle` class.

Now look at the `main()` function:

```
void main(void)
{

// Create an object of class CCircle with radius
// equal to 10.
CCircle MyCircle ( 10 );

// Display the area of the circle
MyCircle.DisplayArea();

}
```

The first statement in `main()` creates an object called `MyCircle` of class `CCircle`:

```
CCircle MyCircle ( 10 );
```

This statement causes the execution of the constructor function. At first glance, the notation for executing the constructor function may look strange. However, this notation makes sense: As stated earlier, the statement creates an object called `MyCircle` of class `CCircle`. The `MyCircle` object is created with a radius equal to 10 because the constructor function `CCircle()` has `radius` as its parameter.

Before continuing to examine the `main()` function, look at the constructor function:

```
// The constructor function
CCircle::CCircle ( int r )
{

// Set the radius
m_Radius = r;

}
```

The constructor function has one parameter, `int r`, as specified in its prototype. In the first line of the function, the function name is preceded by the text `CCircle::`, which means that the `CCircle()` function is a member function of the `CCircle` class:

```
CCircle::CCircle ( int r )
{
...
...
...
}
```

The code in the constructor function consists of a single statement:

```
m_Radius = r;
```

The parameter r is passed to the constructor function. Since you created MyCircle in main(), 10 is passed to the constructor function:

```
CCircle MyCircle ( 10 );
```

The statement in the constructor function sets the value of m_Radius to r:

```
m_Radius = r;
```

In short, the constructor function sets the value of m_Radius to 10. Recall that m_Radius was declared as a data member of the CCircle class, so any member function (public or private) of the CCircle class can read or update m_Radius. At this point, the object MyCircle of class CCircle has been created, and its data member m_Radius has been set to 10. The next statement in main() executes the DisplayArea() member function:

```
MyCircle.DisplayArea();
```

You declared the DisplayArea() function in the public section of the CCircle class declaration; therefore, main() can access the DisplayArea() function. The dot (.) operator separates the name of the object MyCircle and the DisplayArea() function, giving the following instruction to the compiler:

```
"Execute the DisplayArea() function on the MyCircle object."
```

The DisplayArea() function displays the area of the MyCircle object. Look at the code of the DisplayArea() function:

```
void Circle::DisplayArea ( void )
{

float fArea;

fArea = CalculateArea ( );

// Print the area
cout << "The area of the circle is: " << fArea;
cout << "\n";

}
```

Again, the compiler knows that this function is a member function of the CCircle class because the first line uses the CCircle:: notation. The function declares a local float variable called fArea:

```
float fArea;
```

Then the CalculateArea() function is executed:

```
fArea = CalculateArea ( );
```

CalculateArea() is a member function of the CCircle class; therefore, DisplayArea() can call the CalculateArea() function. The CalculateArea() function returns the area of the circle as a float number. The next statement in DisplayArea() uses cout to display the value of fArea:

```
cout << "The area of the circle is: " << fArea;
cout << "\n";
```

This statement streams the value of fArea and the string The area of the circle is: onto the screen.

> **Note:** You can use a single cout statement to display more than one string, as shown in this example:
>
> ```
> cout << "The area of the circle is: " << fArea;
> ```
>
> The preceding statement produces the same result as the following two statements:
>
> ```
> cout << "The area of the circle is: ";
> cout << fArea;
> ```

Now examine the CalculateArea() function. The first line of the CalculateArea() function uses the CCircle:: text to indicate that this function is a member function of the CCircle class:

```
float CCircle::CalculateArea ( void )
{

float f;

f = (float) (3.14 * m_Radius * m_Radius);

return f;

}
```

The CalculateArea() function declares a local variable called f:

```
float f;
```

Then the area of the circle is calculated and assigned to the f variable:

```
f = (float) (3.14 * m_Radius * m_Radius);
```

The text (float) is called *cast.* The number 3.14 is a float number (number with fractions), and m_Radius is an integer. The preceding statement multiplies an integer by an integer, then the result is multiplied by the float number 3.14. What is the data type of the result? You must assign a float number to f, because f was declared as float. Therefore, you cast the result of the multiplication with the (float) text. *Casting* is the process of converting the result to the desired data type.

CalculateArea() does not have any parameters. How, then, does this function know to substitute 10 for m_Radius? During the execution of the Circle program, the history of executing functions is traced. First, main() creates the MyCircle object:

```
Circle MyCircle ( 10 );
```

This code causes the execution of the constructor function, which causes the m_Radius variable of the MyCircle object to be equal to 10. Then main() executes the DisplayArea() function on the MyCircle object:

```
MyCircle.DisplayArea();
```

DisplayArea() executes the CalculateArea() function:

```
fArea = CalculateArea ( );
```

CalculateArea() knows to use 10 for the value of m_Radius since CalculateArea() is executed because DisplayArea() was executed on the MyCircle object. CalculateArea() can access m_Radius because CalculateArea() is a member function of the CCircle class and m_Radius is a data member of the CCircle class.

The last statement in CalculateArea() returns the calculated area:

```
return f;
```

The destructor function looks like this:

```
CCircle::~CCircle ()
{

}
```

The first line of the destructor function starts with the CCircle:: text, an indication that this function is a member function of the CCircle class. No further code is used in the destructor function. You should know, however, that the destructor function is executed automatically whenever the MyCircle object is destroyed—in this program, it's destroyed when the program terminates.

Notice that the SetRadius() function was not used in the program.

Compiling and Linking the Circle Program

You'll now compile and link the Circle.cpp program.

☐ Select Build Circle.EXE from the Build menu.

Visual C++ responds by displaying a dialog box that asks whether you want to create a project.

☐ Click the Yes button.

Visual C++ responds by compiling and linking the Circle.cpp program.

☐ Execute the Circle.EXE program.

The Circle.EXE program displays this message:

```
The area of the circle is: 314.
```

The Circle2 Program

So far, you have declared a class called CCircle, you have created the object MyCircle of class CCircle, and you have calculated and displayed the area of the MyCircle object.

Although main() looks very elegant and short, it doesn't demonstrate the object-oriented nature of C++. The Circle2 program shows how you can create more than one object of class CCircle.

Writing the Code of the Circle2 Program

You'll now write the code of the Circle2.cpp program by following these steps:

☐ Select Close Project Workspace from the File menu.

☐ Select New from the File menu, select Text File from the New dialog box, then click the OK button.

Visual C++ responds by displaying an empty window called Text1.

☐ Select Save As from the File menu and save the new empty text file as Circle2.cpp in the C:\TYVCProg\Programs\AppendB directory.

☐ Type the code of the Circle2.cpp program as it appears in Listing B.2.

Listing B.2. The code of the Circle2.cpp program.

```cpp
// Program Name: Circle2.CPP

// #include files
#include <iostream.h>

// Declare the Circle class
class CCircle
{
public:
CCircle( int r);      // Constructor
void    SetRadius(int r);
void    DisplayArea(void);
~CCircle();           // Destructor
private:
float CalculateArea(void);
int m_Radius;
int m_Color;
};

// The constructor function
CCircle::CCircle ( int r )
{

// Set the radius
m_Radius = r;

}

// The destructor function
CCircle::~CCircle ()
{

}

// Function Name: DisplayArea()
void CCircle::DisplayArea ( void )
{

float fArea;

fArea = CalculateArea ( );

// Print the area
cout << "The area of the circle is: " << fArea;

}

// Function Name: CalculateArea()
float CCircle::CalculateArea ( void )
{

float f;

f = (float) (3.14 * m_Radius * m_Radius);
```

```
    return f;

}

void main(void)
{
// Create an object of class CCircle with
// radius equal to 10.
CCircle MyCircle ( 10 );

// Create an object of class CCircle with
// radius equal to 20.
CCircle HerCircle ( 20 );

// Create an object of class CCircle with
// radius equal to 30.
CCircle HisCircle ( 30 );

// Display the area of the circles
MyCircle.DisplayArea();
cout << "\n";
HerCircle.DisplayArea();
cout << "\n";
HisCircle.DisplayArea();
cout << "\n";

}
```

Examining the Code of the Circle2 Program

In this section, you'll examine the code of the Circle2.cpp program. First, because the Circle2 program uses cout, you need to include the iostream.h file:

```
#include <iostream.h>
```

Then the class declaration of the CCircle class appears:

```
class CCircle
{
public:
    CCircle( int r);     // Constructor
    void    SetRadius(int r);
    void    DisplayArea(void);
    ~CCircle();          // Destructor
private:
    float CalculateArea(void);
    int m_Radius;
    int m_Color;
};
```

This class declaration is identical to the one in the Circle.cpp program. The constructor function of the CCircle class, the destructor function, the DisplayArea() function, and the CalculateArea() function are also the same as those for the Circle.cpp program. The code in the main() function is the only difference in the Circle2.cpp program:

```
void main(void)
{

// Create an object of class Circle with
// radius equal to 10.
CCircle MyCircle ( 10 );

// Create an object of class Circle with
// radius equal to 20.
CCircle HerCircle ( 20 );

// Create an object of class Circle with
// radius equal to 30.
CCircle HisCircle ( 30 );

// Display the area of the circles
MyCircle.DisplayArea();
cout << "\n";
HerCircle.DisplayArea();
cout << "\n";
HisCircle.DisplayArea();
cout << "\n";

}
```

The first statement in main() creates an object called MyCircle of class CCircle with its m_Radius data member equal to 10:

```
CCircle MyCircle ( 10 );
```

The next two statements create two more objects:

```
CCircle HerCircle ( 20 );
CCircle HisCircle ( 30 );
```

The HerCircle object is created with its m_Radius data member equal to 20, and the HisCircle object is created with its m_Radius data member equal to 30.

Note: C++ is known as an OOP (object-oriented programming) language because it deals with objects.

Now that these three objects have been created, main() displays the circles' areas by using the DisplayArea() member function on the corresponding circle objects:

```
MyCircle.DisplayArea();
cout << "\n";
HerCircle.DisplayArea();
cout << "\n";
HisCircle.DisplayArea();
cout << "\n";
```

Between the execution of the `DisplayArea()` functions, `cout` is used to print a carriage-return/line-feed character (\n) so that an empty line will appear between the messages.

When the first `DisplayArea()` function is executed, its code executes the `CalculateArea()` function:

```
MyCircle.DisplayArea();
```

`CalculateArea()` makes use of the `m_Radius` data member, but which `m_Radius` will be used? The `m_Radius` of the `MyCircle` object is used because `DisplayArea()` works on the `MyCircle` object.

Similarly, when the `CalculateArea()` function is executed from within the `DisplayArea()` function, the `m_Radius` of the `HerCircle` object is used:

```
HerCircle.DisplayArea();
```

When the area of the `HisCircle` object is displayed, the `m_Radius` of `HisCircle` is used to calculate the area.

Compiling, Linking, and Executing the Circle2 Program

To see your code in action, follow these steps:

☐ Select Save All from the File menu to save your work.

☐ Select Build Circle2.EXE from the Build menu.

Visual C++ responds by compiling and linking the Circle2 program.

☐ Select Execute Circle2.EXE from the Build menu.

Visual C++ responds by executing the Circle2.EXE program.

The Circle2 program should report the areas corresponding to the three circle objects: `MyCircle` has an area of 3.14*10*10=314, `HerCircle` has an area of 3.14*20*20=1256, and `HisCircle` has an area of 3.14*30*30=2826.

In the preceding section, you entered the code of the Circle2.cpp program from Listing B.2; however, most of the code had been typed already in the Circle.cpp file. As you're probably starting to realize, that's the idea of object-oriented programming. You created the class during the development of the Circle.cpp program. From now on, you can develop other programs

(such as the Circle2.cpp program) with a minimum of typing because you did most of the work during the development of the Circle.cpp program. In fact, the only thing you have to do to the Circle.cpp program to convert it to the Circle2.cpp program is to modify its `main()` function.

Reusing the *CCircle* Class

Notice how short and elegant the `main()` function of the Circle2 program is. This function is easy to read and, more important, easy to maintain. If you decide you need more accuracy in calculating the circle areas, you can simply change the code of the `CalculateArea()` member function. (You can change 3.14 to 3.1415, for example.)

If you type the class declaration in a file called CCircle.h, you can remove the `CCircle` class declaration from the Circle.cpp and Circle2.cpp files, then add the following statement at the beginning of the Circle.cpp and Circle2.cpp files:

```
#include "CCircle.h"
```

Note: Notice that in both Circle.cpp and Circle2.cpp, `m_Radius` was set by the constructor function. You cannot change the value of `m_Radius` from within `main()` because `m_Radius` was declared in the `private` section of the class declaration.

Follow these steps to see the advantage of using classes in action:

☐ While the Circle2 project is open, select New from the File menu, select Text File from the New dialog box, then click the OK button of the New dialog box.

Visual C++ responds by displaying a new empty text file.

☐ Make sure the new empty text window is selected, then select Save File As from the File menu and save the file as CCircle.h in the C:\TYVCProg\Programs\AppendB directory.

☐ Type the `CCircle` class declaration and its member functions in the CCircle.h file. (You can use the Copy and Paste tools from the Edit menu to copy the `CCircle` class declaration from the Circle2.cpp file into the CCircle.h file.) Make sure the CCircle.h file looks like the one in Listing B.3.

☐ Make sure the CCircle.h window is selected, then select Save from the File menu.

Listing B.3. The listing of the CCircle.h file.

```
// CCircle.h

// Declare the CCircle class
class CCircle
   {
```

```
public:
CCircle( int r);      // Constructor
void    SetRadius(int r);
void    DisplayArea(void);
~CCircle();           // Destructor
private:
float CalculateArea(void);
int m_Radius;
int m_Color;
};

// The constructor function
CCircle::CCircle ( int r )
{

// Set the radius
m_Radius = r;

}

// The destructor function
CCircle::~CCircle ()
{

}

// Function Name: DisplayArea()
void CCircle::DisplayArea ( void )
{

float fArea;

fArea = CalculateArea ( );

// Print the area
cout << "The area of the circle is: " << fArea;
cout << "\n";

}

// Function Name: CalculateArea()
float CCircle::CalculateArea ( void )
{

float f;

f = (float) (3.14 * m_Radius * m_Radius);

return f;

}
```

☐ Modify the code in the Circle2.cpp file:

```
// Program Name: Circle2.CPP

// #include files
```

```
#include <iostream.h>
#include "CCircle.h"

void main(void)
{
// Create an object of class CCircle with
// radius equal to 10.
CCircle MyCircle ( 10 );

// Create an object of class CCircle with
// radius equal to 20.
CCircle HerCircle ( 20 );

// Create an object of class CCircle with
// radius equal to 30.
CCircle HisCircle ( 30 );

// Display the area of the circles
MyCircle.DisplayArea();
cout << "\n";
HerCircle.DisplayArea();
cout << "\n";
HisCircle.DisplayArea();
cout << "\n";

}
```

Note that you deleted the CCircle class declaration from the Circle2.cpp file. Instead, you included the CCircle class declaration by including the CCircle.h file.

Note: When you included the iostream.h file, you used the following statement:

```
#include <iostream.h>
```

When you included the CCircle.h file, you used the following statement:

```
#include "CCircle.h"
```

One h file is enclosed with the < > characters, and the other h file is enclosed with the " " characters.

One of the settings of Visual C++ is the Include path, which sets a path to the directory where several h files reside. iostream.h resides in the directory mentioned in the Include path of Visual C++; therefore, you can enclose the filename with the < > characters. Specifically, the iostream.h file resides in the \Include directory of Visual C++, which is also the default setting of the Include path.

On the other hand, the CCircle.h file resides in the C:\TYVCProg\Programs\ AppendB directory, which isn't mentioned in the Include path. This means you have to enclose the filename CCircle.h with the " " characters so the compiler will know to look for the CCircle.h file in the current directory.

☐ Make sure the Circle2.cpp window is selected, then select Save from the File menu.

☐ Select Build Circle2.cpp from the Build menu.

Visual C++ responds by compiling and executing the Circle2 program.

☐ Select Execute Circle2.EXE from the Build menu.

Visual C++ responds by executing the Circle2.EXE program. Check that the areas reported by the Circle2 program are correct.

In a similar manner, you can modify the Circle.cpp program so that it will look like the following:

```
// Program Name: Circle.CPP

// #include files
#include <iostream.h>
#include "CCircle.h"


void main(void)
{
// Create an object of class Circle with
// radius equal to 10.
CCircle MyCircle ( 10 );

// Display the area of the circle
MyCircle.DisplayArea();

}
```

In the above code, you deleted the class declaration of `CCircle` from the Circle.cpp file. Instead, you included this statement:

```
#include "CCircle.h"
```

Overloaded Functions

In C++ (but not in C), you can use the same function name for more than one function. For example, you can declare two `SetRadius()` functions in the class declaration of the `CCircle` class. Such functions are called *overloaded functions*. Modify the `CCircle` class declaration to include an overloaded function:

☐ Select Open from the File menu and load the CCircle.h file from the C:\TYVCProg\ Programs\AppendB directory.

☐ Modify the `CCircle` class declaration in the CCircle.h file:

```
// Declare the CCircle class
class CCircle
{
```

747

```
public:
CCircle( int r);      // Constructor

void    SetRadius(int r);           // Overloaded
void    SetRadius(int r, int c );   // Overloaded

void    DisplayArea(void);
~CCircle();               // Destructor

int m_Color;
int m_Radius;

private:
float CalculateArea(void);
//int m_Radius;
// int Color;
};
```

This modified CCircle class is similar to the original CCircle class. However, now the int m_Radius and int m_Color data members have been moved from the private section to the public section so you could access m_Color from main(). As you can see, now the CCircle class has two SetRadius() member functions:

```
void    SetRadius(int r);           // Overloaded
void    SetRadius(int r, int c );   // Overloaded
```

The first SetRadius() member function has one parameter, and the second SetRadius() has two parameters.

☐ Add the following code to the end of the CCircle.h file:

```
// Function Name: SetRadius()
void CCircle::SetRadius ( int r)
{

m_Radius = r;
m_Color = 255;

}
```

The code of the SetRadius() function sets the m_Radius data member to r, the parameter that was passed to SetRadius(). The code also sets the m_Color data member to 255.

☐ Add the following code to the end of the CCircle.h file:

```
// Function Name: SetRadius()
void CCircle::SetRadius ( int r, int c)
{

m_Radius = r;
m_Color = c;

}
```

The code of this second `SetRadius()` function sets the `m_Radius` data member to r. The code also sets the `m_Color` data member to c, the second parameter that was passed to `SetRadius()`.

☐ Select Save All from the File menu to save your work.

☐ Open the Circle.cpp file and modify the code of the main() function as follows:

B

```
// Program Name: Circle2.CPP

// #include files
#include <iostream.h>
#include "CCircle.h"

void main ( void)
{
// Create the MyCircle object with radius equal to 10
CCircle MyCircle (10);

// Display the radius of the circle
cout << "The Radius is: " << MyCircle.m_Radius;
cout << "\n";

//Set the radius of MyCircle to 20.
MyCircle.SetRadius (20);

// Display the radius of the circle
cout << "The Radius is: " << MyCircle.m_Radius;
cout << "\n";

// Display the color of the circle
cout << "The Color of the circle is: " << MyCircle.m_Color;
cout << "\n";


// Use the other SetRadius() function
MyCircle.SetRadius (40, 100);

// Display the radius of the circle
cout << "The Radius is: " << MyCircle.m_Radius;
cout << "\n";

// Display the color of the circle
cout << "The Color of the circle is: " << MyCircle.m_Color;
cout << "\n";

}
```

☐ Select Save All from the File menu to save your work.

Examining the Modified *main()* Function of the Circle2 Program

This CCircle class is similar to the CCircle class used in the previous programs, except that the int m_Color data member has been moved from the private section to the public section. Also, the CCircle class declaration now has the following set of overloaded functions:

```
void    SetRadius(int r);           // Overloaded
void    SetRadius(int r, int c );   // Overloaded
```

The CCircle class has two SetRadius() functions: one with a single parameter (int r) and the other with two parameters (int r and int c). The first SetRadius() member function sets m_Radius to the value that was passed to it and also sets m_Color to 255:

```
void CCircle::SetRadius ( int r )
{

m_Radius = r;
m_Color = 255;


}
```

The second SetRadius() member function sets m_Radius and m_Color to the values that were passed to them:

```
void CCircle::SetRadius ( int r, int c )
{

m_Radius = r;
m_Color = c;


}
```

The main() function starts by creating the MyCircle object:

```
CCircle MyCircle (10);
```

The radius of MyCircle is then displayed:

```
// Display the radius of the circle
cout << "The Radius is: " << MyCircle.m_Radius;
cout << "\n";
```

The radius of MyCircle is changed to 20:

```
//Set the Radius of MyCircle to 20.
MyCircle.SetRadius (20);
```

And the new radius is displayed:

```
// Display the radius of the circle
cout << "The Radius is: " << MyCircle.m_Radius;
cout << "\n";
```

In the preceding statements, the first `SetRadius()` was used. This means that only one parameter was passed to `SetRadius()`, which set `m_Color` to `255`. The value of `m_Color` is then displayed:

```
// Display the color of the circle
cout << "The Color of the circle is: " << MyCircle.m_Color;
cout << "\n";
```

Next, you used the second `SetRadius()` function:

```
// Use the other SetRadius() function
MyCircle.SetRadius (40, 100);
```

In the preceding statement, you set the radius to `40` and the color to `100`. Next, you display the radius and the color:

```
// Display the radius of the circle
cout << "The Radius is: " << MyCircle.m_Radius;
cout << "\n";
```

```
// Display the color of the circle
cout << "The Color of the circle is: " << MyCircle.m_Color;
cout << "\n";
```

☐ Select Build Circle2.cpp from the Build menu.

☐ Select Execute Circle2.EXE from the Build menu.

Check that the Circle2 program reports the radius and color of the `MyCircle` object as dictated in `main()`.

How does the program know which `SetRadius()` function to use? By noticing the number of parameters you supplied to the function.

Note: The Circle2.cpp program illustrates how to set up and use overloaded functions, but it doesn't demonstrate how overloaded functions are used in practice. To understand the practical use of overloaded functions, consider a program that calculates the area of a circle and the area of a rectangle. As you know, the area of a circle is calculated in the following way:

```
Circle Area = Radius * Radius * 3.14
```

You also know that the area of a rectangle is calculated like this:

```
Rectangle Area = SideA * SideB
```

One way to write a program that calculates the area for both the circle and the rectangle is to write the following two functions:

```
CalculateCircleArea(Radius)
CalculateRectangleArea(SideA, SideB)
```

With overloaded functions, however, you can use a single function from within your program: `CalculateArea()`. The `CalculateArea()` function is an overloaded function. When only one parameter is supplied to the `CalculateArea()` function, the program calculates the circle's area; when two parameters are supplied to the `CalculateArea()` function, the program calculates the rectangle's area.

At first glance, this business of overloaded functions seems to be no help at all. After all, you have to write two separate functions; one function calculates the circle's area, and the other function calculates the rectangle's area. So what's the big deal about overloaded functions?

Consider what your main program looks like. Instead of remembering that the program has one function for calculating the circle's area and another function for calculating the rectangle's area, all you have to remember is that the program has one function—`CalculateArea()`—that takes care of both the circle and the rectangle. You have to know how to use the function, of course, which means you have to know what parameters, and how many, you should supply to the function.

Still, you may not agree that overloaded functions really help when it comes to calculating the areas of circles and rectangles. You'll learn to appreciate overloaded functions, however, when you create Windows applications. As you'll see in this book, Visual C++ comes with hundreds of useful Windows functions, many of which are overloaded functions. When you use these functions, your programs are easy to write, easy to read, and easy to maintain.

Declaring Variables in C++ Versus C

In C, you declare your variables at the beginning of the function. The following `main()` function declares the variable i at its beginning; then, 1000 lines later, it uses the variable i:

```
void main(void)
{
i = 3;
.....
.....
.....
// 1,000 lines of code
.....
.....
.....
```

```
i =i + 1;
...
...
...
}

}
```

In C++, however, you don't have to declare your variables at the beginning of the function. The preceding C main() function can be written in C++:

```
void main(void)
{
.....
.....
.....
// 1,000 lines of code
.....
.....
.....
int i = 3;
i = i + 1;
...
...
...
}

}
```

Therefore, the variable i is declared closer to the code that uses it. Don't try to use the i variable before it's declared, of course.

Default Parameters

Another convenient feature of C++ that doesn't exist in C is default parameters. In C, you can declare the following function prototype:

```
int MyFunction (int a,
                int b,
                int c,
                int d);
```

The actual function may look like this:

```
int MyFunction (int a,
                int b,
                int c,
                int d)
{
...
...
...
}
```

If you execute MyFunction() from within main(), you must supply four parameters because that's what you specified in the prototype of the function. So from within main(), you can execute MyFunction() as follows:

```
MyFunction (int 1,
            int 4,
            int 3,
            int 7);
```

C++ is more liberal than C. The designers of C++ knew that although you specified four parameters for MyFunction(), in most cases, you'll use the same values for some of the parameters of the function. Therefore, C++ enables you to specify default parameters in the prototype of MyFunction(), as in the following example:

```
MyFunction ( int a = 10,
             int b = 20,
             int c = 30,
             int d = 40 );
```

From main(), you can execute MyFunction():

```
main()
{
...
...
...
int iResult;
iResult = MyFunction();
...
...
...
}
```

Because you did not supply any parameters for MyFunction(), the compiler automatically interprets your statement this way:

```
main()
{
...
...
...
int iResult;
iResult = MyFunction(10,
                     20,
                     30,
                     40);
...
...
...
}
```

In addition, you can override some of the default parameters as follows:

```
main()
{
...
...
...
int iResult;
iResult = MyFunction(100, 200);
...
...
...
}
```

Since you didn't supply any third and fourth parameters to MyFunction(), the compiler automatically interprets your statement in the following way:

```
main()
{
...
...
...
int iResult;
iResult = MyFunction(100, 200, 30, 40);
...
...
...
}
```

In other words, you overrode the first and second parameters, and the compiler automatically substituted the third and fourth parameters (as indicated in the prototype of the function).

> **Note:** When using a default parameter, you must use all the default parameters that appear after that parameter. For example, the following is not allowed:
>
> ```
> void main(void)
> {
> ...
> ...
> ...
> int iResult;
> iResult = MyFunction(100,
>                         ,     // Not allowed
>                      300
>                      400);
> ...
> ...
> ...
> }
> ```
>
> Since you overrode the third parameter, you must specify a value for the second parameter as well.

Summary

In this chapter, you have learned about classes and objects in C++ and the major differences between C and C++. C++ concepts are not difficult; they represent the natural evolution of the C programming language. C++ enables you to write complex programs that are easy to read and understand.

Consider the following declaration of the CPersonGoToWork class:

```
class CPersonGoToWork
{
public:
CPersonGoToWork(); // The constructor
void WakeUp(void);
void Wash(void);
void Dress(void);
void Eat(void);
void TakeBus(void);
void TakeCar(void);
void TakeSubway(void);
void TurnPCon(void);
void TurnIrrigationOn(void);
void CalibrateRadar(void);
~CPersonGoToWork(); // The destructor

private:
.....
.....
.....
}
```

This class contains member functions that display cartoon characters doing something during the course of going to work. The TakeCar() function displays a person getting into a car, for example, and the TakeSubway() function displays a person taking a subway to work.

Consider the following main() program:

```
void main(void)
{
// Create an object called Jim
// for Mr. Jim Smart the programmer.
CPersonGoToWork Jim;

// Show Jim going to work.
Jim.WakeUp(void);
Jim.Wash(void);
Jim.Dress(void);
Jim.Eat(void);
Jim.TakeCar(void);
Jim.TurnPCon(void);

// Create an object called Jill
// for Ms. Jill Officer the policewoman.
CPersonGoToWork Jill;
```

```
// Show Jill going to work.
Jill.WakeUp(void);
Jill.Wash(void);
Jill.Dress(void);
Jill.Eat(void);
Jill.TakeCar(void);
Jill.CalibrateRadar();

// Create an object called Don
// for Mr. Don Farmer the farmer.
CPersonGoToWork Don;

// Show Don going to work.
Don.WakeUp(void);
Don.Wash(void);
Don.Dress(void);
Don.Eat(void);
Don.TurnIrrigationOn(void);

}
```

As you can see, `main()` can be written in a matter of minutes and can be easily understood and maintained. The real work of writing such a program, of course, is writing the member functions of the `CPersonGoToWork` class. When the class is ready, however, writing `main()` is very easy—this is the main advantage of using Visual C++ for writing Windows applications.

MFC is a group of C++ functions supplied with the Visual C++ package. As you'll see during the course of this book, most of your program is written already! All you have to do is understand the powerful member functions that exist in the MFC and apply them to your Windows applications.

In the next appendix (the third and last part of the tutorial), you'll learn about the inheritance topic of C++.

> **Note:** As you'll see during the course of this book, writing Visual C++ Windows programs is actually very easy. Why? Because during the creation of your Visual C++ programs, you'll use C++ functions that were supplied with the Visual C++ package. You could say that knowing Visual C++ amounts to knowing how to use the C++ member functions and classes supplied with Visual C++.

Learning C/C++
Quickly (Part III)

In this part of the tutorial, you'll learn about the important topics of inheritance and hierarchy in C++.

The Rect Program

You'll begin by writing the Rect.cpp program.

☐ Create the C:\TYVCProg\Programs\AppendC directory (you'll save the programs of this appendix in this directory).

☐ Start Visual C++.

☐ Select Close Project Workspace from the File menu to close all the open windows in the Visual C++ desktop (if there are any).

☐ Select New from the File menu.

Visual C++ responds by displaying the New dialog box.

☐ Select Text from the list of items in the New dialog box, then click the OK button.

☐ Select Save As from the File menu, and save the new (empty) file as Rect.cpp in the directory C:\TYVCProg\Programs\AppendC.

☐ In the Rect.cpp window, type the code shown in Listing C.1.

☐ Select Rebuild All from the Build menu.

☐ Click the Yes button in the dialog box that Visual C++ displays. (You are telling Visual C++ "Yes, create the project.")

Visual C++ responds by compiling and linking the Rect program.

☐ Select Execute Rect.EXE from the Build menu.

As you can see, the Rect.EXE program displays a message that tells you the area of a rectangle.

Listing C.1. The Rect.cpp program.

```
// Program Name: Rect.CPP

// #include
#include <iostream.h>

// The CRectangle class declaration

class CRectangle
{
public:
CRectangle(int w, int h);  // Constructor
```

```
void DisplayArea (void);    // Member function

~CRectangle();              // Destructor

int m_Width;   // Data member
int m_Height;  // Data member

};

// The constructor function

CRectangle::CRectangle( int w, int h)
{

m_Width = w;
m_Height = h;

}

// The destructor function
CRectangle::~CRectangle()
{

}

// Function Name: DisplayArea()

void CRectangle::DisplayArea(void)
{

int iArea;

iArea = m_Width * m_Height;

cout << "The area is: " << iArea << "\n";

}

void main(void)
{

CRectangle MyRectangle ( 10, 5 );

MyRectangle.DisplayArea();

}
```

The Rect Program's Code

In this section, you'll go over the code of the Rect.cpp program. The program starts by including the iostream.h file because the cout statement is used:

```
#include <iostream.h>
```

Then the program declares the CRectangle class:

```
class CRectangle
{
public:
CRectangle(int w, int h);   // Constructor

void DisplayArea (void);    // Member function

~CRectangle();              // Destructor

int m_Width;    // Data member
int m_Height;   // Data member

};
```

The CRectangle class declaration contains the constructor function, the destructor function, the DisplayArea() member function, and two data members The constructor function simply initializes the data members:

```
CRectangle::CRectangle( int w, int h )
{

m_Width = w;
m_Height = h;

}
```

No code appears in the destructor function, and the DisplayArea() function calculates the area of the rectangle and then displays it:

```
void CRectangle::DisplayArea(void)
{

int iArea;

iArea = m_Width * m_Height;

cout << "The area is: " << iArea << "\n";

}
```

The main() function creates an object called MyRectangle of class CRectangle:

```
CRectangle MyRectangle ( 10, 5 );
```

Because (10, 5) is passed to the constructor function, the MyRectangle object has its width equal to 10 and height equal to 5.

main() then displays the area of MyRectangle:

```
MyRectangle.DisplayArea();
```

As you can see, the CRectangle class enables you to calculate the area of the rectangle. Suppose you want to calculate the area of a rectangle with its width equal to 20 and height equal to 5.

What would you do? You could add `SetWidth()` and `SetHeight()` member functions that set the values of `m_Width` and `m_Height`. Therefore, the `CRectangle` class declaration would look like this:

```
// The CRectangle class declaration

class CRectangle
{
public:
CRectangle(int w, int h);   // Constructor

void DisplayArea (void);

void SetWidth  ( int w );
void SetHeight ( int h );

~CRectangle();              // Destructor

int m_Width;
int m_Height;
};
```

The `SetWidth()` and `SetHeight()` member functions would look like this:

```
// Function Name: SetWidth()

void CRectangle::SetWidth(int w)
{

m_Width = w;

}


// Function Name: SetHeight()

void CRectangle::SetHeight(int h)
{

m_Height = h;

}
```

Your `main()` function would look like this:

```
void main(void)
{

// Create the MyRectangle with width equal to 10
// and height equal to 5
CRectangle MyRectangle (10,5);

// Display the area
MyRectangle.DisplayArea();

// Change the width and height
MyRectangle.SetWidth(20);
MyRectangle.SetHeight(5);
```

```
// Display the area
MyRectangle.DisplayArea();

}
```

Adding Member Functions

There is nothing wrong with the preceding program's design, but it assumes you own the source code of the CRectangle class and therefore can modify it at any time. In many cases, software vendors don't give you the source code of the class; for one thing, they don't want you to have the source code because they worked hard to develop it. Also, they don't want you to mess with the source code of the class, because you could accidentally damage the class.

Nevertheless, in many cases you need to add some of your own member functions, just as you needed to add the SetWidth() and SetHeight() functions to the CRectangle class.

Class Hierarchy

To solve the problem of adding member functions, you can use the *class hierarchy* concept of C++, which enables you to create a new class from the original class. The original class is called the *base class*, and the class you create is called the *derived class*. The derived class inherits data members and member functions from its base class. When you create the derived class, you can add member functions and data members to it.

In this section, you create a class called CNewRectangle from the CRectangle class. The base class is CRectangle, and the derived class is CNewRectangle. Listing C.2 shows the code of the Rect2.cpp program that creates the derived class.

Listing C.2. The Rect2.cpp program.

```
// Program Name: Rect2.CPP

// #include
#include <iostream.h>

// The CRectangle class declaration (base class)
class CRectangle
{
public:
CRectangle(int w, int h);   // Constructor

void DisplayArea (void);

~CRectangle();              // Destructor

int m_Width;
int m_Height;
```

```
};

// The declaration of the derived class CNewRectangle
class CNewRectangle : public CRectangle
{

public:
CNewRectangle(int w, int h);   // Constructor

void SetWidth (int w);
void SetHeight (int h);

~CNewRectangle();              // Destructor

};
// The constructor function of CRectangle (base)
CRectangle::CRectangle( int w, int h)
{

cout << "In the constructor of the base class" << "\n";

m_Width = w;
m_Height = h;

}

// The destructor function of CRectangle (base)

CRectangle::~CRectangle()
{

cout << "In the destructor of the base class" << "\n";

}

// Function Name: DisplayArea() (base)
void CRectangle::DisplayArea(void)
{

int iArea;

iArea = m_Width * m_Height;

cout << "The area is: " << iArea << "\n";

}

// The constructor function of CNewRectangle (derived)
CNewRectangle::CNewRectangle( int w,int h):CRectangle( w, h)
{

cout << "In the constructor of the derived class" << "\n";

}
```

continues

Listing C.2. continued

```cpp
// The destructor function of CNewRectangle (derived)
CNewRectangle::~CNewRectangle()
{

cout << "In the destructor of the derived class" << "\n";

}

// Function Name: SetWidth() (derived)
void CNewRectangle::SetWidth(int w)
{

m_Width = w;

}

// Function Name: SetHeight() (derived)
void CNewRectangle::SetHeight(int h)
{

m_Height = h;

}

void main(void)
{

CNewRectangle MyRectangle (10, 5);

MyRectangle.DisplayArea();

MyRectangle.SetWidth (100);
MyRectangle.SetHeight (20);

MyRectangle.DisplayArea();

}
```

The Rect2 Program's Code

The Rect2.cpp program declares the CRectangle class exactly as it was declared in the Rect.cpp program:

```cpp
class CRectangle
{
public:
CRectangle(int w, int h);  // Constructor

void DisplayArea (void);

~CRectangle();             // Destructor
```

```
int m_Width;
int m_Height;

};
```

The Rect2.cpp program then declares a class called `CNewRectangle`, which is derived from the `CRectangle` class:

```
// The declaration of the derived class CNewRectangle
class CNewRectangle : public CRectangle
{

public:
CNewRectangle(int w, int h);   // Constructor

void SetWidth (int w);
void SetHeight (int h);

~CNewRectangle();              // Destructor

};
```

In the first line of the declaration of the derived class, the text `: public CRectangle` indicates that `CNewRectangle` is derived from `CRectangle`:

```
class CNewRectangle : public CRectangle
{
....
....
....
};
```

The derived class has a constructor function, a destructor function, the `SetWidth()` function, and the `SetHeight()` function. As you'll see, the `CNewRectangle` class has all the features of the `CRectangle` class. For example, even though the data members `m_Width` and `m_Height` don't appear as data members of `CNewRectangle`, `CNewRectangle` inherited these data members from `CRectangle`. Also, even though `CNewRectangle` doesn't have `DisplayArea()` as one of its member functions, for all practical purposes it does because `CNewRectangle` inherited the `DisplayArea()` function from its base class.

The constructor function of the base class simply sets the values for the data members of the class:

```
CRectangle::CRectangle( int w, int h)
{

cout << "In the constructor of the base class" << "\n";

m_Width = w;
m_Height = h;

}
```

The `cout` statement is used in the preceding constructor function so you can tell during the program's execution that this constructor function was executed.

Following is the destructor function of the base class:

```
CRectangle::~CRectangle()
{

cout << "In the destructor of the base class" << "\n";

}
```

Again, the `cout` statement is used so you'll be able to tell this function was executed.

The `DisplayArea()` function of the base class calculates and displays the area:

```
void CRectangle::DisplayArea(void)
{

int iArea;

iArea = m_Width * m_Height;

cout << "The area is: " << iArea << "\n";

}
```

Now look at the constructor function of the derived class:

```
CNewRectangle::CNewRectangle(int w,int h):CRectangle(w,h)
{

cout << "In the constructor of the derived class" << "\n";

}
```

The first line of the preceding function includes this text:

```
:CRectangle(w,h)
```

This code means that when an object of class `CNewRectangle` is created, the constructor function of the base class is executed and the parameters (w and h) are passed to the constructor function of the base class.

The code in the constructor function of the derived class uses the `cout` statement so that during the program's execution you'll be able to tell that this function was executed.

Following is the destructor function of the derived class:

```
CNewRectangle::~CNewRectangle()
{

cout << "In the destructor of the derived class" << "\n";

}
```

Again, the cout statement is used so you'll be able to tell when this function is executed.

Following are the SetWidth() and SetHeight() functions of the derived class:

```
void CNewRectangle::SetWidth(int w)
{

m_Width = w;

}

void CNewRectangle::SetHeight(int h)
{

m_Height = h;

}
```

main() starts by creating an object of class CNewRectangle:

```
CNewRectangle MyRectangle (10, 5);
```

The preceding statement creates the MyRectangle object of class CNewRectangle. Because CNewRectangle is derived from CRectangle, however, you can use member functions from the base class:

```
MyRectangle.DisplayArea();
```

The preceding statement executes the DisplayArea() member function on the MyRectangle object. Even though the CNewRectangle class doesn't have the DisplayArea() member function in its class declaration, CNewRectangle inherited the DisplayArea() member function of the base class CRectangle.

The main() function then uses the SetWidth() and SetHeight() member functions to set new values for m_Width and m_Height:

```
MyRectangle.SetWidth (100);
MyRectangle.SetHeight (20);
```

Finally, main() uses the DisplayArea() function to display the area of the rectangle:

```
MyRectangle.DisplayArea();
```

Now that you understand the code of the Rect2.cpp program, you're ready to see it in action.

☐ Select Close Project Workspace from the File menu.

☐ Select New from the File menu, select Text in the New dialog box, then click the OK button.

☐ Save the new empty text file as Rect2.cpp in the C:\TYVCProg\Programs\AppendC directory.

☐ In the Rect2.cpp window, type the code shown in Listing C.2 earlier in this chapter.

You now can compile, link, and execute the Rect2.cpp program, as follows:

☐ Select Rebuild All from the Build menu.

> *Visual C++ displays a dialog box that asks whether you want to create a default project.*

☐ In the dialog box, click the Yes button.

☐ Select Execute Rect2.EXE from the Build menu.

The Rect2.cpp program first executes the constructor function of the base class, then executes the constructor function of the derived class because of the following statement in `main()`:

```
CNewRectangle MyRectangle(10, 5);
```

The Rect2.cpp program then displays the area of a rectangle with its width equal to 10 and height equal to 5. Next, the program displays the area of a rectangle with its width equal to 100 and height equal to 20.

Finally, when the `main()` function is done, the `MyRectangle` object is destroyed. The destructor function of the derived class is executed, then the destructor function of the base class is executed.

When the object is created, the constructor function of the base class is executed, then the constructor function of the derived class is executed. When the object is destroyed, the destructor function of the derived class is executed, then the destructor function of the base class is executed.

Illustrating Class Hierarchy

Figure C.1 shows the class hierarchy relationship between `CRectangle` and `CNewRectangle`.

Figure C.1.
The class hierarchy of `CRectangle` *and* `CNewRectangle`.

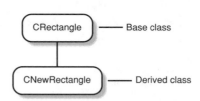

The relationship shown in Figure C.1 is simple, but the class hierarchy can be as complex as you want it to be. For example, you may want to construct another derived class, called

`CNewNewRectangle`, derived from the `CNewRectangle` class. Its class declaration would look like this:

```
class CNewNewRectangle: public CNewRectangle
{
....
....
....
};
```

In the preceding declaration, `CNewNewRectangle` serves as the derived class and `CNewRectangle` serves as the base class. You can now declare another derived class for which `CNewNewRectangle` serves as the base class.

Figure C.2 shows a complex class hierarchy, which isn't shown just for educational purposes. In fact, as you'll see later in this book, the class hierarchy of MFC is far more complex than the one shown in the figure.

How can you use this illustration of a class hierarchy? You can tell which member functions you can execute. By looking at Figure C.2, you can tell that you can execute a member function that exists in class A on objects of classes B, C, D, E, F, G, and H. You also can execute a member function in class F on an object of clases G, E, and H, but you cannot execute a member function in class F on objects of classes A, B, C, D, and E.

Figure C.2.

A complex class hierarchy.

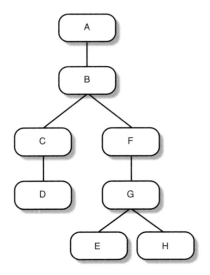

Overriding a Member Function

Sometimes, you may find it necessary to override a particular member function. Suppose you purchase the CRectangle class; you like this class, and you want to use it in your applications. The only problem is you don't like the way the author of the CRectangle class wrote the DisplayArea() function. Can you override that function? Sure. The Rect3.cpp program, which is very similar to the Rect2.cpp program, demonstrates how to do this. Follow these steps to create the Rect3.cpp program:

☐ Select New from the File menu, select the Text item from the New dialog box, then click the OK button of the New dialog box.

> *Visual C++ responds by opening the new empty Text 1 text window.*

☐ Select Save As from the File menu and save the file as Rect3.cpp in the C:\TYVCProg\Programs\AppendC directory.

☐ Select Open from the File menu and open the C:\TYVCProg\Programs\AppendC\Rect2.cpp file.

☐ Use the Edit menu items to copy the contents of the Rect2.cpp file into the Rect3.cpp file.

☐ Make sure the Rect2.cpp window is selected, then select Close from the File menu.

Now the Visual C++ desktop contains the Rect3.cpp file.

☐ Modify the first line in the Rect3.cpp file as follows:

```
// Program Name: Rect3.CPP

// #include
#include <iostream.h>
...
...
...
```

☐ Add another prototype function to the declaration of the CNewRectangle class in the Rect3.cpp file as follows:

```
// The declaration of the derived class CNewRectangle
class CNewRectangle : public CRectangle
{

public:
CNewRectangle(int w, int h);  // Constructor

void SetWidth (int w);
void SetHeight (int h);
```

```
void DisplayArea();

~CNewRectangle(); // Destructor

};
```

In the preceding example, the prototype of the DisplayArea() function was added to the class declaration of the CNewRectangle derived class.

☐ Add the code of the DisplayArea() function of the derived class to the Rect3.cpp file:

```
// Function Name: DisplayArea() (derived)
void CNewRectangle::DisplayArea(void)
{

int iArea;

iArea = m_Width * m_Height;

cout << "================ \n";
cout << "The area is: " << iArea << "\n";
cout << "================ \n";

}
```

As you can see, the Rect3.cpp program now has two DisplayArea() functions. One is a member function of the CRectangle class (the base class), and the other is a member function of the CNewRectangle class (the derived class).

The main() function remains exactly as it was in the Rect2.cpp program:

```
void main(void)
{

CNewRectangle MyRectangle (10, 5);

MyRectangle.DisplayArea();

MyRectangle.SetWidth (100);
MyRectangle.SetHeight (20);

MyRectangle.DisplayArea();

}
```

☐ Save your work by selecting Save All from the File menu.

☐ Select Rebuild All from the Build menu, then click the Yes button in the dialog box.

Visual C++ responds by compiling and linking the Rect3.cpp program.

☐ Select Execute Rect3.EXE from the Build menu.

The output of Rect3.cpp is the same as the output of Rect2.cpp, except that the areas are displayed with the `DisplayArea()` function of the derived class. This means that when the following statement is executed, the `DisplayArea()` of the derived class, not the base class, is executed:

```
MyRectangle.DisplayArea();
```

Using Pointers to Objects

In many cases, it is convenient to use pointers to objects. The Rect4.cpp program demonstrates this concept.

☐ Select Close Project Workspace from the File menu.

☐ Select New Project Workspace from the File menu, select the Text item of the New dialog box, then click the OK button of the New dialog box.

Visual C++ responds by displaying the new empty Text1 window.

☐ Save the Text1 window as Rect4.cpp in the C:\TYVCProg\Programs\AppendC directory.

☐ Select Open from the File menu and select the Rect3.cpp file from the C:\TYVCProg\Programs\AppendC directory.

☐ Use the Edit menu items to copy the contents of the Rect3.cpp file to the Rect4.cpp file.

☐ Make sure the Rect3.cpp window is selected, then select Close from the File menu.

☐ Modify the first line of the Rect4.cpp file as follows:

```
// Program Name: Rect4.CPP

// #include
#include <iostream.h>
...
...
...
```

☐ Modify the `main()` function of Rect4.cpp:

```
void main(void)
{

CNewRectangle MyRectangle (10, 5);

CNewRectangle* pMyRectangle = &MyRectangle;

pMyRectangle->DisplayArea();


pMyRectangle->SetWidth (100);
pMyRectangle->SetHeight (20);
```

```
    pMyRectangle->DisplayArea();

    }
```

As you can see, main() creates an object MyRectangle of class CNewRectangle:

```
CNewRectangle MyRectangle (10, 5);
```

Then main() declares a pointer pMyRectangle of type CNewRectangle:

```
CNewRectangle* pMyRectangle = &MyRectangle;
```

In the preceding statement, the address of the MyRectangle object is assigned to pMyRectangle.

The rest of the statements in main() are similar to the ones in the Rect3.cpp program. Unlike the main() function in Rect3.cpp, however, the main() function in Rect4.cpp uses the pointer of the MyRectangle object to execute the member function.

The DisplayArea() function is executed as follows:

```
pMyRectangle->DisplayArea();
```

You execute the SetWidth() and SetHeight() functions this way:

```
pMyRectangle->SetWidth (100);
pMyRectangle->SetHeight (20);
```

The name of the member function is separated from the pointer of the object with the -> characters.

☐ Compile and link the Rect4.cpp program (select Rebuild All from the Build menu, then click the Yes button when Visual C++ asks whether you want to create the default project).

☐ Execute the Rect4.EXE program (select Execute Rect4.EXE from the Build menu).

☐ Check that the results of the Rect4.EXE program are identical to those of the Rect3.EXE program.

The New and Delete Operators

In the Rect4.cpp program, you created the MyRectangle object in main():

```
void main(void)
{

CNewRectangle MyRectangle (10, 5);

CNewRectangle* pMyRectangle = &MyRectangle;

pMyRectangle->DisplayArea();
```

```
   ...
   ...
   ...

}
```

In the preceding `main()` function, the object is destroyed when `main()` terminates. If you create the object from within a function, however, the memory used for storing the `MyRectangle` object is freed automatically when `MyFunction()` terminates:

```
void MyFunction(void)
{

CNewRectangle MyRectangle (10, 5);

CNewRectangle* pMyRectangle = &MyRectangle;

pMyRectangle->DisplayArea();

   ...
   ...
   ...

}
```

The object is created with the following statement:

```
CNewRectangle MyRectangle (10, 5);
```

Then the pointer to the object is created:

```
CNewRectangle* pMyRectangle = &MyRectangle;
```

You can also use the new operator, which is equivalent to C's `malloc()` function. (The `malloc()` function allocates memory.) The Rect5.cpp program demonstrates how you can use the new operator.

☐ Select Close Project Workspace from the File menu.

☐ Select New from the File menu, select Text from the New dialog box, then click the OK button of the New dialog box.

   Visual C++ responds by displaying the new empty Text1 window.

☐ Select Save As from the File menu to save the file as Rect5.cpp in the C:\TYVCProg\Programs\AppendC directory.

☐ Select Open from the File menu and load the C:\TYVCProg\Programs\AppendC\Rect4.cpp file.

☐ Use the Copy and Paste menu items of the Edit menu to copy the contents of the Rect4.cpp file into the Rect5.cpp file.

☐ Make sure the Rect4.cpp window is selected, then select Close from the File menu.

☐ Modify the first line of the Rect5.cpp file as follows:

```
// Program Name: Rect5.CPP

// #include
#include <iostream.h>
...
...
...
```

☐ Modify the main() function of Rect5.cpp:

```
void main(void)
{

CNewRectangle* pMyRectangle;
pMyRectangle = new CNewRectangle(10,5);

pMyRectangle->DisplayArea();


pMyRectangle->SetWidth (100);
pMyRectangle->SetHeight (20);


pMyRectangle->DisplayArea();

delete pMyRectangle;
}
```

☐ Select Save All from the File menu to save your work.

☐ Select Rebuild from the Build menu.

☐ Select Execute Rect5.EXE from the Build menu.

As you can see, the output of Rect5.EXE is identical to the output of the Rect4.EXE program.

Now look at the code of the main() function of the Rect5.cpp program. The pointer pMyRectangle is declared. This pointer is declared as a pointer to an object of class CNewRectangle:

```
CNewRectangle* pMyRectangle;
```

Then the new operator is used to create a new object of class CNewRectangle. The address of this new object is stored in the pointer pMyRectangle:

```
pMyRectangle = new CNewRectangle(10,5);
```

The rest of the code in main() remains the same as it was in the Rect4.cpp program. To execute the DisplayArea() member function on the object, for example, you use this statement:

```
pMyRectangle->DisplayArea();
```

777

The last thing `main()` does is free the memory occupied by the object:

```
delete pMyRectangle;
```

The `delete` operator must be used to free objects created with the `new` operator.

Note: If you use the `new` operator from within a function, the memory occupied by the pointer is freed automatically when the function terminates (because the pointer is just a local variable to the function). The pointer holds a memory address where the actual object is stored; that memory is not freed when the function terminates. You must use the `delete` operator to free the memory occupied by the object.

Note: In the Rect5.cpp program, you created the object by using two statements in `main()`:

```
CNewRectangle* pMyRectangle;
pMyRectangle = new CNewRectangle(10,5);
```

In Visual C++, you typically see these statements combined in one statement:

```
CNewRectangle* pMyRectangle = new CNewRectangle(10,5);
```

This statement is identical to the preceding two statements.

Summary

Congratulations! You've finished the quick C++ tutorial. Starting in Chapter 1, "Writing Your First Visual C++ Application," you'll write true C++ Windows applications. Visual C++ enables you to write professional applications in a very short time. This is possible because Microsoft ships Visual C++ with a set of powerful classes called the MFC library. Learning Visual C++ amounts to knowing how to use the member functions of the MFC.

Visual C++ enables you to design your windows, dialog boxes, menus, bitmaps, and icons visually—you use the mouse and the visual tools to design these objects. Visual C++ also includes a wizard program called AppWizard, which writes the overhead code for you. A Windows application usually requires several overhead files; they appear in every Windows application you'll write. Instead of typing these repetitive, boring overhead files yourself, you can use AppWizard to generate and write them for you.

Finally, Visual C++ is equipped with a wizard program called ClassWizard. As you learned in this chapter, when you know that a certain class is available, you can derive other classes that inherit the data members and member functions of the base class.

Unlike the CRectangle and CNewRectangle classes discussed in this appendix, the MFC classes are very powerful. Deriving classes from the MFC requires a great deal of typing. Don't worry, though—ClassWizard takes care of this task. ClassWizard inserts the prototypes of the member functions into the declaration of the derived classes and even starts writing the functions for you. All you have to do is type your own specific code in the functions ClassWizard prepares for you.

These wizards are what Visual C++ is all about. Throughout this book, you'll use these wizards extensively.

Index

functions

Add to Your Sams Library Today with the Best Books for Programming, Operating Systems, and New Technologies

The easiest way to order is to pick up the phone and call
1-800-428-5331
between 9:00 a.m. and 5:00 p.m. EST.
For faster service please have your credit card available.

ISBN	Quantity	Description of Item	Unit Cost	Total C
0-672-30787-1		Essential Visual C++ 4	$25.00	
0-672-30743-X		Gurewich OLE Controls for Visual Basic 4 (Book/CD-ROM)	$39.99	
0-672-30605-0		Borland C++ 4.5 Object-Oriented Programming, 4E (Book/Disk)	$45.00	
0-672-30727-8		Teach Yourself Turbo C++ 4.5 for Windows in 21 Days	$29.99	
0-672-30715-4		Teach Yourself Visual Basic 3 in 21 Days, Bestseller Edition	$35.00	
0-672-30495-3		Teach Yourself More Visual Basic 3 in 21 Days, (Book/Disk)	$35.00	
0-672-30593-3		Develop a Professional Visual C++ Application in 21 Days (Book/CD-ROM)	$35.00	
0-672-30462-7		Teach Yourself Microsoft Foundation Class Library Programming in 21 Days	$29.99	
0-672-30663-8		Visual C++ 2 Developer's Guide, 2E (Book/Disk)	$49.99	
0-672-30613-1		Database Developer's Guide with Visual C++ (Book/Disk)	$49.99	
0-672-30292-6		Programming Windows Games with Borland C++ (Book/Disk)	$34.95	
❏ 3 ½" Disk		Shipping and Handling: See information below.		
❏ 5 ¼" Disk		TOTAL		

Shipping and Handling: $4.00 for the first book, and $1.75 for each additional book. Floppy disk: add $1.75 for shippin handling. If you need to have it NOW, we can ship the product to you in 24 hours for an additional charge of approxim $18.00, and you will receive your item overnight or in two days. Overseas shipping and handling adds $2.00 per book $8.00 for up to three disks. Prices subject to change. Call for availability and pricing information on latest editions.

201 W. 103rd Street, Indianapolis, Indiana 46290

1-800-428-5331 — Orders   1-800-835-3202 — FAX   1-800-858-7674 — Customer Ser

Book ISBN 0-672-3079

PLUG YOURSELF INTO...

MACMILLAN INFORMATION SUPERLIBRARY™

que • SAMS PUBLISHING • Hayden Books • que COLLEGE • NRP • alpha books • Brady • ADOBE PRESS

THE MACMILLAN INFORMATION SUPERLIBRARY™

Free information and vast computer resources from the world's leading computer book publisher—online!

FIND THE BOOKS THAT ARE RIGHT FOR YOU!

A complete online catalog, plus sample chapters and tables of contents give you an in-depth look at *all* of our books, including hard-to-find titles. It's the best way to find the books you need!

- ● STAY INFORMED with the latest computer industry news through our online newsletter, press releases, and customized Information SuperLibrary Reports.

- ● GET FAST ANSWERS to your questions about MCP books and software.

- ● VISIT our online bookstore for the latest information and editions!

- ● COMMUNICATE with our expert authors through e-mail and conferences.

- ● DOWNLOAD SOFTWARE from the immense MCP library:
    - Source code and files from MCP books
    - The best shareware, freeware, and demos

- ● DISCOVER HOT SPOTS on other parts of the Internet.

- ● WIN BOOKS in ongoing contests and giveaways!

TO PLUG INTO MCP: ➔ WORLD WIDE WEB: **http://www.mcp.com**

GOPHER: gopher.mcp.com

FTP: ftp.mcp.com

Home Page | What's New | Bookstore | Reference Desk | Software Library | Macmillan Overview | Talk to Us

Special Disk Offer

The Full Version TegoSoft OCX Control Kit

You can order the full version of the TegoSoft OCX Control Kit directly from TegoSoft Inc. It includes a variety of powerful OCX controls for Visual C++ (as well as for Visual Basic and other programming languages that support OCX controls).

The TegoSoft OCX Control Kit includes the following controls:

- Advanced Multimedia OCX control (to play WAV, MIDI, CD audio, and movie files).
- 3-D Virtual Reality OCX control (lets you use the mouse and keyboard to travel inside your 3-D pictures).
- Advanced Animation OCX control and Sprite OCX control.
- 3-D Controls (for example, 3-D buttons, 3-D spin).
- Spy OCX control (lets you intercept Windows messages of other applications).
- Gadget OCX controls.
- PC Speaker OCX control (enables you to play WAV files through the PC speaker without a sound card and without any drivers).
- Other OCX controls, such as WinG, DirectDraw, and WAV Control.

The price of the TegoSoft OCX Control Kit is $29.95. Please add $5.00 for shipping and handling. New York State residents, please add appropriate sales tax. When ordering from outside the United States, check or money order must be in U.S. dollars drawn from a U.S. bank.

To order, send check or money order to:

TegoSoft Inc.
Attn: OCX-Kit-TYVC4
Box 389
Bellmore, NY 11710
Phone: (516)783-4824
WORLD WIDE WEB: http://www.tegosoft.com

Free Online Code Offer

The last two chapters of the book, Chapter 20 and Chapter 21, use OLE controls from TegoSoft. These controls may be downloaded from our Internet site or from CompuServe.

Instructions for Internet Users

To retrieve the supplemental files from the Internet, here's what to do:

1. Point your web browser at http://www.mcp.com/sams.
2. Click on the "easy-to-use web page" link.
3. Click on the "programming titles" link.
4. Locate *Teach Yourself Visual C++ 4 in 21 Days* in the list of titles. Then click on the tyvcprog.exe link.
5. Save the file to your hard disk and run tyvcprog.exe to decompress the files.

Instructions for CompuServe Users

To retrieve the supplemental files from CompuServe, here's what to do:

1. Log in to CompuServe and GO PHCP to enter the Macmillan Publishing forum.
2. Enter the "Programming" section (Library 9).
3. Retrieve the file titled *Teach Yourself Visual C++ 4 in 21 Days*. Then run tyvcprog.exe to expand the files.